ANIMALLIFE

ANIMALLIFE

CHARLOTTE UHLENBROEK

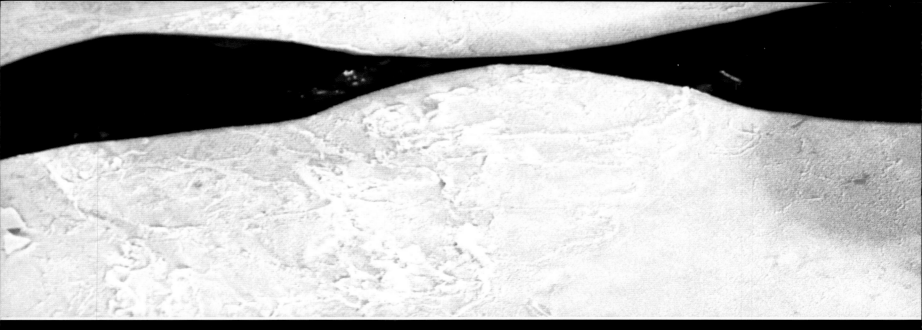

LONDON, NEW YORK, MELBOURNE,
MUNICH, AND DELHI

DORLING KINDERSLEY

Senior Art Editors
Maxine Lea, Ina Stradins

Senior Editors
Peter Frances, Angeles Gavira Guerrero
US Senior Editor Jill Hamilton

Project Art Editors
Alison Gardner, Samantha Richiardi,
Hugh Schermuly, Francis Wong,
Steve Woosnam-Savage

Project Editors
Rob Houston, Nathan Joyce, Cathy Meeus,
Ruth O'Rourke, Gill Pitts, David Summers,
Rebecca Warren, Victoria Wiggins

Designers
Sonia Barbate, Julian Barford,
Mark Lloyd

Editors
Polly Boyd, Tamlyn Calitz, Salima Hirani,
Ben Hoare, Claire Tennant-Scull,
Miezan van Zyl, Ed Wilson

Production Editor
Tony Phipps

US Editor Jane Perlmutter

First American Edition, 2008

Published in the United States by
DK Publishing
375 Hudson Street
New York, New York 10014

08 09 10 11   10 9 8 7 6 5 4 3 2 1

Contributors

Richard Beatty
Glossary

Dr. Frances Dipper
Fishes, Defence

Dr. Kim Dennis-Bryan
Mammals

Professor Tim Halliday
*Amphibians, Sex and Reproduction,
Reproducing without a Mate,
Finding a Mate, Sexual Rivalry,
Mating*

Rob Hume
Birds

Chris Mattison
Amphibians

Dr. George C. McGavin
Invertebrates, Predation, Scavenging

Dr. Sanjida O'Connell
Intelligence

Dr. Douglas Palmer
Evolution

Steve Parker
*Skeletons and Muscles, Movement,
Body Coverings, Body Systems*

Dr. Katie Parsons
Senses, Living Space, Life Histories

Dr. Sean Rands
Society

Dr. Graham Scott
*Feeding, Feeding on Plants, Omnivores, Feeding
Partnerships*

Dr. Charlotte Uhlenbroek
Communication

Dr. Elizabeth White
*Vision, Birth and Development,
Raising Young*

John Woodward
Courtship

Consultants

Dr. Juliet Clutton-Brock
Mammals

Dr. Frances Dipper
Fishes

Professor Tim Halliday
Reptiles

Rob Hume
Birds

Chris Mattison
Amphibians

Dr. George C. McGavin
Invertebrates

American Museum of Natural History

Dr. Christopher J. Raxworthy
Chief consultant

Dr. George F. Barrowclough

Dr. Randall T. Schuh

Dr. Mark E. Siddall

Dr. John S. Sparks

Dr. Robert S. Voss

Animal data

The behavior profiles in this book contain summary
information about the animals being described.
This information usually covers a species, but in some
cases it refers to a group, such as family or genus.
The symbols used in the summary panel are as follows:

◨ In most cases (and unless otherwise stated), this
refers to the length of the adult animal, with the
following dimensions given for different groups:

Mammals: head and body
Birds: tip of bill to tip of tail
Reptiles, Amphibians, and Fishes: head and body,
including tail
Invertebrates: head and body, including tail but not
including antennae

⊙ Occurrence, including both habitat and geographical
distribution

▥ A brief description of the animal's main physical
features

≫ Cross-references to other behavioral profiles about
the same species or group

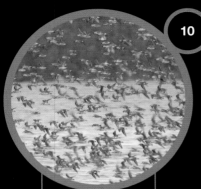

(10)

Animals have lived on Earth for more than a billion years, and have evolved a staggering array of forms.

A N I M A L
KINGDOM

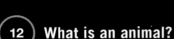

(78)

Animals' bodies allow them to maintain a stable shape, move around, and sense and react to their surroundings.

A N I M A L
ANATOMY

contents

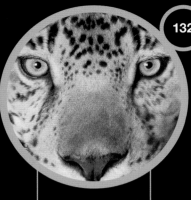

(132)

An animal's behavior encompasses all the things it does, from competing for food to forming societies.

ANIMAL
BEHAVIOR

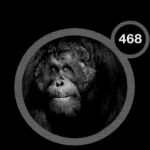

foreword

I am thrilled to have worked on this book. It is unique, so far as I am aware, in exploring the richness and diversity of animal behavior across the animal kingdom.

The essentials of animal life are relatively simple— finding food, self-defense, reproduction, and dispersal—but the ways in which animals achieve these things are extraordinarily complex and varied. From amazing hunting strategies and extraordinary defenses to stunning mating rituals and complex relationships, the wealth of different behaviors reflects the diversity of animals and the huge range of physical and social environments in which they live. Animals populate every corner of the globe from the bottom of the sea to mountain peaks and from the Equator to the poles; they may live in groups of thousands or meet others of their kind just once in a lifetime.

An animal's behavior depends to a large extent on its form and evolutionary history, and the first two parts of this book provide a clear and comprehensive description of the major groups of animals and their evolution, anatomy, and senses. The main part of this book then looks at animals in action. It is divided into eight chapters that look at different aspects of animals' lives, although these are not always mutually exclusive. It doesn't attempt to provide a complete catalog of all animal behavior—that would run to many volumes and is expanding all the time. Nevertheless, it is an extensive overview of our current knowledge of animal behavior, including typical and unusual behaviors in different animal groups, classic studies, and new discoveries.

It is an exciting time to be writing about animal behavior. Advances in neurobiology, anatomy, and physiology have revolutionized our understanding of behavioral mechanisms; the rapidly expanding field of ecology is revealing the extraordinary web of relationships between species; and the maturation of long-term studies of social behavior is providing intimate views of animal societies. Many discoveries are blurring the boundaries between human and animal behavior, such as the use of symbolic signals to communicate, intense sociality, and problem solving. Meanwhile, new technology has taken us into realms utterly alien to our experience such as the use of polarized light and magnetism to navigate, electricity to hunt, or minute vibrations to communicate.

This book reflects the extraordinary body of work carried out by biologists who have devoted years, often whole lifetimes, to the patient observation of animals in the field and in the lab and to designing ingenious experiments to learn why animals behave in the ways they do. Some species have been very well studied and we know an extraordinary amount of detail about their behavior; others are barely known and as yet we only have tantalizing glimpses into their lives.

Written by a team of respected biologists and illustrated with fantastic photography that jumps off the page at you, this book really puts the "life" into wildlife. The great biologist E.O. Wilson said, "Once you know an animal's behavior... you know its essence." I hope that this book helps capture the essence of animal life on this planet and makes us ever more determined and equipped to protect it.

CHARLOTTE UHLENBROEK

What is an animal?

There are at least two million living species of animals on Earth. They range from microscopic worms to huge whales, but they all share a few key characteristics which, when combined, distinguish them from all other forms of life. These defining characteristics include both physiological features and the behavior that makes animals so intriguing.

Life on Earth is traditionally divided into five "kingdoms." Two of these, consisting mostly of bacteria and protists, are mainly microscopic, so we are rarely aware of them. The other three are more familiar—the fungi, plants, and animals. The essential differences between fungi and plants may not be obvious at first sight, but most animals are easy to recognize by the way they move and react to their environment. Some aquatic animals move very little, and may look a lot like plants, but animals and plants function in very different ways.

VERTEBRATES 2.6%	
	Mammals 9%
	Birds 19%
	Reptiles 13.5%
	Amphibians 10%
	Fishes 48.5%
INVERTEBRATES 97.4%	
	Arthropods 60.5%
	Cnidarians 0.5%
	Worms 3%
	Echinoderms 0.5%
	Mollusks 5%
	Other 30.5%

SPECIES DIVERSITY
Scientists believe that there may be more than ten million species of animals, although fewer than two million have been described scientifically. Of these, less than 3 percent are vertebrates, such as mammals, birds, and fishes. The arthropods make up by far the largest group of animals on Earth.

Energy and food

Plants, and many bacteria and protists, use the energy of sunlight to make food. They combine carbon dioxide with water to form a sugar called glucose—a simple carbohydrate—in a process known as photosynthesis. The glucose stores energy, which plants use to fuel their growth. They can also convert glucose into other carbohydrates, such as the tough cellulose that reinforces their structure. As they absorb the water they need, plants also acquire dissolved chemicals such as nitrates and phosphates, which they turn into proteins.

Animals cannot make their own food from simple chemicals. A few, such as reef corals, live in partnership with organisms that can produce food like this, but most get their nourishment by eating plants or other living things. They digest the living tissue to break it down into simpler ingredients, such as glucose, and use these to fuel and build their own bodies. Their need to find food is one reason why animals have evolved mobility and senses.

MOBILE FEEDERS
Gerenuks are superbly adapted to reach the most succulent young shoots on trees. Standing on their hind legs, they can stretch their long, muscular necks in among the branches.

Unique embryos

Some simple creatures, such as jellyfish, sea anemones, and corals, can multiply asexually by growing buds that turn into new animals. Many insects and other invertebrates, such as water fleas and some aphids, can develop from unfertilized eggs—a process known as parthenogenesis. In both cases the young are clones of their parent.

However, most animals produce single-celled eggs, each fertilized by the sperm cell of another individual to create a "zygote" that contains the DNA of both parents. This single fertilized cell develops into a ball of cells called a blastula, which is unique to animals. Through a process of cell division, the blastula becomes a multicellular embryo (see p.379). Having inherited a mixture of genes from each parent, the embryos produced in this way are genetically different (except in the case of identical twins). Combined with gene mutation and natural selection (see pp.14–15), this genetic mixing creates the variation that has enabled animals to evolve into such a dazzling variety of species.

Multicellular

Animals are built up from many microscopic cells which, unlike those of plants or fungi, do not have rigid cell walls. In all animals, except sponges, the cells are organized into different types of living tissue such as muscles and nerves. These tissues may form specialized organs such as the heart, brain, and lungs. The body plan usually becomes fixed early in life, but the bodies of some animals, such as butterflies, undergo a radical rebuild, called metamorphosis (see p.386), when they become adults.

Feeding

All animals obtain nutrition from other living organisms or from the remains of dead organisms. Parasitic worms that live inside other animals absorb simple nutrients through their skins. Other animals have ways of ingesting food into gut cavities, which are specialized for digesting it and turning it into useful nutrients such as glucose. Some aquatic animals simply filter food particles from the water, but most animals have well-defined, mobile mouths that they can use to seize and even chew their food.

Gas exchange

All animals need oxygen to turn carbohydrate food into energy, a process that releases carbon dioxide. This is the reverse of photosynthesis, which produces oxygen, so animals are oxygen consumers, not producers. They exchange gases through thin-walled gills in water (as in fishes), through their moist skins (as in amphibians), through branched tube systems (insects), or through lungs. Many types of animal have bloodstreams of some description that carry these gases around the body, along with food, such as blood sugar.

Sensory systems

Nearly all animals, except sponges, have networks of nerve cells that respond to external stimuli. Touch a simple animal like a sea anemone (a cnidarian), and it will twitch. More complex animals have sense organs that react to light, sound, pressure, scent, taste, and even electricity. They also have brains that can memorize and recognize the stimuli, enabling many animals to learn by experience. Most of these sensory organs are concentrated at the head of a typical animal, near its mouth.

Mobility

The most distinctive feature of animals is their mobility. Some aquatic animals, such as mussels, spend their adult lives attached to rocks and may not move visibly, but they do pump water through their bodies. Mussels also open and close their shells as the tide rises and falls. Most other animals are able to slither, crawl, swim, walk, run, and even fly. Combined with their senses and memories, this enables them to seek out food, escape enemies, and find breeding partners. In other words, they display behavior.

Evolution

Charles Darwin's definition of evolution was "descent with modification," a term he used in his book *The Origin of Species* to describe how successive generations of a species adapt to their changing environments over time to eventually form entirely new species.

What is evolution?

Evolution is the process of change in the inherited characteristics of populations of animals over time. The crux of the theory is that all life today has evolved and diverged from simple ancestors that lived in the oceans over 3 billion years ago. This means that all animals are related to each other. Accumulated evidence from biology, genetics, and fossils supports evolution as the unifying theory that directs our understanding of life and its history.

PEPPERED MOTH VARIATION
These three moths are members of the same species. The variations originally occurred as a result of genetic mutations. Natural selection led to the darkest moth becoming more abundant, since industrial pollution made them blend in better to the blackened trees that the moths rest on during the day.

Macroevolution and microevolution

The large-scale pattern of change is known as "macroevolution." Macroevolution refers to large-scale changes, such as the evolution of limbed vertebrates from those with fins. Other examples of macroevolution are the emergence of the shelled egg, freeing some land-living, four-limbed animals from dependence upon water for reproduction and the divergence of egg-laying reptiles into other major groups, including turtles and crocodiles. This occurs as a result of small-scale descent with modification, known as "microevolution." For example, since their introduction to the United States, house sparrow populations in the north and south of the continent have developed differences, with the northern variant becoming bigger—probably as an adaptation to the colder climate.

NATURAL SELECTION

NATURAL SELECTION
This is often described as "the survival of the fittest." This species of butterfly varies in color and reproduces in large numbers, not all of which survive, due to limited resources in the environment. Predators eat more of the purples, which are less camouflaged than the yellows. The surviving yellows produce more of their own kind. With continued predator preference over time, the yellow butterflies become dominant.

GENETIC DRIFT
Randomly occurring change in the genetic makeup of a population over time is known as genetic drift. For example, a forest fire wipes out most of the purple butterflies in the population. The next generation contains the genes of the lucky survivors, not necessarily the "fitter" ones. Despite being unlikely, it is even possible for a series of chance events to lead to the total loss of the purple population.

GENE FLOW
Gene flow (or migration) results from the movement of genes from one population to another. For instance, genes are carried from one population and introduced to another by the migration of an adult organism. In this example, a

GENETIC DRIFT

GENE

SHARKS

RAY-FINNED FISHES

AMPHIBIANS

TURTLES

SNAKES AND LIZARDS

CROCODILES

BIRDS

MAMMALS

SHARING A COMMON ANCESTOR
To the left is a cladogram—a diagram showing a group of organisms descended from a common ancestor. The animal groups in the diagram are all related to the first vertebrate, which appeared around 540 million years ago. The branching patterns occur as a result of divergent evolution. These branching patterns form a "family tree"(or phylogeny).

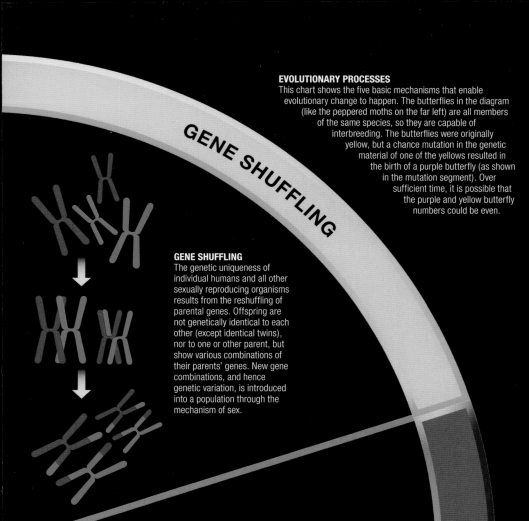

GENE SHUFFLING

EVOLUTIONARY PROCESSES
This chart shows the five basic mechanisms that enable evolutionary change to happen. The butterflies in the diagram (like the peppered moths on the far left) are all members of the same species, so they are capable of interbreeding. The butterflies were originally yellow, but a chance mutation in the genetic material of one of the yellows resulted in the birth of a purple butterfly (as shown in the mutation segment). Over sufficient time, it is possible that the purple and yellow butterfly numbers could be even.

GENE SHUFFLING
The genetic uniqueness of individual humans and all other sexually reproducing organisms results from the reshuffling of parental genes. Offspring are not genetically identical to each other (except identical twins), nor to one or other parent, but show various combinations of their parents' genes. New gene combinations, and hence genetic variation, is introduced into a population through the mechanism of sex.

DNA AND GENES

Every life form is made up of a specific series of molecules, and the order of molecules is contained in a chemical code. This code is extremely complex and is encased in spiral-shaped molecules of deoxyribonucleic acid (DNA). Chemicals, known as bases, link each molecule of DNA. There are four different kinds—adenine, cytosine, guanine, and thymine. They are always linked up in pairs—adenine always fuses with thymine, and cytosine with guanine. The sequence of these bases makes up the cell's genetic code. The code found in each human cell consists of 20,000–25,000 separate instructions. Each of these instructions is known as a gene, and each gene is responsible for controlling particular characteristics. For example, there is a single gene that is responsible for the color of eyes. Genetics is the study of how these characteristics are inherited and is one of the central pillars of biology.

each DNA molecule forms a threadlike structure, known as a chromosome

the DNA molecule forms a spiral shape (a double helix), and is linked by the 4 different bases

MUTATION
A mutation is brought about by change in the genetic material of an organism that is subsequently inherited by its offspring. This chance alteration can happen through deletion or insertion of a single base in a DNA molecule (see panel, right). Occasionally, single mutations may produce large effects but generally, evolutionary change is the result of many mutations.

purple butterfly leaves a purple population and joins a yellow population. The migrant interbreeds with members of the yellows and, in doing so, introduces its purple genes into the yellow population.

Speciation
Among other meanings, a species can be defined as a group of similar organisms that can interbreed to produce fertile offspring. Speciation is the process whereby new species evolve from a single ancestral species. This occurs for a number of reasons, including geographical isolation arising from habitat fragmentation. If a small population is isolated from the main group and its members can only share genes with each other, over time they will evolve independently to the point where, if they came back in contact with the original group, they could not interbreed.

DARWIN'S FINCHES
Isolated gene pools in islands such as the Galapagos create unique traits. This woodpecker finch has evolved to use tools to catch prey.

Divergent evolution
Over vast periods of time, repeated speciation has led to evolutionary divergence, where new descendent species become significantly different from their common ancestors. For instance, all life on land has diverged from water-living ancestors, and all living species of mammal have diverged from a common ancestral mammal that lived alongside the dinosaurs. These series of changes arise as a product of Earth's dynamic environments, which vary from place to place and from time to time.

Convergent evolution
Sometimes, different organisms will evolve similar characteristics to adapt to the environment that they inhabit. For example, the similarity in body forms of whales, seals, and penguins is the result of similar adaptations to similar ways of life. The common factor is the adaptation of a streamlined body shape, with reduced limbs for a more efficient swimming motion. In a similar way, wings have evolved independently in birds and bats for flight.

COEVOLUTION AND MUTUAL DEPENDENCY
Some flowers rely on hummingbirds for pollination, while some hummingbirds rely on specific flowers for nectar. They have coevolved in terms of shape and color to accommodate each other's survival.

MUTATION

FLOW

Animal history

The evolution and expansion of animal life on Earth is a remarkable story. From microscopic beginnings billions of years ago, animal life evolved in the protective and supportive medium of ocean water. Fossilized remains show us that the earliest multicellular creatures evolved in the Ediacaran period, around 630 million years ago (MYA). However, the fossil record is by no means complete. We know surprisingly little about the origins of some groups, such as sharks and rays, but with each new fossil discovery, we move a step closer to answering the questions that have puzzled paleontologists for years.

Diversification and proliferation

Early in the Cambrian, marine invertebrates underwent a period of expansion and diversification. Many familiar living invertebrate groups evolved in this period, along with now extinct groups. The first vertebrate animals also evolved in the Cambrian. These diversified into several fish-related groups, some of which are now extinct. After the arthropods moved into the terrestrial environments, they proliferated and rapidly diversified. By late Devonian times, tetrapod (four-limbed) vertebrates had left the water and the next stage in vertebrate evolution had begun. The airways were the last environment for animal life to conquer, with insects first achieving this in the Carboniferous period. Many animal groups have members that have evolved and adapted to life in each environment. For example, reptiles first evolved on land, then evolved water-living members before finally taking to the air.

Extinction events

The history of animal evolution was not one of simple expansion and diversification. As animal groups evolved and died away, changing environments and events impacted upon their evolution, sometimes disastrously. There were several major extinction events that reset the evolutionary clock. The most devastating of these—the Permian–Triassic extinction—wiped out 96 percent of all marine species.

How this chart works

This chart separates animal life into three major habitats—sea, land, and air. The major animal groups are individually colored. Their relative abundance through time is represented by an expanding and contracting band. The evolution of each group is signified by tie lines that link them to their ancestral group. Th[e] invertebrate bands are shown o[n] scale to the vertebrates due to t[he] estimating their numbers (they a[re] account for 97 percent of all spe[cies] of their strands are relative to ea[ch]

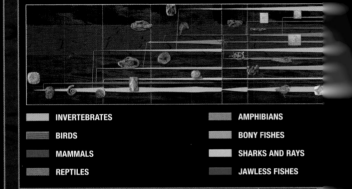

- INVERTEBRATES
- BIRDS
- MAMMALS
- REPTILES
- AMPHIBIANS
- BONY FISHES
- SHARKS AND RAYS
- JAWLESS FISHES

ORDOVICIAN–SILURIAN EXTINCTION 440 MYA
One third of all brachiopod and bryozoan families, and many groups of conodonts and trilobites were rendered extinct. Overall, around 100 families of marine invertebrates were wiped out.

Earliest terrestrial arthropod groups (centipedes, millipedes, and others) evolve around 450 MYA.

Earliest jawed fishes evolve around 450 MYA.

EVOLUTION OF ANIMAL LIFE
The first complex multicellular organisms began to appear in the Ediacaran period, around 630 MYA. This fossil of a *Mawsonites* species is thought to be an early jellyfish or a primitive worm.

MAWSONITES

Evolution of coral

ESTONIOCERAS NAUTILUS

The Cambrian "Explosion," around 540 MYA, saw the rapid evolution of groups of marine invertebrates, and the evolution of the

OLENELLUS TRILOBITE

Primitive nautiloids (marine cephalopods) become abundant around 475 MYA

Coral reefs become widespread in the mid-Ordovician period, around 470 MYA

PALEOZOIC

400   350   300

LATE DEVONIAN EXTINCTION 365 MYA
This event mostly affected marine organisms. Coral reefs, brachiopods, and trilobites were all severely reduced in number. Most terrestrial animals were unscathed, but some early amphibians were wiped out.

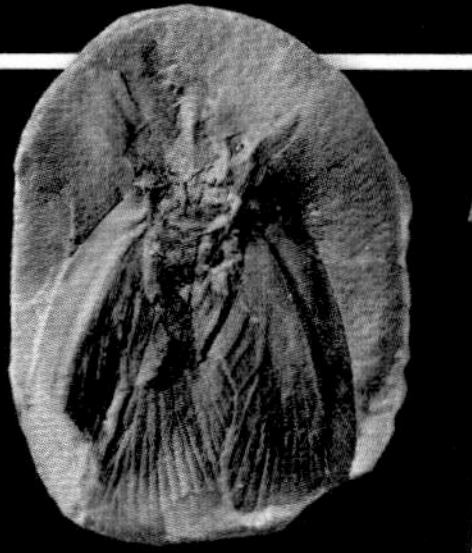

ARCHIMYLACRIS

AERIAL INVERTEBRATES

Late Carboniferous insects begin to appear around 320 MYA, including roaches and dragonflies. *Archimylacris* was an early cockroach with folded wings.

This fossil of *Westlothiana lizziae* was hailed as the first true reptile due to its superficial reptilelike features, but it is now thought to be an amniote ancestor (340 MYA).

ACANTHOSTEGA

WESTLOTHIANA LIZZIAE

Evolving from fishes, the first tetrapods (four-legged vertebrates) rose up out of the water and started colonizing the land around 370 MYA. *Acanthostega* had both lungs and gills, eight digits on each limb, and webbed feet.

Amniote ancestors are thought to branch out from the amphibians around 340 MYA.

REPTILES

The amniotes split into two groups around 315 MYA—the synapsids (eventually leading to living mammals) and the sauropsids (eventually leading to living reptiles).

Earliest known scorpions evolve around 418 MYA.

Early land snails evolve in the Carbonifeous, around 320 MYA.

AMPHIBIANS

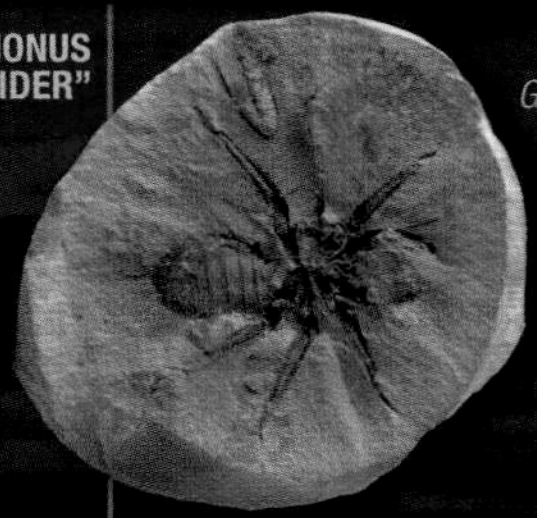

GRAEOPHONUS "SPIDER"

Arthropods continue to diversify. *Graeophonus* was a true spider relative.

TERRESTRIAL INVERTEBRATES

CHEIRACANTHUS JAWED FISH

Acanthodians (early jawed fishes), such as *Cheiracanthus*, expand early in the Devonian period, around 410 MYA.

HELIOCOPRION TOOTH SPIRAL

Colossal early Permian sharks, such as *Heliocoprion*, become the dominant predators in the seas, around 298 MYA.

BONY FISHES

SHARKS AND RAYS

JAWLESS FISHES

PTERASPIS JAWLESS FISH

Early jawless fishes are common around 405 MYA. *Pterapsis* had a distinctive flattened head, enclosed by massive bony plates.

Extensive development of Carboniferous coral reefs, around 350 MYA.

MARINE INVERTEBRATES

CONTINUED OVERLEAF »

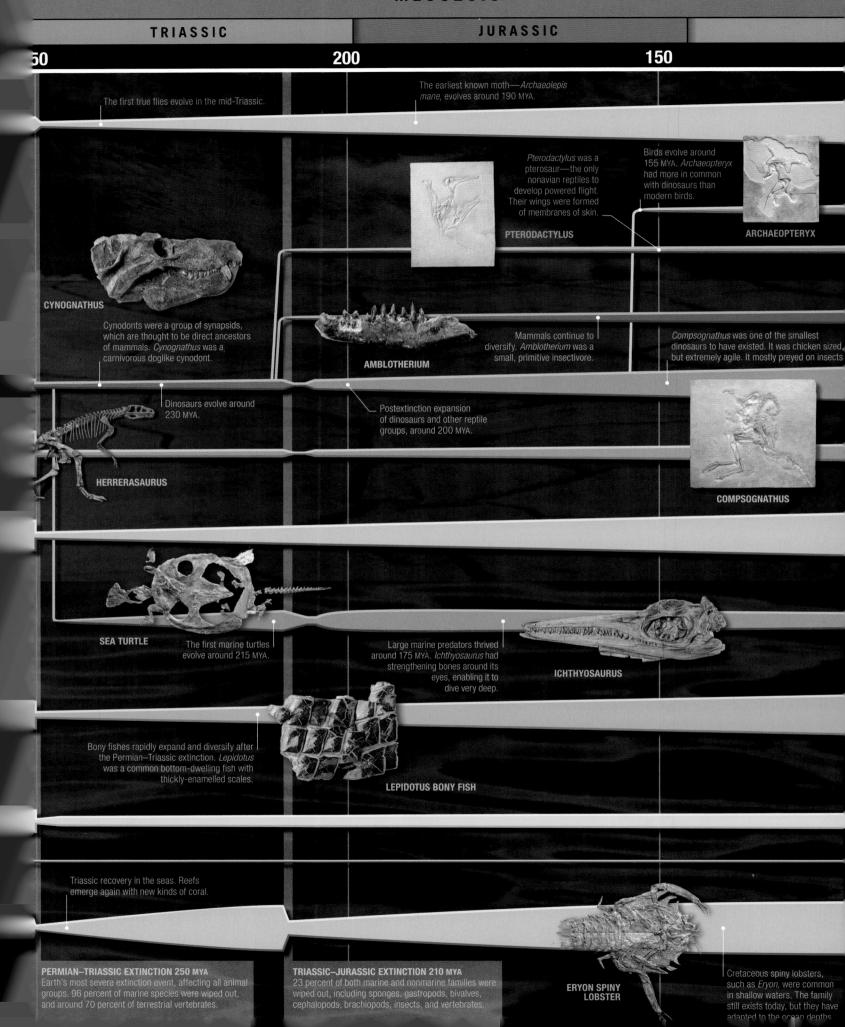

MESOZOIC

TRIASSIC

JURASSIC

50

200

150

The first true flies evolve in the mid-Triassic.

The earliest known moth—*Archaeolepis mane*, evolves around 190 MYA.

Pterodactylus was a pterosaur—the only nonavian reptiles to develop powered flight. Their wings were formed of membranes of skin.

PTERODACTYLUS

Birds evolve around 155 MYA. *Archaeopteryx* had more in common with dinosaurs than modern birds.

ARCHAEOPTERYX

CYNOGNATHUS

Cynodonts were a group of synapsids, which are thought to be direct ancestors of mammals. *Cynognathus* was a carnivorous doglike cynodont.

AMBLOTHERIUM

Mammals continue to diversify. *Amblotherium* was a small, primitive insectivore.

Compsognathus was one of the smallest dinosaurs to have existed. It was chicken sized, but extremely agile. It mostly preyed on insects

Dinosaurs evolve around 230 MYA.

Postextinction expansion of dinosaurs and other reptile groups, around 200 MYA.

HERRERASAURUS

COMPSOGNATHUS

SEA TURTLE

The first marine turtles evolve around 215 MYA.

Large marine predators thrived around 175 MYA. *Ichthyosaurus* had strengthening bones around its eyes, enabling it to dive very deep.

ICHTHYOSAURUS

Bony fishes rapidly expand and diversify after the Permian–Triassic extinction. *Lepidotus* was a common bottom-dwelling fish with thickly-enamelled scales.

LEPIDOTUS BONY FISH

Triassic recovery in the seas. Reefs emerge again with new kinds of coral.

PERMIAN–TRIASSIC EXTINCTION 250 MYA
Earth's most severe extinction event, affecting all animal groups. 96 percent of marine species were wiped out, and around 70 percent of terrestrial vertebrates.

TRIASSIC–JURASSIC EXTINCTION 210 MYA
23 percent of both marine and nonmarine families were wiped out, including sponges, gastropods, bivalves, cephalopods, brachiopods, insects, and vertebrates.

ERYON SPINY LOBSTER

Cretaceous spiny lobsters, such as *Eryon*, were common in shallow waters. The family still exists today, but they have adapted to the ocean depths.

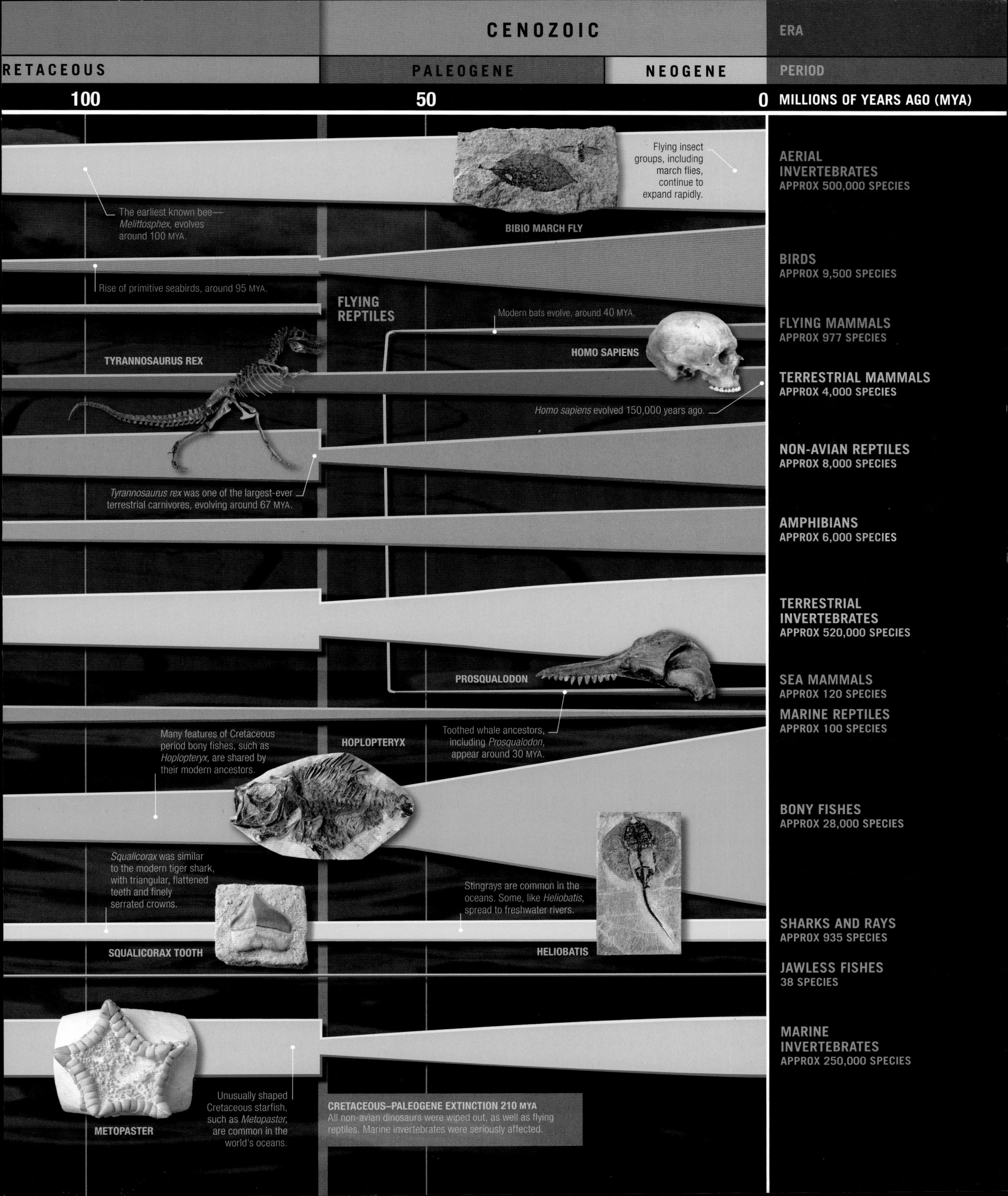

CENOZOIC		ERA
CRETACEOUS	PALEOGENE	NEOGENE	PERIOD
100	50	0	MILLIONS OF YEARS AGO (MYA)

Flying insect groups, including march flies, continue to expand rapidly.

AERIAL INVERTEBRATES
APPROX 500,000 SPECIES

The earliest known bee— *Melittosphex*, evolves around 100 MYA.

BIBIO MARCH FLY

BIRDS
APPROX 9,500 SPECIES

Rise of primitive seabirds, around 95 MYA.

FLYING REPTILES

Modern bats evolve, around 40 MYA.

FLYING MAMMALS
APPROX 977 SPECIES

TYRANNOSAURUS REX

HOMO SAPIENS

TERRESTRIAL MAMMALS
APPROX 4,000 SPECIES

Homo sapiens evolved 150,000 years ago.

Tyrannosaurus rex was one of the largest-ever terrestrial carnivores, evolving around 67 MYA.

NON-AVIAN REPTILES
APPROX 8,000 SPECIES

AMPHIBIANS
APPROX 6,000 SPECIES

TERRESTRIAL INVERTEBRATES
APPROX 520,000 SPECIES

PROSQUALODON

SEA MAMMALS
APPROX 120 SPECIES

MARINE REPTILES
APPROX 100 SPECIES

Many features of Cretaceous period bony fishes, such as *Hoplopteryx*, are shared by their modern ancestors.

HOPLOPTERYX

Toothed whale ancestors, including *Prosqualodon*, appear around 30 MYA.

BONY FISHES
APPROX 28,000 SPECIES

Squalicorax was similar to the modern tiger shark, with triangular, flattened teeth and finely serrated crowns.

Stingrays are common in the oceans. Some, like *Heliobatis*, spread to freshwater rivers.

SHARKS AND RAYS
APPROX 935 SPECIES

SQUALICORAX TOOTH

HELIOBATIS

JAWLESS FISHES
38 SPECIES

MARINE INVERTEBRATES
APPROX 250,000 SPECIES

Unusually shaped Cretaceous starfish, such as *Metopaster*, are common in the world's oceans.

METOPASTER

CRETACEOUS–PALEOGENE EXTINCTION 210 MYA
All non-avian dinosaurs were wiped out, as well as flying reptiles. Marine invertebrates were seriously affected.

Classification

Before 1650, the study of living organisms was much more localized than it is today. However, when the early explorers started to send home vast collections of exotic plants and animals previously unknown to science, it soon became evident that without some sort of ordered system, the situation would rapidly become chaotic.

Order from chaos

John Ray (1628–1705) was the first person to attempt to classify the natural world. He organized organisms based on their form and structure, or morphology, using lengthy names that incorporated a brief anatomical description. But it was Carl Linnaeus who devised the system of classification that we still use today. Like Ray, Linnaeus made use of morphological features, but used them to group things together rather than to describe them. He set up formal categories on the basis of shared morphological features, creating a hierarchy of increasing exclusiveness that extends from kingdom to species (see diagram, right). Over time, scientists have expanded the system, adding levels such as domain and cohort, and subdividing others into infra-, super-, and sub- categories to accommodate our increasing knowledge of different animals. Despite these revisions, the Linnaean system has remained fundamentally the same since its inception 250 years ago.

Nomenclature

In formulating his hierarchical system, Linnaeus also streamlined the names of individual organisms—species were previously referred to by a common name or descriptive anatomical phrase. He adopted Latin as the universal language of taxonomy, and gave each taxon a unique two-word name, called a binomial, by combining the genus and species names. *Homo sapiens*, for example, is the scientific name for humans. What makes the name unique is the species part—all humans carry the generic name *Homo*, including fossil humans such as *Homo habilis*, but only modern humans are referred to as *Homo sapiens*, or "knowing man." Binomial names can still be descriptive but, more crucially, the unique name avoids confusion.

MISLEADING NAMES
The common name "robin" is applied to very different birds, but using their Latin names readily distinguishes them. The American robin (left) is *Turdus migratorius*, while the European robin (right) is *Erithacus rubecula*.

LINNAEAN SYSTEM
The Linnaean classification system is shown here in its original form. To demonstrate how this system works, the highlighted boxes trace the systematic position of the Indian rhinoceros, from the broadest grouping of kingdom to the narrowest grouping of species, which comprises only Indian rhinoceroses.

PLANTAE
Plants
12 phyla

PORIFERA
Sponges
4 classes

CHORDATA
Chordates
12 classes

CNIDARIA
Cnidarians
4 classes

MAMMALIA
Mammals
28 orders

AVES
Birds
29 orders

REPTILIA
Reptiles
4 orders

SCANDENTIA
Tree shrews
2 families

CHIROPTERA
Bats
18 families

PHOLIDOTA
Pangolins
1 family

CARL LINNAEUS
Carl Linnaeus (1707–1778) was a Swedish botanist. Often referred to as the father of taxonomy, Linnaeus published the first edition of the *Systema Naturae*, his classification of living organisms, in 1735. The resulting system remains in use today.

"Nature does not proceed by leaps and bounds."
CARL LINNAEUS

RHINOCEROS
One-horned rhinoceroses
2 species

RHINOCEROS UNICORNIS
Indian rhinoceros

RHINOCEROS SONDAICUS
Sumatran rhinoceros

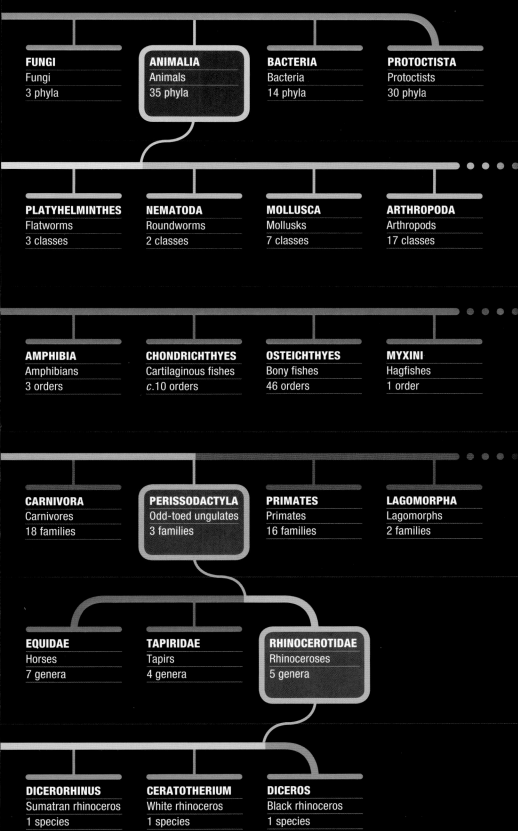

Kingdom

This is the highest level of Linnaeus's hierarchy. Each contains living organisms that work in fundamentally the same way. Initially, there were only two kingdoms, plant and animal, but today there are five.

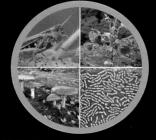

FUNGI
Fungi
3 phyla

ANIMALIA
Animals
35 phyla

BACTERIA
Bacteria
14 phyla

PROTOCTISTA
Protoctists
30 phyla

Phylum

A major subdivision of the animal kingdom, made up of classes. Phylum Chordata, for example, comprises all animals that possess a precursor of the backbone, called a notochord, at some time during their lives.

PLATYHELMINTHES
Flatworms
3 classes

NEMATODA
Roundworms
2 classes

MOLLUSCA
Mollusks
7 classes

ARTHROPODA
Arthropods
17 classes

Class

A taxonomic level made up of orders and their respective subgroups. Class Mammalia, for example, comprises those chordates that have a single jaw bone (the dentary), fur, and mammary glands.

AMPHIBIA
Amphibians
3 orders

CHONDRICHTHYES
Cartilaginous fishes
c.10 orders

OSTEICHTHYES
Bony fishes
46 orders

MYXINI
Hagfishes
1 order

Order

More exclusive are the different orders into which a class is subdivided. Each order contains one or more families and their subgroups. The Perissodactyla, for example, are plant-eating mammals that walk on an odd number of toes.

CARNIVORA
Carnivores
18 families

PERISSODACTYLA
Odd-toed ungulates
3 families

PRIMATES
Primates
16 families

LAGOMORPHA
Lagomorphs
2 families

Family

A family is a subdivision of an order, and it contains one or more genera and their subgroups. Family Rhinocerotidae, for example, comprises those perissodactyls (odd-toed ungulates) that have horns on their noses.

EQUIDAE
Horses
7 genera

TAPIRIDAE
Tapirs
4 genera

RHINOCEROTIDAE
Rhinoceroses
5 genera

Genus

Aristotle (384–322 BCE) was the first to use the term genus to group things together. It was later adopted by Linnaeus to identify a subdivision of a family. The genus *Rhinoceros* contains the one-horned rhinoceroses.

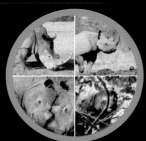

DICERORHINUS
Sumatran rhinoceros
1 species

CERATOTHERIUM
White rhinoceros
1 species

DICEROS
Black rhinoceros
1 species

Species

This group comprises similar individuals able to interbreed in the wild. Indian rhinoceroses, for example, breed only with one another and not with other types of rhinoceroses. Their species name *unicornis* refers to the single horn.

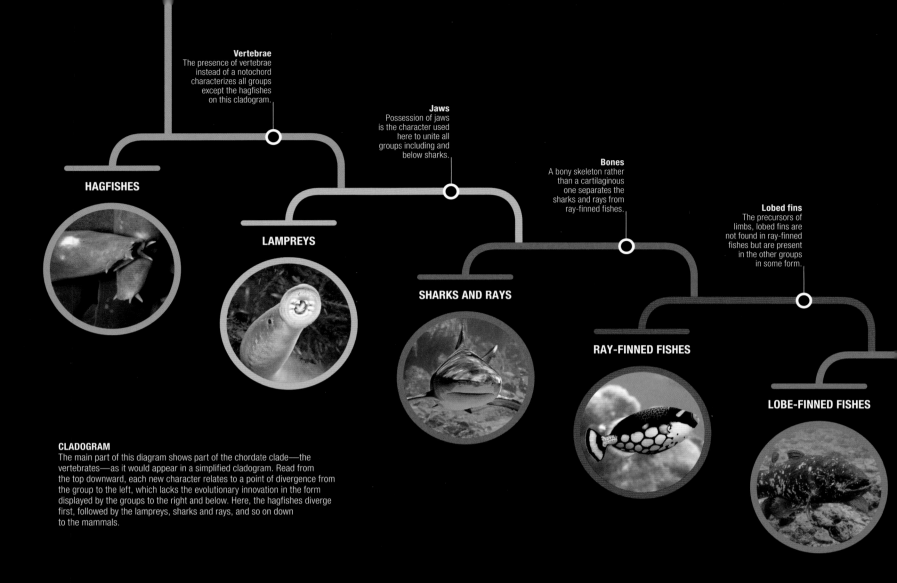

Vertebrae
The presence of vertebrae instead of a notochord characterizes all groups except the hagfishes on this cladogram.

Jaws
Possession of jaws is the character used here to unite all groups including and below sharks.

Bones
A bony skeleton rather than a cartilaginous one separates the sharks and rays from ray-finned fishes.

Lobed fins
The precursors of limbs, lobed fins are not found in ray-finned fishes but are present in the other groups in some form.

HAGFISHES

LAMPREYS

SHARKS AND RAYS

RAY-FINNED FISHES

LOBE-FINNED FISHES

CLADOGRAM
The main part of this diagram shows part of the chordate clade—the vertebrates—as it would appear in a simplified cladogram. Read from the top downward, each new character relates to a point of divergence from the group to the left, which lacks the evolutionary innovation in the form displayed by the groups to the right and below. Here, the hagfishes diverge first, followed by the lampreys, sharks and rays, and so on down to the mammals.

PHYLOGENETIC SYSTEMATICS

A relatively new system for classifying living organisms, which arose in the 1950s, is called phylogenetics, or cladistics. Based on the work of German entomologist Willi Hennig (1913–1976), it unites organisms in groups called clades on the basis of morphology (form and structure) and genetic characters. The system assumes that a character shared by a group of organisms but not by others indicates that they have a closer evolutionary relationship to each other and therefore a more recent ancestor in common. Like the Linnaean system (see pp.20–21), this method of classification is hierarchical, but, unlike those created by Linnaeus, the groupings are used to construct taxonomic trees using evolutionary relationships.

Primitive and derived characters

The characters that are important in cladistic classification are referred to as "derived" because they have altered in some way from what is considered the ancestral "primitive" condition. They also need to be present in at least two groups, or taxa, to be informative about relationships. For example, in the rhinoceroses, the character of a hairy body is found only in the Sumatran rhino (*Dicerorhinos sumatrensis*) and therefore it tells you nothing about its relationship with the rest of the rhino species, whereas a single horn (see character 4 in the diagram, opposite) is unique to both the Indian (*Rhinoceros unicornis*) and

Javan rhinoceroses (*Rhinoceros sondaicus*), suggesting that they inherited it from an ancestor they shared in the past. Derived characters, such as a single horn, that are shared among taxa are referred to as synapomorphies. Although, for simplicity, only single characters are shown in the rhinoceros diagram opposite, the number of characters used to create a cladistic hierarchy, or cladogram, is usually very large—so large that it takes a computer to analyze the data and generate the cladogram.

Common ancestry

Cladistics assumes that the more derived characters species have in common, the more closely related they are to each other than to anything else. This being the case, it also then follows that they have a more recent ancestor in common than they do with other taxa. This can be confirmed by examining the fossil record for taxa or characters once a cladogram has been generated. Brothers, for example, share more characters with each other than they do with their cousins because they have the same parents—parents being their common ancestors. They also have features in common with their cousins because they share the same grandparents—so the whole family would be placed within the same clade, but with the cousins branching off earlier from the line leading to the brothers. In the same way, rhinoceroses form a clade within the odd-toed ungulates.

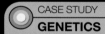
CASE STUDY
GENETICS

Until recently, systematics was based on morphological characters, because investigation of evolutionary history involves looking at fossils in which DNA is not preserved. Today, cladistics is being used increasingly to examine the relationships of living animals. For these organisms, relationships can be established using DNA analysis. Such work has led to major revisions in some of the "traditional" groupings. For example, whales are now grouped with even-toed ungulates and more specifically with hippopotamuses.

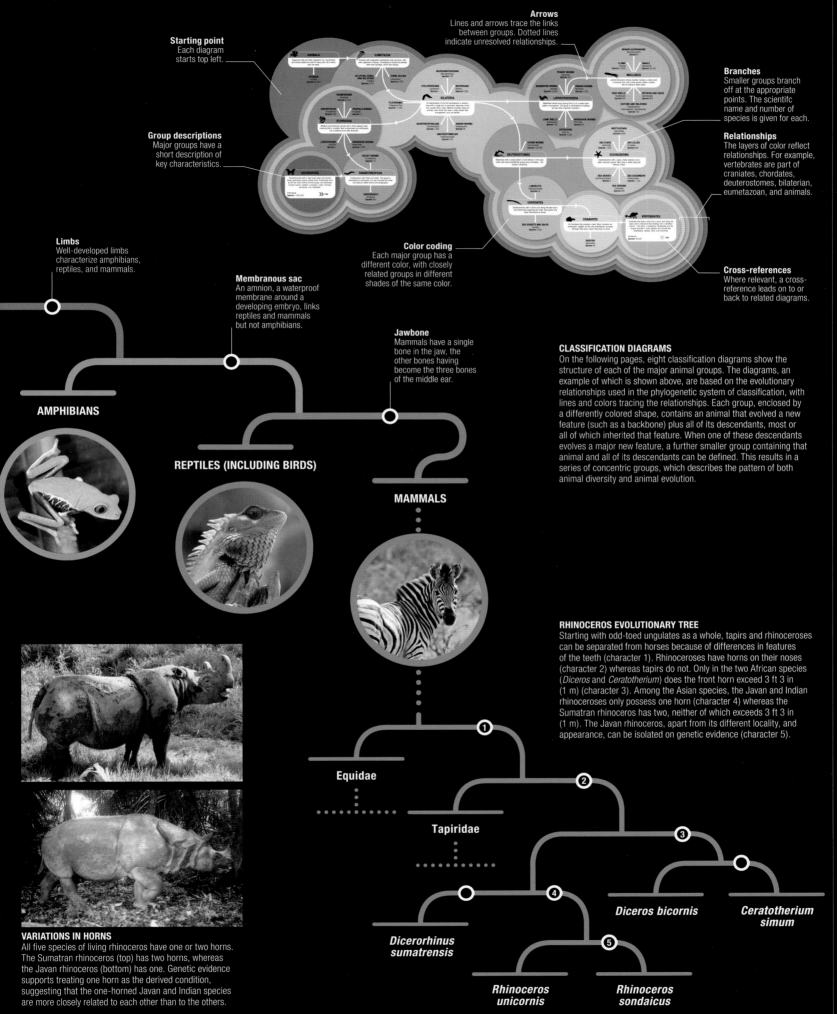

Starting point
Each diagram starts top left.

Arrows
Lines and arrows trace the links between groups. Dotted lines indicate unresolved relationships.

Branches
Smaller groups branch off at the appropriate points. The scientifc name and number of species is given for each.

Group descriptions
Major groups have a short description of key characteristics.

Relationships
The layers of color reflect relationships. For example, vertebrates are part of craniates, chordates, deuterostomes, bilaterian, eumetazoan, and animals.

Color coding
Each major group has a different color, with closely related groups in different shades of the same color.

Cross-references
Where relevant, a cross-reference leads on to or back to related diagrams.

Limbs
Well-developed limbs characterize amphibians, reptiles, and mammals.

Membranous sac
An amnion, a waterproof membrane around a developing embryo, links reptiles and mammals but not amphibians.

Jawbone
Mammals have a single bone in the jaw, the other bones having become the three bones of the middle ear.

AMPHIBIANS

REPTILES (INCLUDING BIRDS)

MAMMALS

CLASSIFICATION DIAGRAMS
On the following pages, eight classification diagrams show the structure of each of the major animal groups. The diagrams, an example of which is shown above, are based on the evolutionary relationships used in the phylogenetic system of classification, with lines and colors tracing the relationships. Each group, enclosed by a differently colored shape, contains an animal that evolved a new feature (such as a backbone) plus all of its descendants, most or all of which inherited that feature. When one of these descendants evolves a major new feature, a further smaller group containing that animal and all of its descendants can be defined. This results in a series of concentric groups, which describes the pattern of both animal diversity and animal evolution.

RHINOCEROS EVOLUTIONARY TREE
Starting with odd-toed ungulates as a whole, tapirs and rhinoceroses can be separated from horses because of differences in features of the teeth (character 1). Rhinoceroses have horns on their noses (character 2) whereas tapirs do not. Only in the two African species (*Diceros* and *Ceratotherium*) does the front horn exceed 3 ft 3 in (1 m) (character 3). Among the Asian species, the Javan and Indian rhinoceroses only possess one horn (character 4) whereas the Sumatran rhinoceros has two, neither of which exceeds 3 ft 3 in (1 m). The Javan rhinoceros, apart from its different locality, and appearance, can be isolated on genetic evidence (character 5).

Equidae

Tapiridae

Diceros bicornis

Ceratotherium simum

Dicerorhinus sumatrensis

Rhinoceros unicornis

Rhinoceros sondaicus

VARIATIONS IN HORNS
All five species of living rhinoceros have one or two horns. The Sumatran rhinoceros (top) has two horns, whereas the Javan rhinoceros (bottom) has one. Genetic evidence supports treating one horn as the derived condition, suggesting that the one-horned Javan and Indian species are more closely related to each other than to the others.

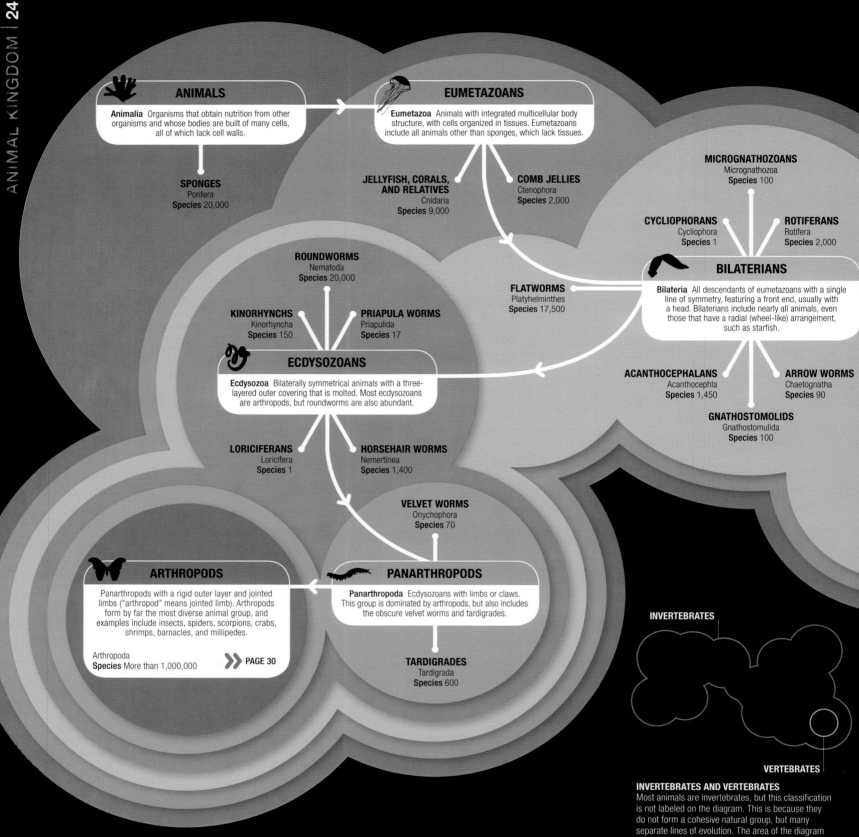

ANIMALS

Animalia Organisms that obtain nutrition from other organisms and whose bodies are built of many cells, all of which lack cell walls.

SPONGES
Porifera
Species 20,000

EUMETAZOANS

Eumetazoa Animals with integrated multicellular body structure, with cells organized in tissues. Eumetazoans include all animals other than sponges, which lack tissues.

JELLYFISH, CORALS, AND RELATIVES
Cnidaria
Species 9,000

COMB JELLIES
Ctenophora
Species 2,000

MICROGNATHOZOANS
Micrognathozoa
Species 100

CYCLIOPHORANS
Cycliophora
Species 1

ROTIFERANS
Rotifera
Species 2,000

ROUNDWORMS
Nematoda
Species 20,000

FLATWORMS
Platyhelminthes
Species 17,500

BILATERIANS

Bilateria All descendants of eumetazoans with a single line of symmetry, featuring a front end, usually with a head. Bilaterians include nearly all animals, even those that have a radial (wheel-like) arrangement, such as starfish.

KINORHYNCHS
Kinorhyncha
Species 150

PRIAPULA WORMS
Priapulida
Species 17

ECDYSOZOANS

Ecdysozoa Bilaterally symmetrical animals with a three-layered outer covering that is molted. Most ecdysozoans are arthropods, but roundworms are also abundant.

ACANTHOCEPHALANS
Acanthocephla
Species 1,450

ARROW WORMS
Chaetognatha
Species 90

GNATHOSTOMOLIDS
Gnathostomulida
Species 100

LORICIFERANS
Loricifera
Species 1

HORSEHAIR WORMS
Nemertinea
Species 1,400

VELVET WORMS
Onychophora
Species 70

ARTHROPODS

Panarthropods with a rigid outer layer and jointed limbs ("arthropod" means jointed limb). Arthropods form by far the most diverse animal group, and examples include insects, spiders, scorpions, crabs, shrimps, barnacles, and millipedes.

Arthropoda
Species More than 1,000,000
➤➤ PAGE 30

PANARTHROPODS

Panarthropoda Ecdysozoans with limbs or claws. This group is dominated by arthropods, but also includes the obscure velvet worms and tardigrades.

TARDIGRADES
Tardigrada
Species 600

INVERTEBRATES

VERTEBRATES

INVERTEBRATES AND VERTEBRATES
Most animals are invertebrates, but this classification is not labeled on the diagram. This is because they do not form a cohesive natural group, but many separate lines of evolution. The area of the diagram occupied by invertebrates is outlined in blue. Having evolved from invertebrates, vertebrates also lie within the blue outline, but have their own discrete section reflecting their distinctive evolved feature.

ANIMAL GROUPS

Just over a million animal species have been identified by scientists, but the total is probably several million. The vast majority of these are invertebrates—animals without a backbone—from simple sponges and jellyfish to sophisticated honey bees. The vast array of invertebrate groups occupies most of the animal evolutionary tree. Although relatively few vertebrates have been identified, they comprise a diverse group ranging in size from tiny fishes less than 3/8 in (1 cm) long to the blue whale, at more than 98 ft (30 m) long, the largest animal to have ever lived.

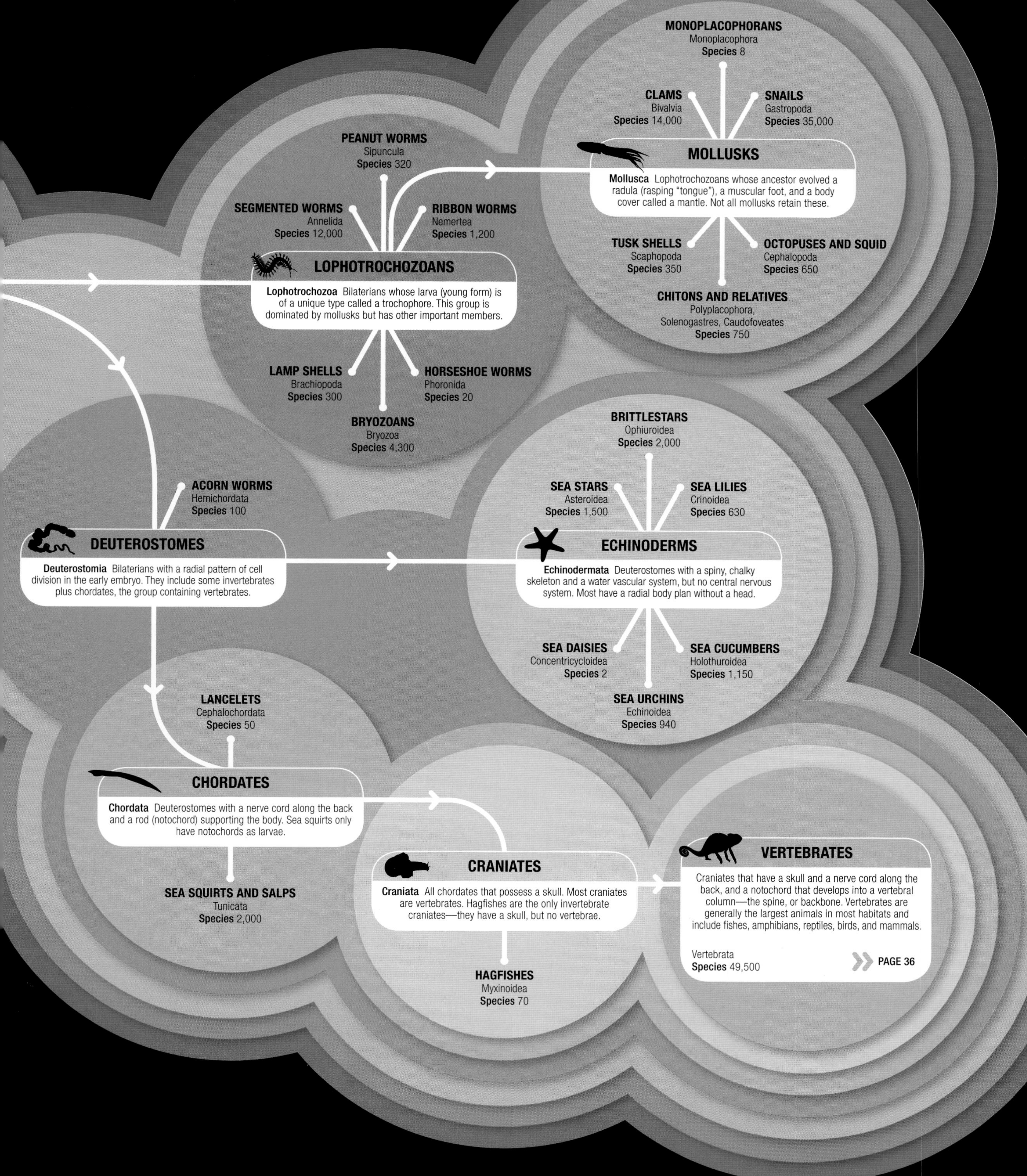

MONOPLACOPHORANS
Monoplacophora
Species 8

CLAMS
Bivalvia
Species 14,000

SNAILS
Gastropoda
Species 35,000

MOLLUSKS

Mollusca Lophotrochozoans whose ancestor evolved a radula (rasping "tongue"), a muscular foot, and a body cover called a mantle. Not all mollusks retain these.

TUSK SHELLS
Scaphopoda
Species 350

OCTOPUSES AND SQUID
Cephalopoda
Species 650

CHITONS AND RELATIVES
Polyplacophora,
Solenogastres, Caudofoveates
Species 750

PEANUT WORMS
Sipuncula
Species 320

SEGMENTED WORMS
Annelida
Species 12,000

RIBBON WORMS
Nemertea
Species 1,200

LOPHOTROCHOZOANS

Lophotrochozoa Bilaterians whose larva (young form) is of a unique type called a trochophore. This group is dominated by mollusks but has other important members.

LAMP SHELLS
Brachiopoda
Species 300

HORSESHOE WORMS
Phoronida
Species 20

BRYOZOANS
Bryozoa
Species 4,300

BRITTLESTARS
Ophiuroidea
Species 2,000

SEA STARS
Asteroidea
Species 1,500

SEA LILIES
Crinoidea
Species 630

ACORN WORMS
Hemichordata
Species 100

DEUTEROSTOMES

Deuterostomia Bilaterians with a radial pattern of cell division in the early embryo. They include some invertebrates plus chordates, the group containing vertebrates.

ECHINODERMS

Echinodermata Deuterostomes with a spiny, chalky skeleton and a water vascular system, but no central nervous system. Most have a radial body plan without a head.

SEA DAISIES
Concentricycloidea
Species 2

SEA CUCUMBERS
Holothuroidea
Species 1,150

SEA URCHINS
Echinoidea
Species 940

LANCELETS
Cephalochordata
Species 50

CHORDATES

Chordata Deuterostomes with a nerve cord along the back and a rod (notochord) supporting the body. Sea squirts only have notochords as larvae.

CRANIATES

Craniata All chordates that possess a skull. Most craniates are vertebrates. Hagfishes are the only invertebrate craniates—they have a skull, but no vertebrae.

VERTEBRATES

Craniates that have a skull and a nerve cord along the back, and a notochord that develops into a vertebral column—the spine, or backbone. Vertebrates are generally the largest animals in most habitats and include fishes, amphibians, reptiles, birds, and mammals.

Vertebrata
Species 49,500

>> PAGE 36

SEA SQUIRTS AND SALPS
Tunicata
Species 2,000

HAGFISHES
Myxinoidea
Species 70

Invertebrates

The vast majority of the world's animals are invertebrates—species without a backbone. Vertebrates—such as birds, fish, mammals, reptiles, and amphibians—make up less than three percent of all known species.

While vertebrates make up a single group within the phylum Chordata, invertebrates are arranged scientifically into 30 or so separate phyla, ranging from simple organisms such as sponges, flatworms, and roundworms to more complex creatures such as arthropods (see pp.38–41) and mollusks. Asexual reproduction is widespread among invertebrates, but sexual reproduction is typical. Hermaphrodites, where male and female sexual organs occur in the same individual, are common. In species where there are separate sexes, the male and the female do not always have to meet, since fertilization can take place externally.

Support

Invertebrates do not have bony skeletons, but many have an internal or external skeleton of some sort. These skeletons are made from a variety of materials: hard structures often consist of crystalline minerals, while the outer covering (called a cuticle) of arthropods is made of chitin (see p.85). In some groups, body shape is maintained by means of a tough, flexible cuticle and high internal pressure. One of the main differences between invertebrate groups is in body symmetry. Some groups, such as cnidarians, have radial symmetry, their bodies being arranged in the same way as the spokes of a wheel. Invertebrates showing bilateral symmetry, such as the arthropods, can be divided down the midline into two equal parts.

Senses

Invertebrate senses can range from simple systems in sedentary species to complex organs such as the highly developed eyes of predators. Many invertebrates can sense dissolved or airborne chemicals, changes in pressure, gravity, and portions of the electromagnetic spectrum including infrared and ultraviolet radiation.

Sponges

Phylum Porifera

Sponges are the simplest of all living animals and lack true tissues or organs. They live attached to solid surfaces, and feed on nutrients that they filter from the water using specialized cells and a system of canals and pores. The soft parts are supported by a skeleton of spicules (slivers of carbon carbonate or silica).

Demosponge
Niphates digitalis 12 in (30 cm)

Flatworms

Phylum Platyhelminthes

These worms are simple, bilaterally symmetrical animals with distinct heads and flattened, elongate, unsegmented bodies. They contain no respiratory system and no circulatory system. Most species, such as tapeworms, are parasitic, but some are free-living predators in freshwater and marine habitats, and others rely on symbiotic algae.

Terrestrial flatworm
Bipalium sp.
14 in (35 cm) long

Marine flatworm
Pseudobiceros zebra
2 in (5 cm) long

Roundworms

Phylum Nematoda

These small, free-living or parasitic, wormlike animals are among the most abundant creatures on the planet. Their unsegmented, cuticle-covered bodies are round in cross section and taper toward both ends. They have no circular muscles and maintain their shape by high internal pressure. They move by thrashing their bodies around in characteristic C- or S-shapes using longitudinal muscle bands.

Intestinal nematode of rats
Nippostrongylus brasiliensis 3/16 in (4 mm)

Jellyfish, corals, and sea anemones

Phylum Cnidaria

Members of this group of aquatic animals have radially symmetrical bodies that are essentially tubes, open at one end. The tube is either flattened into a bell shape (a medusa) or elongate with the closed end attached to a hard surface (a polyp). All cnidarians have tentacles around their mouths that contain stinging cells for prey capture and defense. Most species reproduce asexually by budding. In some species, such as corals, the new creatures remain joined to form a colony.

Bushlike soft coral
Dendronephthya sp.
3ft 3in (1 m) tall

Atlantic snakelocks anemone
Anemonia viridis Tentacles up to 4 in (10 cm) long

Upside-down jellyfish
Cassiopea xamachana
12 in (30 cm) across

Lion's mane jellyfish
Cyanea capillata
6½ ft (2 m) across

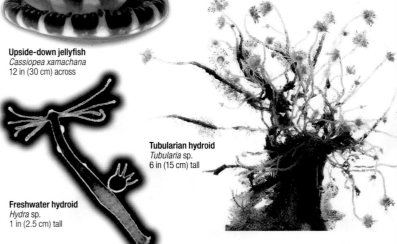

Freshwater hydroid
Hydra sp.
1 in (2.5 cm) tall

Tubularian hydroid
Tubularia sp.
6 in (15 cm) tall

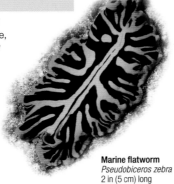

Segmented worms

Phylum Annelida

The bodies of annelids differ from other worms in being divided into a series of linked, but partly independent, functional sections. Each section contains a set of some of the same organs. The head is often well developed, with sense organs, a brain, and a mouth. Locomotion by expansion and contraction of the body is made possible by circular and longitudinal muscles.

Ragworm
Nereis virens
20 in (50 cm)

Parchment worm
Chaetopterus variopedatus
10 in (25 cm)

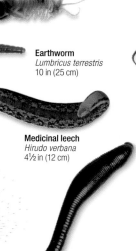

Earthworm
Lumbricus terrestris
10 in (25 cm)

Peacock worm
Sabella pavonina
12 in (30 cm)

Medicinal leech
Hirudo verbana
4½ in (12 cm)

Horse leech
Haemopsis sanguisuga
2¼ in (6 cm)

Starfish, sea urchins, sea cucumbers

Phylum Echinodermata

The bodies of these marine invertebrates are typically spiny, and usually divided into five equal parts arranged symmetrically around a central point. Their bodies may be drawn out into arms (as in starfish), feathery (as in sea lilies), or spherical to cylindrical (as in sea urchins). A unique internal network, called the water-vascular system, helps them move, feed, and exchange gases.

Sunstar
Crossaster papposus
10 in (25 cm) across

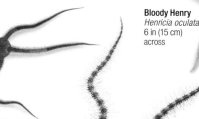

Bloody Henry
Henricia oculata
6 in (15 cm)
across

Red cushion star
Porania pulvillus
4½ in (12 cm) across

Black brittlestar
Ophiocomina nigra
arms up to 1 in (2.5 cm)

Sea cucumber
Pseudocolochirus tricolor
4 in (10 cm)

Northern brittlestar
Ophiothrix fragilis
arms up to 6 in (15 cm)

Edible sea urchin
Echinus esculentus
8 in (20 cm) across

Mollusks

Phylum Mollusca

Mollusks have one of the widest ranges of body forms of all invertebrates, but most species have a head, a soft "body" mass, and a muscular foot, which is used for locomotion. In the most advanced mollusks, the cephalopods, which includes the octopus, the head is well developed and has sophisticated sense organs, and parts of the head and foot are modified to form prey-capturing arms. All mollusks have one or all of the following features: a horny, toothed ribbon (the radula) used for rasping food; a calcium carbonate shell or other structure covering the upper surface of the body; and a mantle, which is an outer fold of skin covering the mantle cavity. Mollusks are adapted to life on land, and in fresh or sea water.

Giant clam
Tridacna gigas
up to 5 ft (1.5 m) across

Queen scallop
Aequipecten opercularis
3½ in (9 cm)

Cat's tongue oyster
Spondylus linguaefelis 3 in (7.5 cm)

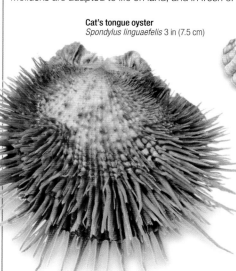

Thickened cardita
Megacardita incrassata
1½ in (4 cm)

Lazarus jewel box
Chama lazarus
3 in (7.5 cm)

Stepped venus
Chione subimbricata
1¼ in (3 cm)

Common limpet
Patella vulgata
2¼ in (6 cm) across

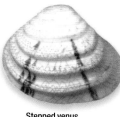

Precious turban
Turbo petholatus
2¼ in (6 cm)

Triumphant star turban
Guilfordia triumphans
2 in (5 cm)

Precious wentletrap
Epitonium scalare
2¼ in (5.7 cm)

Snipe's bill murex
Haustellum haustellum
5 in (13 cm)

Trapezium horse conch
Pleuroploca trapezium
5 in (13 cm)

Tent olive
Oliva porphyria
3½ in (9 cm)

Imperial harp
Harpa costata
3 in (7.5 cm)

The junonia
Scaphella junonia
4½ in (11 cm)

Tusk shell
Pictodentalium formosum
3 in (7.5 cm)

Great pond snail
Lymnaea stagnalis
2 in (5 cm)

Violet snail
Janthina janthina
1½ in (4 cm)

Common snail
Cepaea nemoralis
shell 1 in (2.5 cm) across

Polynesian tree snails
Partula sp.
shell 1¼ in (3 cm)

Giant African snail
Achatina fulicula
12 in (30 cm)

European striped snail
Helix aspersa
shell 1½ in (4 cm) across

Black slug
Arion ater
6 in (15 cm)

Green-blue lettuce sea slug
Elysia crispata
2 in (5 cm)

Marbled chiton
Chiton marmoratus
2¼ in (6 cm)

Squid
Loligo paelei
12 in (30 cm)

Cuttlefish
Sepia officinalis
15½ in (40 cm)

Common octopus
Octopus vulgaris
3ft 3in(100 cm)

Blue-ringed octopus
Hapalochlaena lunulata
4 in (10 cm)

SEA SLUG
This brightly colored neon sea slug (*Nembrotha* sp.) is a marine mollusk of the order Nudibranchia. The slug is moving among a colony of sea squirts, on which it feeds.

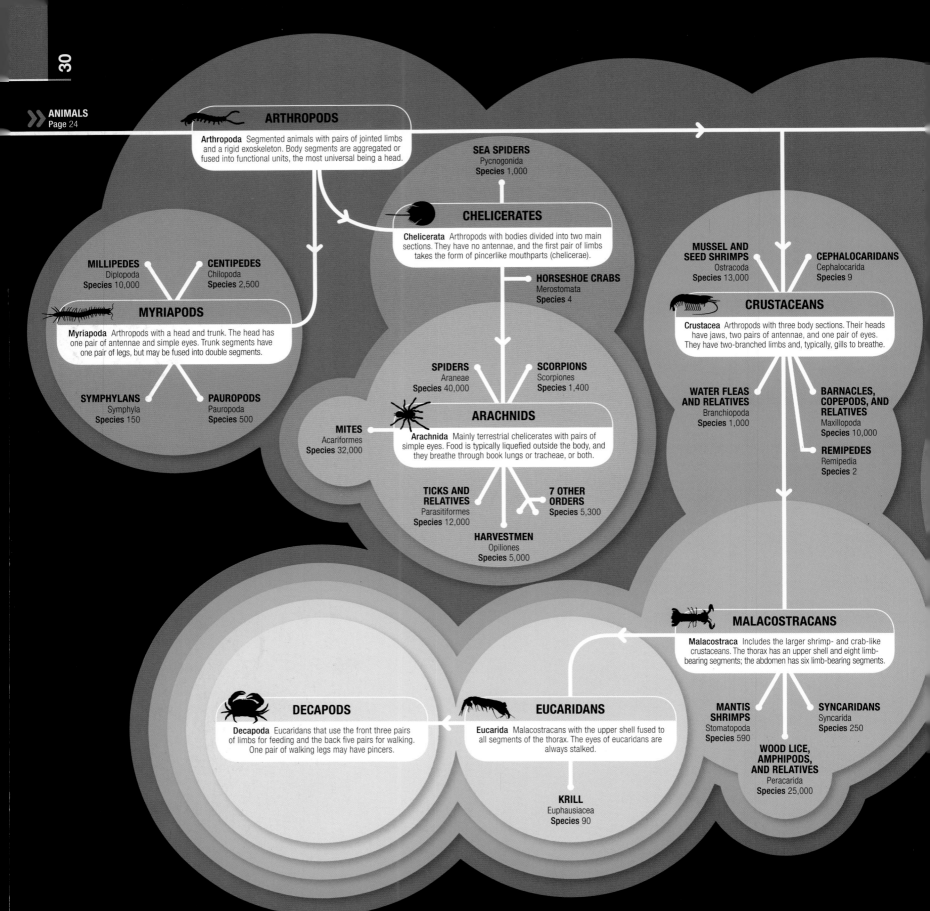

Arthropod groups

Arthropods appeared in the seas more than 540 million years ago. There are four main groups of living species: chelicerates, myriapods, crustaceans, and hexapods. The relationship between these groups has been the subject of debate. For example, the common view that hexapods and myriapods are most closely related to each other has been challenged by recent studies, which have suggested that hexapods are more closely related to crustaceans.

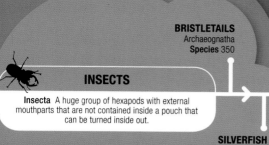

SPRINGTAILS
Collembola
Species 6,000

PROTURANS
Protura
Species 400

BRISTLETAILS
Archaeognatha
Species 350

DRAGONFLIES
Odonata
Species 5,500

MAYFLIES
Ephemeroptera
Species 2,500

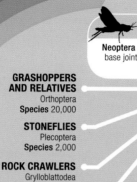

HEXAPODS

Hexapoda Arthropods with a fused thorax comprising three segments, each bearing a pair of legs. Their heads have one pair of antennae.

INSECTS

Insecta A huge group of hexapods with external mouthparts that are not contained inside a pouch that can be turned inside out.

WINGED INSECTS

Pterygota Insects that have wings in addition to legs. The second and third segments of the thorax typically each carry a pair of wings.

SILVERFISH
Thysanura
Species 370

DIPLURANS
Diplura
Species 800

NEOPTERANS

Neoptera Winged insects in which special muscles and base joints allow the wings to be folded back along the body when not in use.

LACEWINGS AND ANTLIONS
Neuroptera
Species 4,000

SNAKEFLIES
Rapdhidioptera
Species 150

ALDERFLIES, FISHFLIES, AND DOBSONFLIES
Megaloptera
Species 300

GRASHOPPERS AND RELATIVES
Orthoptera
Species 20,000

STONEFLIES
Plecoptera
Species 2,000

ROCK CRAWLERS
Grylloblattodea
Species 25

MANTOPHASMATODEANS
Mantophasmatodea
Species 14

EARWIGS
Dermaptera
Species 1,900

STICK INSECTS
Phasmatodea
Species 2,500

NEUROPTERIDS

Neuropterida The least advanced group of holometabolans with net- or lace-like wing veining and a simple pupal stage.

BEETLES
Coleoptera
Species 370,000

HOLOMETABOLANS

Holometabola Neopterans that develop with complete metamorphosis by means of a pupal stage. Larvae and adults are dissimilar and have different lifestyles.

TWISTED-WING PARASITES
Strepsiptera
Species 560

BARKLICE
Psocoptera
Species 3,000

LICE
Phthiraptera
Species 6,000

THRIPS
Thysanoptera
Species 5,000

BEES, ANTS, AND WASPS
Hymenoptera
Species 198,000

MANTIDS
Mantodea
Species 2,000

TERMITES
Isoptera
Species 2,800

BUGS
Hemiptera
Species 82,000

COCKROACHES
Blattodea
Species 4,000

ZORAPTERANS
Zoraptera
Species 30

MOTHS AND BUTTERFLIES
Lepidoptera
Species 165,000

FLEAS
Siphonaptera
Species 2,000

FLIES
Diptera
Species 122,000

WEBSPINNERS
Embioptera
Species 300

CADDIS FLIES
Trichoptera
Species 8,000

SCORPIONFLIES
Mecoptera
Species 550

Arthropods

This group of invertebrates forms the largest phylum of all living organisms and accounts for more than three out of four known species of animal. Their collective biomass far outweighs that of the vertebrates.

Arthropods share several common features. All species have a bilaterally symmetrical body that is divided into segments. Over evolutionary time these segments have become fused into functional groups (tagma); one of these tagma always includes a head. Myriapods have a head and a body trunk that is made up from a number of similar segments. In arachnids the head and thorax are fused, forming a cephalothorax, and the remaining body segments are fused to form the abdomen. In insects, a very advanced group of arthropods, the head is comprised of six fused segments; a thorax, three segments, and an abdomen, typically with 11 segments.

Exoskeleton

The body is covered by the cuticle—a tough, lightweight exoskeleton made of protein and chitin—which is secreted by the epidermal cells. To permit movement, the exoskeleton has joints and hinges where the cuticle is soft and flexible. In large marine species the exoskeleton is strengthened by calcium carbonate, while in terrestrial species it is topped by a thin layer of waterproof wax to prevent them from drying out. As an individual grows, it must shed its cuticle periodically. Arthropods have a number of jointed limbs, from three pairs in insects to many hundreds of pairs in myriapods.

Internal systems

All arthropods have an open circulatory system: their internal organs are bathed in a fluid known as hemolymph, which is moved to the front of the animal by a dorsal, tubelike heart. Gaseous exchange is carried out by means of gills, leaflike book lungs, or a branching system of minute, air-filled tubes called tracheae. The central nervous system consists of a brain, situated in the head, connected to paired nerve cords running along the underside of the body.

Sea spiders

Class Pycnogonida

Sea spiders are marine arthropods with a small, segmented body and long, slender legs that give them a superficial resemblance to terrestrial spiders. All species have a small head and three trunk segments.

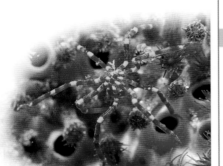

Sea spider
Styllopalene longicauda
¼ in (7.5 mm)

Horseshoe crabs

Class Merostomata

Horseshoe crabs are large, marine arthropods that are survivors of a diverse group that flourished in the seas 300 million years ago. They have a fused head and thorax, and six pairs of limbs, which are covered by a tough carapace.

Horseshoe crab
Limulus polyphemus
up to 23½ in (60 cm)

Arachnids

Class Arachnida

This diverse group of largely terrestrial arthropods includes spiders, scorpions, harvestmen, ticks, mites, pseudoscorpions, whip-scorpions, and whip-spiders. The body is divided into two sections. The head and thorax are fused to form the cephalothorax, which is joined to the abdomen, in some species by a narrow stalk. In scorpions, the abdomen has a tail-like extension bearing a sting. The cephalothorax carries a pair of pincerlike chelicerae used for consuming prey, a pair of limblike pedipalps, and four pairs of normal walking legs. Arachnids are mostly predatory, although a few are scavengers and some mites are parasitic. They have narrow mouths and cannot eat large pieces of food, so they rely on enzymes to predigest their prey outside the body or in a preoral cavity.

Yellow scorpion
Buthus occitanus
1½–4 in (4–10 cm)

Chilean scorpion
Centromachetes pococki
1–4½ in (2.5–12 cm)

Pseudoscorpion
Dactylochelifer sp.
1⁄16– 3⁄16 in (2–4 mm)

Soft tick
Argas persicus ¼ in (6 mm)

Vinegaroon
Thelyphonus sp.
1–1½ in (2.5–3.5 cm)

Whip-spider
Phyrnus sp.
1¼–1½ in (3–4 cm)

House spider
Tegenaria duellica
3⁄8–½ in (1–1.5 cm)

Funnel-web spider
Atrax robustus
¾–1½ in (2–4 cm)

Red-kneed tarantula
Brachypelma smithi 4 in (10 cm)

Jumping spider
Salticus sp. 3⁄16–5⁄16 in (5–8 mm)

Crustaceans

Superclass Crustacea

Crustaceans are a very diverse group, ranging from tiny copepods—barely visible to the naked eye—to heavy-bodied crabs and lobsters. They have two pairs of antennae, compound eyes on stalks, and a cuticle that is often strengthened with calcium carbonate. The head and thorax are often covered by a shieldlike shell or carapace, which extends forward to form a projection called the rostrum. The thoracic limbs are two-branched and specialized to carry out a range of functions, such as feeding, locomotion, sensing the environment, and respiration by mean of basal gills. The first pair of legs may be enlarged to form chelipeds with strong claws for food handling, defense, and signaling. The vast majority of species live in freshwater or the sea.

Barnacle
Chthamalus sp.
½ in (1.5 cm)

Brine shrimp
Artemia sp.
⅜ in (1 cm)

FISH CLEANER
The fire shrimp (*Lysmata debelius*) is known to feed on small parasites and dead skin found on fish. It can grow up to 2 in (5 cm) in length.

Common shrimp
Crangon crangon
3½ in (9 cm)

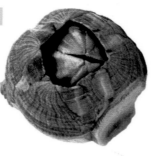

Antartic krill
Euphausia superba
2¼ in (6 cm)

Common prawn
Palaemon serratus
4½ in (11 cm)

Decorater crab
Naxia tumida
carapace up to 1½ in (4 cm)

Brown crab
Cancer pagurus
carapace 12 in (30 cm)

Spiny spider crab
Maja squinado
carapace 6 in (15 cm)

Blue crab
Callinectes sapidus
carapace 7 in (18 cm)

Common hermit crab
Pagurus bernhardus 4 in (10 cm)

Squat lobster
Munida quadrispina
2¾ in (7 cm)

Common lobster
Homarus gammarus 23½ in (60 cm)

Centipedes and millipedes

Superclass Myriapoda

Myriapods are terrestrial arthropods with biting mandibles and a single pair of antennae. They are confined to moist habitats because they do not have a waterproof cuticle. Centipedes are fast moving and carnivorous with elongate, slightly flattened bodies. The trunk segments each bear a single pair of legs, the first pair modified as poison claws used to subdue prey. Millipedes are mostly herbivorous or scavenging species with elongate, cylindrical or flattened bodies. The first three segments of the trunk have no legs, but the remaining segments are fused in pairs, known as diplosegments, each bearing two pairs of legs. Despite their common name they never have a thousand legs.

Lithobiid centipede
Lithobius fortificatus
¼–1½ in (0.6–3.8 cm)

Pill millipede
Glomeris marginata
¹⁄₁₆–¾ in (0.2–2 cm)

Flat-backed millipede
Polydesmus sp.
³⁄₁₆–1¼ in (0.5–3.2 cm)

Insects

Class Insecta

Insects are the most abundant animals on Earth, and they have evolved many diverse lifestyles. Although they are mainly terrestrial, there are a significant number of aquatic species. The body of an insect is divided into three main sections—the head, thorax, and abdomen. The head bears external mouthparts, one pair of antennae, and a pair of compound eyes. The thorax bears three pairs of legs and, typically, two pairs of wings. The abdomen contains the major organ systems for digestion and reproduction. The immature stages of some aquatic species have gills, but all adult insects breathe air and have a well-developed tracheal system joined to the outside through a number of small holes called spiracles. Insects are the only invertebrates capable of powered flight and this, together with their small size and waterproof cuticle, has allowed them to colonize a vast range of habitats.

Jumping bristletail
Dilta littoralis ⅜ in (1.2 cm)

Silverfish
Lepisma saccharina
³⁄₁₆–⅜ in (0.5–1 cm)

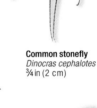

Siphlonurid mayfly
Siphlonurus lacustris ⅜ in (1 cm)

Southern hawker dragonfly
Aeshna cyanea
wingspan 4 in (10 cm)

Mountain grasshopper
Stauroderus scalaris
1 in (2.5 cm)

Speckled bush cricket
Leptophyes punctatissima
¾ in (2 cm)

Common stonefly
Dinocras cephalotes
¾ in (2 cm)

Earwig
Forficula auricularia
⅜–½ in (1–1.5 cm)

Stick insect
Pharnacia sp.
up to 11½ in (29 cm)

Green leaf insect
Phyllium bioculatum
2–3½ in (5–9 cm)

Praying mantis
Mantis religiosa
¾ in (7 cm)

American cockroach
Periplaneta americana
1–1½ in (2.5–4 cm)

Rottenwood termite
Zootermopsis sp.
⅜–¾ in (1–2 cm)

Bird louse
Menacanthus stramineus
⅛–³⁄₁₆ in (3–4 mm)

Giant water bug
Lethocerus grandis
3¼–4 in (8–10 cm)

Shield bug
Graphosoma italicum
⅜ in (1 cm)

Thorn bug
Umbonia crassicornis
½ in (1.5 cm)

Cicada
Angamiana aetherea
1¼–2¼ in (3–5.5 cm)

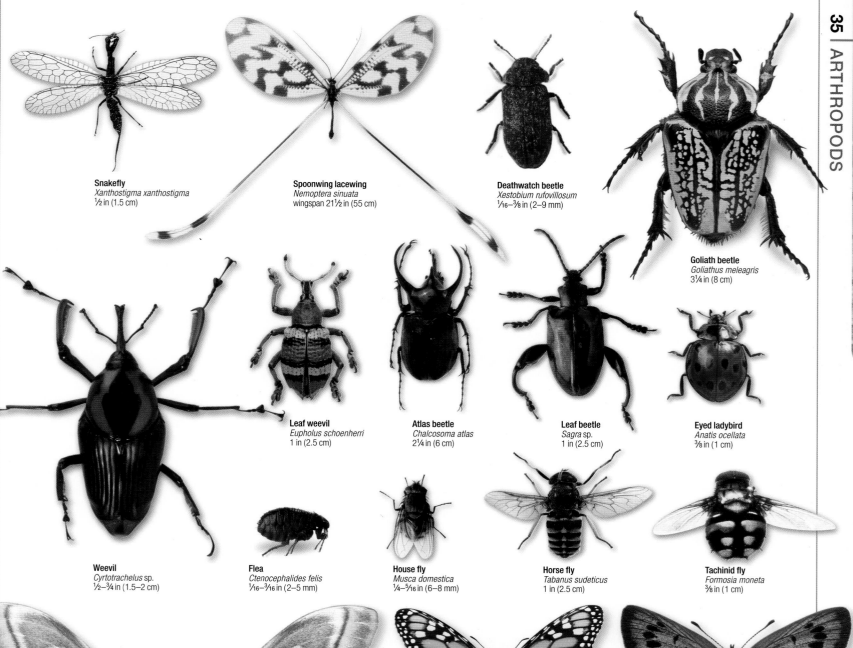

Snakefly
Xanthostigma xanthostigma
½ in (1.5 cm)

Spoonwing lacewing
Nemoptera sinuata
wingspan 21½ in (55 cm)

Deathwatch beetle
Xestobium rufovillosum
¹⁄₁₆–³⁄₈ in (2–9 mm)

Goliath beetle
Goliathus meleagris
3¼ in (8 cm)

Leaf weevil
Eupholus schoenherri
1 in (2.5 cm)

Atlas beetle
Chalcosoma atlas
2¼ in (6 cm)

Leaf beetle
Sagra sp.
1 in (2.5 cm)

Eyed ladybird
Anatis ocellata
³⁄₈ in (1 cm)

Weevil
Cyrtotrachelus sp.
½–¾ in (1.5–2 cm)

Flea
Ctenocephalides felis
¹⁄₁₆–³⁄₁₆ in (2–5 mm)

House fly
Musca domestica
¼–⁵⁄₁₆ in (6–8 mm)

Horse fly
Tabanus sudeticus
1 in (2.5 cm)

Tachinid fly
Formosia moneta
³⁄₈ in (1 cm)

Pine emperor moth
Nudaurelia cytherea
wingspan 3½–5 in (9–13 cm)

Monarch butterfly
Danaus plexippus
wingspan 3¼–4½ in (8.5–12 cm)

Reakirt's blue butterfly
Hemiargus isola
wingspan ¾–1¼ in (2–3 cm)

Giant sphinx moth
Cocytius antaeus
wingspan 5–7 in (13–18 cm)

Basker moth
Euchromia lethe
wingspan 1½–2 in
(4–5 cm)

Bumble bee
Bombus terrestris
½–¾ in (1.5–2 cm)

Jewel wasp
Parnopes carnea
³⁄₈–½ in (1–1.5 cm)

German wasp
Vespula germanica
½ in (1 cm)

Wood ant
Formica rufa
⁵⁄₁₆–³⁄₈ in (0.8–1 cm)

ANIMALS
Page 25

VERTEBRATES

Vertebrata All animals with a vertebral column (backbone or spine). Vertebrates include all fishes except hagfishes, plus mammals, birds, reptiles, and amphibians.

LAMPREYS
Petromyzontida
Species 38

JAWED VERTEBRATES

Gnathosomata Vertebrates with jaws. They include all land vertebrates and all fishes except lampreys, which are jawless, and hagfishes, which lack jaws and vertebrae.

RAY-FINNED FISHES

Bony fishes with ray fins built from a fan of narrow bone or cartilage rods. Because ray-finned fishes are so diverse, they represent the majority of vertebrate species. They range from tiny guppies to giant sturgeons, and from sea horses to swordfish.

Actinopterygii
Species 28,000   **PAGE 38**

BONY VERTEBRATES

Osteichthyes Bony fishes and all descendants. They include all vertebrates with a mineralized skeleton— mammals, birds, reptiles, amphibians, and most fishes.

SHARKS AND RAYS
Elasmobranchii
Species 1,080

CARTILAGINOUS FISHES

Chondrichthyes Jawed fishes with a skeleton made of cartilage rather than bone.

LOBE-FINNED FISHES AND TETRAPODS

Sarcopterygii Vertebrates with either lobed fins or limbs (tetrapods), which arose from lobed fins.

COELACANTHS
Crossopterygii
Species 2

LUNGFISHES
Dipnoi
Species 6

CHIMAERAS
Holocephali
Species 34

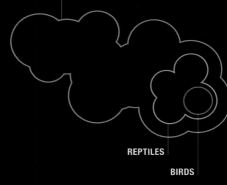

VERTEBRATES

REPTILES

BIRDS

REPTILES AND BIRDS
Under the traditional or Linnaen classification system, which groups animals by overall similarity, reptiles and birds form two separate "classes" of vertebrates (see pp.20–21). Through the phylogenetic classification system, which recognizes the evolutionary relationships between animals, birds are grouped within reptiles. This is due to the fact that they share a common ancestor with the other groups that comprise "reptiles," including lizards and snakes, turtles, crocodilans, and tuataras.

MAMMALS

Animals with three middle-ear bones and a unique jaw hinge. Today's mammals also have fur and mammary glands, but we cannot be sure about the many fossil forms. The early ancestors of mammals diverged from reptilelike amniotes more than 200 million years ago.

Mammalia
Species 5,000   **PAGE 68**

VERTEBRATE GROUPS

Although vertebrates are a very diverse group of animals, only about 50,000 species have been identified—a tiny fraction of all animal species. The first vertebrates were primitive fishes, and fishes make up more than half of all living vertebrate species. This evolutionary tree has tetrapods at its center, and it was the earliest tetrapods that first grew limbs and left the water for land. These are the common ancestors from which the vast array of amphibians, reptiles, birds, and mammals evolved, populating the land, taking to the sky, and, in some cases, returning to the sea.

AMPHIBIANS

Cold-blooded tetrapods with porous, glandular skin. Today's amphibians (frogs and toads, salamanders and newts, and caecilians) are descendants of early tetrapods that did not develop an amnion (waterproof egg membrane).

Amphibia
Species 6,000   » **PAGE 44**

TETRAPODS

Tetrapoda Bony vertebrates with four limbs or limblike appendages. The first land-living vertebrates, tetrapods include the earliest limbed vertebrate and all of its descendants, including those that have since lost their limbs, such as snakes.

TUATARAS
Sphenodontida
Species 2

LEPIDOSAURS

Lepidosauria Reptiles that shed skin in large pieces or as a whole. Lepidosaurs include tuataras, snakes, lizards, as well as worm lizards (amphisbaenians).

TURTLES
Testudines
Species 300

AMNIOTES

Amniota Tetrapods whose embryo grows inside a waterproof membrane called an amnion, enabling life outside bodies of water.

REPTILES

Amniotes with thick skin, horny epidermal (skin surface) scales, and whose eggs have a mineralized shell. This group includes warm-blooded birds, and other, scaly, cold-blooded reptiles.

Reptilia
Species 17,500   » **PAGE 50**

SNAKES AND LIZARDS
Squamata
Species 7,800

BIRDS

Archosaurs with asymmetrical flight feathers (lost in some flightless species). Many dinosaurs had feathers, but they were not flight feathers. More recently evolved birds—not including the primitive tinamous and ratites—have many more shared features, including a horny, toothless bill, and a keeled breastbone.

Aves
Species 9,500   » **PAGE 56**

ARCHOSAURS

Archosauria Reptiles whose teeth are sunk into sockets. Their living representatives include only crocodiles and birds, which are dinosaurs.

CROCODILIANS
Crocodylia
Species 23

RAY-FINNED FISHES

Actinopterygii Bony fishes with ray fins built from a fan of narrow bone or cartilage rods. This very diverse group includes more than 28,000 species.

BICHIRS, REEDFISHES, AND RELATIVES
Cladistia
Species 16

STURGEONS AND PADDLEFISHES
Chondrostei
Species 27

GARS
Ginglymodi
Species 7

BOWFINS
Halecomorphi
Species 1

HAGFISHES

Myxinoidea The only craniates that are not vertebrates, hagfishes have a skull but no vertebral column (backbone).

LAMPREYS

Petromyzontia The only jawless vertebrates, lampreys form the sister group to all jawed vertebrates. There are about 40 species of living lampreys.

TELEOSTS

Teleostei Ray-finned fishes with mobile mouths, due to moveable upper jaws, and symmetrical (homocercal) tail fins.

BONY TONGUES
Osteoglossiformes
Species 220

EELS, TARPONS, AND RELATIVES
Elopomorpha
Species 856

HERRINGS AND RELATIVES
Clupeomorpha
Species 397

CATFISHES AND RELATIVES
Ostariophysi
Species 8,000

EUTELEOSTS

Euteleostei Modern ray-finned fishes—the majority of teleosts. Each of the other four teleost groups show various primitive features.

PIKES AND RELATIVES
Protacanthopterygii
Species 366

DRAGONFISHES AND RELATIVE
Stenopterygii
Species 400

LIZARDFISHES AND RELATIVES
Cyclosquamata
Species 240

LANTERNFISHES
Scopelomorpha
Species 250

BONY FISHES

Osteichthyes Jawed fishes with bony, calcified skeletons. This group includes all fishes except for hagfishes, lampreys, and cartilaginous fishes.

LOBE-FINNED FISHES AND TETRAPODS

Sarcopterygii Bony fishes with lobed fins. These fishes were the ancestors of all limbed land vertebrates (tetrapods).

COELACANTHS
Crossopterygii
Species 2

LUNGFISHES
Dipnoi
Species 6

TETRAPODS
Tetrapoda
Species 38,000

Fish groups

The earliest fishes evolved from primitive jawed vertebrates more than 500 million years ago, and from these, two main groups emerged. Cartilaginous fishes remain largely unchanged as modern-day sharks, rays and skates, and chimaeras. Bony fishes diverged into lobe-finned fishes

and ray-finned fishes. The former gave rise to tetrapods, the first limbed vertebrates and the ancestors of amphibians, reptiles, birds, and mammals. Ray-finned fishes evolved into a diverse group that includes more than half of all vertebrate species, and the vast majority of living fishes.

SPINY-RAYED FISHES

Acanthomorpha Euteleosts with true bony spines in their dorsal, anal, and pelvic fins.

OPAHS AND OARFISHES
Lampridiomorpha
Species 21

BEARDFISHES
Polymixiomorpha
Species 10

COD, ANGLERFISHES, AND RELATIVES
Paracanthopterygii
Species 1,400

ACANTHOPTERYGIANS

Acanthopterygii Spiny-rayed fishes with jaws that can be protruded when feeding. This group includes about half of all fish species.

MULLETS
Mugilomorpha
Species 70

SILVERSIDES
Atherinomorpha
Species 315

DORIES AND RELATIVES
Zeiformes
Species 32

STICKLEBACKS
Gasterosteiformes
Species 285

FLATFISHES
Pleuronectiformes
Species 680

PERCOMORPHS

Percomorpha The largest and most diverse group of fishes and the most advanced spiny-rayed fishes. Percomorphs share several structural features.

TRIGGERFISHES
Tetraodontiformes
Species 360

SWAMP EELS
Synbranchiformes
Species 100

SCORPIONFISHES
Scorpaeniformes
Species 1,500

CARTILAGINOUS FISHES

Chondrichthyes Jawed fishes with internal skeletons made of cartilage, rather than bone.

CHIMAERAS
Chimaeriformes
Species 34

PERCHLIKE FISHES

Perciformes Percomorphs with spines and soft rays in their dorsal and anal fins. They include 10,000 diverse species of marine and freshwater fishes.

ELASMOBRANCHS

Elasmobranchii The largest group of cartilaginous fishes, including sharks and rays.

SHARKS
Selachimorpha
Species 400

RAYS AND SKATES
Batoidea
Species 535

Fishes

Fishes are vertebrate animals that are adapted to live, swim, and breathe in fresh or salt water. They are the most numerous and diverse vertebrate animals on Earth and can be found in every conceivable aquatic habitat.

Fishes do not form a natural group. The general term "fishes" includes four groups of vertebrates that are as different from one another as mammals, reptiles, and birds. The largest group is the bony fishes, which includes familiar species such as cod, salmon, and trout. Sharks, rays, and chimaeras make up the second group, the cartilaginous fishes. The remaining two small groups are the jawless marine hagfishes and the lampreys. Land vertebrates (tetrapods) and bony fishes share a common ancestry—primitive bony fishes, the lobe-finned coelacanths, and lungfishes are grouped together with the tetrapods in modern classification systems. Lobe-finned fishes are the most likely ancestors of the first land vertebrates.

Characteristics

Fishes from all these groups typically breathe using gills to extract oxygen from the water, swim using fins, are covered with protective scales or bony plates, and are cold-blooded.

However, there are also lungfishes that breathe air, fishes with no scales, and sharks, such as the salmon shark, that can control their body temperature. The familiar vertebrate senses of vision, hearing, touch, taste, and smell are used by all fishes to gather information about their environment. Most fishes have a system of sensory organs called the lateral line running along both sides of the body, which detects vibrations made by other fishes and animals moving through the water. Fins are also characteristic of most, but not all, fishes. These usually consist of two sets of paired fins (pectoral and pelvic), one, two, or rarely three dorsal fins, an anal fin, and a caudal (tail) fin. The fins are used for propulsion, maneuverability, and stability. Some fishes, such as the gurnard, even use their fins to walk along the seabed, and flying fishes use theirs like wings to glide above water.

Jawless fishes

Classes Myxini, Petromyzontia

Hagfishes and lampreys are long, slimy, eel-like fishes with no biting jaws. Lampreys have a round sucker mouth surrounded by horny, rasping teeth and are mostly parasitic on other fishes. Hagfishes have a slitlike mouth surrounded by four pairs of tentacles and are mostly scavengers. They do not have a true backbone; instead, a simple flexible rod called a notochord runs the length of the body.

Lampern
Lampetra fluviatilis
up to 19½ in (50 cm)

Hagfish
Myxine glutinosa up to 31 in (80 cm)

Cartilaginous fishes

Class Chondrichthyes

Cartilaginous fishes comprise sharks, rays, and deep-water chimaeras. These fishes have an internal skeleton made principally of flexible cartilage. Males have a copulatory organ called a clasper and females give birth to live young or lay large egg capsules. Special sense organs, called ampullae of Lorenzini, allow cartilaginous fish to track other animals by detecting their electrical fields. Sharks have strong, replaceable teeth and rough skin covered in tiny, toothlike dermal denticles. Skates and rays are flat with winglike pectoral fins and a long, thin tail. The chimaeras are scaleless with a large head and ratlike tail.

Blonde ray
Raja brachyura
up to 4 ft (1.2 m)

Electric ray
Torpedo californica
up to 4½ ft (1.4 m)

SAWSHARK
Pristiophorus japonicus grows to a length of up to 5 ft (1.5 m). A pair of barbels on the distinctive saw-shaped snout are used in combination with taste sensors to locate prey, such as small fishes and invertebrates, on the seabed.

Leopard shark
Triakis semifasciata
up to 7 ft (2.1 m)

White-spotted bambooshark
Chiloscyllium plagiosum up to 3 ft 1 in (95 cm)

Great white shark
Carcharodon carcharias
up to 26 ft (8 m)

Horn shark
Heterodontus francisci
up to 3 ft 2 in (97 cm)

Frill shark
Chlamydoselachus anguineus
up to 6½ ft (2 m)

Spotted ratfish
Hydrolagus colliei
up to 3 ft 1 in (95 cm)

Bony fishes

Class Osteichthyes

All bony fishes have an internal skeleton of hard, calcified bone, though in some primitive species this may be part cartilage. With the exception of the lobe-finned fishes, the skeleton extends into the fins as flexible, movable rays and spines. This system allows the fish to maneuver with far greater precision than sharks and rays. Most bony fishes also have a gas-filled swim bladder, which is used to adjust their buoyancy and is covered in overlapping flexible scales. While most cartilaginous fishes can be easily recognized as such, bony fishes have evolved many different and sometimes bizarre body shapes and fin functions that enable them to survive in almost every aquatic habitat.

COELACANTH
Latimeria chalumnae is 5–6 ft (1.5–1.8 m) long. It is found on steep, rocky reefs at depths of 500–2,300 ft (150–700 m).

American paddlefish
Polyodon spathula
4–6 ft (1.2–1.8 m)

Longnose gar
Lepisosteus osseus
up to 5¼ ft (1.5 m)

Barred bichir
Polypterus delhezi
up to 17½ in (44 cm)

Clown knifefish
Notopterus chitala
up to 4 ft (1.2 m)

Freshwater butterflyfish
Pantodon buchholzi
up to 4 in (10 cm)

Longnosed elephant fish
Gnathonemus petersii
up to 14 in (35 cm)

Tarpon
Megalops atlanticus
up to 4½–8¼ ft (1.3–2.5 m)

Ringed snake eel
Myrichthys colubrinus
up to 35 in (88 cm)

Jewel moray eel
Muraena lentiginosa up to 23½ in (60 cm)

Blue ribbon eel
Rhinomuraena quaesita up to 4¼ ft (1.3 m)

Sea gulper eel
Eurypharynx pelecanoides
23½–39 in (60–100 cm)

Milkfish
Chanos chanos
up to 6 ft (1.8 m)

Elegant corydoras
Corydoras elegans
up to 2¼ in (6 cm)

Black angel catfish
Synodontis angelicus
up to 21½ in (55 cm)

Walking catfish
Clarias batrachus
up to 21½ in (55 cm)

Red-bellied piranha
Pygocentrus nattereri
up to 12 in (30 cm)

Silver hatchetfish
Gasteropelecus sternicla
up to 2¼ in (6 cm)

Rust-colored rudd
Scardinius erythrophthalmus
up to 4 in (10 cm)

Rainbow trout
Oncorhynchus mykiss up to 4 ft (1.2 m)

Sockeye salmon
Oncorhynchus nerka
up to 33 in (84 cm)

Northern pike
Esox lucius up to 4¼ ft (1.3 m)

Marine hatchetfish
Argyropelecus aculeatus
up to 2½ in (7 cm)

Berndt's beardfish
Polymixia berndti
up to 18¼ in (47.5 cm)

Atlantic cod
Gadus morhua
up to 6½ ft (2 m)

Splendid toadfish
Sanopus splendidus up to 9½ in (24 cm)

Sargassum fish
Histrio histrio
up to 7 in (18.5 cm)

Crimson soldierfish
Myripristis murdjan
up to 23½ in (60 cm)

John Dory
Zeus faber
up to 35 in (90 cm)

Silver needlefish
Xenentodon cancila up to 12 in (30 cm)

Threadfin rainbowfish
Iriatherina werneri
up to 1½ in (4 cm)

Madagascar rainbowfish
Bedotia geayi
up to 4 in (10 cm)

Three-spined stickleback
Gasterosteus aculeatus
up to 3½ in (8 cm)

Sea horse
*Hippocampus
guttulatus*
up to 6 in (15 cm)

Weedy seadragon
Phyllopteryx taeniolatus
up to 18 in (46 cm)

Talibar lionfish
Pterois radiata up to 10 in (25 cm)

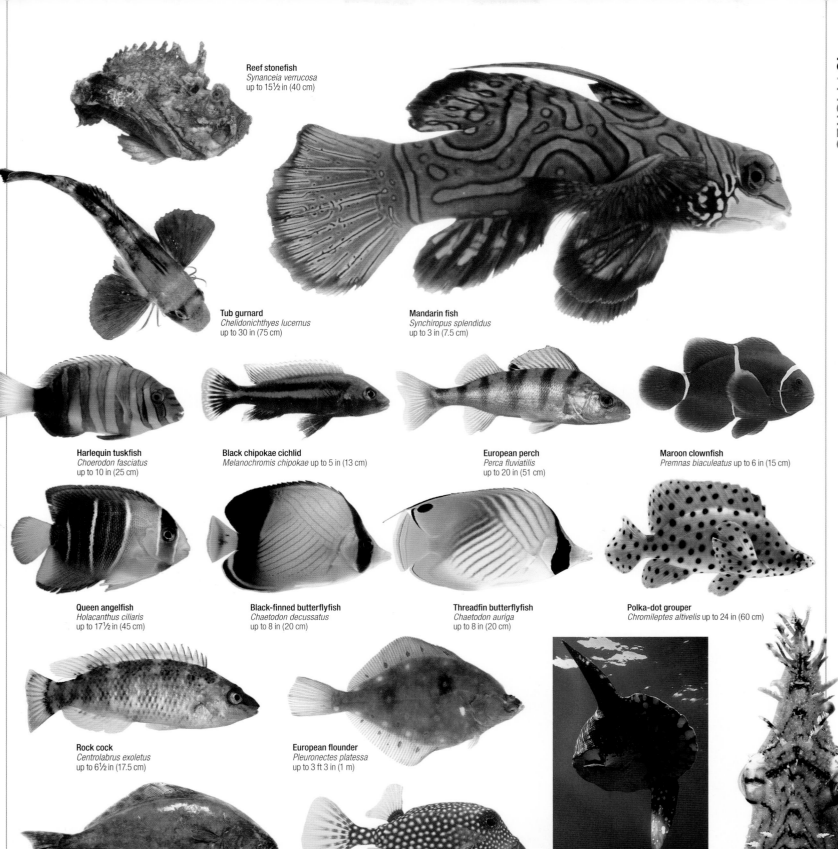

Reef stonefish
Synanceia verrucosa
up to 15½ in (40 cm)

Tub gurnard
Chelidonichthyes lucernus
up to 30 in (75 cm)

Mandarin fish
Synchiropus splendidus
up to 3 in (7.5 cm)

Harlequin tuskfish
Choerodon fasciatus
up to 10 in (25 cm)

Black chipokae cichlid
Melanochromis chipokae up to 5 in (13 cm)

European perch
Perca fluviatilis
up to 20 in (51 cm)

Maroon clownfish
Premnas biaculeatus up to 6 in (15 cm)

Queen angelfish
Holacanthus ciliaris
up to 17½ in (45 cm)

Black-finned butterflyfish
Chaetodon decussatus
up to 8 in (20 cm)

Threadfin butterflyfish
Chaetodon auriga
up to 8 in (20 cm)

Polka-dot grouper
Chromileptes altivelis up to 24 in (60 cm)

Rock cock
Centrolabrus exoletus
up to 6½ in (17.5 cm)

European flounder
Pleuronectes platessa
up to 3 ft 3 in (1 m)

OCEAN SUNFISH
The ocean sunfish (*Mola mola*) is up
to 13 ft (4 m) in length, and is the heaviest
bony fish, weighing up to 2.2 tons.

Atlantic halibut
Hippoglossus hippoglossus
up to 14¾ ft (4.5 m)

Spotted trunkfish
Lactophrys triqueter
up to 18½ in (47 cm)

Silver sailfin molly
Poecilia latipinna up to 4 in (10 cm)

Amiet's killifish
Fundulopanchax amieti up to 2¾ in (7 cm)

Dwarf Argentine pearlfish
Austrolebias nigripinnis up to 2 in (5 cm)

Tasselled filefish
Chaetodermis pencilligerus
up to 10 in (25 cm)

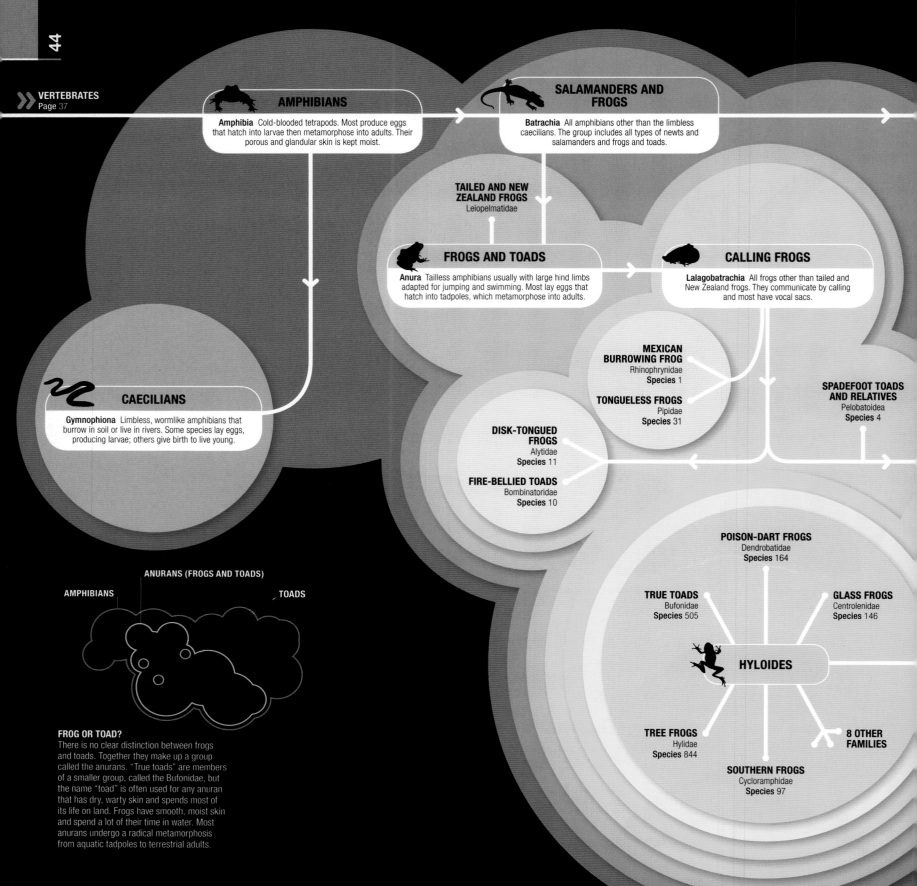

VERTEBRATES
Page 37

AMPHIBIANS

Amphibia Cold-blooded tetrapods. Most produce eggs that hatch into larvae then metamorphose into adults. Their porous and glandular skin is kept moist.

SALAMANDERS AND FROGS

Batrachia All amphibians other than the limbless caecilians. The group includes all types of newts and salamanders and frogs and toads.

TAILED AND NEW ZEALAND FROGS
Leiopelmatidae

FROGS AND TOADS

Anura Tailless amphibians usually with large hind limbs adapted for jumping and swimming. Most lay eggs that hatch into tadpoles, which metamorphose into adults.

CALLING FROGS

Lalagobatrachia All frogs other than tailed and New Zealand frogs. They communicate by calling and most have vocal sacs.

CAECILIANS

Gymnophiona Limbless, wormlike amphibians that burrow in soil or live in rivers. Some species lay eggs, producing larvae; others give birth to live young.

MEXICAN BURROWING FROG
Rhinophrynidae
Species 1

TONGUELESS FROGS
Pipidae
Species 31

SPADEFOOT TOADS AND RELATIVES
Pelobatoidea
Species 4

DISK-TONGUED FROGS
Alytidae
Species 11

FIRE-BELLIED TOADS
Bombinatoridae
Species 10

POISON-DART FROGS
Dendrobatidae
Species 164

TRUE TOADS
Bufonidae
Species 505

GLASS FROGS
Centrolenidae
Species 146

HYLOIDES

TREE FROGS
Hylidae
Species 844

8 OTHER FAMILIES

SOUTHERN FROGS
Cycloramphidae
Species 97

ANURANS (FROGS AND TOADS)

AMPHIBIANS

TOADS

FROG OR TOAD?
There is no clear distinction between frogs and toads. Together they make up a group called the anurans. "True toads" are members of a smaller group, called the Bufonidae, but the name "toad" is often used for any anuran that has dry, warty skin and spends most of its life on land. Frogs have smooth, moist skin and spend a lot of their time in water. Most anurans undergo a radical metamorphosis from aquatic tadpoles to terrestrial adults.

Amphibian groups

Amphibians have existed for at least 230 million years, when they evolved from fishes. It is not clear whether the three main groups—caecilians, salamanders and newts, and frogs and toads—are descended from a common ancestor or whether they evolved from different groups.

Amphibians are often erroneously seen as an intermediate group between fishes and reptiles. In fact they have evolved adaptations for living in moist habitats around freshwater. This diagram represents a recent hypothesis of amphibian relationships, and not all families are shown here.

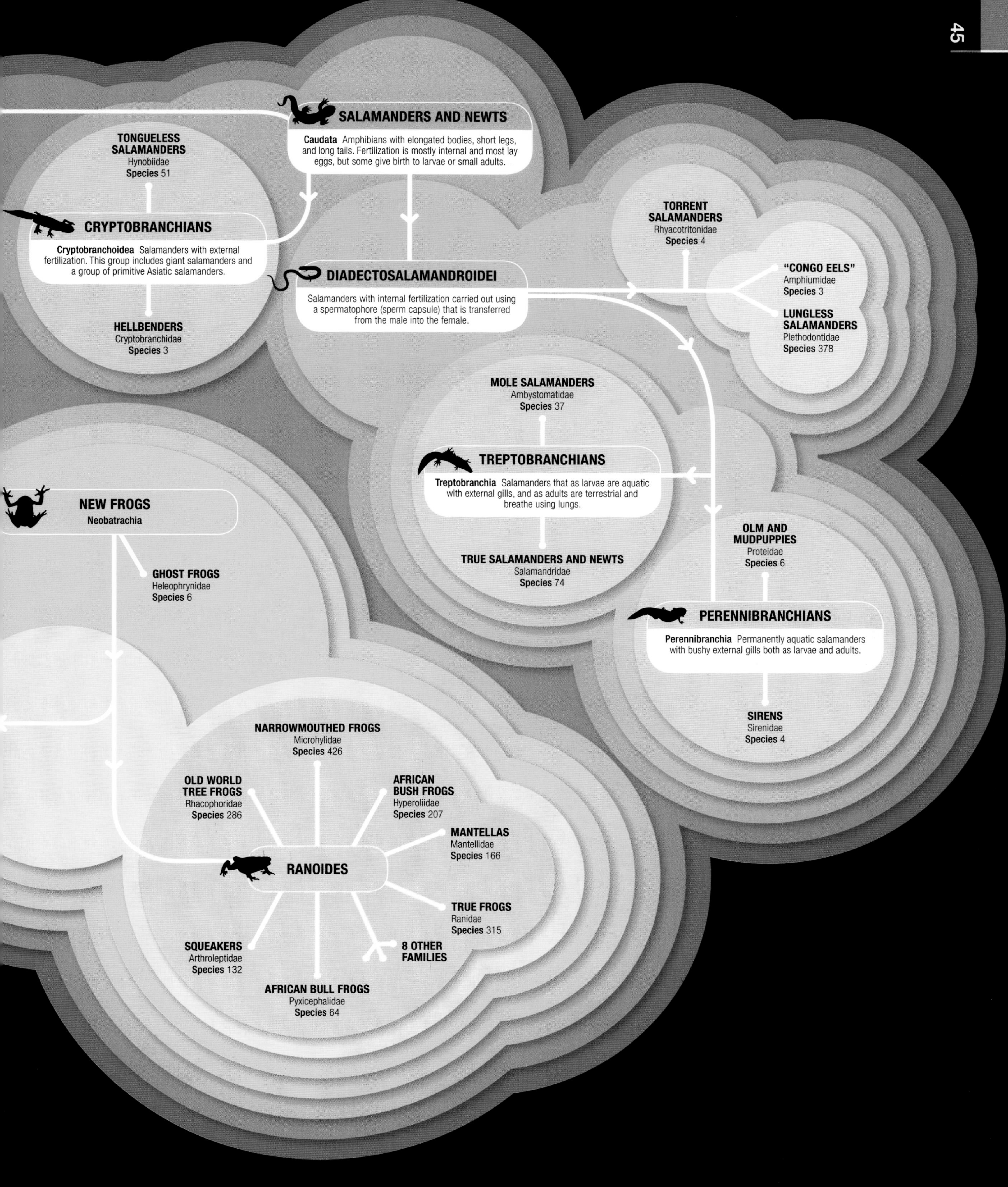

SALAMANDERS AND NEWTS

Caudata Amphibians with elongated bodies, short legs, and long tails. Fertilization is mostly internal and most lay eggs, but some give birth to larvae or small adults.

TONGUELESS SALAMANDERS
Hynobiidae
Species 51

 CRYPTOBRANCHIANS

Cryptobranchoidea Salamanders with external fertilization. This group includes giant salamanders and a group of primitive Asiatic salamanders.

HELLBENDERS
Cryptobranchidae
Species 3

DIADECTOSALAMANDROIDEI

Salamanders with internal fertilization carried out using a spermatophore (sperm capsule) that is transferred from the male into the female.

TORRENT SALAMANDERS
Rhyacotritonidae
Species 4

"CONGO EELS"
Amphiumidae
Species 3

LUNGLESS SALAMANDERS
Plethodontidae
Species 378

MOLE SALAMANDERS
Ambystomatidae
Species 37

TREPTOBRANCHIANS

Treptobranchia Salamanders that as larvae are aquatic with external gills, and as adults are terrestrial and breathe using lungs.

TRUE SALAMANDERS AND NEWTS
Salamandridae
Species 74

OLM AND MUDPUPPIES
Proteidae
Species 6

PERENNIBRANCHIANS

Perennibranchia Permanently aquatic salamanders with bushy external gills both as larvae and adults.

SIRENS
Sirenidae
Species 4

NEW FROGS

Neobatrachia

GHOST FROGS
Heleophrynidae
Species 6

NARROWMOUTHED FROGS
Microhylidae
Species 426

OLD WORLD TREE FROGS
Rhacophoridae
Species 286

AFRICAN BUSH FROGS
Hyperoliidae
Species 207

MANTELLAS
Mantellidae
Species 166

RANOIDES

TRUE FROGS
Ranidae
Species 315

SQUEAKERS
Arthroleptidae
Species 132

8 OTHER FAMILIES

AFRICAN BULL FROGS
Pyxicephalidae
Species 64

Amphibians

Amphibians are ectothermic (cold-blooded) vertebrates that derive body heat from their environment. They have four limbs, smooth skin, and are divided into three groups: caecilians, newts and salamanders, and frogs and toads.

Amphibians are typically aquatic as larvae and terrestrial as adults. They are highly dependent on water and are associated with freshwater habitats—none live in the sea. They typically produce eggs that lack shells to prevent water loss and have to be laid in water. Eggs hatch into larvae (called tadpoles in frogs and toads) that live in water for an extended period. Larvae undergo a complex transformation, called metamorphosis, in which a number of changes in body form equip them for life as adults in terrestrial habitats. Most importantly, the larval gills are lost and replaced by air-breathing lungs. In frogs and toads, the tail is reabsorbed during metamorphosis and the limbs develop.

Skin

The skin of amphibians contains glands, is commonly moist, and lacks scales, feathers, or hair. Most amphibians have lungs but all, to a greater or lesser extent, take in oxygen through their skin. The skin is also important for taking in water from the environment and contains numerous pigment cells that give it color. Many amphibians are brightly colored; this is especially common in poisonous species, in which striking colors and skin patterns serve as a warning. In other species, skin coloration provides camouflage or plays a role in mate selection.

Parental care

Amphibians have diverse life histories. While many produce very large numbers of eggs that they do not care for, others have evolved parental care in which a small number of eggs are protected by one or both parents. Parental care is usually provided by the female in caecilians, newts, and salamanders, but in many frogs it is provided by the male. Lacking a shell, amphibian eggs need protection against dehydration and infection by fungae, as well as from predators.

Caecilians

Order Gymnophiona

With a total of 175 species in three families, caecilians form the smallest of the three major groups of amphibians. They are limbless, wormlike animals that burrow in the soil in forested habitats, although some species live in rivers and streams. Confined to tropical habitats in South America, Africa, and Southeast Asia, caecilians vary in length from several centimetres to more than 1.5m (5ft). Fertilization is internal. Some species lay eggs, from which free-living larvae emerge, while in others development through metamorphosis occurs within the mother, who gives birth to small adults. Caecilians are difficult to observe and their biology is less well known than that of other amphibians.

SRI LANKAN CAECILIAN
Ichthyophis glutinosus, seen protecting its eggs, is 12–15½ in (30–40 cm) long. It lives underground and feeds on worms and other invertebrates.

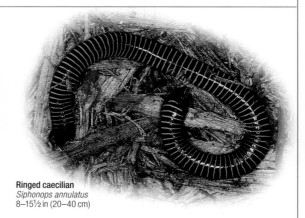

Ringed caecilian
Siphonops annulatus
8–15½ in (20–40 cm)

Salamanders and newts

Order Caudata

These tailed amphibians generally lead secretive lives. They live in cool, shady places and are typically active at night. Absent from most of Africa and Australia, salamanders and newts occur in temperate and tropical habitats in North and South America, Europe, and Asia. There are 563 species in nine families, and few are more than 6 in (15 cm) long. Fertilization is usually internal. Most species lay eggs but in some the eggs hatch inside the mother, who gives birth to larvae or small adults. The male lacks a penis and sperm is transferred to the female in a special structure called a spermatophore. Some species are aquatic, others are wholly terrestrial, and others spend their lives partly in water and partly on land.

Hellbender
Cryptobranchus alleganiensis
12–30 in (30–75 cm)

Mudpuppy
Necturus maculosus 8–19½ in (20–50 cm)

GREATER SIREN
One of the longest amphibians in North America, *Siren lacertina* is 19½–35 in (50–90 cm) long. This species has only one pair of small legs, situated behind the feathery external gills.

Mexican axolotl
Ambystoma mexicanum
4–8 in (10–20 cm)

Fire salamander
Salamandra salamandra
3¼–11 in (8–28 cm)

Great crested newt
Triturus cristatus
4–6 in (10–15 cm)

Californian newt
Taricha torosa
4½–8 in (12–20 cm)

Himalayan newt
Tylototriton verrucosus
4½–7 in (12–18 cm)

Pacific giant salamander
Dicamptodon tenebrosus
6½–13½ in (17–34 cm)

Frogs and toads

Order Anura

Frogs and toads lack tails, at least as adults. Their hind limbs are much larger than their front legs and are adapted for jumping, swimming, and digging. Most are active at night and communicate by calling. Frogs and toads occur in temperate and tropical habitats in all continents. There are 5,572 species in 44 families and few are more than 14 in (35 cm) long. Fertilization is external. Most species lay eggs that hatch into free-swimming tadpoles, which then metamorphose into small adults. In some the eggs develop in or on one of the parents. Some species spend their lives partly in water and partly on land, some are aquatic throughout their lives, while others are wholly terrestrial.

Tailed frog
Ascaphus truei
1–2 in (2.5–5 cm)

Mexican burrowing toad
Rhinophrynus dorsalis
2½–3¼ in (6–8 cm)

African clawed frog
Xenopus laevis
2¼–5 in (6–13 cm)

Midwife toad
Alytes obstetricans
1¼–2 in (3–5 cm)

Mallorcan midwife toad
Alytes muletensis
1¼–1¾ in (3–4.5 cm)

Oriental fire-bellied toad
Bombina orientalis
1¼–2 in (3–5 cm)

Parsley frog
Pelodytes punctatus
1¼–2 in (3–5 cm)

Couch's spadefoot toad
Scaphiopus couchii
2¼–3½ in (5.5–9 cm)

Asian leaf frog
Megophrys montana
2¾–5½ in (7–14 cm)

Cape ghost frog
Heleophryne purcelli
1¼–2¼ in (3–6 cm)

Seychelles frog
Sechellophryne gardineri
⅜–½ in (1–1.5 cm)

Sign-bearing froglet
Crinia insignifera
½–1¼ in (1.5–3 cm)

Mountain marsupial frog
Gastrotheca monticola
1½–2¼ in (4–6 cm)

White's treefrog
Litoria caerulea
2–4 in (5–10 cm)

Red-eyed treefrog
Agalychnis callidryas
1½–2¾ in (4–7 cm)

Green treefrog
Hyla cinerea
1¼–2¼ in (3–6 cm)

European treefrog
Hyla arborea 1¼–2 in (3–5 cm)

Surinam horned frog
Ceratophrys cornuta 4–8 in (10–20 cm)

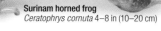

Green poison frog
Dendrobates auratus
1–2¼ in (2.5–6 cm)

BLUE POISON FROG
The electric-blue coloration of *Dendrobates tinctorius* warns predators of its highly poisonous nature. It is 1¼–2in (3–5 cm) long and is found in the tropical forests of South America.

Yellow-banded poison frog
Dendrobates leucomelas
1¼–1½ in (3–3.5 cm)

Green toad
Pseudepidalea viridis
3½–4½ in (9–12 cm)

Marine toad
Rhinella marina
4–9½ in (10–24 cm)

European common toad
Bufo bufo 3¼–8 in (8–20 cm)

Panamanian golden frog
Atelopus zeteki
1½–2¼ in (4–5.5 cm)

Tomato frog
Dyscophus antongilii
3¼–4½ in (8–12 cm)

Boulenger's Asian tree toad
Pedostibes hosii
2–4 in (5–10 cm)

Kassina frog
Kassina senegalensis 1¼–2 in (3–5 cm)

African bullfrog
Pyxicephalus adspersus
3¾–9 in (8–23 cm)

Tinker reed frog
Hyperolius tuberilinguis
1¼–1¾ in (3–4.5 cm)

Green mantella
Mantella viridis ¾–1¼ in (2–3 cm)

Golden mantella
Mantella aurantiaca ¾–1¼ in (2–3 cm)

Solomon Island horned frog
Ceratobatrachus guentheri
2–3¼ in (5–8 cm)

European common frog
Rana temporaria
2–4 in (5–10 cm)

Agile frog
Rana dalmatina
2–3½ in (5–9 cm)

AMERICAN BULLFROG
Lithobates catesbeianus is the largest frog in North America, growing to a length of up to 8 in (20 cm). It lives in lakes, ponds, and slow-flowing streams.

STRAWBERRY POISON FROG
Found in the rain forests of Costa Rica,
Nicaragua, and Panama, the strawberry
poison frog (*Oophaga pumilio*) is
¾–1 in (2–2.5 cm) long and may
exhibit remarkable color variation.

REPTILES

Reptilia Thick-skinned tetrapods with amniotic eggs or internal development of young. They include warm-blooded birds and other scaly, cold-blooded reptiles.

DIAPSIDS

Diapsida All reptiles, other than turtles, including birds. Body forms vary but are often elongated, with scaly or feathered coverings and, commonly, four limbs.

TUATARAS
Rhynchocephalia
Species 2

LEPIDOSAURS

Lepidosauria Diapsids that shed their skin in large pieces or as a whole.

HIDDEN-NECKED TURTLES AND TORTOISES
Cryptodira
Species 255

TURTLES

Testudines Reptiles with bodies contained within upper and lower bony, boxlike shells. There are aquatic, semiaquatic, and terrestrial species.

SIDE-NECKED TURTLES
Pleurodira
Species 54

IGUANAS
Iguanidae
Species 38

ANOLES
Polychrotidae
Species 398

IGUANAS AND RELATIVES

Iguania Lizards that have four functional limbs and use their tongues to capture and grab food.

ARCHOSAURS

Archosauria Reptiles with teeth sunk into sockets. This group includes many extinct dinosaur groups, with birds and crocodilians being the only living archosaurs.

AGAMAS AND CHAMELEONS
Acrodonta
Species 567

6 OTHER FAMILIES
Species 570

BIRDS

Archosaurs with asymmetrical flight feathers (lost in some flightless species). Many dinosaurs had feathers, but they were not flight feathers. More recently evolved birds—not including the primitive tinamous and ratites—have many more shared features, including a horny, toothless bill and a keeled breastbone.

Aves
Species 9,500

>> PAGE 56

CROCODILIANS

Crocodylia Elongated, limbed reptiles covered with thick leathery plates under which are bony plates on their top surface. All are semiaquatic predators.

LIZARDS AND SNAKES
Lizards and snakes are closely related and make up the group Squamata. It is thought that snakes evolved from lizards, possibly from burrowing species, and the differences between them are slight.

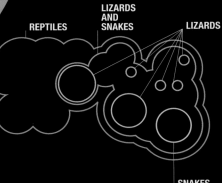

REPTILES

LIZARDS AND SNAKES

LIZARDS

SNAKES

Reptile groups

The oldest groups of reptiles are the turtles and archosaurs, which first appeared about 220 million years ago. Archosaurs include crocodilians and birds, which are feathered reptiles, but also the extinct dinosaurs. Lepidosaurs include the tuataras, relics of a once widespread group of lizardlike reptiles, and the squamates, a huge group that includes all lizards and snakes. This diagram represents one hypothesis of reptile relationships. Controversy surrounds the relations between squamates and the placement of turtles. Not all families are shown here.

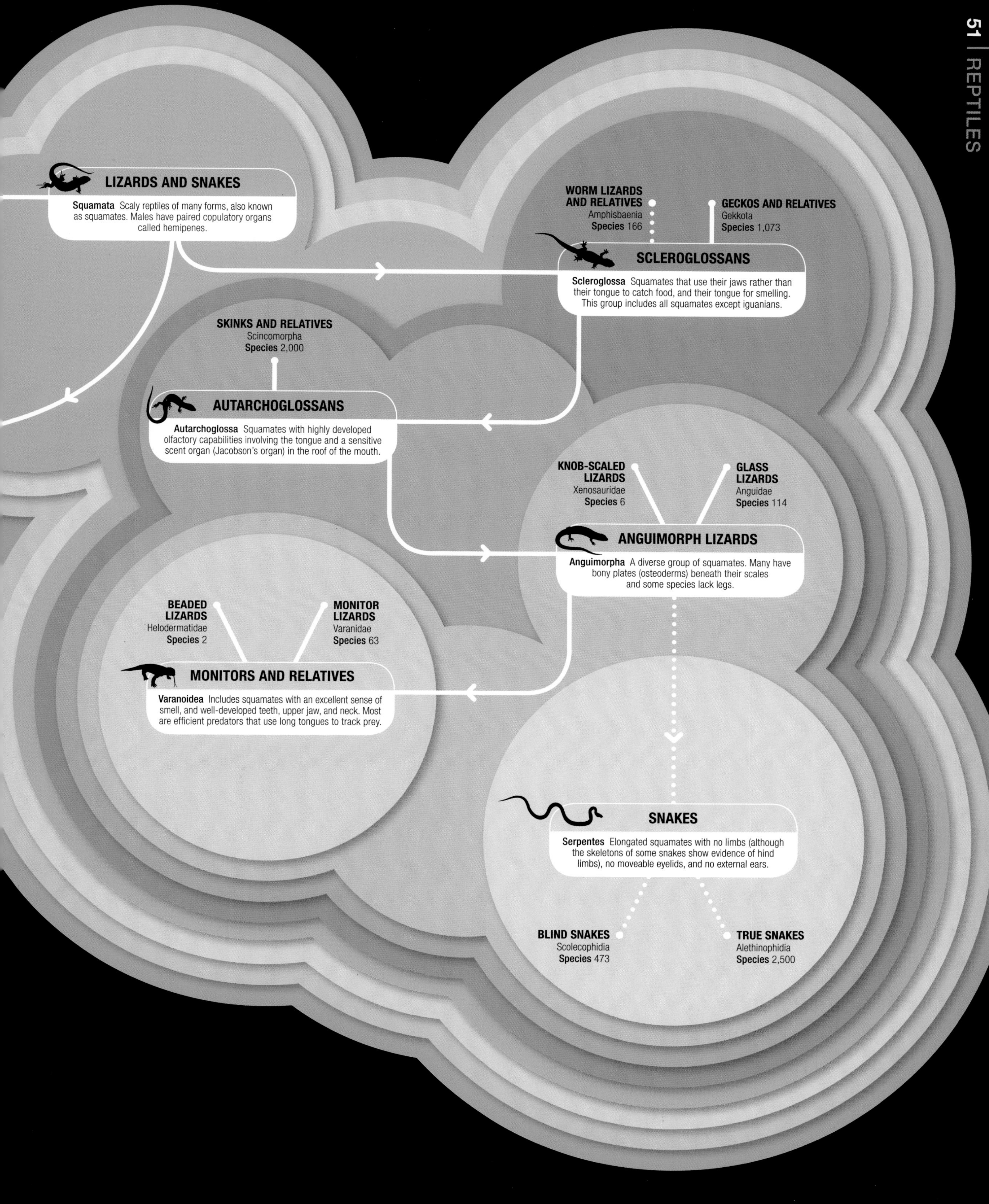

LIZARDS AND SNAKES

Squamata Scaly reptiles of many forms, also known as squamates. Males have paired copulatory organs called hemipenes.

WORM LIZARDS AND RELATIVES
Amphisbaenia
Species 166

GECKOS AND RELATIVES
Gekkota
Species 1,073

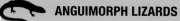

SCLEROGLOSSANS

Scleroglossa Squamates that use their jaws rather than their tongue to catch food, and their tongue for smelling. This group includes all squamates except iguanians.

SKINKS AND RELATIVES
Scincomorpha
Species 2,000

AUTARCHOGLOSSANS

Autarchoglossa Squamates with highly developed olfactory capabilities involving the tongue and a sensitive scent organ (Jacobson's organ) in the roof of the mouth.

KNOB-SCALED LIZARDS
Xenosauridae
Species 6

GLASS LIZARDS
Anguidae
Species 114

ANGUIMORPH LIZARDS

Anguimorpha A diverse group of squamates. Many have bony plates (osteoderms) beneath their scales and some species lack legs.

BEADED LIZARDS
Helodermatidae
Species 2

MONITOR LIZARDS
Varanidae
Species 63

MONITORS AND RELATIVES

Varanoidea Includes squamates with an excellent sense of smell, and well-developed teeth, upper jaw, and neck. Most are efficient predators that use long tongues to track prey.

SNAKES

Serpentes Elongated squamates with no limbs (although the skeletons of some snakes show evidence of hind limbs), no moveable eyelids, and no external ears.

BLIND SNAKES
Scolecophidia
Species 473

TRUE SNAKES
Alethinophidia
Species 2,500

Reptiles

What most people understand by the term "reptile" is an egg-bearing vertebrates that has a tough skin with a covering of hard, dry scales. In fact, the term also includes birds, with their covering of feathers.

Living reptiles include turtles and tortoises, tuatara, squamates (lizards, amphisbaenians, and snakes), crocodilians (crocodiles, alligators, and caimans), and, perhaps somewhat surprisingly, birds. In fact, crocodilians are more closely related to the birds than to the other reptiles, and together they form a group known as the Archosaura ("ruling reptiles"), which also contains several extinct groups of dinosaurs and pterosaurs (flying reptiles). Birds, then, are warm-blooded reptiles with feathers. For the

purposes of this catalog, the birds have been profiled separately from the non-avian reptiles (see pp.58–67)

Temperature control

Reptiles occur throughout the world but are more common in tropical habitats. Most non-avian reptiles are ectothermic, meaning they cannot generate metabolic heat. However, some regulate their internal body temperature through behavior, such as sunning, and can operate at

higher temperatures than endothermic ("warm-blooded") birds and mammals. Some reptiles may also survive temperatures as low as freezing, although in these conditions their bodily functions operate at a very reduced rate.

Extreme habitats

By obtaining all their heat from external sources such as the sun, ectothermic reptiles can survive easily on one-tenth of the amount of food needed by an endothermic animal of the same size—endotherms use up a large proportion of the energy obtained from their food just to maintain a constant body temperature. This gives non-avian reptiles a great advantage in habitats where conditions are extreme and food is in short supply, notably deserts, where lizards are often the most common form of vertebrate life.

Turtles and tortoises

Order Chelonia

Turtles and tortoises comprise the order Chelonia. They are heavily armored reptiles with bony shells that originate from their ribs and cover the top and bottom of their bodies. This gives them excellent protection from predators but limits their speed and agility on land. They all lack teeth and instead use a sharp horny "beak" to break up their food, which may consist of animal or vegetable material, or both, depending on the species. Turtles occur on the land (where they are often known as tortoises), in freshwater, and in the sea. They all lay nearly spherical eggs, with some marine species laying up to 100 in a clutch.

Alligator snapping turtle
Macroclemys temminckii
15½–31 in (40–80 cm)

Big-headed turtle
Platysternon megacephalum
5½–8 in (14–20 cm)

Green sea turtle
Chelonia mydas
31 in–3 ft 3 in (80–100 cm)

Starred tortoise
Geochelone elegans
12–15 in (30–38 cm)

Red-eared turtle
Trachemys scripta elegans
8–11 in (20–28 cm)

Yellow mud turtle
Kinosternon flavescens
4½–6½ in (12–16 cm)

Hermann's tortoise
Testudo hermanni
6–8 in (15–20 cm)

Leopard tortoise
Geochelone pardalis
17½–28 in (45–72 cm)

Chinese soft-shelled turtle
Pelodiscus sinensis
6–12 in (15–30 cm)

Common snake-necked turtle
Chelodina longicollis
8–10 in (20–25 cm)

Tuatara

Order Rhynchocephalia

Both surviving members of the order Rhynchocephalia live on islands off the coast of New Zealand. Despite their lizardlike appearance, they are not squamates and belong to an ancient group of reptiles that was formerly spread over much of the world. Their teeth are fused to their jawbones and those on the tip of their upper jaw are modified into a beaklike arrangement. Tuataras also lack the hemi penis (double penis) unique to squamates. They lay eggs, which take about a year to hatch, and have long life spans.

Tuatara
Sphenodon punctatus
19½–26 in (50–65 cm)

Lizards and snakes

Order Squamata

The lizards, snakes, and amphisbaenians (worm-lizards) comprise the Squamata. This is the largest group of ectothermic reptiles, with the widest distribution. Most squamates lay eggs but a sizable proportion bear live young. Lizards are the most numerous group and are distinguished by the presence of legs, although limblessness has evolved many times among squamates. They also have eyelids and external ear openings. Squamates have adapted to many habitats and filled many ecological niches. The worm-lizards are burrowing squamates restricted to warm climates. Their scales are arranged in annuli (rings) and their skulls are bony, allowing them to force their way through hardened soil. Most worm-lizards have no limbs, but the ajolotes or mole lizards (Bipedidae) have front limbs that they use to dig. Snakes are elongated squamates lacking legs, eyelids, and external ear openings. These constraints have resulted in specialized methods of locomotion and hunting. All snakes are carnivorous, feeding on animals ranging from ants to antelopes.

Australian frilled lizard
Chlamydosaurus kingii
23½–35 in (60–90 cm)

Thai water dragon
Physignathus cocincinus
31–39 in (80–100 cm)

Spiny dab lizard
Uromastyx acanthinurus
12–15½ in (30–40 cm)

Inland bearded dragon
Pogona vitticeps
12–19½ in (30–50 cm)

Common agama
Agama agama
12–15½ in (30–40 cm)

Flying lizard
Draco spilonotus
6–8 in (15–20 cm)

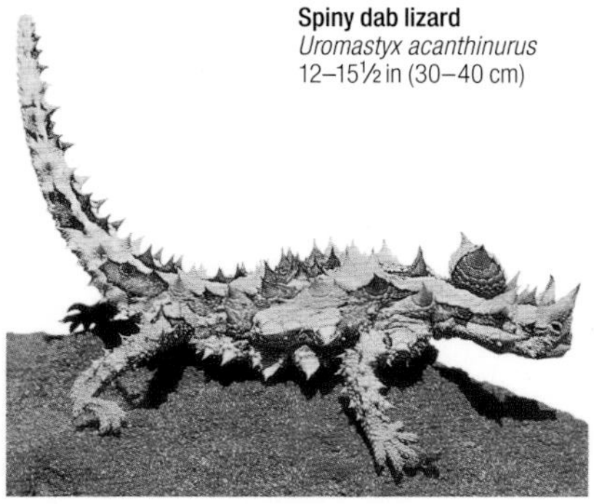

Thorny devil
Moloch horridus
6–7 in (15–18 cm)

Warty chameleon
Furcifer verrucosus
4–10 in (10–26 cm)

Jackson's chameleon
Chamaeleo jacksonii
8–12 in (20–30 cm)

Plumed basilisk
Basiliscus plumifrons
23½–28 in (60–70 cm)

Collared lizard
Crotaphtus collaris
8–14 in (20–35 cm)

Desert horned lizard
Phrynosoma platyrhinos
3¼–4½ in (8–11 cm)

Marine iguana
Amblyrhynchus cristatus
3ft 3in–5½ ft (1–1.7 m)

Green iguana
Iguana iguana
5–6½ ft (1.5–2 m)

Green anolis
Anolis carolinensis
4½–8 in (12–20 cm)

Tokay gecko
Gekko gecko
7–14 in (18–35 cm)

Kuhl's flying gecko
Ptychozoon kuhli
7–8 in (18–20 cm)

Northern leaf-tailed gecko
Phyllurus cornutus
6–8½ in (15–21 cm)

Nicobar blind lizard
Dibamus nicobaricus 4–5 in (10–13 cm)

Armadillo lizard
Cordylus cataphractus
6½–8½ in (16–21 cm)

Rough-scaled plated lizard
Gerrhosaurus major 16–19 in (41–48 cm)

Tegu lizard
Tupinambis teguixin
31–39 in (80–100 cm)

Ocellated lizard
Lacerta lepida
23½–31 in (60–80 cm)

Eyed skink
Chalcides ocellatus
7–12 in (18–30 cm)

Yellow-spotted night lizard
Lepidophyma flavimaculatum
8–12 in (20–30 cm)

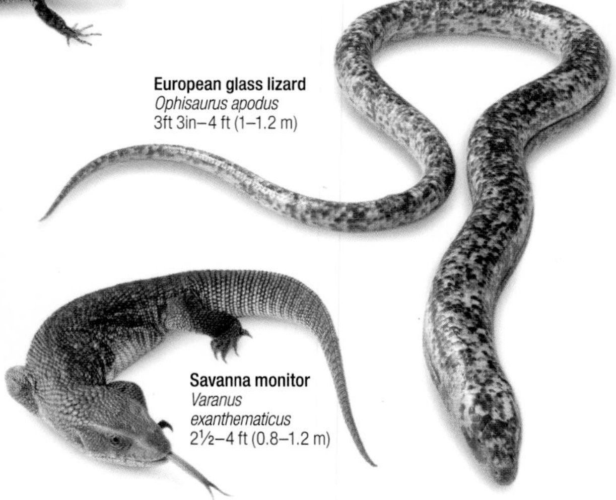

European glass lizard
Ophisaurus apodus
3ft 3in–4 ft (1–1.2 m)

Black-and-pink-striped gila monster
Heloderma suspectum
12–19½ in (30–50 cm)

Savanna monitor
*Varanus
exanthematicus*
2½–4 ft (0.8–1.2 m)

Komodo dragon
Varanus komodoensis
8¼–10¼ ft (2.5–3.1 m)

**Black-and-white
amphisbaenian**
Amphisbaena fuliginosa
12–17½ in (30–45 cm)

TEXAS THREADSNAKE
Leptotyphlops dulcis grows to a length of 6–10½ in (15–27 cm).
It is a member of the Leptotyphlopidae, a family of small,
burrowing snakes that live in the soil and feed mainly on termites.

SOUTH AMERICAN PIPESNAKE
Anilius scytale is 28–35 in (70–90 cm) long. The sole
member of its family, its markings mimic those of
venomous coral snakes that live in the same region.

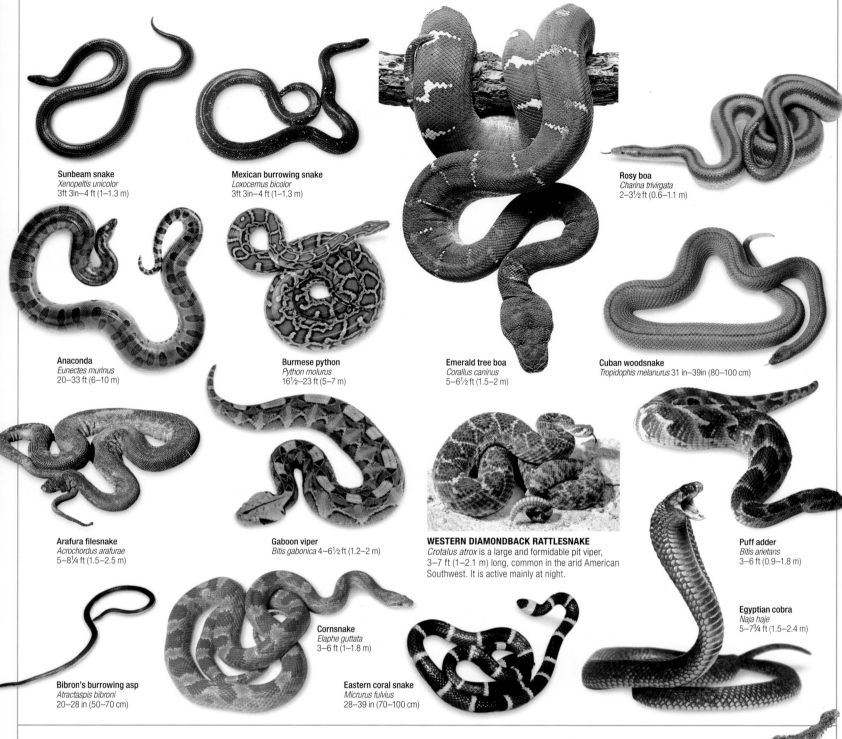

Sunbeam snake
Xenopeltis unicolor
3ft 3in–4 ft (1–1.3 m)

Mexican burrowing snake
Loxocemus bicolor
3ft 3in–4 ft (1–1.3 m)

Rosy boa
Charina trivirgata
2–3½ ft (0.6–1.1 m)

Anaconda
Eunectes murinus
20–33 ft (6–10 m)

Burmese python
Python molurus
16½–23 ft (5–7 m)

Emerald tree boa
Corallus caninus
5–6½ ft (1.5–2 m)

Cuban woodsnake
Tropidophis melanurus 31 in–39in (80–100 cm)

Arafura filesnake
Acrochordus arafurae
5–8¼ ft (1.5–2.5 m)

Gaboon viper
Bitis gabonica 4–6½ ft (1.2–2 m)

WESTERN DIAMONDBACK RATTLESNAKE
Crotalus atrox is a large and formidable pit viper,
3–7 ft (1–2.1 m) long, common in the arid American
Southwest. It is active mainly at night.

Puff adder
Bitis arietans
3–6 ft (0.9–1.8 m)

Bibron's burrowing asp
Atractaspis bibroni
20–28 in (50–70 cm)

Cornsnake
Elaphe guttata
3–6 ft (1–1.8 m)

Eastern coral snake
Micrurus fulvius
28–39 in (70–100 cm)

Egyptian cobra
Naja haje
5–7¾ ft (1.5–2.4 m)

Crocodiles, alligators, and gharials

Order Crocodilia

Crocodilians are one of the two surviving groups from an
evolutionary line that also contained the extinct dinosaurs, the
other survivors being the birds. Crocodilians are covered with
thick bony plates and are semiaquatic predators. Their social
behavior, complex displays, and vocalizations set them apart
from all other reptiles. All species lay eggs, and females show
a high degree of parental care. Most crocodilians live in
freshwater rivers, lakes, and lagoons, while a few species
inhabit tidal reaches and may venture out to sea.

Nile crocodile
Crocodylus niloticus
16½–21 ft (5–6.5 m)

American alligator
Alligator mississippiensis
9¼–16½ ft (2.8–5 m)

Spectacled caiman
Caiman crocodilus
8¼–9¾ ft (2.5–3 m)

Gharial
Gavialis gangeticus
13–23 ft (4–7 m)

VERTEBRATES
Page 37

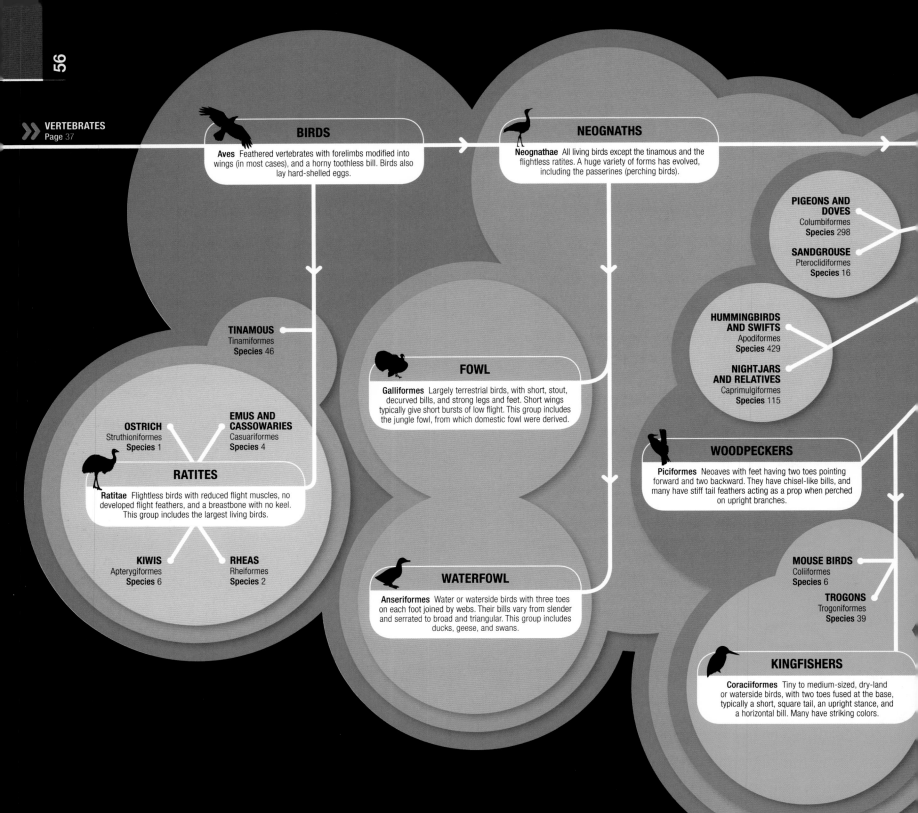

BIRDS

Aves Feathered vertebrates with forelimbs modified into wings (in most cases), and a horny toothless bill. Birds also lay hard-shelled eggs.

NEOGNATHS

Neognathae All living birds except the tinamous and the flightless ratites. A huge variety of forms has evolved, including the passerines (perching birds).

PIGEONS AND DOVES
Columbiformes
Species 298

SANDGROUSE
Pteroclidiformes
Species 16

TINAMOUS
Tinamiformes
Species 46

HUMMINGBIRDS AND SWIFTS
Apodiformes
Species 429

NIGHTJARS AND RELATIVES
Caprimulgiformes
Species 115

FOWL

Galliformes Largely terrestrial birds, with short, stout, decurved bills, and strong legs and feet. Short wings typically give short bursts of low flight. This group includes the jungle fowl, from which domestic fowl were derived.

OSTRICH
Struthioniformes
Species 1

EMUS AND CASSOWARIES
Casuariformes
Species 4

RATITES

Ratitae Flightless birds with reduced flight muscles, no developed flight feathers, and a breastbone with no keel. This group includes the largest living birds.

KIWIS
Apterygiformes
Species 6

RHEAS
Rheiformes
Species 2

WOODPECKERS

Piciformes Neoaves with feet having two toes pointing forward and two backward. They have chisel-like bills, and many have stiff tail feathers acting as a prop when perched on upright branches.

MOUSE BIRDS
Coliiformes
Species 6

TROGONS
Trogoniformes
Species 39

WATERFOWL

Anseriformes Water or waterside birds with three toes on each foot joined by webs. Their bills vary from slender and serrated to broad and triangular. This group includes ducks, geese, and swans.

KINGFISHERS

Coraciiformes Tiny to medium-sized, dry-land or waterside birds, with two toes fused at the base, typically a short, square tail, an upright stance, and a horizontal bill. Many have striking colors.

Bird groups

Birds number close to 10,000 species, ranging from the primitive tinamous and ratites to perching birds, the most recently evolved group. Outward appearances make some groupings such as penguins and hummingbirds obvious, but birds within other groups, such as the cranes and rails, may appear to have little in common. Recent DNA studies have helped resolve some of the relationships, producing dramatically revised groupings. Surprises have included the close relationship between New World vultures and storks, rather than other birds of prey.

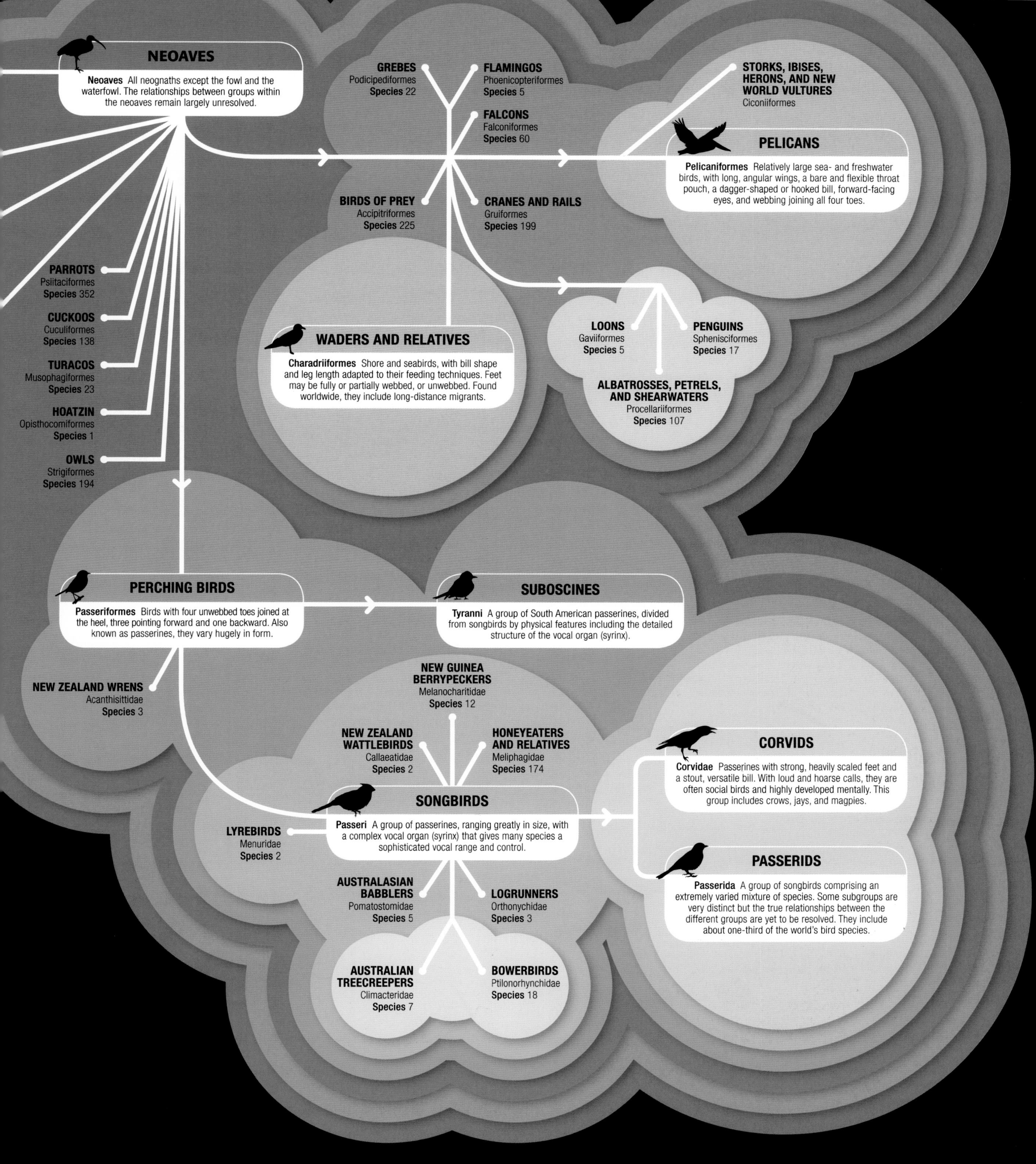

NEOAVES

Neoaves All neognaths except the fowl and the waterfowl. The relationships between groups within the neoaves remain largely unresolved.

GREBES
Podicipediformes
Species 22

FLAMINGOS
Phoenicopteriformes
Species 5

STORKS, IBISES, HERONS, AND NEW WORLD VULTURES
Ciconiiformes

FALCONS
Falconiformes
Species 60

PELICANS

Pelicaniformes Relatively large sea- and freshwater birds, with long, angular wings, a bare and flexible throat pouch, a dagger-shaped or hooked bill, forward-facing eyes, and webbing joining all four toes.

BIRDS OF PREY
Accipitriformes
Species 225

CRANES AND RAILS
Gruiformes
Species 199

PARROTS
Psiitaciformes
Species 352

CUCKOOS
Cuculiformes
Species 138

WADERS AND RELATIVES

Charadriiformes Shore and seabirds, with bill shape and leg length adapted to their feeding techniques. Feet may be fully or partially webbed, or unwebbed. Found worldwide, they include long-distance migrants.

LOONS
Gaviiformes
Species 5

PENGUINS
Sphenisciformes
Species 17

TURACOS
Musophagiformes
Species 23

HOATZIN
Opisthocomiformes
Species 1

ALBATROSSES, PETRELS, AND SHEARWATERS
Procellariiformes
Species 107

OWLS
Strigiformes
Species 194

PERCHING BIRDS

Passeriformes Birds with four unwebbed toes joined at the heel, three pointing forward and one backward. Also known as passerines, they vary hugely in form.

SUBOSCINES

Tyranni A group of South American passerines, divided from songbirds by physical features including the detailed structure of the vocal organ (syrinx).

NEW GUINEA BERRYPECKERS
Melanocharitidae
Species 12

NEW ZEALAND WRENS
Acanthisittidae
Species 3

NEW ZEALAND WATTLEBIRDS
Callaeatidae
Species 2

HONEYEATERS AND RELATIVES
Meliphagidae
Species 174

CORVIDS

Corvidae Passerines with strong, heavily scaled feet and a stout, versatile bill. With loud and hoarse calls, they are often social birds and highly developed mentally. This group includes crows, jays, and magpies.

SONGBIRDS

Passeri A group of passerines, ranging greatly in size, with a complex vocal organ (syrinx) that gives many species a sophisticated vocal range and control.

LYREBIRDS
Menuridae
Species 2

PASSERIDS

Passerida A group of songbirds comprising an extremely varied mixture of species. Some subgroups are very distinct but the true relationships between the different groups are yet to be resolved. They include about one-third of the world's bird species.

AUSTRALASIAN BABBLERS
Pomatostomidae
Species 5

LOGRUNNERS
Orthonychidae
Species 3

AUSTRALIAN TREECREEPERS
Climacteridae
Species 7

BOWERBIRDS
Ptilonorhynchidae
Species 18

Birds

Birds are lightweight but remarkably tough animals, with a high metabolic rate and often fast, high-energy lifestyles. They are found throughout the world, except for the most extreme polar areas, and in nearly every surface habitat.

Modern birds trace their descent back to dinosaurs and have much in common with reptiles, but all bird species are warm-blooded. Most species can fly, but there are some flightless ones. All species lay eggs that are incubated externally, and have horn-sheathed bills. There is, however, another feature that is unique to birds: the feather. Feathers developed from modified scales, and grow in well-defined tracts. On most birds these tracts form a regular pattern, described by such terms as ear coverts, scapulars, primaries, and tail feathers. Overlying the body, smaller contour feathers smooth the bird's outline. On some species, including penguins and kiwis, the tracts are harder to define. Feathers provide insulation, enable flight, and need to be replaced regularly through the process of molting, usually once or twice a year.

Counting toes

By using detailed physical and behavioral features to trace common descent, birds are grouped into 227 families to create an evolutionary family tree. Physical characters include the structure of the feet: most birds have four toes, the majority having three facing forward, one back. A substantial number of species have just three toes and a few, including the ostrich, have just two toes.

Tinamous

Order Tinamiformes

This ancient South American family of ground-living, quail-like birds lives mostly in dense, tropical forest as far north as Mexico. Some species live in open grasslands. Elusive but often heard, they eat insects, seeds, and berries, and range from 6–19½ in (15–50 cm) in length.

Red-winged tinamou
Rhynchotus rufescens
15½ in (40 cm)

Ostrich

Order Struthioniformes

The world's largest birds are flightless and can run at up to 40 mph (65 kph).

Ostrich
Struthio camelus
7–9½ ft (2.1–2.8 m)

Rheas

Order Rheiformes

Rheas are flightless, polygamous birds that are ostrichlike in form but have three toes and are considerably smaller, up to 5 ft (1.5 m) tall. They live in open habitats in South America. They eat leaves, shoots, seeds, and some invertebrates.

Greater rhea
Rhea americana
3–5 ft (0.9–1.5 m)

Cassowaries and emus

Order Casuariiformes

These flightless birds, found in Australia and New Guinea, are somewhat ostrichlike, but with a longer, lower profile and three toes. Cassowaries can reach 6 ft (1.8 m) in height and emus, the world's second-largest birds, can reach 6½ ft (2 m) and weigh up to 100 lb (45 kg).

Southern cassowary
Casuarius casuarius
6 ft (1.8 m)

Kiwi

Order Apterygiformes

Three species of small flightless birds make up this order. Females are larger than males, and their especially large eggs are each up to 25 percent of the female's body weight. They are nocturnal, and find food, especially earthworms, by touch and scent, using facial bristles and nostrils at the tip of a long bill.

Brown kiwi
Apteryx australis
15¼ in (40 cm)

Gamebirds and relatives

Order Galliformes

Gamebirds occur in many habitats, including semi-desert, grassland, savanna, woodland and forest, and even high peaks and northern tundra. They are all small-headed, large-bodied birds with short, stout, arched bills and often marked sexual differences. Some cold-climate species have feathered feet and turn white in winter.

California quail
Callipepla californica
10 in (25 cm)

Chukar
Alectoris chukar
12½–15½ in (32–39 cm)

Northern bobwhite
Colinus virginianus
9½–11 in (24–28 cm)

Western capercaillie
Tetrao urogallus
23½–33 in (60–85 cm)

Wildfowl

Order Anseriformes

This group consists of ducks, geese, swans, and screamers. Wildfowl are mostly water or waterside birds, many of which feed on dry land and retreat to water for safety. Swans are the largest, geese mostly intermediate, and ducks smaller. Ducks can be freshwater, marine, or both, and feed on land and in water.

Mute swan
Cygnus olor
4½–5¼ ft (1.4–1.6 m)

Eurasian wigeon
Anas penelope
30–34 in (75–86 cm)

Plumed whistling-duck
Dendrocygna eytoni 15½–17½ in (40–45 cm)

Red-breasted goose
Branta ruficollis 21–21½ in (53–55 cm)

Grey francolin
Francolinus pondicerianus
13½ in (34 cm)

Temminck's tragopan
Tragopan temminckii
25 in (63 cm)

Penguins

Order Sphenisciformes

Although some species venture as far north as the Equator, these distinctive flightless seabirds are most typically associated with the very cold conditions and rich marine food sources farther south in the Southern Ocean. Most species breed in large colonies, some consisting of hundreds of thousands of birds. Penguins have plump bodies and can weigh between 2½ and 66 lb (1–30 kg). They have short legs, webbed feet, and wings that are flattened to serve as flippers. All species stand upright and waddle on land, but are superb swimmers, reaching speeds of up to 9 mph (14 kph). They are also deep divers, pursuing fish and krill.

Rockhopper penguin
Eudyptes chrysocome
19½ in (50 cm)

Adelie penguin
Pygoscelis adeliae
18–24 in (46–61 cm)

Jackass penguin
Spheniscus demersus
23½–28 in (60–70 cm)

Humboldt penguin
Spheniscus humboldti
23 in (58 cm)

King penguin
Aptenodytes patagonicus
35 in (90 cm)

Loons

Order Gaviiformes

Loons (also called divers) are Northern Hemisphere water birds, nesting by freshwater, but spending much time at sea. Their strong legs, set far back on the body, are ideal for swimming underwater, but make walking on land impossible.

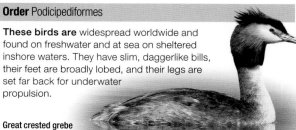

Arctic loon
Gavia arctica
23½–28 in (60–70 cm)

Grebes

Order Podicipediformes

These birds are widespread worldwide and found on freshwater and at sea on sheltered inshore waters. They have slim, daggerlike bills, their feet are broadly lobed, and their legs are set far back for underwater propulsion.

Great crested grebe
Podiceps cristatus
18–20 in (46–51 cm)

Albatrosses, petrels, and shearwaters

Order Procellariiformes

From tiny storm-petrels to the wandering albatross (which has the longest wingspan of any bird), albatrosses, shearwaters, and petrels are all characterized by tubular nostrils. They spend much time over open sea, but come to land to breed. Smaller species, effectively unable to walk, visit nests only under cover of darkness, and even the larger species are weak on land, but all show great mastery of oceanic conditions.

ROYAL PAIR
A breeding pair of royal albatrosses (*Diomedea epomophora*) on their nest.

Northern fulmar
Fulmarus glacialis
17½–19½ in (45–50 cm)

Cory's shearwater
Calonectris diomedea
17½–22 in (45–56 cm)

European storm-petrel
Hydrobates pelagicus
5½–6½ in (14–17 cm)

Flamingos

Order Phoenicopteriformes

Flamingos are tropical and temperate waterside birds that live and breed socially, within very few, large breeding colonies. Tens or hundreds of thousands gather to feed in very restricted areas with favorable conditions. They are long-legged, long-necked, and have remarkable, angled bills used for filtering food from the water as they wade, or sometimes swim.

Greater flamingo
Phoenicopterus ruber
4–4¾ ft (1.2–1.45 m)

Storks, ibises, and herons

Order Ciconiiformes

This is a varied group of waterside birds that includes herons, bitterns, egrets, storks, ibises, and spoonbills. They are widespread, but some species are localized, restricted to tiny areas of suitable habitat such as reed beds. Most are long-legged, long-necked birds, with daggerlike bills for grasping, not stabbing, fish. Spoonbills have flattened bills with sensitive, spoon-shaped tips used to detect food in shallow water.

Black-crowned night-heron
Nycticorax nycticorax
23–63 in (58–65 cm)

European spoonbill
Platalea leucorodia
32–37 in (80–93 cm)

Scarlet ibis
Eudocimus ruber
22–27 in (56–68 cm)

European white stork
Ciconia ciconia
3–3½ ft (0.95–1.1 m)

Cattle egret
Bubulcus ibis
18–20 in (45–50 cm)

Grey heron
Ardea cinerea
35–39 in (90–98 cm)

Pelicans and relatives

Order Pelecaniformes

A widespread group in tropical and temperate regions, these birds all share long, angular wings, flexible throat pouches, and forward-facing eyes. All but the frigatebirds have webbing joining all four toes (unlike ducks or gulls). Many are seabirds, but some are freshwater species. Colonies sometimes number many thousands of pairs.

Great frigatebird
Fregata minor
33–41 in (85–105 cm)

Shoebill
Balaeniceps rex
3½–4½ ft
(1.1–1.4 m)

Brown pelican
Pelecanus occidentalis
3½–5 ft (1–1.5 m)

Northern gannet
Morus bassanus
35–39¾ in (89–102 cm)

Great cormorant
Phalacrocorax carbo
31–39 in (80–100 cm)

Birds of prey

Orders Accipitriformes, Cathartiformes, and Falconiformes

A diverse group, birds of prey include birds smaller than a thrush as well as some of the world's largest flying birds. Many are predatory, others scavengers, and some are largely vegetarian. Most species have muscular legs, sharp talons, and a sharp, hooked bill.

Turkey vulture
Cathartes aura
25–32 in (64–81 cm)

Andean condor
Vultur gryphus
4–4¼ ft (1.2–1.3 m)

Southern caracara
Caracara plancus
19½–23 in (49–59 cm)

Common kestrel
Falco tinnunculus 12–15 in (30–38 cm)

Harris's hawk
Parabuteo unicinctus
30 in (75 cm)

Secretary bird
Sagittarius serpentarius
4¼–4½ ft (1.3–1.4 m)

White-bellied sea eagle *Haliaeetus leucogaster* 28 in (70 cm)

Egyptian vulture (immature) *Neophron percnopterus* 23–28 in (58–70 cm)

Cranes and rails

Order Gruiformes

Characterized by the tall, upright, long-legged, powerful cranes, these birds are strongly migratory and social. The group includes birds as varied as rails and crakes, many of which are waterside birds; the bustards, which inhabit various open grassland habitats; and oddities such as the limpkin and seriemas. The order is widespread, but many species are secretive, and some are relatively little-known.

Great bustard
Otis tarda
3½ ft (1.1 m)

Little bustard
Tetrax tetrax
15½–17½ in (40–45 cm)

Kagu
Rhynochetos jubatus 21½ in (55 cm)

Buff-banded rail
Gallirallus philippensis
11–13 in (28–33 cm)

Water rail
Rallus aquaticus
8½–11 in (22–28 cm)

Purple swamphen
Porphyrio porphyrio
15–19½ in (38–50 cm)

Common moorhen
Gallinula chloropus
12½–14 in (32–35 cm)

Limpkin
Aramus guarauna 22–28 cm (56–71 cm)

Common crane
Grus grus
3–4 ft (0.95–1.2 m)

Waders, gulls, and auks

Order Charadriiformes

This large and varied order, found worldwide, includes some of the greatest long-distance migrants of the bird world. The core groups are wading birds or shorebirds, including plovers and sandpipers; the more marine gulls and terns; and true seabirds, the auks, including guillemots and puffins, which breed in spectacular coastal colonies. Waders show great variation in size, bill shape, and leg length, according to their various foods and habitats. They spend most time close to water, but breed on tundra, moorland, marshland, or even farmed habitats.

Eurasian oystercatcher
Haematopus ostralegus
15½–17½ in (40–45 cm)

Masked lapwing
Vanellus miles 13–15 in (33–38 cm)

Black-necked stilt
Himantopus mexicanus
14 in (35 cm)

Little ringed plover
Charadrius dubius
5½–6 in (14–15 cm)

Wattled jacana
Jacana jacana
6½–10 in (17–25 cm)

Eurasian curlew
Numenius arquata
19½–23½ in (50–60 cm)

Pied avocet
Recurvirostra avosetta
16½–17½ in (42–45 cm)

Common gull
Larus canus
15–17½ in (38–44 cm)

Inca tern
Larosterna inca
15½–16½ in (39–42 cm)

Long-tailed jaeger
Stercorarius longicaudus
19–21 in (48–53 cm)

Atlantic puffin
Fratercula arctica
10 in (25 cm)

Sandgrouse

Order Pteroclidiformes

The sandgrouse are a small group of terrestrial birds found in warm or hot, open steppe or semidesert habitats. These short-legged, stout-bodied, long-winged birds are weak walkers but swift fliers. They often live socially, making regular morning or evening flights to water. They can carry water back to their chicks in their soaked belly feathers.

Pin-tailed sandgrouse
Pterocles alchata
11 in (28 cm)

Parrots and cockatoos

Order Psittaciformes

Widespread tropical birds, which are found mostly in scrub, woodland, or forest. They are often social, and feed on fruit and seeds. All have short legs, strong feet with two toes pointing backward, and stout, hooked bills with bare skin (a "cere") at the base, somewhat like falcons and pigeons.

Kea
Nestor notabilis
18 in (46 cm)

White cockatoo
Cacatua alba
18 in (46 cm)

Brown lory
Chalcopsitta duivenbodei
12½ in (32 cm)

Black-winged lory
Eos cyanogenia
4 in (10 cm)

Pigeons and doves

Order Columbiformes

A large group of species, which is found worldwide on land, except in areas of extreme cold and desert conditions. The order comprises pigeons and doves (there is no clear separation between the two) and includes two well-known extinct families, the dodo and solitaires.

Speckled pigeon
Columba guinea
13½ in (33 cm)

Croaking ground dove
Columbina cruziana
6 in (15 cm)

Mourning dove
Zenaida macroura
9–13½ in (23–34 cm)

Pink-spotted fruit dove
Ptilinopus perlatus
10 in (26 cm)

Red-fronted lorikeet
Charmosyna rubronotata 4 in (10 cm)

St. Vincent parrot
Amazona guildingii 15½ in (40 cm)

Cuckoos and turacos

Order Cuculiformes

This group is found widely around the world, some cuckoos being long-distance migrants between tropical and temperate regions. Turacos are residents of tropical forests, and the hoatzin lives in South American forests. Many cuckoos lay their eggs in the nests of other species and play no part in raising their own young. Cuckoos feed on insects, especially caterpillars.

Red-crested turaco
Tauraco erythrolophus
15½–17 in (40–43 cm)

Common cuckoo
Cuculus canorus 12½–13 in (32–33 cm)

TREE DWELLER
This primitive South American hoatzin (*Opisthocomus hoazin*) lives in trees and feeds almost entirely on leaves. It is 24–28 in (62–72 cm) in length.

Owls

Order Strigiformes

Owls and barn owls are mostly crepuscular or nocturnal, but some feed by day. Most owls have excellent hearing and eyesight; adapted to almost silent flight, they are able to pinpoint prey by sound in near darkness or under snow. They occupy tundra and desert, dense rain forest, and open scrub. Found worldwide, the barn owl is among the most widespread of land birds.

Eagle owl
Bubo bubo
23–29 in (59–73 cm)

Spectacled owl
Pulsatrix perspicillata
17–20½ in (43–52 cm)

Tawny owl
Strix aluco
14½–15½ in (37–39 cm)

Ural owl
Strix uralensis
23–24 in (58–62 cm)

Great grey owl
Strix nebulosa
23–33 in (59–85 cm)

Eurasian pygmy owl
Glaucidium passerinum
6–7½ in (15–19 cm)

Northern hawk-owl
Surnia ulula
14–16 in (36–41 cm)

Barn owl
Tyto alba
11½–17½ in (29–44 cm)

Nightjars and frogmouths

Order Caprimulgiformes

Nightjars and frogmouths are found around the world, together with localized species of Caprimulgiformes, such as the oilbird. They are active at dawn and dusk or in darkness, usually hunting for flying insects. Nightjars and frogmouths are characterized by tiny legs, tiny bills with huge gapes, large eyes, and highly cryptic plumage patterns. By day they rely on their camouflage to hide against bark, in foliage, or on the ground.

European nightjar
Caprimulgus europaeus 10–11 in (26–28 cm)

Tawny frogmouth
Podargus strigoides
13½–21 in (34–53 cm)

Common potoo
Nyctibius griseus
13–15 in (33–38cm)

Hummingbirds and swifts

Order Apodiformes

Swifts are the world's most aerial birds, some not coming to land for two or three years, and then only to nest. They catch insects, despite having tiny bills. The hummingbirds eat nectar, having highly adapted bill shapes. The world's most maneuverable birds, they hover, dash forward, or can even fly backward. This group includes the world's smallest birds.

Pallid swift
Apus pallidus
6½–7 in
(16–18 cm)

Andean hillstar
*Oreotrochilus
estella* 5–6 in
(13–15 cm)

Mousebirds

Order Coliiformes

Just six species, all found in tropical Africa, make up this order. They are characteristic of open bush in the great savanna plains. Mousebirds have small, decurved bills, short but strong feet, and long, slender tail feathers. They are highly social birds, feeding close together. This is one of only two orders of birds exclusively native to Africa. The other is the ostrich.

Blue-naped mousebird
Urocolius macrourus
13–14 in (33–36 cm)

Speckled mousebird
Colius striatus
12–15½ in (30–40 cm)

Trogons

Order Trogoniformes

Despite being found in the widely separated tropical regions of Africa, the Americas, and Indo-China, all trogons are remarkably similar in appearance. They are essentially green above, often barred black-and-white on the tail, and bright red, pink, orange, or yellow below. They have short, stout bills, and short legs. Most species prefer forest or woodland habitats and feed on insects.

Resplendent quetzal
Pharomachrus mocinno
14–15½ in (35–40 cm)

Violaceous trogon
Trogon violaceus
9–10 in (23–26 cm)

Woodpeckers and toucans

Order Piciformes

Puffbirds, barbets, honeyguides, toucans, and woodpeckers form a group with zygodactyl feet—meaning that they have two toes facing forward and two toes facing backward. They have strong bills and often rather bold, noisy behavior. Honeyguides lead other animals to bees' nests and benefit from the other animals breaking into the hives. Toucans are characterized by remarkable, colorful, long but lightweight bills. Woodpeckers use their tails as "props" to support them against upright branches, and "drum" against branches with their bills, using this instrumental communication in place of conventional song. Only the woodpeckers are widespread on several continents.

Toco toucan
Ramphastos toco
21–23½ in (53–60 cm)

D'Arnaud's barbet
Trachyphonus darnaudii
8 in (20 cm)

Greater honeyguide
Indicator indicator
8 in (20 cm)

Northern wryneck
Jynx torquilla
6½ in (16 cm)

Middle spotted woodpecker
Dendrocopos medius
7½–8½ in (19–22 cm)

Rufous-tailed jacamar
Galbula ruficauda
10 in (25 cm)

Kingfishers and relatives

Order Coraciiformes

Kingfishers, motmots, bee-eaters, rollers, hoopoes, and hornbills as a group are represented almost worldwide, but only kingfishers are really widespread. Few kingfishers actually eat fish, many catching insects or reptiles in woodland, as do the Australasian kookaburras. Bee-eaters take insects on the wing; rollers drop from perches to the ground to catch their prey; hoopoes and some hornbills feed on the ground. Kingfishers range from tiny to medium sized, whereas ground hornbills are huge birds. These species all nest in holes of various kinds, either tunneled into earth or ready-made in tree cavities.

European roller
Coracias garrulus
12 in (30 cm)

Laughing kookaburra
Dacelo novaeguineae
16½ in (42 cm)

Common kingfisher
Alcedo atthis 6½ in (16 cm)

Pied kingfisher
Ceryle rudis
10 in (25 cm)

Jamaican tody
Todus todus
4½ in (11 cm)

Blue-crowned motmot
Momotus momota 18½ in (47 cm)

European bee-eater
Merops apiaster
12 in (30 cm)

Common hoopoe
Upupa epops
10–11 in (26–28 cm)

Southern yellow-billed hornbill
Tockus leucomelas
19½–23½ in (50–60 cm)

Great hornbill
Buceros bicornis
5 ft (1.5 m)

Passerines

Order Passeriformes

By far the largest order of birds, all passerines have four unwebbed toes with three pointing forward, one backward. They are otherwise hugely variable in size, form, color, behavior, and habitat. Known as the perching birds, they form two varied suborders. The smaller group, the sub-oscine passeriformes, has 12 families, and the larger, the oscines, often called songbirds, has 70 families. Some songbirds, such as the crows, are not very musical, while others, such as the Australasian lyrebirds, Old and New World thrushes, and various chats, including the nightingale, are among the world's finest songsters.

Rifleman
Acanthisitta chloris
3½ in (3 cm)

Green broadbill
Calyptomena viridis
8 in (20 cm)

African pitta
Pitta angolensis
8 in (20 cm)

Barred antshrike
Thamnophilus doliatus
6½ in (16 cm)

Three-wattled bellbird
Procnias tricarunculatus
10–12 in (25–30 cm)

Sharpbill
Oxyruncus cristatus
6½ in (17 cm)

Eastern kingbird
Tyrannus tyrannus
8 in (20 cm)

Blue manakin
Chiroxiphia caudata
5 in (13 cm)

Buff-fronted foliage-gleaner
Philydor rufum. 7½ in (19 cm)

Wedge-billed woodcreeper
Glyphorynchus spirurus
5½ in (14 cm)

SUPERB LYREBIRD
Despite its extraordinary appearance, the lyrebird (*Menura novaehollandiae*) is elusive. It is known for its remarkable mimicry of natural and artificial sounds.

Red-backed fairy-wren
Malurus melanocephalus
4–5 in (10–13 cm)

Blue-faced honeyeater
Entomyzon cyanotis
12 in (31 cm)

Brown thornbill
Acanthiza pusilla
4 in (10 cm)

Grey-chinned minivet
Pericrocotus solaris
7½ in (19 cm)

Lesser grey shrike
Lanius minor 7½–8 in (19–20 cm)

Tawny-crowned greenlet
Hylophilus ochraceiceps 4½ in (11.5 cm)

Eastern black-headed oriole
Oriolus larvatus 8½ in (22 cm)

Magpie-lark
Grallina cyanoleuca
11½ in (29 cm)

Carrion crow
Corvus corone
20½ in (52 cm)

Blue jay
Cyanocitta cristata
12 in (30 cm)

Scarlet robin
Petroica boodang
4¾–5½ in (12–14 cm)

White-necked picathartes
Picathartes gymnocephalus
15½–19½ in (39–50 cm)

Bohemian waxwing
Bombycilla garrulus 6½ in (17 cm)

Greater bird-of-paradise
Paradisaea apoda
14 in (35 cm)

Palmchat
Dulus dominicus
7 in (18 cm)

Blue tit
Parus caeruleus 4½ in (12 cm)

Bank swallow
Riparia riparia
4½ in (12 cm)

Eurasian skylark
Alauda arvensis
7–7½ in (18–19 cm)

Red-whiskered bulbul
Pycnonotus jocosus
8 in (20 cm)

Dartford warbler
Sylvia undata
4½–5 in (12–13 cm)

Red-billed leiothrix
Leiothrix lutea
6 in (15 cm)

Bearded tit
Panurus biarmicus
4½–6 in (12–15 cm)

Asian fairy-bluebird
Irena puella
10½ in (27 cm)

Cape white-eye
Zosterops pallidus 4½ in (11 cm)

Winter Wren
Troglodytes troglodytes
3½–4 in (9–10 cm)

Eurasian nuthatch
Sitta europaea
4–8 in (10–20 cm)

Eurasian treecreeper
Certhia familiaris
5 in (12.5 cm)

Northern mockingbird
Mimus polyglottos
9–11 in (23–28 cm)

Common starling
Sturnus vulgaris
8½ in (21 cm)

Song thrush
Turdus philomelos
9 in (23 cm)

Rufous-gorgetted flycatcher
Ficedula strophiata
5½ in (14 cm)

Scarlet-chested sunbird
Chalcomitra senegalensis 6 in (15 cm)

House sparrow
Passer domesticus
5½ in (14 cm)

Java sparrow
Lonchura oryzivora
5½–6 in (14–15 cm)

Dunnock
Prunella modularis
5½ in (14 cm)

Richard's pipit
Anthus richardi
6½–8 in (17–20 cm)

Eurasian bullfinch
Pyrrhula pyrrhula
6 in (15 cm)

Hooded warbler
Wilsonia citrina 5½ in (14 cm)

Bullock's oriole
Icterus bullockii
8½ in (21 cm)

Snow bunting
Piectrophenax nivalis
6½ in (16 cm)

Green honeycreeper
Chlorophanes spiza 5½ in (14 cm)

Northern cardinal
Cardinalis cardinalis 8½ in (22 cm)

BEARDED TIT
Related to Asian parrotbills rather than true tits, the bearded tit (*Panurus biarmicus*) is usually confined to reed beds. When numbers are high in fall, some disperse in search of new sites and may be seen in cattails or other marsh plants.

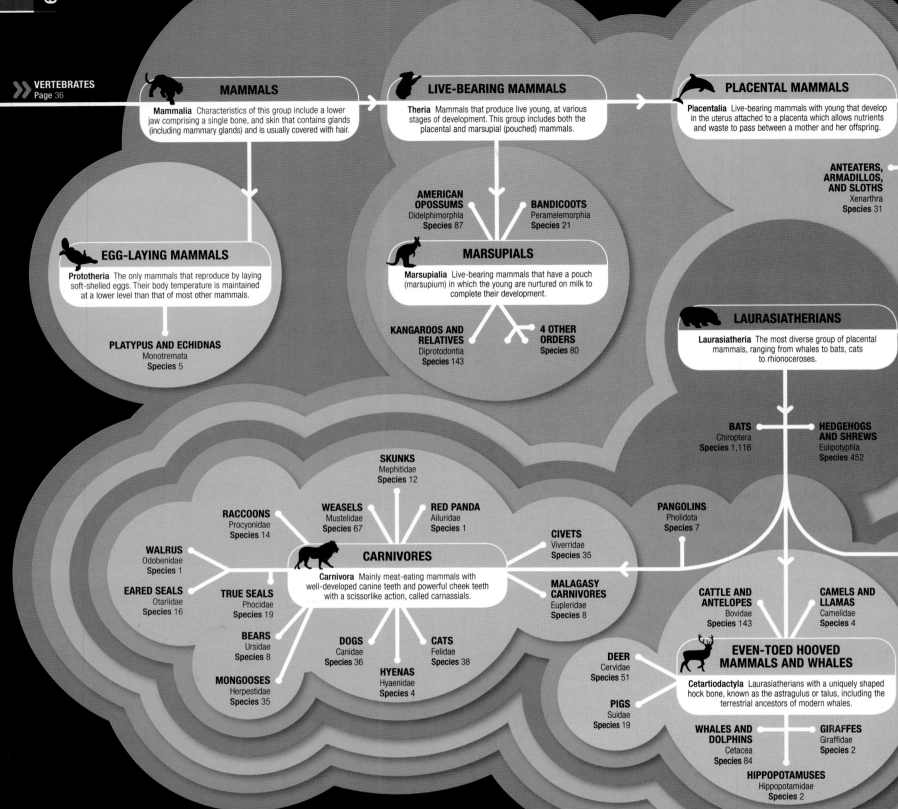

MAMMALS

Mammalia Characteristics of this group include a lower jaw comprising a single bone, and skin that contains glands (including mammary glands) and is usually covered with hair.

LIVE-BEARING MAMMALS

Theria Mammals that produce live young, at various stages of development. This group includes both the placental and marsupial (pouched) mammals.

PLACENTAL MAMMALS

Placentalia Live-bearing mammals with young that develop in the uterus attached to a placenta which allows nutrients and waste to pass between a mother and her offspring.

ANTEATERS, ARMADILLOS, AND SLOTHS
Xenarthra
Species 31

EGG-LAYING MAMMALS

Prototheria The only mammals that reproduce by laying soft-shelled eggs. Their body temperature is maintained at a lower level than that of most other mammals.

AMERICAN OPOSSUMS
Didelphimorphia
Species 87

BANDICOOTS
Peramelemorphia
Species 21

MARSUPIALS

Marsupialia Live-bearing mammals that have a pouch (marsupium) in which the young are nurtured on milk to complete their development.

PLATYPUS AND ECHIDNAS
Monotremata
Species 5

KANGAROOS AND RELATIVES
Diprotodontia
Species 143

4 OTHER ORDERS
Species 80

LAURASIATHERIANS

Laurasiatheria The most diverse group of placental mammals, ranging from whales to bats, cats to rhionoceroses.

BATS
Chiroptera
Species 1,116

HEDGEHOGS AND SHREWS
Eulipotyphla
Species 452

SKUNKS
Mephitidae
Species 12

WEASELS
Mustelidae
Species 67

RED PANDA
Ailuridae
Species 1

PANGOLINS
Pholidota
Species 7

RACCOONS
Procyonidae
Species 14

CIVETS
Viverridae
Species 35

WALRUS
Odobenidae
Species 1

CARNIVORES

Carnivora Mainly meat-eating mammals with well-developed canine teeth and powerful cheek teeth with a scissorlike action, called carnassials.

MALAGASY CARNIVORES
Eupleridae
Species 8

CATTLE AND ANTELOPES
Bovidae
Species 143

CAMELS AND LLAMAS
Camelidae
Species 4

EARED SEALS
Otariidae
Species 16

TRUE SEALS
Phocidae
Species 19

BEARS
Ursidae
Species 8

DOGS
Canidae
Species 36

CATS
Felidae
Species 38

DEER
Cervidae
Species 51

EVEN-TOED HOOVED MAMMALS AND WHALES

Cetartiodactyla Laurasiatherians with a uniquely shaped hock bone, known as the astragulus or talus, including the terrestrial ancestors of modern whales.

MONGOOSES
Herpestidae
Species 35

HYENAS
Hyaenidae
Species 4

PIGS
Suidae
Species 19

WHALES AND DOLPHINS
Cetacea
Species 84

GIRAFFES
Giraffidae
Species 2

HIPPOPOTAMUSES
Hippopotamidae
Species 2

Mammal groups

The primitive egg-laying mammals were the first group to diverge, followed by the marsupials. The placental mammals divided into three broad groups, the laurasiatherians, afrotherians, and euarchontoglires, plus the anteaters and relatives, before evolving into the diverse array of forms and sizes we see today. Although many of the traditional mammal groups, such as primates and carnivores, appear on this diagram, others are less familiar. These include the even-toed hooved mammals and whales, which have been combined quite recently using genetic and fossil evidence.

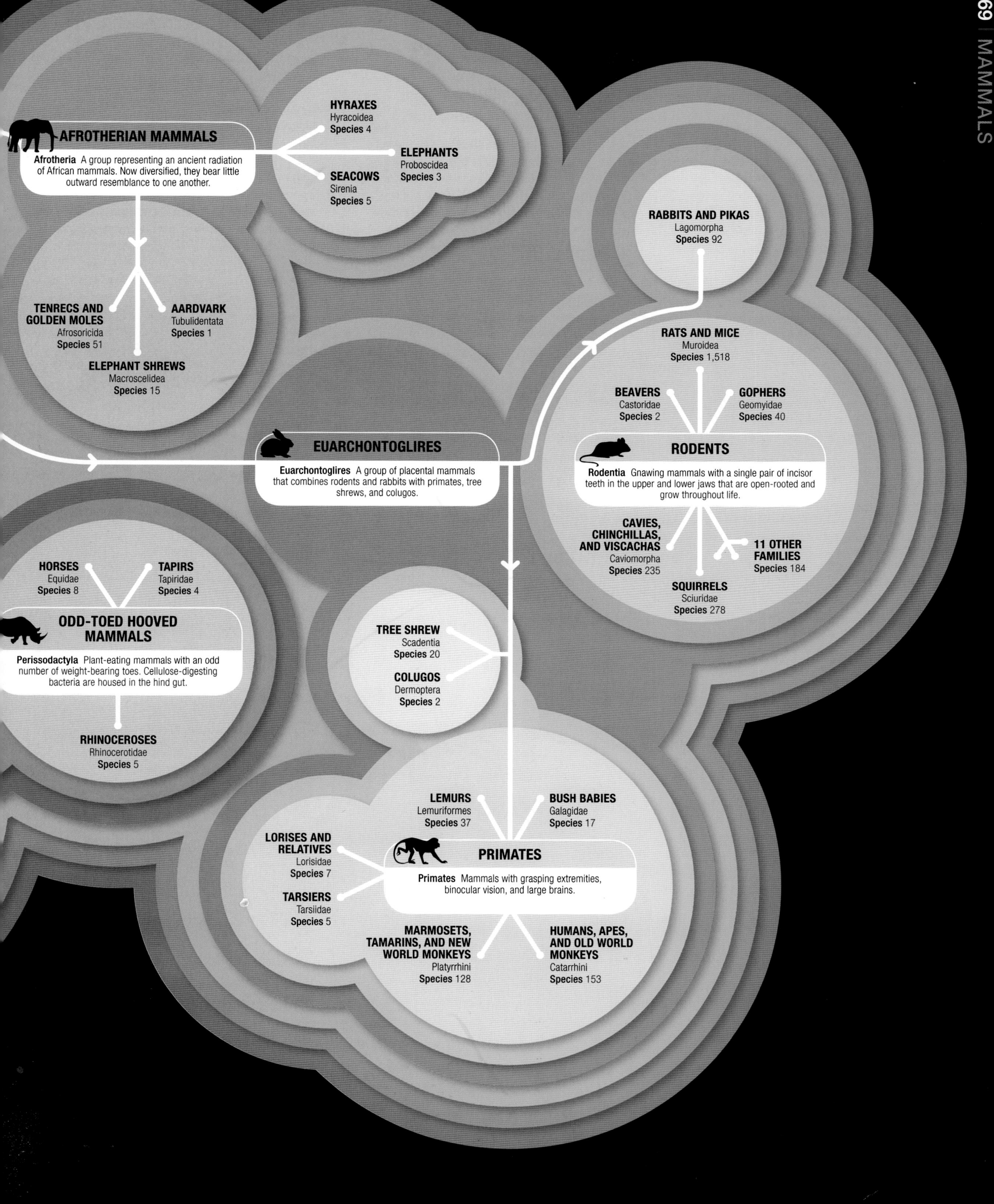

AFROTHERIAN MAMMALS

Afrotheria A group representing an ancient radiation of African mammals. Now diversified, they bear little outward resemblance to one another.

HYRAXES
Hyracoidea
Species 4

ELEPHANTS
Proboscidea
Species 3

SEACOWS
Sirenia
Species 5

TENRECS AND GOLDEN MOLES
Afrosoricida
Species 51

AARDVARK
Tubulidentata
Species 1

ELEPHANT SHREWS
Macroscelidea
Species 15

RABBITS AND PIKAS
Lagomorpha
Species 92

RATS AND MICE
Muroidea
Species 1,518

BEAVERS
Castoridae
Species 2

GOPHERS
Geomyidae
Species 40

EUARCHONTOGLIRES

Euarchontoglires A group of placental mammals that combines rodents and rabbits with primates, tree shrews, and colugos.

RODENTS

Rodentia Gnawing mammals with a single pair of incisor teeth in the upper and lower jaws that are open-rooted and grow throughout life.

CAVIES, CHINCHILLAS, AND VISCACHAS
Caviomorpha
Species 235

11 OTHER FAMILIES
Species 184

SQUIRRELS
Sciuridae
Species 278

HORSES
Equidae
Species 8

TAPIRS
Tapiridae
Species 4

ODD-TOED HOOVED MAMMALS

Perissodactyla Plant-eating mammals with an odd number of weight-bearing toes. Cellulose-digesting bacteria are housed in the hind gut.

RHINOCEROSES
Rhinocerotidae
Species 5

TREE SHREW
Scadentia
Species 20

COLUGOS
Dermoptera
Species 2

LEMURS
Lemuriformes
Species 37

BUSH BABIES
Galagidae
Species 17

LORISES AND RELATIVES
Lorisidae
Species 7

PRIMATES

Primates Mammals with grasping extremities, binocular vision, and large brains.

TARSIERS
Tarsiidae
Species 5

MARMOSETS, TAMARINS, AND NEW WORLD MONKEYS
Platyrrhini
Species 128

HUMANS, APES, AND OLD WORLD MONKEYS
Catarrhini
Species 153

Mammals

Despite their relatively late appearance in the fossil record, mammals have diversified into an astonishing array of shapes and sizes. They are most diverse and widespread on land, but have also colonized air and water.

About 5,000 species of mammal have been described, ranging from the egg-laying duck-billed platypus to humans with their sophisticated brain and hand dexterity, but there are similarities that unite them all in the class Mammalia. Mammals uniquely possess fur, which protects delicate skin, provides camouflage, and helps insulate the body. Mammals also have skin glands, among which are sebaceous glands that allow sweating. Mammals are endothermic, which means that they maintain a constant body temperature—often above that of their surroundings—by producing heat through metabolic processes, such as breaking down fat. Milk-producing mammary glands are also found only in mammals. The milk provides nourishment to offspring, removing the need to expend energy on foraging, and initially contains antibodies, which protect infants from disease.

Key characters
The only characters that can identify all mammals, whether extant (living) or fossil, are skeletal—among these are the possession of a single bone in the lower jaw (dentary) and having three bones (incus, stapes, and malleus) in the middle ear. Any one of these features identifies an animal as a mammal and separates it from all other living things.

Monotremes

Order Monotremata

All other mammals produce live young, but monotremes lay soft-shelled eggs, which hatch after a short incubation period. Monotremes have only a single posterior opening, called the cloaca, into which the urinary, alimentary, and reproductive systems open.

Duck-billed platypus
Ornithorhynchus anatinus
16–24 in (40–60 cm)

Short-beaked echidna
Tachyglossus aculeatus 12–17½ in (30–45 cm)

Marsupials

Supercohort Marsupialia

These are the so-called pouched mammals, although not all of the species have one. The offspring are born after a very limited gestation period, and then make their way to the pouch. Born in almost embryonic form, the young attach to a nipple and suckle milk while completing their development. Marsupialia is divided into seven orders, including: American opossums (Didelphimorphia); bandicoots and bilbies (Paramelemorphia); and koalas, kangaroos, wombats, and possums (Diprotodontia).

Virginia opossum
Didelphis virginiana
15–20 in (38–50 cm)

Tasmanian devil
Sarcophilus harrisii
28–42 in (70–110 cm)

Common brush-tailed possum
Trichosurus vulpecula
14–23 in (35–58 cm)

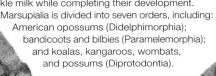
Greater glider
Petauroides volans
14–19 in (35–48 cm)

Feather-tailed possum
Distoechurus pennatus
4½–5½ in (10.5–13.5 cm)

Red-necked wallaby
Macropus rufogriseus
28–41 in (70–105 cm)

Rufus bettong
Aepyprymnus rufescens 14½–20½ in (37–52 cm)

Quokka
Setonix brachyurus
16–21½ in (40–54 cm)

Koala
Phascolarctos cinereus
26–31 in (65–78 cm)

Red kangaroo
Macropus rufus
3¼–5¼ ft (1–1.6 m)

Common wombat
Vombatus ursinus 28–47 in (70–120 cm)

HONEY POSSUM
This tiny Australian marsupial (*Tarsipes rostratus*) is only 2½–3½ in (6.5–9 cm) long, and gathers pollen and nectar ("honey") from flowers.

Tenrecs and golden moles

Order Afrosoricida

This recently recognized group is chiefly supported by genetic evidence, but there are some features of the dentition that are characteristic. Afrosoricids have only one major cusp on each of the upper molars; other placental mammals have several.

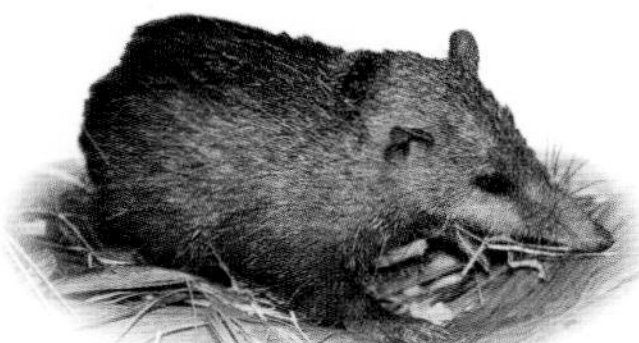

Common tenrec
Tenrec ecaudatus 10–15½ in (25–39 cm)

Elephant shrews (Sengis)

Order Macroscelidea

Elephant shrews, or sengis, are characterized by a long, highly mobile snout, an enlarged cecum (a pouch connected to the large intestine) in the hind gut, and cheek teeth that can grow throughout life since they have open roots.

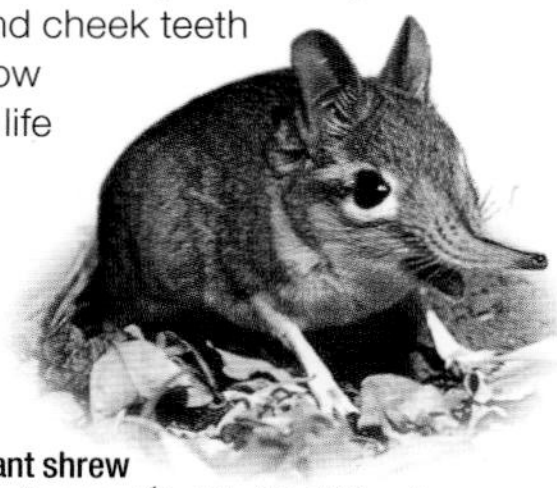

Rufous elephant shrew
Elephantulus rufescens 4½–5 in (12–12.5 cm)

Aardvark

Order Tubulidentata

This monospecific order comprises only the long-eared, long-snouted aardvark. Unlike most other mammals, its teeth lack an outer coating of enamel and are covered instead with cementum, the same tissue that coats tooth roots.

Aardvark
Orycteropus afer
5¼ ft (1.6 m)

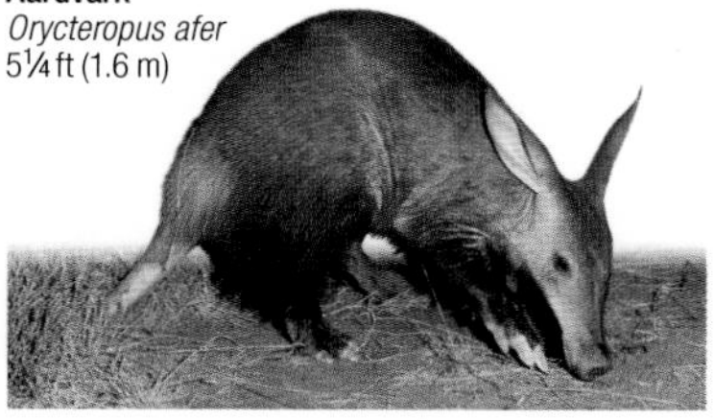

Hyraxes

Order Hyracoidea

These species have a unique eye structure. A part of the iris projects over the pupil. This has the effect of reducing the amount of overhead light entering the eye.

Rock hyrax
Procavia capensis
21–23 in (30–58 cm)

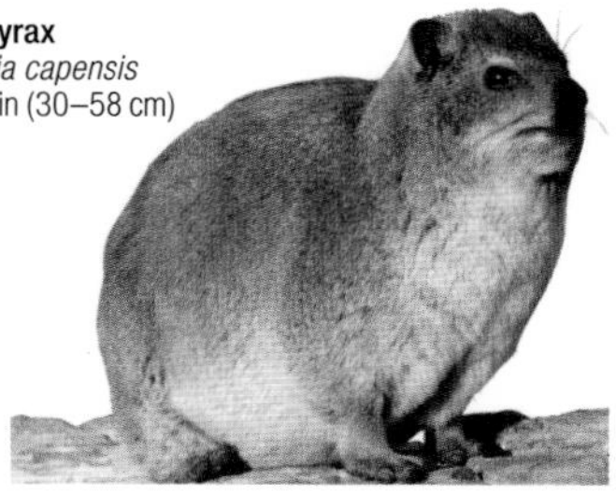

Elephants

Order Proboscidea

An elephant can be easily recognized by its large size, columnar legs, and long trunk. The incisor teeth are modified into continually growing tusks of dentine, while the molar teeth—of which there are six in each half of the upper and lower jaws—erupt at the back of the jaw and migrate forward in a conveyer-belt-like fashion over about 60 years. The large head is made lighter by the presence of air pockets in the skull.

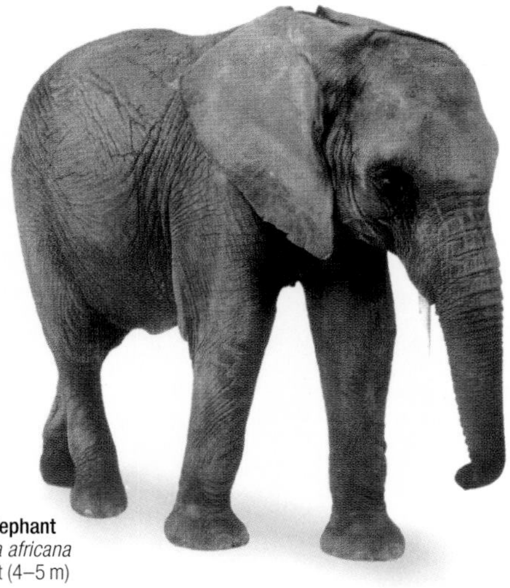

African elephant
Loxodonta africana
13–16½ ft (4–5 m)

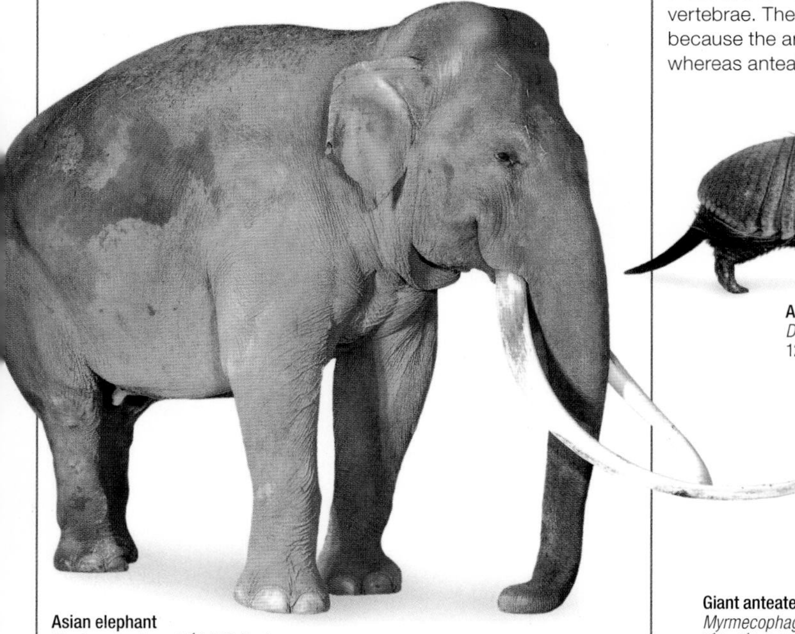

Asian elephant
Elephas maximus 11½ ft (3.5 m)

Dugongs and manatees

Order Sirenia

These large, slow-moving creatures are streamlined for their aquatic lifestyle. Sirenian forelimbs are modified into flippers, while the hindlimbs have been entirely lost. Instead there is a horizontal, spatula-like tail. Manatees have only six neck vertebrae compared to the seven found in most other mammals. Entirely herbivorous, sirenians have unusually long guts, with bacteria for the digestion of cellulose. This bacteria is housed in the cecum in the hind portion of the gut, as it is in horses. They are the only marine mammals that feed purely on plants. Cheek tooth replacement is similar to that of the elephant.

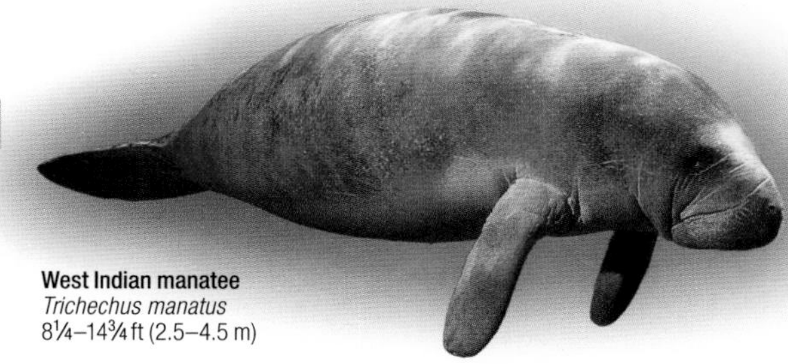

West Indian manatee
Trichechus manatus
8¼–14¾ ft (2.5–4.5 m)

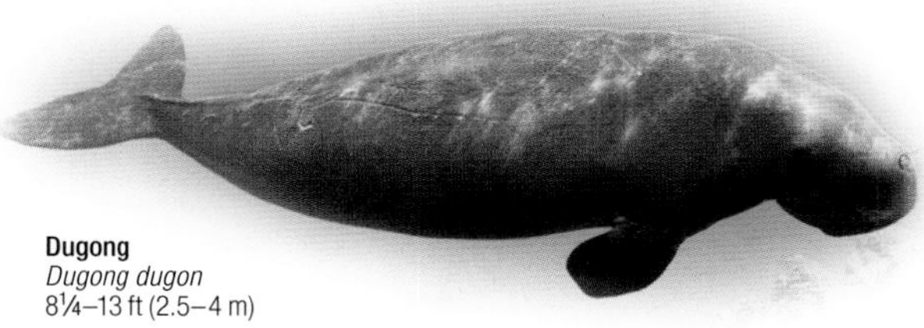

Dugong
Dugong dugon
8¼–13 ft (2.5–4 m)

Anteaters and relatives

Orders Pilosa, Cingulata

The order Pilosa comprises anteaters and sloths, and the order Cingulata contains the armadillos. Both groups are unique in having a double vena cava vein in the lower part of the body and additional moving joints, or articulations—called xenarthrales—on the lower lumbar vertebrae. The two groups can easily be separated because the armadillos have an armored upper body whereas anteaters and sloths have fur.

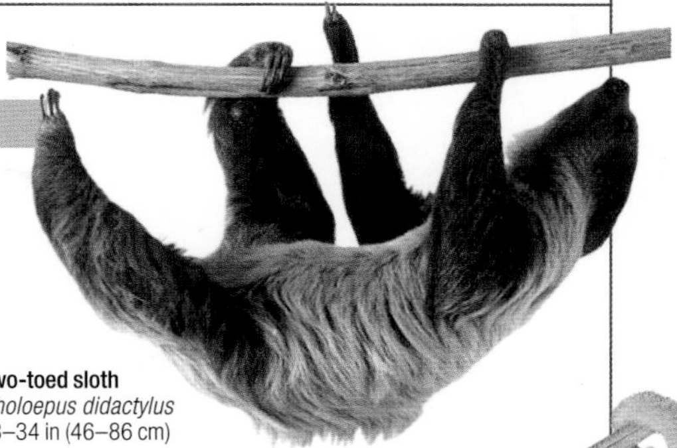

Two-toed sloth
Choloepus didactylus
18–34 in (46–86 cm)

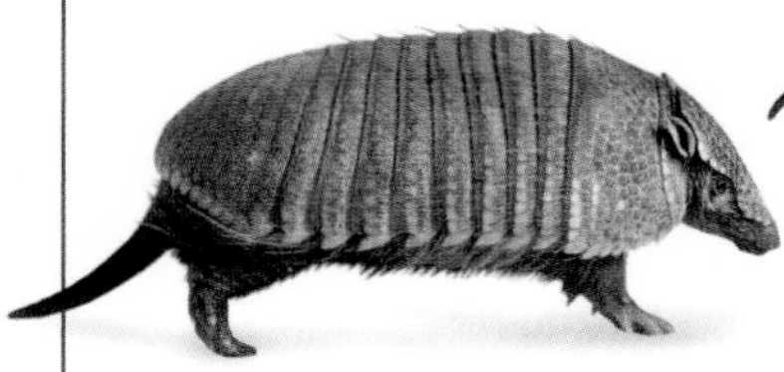

Armadillo
Dasypus sp.
12–15½ in (30–40 cm)

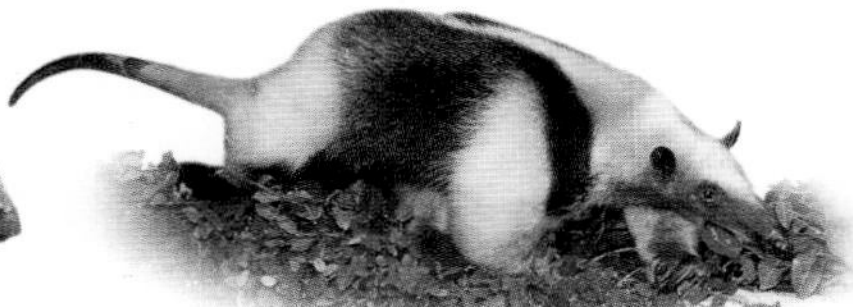

Southern tamandua
Tamandua tetradactyla 21–35 in (53–88 cm)

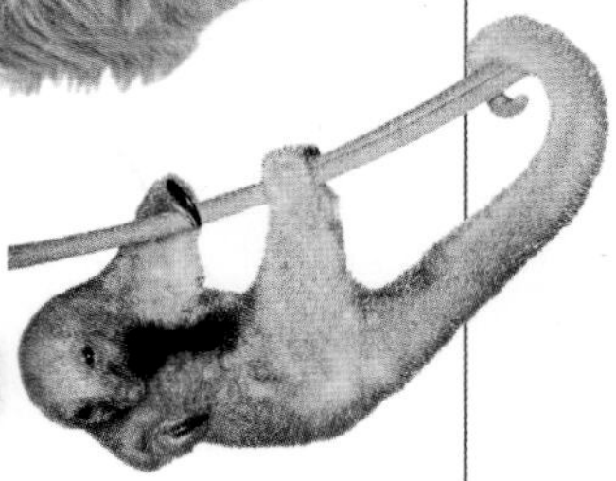

Silky anteater
Cyclopes didactylus
6½–8½ in (16–21 cm)

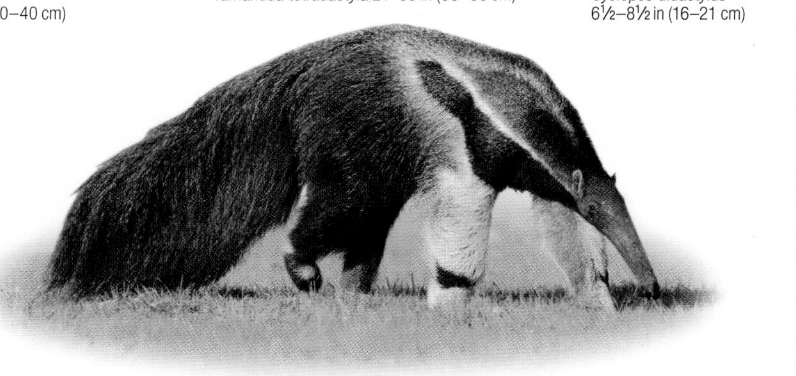

Giant anteater
Myrmecophaga tridactyla
3¼–6½ ft (1–2 m)

Rodents

Order Rodentia

These are the gnawing mammals. Most are small, but all have characteristic teeth. Rodents have a single pair of continually growing incisor teeth in the upper and lower jaws that are sharpened as the lower ones sheer against the inside of the upper ones. Canine teeth are absent, leaving a gap called the diastema. Many species have broad, ridged cheek teeth, which are effective in grinding up vegetation, but some rodents are carnivorous. The cavylike rodents can be separated from the other rodents on the basis of their jaw musculature and longer gestation periods that lead to the birth of smaller numbers of well-developed offspring.

Canadian beaver
Castor canadensis
29–35 in (74–88 cm)

Gray squirrel
Sciurus carolinensis
9–12 in (23–30 cm)

Alpine marmot
Marmota marmota
19½–21½ in (50–55 cm)

Springhare
Pedetes capensis
10½–15½ in
(27–40 cm)

Spiny mouse
Acomys cilicius 6½–7 in (17–18 cm)

Striped grass mouse
Lemniscomys striatus
4–5½ in (10–14 cm)

Malagasy giant rat
Hypogeomys antimena 12–14 in (30–35 cm)

Brown rat
Rattus norvegicus
8½–11½ in (21–29 cm)

Bank vole
Clethrionomys glareolus 3¼–4½ in (8–11 cm)

Red vole
Clethrionomys rutilus 3¼–4½ in (8–11 cm)

Forest dormouse
Dryomys nitedula
3¼–5 in (8–13 cm)

Four-toed jerboa
Allactaga tetradactyla
4–4½ in (10–12 cm)

North American porcupine
Erethizon dorsatum
26–31 in (65–80 cm)

Long-tailed chinchilla
Chinchilla lanigera 8½–9 in (22–23 cm)

Cape porcupine
Hystrix africaeaustralis 19½ in (50 cm)

Naked mole-rat
Heterocephalus glaber
5½–7 in (14–18 cm)

Capybara
Hydrochoerus hydrochaeris
3½–4¼ ft (1.1–1.3 m)

Rabbits, hares, and pikas

Order Lagomorpha

These are herbivorous mammals that gain maximum nutrients from food by ingesting it twice, a behavior called coprophagy. Rabbits and pikas also have very distinctive upper incisor teeth, with a pair of small, nonfunctional, peglike incisors behind the functional pair. Like rodents, they lack canines, which creates a large gap through which the lips can be drawn to prevent debris from entering the mouth while feeding.

Hispid hare
Caprolagus hispidus
15–19½ in (38–50 cm)

Rabbit
Oryctolagus cuniculus
14–19½ in (35–50 cm)

North American pika
Ochotona princeps 6½–8½ in (16–22 cm)

Primates

Order Primates

Members of this order are characterized by an opposable thumb or toe and the ability to rotate the lower arm bones (radius and ulna) around one another. These features allow primates to grasp and manipulate objects. The order is generally subdivided. The lemurs, galagos, and lorises form the strepsirhines, which depend more on their sense of smell than do monkeys and apes. They generally have longer snouts, a glandular (and therefore moist) and naked nasal region, and comma-shaped nostrils. The tarsiers, marmosets, monkeys, and apes form the second group, the haplorhines, which have dry noses with ovate nostrils.

Ring-tailed lemur
Lemur catta
15½–18 in (39–46 cm)

Slender loris
Loris tardigradus
6½–10 in (17–26 cm)

Senegal bushbaby
Galago senegalensis 6–6½ in (15–17 cm)

Golden lion tamarin
Leontopithicus rosalia
8–10 in (20–25 cm)

Gray woolly monkey
Legothrix cana
19½–26 in (50–65 cm)

Red howler monkey
Alouatta seniculus
20–25 in (51–63 cm)

Bolivian squirrel monkey
Saimiri boliviensis
10½–12½ in (27–32 cm)

Patas monkey
Erythrocebus patas
23½–35 in (60–88 cm)

Black and white colobus monkey
Colobus guereza
20½–22½ in (52–57 cm)

Proboscis monkey
Nasalis larvatus 29–30 in (73–76 cm)

Gelada
Theropithecus gelada 28–29 in (70–74 cm)

Lar gibbon
Hylobates lar 16½–23 in (42–59 cm)

Western gorilla
Gorilla gorilla
4¼–6¼ ft (1.3–1.9 m)

Mandrill
Mandrillus sphinx
25–32 in (63–81 cm)

De Brazza's monkey
Cercopithecus neglectus
19½–23 in (50–59 cm)

Chimpanzee
Pan troglodytes
2½–3 ft (0.75–1 m)

Siamang
Hylobates syndactylus
35 in (90 cm)

Orangutan
Pongo pygmaeus 3–3 ft 3 in (0.9–1 m)

Tree shrews

Order Scandentia

These rather squirrel-like mammals have slender bodies and long tails. In the past they have been classified as insectivores and as primates on the basis of characters they have in common with these orders. However, genetic evidence now suggests that tree shrews are an ancient group with an independent evolutionary history.

Lesser tree shrew
Tupaia minor
4½–5½ in (11.5–13.5 cm)

Flying lemurs

Order Dermoptera

Flying lemurs, or colugos, are cat-sized, arboreal mammals. Their distinctive feature is the large gliding membrane, called a patagium, which stretches from the neck to the front and hind digits and onto the very tip of the tail.

Malaysian flying lemur
Cynocephalus variegatus
13–16½ in (33–42 cm)

Insectivores

Order Eulipotyphla

These insect-eating animals have a small brain, which lacks the copious infolding found in other mammals. In common with monotremes and marsupials, they have a cloaca, but unlike them the young develop longer in the womb.

European mole
Talpa europaea
4½–6½in (11–16cm)

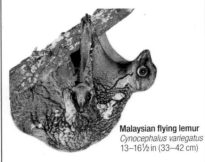

European hedgehog
Erinaceus europaeus
8–12 in (20–30 cm)

Common shrew
Sorex araneus
2¼–3½ in (5.5–9 cm)

Bats

Order Chiroptera

Bats are the only mammals that are capable of powered flight. Their forelimbs have very long finger bones that support the flight membrane. Some bats, known as flying foxes, feed only on fruit and nectar. They do not echolocate because they have excellent vision and sense of smell. Most bats eat insects, which they locate by emitting ultrasound pulses and listening to the returning echoes. To pinpoint the sounds these bats may have large ears with an additional projection called a tragus.

Lesser mouse-tailed bat
Rhinopoma hardwickei
2¼–2¾ in
(5.5–7 cm)

Lesser horseshoe bat
Rhinolophus hipposideros
1½–1¾ in (3.5–4.5 cm)

Rodrigues flying fox
Pteropus rodricensis
14 in (35 cm)

Seba's short-tailed bat
Carollia perspicillata
2–2½ in (5–6.5 cm)

Common vampire bat
Desmodus rotundus 2¾–3½ in (7–9 cm)

Noctule bat
Nyctalus noctula
2¼–3¼ in (6–8 cm)

Daubenton's bat
Myotis daubentonii
1¾–2¼ in (4.5–5.5 cm)

Whiskered bat
Myotis mystacina
1½–2 in (3.5–5 cm)

Brown long-eared bat
Plecotus auritus
1½–2 in (4–5 cm)

Parti-colored bat
Vespertilio murinus
2–2½ in (5–6.5 cm)

Pangolins

Order Pholidota

Distinctive, overlapping body scales provide pangolins with a unique protective armor. Since they feed primarily on ants and termites, they lack teeth and the lower jaw is much reduced. With no teeth to grind up their food, pangolins have a tough, muscular stomach that does this instead.

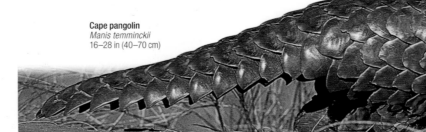

Cape pangolin
Manis temminckii
16–28 in (40–70 cm)

Carnivores

Order Carnivora

A predominantly meat-eating group, carnivora includes terrestrial and aquatic species. The terrestrial carnivores are characterized by their large canine teeth and specialized carnassials—last upper premolar and first lower molar—used for slicing through hide, meat, and bone. In seals and walruses the limbs are modified into flippers and the teeth are less specialized because these animals feed on fish and invertebrates that are swallowed whole. Since meat is relatively easy to digest, the stomach is simple and the intestine short. In all carnivores the clavicle bone is lost, or very reduced, and three of the small bones in the wrist—the scaphoid, centrale, and lunar bones—have fused to form a scapholunar bone.

Least weasel
Mustela nivalis
6½–9½ in (16.5–24 cm)

Eurasian badger
Meles meles
22–35 in (56–90 cm)

Raccoon
Procyon lotor
24–36 in (60–100 cm)

Red panda
Ailurus fulgens
20–25 in (50–64 cm)

California sea lion
Zalophus californianus
7 ft (2.1 m)

Walrus
Odobenus rosmarus
9¾–11¾ ft (3–3.6 m)

Polar bear
Ursus maritimus
up to 8¼ ft (2.5 m)

Brown bear
Ursus arctos
5½–9¼ ft (1.7–2.8 m)

Sand fox
Vulpes rueppellii
16–20½ in (40–52 cm)

Grey wolf
Canis lupus
1–1.5m (3¼–5ft)

Cheetah
Acinonyx jubatus
3½–5 ft (1.1–1.5 m)

Caracal
Caracal caracal
24–36 in (60–91 cm)

Tiger
Panthera tigris
6½–12¼ ft (2–3.7 m)

Lion
Panthera leo
5½–8¼ ft (1.7–2.5 m)

Banded mongoose
Mungos mungo 21½–24 in (55–60 cm)

Meerkat
Suricata suricatta 10–14 in (25–35 cm)

Horses, tapirs, and rhinoceroses

Order Perissodactyla

Odd-toed ungulates are so-called because they bear their weight on either one (equids) or three (rhinoceroses and tapirs) toes. Being plant eaters, they need cellulose-digesting bacteria in their guts to break down plant cell walls. These bacteria are housed in the cecum—a blind-ended sac leading off the small intestine—hence they are referred to as hindgut digesters.

African wild ass
Equus asinus
6½–7½ ft (2–2.3 m)

Brazilian tapir
Tapirus terrestris
5½–6½ ft (1.7–2 m)

White rhinoceros
Ceratotherium simum
12¼–13 ft (3.7–4 m)

Terrestrial even-toed ungulates

Order Cetartiodactyla (part)

The order Cetartiodactyla comprises what used to be recognized as two separate orders, Artiodactyla (terrestrial even-toed ungulates) and Cetacea (whales, dolphins, and porpoises—see opposite). The recent recognition that these two seemingly different groups belong together is based mainly on genetic evidence, but backed up by some fossil evidence. The land-dwelling species are known as even-toed ungulates, because they bear their weight on two toes, each enclosed in a hoof of keratin. Many species ruminate—that is they regurgitate and further chew their plant food. They are also called foregut digesters, as they have digestive bacteria in their rumen, the first of the four chambers of the stomach. A major food source for the larger carnivores, these ungulates have laterally situated eyes for all-round vision and most have elongated lower legs that enable them to be energy efficient when running for long periods.

Warthog
Phacochoerus africanus
3–5 ft (0.9–1.5 m)

Collared peccary
Tayassu tajacu 30–39 in (75–100 cm)

Hippopotamus
Hippopotamus amphibius
10¾–11½ ft (3.3–3.5 m)

Dromedary
Camelus dromedarius
7¼–11¼ ft (2.2–3.4 m)

Guanaco
Lama glama
3–7 ft (0.9–2.1 m)

South African giraffe
Giraffa giraffe
12½–15½ ft (3.8–4.7 m)

Alpine musk deer
Moschus chrysogaster
28–39 in (70–100 cm)

Red deer
Cervus elaphus
5–6½ ft (1.5–2 m)

Okapi
Okapia johnstoni 6½–7¼ ft (2–2.2 m)

American bison
Bison bison
7–11½ ft (2.1–3.5

Scimitar-horned oryx
Oryx dammah 4½–7¾ ft (1.4–2.4 m)

Mouflon
Ovis musimon
3½–4¼ ft (1.1–1.3 m)

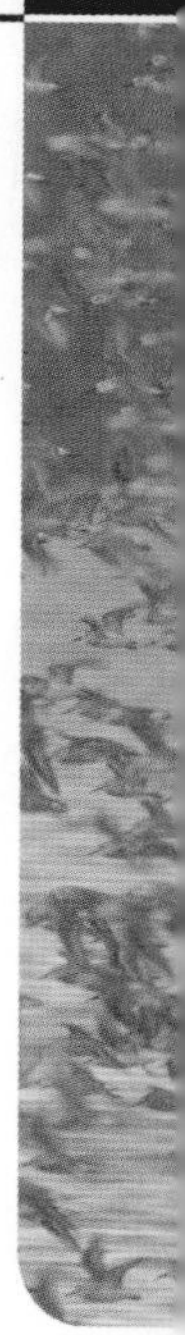

Whales, dolphins, and porpoises

Order Cetartiodactyla (part)

These mammals are perfectly adapted to an aquatic lifestyle, having streamlined bodies with flippers for forelimbs and a large tail fluke instead of legs. The skeleton is much reduced, serving mainly for muscle attachment, and the neck vertebrae may be fused. The whales and dolphins can be divided into two groups— those with teeth and those without. The giant baleen whales filter feed, trapping food particles in two huge baleen plates that hang down from the sides of the upper jaw. Most toothed whales are smaller and some can echolocate to find food.

Ganges river dolphin
Platanista gangetica
7–8¼ ft (2.1–2.5 m)

Franciscana
Pontoporia blainvillei
4¼–5½ ft (1.3–1.7 m)

Common dolphin
Delphinus delphis
7½–8½ ft (2.3–2.6 m)

Killer whale
Orcinus orca up to 26 ft (8 m)

Commerson's dolphin
Cephalorhynchus commersonii
4½–5½ ft (1.4–1.7 m)

Harbour porpoise
Phocoena phocoena 4½–6½ ft (1.4–2 m)

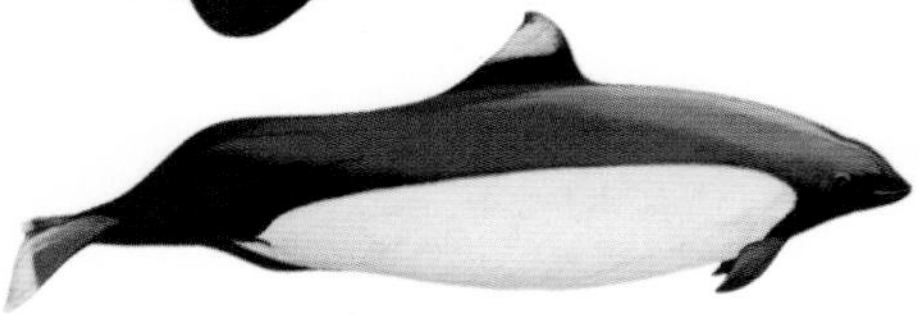

Dall's porpoise
Phocoenoides dalli
7¼–7¾ ft (2.2–2.4 m)

Narwhal
Monodon monoceros
13–14¾ ft (4–4.5 m)

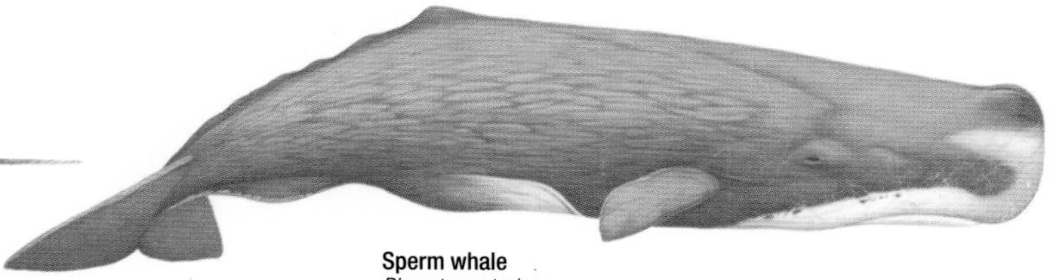

Sperm whale
Physeter catodon
36–66 ft (11–20 m)

Pygmy sperm whale
Kogia breviceps 8¾–9¾ ft (2.7–3 m)

Cuvier's beaked whale
Ziphius cavirostris
23–25 ft (7–7.5 m)

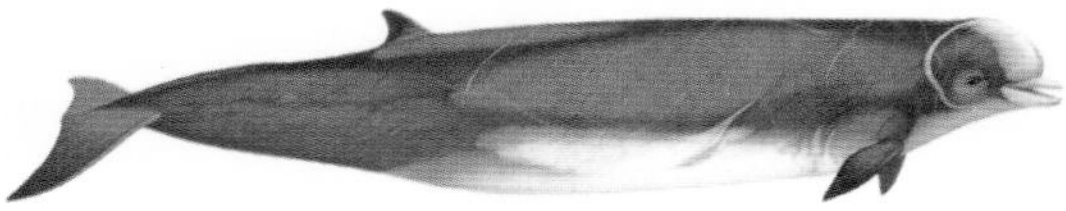

Northern bottlenose whale
Hyperoodon ampullatus
20–33 ft (6–10 m)

Gray whale
Eschrichtius robustus
43–49 ft (13–15 m)

Humpback whale
Megaptera novaeangliae
46–59 ft (14–18 m)

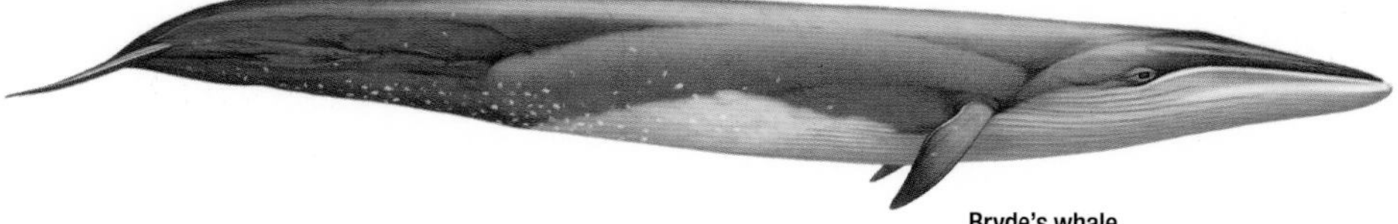

Bryde's whale
Balaenoptera edeni
30–51½ ft (9–15.5 m)

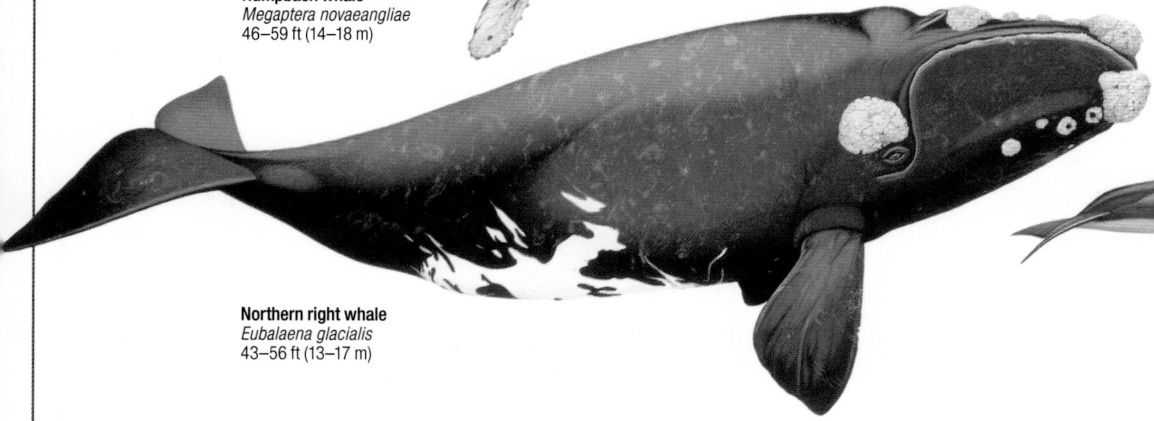

Northern right whale
Eubalaena glacialis
43–56 ft (13–17 m)

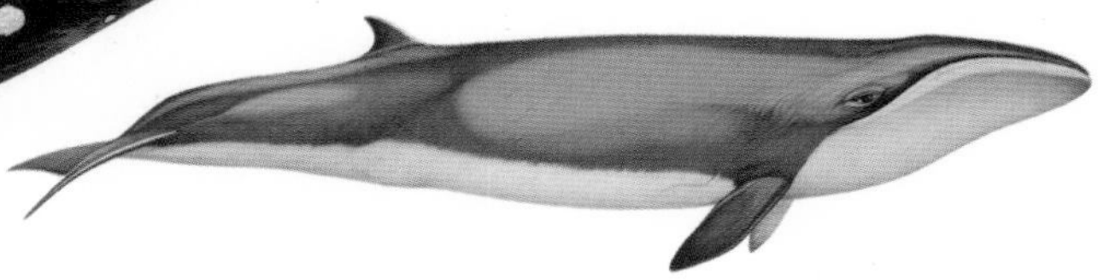

Pygmy right whale
Caperea marginata
18–21 ft (5.5–6.5 m)

ANIMAL

ANAT

ARMORED SUPPORT
Up to 25 percent of a crab's total weight may be its "shell." This is not simply an outer protective casing, it is also its skeleton—a complex set of supporting structures linked at flexible joints, enclosing and moved by intricate sets of muscles.

SKELETONS AND MUSCLES

Most members of the animal kingdom possess some kind of strong body framework, and pulling devices with which to move it. Although the principles and detailed structure of muscles are virtually constant across all major groups of animals, types of skeletons show huge variety in design and construction.

Movement and structure

Muscle tissue is the primary means of movement in almost all animals, except for sponges, allowing an animal to implement its behaviors and actions. Muscle is often the most plentiful tissue in the body, and it has one basic function: to shorten, or contract. As it does so, it moves parts of the skeleton or other body structures. Muscles power not only the movements visible on the outside, they are also the basis of internal activities, such as the pumping of the heart. For invertebrates with a hard outer framework, or exoskeleton, most muscles are positioned on the inside and attached to the skeleton's inner walls. In vertebrates, the situation is reversed, with the muscles attaching to the outside of the endoskeleton. In soft-bodied animals like worms, muscle tissue forms its own fluid-pressurized "water skeleton."

MUSCLE FIBERS
This scanning electron micrograph (SEM) of a skeletal muscle shows striations (bands) of muscle fibers.

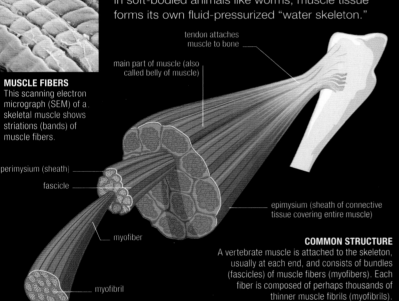

tendon attaches muscle to bone

main part of muscle (also called belly of muscle)

perimysium (sheath)

fascicle

epimysium (sheath of connective tissue covering entire muscle)

myofiber

myofibril

COMMON STRUCTURE
A vertebrate muscle is attached to the skeleton, usually at each end, and consists of bundles (fascicles) of muscle fibers (myofibers). Each fiber is composed of perhaps thousands of thinner muscle fibrils (myofibrils).

EXTENSION
biceps relaxes
triceps contracts

OPPOSITE CONTRACTION
Two muscles in a vertebrate forelimb demonstrate a simple antagonistic system, where each muscle opposes the pull of the other. If both muscles exert tension, the joint can be held steady in any position through its range.

biceps contracts
triceps relaxes

FLEXION

teams. In the simplest arrangement, one muscle pulls a skeletal element or body part one way, while its opposing partner on the other side relaxes. To move the part the other way, the opposing muscle contracts while the first muscle relaxes. However, this two-way action is given greater range since there are usually several muscles involved, attached to the skeleton at varying places and angles, to give differing lines of pull. This allows for movement with close control in several directions.

Joints

Most animals have a skeleton or similar framework made up of numerous parts, which move in relation to each other at joints. In arthropods, the joints are relatively simple thinnings of the exoskeleton. The cuticle forms a flexible articular membrane, but the harder, rigid layers of chitin or mineralization are almost absent. In most vertebrates, the bones of the skeleton are covered in their joints by cartilage, which reduces friction and wear. The joint is enclosed in a joint capsule, inside which there is a lubricating liquid, synovial fluid, to further reduce rubbing. Strong, stretchy ligaments are attached to the bones and allow the joint to flex.

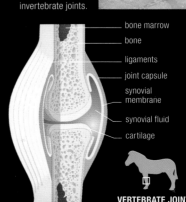

FLEXIBLE JOINTS
The frog's tiny joints have a greater range of movement than invertebrate joints.

Muscle arrangement

A typical mammal has more than 600 individual muscles, while some insects have three times that number. The inner structure of a typical muscle is based on cellular components known as muscle fibers or myofibers. In larger animals, some myofibers exceed 3 ft 3 in (1 m) in length, yet each is thinner than a human hair. Contraction occurs when bundles of overlapping protein filaments in the fibers slide past each other. Because muscles only contract and pull, they are arranged in opposing

INVERTEBRATE MUSCLES
In arthropods the muscle structure can be quite similar to that of vertebrates, but the arrangement differs in that the muscles connect to the inner walls of the exoskeleton.

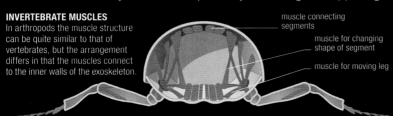

muscle connecting segments
muscle for changing shape of segment
muscle for moving leg

extensor muscle
flexor muscle
cuticle
articular membrane
bearing surface or pivot

INVERTEBRATE JOINT

POINTS OF MOVEMENT
The exoskeleton is flexible at an invertebrate joint, and the shape of the bearing surfaces usually allows movement in only one plane or direction. In a vertebrate joint, a thin layer of synovial fluid helps prevent friction between the connecting bones.

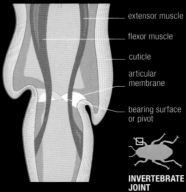

bone marrow
bone
ligaments
joint capsule
synovial membrane
synovial fluid
cartilage

VERTEBRATE JOINT

Water skeletons

Fluid-based skeletons are found in a huge variety of invertebrates, especially worms and similar "soft-bodied" animals. Far from being soft and floppy, many of these can become rigid and resistant when muscular action compresses fluid inside an animal's body.

Support

An animal's hydrostatic skeleton, or hydroskeleton, employs similar principles to hydraulic systems in machinery. In animals, a liquid in some sort of chamber or container is pressurized by contraction of the muscular walls around it. The liquid is the internal body fluid of the animal. Its compression makes the structure become hard and rigid, forming a firm skeletal unit. The skeleton then gives support and protection to the animal's body parts. In simpler animals the whole body covering acts as the hydroskeleton. In more complex ones, especially segmented (annelid) worms, the pressure can be limited to selected body compartments.

LIMITED MOVEMENT
Most nematode worms, such as this parasitic roundworm, have only longitudinal muscles in the body wall. As these contract on each side alternately, they produce characteristic C- or S-like thrashing movements.

PULSES FOR SWIMMING
Muscle fibers compress fluid within a jellyfish's main body, causing contractions to run from the center of the bell to its edges. This produces a pulsing movement for swimming.

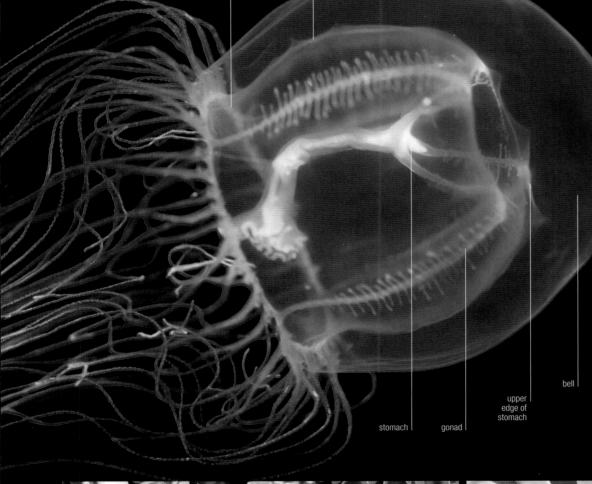

edge of gastric pouch

ring canal

stomach   gonad

upper edge of stomach

bell

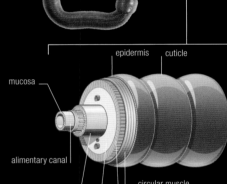

epidermis   cuticle

mucosa

alimentary canal

visceral peritoneum

circular muscle

longitudinal muscle

coelem

SEGMENTED WORM ANATOMY
Each worm segment has a set of circular muscles around it. Some longitudinal muscles span a segment, while others run along many segments. This allows the worm to stretch some parts, while shortening others.

Movement

In a hydroskeleton, changes in muscle tone and the arrangement of muscles can alter the pressure within its chambers, thereby changing the skeleton's shape, and causing the structure to become rigid. This provides a stiff base against which movements can occur, and also produces the movements themselves. In many worms, for example, there are two layers of muscle in the outer body wall: ringlike circulars; and strap-shaped, longitudinal (lengthwise) muscles. Contraction of circular muscles squeezes the body, making it longer and thinner; longitudinal muscle contraction makes it shorter and fatter; and when both sets contract, the body becomes tense, stiff, and rigid. Other combinations of contractions permit further movements. If the longitudinal muscles along one side shorten, the body curves to that side. Using such a system of contractions, burrowing earthworms are able to push their way between tightly packed soil particles with great force.

BENDY APPENDAGES
Apart from whole body movements, hydrostatic and hydraulic principles can also be used to move smaller body parts or individual appendages. Such movements allow animals to perform tasks such as self defense and capturing prey.

Octopus suckers are able to grasp objects firmly

Sea cucumber tentacles rely on internal pressure.

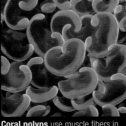
Coral polyps use muscle fibers in the stalks to "lean" in any direction.

Anemone tentacles bend to the side on which the muscle contracts.

Horny skeletons

"Horny" describes substances that are strong, tough, and resilient, yet which can also be slightly compressed and flexed. In arthropods, the main horny substance is chitin. This forms the basis of the outer body covering or cuticle, which is the main component of the animal's exoskeleton.

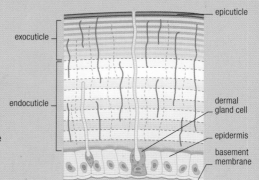

STICKY FEET
A jumping spider has two foot claws and a pad of tufted hairs that are formed by tiny, supple extensions of the cuticle. These can stick to a wide variety of surfaces.

Tough exoskeleton

Chitin is light, strong, translucent, and pliable, and has been compared to plastic. The substance is chemically a polysaccharide (carbohydrate), consisting of glucoselike sugar units. In most land arthropods chitin is accompanied by various proteins, the molecules of which may take many shapes, including fibrous, sheetlike, and helical. Many hundreds of these proteins are known in the insect group alone. In some aquatic arthropods, such as crabs and other crustaceans, the chitin and protein are accompanied by minerals, especially chalky crystals of calcium carbonate. These make the exoskeleton or shell harder for protection. It also makes it heavier—which is of less hinderance to aquatic animals whose weight is supported by water— and consequently also more brittle and liable to fracture.

NEW ARMOR
A spider crab's heavily mineralized shell is hard and rigid, except for where it thins at the joints. During the few hours after each molt, the soft new cuticle enlarges rapidly before it hardens. At this time the crab hides away because of its increased vulnerability until its new shell is ready.

Structure and layering

A typical cuticle has several main layers. The outermost layer, the epicuticle, is the barrier to the outside world—repelling microbes, coping with physical wear, and reducing water loss. The procuticle is formed from chitin fibers and mineral crystals embedded in a variable matrix of proteins. Neither of these layers contains living cells. The epidermis beneath these is the layer of living cells that manufactures the top two layers. Under the epidermis, the basement membrane forms a firm support with fibers of the protein collagen. The relative proportions, compositions, and strengths of these layers vary between arthropod species, and also on different body parts.

A wasp has a typical insect exoskeleton—with a head, thorax, and abdomen.

thorax
head
abdomen

A caterpillar's thinned body cuticle allows each segment to flex and change shape.

many segments make up caterpillar's body
spiny bristles deter predators

Wood lice are terrestrial crustaceans with a shieldlike segmented exoskeleton for protection.

platelike cuticle

A rhinoceros beetle's "horn" is formed from thickened, stiff cuticle.

forewings modified as rear-wing covers

CUTICLE
The procuticle layer is divided into the hardened exocuticle, which has many compacted fibers, and the more flexible endocuticle. Dermal glands in the epidermis can produce chemical repellents to deter predators.

epicuticle
exocuticle
endocuticle
dermal gland cell
epidermis
basement membrane

Chalky skeletons

The bodies of some invertebrates are supported by chalky frameworks. These can take two forms. Mollusks, such as snails, tend to have shell-like coverings, while echinoderms (including starfish and sea urchins) are more likely to have what can be termed a true skeleton. In both groups, a distinctive feature of their structure is calcium carbonate, the main constituent of rocks such as chalk and limestone.

Composition

Chalky body structures are usually laid down in the form of calcium crystals embedded in a matrix, which is usually protein based. Calcium carbonate may be joined by allied minerals such as calcium phosphate, magnesium carbonate, and silicates. Also, calcium carbonate itself crystallizes in a variety of forms, such as angled, prismlike calcite and more rectangular aragonite. Marine mollusks tend to have calcite crystals, while argonite is more common in terrestrial mollusks, such as land snails. The predominant material in echinoderm skeletons is calcite, whose crystals tend to lie in the same orientation within each of the small skeletal elements, called ossicles. These are almost bony in texture, being hard and stiff, and spongy rather than solid.

CALCIUM DIET
This triton trumpet is seen feeding on a crown-of-thorns starfish. The shell of this sea snail is made of calcium carbonate, which it gets from its diet and the surrounding seawater.

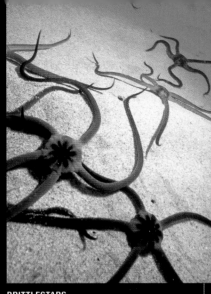

BRITTLESTARS
The flexible arms of the snake starfish, a type of brittlestar, writhe like worms because their ossicles are loosely bound into the pliable body wall.

SPINY SKELETON
Echinoderm means "spiny skin," as exemplified by the crown-of-thorns starfish, shown here feeding at night on coral in the Red Sea.

Echinoderms

The standard echinoderm arrangement is a thick outer body layer containing many embedded calcium-based ossicles. These vary greatly in shape and size—from microscopic to palm-sized, depending on not only the species but also on the body part concerned. This type of skeletal structure is technically defined as an endoskeleton since it is not produced by the outermost body layers. But it functions as an exoskeleton because it encloses the main body parts. In urchins the skeletal plates are large and locked together to form a rigid covering. In more flexible types of echinoderms, such as sea cucumbers and brittlestars, the ossicles are embedded in a matrix of proteins and other substances.

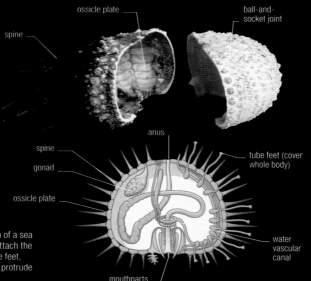

SEA URCHIN
The inflexible ball-shaped skeleton of a sea urchin is known as a test. Joints attach the spines to the test. The waving tube feet, part of the water vascular system, protrude through small holes in the plates.

OSSICLES AND SPICULES
This microscope image shows a collection of sea cucumber ossicles (shaped like sheets, wheels, spines, buckles, and crosses) and silica-based slivers (called spicules) from a sponge's skeleton.

Mollusks

A mollusk shell is secreted by a gland in the mantle, which is the animal's fleshy, cloaklike body covering. Shell form varies hugely, with segmentlike plates in chitons; two-part shells in bivalves, such as mussels and clams; a winding helix in gastropods; and a much reduced internal structure in cephalopods, such as squid, or no shell at all in octopuses. The shell includes a thick central layer, the ostracum, itself composed of two layers of calcium carbonate crystals. On the outside of the ostracum is the protein-rich periostracum that protects the calcium carbonate layers of the ostracum from dissolving or chemical attack. The innermost shell layer is the aragonite-rich hypostracum, which in some mollusks has a lustrous sheen and is commonly known as mother-of-pearl, or nacre.

CALCIUM CARBONATE
The highly magnified ostracum of an abalone shell reveals layers of overlapping, platelike aragonite crystals.

CHITON SHELL

NAUTILUS SHELL

MUREX SHELL

SHELL SHAPES
The nautilus adds inner walls, or septa, to its shell, and lives in the last, largest chamber. Chitons, or coat-of-mail shells, have eight sectional plates and a surrounding girdle "skirt." Murex shells are among the most complex of gastropods and of all mollusk shapes.

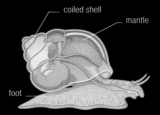

GASTROPOD
A snail shell gradually grows in diameter as new material is added, and its size reflects the snail's age and food supply.

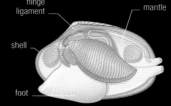

BIVALVE
A bivalve shell grows as the soft, fleshy mantle adds new carbonates and other substances around the edge.

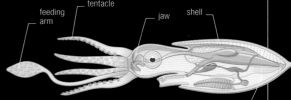

SQUID
A squid's shell is wholly internal and known as a pen. It is thin, lightweight, and pliable.

INTERNAL SUPPORT
A squid's internal shell serves as an endoskeleton, helping the body stay relatively stiff and giving the muscles of its water-jet propulsion system a firm base for their contractions.

Bony skeletons

Most vertebrate animals have an internal framework (or endoskeleton) consisting chiefly of the hard, mineralized tissue known as bone. It is divided into the axial skeleton and the appendicular skeleton. The axial skeleton runs along the middle axis of the body, from head to tail. The appendicular consists of the bones attached to the axial skeleton.

CARTILAGE SKELETON
Sharks, skates, and rays have skeletons, but these are made mainly of cartilage rather than heavier bone. As a result, swimming is more energy-efficient.

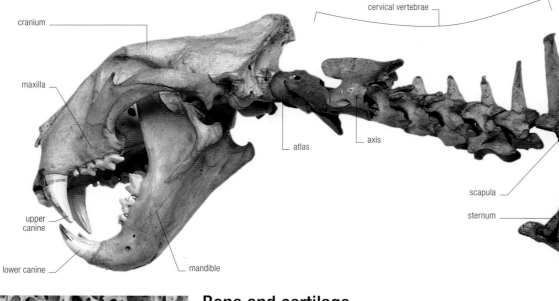

cranium

maxilla

upper canine

lower canine

mandible

atlas

axis

cervical vertebrae

thoracic vertebrae

scapula

sternum

humerus

ulna

radius

carpal

phalanx

metacarpal

Bone and cartilage

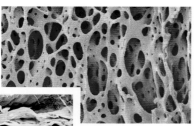

HARD AND SOFT
Under a bone's outer hard layer, cancellous bone tissue (above) has many tiny chambers. Cartilage (here colored green) is light and pliant, forming support for body parts such as the ears.

Bone is a complex tissue, composed of mineral crystals (mainly calcium phosphates) along with fibrous proteins, principally collagen, embedded in a ground tissue or matrix of carbohydrates, salts, and other substances. It is continually maintained by cells known as osteocytes, which can also repair damage, such as fractures. A typical bone has a dense, hard outer layer of compact bone tissue; a layer of cancellous bone tissue beneath this, which is more spongy or honeycomb-like; and a central cavity of jellylike marrow, which stores fat and manufactures new blood cells. Cartilage is similar to bone, with protein fibers, carbohydrates, and other substances encased in a matrix. However, it lacks the hard calcifying minerals of bone, making it somewhat lighter, softer, more pliable, and less brittle.

Skeletal appendages

In addition to an internal skeleton, some vertebrates have associated bony parts and appendages that develop in the same way as the skeleton, but elsewhere in the body. Some fishes, such as armored catfishes, have stiff, bony plates in their skin. Their decreased mobility and increased weight are offset by greater physical protection. Reptiles such as the draco, or "flying dragon," have long, thin rods of bone that hold out flaps of skin. Among mammals, physical protection in armadillos is achieved by hard bony plates. These form crosswise bands around the body and consist of dermal bone, which has no links with the endoskeleton. It forms within the thickness of the skin and is covered by a layer of horn-coated, bone-based scales, known as scutes.

EXTRA BONE
Each of these animals possess bony parts or appendages that have developed for varying functions, such as protection and self-defense. The sea horse has developed bony plates in its skin for protection against predators. The neck frill of the frilled lizard is spread out when the lizard feels threatened, and the bony plates and scutes of an armadillo can protect its whole body.

Sea horses have an outer layer of bony plates covered by thin skin.

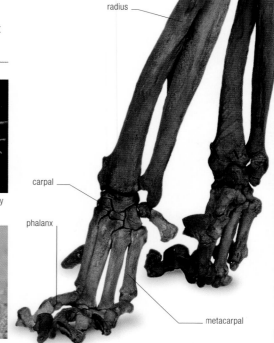

The frilled lizard spreads out its wide neck frill to deter enemies.

Three-banded armadillos roll into balls for all-over body protection.

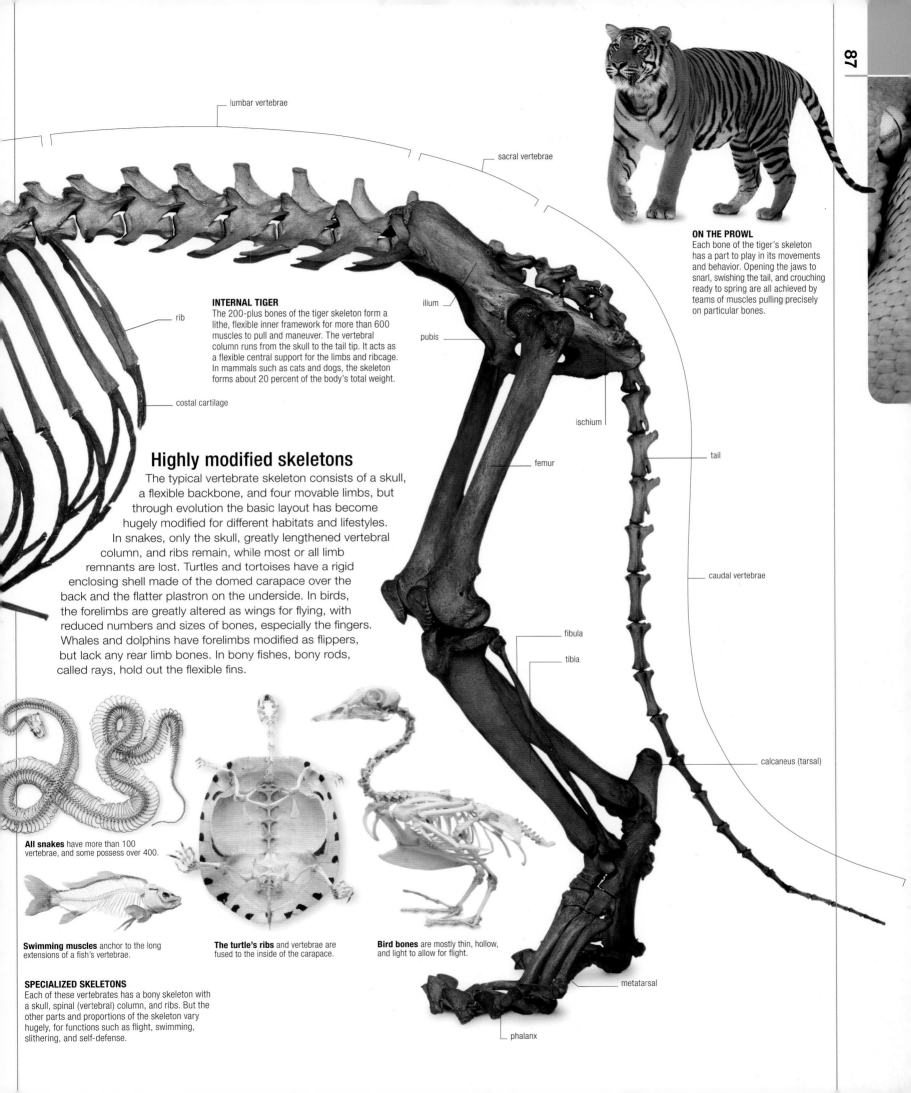

lumbar vertebrae

sacral vertebrae

ON THE PROWL
Each bone of the tiger's skeleton
has a part to play in its movements
and behavior. Opening the jaws to
snarl, swishing the tail, and crouching
ready to spring are all achieved by
teams of muscles pulling precisely
on particular bones.

ilium

rib

INTERNAL TIGER
The 200-plus bones of the tiger skeleton form a
lithe, flexible inner framework for more than 600
muscles to pull and maneuver. The vertebral
column runs from the skull to the tail tip. It acts as
a flexible central support for the limbs and ribcage.
In mammals such as cats and dogs, the skeleton
forms about 20 percent of the body's total weight.

pubis

costal cartilage

ischium

tail

Highly modified skeletons

The typical vertebrate skeleton consists of a skull,
a flexible backbone, and four movable limbs, but
through evolution the basic layout has become
hugely modified for different habitats and lifestyles.
In snakes, only the skull, greatly lengthened vertebral
column, and ribs remain, while most or all limb
remnants are lost. Turtles and tortoises have a rigid
enclosing shell made of the domed carapace over the
back and the flatter plastron on the underside. In birds,
the forelimbs are greatly altered as wings for flying, with
reduced numbers and sizes of bones, especially the fingers.
Whales and dolphins have forelimbs modified as flippers,
but lack any rear limb bones. In bony fishes, bony rods,
called rays, hold out the flexible fins.

femur

caudal vertebrae

fibula

tibia

calcaneus (tarsal)

All snakes have more than 100
vertebrae, and some possess over 400.

Swimming muscles anchor to the long
extensions of a fish's vertebrae.

The turtle's ribs and vertebrae are
fused to the inside of the carapace.

Bird bones are mostly thin, hollow,
and light to allow for flight.

metatarsal

SPECIALIZED SKELETONS
Each of these vertebrates has a bony skeleton with
a skull, spinal (vertebral) column, and ribs. But the
other parts and proportions of the skeleton vary
hugely, for functions such as flight, swimming,
slithering, and self-defense.

phalanx

NEED FOR SPEED
Cheetahs require fast, brief bursts of speed to
catch their prey. They have an extremely flexible
spine, which coils and uncoils with every
movement, propelling the animal forward. The
cheetah can reach speeds of 70 mph (113 kph),
but they are not built for stamina. They become
breathless and overheated within 30 seconds.

MOVEMENT

Animals display an incredible variety of movements, from the hovering of hummingbirds to the slithering of snakes. Locomotion occurs when an animal's entire body moves from one place to another, as when walking, running, swimming, flying, leaping, or crawling. In addition to utilizing muscle power, animals can also harness a number of environmental features, such as the wind, water currents, and gravity, to aid movement.

CARTWHEELING TO SAFETY
The desert arachnid called the solifuge (also known as the sun spider) has a clever method of escaping predators. It curls its legs around to form a wheel shape and rolls down sand dunes.

Land, air, water, and soil

Methods of locomotion vary dramatically, according to the substances or "media" an animal is traveling through. Moving across the land necessitates contact with the ground, using body parts that range from legs and feet, to scales in snakes, and a slimy undersurface or "foot" in snails. Grip against the surface provides the required forward thrust.

The huge variety of surface consistencies requires numerous specializations. For example, desert dwellers such as kangaroo rats have enormous feet and toes as well as hairy soles to help them jump in the soft, shifting sand. Moving through air requires large aerodynamic surfaces, such as wings in true fliers (birds, bats, and insects), or flaps

BARN SWALLOW **COMMON EARTHWORM** **BROWN SEA NETTLE JELLYFISH** **EASTERN GREY KANGAROO**

of skin in gliders, such as colugos and "flying" squirrels. Animals have to expend a lot of energy to provide both lift (to counteract gravity) and thrust for forward movement.

Water is a much more resistant medium than air. In general, it requires at least twice the amount of energy to attain the same speed in water as it does on land. A smoothly contoured, streamlined shape becomes extremely important in water. Aquatic creatures generally have large, flat surfaces such as tails and fins to push against the heavy, fluid medium. Locomotion in soil, sand, and mud is by far the slowest and most energy-intensive. However, as in all forms of locomotion, there

SHAPED TO TRAVEL
Swallows have scythelike wings for speedy, acrobatic pursuit of food. Earthworms are long and slim, to push between soil particles. The jellyfish's shape exploits sea currents, and the kangaroo's hops are energy-efficient on soft ground.

are benefits to offset even the most arduous movement. For example, burrowing animals are usually less visible to predators and are sheltered from the weather. They may also be surrounded by their common food source, such as plant roots in the case of naked mole rats.

MULTISKILLED FISH
Some appendages are a compromise between various forms of locomotion. The mudskipper's muscular pectoral fins can help this fish burrow, swim, wiggle, waddle, and leap.

Gravity-assisted

Various animals take advantage of gravity, by tumbling or sliding down slopes, or simply falling through the air. These methods are generally used as emergency measures to escape predators. A number of animals possess the ability to curl into a ball and roll away from danger, including millipedes and wood lice. Tree-living insects, such as beetles and stick insects, simply let go and drop to the ground. Their survival is ensured by their small size, tough body casing, and soft landing site (leaf litter).

Metabolic rate

There is a close connection between metabolic rate (the speed of essential biochemical processes within an animal's body) and locomotive ability. Birds and mammals are homeothermic (warm-blooded)—that is, they maintain a constant high body temperature. This makes their muscles ready for action at any time. Most other animals are ectothermic (cold-blooded), so their temperatures vary according to the environment. When the temperature cools, their muscle metabolism becomes less effective. At very low temperatures, they are actually unable to move at all.

WARMING UP FOR TAKE OFF
On cool evenings, some hawkmoths have to "shiver" their flight muscles to generate enough heat to take off.

SPRINTING ABILITY
The swordfish is able to channel natural low-level heat within its body along certain blood vessels to warm its muscles, enabling short bursts of speed.

⊙ ENERGY EFFICIENCY

This chart shows four mammals of similar masses—about 1¾ oz (50 g)—that move through land (field mouse), air (bat), water (desman), or soil (mole). It plots how far each travels in one second and how much energy it expends (for comparison, the field mouse's energy expenditure is shown as one unit). The bat uses energy most efficiently, and the mole the least.

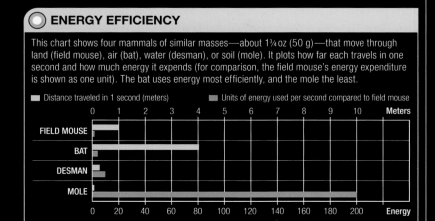

■ Distance traveled in 1 second (meters)   ■ Units of energy used per second compared to field mouse

Walking and running

With the exception of a few extraordinary animals that are able to walk on water or along the ocean floor, walking and running are confined to land animals and require the use of legs. There are many different limb actions that animals employ to achieve locomotion on land, which are known as gaits. Individual animals often exhibit a broad variety of gaits. These methods of locomotion are most obvious in larger mammals, but they also occur in the smallest invertebrates.

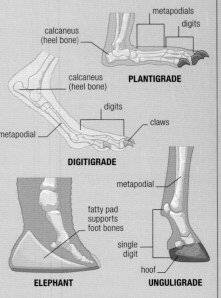

PLANTIGRADE

calcaneus (heel bone)

metapodials

digits

DIGITIGRADE

metapodial

calcaneus (heel bone)

digits

claws

ELEPHANT

fatty pad supports foot bones

UNGULIGRADE

metapodial

single digit

hoof

Numbers of legs

The numbers of legs varies greatly through the animal kingdom, from two in birds and kangaroos, to the standard vertebrate number of four in most mammals, amphibians, and reptiles. Insects have six legs, while arachnids and some crustaceans have eight. Centipedes often possess well over 100 legs. Despite their name, millipedes do not ever have a thousand legs. Most species have between 100–400 legs, but one—the *Illacme plenipes*—has an incredible 750. In centipedes and millipedes, the sheer number of legs is an arthropod adaptation to a part-burrowing way of life. The many tiny limbs allow these creatures to push powerfully through loose material, leaf debris, and soil, without the individual limbs needing a lot of space for their actions. The legs move mainly to and fro rather than out to the side, which keeps their movement efficient.

Different gaits

Many mammals use different gaits, from a slow walk to a full-speed run. These gaits are especially clear in hoofed mammals, such as horses, which alter their leg movement from walk to trot, canter, and gallop. The trot is used to cover long distances efficiently, while the gallop is used to evade predators. Unusual gaits include camel "pacing," where both legs on one side move simultaneously, to give a side-to-side swaying motion.

MAMMAL WALKING GAITS
Plantigrades, such as bears, walk with their heel bone, metapodials, and digits on the ground. Digitigrades, such as dogs, move with only their digits touching the ground. Unguligrades stand on one or more toe tips. Externally, elephants appear plantigrade, but are actually digitigrades, since the heel bone is raised and only their digits touch the ground.

UNUSUAL WALKERS
A crab's sideways walk is due to the direction in which its leg joints bend. A millipede's legs move in coordinated "waves"— a single wave involves lifting around a dozen legs up, lowering them, and then pushing backward.

Specialized movements

In many creatures, specialized body movements aid locomotion. For example, the flexible backbone of the cheetah arches up and down to extend its stride. In salamanders, newts, and lizards (among others), "S"-shaped sideways curves pass along the body from head to tail. This gives added swinging motion to the limbs, which splay out to the sides.

S-SHAPED WALK
A tiger salamander's body curls from side to side as it walks, in a series of "S"-shaped waves. This pattern is derived from the movements of fishy ancestors of amphibians.

Leg design

In general, longer limbs allow longer strides and greater speed. With fast runners, the muscle bulk that moves the limb is near the main body, often in the shoulder or hip region. This reduces the weight of the limb toward its end, making it easier to move to and fro at speed. Many invertebrates have unjointed legs, which often utilize hydraulic pressure. Caterpillars have both jointed and unjointed legs. The latter help the caterpillar to grip, since they contain tiny hooks that act like suction cups.

Rhinoceroses have thick, sturdy limbs to carry their great bulk. In spite of this, they are able to sprint surprisingly quickly.

MODES OF MOVEMENT
Rhinoceroses and ostriches rely on their muscle mass close to their main body to achieve locomotion. Starfish locomote by hydraulic pressure. They squeeze water into each of their tiny-tubed feet to extend them.

● **COMPROMISE LIMBS**

Animals that move both on land and in water have compromise limb designs. Inter-toe webbing is an enhanced version of the standard five-toed land vertebrate foot. It provides a broad, finlike surface for pushing against water and is found in a wide variety of semiaquatic walker-swimmers, including otters and desmans among mammals, many kinds of seabirds and waterfowl from albatrosses to ducks, and many amphibians. The degree of webbing reflects the proportion of time spent in water— for example, tree frogs have virtually none.

Ostriches contain their main musculature in their hips and thighs. They can also use their wings as rudders to help change direction.

Starfish have tiny "tubes" on the underside of their five or seven arms, which lift up and move forward.

Ostriches can sustain a speed of **45 mph (70 kph)** for up to **30 minutes**, covering up to **16½ ft (5 m)** in a single stride.

ZEBRA "FLIGHT"
As a zebra gallops, all four hooves are off the ground for more than half of the time taken for each complete stride. Such minimal contact reduces friction with the ground and allows the zebra to "fly" in a succession of long leaps, at speeds exceeding 35 kph (55 kph).

Climbing and leaping

There is a huge diversity of climbing animals, some of which have developed extraordinary specializations, such as the acrobatic skills of gibbons or the ability of geckos to stick to almost any surface. Leaping involves progression by alternately speeding and slowing, in a series of jerky actions. Most animals use the same limbs for leaping as they do for walking and running, although some invertebrates use additional body parts specifically to leap.

Getting a grip

Moving through tree branches, and up cliffs, rocks, and walls requires strong, mobile limbs and an excellent grip. Most climbers have muscular limbs that can haul their body weight upward. Since it is necessary to hang on while the other limbs are moved to new positions, some climbing animals can support their body weight with only two or even one limb gripping. Powerful claws, fingers, toes, and tails contain various specializations to achieve grip. For example, a chameleon's five toes are grouped as two sets, of three and two, to form a "pincer" that clings onto a twig with a vicelike hold. Some animals, including a number of monkeys, possess "prehensile" tails, which are able to grasp and hold objects.

MADAGASCAN DAY GECKO

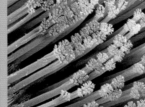

RIDGES, STALKS, AND SPOONS
Geckos have ridged toes (left) with thousands of minuscule stalklike bristles, dividing into billions of microscopic spoonlike hairs (right). These hairs mesh with the tiny irregularities of the surface the gecko is climbing and provides it with grip.

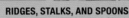

SPIDER SPECIALIZATION
The tip of a tarantula's foot has two claws, a hook, and serrated hairs, all of which grip strongly to most surfaces.

MEXICAN RED-KNEED TARANTULA

⦿ PRIMATE HANDS AND FEET

Primates have adapted limbs not just for locomotion—chiefly in trees—but also for feeding and grooming. The chimpanzee's muscular, semi-opposable toe and thumb grip branches very well. The greatly elongated middle fingers of the aye-aye pick out grubs from under bark. The indri lemur has evolved a grooming claw on its second toe.

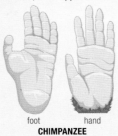

foot   hand
CHIMPANZEE

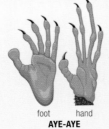

foot   hand
AYE-AYE

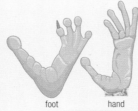

foot   hand
INDRI LEMUR

A proboscis monkey's feet are **partially webbed**, making them very effective swimmers.

Brachiation

Locomotion by brachiation (arm-over-arm swinging) occurs chiefly in tree-living primate mammals, and most spectacularly in gibbons. There are 14 different species of gibbons, which are found in the tropical rain forests of Southeast Asia. The siamang (right) is the largest of them. It is perfectly equipped for brachiation, having long-palmed, hooklike hands with much-reduced thumbs, elongated, powerful arms, muscular shoulders, and flexible joints. This is aided by stereoscopic distance-judging vision, which helps locate the next handhold. When swinging, the siamang's body moves forward in a series of arcs, like a traveling pendulum. It is an energy-efficient form of locomotion because it involves maintaining momentum.

STEP 1   **STEP 2**   **STEP 3**   **STEP 4**

KING OF THE SWINGERS

1 At the start of each swing, the siamang's body gains speed and energy as it swings forward.
2 Its body swings around to allow the free hand to grab the next branch.   **3** The long, muscular arms and the momentum from the swing propel the siamang to the next branch.   **4** The grasping feet reach for a lower branch as it comes to a halt.

Energy-efficient locomotion

The energy efficiency of leaping is improved by structures in the limbs, such as ligaments around joints, and tendons, which anchor muscles to the skeleton. These structures contain rubbery, elastic substances, including the proteins elastin and resilin. As ligaments and tendons stretch or compress in preparation for the leap, they store energy like a coiled spring. The energy is then released during the leap, in a catapult action that assists the muscles. As a kangaroo lands after even a small hop, its body weight stretches its leg tendons and ligaments, storing energy for the next hop.

BACK FLIP TAKEOFF
Before a jump, this cat flea compresses blocks of resilin at the bases of its legs.

EMERGENCY EXIT

Some species of monkey, including the proboscis monkey, make their longest leaps to escape danger. Both fingers and toes are adapted for grasping, and the tail functions as a balancing rudder.

How animals leap

Prodigious leapers, including, hares, kangaroos, frogs, fleas, and grasshoppers, usually have one pair of specially adapted limbs that are larger and stronger than the others. Each limb unfolds sequentially at its joints as a series of levers, from the hip and thigh, to the knee and shin, to the ankle and foot, and lastly, to the toes. This flings the animal up and forward in a series of leveraged pushes, achieving a rapid gain in momentum. In addition to avoiding predators and other dangers, leaps are used in many other contexts—for example, to clear obstacles, reach a nearby branch, or as a display of fitness when courting or defending territory. Desert-dwelling animals often use short, quick leaps as an efficient way to move over soft, shifting sand.

13 in The leap of a ¹⁄₁₆ in (2 mm) cat flea—170 times its own body length.

⬤ PRONKING

Certain hoofed mammals perform stiff-limbed, springlike vertical leaps, as though bouncing along with their legs held straight. This motion is known as "pronking" and is derived from the Afrikaans word "pronk," meaning "to boast." It occurs particularly in antelopes, such as the springbok (shown here) and impala, as well as many gazelles. This behavior is thought to be a display of fitness, showing predators that the individual is healthy, and not worth targeting.

BOUNDING SIFAKA

When on the ground, some lemurs and sifakas, such as this Verreaux's sifaka, move with sideways bounds of their long, muscular legs. They raise their arms up and outward for balance. This remarkable form of locomotion can propel the sifaka over 16½ ft (5 m) in a single leap.

Burrowing, slithering, and sliding

Some forms of locomotion involve progress in tiny, often continuous stages, with a large area of body in contact with the surface. These movements include sliding and slithering, which are undertaken mainly by limbless creatures. Many animals are capable of burrowing and this occurs through many different types of terrain.

Burrowing and tunneling

There are many subterranean animal species that employ a variety of methods and body parts to push aside particles of soil, mud, sand, or similar material and force themselves forward. This is by far the slowest and most energy-expensive method of animal locomotion. However, there are benefits of the fossorial (underground) mode of life for creatures that habitually spend their lives tunneling or burrowing. A truly fossorial animal is relatively safe, since it is out of sight, hearing, and scent of surface predators. It is also sheltered from extreme conditions, such as droughts and blizzards. Also, many burrowing creatures exploit underground food sources such as roots, bulbs, and other subterranean plant parts.

BURROWING THROUGH DIFFERENT SUBSTANCES
Some animals use specialized body parts to burrow through hard surfaces, such as wood and rock. Softer substances also present challenges. Sand collapses as the burrower passes, leaving no permanent tunnel. This means that creatures like sandfish must continually expend energy as they go.

Piddocks are bivalve mollusks that have shells with ridged "teeth" to rasp into rock.

Shipworms are bivalve mollusks that possess tiny, serrated shells, which enable them to bore into wood.

Sandfish (a species of skink) wiggle like fishes to "swim" through loose sand and soil.

Naked mole rats use their large, constantly growing incisor teeth to bite through dry soil.

65ft The length of tunnel an average European mole excavates in a single day.

DIGGING SPECIALIST
The sharp claws on the European mole's enormous front feet work like shovels. The mole anchors itself with its back feet and scoops soil sideways and backward. When it nears the surface, this shoveling action pushes the soil up, forming a "molehill."

Burrowing methods

A typical burrower needs to push aside particles of the surrounding ground, using muscle-powered pressure from one part of its body, while at the same time anchoring another part of its body to generate sufficient burrowing force. Vertebrates, such as moles, have powerful limbs that work like shovels to shift soil. Many invertebrates, such as subterranean termites, have saw-toothed mouthparts, which they use to cut through the soil. Some bivalve mollusks, such as the razor shell, have muscular feet, which expand and contract to enable it to burrow through mud and sand. Aided by its streamlined shape, which minimizes resistance, this burrowing method allows the razor shell to dig 3 ft 3 in (1m) in under 10 seconds.

FOOT EXTENDED
The razor shell pushes its valves (shell halves) slightly open and extends its long, fleshy foot into the sand to thrust downward.

FOOT CONTRACTED
The foot swells at the tip to form a lower anchor point, then the foot contracts, the valves close together, and the shell slides down.

Slithering and sliding

Snakes, slugs, snails, flatworms, and similar animals move smoothly and continuously along a surface, as a result of many tiny muscular contractions. Some snakes tilt their scales to gain purchase against objects and undulations on the surface. Gastropod mollusks, such as snails, slugs, and limpets, slide on a film of mucus using rhythmic actions of their foot muscle layers. These actions move the foot along in undulating waves. The suction achieved by the sticky mucus allows them to grip onto many different surfaces, including rocks and loose soil. It even enables them to travel upside down.

CONVEYOR BELT
A slug travels using small waves of muscle contraction, passing from head to tail along its broad, slime-coated foot, pushing it forward like a conveyor belt.

SLOW PROGRESS
If this garden snail moved continuously, it would take it over a week to cover 0.6 miles (1 km).

⚪ SNAKE LOCOMOTION

In contrast to animals with legs, snakes have no concentrated point to push off from. Instead, they have a complex system of muscles, which allows them to move using four distinct methods. Often, the method used varies according to the size of the snake, the kind of surface they are traveling on, and how quickly they need to move. Most snakes can perform each of these types of locomotion as the situation arises. Sidewinding is the only exception, which is unique to the caenophidian family of snakes.

In sidewinding, the snake lifts its head and extends it forward. The rear of the snake's body lies side-on to the direction of movement, allowing for better leverage. This is employed on smooth or slippery surfaces.

In rectilinear locomotion, the belly scales are lifted, tilted to grip the surface, then pulled forward, in a succession of waves along the body. This method is mainly used by heavy snakes.

In concertina locomotion, the rear body folds in sideways curves, which act like a frictional anchor. The head then extends forward, and the rear is drawn along.

In lateral undulation, the snake exploits surface irregularities, such as rocks, tree trunks, and hillocks, by adjusting the angle of contact to gain forward thrust.

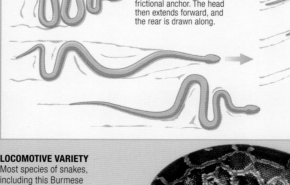

LOCOMOTIVE VARIETY
Most species of snakes, including this Burmese python, are able to vary their style of locomotion according to the terrain they are traveling on. This python is utilizing concertina locomotion, most often used when climbing, or traveling through tunnels.

The three main animal groups to have mastered the air are insects, birds, and bats. They are considered to be "true fliers," since they all capable of staying airborne by flapping their wings. Some other animals are able to employ temporary airborne locomotion but they are considered gliders because they are not capable of powered "flapping" flight. Gliding is also employed by some of the true fliers as an energy-efficient method of locomotion. Some birds are able to use thermals (columns of warm air) to soar for hundreds of miles. This means that they hardly ever need to flap their wings.

Insect flight

Almost all the main insect groups have the power of flight. Typically they are four-winged, such as dragonflies, mayflies, butterflies, caddis flies, moths, bees, and wasps. In the true flies—more than 120,000 species of houseflies, blowflies, gnats, midges, mosquitoes, hoverflies, crane flies, and others—the hindwings have actually become tiny, drumsticklike secondary wings. These vibrate or twirl rapidly, adding stability and control, while the forewings actually provide lift and thrust. The flight muscles are located in the thorax (middle body section). Some insects directly contract and relax these muscles to pull the wing bases up and down. Other insects actually change the shape of their thorax in order to move their wings up and down. For both techniques, muscles at the wing bases determine the direction of flight by adjusting the angle of each stroke. Wing motion is not just up or down, but also to and fro, to generate both lift and thrust.

AEROBATIC FLIERS
Among the fastest, most aerobatic insects are dragonflies. They can rapidly accelerate to speeds of more than 40 mph (65 kph). Dragonflies are also able to beat their two sets of wings alternately, which increases maneuverability.

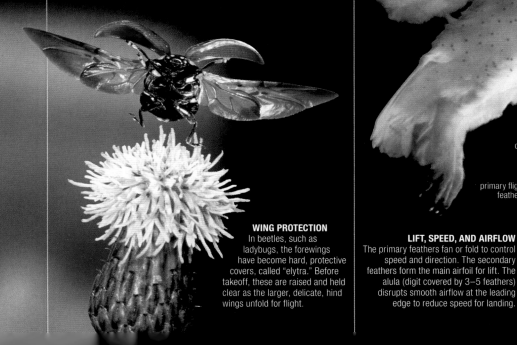

WING PROTECTION
In beetles, such as ladybugs, the forewings have become hard, protective covers, called "elytra." Before takeoff, these are raised and held clear as the larger, delicate, hind wings unfold for flight.

Bird flight

Bird wings create much of their lifting force by forward movement through the air, using the airfoil design (see panel, right). The main power for flapping comes from the pectoralis major (breast) muscles in the chest. These anchor to the sternum (breastbone) at the center of the chest, and at the other end to the inner wing bones. As these muscles contract, they pull the whole wing down and back. Muscles within the wing, aided by long tendons running out through the leading edge, can flex or warp the whole wing, change the angle of the feathers, and alter the wing's curvature for precise control.

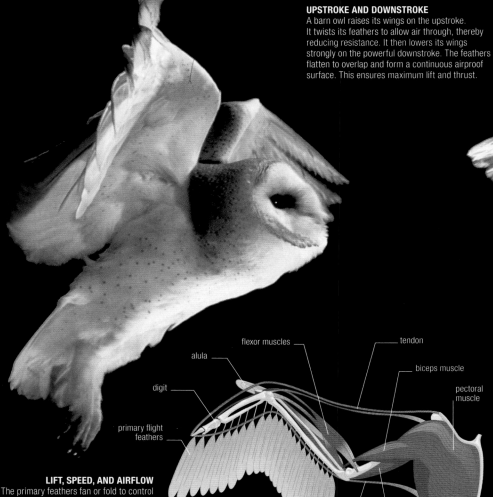

LIFT, SPEED, AND AIRFLOW
The primary feathers fan or fold to control speed and direction. The secondary feathers form the main airfoil for lift. The alula (digit covered by 3–5 feathers) disrupts smooth airflow at the leading edge to reduce speed for landing.

flexor muscles
tendon
alula
digit
biceps muscle
pectoral muscle
primary flight feathers
secondary flight feathers
tendon
triceps muscle

AERODYNAMICS

A bird's wing forms a curved shape along its upper surface, known as an airfoil. Air passing over the upper surface has to travel slightly farther at a faster pace than the air passing along the lower surface. The slow-moving air beneath the wing exerts a greater pressure, which effectively pushes up the wing from below. The faster-moving air above the upper surface of the wing produces lower air pressure and sucks the wing up from above. This creates a continuing force of lift that true fliers need to counteract the downward pull of gravity.

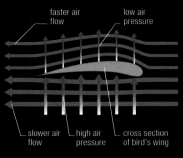

faster air flow
low air pressure
slower air flow
high air pressure
cross section of bird's wing

UPSTROKE AND DOWNSTROKE
A barn owl raises its wings on the upstroke. It twists its feathers to allow air through, thereby reducing resistance. It then lowers its wings strongly on the powerful downstroke. The feathers flatten to overlap and form a continuous airproof surface. This ensures maximum lift and thrust.

Gliding specialists

There are a number of animals—such as flying squirrels, flying possums, flying lizards, flying frogs, and flying fishes—whose names suggest they can fly. They are not, in fact, true fliers, since they cannot remain airborne in a sustained way and gain height under their own power. These remarkable creatures employ winglike structures with large surface areas, which function as parachutes to increase air resistance. They can also generate small amounts of lift that reduce descent speed. Tilting or changing the shapes of these surfaces gives a certain amount of control over distance and direction. The most impressive mammal gliders are the flying lemurs (neither true fliers nor true lemurs) of Southeast Asia, which can travel more than 330 ft (100 m) and land with pinpoint accuracy.

CALIFORNIA FLYING FISH

SOARING
When the sun warms the ground, the air above it also warms. This creates columns of warm air, known as "thermals." "Updrafts" are formed in mountainous terrain by deflected wind. Both thermals and updrafts enable birds to soar with minimal need to flap their wings. This energy-efficient method of locomotion is used by eagles, vultures, condors, and storks among others.

WALLACE'S FLYING FROG

ASTONISHING GLIDERS
California flying fish use their pectoral and pelvic fins as gliding surfaces. Wallace's flying frog extends its webbed toes as four mini-parachutes to slow its fall, as it jumps from a tree.

Wing aspect ratio

A wing's aspect ratio refers to the relative proportion of its span (length from the body to the wing tip) to its width (from leading to trailing edge). Long, narrow wings have a high aspect ratio and are most effective for long-distance gliding and soaring. Flapping is minimized, since the air currents provide much of the lift needed to sustain flight. Many birds feature this wing design, including albatrosses, gulls, and to a lesser extent condors and eagles. Low aspect-ratio wings are shorter and wider. These are used for rapid acceleration, fast turns, and precise control, as in sparrowhawks. Curved, scythelike wings with tapering, drag-reducing tips are used for sustained, speedy aerobatics, as seen in swallows and swifts.

EUROPEAN SPARROWHAWK

FIGURE-EIGHT FLIGHT
Hummingbirds flap their wings in a figure-eight pattern, providing the necessary downflow of air to allow them to hover. With slight adjustments, they can fly sideways and even backward.

SPARKLING VIOLET-EAR HUMMINGBIRD

ANDEAN CONDOR

Swimming

Swimming is remarkably similar to flying in a number of respects. Both air and water are fluid media, and many of the same principles apply to fins as to wings, such as the need to push broad surfaces backward in order to propel an animal forward. One significant difference is that water is 1,000 times denser than air, bringing many drawbacks, but also benefits.

SCHOOL SWIMMERS
Juvenile blackfin barracudas often swim in large schools. They have long, streamlined bodies with very powerful tails, which allow them to accelerate rapidly.

Staying afloat

An advantage of water over air is that it provides plenty of support, so unlike aerial animals, aquatic species do not need to generate powerful lift. However, they do need buoyancy control, as well as propulsion, in order to rise, descend, or "hover" in the water at a certain depth. Bony fishes adjust their buoyancy using an organ called the swim bladder, the gas content of which can be adjusted. Cartilaginous fishes, such as sharks and rays, lack a swim bladder. Their angled fins provide them with hydrodynamic lift as they move

forward, offsetting a tendency to sink. Sharks also have a large, oil-rich liver that adds to their buoyancy, since oil is lighter than water. In cephalopods, such as nautiluses, cuttlefish, and squid, the shell (which is internal in the latter two) contains gas-filled spaces that can be filled or emptied to adjust buoyancy. Diving and swimming birds have adaptations that enable them to sink quickly in order to catch food. Cormorants, for example, have feathers that can hold a lot of water, reducing the air trapped in their plumage.

siphuncle

gas-filled chamber

BUOYANCY CHAMBERS
Each chamber of a nautilus's shell is filled with fluid, which is absorbed and replaced by gas. An opening in each chamber allows the nautilus to control the volume of gas inside, and therefore regulate its buoyancy. The siphuncle removes excess water.

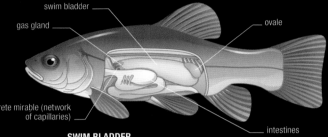

swim bladder

gas gland

ovale

rete mirable (network of capillaries)

intestines

SWIM BLADDER
A bony fish regulates its buoyancy by exchanging gas between its bloodstream and its swim bladder. Gas is secreted into the swim bladder from the gas gland, which is supplied by the rete mirabile. The gas is removed and reabsorbed into the blood by the ovale.

Swimming styles

Most large aquatic animals, such as marine mammals and big fishes, swim using the muscles in their bodies and tails to push against the water. Some cartilaginous fishes, bony fishes such as eels, and sea snakes swim with an undulating or wriggling motion, as "S"-shaped waves travel along the entire body. Most bony fishes swim by moving their rear body and tail (caudal fin) from side to side. The other fins—dorsal on the back, anal on the underside, the paired pectorals at the front, and pelvics toward the rear—are generally used for

steering and to provide stability. However, some fishes use them for their main propulsion, including seahorses, which swim by rippling the dorsal fin, and rays, which undulate their large, winglike pectoral fins. A fish's body shape usually reflects its swimming style. Powerful, fast movers have muscular, torpedo-shaped bodies that are elongated and tapered at both ends. Fishes that live in quiet waters and do not need to move at high speeds, except in short bursts, tend to be laterally compressed (narrow from side to side). Bottom dwellers are usually vertically compressed, (narrow from top to bottom) for example flatfishes and angel sharks.

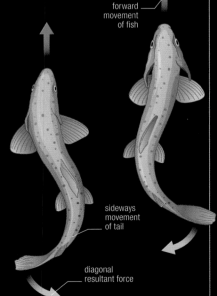

forward movement of fish

sideways movement of tail

diagonal resultant force

BODY PROPULSION
As a fish's tail moves, it generates both sideways and backward thrust in the water. The resultant force acts diagonally halfway between the two. As the fish moves its tail from side to side, the resultant diagonal thrusts to left and right produce a net backward thrust, so the fish will swim in a straight line.

TRUNK SWIMMERS
Seals like the Hawaiian monk seal move by undulating the rear body and "kicking" with their rear flippers. Eels, such as the white-margined moray, utilize serpentine locomotion —moving in a series of muscular waves passing from head to tail. This is aided by a flattened tail, which generates more thrust.

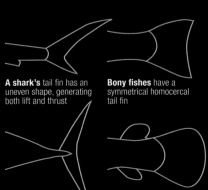

A shark's tail fin has an uneven shape, generating both lift and thrust

Bony fishes have a symmetrical homocercal tail fin

A tuna's tail fin lowers drag for fast cruising

A pike's tail fin has a large surface area for fast acceleration

TAIL FINS
The shape of a fish's tail reveals the swimming style of its owner. Most bony fishes have a "homocercal" tail shape, with upper and lower tail lobes approximately equal.

Some smaller animals propel themselves through water using tiny hairlike structures. Comb jellies have eight rows of tiny hairlike "cilia" that beat in coordinated action, like miniature oars. Some diving beetles (below) swim with their hind legs working simultaneously to push water backward. Their legs are fringed with hairs, which open out to effectively form two paddles.

Legs and limbs

Many vertebrates other than fishes swim using their limbs. Seals propel themselves by wiggling the body and "clapping" their broad, well-webbed hind flippers together, while sea lions use mainly their front flippers. Birds swim by flapping or rowing with their wings or kicking with their feet, or both. Penguins, however, possess unique wings. Their bones are solid instead of hollow, increasing their density and strength. They do not row as with oars, but flap their wings and "fly" underwater. Marine turtles swim in a similar way, but they use their front limbs solely for propulsion and their hind limbs to steer. Some species of turtle can reach up to 18 mph (30 kph).

KITTIWAKE

WEBBED FEET
Aquatic species like the kittiwake and caiman have webbing between their digits, which increases thrust due to the larger surface area.

CAIMAN

FROG "BREASTSTROKE"

Frogs swim by pushing against the water with a synchronized motion of their hind limbs and webbed feet. The whole process happens quite slowly. The frog draws its legs up to its body by bending the hips, knees, ankles, and toes. Then is straightens its legs, with its webbed toes spread, to ensure maximum thrust. The human swimming style breaststroke may have actually originated as an imitation of the way a frog swims.

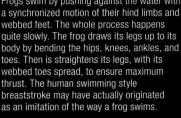

Jet propulsion

A specialized form of aquatic locomotion known as jet propulsion is seen in various cephalopod mollusks, including octopuses, squid, cuttlefish, and nautiluses, and some species of jellyfish. In a squid, the mantle muscles relax, slowly drawing the water into a chamber called the mantle cavity between the animal's main body and its fleshy, cloaklike mantle. The mantle cavity expands to accommodate the water. Muscle contraction prevents water from escaping the way that it entered. A powerful muscular action then squirts the water out very quickly through a funnel-like valve, called the siphon. The cephalopod is pushed forwards as the water jets out.

FAST ESCAPE
Cephalopods like this bigfin reef squid use jet propulsion primarily to escape danger. They can also move slowly by rippling the fins along the sides of their bodies.

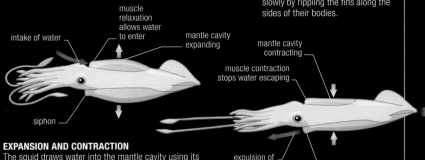

intake of water

muscle relaxation allows water to enter

mantle cavity expanding

mantle cavity contracting

muscle contraction stops water escaping

siphon

expulsion of water

siphon

EXPANSION AND CONTRACTION
The squid draws water into the mantle cavity using its mantle muscles. The cavity expands to accommodate the water. Sudden muscle contractions thrust the water out through the siphon and propel the squid through the water.

INTRICATE PATTERNS
The exquisite layout and patterning of the differently sized scales around the eyes of a reptile, in this case, a green iguana, allow sufficient flexibility for the eyes to blink but still provide a high degree of protection.

BODY COVERINGS

Animals and their environments are endlessly varied, and so are the interfaces between them—their body coverings. The outer surfaces, casings, or skins of animals are highly adapted to their surroundings and vary from microscopically thin and fragile to thicker and more durable than a brick.

HEAVY ARMOR
The shells of tortoises, turtles, and terrapins provide excellent protection but are heavy, limit movement, and restrict lifesyle.

Types and functions

An animal's outer layers are known as its integument, or integumentary system. These coverings range from basic skin and its outgrowths—scales, feathers, hairs, and bristles—to horny sheaths and rock-hard shells. Each covering is a complex compromise for a wide range of functions. Among the most important are the containment and protection of soft inner tissues, and the retention of body fluids to maintain the internal environment. The covering may also be involved in temperature regulation, nutrient uptake, waste removal, gas exchange for respiration, touch and other sensations, and features of appearance, such as camouflage, warning colors, or mating displays. These functions are mixed and matched for each animal.

VARIETY OF COVERINGS
Apart from hard-shelled animals, chiefly mollusks, most body coverings have some degree of flexibility, even if it is limited to small areas around joints, as in insects and crustaceans. This flexibility allows the animal to move around, feed, and avoid danger. Hairy, furry, or bristly coverings occur in a wide variety of animals. Such coverings are characteristic of mammals but are also found in worms, certain insects, such as caterpillars (larvae of butterflies and moths) and bees, and some spiders.

Chimpanzees have the flexible pinkish skin and outgrowths of hair that are typical of mammals.

protection but fulfill few other functions. Some coverings are more temporary, such as the outer casings of crustaceans and developing insects, and bird feathers. These are shed or molted at intervals, taking any damage with them, and are replaced by new, intact coverings. Very temporary coverings, which are not part of the body itself but are bodily products, include the bubbly froth or "cuckoo spit" secreted by froghopper bugs.

Temperature regulation and respiration

In some animal groups, the body covering can be adjusted to aid control of body temperature. This is especially important in homeothermic, or "warm-blooded," animals, which maintain a relatively high body temperature. In cold weather, birds fluff out their feathers and mammals plump up their fur to trap more insulating air and reduce heat loss. A body covering may also function in respiration by absorbing oxygen and giving off carbon dioxide. This function may supplement organs, such as lungs or gills, that are specialized for respiration, as in amphibians. The body covering may also be the sole means of respiration, as in some worms.

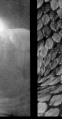

SKIN BREATHING
A typical amphibian's skin is moist and thin enough to allow gases to pass through it. This is important in the Surinam toad, which stays underwater for long periods and so cannot use its lungs for breathing.

INSULATING LAYER
Walruses have a fatty blubber layer under the skin to insulate against the cold; in hot conditions, extra blood flows to the skin surface to help lose excess body heat.

Birds, such as this whooper swan, are the only living animals to have a covering of feathers.

The African bush viper snake, like most reptiles, has a flexible scaly covering over its skin.

The sea mouse, a polychaete worm, has bristles known as chaetae projecting from its surface.

A feather star's arms are covered with flexible projections, called tube feet, that gather food particles.

Protection

A primary function of the body covering is defense. The external surface is the first point of impact for "insults" against a creature, which include physical damage, destructive chemicals or toxins, harmful microbes, parasites, and radiation. The covering may be extremely tough and durable and able to resist these problems long-term, as in the shells of mollusks and tortoises. These shells provide extra strong, extra rigid

Skin

Skin—as distinct from most animal shells or similar hard body coverings—generally provides all, or almost all, of the outer surface of an animal's body, forming a continuous, flexible, protective body covering. Typically, skin is made up of several layers and it may produce appendages and outgrowths, such as hairs, scales, horny or bony plates, or feathers.

Types of skin

In everyday use, the term "skin" usually refers to the flexible outer coverings of animals, especially vertebrates (fishes, amphibians, reptiles, birds, and mammals), rather than the rigid outer casing of invertebrates such as crabs. In many animals, much of the actual skin is under a layer produced by the skin itself, such as scales in reptiles, feathers in birds, or fur in mammals. Apart from the face, large areas of exposed skin are uncommon, occurring only in a few fishes, amphibians, and certain mammals such as whales, hippopotamuses, walruses, naked mole-rats, and humans.

SKIN VARIATIONS
The skin of an animal is adapted to its environment and lifestyle. For example, aquatic animals tend to have smooth skin to reduce friction with the water. Terrestrial animals tend to show greater variation in skin texture, and often have specialized areas of skin on different parts of the body, such as the featherless, waxy cere on the heads of some birds.

Caterpillars have a thin, flexible outer cuticle (an exoskeleton) that is made mainly of chitin.

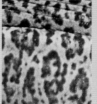
Moray eel skin is smooth and has no scales.

Whale shark skin is up to 4in (10cm) thick.

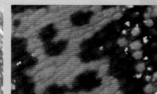
The fire-bellied newt has red patches on its underside that may startle predators.

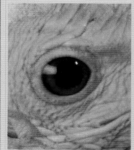
The Egyptian vulture's face is covered in yellow skin.

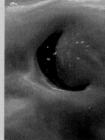
Whale skin is almost hairless, especially around the blowhole.

A gorilla's facial skin can reveal complex expressions.

Hippopotamus skin produces mucus to keep it moist on land.

Basic structure

The skin of all vertebrates has a similar basic microscopic structure, even though it may be thinner than this page or thicker than this book. There are three basic layers: the outermost epidermis, which is made up largely of keratin (a tough, fibrous protein) and continually renews itself; the dermis under this, which consists mainly of collagen and elastin fibres and contains sensory nerve endings, sweat glands, and blood vessels; and an innermost subcutaneous layer. The relative thickness and consistency of each layer varies from species to species, giving each one its unique skin features. For example, in cold-adapted birds and mammals, such as penguins, whales, and seals, the subcutaneous layer is thickened with fatty deposits that form insulating blubber to keep in body heat.

SLIMY SKIN
Hagfishes have many mucus-secreting cells in their skin. In just a few seconds, these cells produce so much slimy mucus that, when mixed with water, it would fill a bucket.

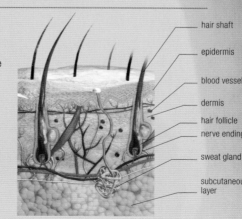

hair shaft
epidermis
blood vessel
dermis
hair follicle
nerve ending
sweat gland
subcutaneous layer

MAMMALIAN SKIN
The skin of all mammals is fundamentally similar. It has three main layers (epidermis, dermis, and the subcutaneous layer) and contains many specialized structures, such as blood vessels and nerve endings.

Defense

One of the most important roles for skin is defense of the body and its delicate internal structures. This defense may be physical, chemical, visual, or a combination of the three. In mammals such as elephants and rhinoceroses, the main physical defensive barrier is the epidermis, which is hugely thickened and strengthened with keratin. This tough protein occurs in various forms in many vertebrates (as well as some invertebrates), and is also the main component of hairs, claws, hooves, nails, horns, bills, and feathers. Chemical defense is particularly common in amphibians; in many species, the skin has tiny glands that ooze unpleasant or poisonous secretions. Visual defense may take the form of vivid coloration, which may prevent predation, or camouflage to help an animal conceal itself by blending into the surroundings.

CANE TOAD

WOMBAT

SKIN DEFENSES
The cane toad's skin secretes a poisonous chemical. The wombat uses its leathery, thick-skinned rump to block its burrow against predators.

Nutrients and wastes

In some animals, especially soft-bodied invertebrates, the skin acts as a selective two-way, in-out barrier. It absorbs nutrients, oxygen, and other useful substances as part of nutrition and respiration, and removes wastes and unwanted substances as part of excretion. These dual functions are especially important in various types of worms, such as segmented worms, flatworms, flukes, and tapeworms, because many of them lack a well-developed respiratory or circulatory system. As a result, they rely on their selectively permeable skin to absorb oxygen and remove carbon dioxide and wastes in direct exchange with the environment. In the sea, arrow worms have no excretory system and expel their body wastes through the skin.

PERMEABLE SKIN
Parasitic tapeworms have no mouth or digestive system. Instead, their very thin skin absorbs nutrients from the semidigested gut contents of their hosts.

Slippery skin

In aquatic animals a specialized function of skin—in addition to its many standard functions—is to minimize drag, turbulence, and eddying for fast, energy-efficient movement through the water. For example, dolphin skin sheds tiny particles of skin into the water flowing past, which greatly reduces drag. The sloughing skin layer replaces itself every two to four hours. In addition, the skin has microscopic ridges that hold a thin layer of water between them. So, in effect, the dolphin's outer skin layer consists partly of water as it swims, thereby reducing drag even more, as water slips past water. A third adaptation is the dolphin's very flexible skin. As the dolphin swims, the skin distorts, bending and rippling into contours that yield least resistance to the flow of water, which again minimizes drag.

REDUCED DRAG
A dolphin's skin adapations mean that drag is reduced more than 100-fold compared to "standard" mammalian skin, which enables bottlenose dolphins to swim faster than 19 mph (30 kph).

THICK HIDE
The skin of the African elephant is up to 2 in (5 cm) thick in places and is very tough. In some areas, such as the tip of the trunk, the skin is much thinner and is highly sensitive.

TOUGH SQUIRT
Sea squirts have a slippery, leathery skin that forms a tough, overall covering. Unlike most animals, the skin is composed of a type of carbohydrate (known as tunicin) that is simlar to the cellulose found in plant cells.

Scales

Most scales are small, platelike outgrowths from an animal's skin or body covering. They provide protection while allowing flexibility, and partly determine visual appearance. Various behaviors, including parasite removal, self defense, camouflage, and courtship are linked to the structure and appearance of scales.

AUSTRALASIAN RAINBOWFISH

Origins of scales

Several groups of animals have scales or scalelike coverings, from worms and certain insects to fishes, reptiles, and birds. There are also scaly-looking mammals such as armadillos and pangolins. In most of these animal groups, scales have evolved independently. Others show an evolutionary progression; for example, the scaly legs and feet of birds may be derived from their reptile ancestors, specifically small, meat-eating dinosaurs.

Invertebrate scales

Among invertebrates, scales are found in a group of segmented worms called scaleworms. They have 12 or more pairs of leathery scales or elytra that overlap like roof tiles. These form a protective outer covering for these stout, free-swimming, predatory worms, but also form channels for water currents that help them breathe.

Butterflies and moths form the major insect group Lepidoptera (the name means "scaly winged"). Their wing scales are flattened versions of

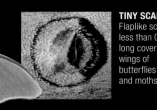

TINY SCALES Flaplike scales less than 0.1mm long cover the wings of butterflies and moths.

AMERICAN MOON MOTH

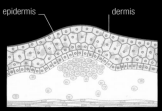

insect hairs called setae. Numbering thousands per wing, these tiny scales are arranged in rows, and their layout and colors produce the wings' overall appearance. They also aid air flow, which improves aerodynamics and helps maintain body temperature. The males of some species have scent scales on the forewings that release pheromones to attract females.

Vertebrate scales

Although some birds have scaled legs and feet, and mammals are represented by the unrelated armadillos and pangolins, the vast majority of scaled vertebrates are fishes and reptiles.

There are several types of fish scale. Cartilaginous fishes, such as sharks and rays, have teethlike placoid scales. Each consists of a plate of enamel embedded in the skin, a main body of dentine, and a pointed cap or spine of enamel. Ganoid scales are found in primitive ray-finned fishes such as sturgeons. These also have dentine, as well as enamel-like ganoine surface layers. In the gar, diamond-shaped ganoid scales fit closely to form a complete covering. In sturgeons the scales are large, platelike, and thickened with bone, forming scutes. Fishes that are more advanced in evolutionary terms

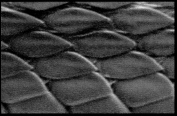 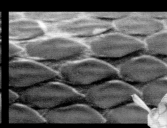

have thin, smooth, overlapping cycloid scales, as in cod, and rough-surfaced ctenoid scales, as in perches. The scales consist of a calcium-rich base with collagen fibres, similar to bone, covered by a thin outer layer.

Among reptiles, lizards and snakes have scales made of horny, flaplike, overlapping extensions of the outer skin, made chiefly of keratin (the tough protein that forms bird scales and feathers, and mammalian skin, horns, hoofs, claws, and nails). These contrast with the solid, fused, bone-reinforced scutes embedded in the outer skin, as seen in crocodiles and alligators, and especially in turtles and tortoises.

MADAGASCAN DAY GECKO

TEMMINCK'S PANGOLIN

VARIED FORM AND FUNCTION
From microscopic flakes to cumbersome plates of armor, the variety of scale types in vertebrates reflects the diversity in form and behavior of the animals that bear them.

FLEXIBLE ARMOUR
A major advantage of a scaly covering is that it combines protection with flexibility for movement. The junctions between the scales are made of proteins such as collagen or keratin and are tough yet bendable.

old skin and scales

new scales revealed beneath

SHEDDING SCALES
Most lizards and snakes shed their skin and scales several times yearly. The epidermis and scales come away to reveal newer, larger scales beneath.

⊙ SCALE DEVELOPMENT

HOW FISH SCALES GROW Most fish scales originate in the dermis, the inner of the skin's two layers. Although the materials they contain differ, most scales develop in a similar way. The placoid scales of sharks (shown here) begin as small clumps of dermal cells, which form tiny mounds. As these mounds grow taller, they tilt backward and the cells on the upper surface secrete a hard dentine layer with a cap of even harder enamel above it. This produces a tough and abrasive skin surface. These scales do not enlarge as the shark grows—it will grow more scales to cover the expanding body surface.

HOW REPTILE SCALES GROW In lizards and snakes, scales begin as pointed mounds in both the dermis (inner) and epidermis (outer) skin layers. As the dermis ages, it leaves the epidermal scale, which is hardened with a protein called keratin.

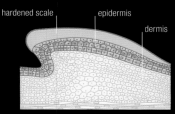

epidermis dermis	mound has tilted dentine row of enamel-secreting cells	enamel dentine pulp basal plate	hardened scale epidermis dermis
MOUND FORMS IN SKIN	**MOUND SECRETES DENTINE**	**FULLY FORMED SCALE**	**COMPLETED REPTILE SCALE**

Scale variety

FISH SCALES

In more primitive fishes, scales develop as thickened areas of skin that are arranged side by side, limiting flexibility. Advanced fish have much thinner, lighter scales growing from pockets of skin. These have free edges that can be lifted or tilted, enabling flexibility and free movement.

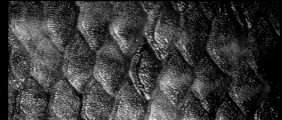

Coelacanths have modified overlapping cosmoid scales, with tiny toothlike spines, or denticles, on each exposed portion.

REPTILE SCALES

Most lizards and snakes have overlapping scales arranged in diagonal rows. There are also various modified scales forming flaps, spines, frills, and spikes. In addition to providing protection, scales help retain moisture. By emphasizing skin color, they play a role in defense, courtship, and territorial displays.

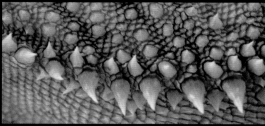

The bearded dragon has rows of spiked scales along the sides of its body, which it uses for defensive displays.

The gar's thick scales have a layer of very hard ganoine.

The marine iguana has differently shaped scales forming knobs, spikes, and cones, used especially in visual displays.

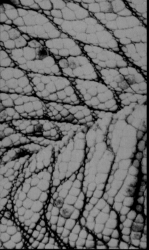

In many sharks, pointed placoid scales produce a rough, abrasive surface. A shark's teeth are actually larger versions of its placoid scales.

A rattlesnake's rattle is made of unshed scales.

The Cape legless skink burrows with a strong snout scale.

Reptile scales are mostly transparent, allowing the skin pigment to be displayed.

Ctenoid scales, like those of the garibaldi, have a surface with minute ridges or toothlike projections.

Cycloid scales have smooth surfaces and edges, as in the trout.

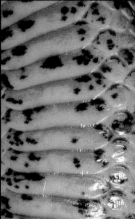

Wide scales on a snake's underside aid in locomotion.

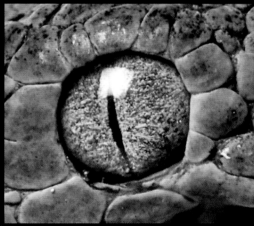

A snake's eye is covered by a single clear scale, the spectacle or "brille."

Most fish scales are transparent, allowing skin color to show through.

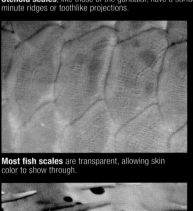

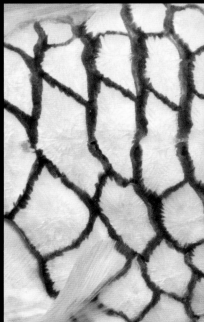

Modified scales form many kinds of accessory skin structures, such as the porcupine fish's spines.

Scales thickened with bone, forming scutes, offer extra protection to the pineapple fish.

The horned viper's horns are scales that may work as camouflage by breaking up the outline of its head.

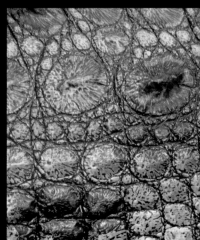

The skin of crocodiles and alligators is covered with nonoverlapping scales embedded with bony scutes.

Feathers

Of all living animals, only birds have feathers, which are made from the tough, fibrous protein keratin. In addition to being used for flying or swimming, feathers have many other functions, including protection, insulation, waterproofing, camouflage, and display.

Feather types

Most birds have different types of feathers on different parts of the body. The main flight feathers (sometimes called remiges) are the primary feathers; they are located toward the wing tips and can spread out like vanes of a fan. On the inner wing are the secondary flight feathers. Tail feathers, like the primaries, can also move and spread. Contour feathers form a streamlined surface over the body and where the wings join the chest. Beneath the contour feathers are fluffy down feathers, which trap air to provide insulation.

FLUFFY TO SMOOTH
The contour feathers form a smooth surface over the body but may have downy, flexible plumes at their bases. These plumes do not interlock and provide insulation and cushioning. The flight feathers have little or no downy base.

CONTOUR FEATHER

SECONDARY FLIGHT FEATHER

PRIMARY FLIGHT FEATHER

⦿ FEATHER STRUCTURE

Feathers grow from the epidermis of the skin and typically have a long, hollow shaft (the quill, or rachis), supporting a large flat surface, the vane. The vane is made up of small parallel strips called barbs, which are like the teeth of a comb. The barbs bear even smaller branches, barbules, some of which have interlocking hooks. As a bird preens, it arranges the barbs into neat rows to form an air-proof surface, which is essential for efficient flight and also provides insulation.

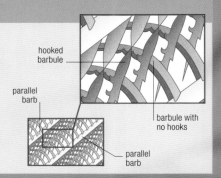

hooked barbule

parallel barb

barbule with no hooks

parallel barb

Flight control

The primary feathers at the wing tip can be fanned out and twisted to adjust their resistance to airflow. This action provides the bird's main form of aerial control, allowing it to slow down, rise, descend, and bank. At slower speeds the tail is also important, used as a rudder for maneuvering and as a fanned-out air brake for landing. The secondary feathers are less adjustable, but form an arched, airfoil surface that generates lift as it moves through the air. A small tuft of feathers at the leading edge, the alula or bastard wing, can be used for low-speed maneuvering.

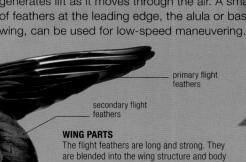

primary flight feathers

secondary flight feathers

inner wing coverts

WING PARTS
The flight feathers are long and strong. They are blended into the wing structure and body by smaller covert feathers on the inner wing, as shown on the wing of this shoveler.

Protection and conditioning

The outer feathers give physical protection, while the down feathers beneath provide cushioning. Feathers also provide waterproofing, which is particularly important for birds that spend time in water, such as seabirds, wildfowl, and waders. As a bird preens, it cleans and tidies the feathers, removes dirt and parasites, and arranges the barbs into neat rows. The bird also spreads oils from its skin oil glands over the feathers, so that they resist water absorption and shed moisture easily. Many birds molt twice yearly and replace the shed feathers with new plumage. This gets rid of damaged feathers and also alters the bird's appearance, for example, for a spring breeding display or fall camouflage.

PREENING
In addition to feeding, nest making, and defense, a bird's bill is used for cleaning and combing through the feathers, arranging them correctly, and waterproofing them, as this roseate spoonbill is doing.

SLOW FLIER
This waxwing demonstrates control at slow speed as its primary wing feathers and tail feathers fan out to increase air resistance and the tuftlike alula feathers are raised to give better lift and prevent stalling.

Fur, hair, and bristles

True fur or hair is found only in mammals. It is composed of strands of the fibrous protein alpha-keratin, which is made by specialized structures in the skin's epidermis. Fur, hair, and bristles also occur in other animals but they are made of different materials.

long, coarse hairs of outer guard coat

short, dense hairs of inner undercoat

TWO LAYERS
Seal fur has the two layers typical of mammalian fur. Long, coarse hairs form the protective outer guard coat and shorter, denser hairs constitute the insulating undercoat.

Functions

Mammalian fur has a wide range of different functions: physical protection and defense; insulation of the warm-blooded body; camouflage or bright-colored display in some species or at certain times of the year; waterproofing in semiaquatic mammals; and various sensory functions. Each hair grows from a hair follicle, a small pocketlike pit in the dermis. Insulation is improved by "fluffing up" the hairs using the tiny arrector pili muscle attached to the base of each hair follicle. This same action is used in aggressive or defensive behavior to make the mammal look larger, as when a dog or wolf raises its hackles.

THE FUR TRADE

Many animals with attractively colored or patterned fur coats have become endangered from being hunted for their pelts. Species include big and medium cats, for example, tigers, ocelots, and jungle cats, as well as foxes, minks, chinchillas, coypu (nutria), beavers, and fur seals. Captive breeding on fur farms and restriction of trade in furs and skins by the CITES agreement have reduced the need for wild kills.

WOOLLY CATERPILLAR
The bristles of "woolly" caterpillars like this sycamore moth larva are made of chitin rather than keratin. In many species, the bristles break easily when touched to release noxious chemicals as a defense mechanism.

HEAT AND COLD
Fur insulates against cold, as in seal pups (top), and against heat, as in bactrian camels that live in the hot desert of Central Asia (above).

Touch and sensation

Hair or fur shafts are almost entirely dead, except at the root in the base of the follicle, where cells accumulate to increase length. The cells quickly fill with keratin, cement together, and die to form a rod or tube shape as they move up the follicle with the growing shaft. The nerve endings wrapped around the follicle are sensitive to a hair's movement when it is tilted or bent. Mammals use this sense to detect direct physical contact, and they also use the hair movements to gauge wind or water currents. Some animals have whiskers, extra-large hairs with follicles that are specialized for touch. Whiskers are especially important in nocturnal animals such as cats and rats, where they extend the width of the head, thereby enabling the animal to feel its way and assess if gaps are big enough to pass through, even in darkness.

USEFUL WHISKERS
Aquatic mammals, such as this beaver, and also otters, seals, sea lions, and walruses, tend to have many whiskers. They enable the animal to feel its way in murky water, especially at night, and to locate food by touch.

Grooming

A mammal relies on its fur for survival, so it must be kept in good condition. Grooming, carried out with the teeth, claws, or nails, gets rid of dirt, mud, pests, such as lice and fleas, and tangles in the fur. It also spreads natural skin oils (sebum) from the sebaceous glands of the hair follicles, to keep the hairs smooth, pliable, and water-resistant. In some groups of mammals, mutual grooming occurs not only for hygiene but also for social reasons. It is part of the parental care of offspring and also a way of establishing a close bond between a breeding pair or rank in a hierarchy. Usually the animal groomed the most has the higher rank or is dominant and the lower-ranking or submissive animal does most of the grooming.

TOOTH COMB
Some primates, such as this diademed sifaka, have a row of forward-pointing teeth in the lower jaw that are used as a "tooth comb" for self-grooming.

GROOMING HIERARCHY
Chimpanzees show dominance and submissiveness by the relative amounts of time spent grooming each other. Grooming also strengthens alliances between individuals who regularly forage together.

MAINTAINING BALANCE
Jellyfish like the sea nettle seem delicate and relatively simple, with only a few organs. But, like all animals, they need to maintain their internal conditions of dissolved nutrients, salts, minerals, and other substances; otherwise, their physiological processes would grind to a halt.

BODY SYSTEMS

All animal bodies carry out similar inner processes—breaking down food for energy and nutrients, obtaining oxygen for energy release, getting rid of waste, and coordinating internal parts so they work together properly. In some animals, these processes occur in all tissues; others have complex body systems for each.

In, between, and out

The "ins" of living involve taking in essentials such as nutrients—which provide energy and raw materials for growth, maintenance, and repair—and oxygen, which is required chiefly to release energy for useful work. The "outs" involve removing waste, leftovers, and potential toxins from the body. Between the "ins" and "outs," it is vital to maintain a suitable environment within the body, in terms of the amount and concentration of all kinds of substances, from water to complex organic chemicals. This is the concept of homeostasis—the constancy of the internal environment. It involves physiology—the functional, or biochemical, side of how living things work, usually at molecular level. Physiology complements anatomy, which is the structure of the body and what it is made of. The collective name for all the thousands of biochemical processes in the body is metabolism. All of these processes are under the control of chemicals known as enzymes, each of which regulates a particular reaction.

SIMPLE INVERTEBRATE
A flatworm has a nervous system for coordination, and a digestive system. But it has no proper circulation with a heart and flowing fluid, and no specialized respiratory system.

COMPLEX INVERTEBRATE
Crayfish, like other arthropods, possess all the major body systems of vertebrates such as mammals, but generally in a more simplified form.

VERTEBRATE
In mammals such as the wolf, each system is composed of several main parts, called organs, which may be close together or widely separated around the body.

SYSTEMS KEY
Circulatory	Excretory
Digestive	Nervous
Respiratory	Reproductive

KEEPING COOL
In the scorching desert, air temperatures may rise above 120° F (50° C). The ostrich's body is fine-tuned to stay at about 18° F (10° C) less—any higher disrupts its internal chemistry. So the ostrich uses anatomy, physiology, and behavior to stay cool.

STAYING WARM
As temperatures fall to -22° F (-30° C) or less, the Arctic hare would be in danger of freezing solid. It fluffs its fur to trap insulating air, and shelters from the biting wind, so that its body can remain at a constant warm temperature.

Life chemicals and processes

The energy sources that power most life processes are sugars, especially glucose obtained by digestion. In cellular respiration, glucose is broken apart to release its chemical energy. This is then transferred to "energy carrier" molecules known as adenosine triphosphates (ATPs). In complex animals, oxygen is brought into the body by the respiratory system and then distributed by the blood. Each overall reaction begins with one molecule of glucose and six of oxygen, and yields six molecules each of the waste product carbon dioxide and water, plus released energy.

NO OXYGEN
Animals that hold their breath for a time, like sea snakes, can alter their cellular respiration so it is anaerobic—it does not need oxygen—but only for a while.

CELLULAR RESPIRATION
Red blood cells bring continual supplies of fresh oxygen and glucose. These pass through the thin walls of the smallest blood vessels, the capillaries, into cells. The carbon dioxide produced by cellular respiration diffuses into the blood and is removed by bodily respiration.

Key to major systems

Food is vital for all animals. This is dealt with by the digestive system, which breaks up food with enzymes. Eventually, the pieces of food are small enough for the body's tissues to absorb. In simple animals, the nutrient molecules may just drift through the cells and tissues. In more complex animals, there is a circulatory system that propels a fluid, such as blood, around all body parts to deliver the nutrients. Likewise, oxygen may simply be absorbed at the body surface and pass into the tissues, or it may be taken in through specialized parts, such as the lungs or gills of the respiratory system, and then passed to the circulation for bodywide delivery. In a similar way, waste may diffuse outward to the body surface, or it may be collected and disposed of by an excretory or urinary system. The immune system protects an animal from germs and disease. Coordinating all these systems are the nervous and hormonal systems.

glucose molecule

oxygen combines with glucose

oxygen diffuses out of blood

six water molecules

six carbon dioxide molecules

tissue cell

carbon dioxide diffuses into blood

capillary wall

blood plasma

six oxygen molecules

Breathing

The term "breathing" is usually applied to the physical movements of inhaling and exhaling. It partly overlaps with the broader term "respiration," which can refer to the overall process of taking in oxygen or using it to release the energy from glucose and similar nutrients inside cells.

Breathable skin

Skin can be breathable in the sense that it is a gas-exchange surface—through which oxygen is absorbed into the body from the environment, as carbon dioxide passes the other way. This is known as cutaneous respiration. The skin must be thin to present a minimal barrier to the diffusion of gas. This type of breathing occurs in aquatic animals, where oxygen is dissolved in the water. The amount of dissolved oxygen rises as the water circulates or becomes colder. So cool, fast-flowing streams have abundant dissolved oxygen, while tropical swamps have much less. Swamp-dwelling fish can absorb oxygen through their skin as well as their gills, and some, like lungfish, gulp oxygen into their lungs.

PLENTY OF SURFACE
Flatworms, like this marine turbellarian, lack a circulatory system to distribute oxygen. They also have no specialized respiratory parts such as gills. The leaflike body shape allows tissues to be a minimal distance from the skin surface, to receive dissolved oxygen as easily as possible.

 CASE STUDY

LUNGLESS FROG

Most frogs respire through their skin and also have lungs to breathe air. The recently discovered Bornean lungless frog, the first-known frog species without lungs, shows that under suitable conditions, enough oxygen can be absorbed through the skin alone—in this case, in a habitat of cool streams. Amphibians evolved true lungs more than 300 million years ago. The lungless frog and several species of lungless salamanders have reversed this trend.

Invertebrate breathing systems

Some terrestrial invertebrates, especially insects, have a respiratory network of air tubes (trachea) branching throughout the body. The tubes open at holes in the body covering called spiracles. Air movement through the spiracles, into and out of the trachea, is much more limited than the forced airflow in true lungs. It occurs mainly when the insect moves, making the trachea compress and stretch, or from air currents. However, even in still air, oxygen can diffuse to areas inside the trachea where there is less oxygen, while carbon dioxide does the reverse and is removed. Most spiders have book lungs in a chamber in the base of the abdomen. Book lungs consist of many thin, leaflike structures into which oxygen can easily diffuse.

spiracle

INSECT SPIRACLES
Spiracles are seen clearly along the sides of insect larvae such as this sphinx moth caterpillar. They may be incorporated into coloration, perhaps as a form of disruptive camouflage that breaks up the body outline.

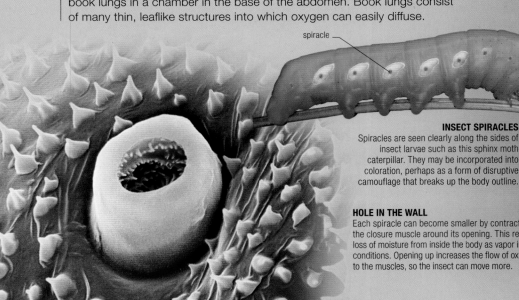

HOLE IN THE WALL
Each spiracle can become smaller by contraction of the closure muscle around its opening. This reduces loss of moisture from inside the body as vapor in dry conditions. Opening up increases the flow of oxygen to the muscles, so the insect can move more.

Breathing with gills

Gills are body parts specialized for gas exchange in water. Their structure consists of many branching surfaces with a plentiful blood supply, to present the greatest possible area for absorbing oxygen and getting rid of carbon dioxide. Gills of various kinds are found in a wide range of aquatic animals. They form frilly tufts on the backs of sea slugs, and fin- or flap-like tail appendages on aquatic insect larvae such as damselfly and mayfly nymphs. Fish gills are on several bony or cartilaginous arches on the sides of the head. In all cases, the gills must be exposed to flowing water, to bring continuing supplies of dissolved oxygen. The flow also takes away carbon dioxide and other unwanted substances, such as salt and ammonia. This occurs in fishes and some amphibians, where gills have become organs of excretion as well as respiration.

EXTERNAL GILLS
Amphibian larvae, like this newt, have external gills on the sides of the head. These are delicate and easily damaged but regrow well.

feathery gills

gill filaments

oral valve

mouth

direction of water movement

gill arch, attachment point for filaments

esophagus

INTERNAL GILLS
Fish gills are composed of hairlike or feathery filaments protected within gill chambers. In most fishes, water flows in through the mouth, over the filaments—where oxygen is taken into the blood inside them—and out through the gill slits (left). The oxygenating blood gives the gills a strong red color, as in the map pufferfish (above).

Breathing with lungs

Lungs are organs specialized to absorb oxygen from air and remove carbon dioxide into air. Most vertebrates except most fishes have lungs (some fishes, such as lung fishes, take in oxygen from swallowed air). Typical vertebrate lungs are paired in the chest, on either side of the heart. Their branching airways connect to the trachea (windpipe), pharynx (throat), and mouth, forming a passage along which air moves. The flow is caused by respiratory muscles in the chest and the sheetlike diaphragm between the chest and abdomen. These muscles contract to expand the lungs and suck in fresh air during inhalation, then relax so the stale air pushes out. Lungs contain millions of tiny bubblelike alveoli surrounded by blood capillaries, which absorb oxygen from the air.

ONE-WAY LUNGS
Mammal lungs are "dead ends" in that air flows in, then back out. Birds have expandable air sacs that draw air down the windpipe and right through the lungs. This allows more oxygen to be absorbed, for the bird's energy-hungry flight muscles.

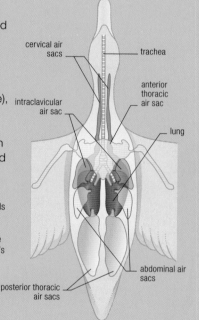

cervical air sacs

trachea

intraclavicular air sac

anterior thoracic air sac

lung

posterior thoracic air sacs

abdominal air sacs

LAND CRAB
The coconut or robber crab has a combined "gill-lung" known as the branchiostegal organ in its rear abdomen. If moistened with sea water, this can take in oxygen from air for long periods, allowing the crab to move considerable distances on land.

HOLDING BREATH
Most seals, such as this Antarctic fur seal, for example, and sea lions can hold their breath for at least several minutes, and some for over one hour. The body uses oxygen stored not only in the lungs, but in the blood and muscles, by the pigments hemoglobin and myoglobin.

CASE STUDY

RECORD DIVE

Cuvier's beaked whale has been tracked to almost 6,200 ft (1,900 m) below the surface on a single dive of 85 minutes. Compared to land mammals, whale blood contains very high amounts of the oxygen-loving pigment hemoglobin, but large quantities of a similar pigment, myoglobin, are found in the muscles. These store plenty of oxygen for diving. Blood vessels to less important body parts like the intestines constrict on the dive, saving oxygen usage, while the vessels to the muscles, heart, and brain stay open for a plentiful flow.

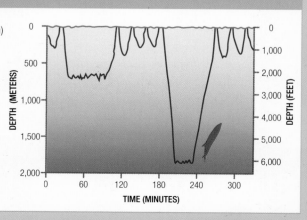

DEPTH (METERS)

DEPTH (FEET)

TIME (MINUTES)

ASSISTED BREATHING
As large animals such as the pronghorn run, the continual acceleration-deceleration of each stride makes the abdominal contents move to and fro within the body. This aids normal breathing by alternately compressing and stretching the chest.

Circulation

In complex animals, the circulatory system sends blood around the body, through a network of tubes or vessels, pumped by the heart. The circulatory systems of other animals use a different fluid, or have few vessels, or no heart—and sometimes they have all these variations.

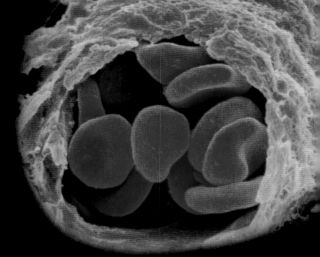

NONSTOP PUMP
The throbbing heart of a water-flea (a small crustacean) is visible through its body wall.

Types of circulation

A dedicated circulation system is much more efficient than simple diffusion, where substances flow at random through tissues and cells. The two main types of circulation are open and closed. In the former, found in invertebrates such as insects, the circulating fluid is usually called hemolymph. For part of its journey, it permeates and oozes through the general body cavity, the hemocoel or celom, unconstrained by vessels, before returning to the heart(s). In the closed system, as seen in most vertebrates, the circulating medium—blood—is within vessels for all of its journey. It exchanges nutrients, oxygen, waste, and other substances through their walls.

heart

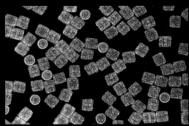

BLUE BLOOD
Red blood has the iron-based pigment hemoglobin carried in red cells (above). Some crustaceans and mollusks have copper-containing pigments, like hemocyanin, so the hemolymph is green or blue, as in a whelk (left).

Blood, lymph, and hemolymph

The blood of vertebrates, and the hemolymph of invertebrates, carries out dozens of functions. It transports nutrients and oxygen to the cells, and gathers unwanted by-products for excretion. It carries hormones to coordinate inner processes. It gets sticky or clots to seal wounds and leaks. In "warm-blooded" animals—mainly mammals and birds—it distributes heat around the body. In a typical vertebrate, about half the blood is a pale fluid (plasma) containing hundreds of dissolved substances. Most of the rest is red blood cells (erythrocytes), which hold onto oxygen or carbon dioxide. Lymph is a circulating fluid that has important roles in the immune system. It is carried inside vessels called lymphatics. It has no pump but oozes slowly, massaged by body movements.

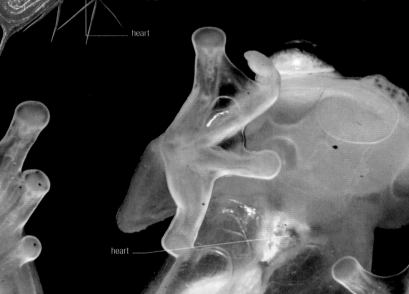

heart

ventral abdominal vein

Immune system

The immune system has major roles in resisting disease and fighting illness. It involves various categories of white cells. Those called macrophages hunt down, engulf, and "eat" microbes such as bacteria. There are also various kinds of lymphocytes. Some are able to recognize microbes and other alien items. They instruct other types of lymphocytes to produce substances known as antibodies, which stick onto the microbes and disable or kill them. In vertebrates, all of these cells travel in the blood and the lymph.

SEE-THROUGH FROG
A glass frog reveals its heart at the front of the chest cavity. The thick muscular walls obscure the red blood inside, but blood can be seen in the

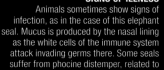

SIGNS OF ILLNESS
Animals sometimes show signs of infection, as in the case of this elephant seal. Mucus is produced by the nasal lining as the white cells of the immune system attack invading germs there. Some seals suffer from phocine distemper, related to

Digestion

Consuming food for internal digestion and absorption distinguishes most members of the animal kingdom from those in other major groups of organisms, such as plants and fungi. Food provides raw materials for growth and repair, health-giving substances like vitamins, and the energy for life.

Digestive systems

After an animal captures food it is taken in through the oral opening, or mouth, into the digestive tract. In simple animals, this is a hollow chamber or branching system with just one opening, so the undigested waste comes out the same way and the mouth functions as the anus. In complex animals, the digestive tract is a long tube or convoluted passageway with the anus or cloaca at the other end. General names are given to sections of the tract in various animals. After the mouth is the gullet or esophagus, perhaps leading to a "crop" which is specialized for storage. The stomach is the main digestion site, the intestine the chief area for absorbing nutrients, and the rectum, or large bowel, stores waste until it is expelled.

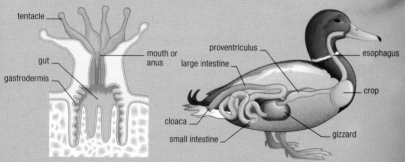

tentacle
gut
gastrodermis
mouth or anus

proventriculus
large intestine
cloaca
small intestine
esophagus
crop
gizzard

DUAL PURPOSE
Cnidarians such as coral polyps (above), jellyfish, and anemones have a single digestive opening that is the mouth when eating and the anus when expelling leftovers. Nutrients diffuse through the gastrodermis (gut lining) into the tissues.

TWO OPENINGS
In some invertebrates and all vertebrates, the gut is a through-tube. Birds, some fishes, and some invertebrates have a gizzard—a muscular grinding chamber following the proventriculus (the stomach area) that secretes digestive enzymes.

Specialist diets

Some animals are omnivorous, with a digestive system that can deal with many kinds of foods. Others are adapted to survive on a narrow range of foods, especially those that are very low-nutrient, or distasteful, or contain chemicals that are toxic to other animals. This means the specialist feeder faces little competition for its meals, but also limits its range to the geographical distribution of its foodstuffs, and its survival to that of the food. Some specializations are physical, for example, the manipulation of bamboo shoots by the giant panda. Others are biochemical, where a unique enzyme allows an animal to deal with a particular food part or a toxin.

UNIQUE FOODS
The golden bamboo lemur's staple diet of giant bamboo (left) contains levels of cyanide that would kill most other mammals, while the creosote bush katydid (above) is not put off by the unpalatable taste of an acid that is found in creosote bush leaves.

PREDIGESTED
In animals such as flies, spiders, and starfish, early digestion is outside the body. The mouth pours digestive juices onto the food, which turns it into a "soup" that is sucked up.

Food breakdown and disposal

Digestion involves breaking food into tinier pieces, until they are small enough for absorption. Physical digestion includes crushing in the mouth and mashing in the stomach or gizzard. In chemical digestion, juices containing enzymes are secreted onto the food by the gut lining. Different enzymes attack different dietary constituents—proteases split apart proteins in meaty food, while lipases break down oils and fats in fatty food. This process may take months, as when a python digests a wild pig. In most cases, undigested material passes out through the anus as droppings or feces, but some animals bring up or regurgitate leftovers via the mouth.

hair and bones matted together

vole leg bone

Worm casts, like that of the lugworm, consist of sand and mud particles that have passed through the gut.

Owl pellets are regurgitated and contain undigestible bits of prey such as bones, teeth, fur, and beaks.

Fluids and temperature control

The control of an animal's bodily internal environment includes regulating the concentrations of hundreds of salts, minerals, and other substances. Called osmoregulation, this involves the delicate processes of water balance. The body temperature must also be maintained within suitable limits so that biochemical reactions can take place efficiently.

Water and salt balance

Living on land, in freshwater, and in seawater pose different problems. Land animals tend to lose water as vapor from permeable body coverings, from moist respiratory surfaces, and in excreted urine and droppings. This must be replaced by drinking, by water contained in foods, and by water made in the body by metabolic processes. In freshwater, an animal's internal environment has a relatively high concentration of salts compared to its surroundings. Water tends to diffuse into the body and so must be removed—in urine and by being actively "pumped" out. In saltwater, the opposite may occur, so water must be prevented from leaving the body.

SLEEPING BAG
The desert-dwelling water-holding frog buries itself in moist soil during drought. It forms a watertight cocoon from shed layers of skin, storing water under its skin and as dilute urine in its large bladder. The frog remains inside its fluid sleeping bag until wet weather returns.

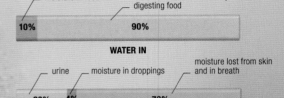

moisture in food | metabolic water released by digesting food

10% | 90%

WATER IN

urine | moisture in droppings | moisture lost from skin and in breath

23% | 4% | 73%

WATER OUT

DESERT DWELLER
Desert animals such as the banner-tailed kangaroo rat have adapted to produce very concentrated urine, which reduces water loss. This kangaroo rat is nocturnal, and it seals its burrow by day, which traps moisture in its breath.

WATER BALANCE IN A KANGAROO RAT
There is little moisture in the kangaroo rat's main diet of seeds. But water is actually made in the body by metabolic processes such as cellular respiration. As well as concentrated urine, the droppings are also dry, to conserve moisture.

Waste disposal

Filtering blood, hemolymph, or other body fluids is a common method of regulating water, salts, and toxins. In vertebrates, the main organs involved are the two kidneys. They remove waste products dissolved in water through microscopic filters known as nephrons. Then the required amount of water is reabsorbed into the bloodstream to maintain water balance. In mammals, the resulting fluid, urine, is stored in the bladder until it can be expelled. Urine contains various hormones and similar substances, which often have distinctive scents, so it has a secondary role as a means of communication, for example, as a sign of readiness to breed. Invertebrates have similar methods of excretion, involving filtering body fluids such as hemolymph, but the main organs have different structures. Worms or flatworms possess nephridia, while the excretory system of an insect is based on malpighian tubules.

USEFUL DROPPINGS
A bird's urine, produced by its kidneys, is combined with digestive wastes from its intestine, and leaves the cloaca as semiliquid droppings. Thick accumulations known as guano from seabirds such as the blue-footed booby are collected for fertilizers and mineral extraction.

USEFUL URINE
Behavioral aspects of waste disposal include the use of urine to scent-mark territories and warn away intruders of the same species, as seen in lions, rhinoceroses, and many other mammals.

Behavior and temperature control

Mammals and birds maintain a constant high body temperature by "burning" energy-containing nutrients—to release heat. Keeping body temperature constant is termed homeothermy, popularly known as being "warm-blooded," and generating warmth in this way is termed endothermy. Such animals can stay active even in cold conditions, but the process requires energy, which must come from increased food consumption. Most other animals are ectothermic, meaning that warmth for their bodies comes from outside. A popular term for this is "cold-blooded." However, a reptile in a scorching desert may have a warmer body than a mammal next to it. Also, ectothermy does not mean having no control—by using behavior such as resting in the shade to cool down, an ectotherm can alter its temperature.

COOL EARS
Elephants have large ears, not only for acute hearing, but to help control their body temperature. The ears have a plentiful blood supply, and when the body temperature rises, the ears flap back and forth to work like radiators and lose heat to the surrounding air. Animals with similar adaptations for hot climates include jackrabbits and the fennec fox.

WARMING UP
In the early morning, a southern rock agama seeks out dark rocks to warm itself. These rocks have held the sun's heat from the previous day and are also absorbing more solar heat in the new dawn.

CONSERVING WARMTH

Mammals and birds in cold places, such as penguins in the Antarctic, have a specialized blood flow called the countercurrent mechanism to conserve body heat. Extremities such as feet and flippers tend to cool fastest. Warm blood flowing from the body core to the extremity passes close to cool blood returning from it, and transfers some heat to warm this blood, while itself cooling. The extremity is kept colder and so loses heat at a slower rate than if warm blood circulated through it.

direction of blood flow

warm blood returns to body

warm blood from body transfers heat to cold blood

cold blood circulates in penguin's foot

Hibernation and torpor

True hibernation is limited to certain mammals such as bats, dormice and other rodents, insectivores including hedgehogs, and some lemurs. It is a strategy to survive adverse conditions, usually winter, by "shutting down" the body's activity and metabolic processes to save energy. Heart and breathing rates fall to a fraction of their usual levels, and body temperature drops to a few degrees above freezing. To prepare, the animal feeds well to lay down reserves of food as body fat, then finds a sheltered, safe place. Once in hibernation, it is unable to rouse quickly. Torpor is a less extreme, short-term slowing of body processes, usually just for a few hours. Some small bats and hummingbirds enter torpor overnight to survive the cold.

FAT RESERVES
The fat-tailed lemur stores food as fat in its tail to survive Madagascar's dry season, which it spends in a state of torpor in a hollow in a tree.

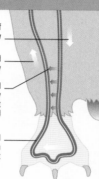

SAFE CAVE
Hibernating bats, such as the whiskered bat, choose sites that are safe from predators, and which also have constant conditions and do not freeze, for example, deep inside a cave.

CASE STUDY
LIZARD ACTIVITY PATTERNS

Terrestrial ectotherms, such as lizards, have an array of behaviors to help them warm up by day, and then keep their body temperature relatively constant so that they can remain active. They move from shelter to sunshine and bask on dark rocks, which soak up the sun's heat better than light-colored ones. To cool down, they seek out shade or a breeze, gape the mouth to breathe out warm air, or enter a burrow.

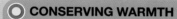

TIME OF DAY

TEMPERATURE °C — 45, 30, 15, 0
TEMPERATURE °F — 110, 90, 70, 50, 32
06:00 09:00 12:00 15:00 18:00 20:00

KEY
— Air temperature
— Lizard's body temperature
▢ Sheltering to avoid cold
▢ Basking
▢ Normal activity
▢ Sheltering to avoid heat

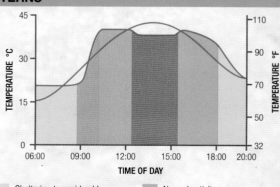

Brains, nerves, and hormones

The nervous and hormonal systems of animals are vital for the control and coordination of internal body parts, ensuring they work together effectively. These systems also control the whole animal as it sees, hears, and otherwise senses its surroundings, moves around, selects a range of behaviors according to circumstances, and prepares to molt or breed.

Nerves

Most animals possess a system of nerves that branch into all body parts and come together at one site, known as the brain, or at several locations, where they form ganglia. The nervous system uses tiny pulses of electricity, or nerve signals, and is concerned with the whole animal sensing and reacting to the environment, instincts, memory, and learning. Its basic components are some of the most specialized of all cells—neurons, or nerve cells. They have thin branches that carry nerve signals at speeds in excess of 330 ft/s (100 m/s) in some species. The branches almost touch those of other neurons, but are separated by tiny gaps known as synapses, which the nerve signals cross in the form of chemicals called neurotransmitters released by the neurons. Not all animals have a nervous system and brain. Sponges lack any nerves and jellyfish are "brainless," with only a simple nerve net.

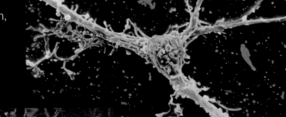

SUPPORT CELLS
As part of the nervous system, millions of cells give physical and nutritional support to neurons, without carrying any nerve signals themselves. Astrocytes (left) are named after their starlike shape, and pass nutrients to neurons. Oligodendrocytes (above) form a type of living scaffolding to hold the neurons firmly.

NEURON
A typical neuron has a rounded cell body with short, thin branches called dendrites. These gather signals from other neurons and process them—the resulting signals travel along a thicker, longer projection, the axon (nerve fiber), to the terminal, which links to other neurons. Some axons have wrappings of fatty insulation (myelin) made by Schwann cells.

Schwann cell

axon terminal fiber

node of Ranvier

nucleus

cell body

dendrite

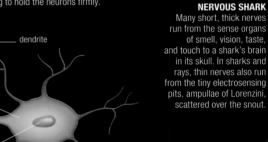

brain

NERVOUS SHARK
Many short, thick nerves run from the sense organs of smell, vision, taste, and touch to a shark's brain in its skull. In sharks and rays, thin nerves also run from the tiny electrosensing pits, ampullae of Lorenzini, scattered over the snout.

Invertebrate nervous systems

Invertebrates show a range of nervous system designs, from simple nerve nets to centralized networks, which have "lumps" of neurons called ganglia or a single brain. These structures contain concentrations of neuron cell bodies with many short, interconnected dendrites and axons. This makes the exchange and processing of information more efficient than in a diffuse network.

Sensory nerves bring incoming signals from the sense organs. This information is analyzed in the brain or ganglia and appropriate signals are then sent out along motor nerves to muscles, which effect movements and behavior, and to body parts such as glands, telling them to release their chemical secretions.

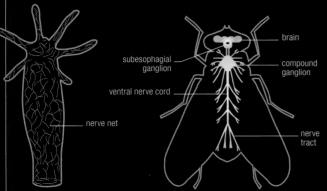

nerve net

subesophagial ganglion

ventral nerve cord

brain

compound ganglion

nerve tract

HYDRA

HOUSE FLY

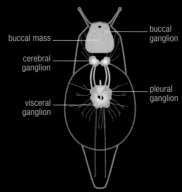

buccal mass

cerebral ganglion

visceral ganglion

buccal ganglion

pleural ganglion

ROMAN SNAIL

DIFFERENT DESIGNS
The nerve net of cnidarians such as the hydra, a tiny pond animal, consists of nerve fibers connected in a simple netlike fashion. Arthropods such as flies and other insects have a frontal brain, ganglia at various sites, and a ventral nerve cord along the base of the body. Mollusk nervous systems, shown here in the snail, have several ganglia linked by thick tracts of nerve fibers that carry signals at very fast speeds.

Vertebrate nervous system

The typical layout of a vertebrate's central nervous system consists of a brain and spinal cord, and branches from these to all body parts, forming the peripheral nervous system. The presence of a spinal column made of vertebra (backbones), which support and protect the spinal cord, is a characteristic of vertebrates. Different lobes, centers, and other parts of the brain deal with specific functions. For example, the optic lobes receive nerve signals from the eyes, while the olfactory lobes process information about smell from the nose, and the motor centers organize nerve signals going out to the muscles for movement. There is also an autonomic nervous system, partly with its own nerves such as sympathetic ganglia chains, and partly using nerve fibers from the other systems. This system is concerned with the "automatic running" of essential actions inside the body, such as breathing and the passage of food through the gut. The sympathetic part of the autonomic system makes body parts more active and ready to cope with stress, while the parasympathetic part restores calm and normal working.

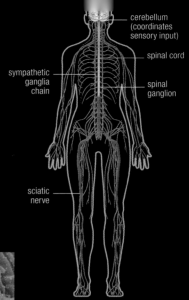

cerebellum
(coordinates
sensory input)

spinal cord

sympathetic
ganglia
chain

spinal
ganglion

sciatic
nerve

DOG BRAIN
The vertebrate brain, colored green in this image, is well protected inside the cranium, a bony chamber at the rear of the skull. Its wrinkled surface provides a large area for billions of neurons.

spinal column

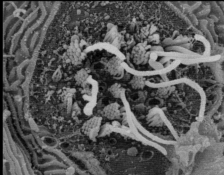

SENSORY CELLS
Many types of sensory cells have microscopic hairs that are moved by outside forces such as sound vibrations in the ear, or water currents in the neuromast organs found in a fish's lateral line (right). As the hairs move, their cells produce nerve signals that travel to the brain.

HUMAN NERVOUS SYSTEM
The spinal cord runs along a tunnel formed by aligned holes in the vertebrae, which protect it against knocks and prevent kinks. Spinal nerves, such as the sciatic nerve, branch from it into the torso and limbs. Cranial nerves branch directly from the brain to the eyes, ears, and other sense organs in the head, and to the head and face muscles.

Hormones

In general, the hormone system works more slowly than the nervous system. Hormones are chemicals made by groups of endocrine cells scattered through various tissues or in separate endocrine glands. Each type of hormone—some animals have more than 100—spreads around the body in the blood. It works as a chemical messenger to affect certain parts known as its target organs or tissues, usually making them work faster or release their products. Hormones maintain internal conditions such as water balance and control growth and development, the reproductive cycle, molting or shedding of body coverings, and in some animals, metamorphosis (drastic change in body shape).

RISING LEVELS
The breeding behavior of brown hares in spring is triggered by rising levels of reproductive hormones from the sex glands— ovaries in females, testes in males. Here, an unreceptive female is boxing to fend off a male.

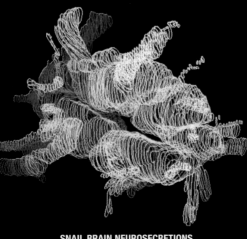

SNAIL BRAIN NEUROSECRETIONS
Neurosecretions are made by nerve cells and trigger actions such as hormone release or muscle activity. A snail's brain shows varying levels of neurosecretion (yellow, red, and white) in response to light levels sensed by the eyes, which makes the snail active at night and restful by day.

ELEPHANT EYE
Vertebrate eyes are remarkably similar in form and
function. Light enters the eye through the central
pupil, the size of which is controlled by muscles
around the colored iris. The light is received and
processed by the retina at the back of the eyeball.

SENSES

Being able to sense what is happening around them is vital for animals' survival. Among a myriad of other things, sensory information helps them find food and avoid predators; to know when they are too hot or too cold, or are hurt; and to improve their reproductive success by aiding the location and selection of mates.

What are senses?

A sense is the reception of a stimulus that is interpreted by the brain to gain information about the external or internal environment. For example, light is gathered by the eye and interpreted by the brain into an image. The five senses most familiar to humans are hearing, sight, taste, smell, and touch. Most animals possess some or all of these senses to varying degrees, but they may also have other senses, most notably echolocation (the use of sound to locate objects), and electroreception and magnetoreception (the abilities to detect electric and magnetic fields respectively). In addition to being able to sense their surroundings, animals require information about their own bodies, such as their position and movement, which is sensed by special cells. For example, thermoreceptors in the skin enable perception of temperature.

POWERFUL EYESIGHT
Steller's sea eagle hunts by sight. Its powerful binocular vision allows it to spot prey and accurately judge distance.

demands of their environment and behavior. Dogs have a well-developed sense of smell, which they use to locate prey and communicate with one another; bats can hunt at night in total darkness because of their ability to use ultrasound for echolocation; many insects and birds can see ultraviolet light, allowing them to detect patterns on flowers and plumage that are invisible to the human eye; and elephants can produce and hear infrasound, permitting them to communicate over many miles. The brain integrates information from all of the senses so that an animal has a mental picture of the world around it, enabling it to react accordingly. For example, a predator spotting possible prey will use sensory information to decide whether or not to launch an attack.

GREETING CEREMONY
Black-backed jackals greet one another by smelling scent glands located in the anal region. Smell is important in identifying members of the pack.

HEARING

SIGHT

TASTE

SMELL

TOUCH

THE FIVE MAJOR SENSES
Jackrabbits have an acute sense of hearing thanks to their huge ears. Deep-sea squid have large eyes that are sensitive to light produced by bioluminescent organisms. Butterflies have taste receptors on their feet as well as their mouthparts. Humpback salmon have a keen sense of smell that helps them find the stream they hatched in. Lobsters have long antennae and tiny hairs all over their body that are receptive to touch.

Sensory systems

Each sensory system comprises sensory receptors, neural pathways, and parts of the brain involved in sensory perception. Examples in vertebrates include the visual system, where receptors of color and brightness in the retina trigger nervous impulses in the optic nerve, which travel to the primary visual cortex for processing; and the auditory system, whereby hair cells in the inner ear receive vibrations caused by sound waves, triggering nervous impulses in the auditory nerve, which travel to the primary auditory cortex. The somatosensory system detects pressure and touch; the gustatory system senses taste; and the olfactory system receives and processes information about smell. Each neuron has a threshold, above which a stimulus will cause it to fire an impulse. The nature of the nervous impulses triggered by the receptors provides the brain with information about the location of the stimulus, its intensity, and its duration. For example, the longer an object touches part of the body, the more the receptor cells will trigger the nerves.

brain

spinal cord

NERVOUS SYSTEM
In vertebrates, such as this seahorse, the central nervous system comprises the spinal cord and the brain.

Senses and behavior

The senses play a vital role in animal behavior. Senses are required for communication between animals—for example, to hear and see sound and visual signals, and to smell scent marks. They are needed to locate prey— for example, by sight, echolocation, or electroreception; to find mates, such as by homing in on pheromones or a mating call; and for navigation, which may be mediated by sight, smell, or magnetoreception of the Earth's magnetic field, or a combination of such cues. Animals may have evolved particularly acute senses, or senses in specific ranges, according to the

Touch and vibration

Animals learn a great deal about their environment by using touch and sensing vibration. They can feel for their food and communicate without the need for sight or sound, skills that are especially helpful in the dark. The sense of touch is facilitated by structures called mechanoreceptors that respond to stimulation. Mechanoreceptors also provide feedback about an animal's movement and orientation so that it can adjust its position as necessary.

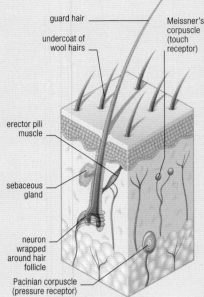

guard hair

undercoat of wool hairs

Meissner's corpuscle (touch receptor)

erector pili muscle

sebaceous gland

neuron wrapped around hair follicle

Pacinian corpuscle (pressure receptor)

FOLLOWING ITS NOSE
As the star-nosed mole hunts for soil-based or aquatic prey, the 22 sensitive, fleshy tentacles around its nostrils wiggle in constant motion.

HAIRY LEGS
A spider's leg is covered in hairs that respond to touch and airborne vibrations. The base of each sensillum connects with the dendrite of a neuron, which transfers a stimulus to the brain for processing when the hair is touched.

Touch receptors

Most arthropods detect touch and vibration through sensory hairs called sensilla. These filaments protrude through the exoskeleton from where they are anchored in the epidermal layer below. Movement of the hair triggers a nerve impulse in an adjacent receptor cell. Vertebrate hairs work in much the same way: the base of the hair is located in a follicle with the tip of a sensory neuron wrapped around the hair shaft to receive and transmit the stimulus. In addition to hairs, the epidermal (top) and dermal (lower) layers of the skin contain a variety of different structures for detecting touch, pressure, and vibration. Mechanoreceptors may be concentrated to create a particularly sensitive area, for example, on the nose of a star-nosed mole.

MAMMALIAN SKIN
Meissner's corpuscles in the upper dermis respond to light touches, while the larger Pacinian corpuscles, located deep in the dermis, detect heavy, more sustained pressure and vibrations.

MULTIPLE HAIRS
The hairs that protrude above a mammal's skin have a variety of functions, including sensitivity to touch, insulation, camouflage, and communication.

Motion detectors

Arthropod sensilla also detect movements of air or water around them, as do vertebrate whiskers (vibrissae). These stiff, long hairs are usually located around the nose and mouth or above the eyes. They are anchored in special follicles called blood sinuses, which allow even a tiny deflection of the whisker, such as might be caused by a whisper of wind, to be amplified and stimulate mechanoreceptor cells. Fishes and larval amphibians have a different system to detect movements in water. The lateral line is composed of receptors called neuromasts, each of which has several hair cells projecting into a gel-filled cap called a cupula. The cupula bends in response to water movement, allowing the animal to detect the direction of water currents.

 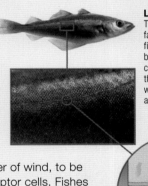

LATERAL LINE
The lateral-line system is visible as a faint line running down each side of a fish's body. In sharks, rays, and many bony fishes, the neuromast receptor cells are located in a canal beneath the skin's surface. The canal connects with the external environment through a series of pores.

water-filled canal

gelatinous cupula

nerve

hair cell

hairs

pore

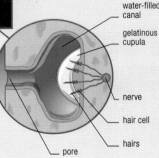

SYNCHRONIZED SWIMMING
Many species of small bony fishes, such as the white salemas (grunts) seen here, form large, dense schools as a means of protection against predators. Their lateral-line system enables the fish to move in unison, and predators find it hard to pick out an individual target since the school constantly moves and makes sudden changes in direction.

Gravitational detectors

Many invertebrates possess structures called statocysts that sense changes in orientation and movement. A statocyst comprises a relatively heavy ball, the statolith, inside a hollow sphere. The statolith may be secreted by the statocyst or, as in lobsters, it may be formed of sand grains collected from the environment. The vertebrate inner ear also operates like a statocyst. Otoliths, the equivalent of statoliths, move against hair cells called cristae inside fluid-filled ducts (ampullae) to detect gravity and acceleration.

SCALLOPS IN MOTION
Scallops propel themselves along by expelling jets of water from their shells. A statocyst provides the scallop with information on its orientation, prompting it to adjust its path accordingly.

hollow cavity

statolith

sensory hairs

BIVALVE STATOCYST
As the animal moves, gravity acts on the statolith in the center of the statocyst, causing it to stimulate the sensory hairs of the receptor cells against which it rests.

nerve

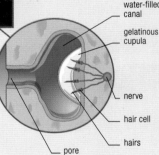

Vibration

Vibration receptors are attuned to vibrations that are transmitted through a surface, usually the ground, but also other surfaces such as tree trunks, leaves, or spiders' webs. The detection of vibrations felt through the environment is often a precursor to hearing the vibrations of sound waves transmitted through the air. In animals that lack a tympanic membrane (see p.126), such as some amphibians and reptiles, sound vibrations are transmitted through the body to the inner ear. Animals that lack ears are able to "feel" sound by detecting its vibrations, rather than hearing it. Many mechanoreceptors, including insect sensilla and

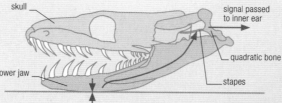

skull
signal passed to inner ear
lower jaw
quadratic bone
stapes

BONE CONDUCTION
Snakes receive ground-borne vibrations by pressing their lower jaw to the ground. The vibrations are conducted to the stapes bone and on to the inner ear.

Pacinian corpuscles, detect vibrations. Other vibration sensors include lyriform organs on spiders' legs, which detect the vibrations of struggling prey trapped in their webs, and Herbst corpuscles in the bills of wading birds, which detect the vibrations of prey moving in the sand. The ability to sense vibration is particularly useful underground, where sound does not travel very far and visual signals are of no use (see panel, right).

SENSITIVE FEET
This raft spider can detect aquatic prey by placing its front two pairs of legs on the surface of a pool of water.

THE CAT'S WHISKERS
Whiskers are incredibly sensitive to touch and air movement. They permit animals, such as this leopard, to feel their way and hunt in conditions of poor visibility.

CASE STUDY
SEISMIC SIGNALING

Cape mole-rats communicate by drumming their hind legs on the floor of their individual burrows to create vibrations. During a typical foot-thumping interaction, a male and a female mole-rat will drum together in synchrony. Their seismic signals travel through the ground to neighboring burrows more efficiently than sound.

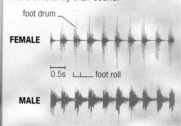

foot drum
FEMALE
0.5s   foot roll
MALE

FOOT-THUMPING SESSION
When ready to breed, Cape mole-rats signal their sex by drumming at different tempos in order to locate a mate.

Taste and smell

Taste and smell are important senses for many animals, helping them find food and mates, communicate, and navigate. Both senses are mediated by special cells called chemoreceptors, which bind with specific chemicals then send a nervous impulse to the brain, where the taste or smell is processed.

CATFISH WHISKERS
The whiskerlike barbels around the mouths and noses of catfishes are covered with taste buds. The barbels are used to locate food in the murky waters at the bottoms of streams and rivers.

Taste

The sense of taste allows an animal to detect and identify molecules from objects that come into contact with its gustatory (taste) receptors. These sensory cells may be concentrated in different regions, for example, in the mouth or on mouthparts, in the skin, or on the feet, depending on the animal. They can be used to find food and check that it is good to eat. For example, flies have gustatory sensilla (hairs) on their feet with which they taste things they land on. The sensilla are sensitive to different substances, such as sugars, salts, or water. Taste is also used by some animals as a means of chemical communication.

pore leading to taste bud

sensory papilla

TASTING WITH CARE
The surface of a mammal's tongue (above) is covered with sensory papillae, which surround small pores that lead to barrel-shaped taste buds beneath. Mammals detect flavors with their tongues and some, such as the brown hyena (left), will taste scent marks to gain information about another individual.

Smell

The sense of smell is governed by olfactory receptors, which detect odor molecules from objects at a distance. The molecules may be carried on the air or in the water. On reaching an animal, the molecules bind to the membrane of olfactory hairs (cilia). In arthropods, these are usually located in pits within the exoskeleton or on bristly extensions of the exoskeleton. In vertebrates, the cilia are usually located on the surface of the olfactory tissue (epithelium) in the nasal cavity of the nose. Glands within the epithelium secrete mucus that keeps the surface moist, helping trap the odor molecules. Mammals, particularly rodents and carnivores, have a good sense of smell. They use it to find food, and many use scent as a means of communication—to mark their territory, for example.

Southern giant petrels have long tubular nostrils with which they can locate food by day or night.

Emperor moth males can detect the scent of a female 6 miles (11 km) away using their antennae.

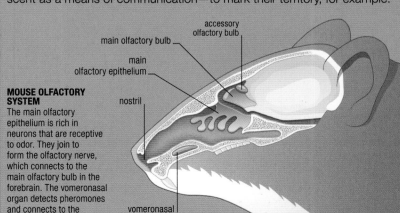

accessory olfactory bulb

main olfactory bulb

main olfactory epithelium

nostril

MOUSE OLFACTORY SYSTEM
The main olfactory epithelium is rich in neurons that are receptive to odor. They join to form the olfactory nerve, which connects to the main olfactory bulb in the forebrain. The vomeronasal organ detects pheromones and connects to the accessory olfactory bulb.

vomeronasal organ

Eurasian water shrews have poor eyesight, but this is compensated for by their acute sense of smell.

CASE STUDY
SNIFFING OUT CANCER

Dogs are renowned for having a good sense of smell. Their sensitive noses have long been employed by humans to assist in various tasks, such as tracking missing people and detecting illegal substances. Recent research has shown that dogs can sense whether or not a person has breast or lung cancer according to the smell of their breath. Cancerous cells produce different metabolic waste products to normal cells, and it is these products that the dogs are able to identify. The advantage of canine help is that cancers may be identified and diagnosed earlier, leading to more effective treatment.

Tasting the air

Many vertebrates have a Jacobson's or vomeronasal organ, a patch of specialized olfactory epithelium, situated in the roof of the mouth at the base of the nasal cavity. This organ is particularly sensitive to airborne molecules contained in scents such as pheromones, which are used for chemical communication between animals of the same species. Some mammals, including most ungulates and felids, such as lions and tigers, raise their heads and grimace when testing the sexual receptivity of a female, a behavior known as the Flehmen response. Lizards and snakes use the Jacobson's organ to detect chemicals such as those produced by potential prey or a possible predator, transferring the molecules from the air with their tongues. This is why they constantly flick their tongues when exploring their surroundings or when they have been disturbed.

FLEHMEN RESPONSE
Ungulates such as zebras (right) and giraffes (below), show a characteristic behavior when tasting the air for pheromones. They pull the upper lip back and draw air across the vomeronasal organ. Through its use a male is able to tell whether a female is ready to mate.

Jacobson's organ

nostril

extended tongue

retracted tongue

JACOBSON'S ORGAN
In snakes, the Jacobson's organ has two small openings in the roof of the mouth into which the tips of the snake's forked tongue are inserted when it is withdrawn.

FORKED TONGUE
Snakes flick their tongues in and out to transfer odor-bearing molecules from the air, water, or ground to the Jacobson's organ. Elephants do the same thing, but instead use the fleshy "finger" at the tip of their trunks.

Vision, or visual perception, is the way in which animals interpret information about their environment using visible light. Some animals are only sensitive to the presence or absence of light, while others can determine differences in the wavelength of light, an ability known as color vision. The visual ability of an animal influences many aspects of its behavior, including feeding, defense, and courtship.

ommatidia

optic nerve carries signals to brain

light-sensitive cell converts image into a signal

OMMATIDIA
Each ommatidium sees a single image, which the animal's brain puts together, forming a blurred mosaic.

What is an eye?

Light is effectively parcels of energy called photons, which travel in a wave, the frequency (or wavelength) of which is proportional to the energy they contain. An eye is an organ that detects this light and translates it via nervous impulses to the brain, where the information is processed further. There is a wide variety of eye designs across the animal kingdom, relating to the different types of environments that animals inhabit and the different behavioral tasks they undertake.

African land snail eyes can only distinguish between light and dark.

Compound eyes

Most arthropods have eyes formed from multiple units called ommatidia. Each of these consists of a lens to focus light into a cell, a transparent crystalline cone to funnel the light, and visual cells that absorb the light and trigger a nervous impulse. The more ommatidia an eye has, the more refined the resulting image. Each cell is angled in a slightly different way, collecting light from a slightly different area of the visual scene. This makes compound eyes excellent at detecting motion, since the ommatidia are consecutively turned on and off as an object passes across the field of vision.

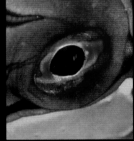

Cuttlefish have excellent eyesight and distinctive w-shaped pupils.

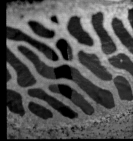

Mandarin fishes, like most tropical fishes, have good color vision.

Red-eyed treefrogs have a third eyelid that helps keep the eye clean.

Chameleons can move their eyes independently of each other.

Southern ground hornbill eyes have long eyelashes that act as sunshades.

Tigers can see well at night because of a mirrorlike layer in their eyes.

MONOCULAR AND BINOCULAR VISION

There are many benefits to having two eyes, both as a backup system should one become damaged, and as a way to increase the field of view. But perhaps the greatest benefit is that they can be used together to gather information about distance. Eye position relates to an animal's behavioral need. Many animals have eyes positioned on the sides of their head, offering a very wide field of view, of up to 360°, from which to watch for predators. Most of this field is monocular, with little sense of depth. Predators, however, typically have forward-facing eyes, with a comparatively wide overlap of the visual fields. This binocular vision enables predators to judge distances with great accuracy.

rear field of binocular vision

blind spot

field of monocular vision

forward field of binocular vision

MONOCULAR

field of monocular vision

field of binocular vision

BINOCULAR

HOVERFLY EYES
The multifaceted compound eyes of the hoverfly are composed of many thousands of tightly packed ommatidia. Different ommatidia have different visual pigments, which allow the fly to see different colors of light.

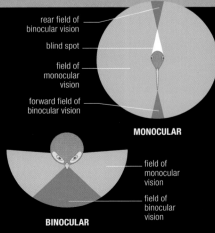

Vertebrate eyes

Light enters a vertebrate eye through the transparent cornea, which bends the rays. The light rays pass through a fluid-filled space to the iris, a pigmented, muscular layer that can alter the diameter of its central hole, the pupil, to control light entering the eye. The light rays reach the crystalline lens, which can be squeezed or relaxed to bend and focus the light rays onto the retina at the rear of the eye, where an upside-down image is formed. The retina is a layer of light-sensitive cells, which convert the information from the light rays into nerve signals. The optic nerve carries the signals to the brain, where an upright image is formed.

ciliary muscle alters shape of lens

light rays reflected from tree enter eye

cornea bends incoming light rays

lens changes shape to focus light on retina

eye muscle moves eye in socket

retina contains light-sensitive cells

light rays cross inside eye

crossed-over rays produce an upside-down image on retina

optic nerve

CAMERA EYE
The eyes of all vertebrates share a common design, which works like a camera, using a lens to focus light and form an image.

RODS AND CONES
There are two types of photoreceptor in the retina. Rods (stained yellow) are sensitive in low light while cone cells (stained blue) are involved in color vision.

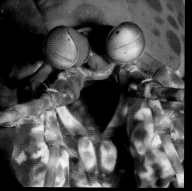

MOST COMPLEX EYE
Mantis shrimp have 12 different spectral receptor types in their compound eyes, sensitive to wavelengths ranging from ultraviolet to infrared.

Color vision

Color vision is the ability of an animal to differentiate between objects based upon the wavelength of light they emit or reflect. Cone cells contain pigments that are "tuned" to absorb light from different regions of the visible spectrum (see below), which the brain detects and translates as color. The more cone pigments an animal has, the more colors it can tell apart. Old World monkeys and primates (including humans) have three types of cone cell, while many fishes and birds have four. Most mammals have just two cones and see in a similar way to a "color-blind" human.

ABSORPTION RANGES OF THREE CONE PIGMENTS

Cone pigments are classified by the wavelength of light they are most sensitive to, for example short-wave (or "blue" light), medium-wave ("green" light), or long-wave ("red" light).

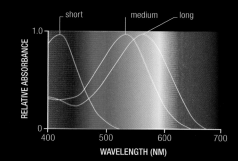

short medium long

RELATIVE ABSORBANCE

1.0

0

400   500   600   700
WAVELENGTH (NM)

MANDRILL
In the animal kingdom, color is widely used for sexual signaling. The red color of a male mandrill's face conveys information about his age, rank, and testosterone levels.

2 million The number of **different surface** colors that Old World Monkeys, apes, and humans can see.

Beyond the visible spectrum

Humans are sensitive to wavelengths of light in the range 400–700 nanometers (nm), but many animals, including birds, insects, reptiles, and fishes, can detect short-wavelength light in the near-ultraviolet (UV) range (320–400nm). UV sensitivity is used in many behaviors, including courtship (see p.333) and predation (see p.228). An unrelated ability is that of many animals, including insects, birds, and cephalopods, to perceive polarized light. Polarization occurs when, for example, sunlight is scattered by atmospheric particles to vibrate in a specific plane. The way in which sunlight is polarized is related to the sun's position, so animals can use it to navigate.

ULTRAVIOLET LIGHT

VISIBLE LIGHT

NECTAR GUIDES
To human eyes, this flower is yellow, but a UV-sensitive camera reveals the patterns that guide insects to the nectar at its center.

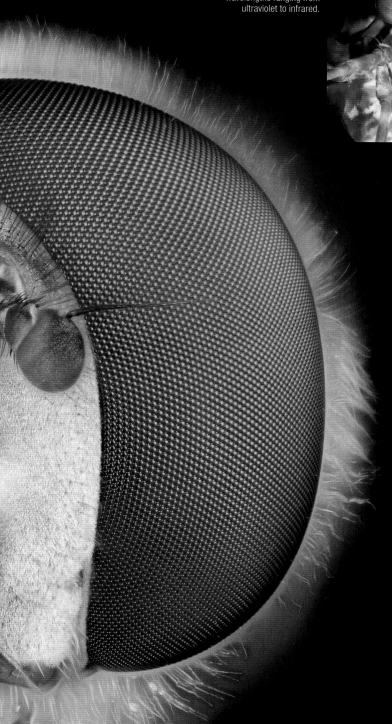

Hearing

The ability to hear allows animals to sense the rustles of approaching prey or respond to a mating call. In order to hear, an animal must have a mechanism for detecting the vibration of sound waves; sound receptor cells have tiny hairs that are deflected by sound waves, triggering nervous impulses that are processed in the brain.

Sound

Sound is produced by pressure waves that create disturbance in a medium (usually air or water) detectable by hearing apparatus. Pressure waves that are transmitted through a solid medium, such as the ground, are usually referred to as vibrations. The number of oscillations or vibrations per second is called the frequency of the sound and is measured in hertz (Hz). The frequency of the sound wave determines its pitch: a high-pitched sound, such as a bird whistling, makes the air molecules vibrate backward and forward more times each second than a low-pitched sound, such as the croak of a bullfrog.

HEARING RANGES
There is a vast array of hearing ranges across the animal kingdom. Humans can only hear sounds with a frequency above 20 hertz and below 20,000 hertz (this sound range is called sonic).

FREQUENCY (HERTZ)

175,000

150,000

125,000

100,000

75,000

Noctuid moth 1,000–240,000

Dolphin 110–150,000

Bat 10–100,000

Cat 70–64,000

Dog 20–45,000

KEY

ULTRASONIC Above 20,000 hertz

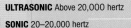
SONIC 20–20,000 hertz

INFRASONIC Below 20 hertz

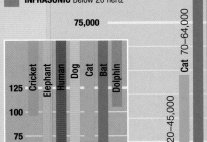

Cricket | Elephant | Human | Dog | Cat | Bat | Dolphin

125
100
75
50
25
0

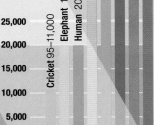

Cricket 95–11,000

Elephant 1–20,000

Human 20–20,000

25,000
20,000
15,000
10,000
5,000
0

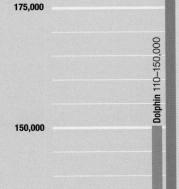

Sound detection
Movement-sensitive sensilla (hairs) in insects detect the vibrations of sound waves. Some insects, including grasshoppers and some moth species, have tympanic ears, which are more similar in structure to those of frogs, some reptiles, birds, and mammals (although grasshoppers have eardrums in their abdomen rather than their head). Tympanic ears have a thin membrane that transmits sound vibrations. In many frogs, the membrane is visible on the sides of the head, while in other animals it is obscured by elaborate ear structures that improve sound reception. Some fish use their swim bladder as a hydrophone to transmit sound waves through small bones that connect it to the inner ear. To communicate over long distances, elephants make infrasonic rumbles that they can detect through their feet and trunks as well as with their ears (see p.467).

LARGE EARDRUM
For each species of frog, the size of the tympanic membrane (behind the eye), and the sensitivity of the female's ear, is related to the frequency of the male's call.

MOSQUITO ANTENNA
The antenna of the male mosquito is most sensitive to sound around 380 hertz, the frequency produced by a female mosquito in flight. Movement of the antenna in response to a sound wave stimulates the auditory sense organ at the antenna's base.

MAMMALIAN EAR STRUCTURE
A typical mammalian ear comprises the external ear (pinna or auricle), which leads to the tympanic membrane; the middle ear, an air-filled cavity across which sound is transferred by the auditory ossicles; and the inner ear, where the sound receptor cells are located.

SOUND WAVES
Sounds emitted and perceived by animals can be broadly separated according to frequency into infrasonic (very low frequency), sonic, and ultrasonic (very high frequency).

ULTRASONIC Above 20,000 hertz (20kHz)

SONIC 20–20,000 hertz

INFRASONIC Below 20 hertz (Hz)

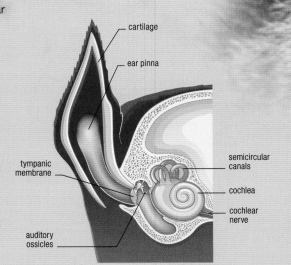

cartilage

ear pinna

tympanic membrane

semicircular canals

cochlea

cochlear nerve

auditory ossicles

Sound localization

The presence of two ears allows an animal to determine the origin of a sound through localization. Unless the animal is facing directly toward the sound source there is a delay between the sound arriving at the ear closest to and farthest from the source. The brain uses this split-second delay to calculate the direction from which the sound came. To gain information about the height of a sound, the two ears must be asymmetrically placed, as in the barn owl. Its heart-shaped facial disk of feathers acts like a radar dish, collecting sound and guiding it to the eardrums within the skull.

ASYMMETRIC EARS

In some species of owls, the right ear cavity is usually higher (and larger) than the left, so a sound coming from below the owl's line of sight will arrive sooner at the left ear.

internal cavity of right ear

internal cavity of left ear

PINPOINTING PREY

A barn owl localizes sound so well that it can hunt in total darkness by listening for the movement of its prey, usually small rodents, rustling through the undergrowth.

SOUND RECEPTION TIME LAG

A barn owl can detect a time lag of 30 msec between sound reaching each of its ears. This information is processed by 10,000 space-specific neurons. To pinpoint its prey, the owl moves its head until the sound reaches both ears as the same time.

sound level

LEFT EAR

RIGHT EAR

30 msec

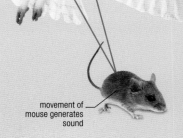

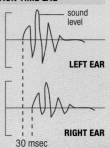

movement of mouse generates sound

COLLECTING SOUND

The huge ears of the bat-eared fox gather and amplify the sounds of its insect prey moving beneath the surface of the soil.

Wrens are tiny, but their songs can be heard from hundreds of yards.

The loudest animal on the planet is the blue whale, with a call of up to 188 decibels. A jet engine reaches only 140 decibels.

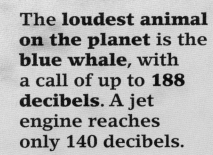

Rattlesnakes shake the modified scales at the tip of their tails.

trachea

muscle

cartilage ring

pessulus

internal tympaniform membrane

clavicular air sac

bronchus

BIRD'S SYRINX

The syrinx is located where the trachea branches into the two bronchi. Air passing over the pessulus and the external and internal tympaniform membranes causes them to vibrate, producing sound.

external tympaniform membrane

bronchi lead downward to lungs

Sound generation

Animals produce sounds in many different ways. Perhaps the simplest form of sound production is hitting something, often the ground, with a body part. For example, ants stamp their feet, fiddler crabs bang their claws, and mole-rats thump with their heads or feet. Many insects and some other arthropods generate sound by rubbing parts of their body together, a method called stridulation (see p.457). Terrestrial vertebrates make vocalizations by using the movement of air in the respiratory system. For example, vibrations of the vocal cords of the larynx produce a wolf's howl, while bird calls and songs are produced by the syrinx (see left).

Wolves howl to signal ownership of their territory to other wolf packs.

Echolocation

Echolocation, also called biosonar, is the ability to locate objects through the use of sound. Animals that echolocate form an image of their surroundings from returning echoes, allowing them to pick a path through vegetation or a cave system, or to home in on their prey in the dark. The majority of bats use very high-frequency (ultrasonic) calls to echolocate, whereas dolphins and most other echolocators use clicks.

Echolocation calls

Echolocation calls can be sonic, that is within the range of human hearing, but most echolocators use very high-frequency, or ultrasonic, calls, which are measured in kilohertz (kHz) . The types of calls are incredibly diverse. Different bat species produce different calls according to the habitats in which they forage. A fast-flying species that hunts in the open air uses relatively low-frequency calls that travel farther ahead of the bat, whereas a slower-flying species feeding in a cluttered habitat, such as among trees, requires detailed resolution gained from higher-frequency calls. Bat echolocation calls typically range from 20 to 100kHz, whereas some species of toothed whales use even higher-frequency clicks, with those of bottlenose dolphins reaching 220kHz. Sperm whale clicks range from 40Hz to 15kHz.

▶ BAT SONOGRAMS

Sonograms depict the frequency range, duration, repetition rate, and shape of the echolocation call. Calls from common pipistrelle, Daubenton's, and Leisler's bats differ in all of these attributes.

■ Leisler's bat ■ Daubenton's bat ■ Pipistrelle

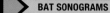
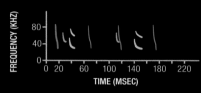

▶ SPERM WHALE SONOGRAM

This sonogram of a single sperm whale echolocating shows it emitting a steady series of clicks while searching for prey. Sperm whales eat mainly octopuses and squid, even giant squid.

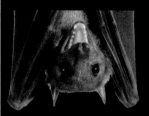

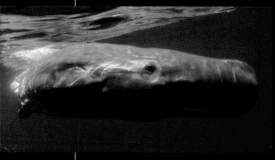

SPERM WHALE
Up to 65 ft (20 m) in length, the sperm whale is the largest toothed whale. Its huge, square-ended head contains a spermaceti organ, a large mass of waxy oil, which focuses echolocation clicks into a beam.

Bats

The majority of bat species are sophisticated echolocators, producing their ultrasonic calls in the larynx. Most of these bats emit the call through the mouth, but some send it out through their nose, which has lead to the evolution of elaborate nose ornamentation. Many bats have large, forward-facing ears with a projecting lobe called the tragus that helps receive returning echoes. Bats usually emit one call for each wing beat when flying. Their calls are so loud that bats risk deafening themselves. To avoid this, muscles in the middle ear contract when the bat calls and then relax to allow the returning echo to be heard before the bat calls again. When potential prey has been located, the rate of calling increases as the bat homes in on its target.

LESSER HORSESHOE BAT
This bat is named for its small size and horseshoe-shaped nose-leaf. Furrows in the nose-leaf help shape and focus the beam of sound as it is emitted through the nose.

EGYPTIAN FRUIT BAT
This species belongs to a genus of Old World fruit bats that echolocate by producing pairs of sharp clicks with their tongue. They have good eyesight and use this relatively crude form of echolocation to find their way in dark caves.

Toothed whales

Echolocation allows toothed whales to pursue agile prey, even in dark or turbid waters. Porpoises and dolphins produce ultrasonic clicks by forcing air between phonic lips in their nasal passages. The lips open and close causing the surrounding tissue to vibrate and form sound waves. These bounce off the bony cribriform plate at the front of the skull and are focused into a beam by the melon, which the hunter aims at its prey. Sperm whales have a different anatomy for producing echolocation clicks. The left nasal passage is used for breathing, while the right is used for sound production. Sound waves pass through an oil-filled spermaceti organ, rebound off an air sac at the rear of the head, and are focused into a beam of sound through several fatty lenses. Experiments with bottlenose dolphins have shown them to be extremely sophisticated echolocators, capable of identifying submerged objects by size, shape, or composition, for example. This enables them to learn the echo signatures of their preferred prey species.

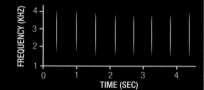

BOTTLENOSE DOLPHINS VOCALIZING
Dolphins produce rapid bursts of ultrasonic clicks to locate prey. They also make an array of other, lower-frequency sounds to communicate with each other, including whistles and squeaks.

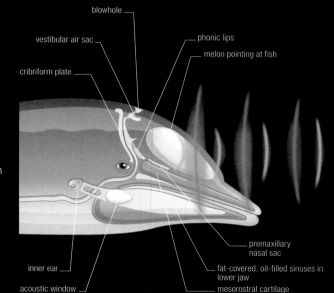

blowhole

vestibular air sac

phonic lips

melon pointing at fish

cribriform plate

inner ear

premaxillary nasal sac

fat-covered, oil-filled sinuses in lower jaw

acoustic window

mesorostral cartilage

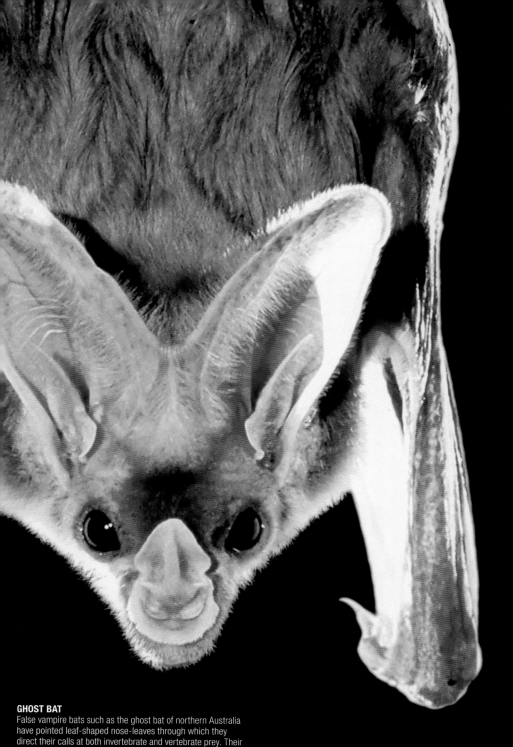

Birds

Only two families of birds are known to echolocate: the cave swiftlets of Southeast Asia and Australia and the oilbirds of South America. Both roost deep inside caves, where the ability to see is not of much use, so instead they use sound to avoid bumping into the rock walls and each other, and to find their nests. They produce low-frequency clicks of less than 15 kilohertz (kHz), by contracting muscles around the vocal organ, or syrinx (see p.127), which cause the tympaniform membranes to vibrate. Their echolocation is low resolution and both groups feed by sight; swiftlets on insects during the day and oilbirds on oil palm and laurel fruits at night.

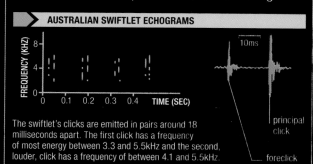

AUSTRALIAN SWIFTLET ECHOGRAMS

The swiftlet's clicks are emitted in pairs around 18 milliseconds apart. The first click has a frequency of most energy between 3.3 and 5.5kHz and the second, louder, click has a frequency of between 4.1 and 5.5kHz.

principal click

foreclick

CAVE BIRD
As the Australian swiftlet flies deeper into the darkness of its cave, it lessens the interval between the pairs of clicks it emits to gain more information from faster-returning echoes.

GHOST BAT
False vampire bats such as the ghost bat of northern Australia have pointed leaf-shaped nose-leaves through which they direct their calls at both invertebrate and vertebrate prey. Their large ears meet in the middle and each has a prominent tragus.

sound wave emitted by the dolphin

echo returning to the dolphin from the fish's swim bladder

swim bladder

fish swimming ahead of dolphin

DETECTING PREY
Dolphins use the melon, an oily lump of tissue behind the forehead, to focus their outgoing sound waves into a beam. Echoes returning from a fish in the dolphin's path are transferred through oil-filled sinuses in the lower jaw to the inner ear.

TONGUE-CLICKING TENREC
The streaked tenrec searches for worms and grubs in the Madagascan rain forest floor, making a series of low-frequency tongue clicks to locate its prey.

Other mammals

Bats and toothed whales have by far the most sophisticated echolocation among mammals, although some nocturnal insectivores also use primitive echolocation to explore their habitats and catch their insect prey. Shrews produce ultrasonic calls from the larynx whereas the tenrecs of Madagascar use less specialized tongue clicks. In addition, both may communicate with other individuals at ultrasonic frequencies. The aye-aye, also from Madagascar, uses sound to locate its prey too, but in a very different manner. It taps a tree trunk with its long, bony middle finger and listens for the larvae of wood-boring beetles moving underneath (see p.247).

Electricity and magnetism

Many animals possess the ability to sense electric and magnetic fields. Some detect the electrical signals generated by the muscles of other animals, while others produce their own electricity, either to use in prey location, navigation, or communication, or as a means of defense or prey capture. Animals with a magnetic sense use the Earth's magnetic field for navigation or orientation.

SENSITIVE BILL
The duck-billed platypus has about 40,000 electroreceptors in its bill, which sense the electric fields of prey concealed in muddy river bottoms.

SHORT-BEAKED ECHIDNA
The short-beaked echidna inhabits drier habitats than the long-beaked echidna and has only around 400 electroreceptors at the tip of its beak. It uses them to locate prey when conditions are wet—for example, when it rains.

Electroreception

Animals that are capable of detecting electrical impulses but do not generate them are said to show "passive" electroreception. Those that both receive and generate electrical signals are capable of "active" electroreception. Electroreception is more common among animals living in water than on land because of the capacity of water to conduct electricity. The majority of electroreceptive animals are fishes, but monotreme mammals also possess the ability. For example, the long-beaked echidna, which lives in wet tropical forest, has around 2,000 electroreceptors in its beak, which it uses to track down earthworms and other soil-dwelling prey. This use of electric fields to find food is known as electrolocation. The structures responsible for electroreception are called ampullary receptors. The electroreceptive sense organs found in sharks and rays are known as ampullae of Lorenzini after the Italian anatomist Stefano Lorenzini, who described their structure in 1678; their function remained a mystery until the 20th century.

ELEPHANTNOSE FISH
Weakly electric fishes, like this elephantnose fish, generate small electrical pulses of less than 1 volt. They then detect distortions in the electrical fields they produce and use these for navigation, location of prey, and communication.

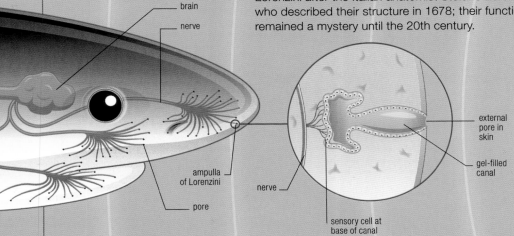

brain
nerve
ampulla of Lorenzini
nerve
pore
sensory cell at base of canal
external pore in skin
gel-filled canal

SENSING ELECTRIC FIELDS
An ampulla of Lorenzini consists of a pore in the skin opening to a gel-filled canal. It works by detecting the difference in voltage between the pore and the base of the canal, allowing the shark to sense electric fields such as those generated by the muscles of a fish.

Electrogenesis

Electrogenesis is the production of an electrical discharge by an animal. Strongly electric fishes, such as the electric eel, electric catfishes, and electric rays, produce much higher voltage pulses than weakly electric fishes. The organs of electrogenesis, called electrocytes or electroplaques, are usually modified muscle cells or occasionally nerve cells. The electric eel has between 5,000 and 6,000 electroplaques stacked in series in its abdomen, enabling it to generate huge shocks of up to 600 volts to stun prey when hunting. The electric eel also uses lower voltage pulses of around 10 volts for navigating and detecting prey. Electric rays use the electric organs in their heads to electrocute prey or stun a potential predator. The size of the electric discharge varies from 8 to 200 volts, depending on the species. The electric catfish produces its electrical discharge in its skin.

STUNNING PREDATOR
Despite its name and appearance, the electric eel is not a true eel but a type of freshwater fish known as a knifefish.

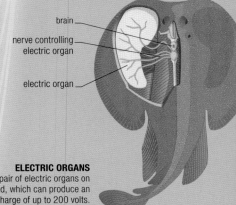

brain
nerve controlling electric organ
electric organ

ELECTRIC ORGANS
The electric ray has a pair of electric organs on either side of its head, which can produce an electrical discharge of up to 200 volts.

MAKO SHARK
Sharks' snouts are covered with electroreceptors called ampullae of Lorenzini, which appear as dark spots. Sharks may also orient themselves relative to the Earth's magnetic field by using their own electric field and those generated by ocean currents.

Sharks can detect tiny electrical signals as weak as 15 billionths of a volt

MAGNETIC MINERAL
This scanning electron micrograph of a particle of magnetite reveals the mineral's classic octahedral shape. It is the most magnetic of all the naturally occurring minerals on Earth.

Magnetoreception

Some animals are able to perceive the Earth's magnetic field and use it for navigation. This ability to detect changes in the magnetic field is called magnetoreception. At least two different mechanisms may be involved. The first involves crystals of magnetite, a magnetic form of iron oxide, which has been found in many species—for example in the upper mandible of pigeons, in the abdomen of honey bees, and in the head of trout. Clusters of the mineral are thought to be sensitive to changes in magnetic intensity. The second mechanism is known as the "radical pair model." It is thought that a magnetic field alters the spin of electrons in a specialized photopigment called cryptochrome, allowing the direction of the field to be determined. It is possible that birds might use both mechanisms simultaneously: magnetite in the bill to sense the intensity of the magnetic field and so locate magnetic north; and cryptochrome in the right eye to sense the direction in which they are flying.

HEADING FOR HOME
Experimental alteration of the magnetic field around the lofts of homing pigeons has been shown to disrupt their homing ability, lending weight to the theory that they use magnetic fields when navigating their way home.

NORTH AND SOUTH
Magnetic termite mounds are aligned north–south so that their broad, flat sides face east and west, which helps keep the mound at 86° F (30° C). Experiments have shown that termites use the Earth's magnetic field to orient their mounds.

ANIMAL

BEHA

LIVING SPACE

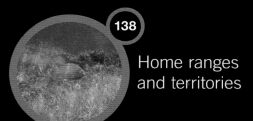

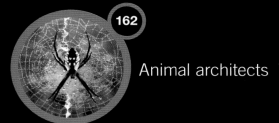

AT HOME ON ICE
The Antarctic ice floes are among the most extreme
habitats on the planet. Temperatures regularly
plunge below freezing, yet chinstrap penguins make
their home in this spectacular landscape with access
to plenty of food in the sea and few predators.

LIVING SPACE

An animal's living space should contain all an animal needs to survive. The living space might be very small if the animal is fixed in position, such as an adult barnacle, or very broad if the animal moves around a lot in the course of feeding or if it is a species that migrates.

Habitat choice

Put simply, an animal's habitat is its living space. Animals choose to live in a habitat that enables them to maximize their fitness by providing all they need to produce offspring and maximize their own survival. Animals show adaptations, both physical and behavioral, to their preferred habitats. For example, coal tits prefer to live in pine forests while blue tits like oak woods. Young coal tits are better adapted to foraging among pine needles, whereas blue tits are more adept at searching for food among oak leaves.

NESTING SITE
An Arctic tern is very protective of its nest and chicks. It will fly at a predator, such as a herring gull, that ventures near its territory, attacking the imposter with its sharp bill.

ADAPTED TO HABITAT
The Arctic fox (left) has thick white fur that provides camouflage and insulation against the cold. By contrast, the fennec fox (above) has sandy brown fur and large ears that dissipate heat to keep it cool.

round or just at certain times. For example, they may guard a mating site during the breeding season, a particular seasonal food source, or a shelter such as den or nest. Territories are often marked to warn neighboring animals of the territory owner's presence. These behaviors—dispersal, migration, and territoriality—have costs in terms of predation risk, energy, and time. In order to be worthwhile, the benefits must outweigh the costs.

Surviving extremes

Around the world, animals cope with an astounding variety of environmental conditions, and they have evolved a wide range of physiological and behavioral adaptations to enable them to survive. Some animals possess a natural antifreeze and can survive being frozen; others have thick insulating blubber, fur, or feathers to avoid becoming chilled. Many animals hibernate during cold periods or estivate during warm ones by reducing their metabolic, heart, and breathing rates to the bare minimum until conditions change and they can be active again. And some species can survive on very little water by storing it or obtaining it only from their food.

Home range, territory, and migration

An animal's home range contains places for it to sleep, breed, and feed. It may spend the majority of its time in one or more core areas of the range and venture to the periphery only occasionally. Animals may disperse from their home range into another or migrate periodically between different home ranges, which can be separated by vast distances. Many animals defend all or part of their home range as a territory, either year

FROM HOME TO HOME
Arctic terns maintain breeding territories in Greenland during the northern summer. A colony's home range extends 1.9 miles (3 km) out to sea, where the birds feed on small fishes. In fall, the terns migrate south to the edge of the Antarctic ice sheet, where they overwinter, moving south with the ice as it melts.

KEY
● Home range
● Territory
→ Migration route

EXTREME PLACES TO LIVE

COLDEST
Emperor penguins live in Antarctica, where temperatures reach -40° F (-40° C). Arctic beetles also withstand -40° F in the wild, but have been chilled to -125° F (-87° C) in a laboratory.

HOTTEST
Pompeii worms live around deep-sea hydrothermal vents in the Pacific Ocean, where water is heated to 570° F (300° C). The worms hold their heads in cooler water than their tails.

DRIEST
Peringuey's desert adder lives in the Namib Desert in Namibia, which receives less than ⅜ in (1 cm) of rain each year. The snake obtains most of its water requirements from the lizards it eats.

HIGHEST ALTITUDE
Yaks roam up to 19,700 ft (6,000 m) and red-billed choughs up to 26,000 ft (8,000 m) above sea level in the Himalayas. Vultures have collided with planes at 36,000 ft (11,000 m).

HIGHEST PRESSURE
The fangtooth fish is found at depths of 16,400 ft (5,000 m). In addition to high pressures, deep-sea fishes must cope with cold water temperatures, reduced oxygen, and little to no ambient light.

HIGHEST SALINITY
Brine shrimps live in hypersaline lakes where salinity may be 25 percent (normal seawater is around 3.5 percent). The shrimps and algal blooms color the water red and green.

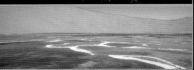

Home ranges and territories

A home range is the place where an animal lives. Whether an animal defends all or part of its home range as a territory or coexists peacefully with others on an undefended home range depends on whether the benefits of being territorial outweigh the costs of territory defense. Some species become territorial for part of the annual cycle and are nonterritorial occupants of a home range for the rest of the year.

Home ranges

A home range contains all areas used by an animal during its everyday movements. It should be large enough to contain food for the animal and its young, and other resources such as shelter and water. Home ranges consequently vary in size according to resource availability. Polar bears, for example, have huge ranges of up to 48,250 square miles (125,000 square km) because their prey is sparsely distributed. An animal's home range might overlap with those of others, or it may travel beyond its own home range to find a mate. Home ranges can be three-dimensional; plankton and fish move up and down within the water column, while bats and vultures soar into the sky.

SPATIAL LEARNING BY A WASP

In 1958, Dutch ethologist Niko Tinbergen showed that digger wasps find their nest entrance by remembering the configuration of objects around it. After emerging from her burrow, the female wasp flies around the landmarks, in this case a circle of pinecones. If the circle is moved once the wasp has left to hunt she will search for her nest in the location indicated by the cones when she returns.

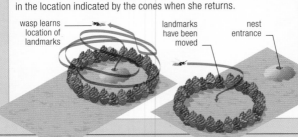

wasp learns location of landmarks

landmarks have been moved

nest entrance

Territories

Many animals defend territories against intruders. Territorial boundaries are often marked to announce the owner's presence, thus avoiding potentially harmful confrontations between neighbors. Marking may involve visual displays, scent, or audible signals. An incursion into another animal's territory can escalate to combat if the intruder persists. In social species, larger groups often win territorial disputes. The advantage of territoriality is that the territory holder can monopolize resources such as food or a good breeding site within the territory.

AGGRESSIVE DEFENSE
A northern gannet's territory comprises its nest and a small space around it. It viciously attacks any bird other than its partner that ventures within reach.

Dispersal

Dispersal occurs when an animal leaves one home range or territory to establish its own elsewhere. It may be forced to depart because changing environmental conditions have rendered its current habitat unsuitable. Alternatively, an animal may leave an area to avoid competition with rivals for food or other resources. Dispersal is also a mechanism whereby animals avoid breeding with close relatives. In many species, the males disperse while the females stay at or close to their birth territory. In some cases, once young animals become independent, they are chased away by their parents. These behaviors ensure that the species does not become inbred.

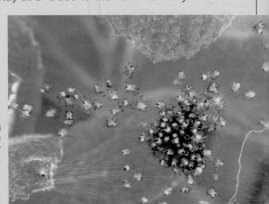

SCENT-MARKING
Adult black bears rub their backs, shoulders, and the backs of their heads on trees to scent-mark their territorial boundaries and to advertise their presence to prospective mates.

SPIDERLINGS DISPERSING
Newly hatched garden spiders disperse in different directions by walking or using a strand of silk to catch the wind.

Home scar
Common limpet

The common limpet grinds circular scars with the edge of its shell into the rocks on which it lives. When covered with seawater at high tide, it moves away from its scar to forage on algae. It returns before the water recedes by following chemical cues in a mucus trail it leaves behind. Settling in the scar helps the limpet create a strong seal to avoid both predation and dehydration when left exposed on the rocks at low tide. Limpets play an important role on rocky shores by keeping the substrate clear of algae, allowing other organisms to colonize.

Patella vulgata
- Up to 2¼ in (6 cm) (shell diameter)
- Temperate rocky shores throughout Europe, from Norway southward to Portugal.
- Conical, gray-white shell, sometimes tinged with yellow or covered in algae. Muscular foot underneath contracts and prevents limpet from being lifted.

Perch patrol
Common whitetail

Mature male common whitetail dragonflies develop a whitish bloom known as pruinescence on their blue abdomens. In territorial displays, dominant males raise their abdomens to intruders as a threat, while less dominant males lower theirs as a sign of submission. Common whitetails guard perches from where they patrol their territory, a 33–98 ft (10–30 m) stretch of water's edge, for several hours a day. Males with larger territories have greater success in mating with females that visit the water to breed. They also defend their territories against other species such as the cardinal meadowhawk, as pictured below.

Libellula lydia
- Up to 2 in (5 cm)
- Wetland habitats throughout North America.
- Males have a light blue abdomen, females a brown abdomen. Dark brown band down center of wings.

Keeping a distance
Dancing white lady spider

The dancing white lady spider inhabits a burrow protected by a trapdoor in the sands of the Namib Desert. Each individual has a territory with a radius of 3¼–9¾ ft (1–3 m), depending on the sex and age of the spider. These spiders will apparently resort to cannibalism in order to defend their territories. It is hardly surprising then that a male spider walking through another male's territory while out searching for a mate will drum the sand to announce his arrival, using all eight of his legs and even his body. A male may travel up to 300 ft (90 m) across the dunes during a nightly excursion, crossing the territories of between one and five other males. However, it may encounter only one or two females on its journey. Immature and female spiders tend to stay put in their foraging territories.

Leucorchestris arenicola
- ½–1½ in (1.5–3.5 cm)
- Namib Desert, Namibia.
- Creamy white spider.

10 ft The maximum radius of a male dancing white lady spider's territory around its burrow.

CONFRONTATION DANCE
Male dancing white lady spiders drum their feet on the sand when they are close to other males, causing rivals to withdraw or keep out of the way of the signaling spider.

Fighting for position
Poplar petiole gall aphid

In spring, female poplar petiole gall aphids hatch from eggs that have overwintered on cottonwood trees. Each aphid selects a leaf and starts feeding at the base, causing a hollow ball of tissue called a gall to form. The female moves into the gall, where she gives birth to a brood of winged females, the result of asexual reproduction. These females disperse and continue to reproduce. The last generation of the year contains both male and female aphids, which reproduce sexually and lay eggs that overwinter. The females are extremely territorial and may spend several hours, or even days, fighting with one another over a leaf. Large leaves are preferred, presumably because they contain more sap on which to feed. Defeated and small females must accept smaller leaves or less favorable positions closer to the center of large leaves.

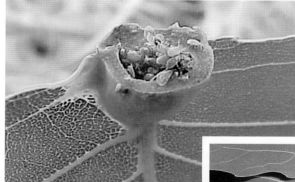

APHIDS AND GALLS
Aphid galls are typically located at the base of the leaf where it joins the petiole (stalk). Each gall contains new aphids, which are produced parthenogenetically by the female that created the gall. They eventually emerge to establish their own galls elsewhere.

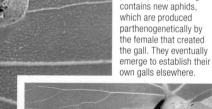

POSITION AND REPRODUCTIVE SUCCESS
Where three females occupy the same leaf, the reproductive success of the female closest to the base is always greater than that of the female farthest away. On average, the female at the base produces 138 young, the middle female 75, and the most distant female 29.

female farthest from base has least young

gall of second female

female at base produces most young

Pemphigus populitransversus
- 1/16–1/8 in (1.5–3 mm)
- Eastern cottonwood trees in Illinois, Missouri, and Utah, US.
- Green insect with a pear-shaped abdomen. There are both winged and wingless forms.

Border guards

Malaysian giant ant

Territorial behavior is well developed in the Malaysian giant ant. Colonies defend their borders against ants of the same species and also enter into violent combat with ants of different species. Colonies of Malaysian giant ants may contain around 7,000 workers divided among 8 to 14 underground nests. A colony's territory extends up into the tree canopy and may cover an area of 86,100 square feet (8,000 square meters). Barrack nests near the territory borders contain a high proportion of major workers—large soldier ants that take part in ritual combat with other Malaysian giant ants during boundary disputes. These fights can take place over a number of days, or even weeks, with majors squaring up to one another repeatedly each night. The majors also patrol trunk trails through the colony's territory, attacking impostors of their own and different species, and serve as sentinels at points known as bridgeheads. These are usually at the base of tree trunks that give access to the canopy.

RAIN FOREST HABITAT
Malaysian giant ants build subterranean nests in the forest floor. A few ants are active on the ground during the day, but hordes of workers travel into the canopy at night to forage.

Camponotus gigas

📏 ¾ in (2 cm) (worker); 1¼ in (3 cm) (soldier)

🌍 Rain forest from lowland peat swamps and mangroves to mountain forests of Southeast Asia, from Sumatra north to Thailand.

📖 Large ant with a black head and thorax and a brown rear abdomen.

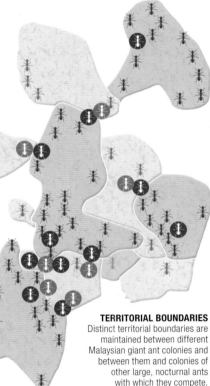

```
0         50 m
0         50 yds
```

KEY

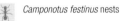 *Camponotus gigas* nests

Camponotus festinus nests

Other *Camponotus* species' nests

Oecophylla smaragdina nests

 Camponotus gigas sentries

 Camponotus festinus sentries

TERRITORIAL BOUNDARIES
Distinct territorial boundaries are maintained between different Malaysian giant ant colonies and between them and colonies of other large, nocturnal ants with which they compete.

Aggressive defense

Titan triggerfish

The titan triggerfish is a large, rhomboid-shaped tropical reef fish that defends its territory aggressively during the breeding season. If approached, it repeatedly swims at the intruder until the intruder retreats. When threatened while feeding on the reef, a triggerfish may hide between rocks and erect the spines on its back, bracing itself in position and thus rendering it immovable. As the largest of the triggerfishes, the titan is usually dominant to other species in competitive encounters.

Balistoides viridescens

📏 Up to 30 in (75 cm)

🌍 Coral reefs of the Indo-Pacific Ocean.

📖 Heavily scaled fish. Main body coloration can include yellow, black, green, and dark gray.

➤➤ 400

NEST SITE
Titan triggerfish typically build their nests in sandy patches of coral rubble on the seabed. They use jets of water to excavate a chamber in the sand in which the female lays her eggs.

NASTY BITE

The titan triggerfish is notorious for attacking divers and snorkelers that enter its territory while it is guarding eggs. It will attempt to escort people away, but it has been known to knock divers unconscious and inflict bites with its strong teeth. The bites can be poisonous if high levels of the ciguatera toxin are present (this accumulates in the fish as a result of eating contaminated prey, including shellfish). The fish's territory encompasses a cone-shaped body of water above the nest, so to retreat safely, intruders should swim away to the side, not upward.

Nesting platform

Garibaldi damselfish

Male garibaldi damselfishes trim algae into a circular nesting platform, to which they entice females by making a loud clicking noise. Females are very selective and tend to choose nests with a thicker layer of algae and that already contain eggs at an early stage of development. This appears to be because male garibaldis often cannibalize a single clutch of eggs and they will guard a large clutch more aggressively than a small one. They vigorously defend the eggs for the two- to three-week period between laying and hatching.

Hypsypops rubicundus

📏 Up to 12 in (30 cm)

🌍 Coastal reefs and kelp forests from central California to southern Baja California, Mexico.

📖 Adults are bright orange with a deeply forked tail. Juveniles have blue spots.

RITUAL COMBAT
Malaysian giant ant majors engage in ritual fights at tournament sites on their territorial boundaries. Two ants stand on their hind legs and box one another with their forelegs. The ant that holds its legs up longest and throws its opponent off balance wins the bout.

Watery crib

Harlequin poison frog

The female harlequin poison frog gives each of her tadpoles its own pool in the base of an aerial plant. Water collects where the leaves join, and the female drops one tadpole into each reservoir. The tadpoles are kept apart because they tend to be cannibalistic. The adult frog returns every other day to deposit an unfertilized egg into the pool as food for her developing offspring. The young frog emerges from its aquatic nursery after three months.

Dendrobates histrionicus

◀▶ 1–1½ in (2.5–4 cm)

◐ Tropical rain forest of western Ecuador and parts of Colombia.

▥ Many color forms exist, including black markings over a base of yellow, orange, white, red, or blue.

Fighting colors

Common side-blotched lizard

Male common side-blotched lizards have three different strategies when it comes to mating. Orange-throated males are territorial and aggressive. They are dominant over both blue- and yellow-throated males, and consequently mate with the most females. Blue-throated males are also territorial and guard their mates carefully. They are able to chase yellow-throated males away, but often lose out to orange-throated males unless they cooperate to protect their mates. Yellow-throated males do not defend territories at all; instead, they attempt to sneak past the territorial males to mate. Early in the breeding season, before the males' coloration has developed, competitions for the best territories are decided on the basis of size rather than color.

Uta stansburiana

◀▶ 1½–2½ in (4–6.5 cm)

◐ Desert and semiarid areas of Pacific North America and north-central Mexico.

▥ Females are patterned brown and white; males are mainly brown/gray but have three color forms (orange, blue, and yellow) during the breeding season.

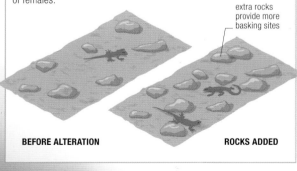

CASE STUDY

● ROCKS COUNT

Researchers tested the theory that male common side-blotched lizards in a high-quality habitat maintain a smaller territory than those in a poor habitat. They altered territories so that some males had valuable, sun-warmed rocks taken away and others were given more. Males in areas with fewer rocks expanded their territories to compensate for the poorer-quality resource, while those with more rocks contracted the size of their territory, but still managed to attract a higher density of females.

extra rocks provide more basking sites

BEFORE ALTERATION   **ROCKS ADDED**

SOAKING UP THE SUN
Male (right) and female (left) common side-blotched lizards bask on a rock that has been warmed by the sun to absorb the heat contained in the rock.

Canyon soaring

Andean condor

The Andean condor soars at altitudes of up to 18,000 ft (5,500 m) while scanning the ground for carcasses to scavenge. It has a large home range and may travel up to 125 miles (200 km) in a day. This bird's excellent eyesight enables it to spot food from several miles away, and it often uses the presence of other vultures to reveal the location of a potential meal, perhaps a dead farm animal, wild deer carcass, or even a beached whale. Condors rarely flap their wings when flying; instead, they ride on updrafts of warm air, circling with their wing tips bent upward. Andean condors nest at 9,850–16,400 ft (3,000–5,000 m) above sea level on rocky ledges. Like their relative, the California condor, they have in the past been subjected to persecution, which has caused their numbers to fall. Captive breeding and raising programs aim to improve their breeding success to secure the bird's future.

white ruff of feathers

MATURE FEMALE
Andean condors become sexually mature at four or five years of age. Females lay one or two eggs in alternate years.

Vultur gryphus

◧ 4–4¼ ft (1.2–1.3 m)

◉ Open grassland and rocky areas of the Andes and Pacific coast of South America.

▥ Large black vulture with featherless black and red head and neck. Males have large white patch on their wings.

The Andean condor has the largest wing area of any bird.

FLYING HIGH
These Andean condors are soaring on an updraft in the Colca Canyon in Peru. They typically hunt in the early morning and late afternoon.

Pecking distance

Black-browed albatross

Like many seabirds, black-browed albatrosses are colonial, coming together in huge nesting colonies during the breeding season. They are forced to nest together because of the limited availability of islands suitable for breeding in the Southern Ocean, and also because communal living decreases the risk of predation of eggs and chicks. The optimal nesting density leaves them just out of pecking reach of the bird next door. The colony therefore appears to be evenly spaced across the tussock-grass plateau, each bird the ruler of its own small territory. When away from their nests, black-browed albatrosses range over hundreds of miles of ocean, feeding on fishes, squid, and octopuses. This species is officially listed as endangered because of the high number of deaths caused by long-line fishing (see p.155).

Immature birds may spend up to seven years at sea before returning to establish a territory of their own.

Thalassarche melanophrys

◧ 31–37 in (80–95 cm)

◉ Islands and open waters of the Southern Ocean.

▥ Mainly white bird with dark gray upper wings. Yellow to dark orange bill and dark eyestripe above each eye.

≫ 253, 403

IN THE NEST
The world's largest breeding colony of black-browed albatrosses is on Steeple Jason Island in the Falklands. A pair raises just one chick each year, so their population is slow to recover from decline.

Controlled supply

New Holland honeyeater

The New Holland honeyeater defends feeding territories containing nectar-producing *Banksia* flowers. In general, birds hold smaller territories in areas with a high density of *Banksia* flower clusters than where these are sparsely distributed. The nectar resource varies over time. When it is scarce, New Holland honeyeaters exhibit more aggression toward intruders in an effort to keep them off their patch, but when the sugar-rich liquid becomes abundant they may relax their hold on territories and become less aggressive since there is enough food to go around. During the breeding season, pairs of New Holland honeyeaters also hold breeding territories. The female is more involved in nest building and incubating of eggs and tends to feed closer to the nest, while the male defends the nest but ranges farther afield—often to the edge of their territory—to feed.

Phylidonyris novaehollandiae

⬦ 7 in (18 cm)

◉ Meadows, woodland, and yards across southern Australia.

▢ Black-and-white bird with yellow wing patch and yellow margin on tail.

Seasonal variation

European robin

The European robin maintains territories in both the breeding and nonbreeding seasons. Spring and summer breeding territories average 1.3 acres (0.55 hectares), while winter territories may be only half that size. The first territories to become colonized in an area are the most resource-rich, wooded habitats, which are favored for breeding. During winter, migrant birds may arrive and colonize territories in less valuable shrub habitats. During the breeding season, males sing and patrol their territories more often; they are also quicker to attack neighboring males, which are more likely to trespass.

SEEING RED
An intruder's red breast triggers territorial defense behavior in a resident male robin. A warning song can quickly escalate into a vicious fight in which one or other of the opponents might die.

CHANGING TERRITORIES
Male and female robins hold separate territories in winter. By the time spring comes around, some birds have died, permitting others to increase the size of their territories. By the following winter, the territories have been recolonized by young birds.

agricultural land · SPRING · territory · backyard · farmhouse · WINTER

Erithacus rubecula

⬦ 4½–5½ in (12–14 cm)

◉ Woodland, parks, yards, and farm hedgerows across Europe.

▢ Songbird with bright orange-red breast and face, gray-brown upperparts, and off-white belly.

≫ 460

Fixed range

Koala

Koalas are mainly solitary animals that occupy distinct home ranges. In wetter forests in the south of their distribution, koalas require only small home ranges of 1.2–7.4 acres (0.5–3 hectares) to meet their needs, while in drier, less productive areas in the west their home ranges can be as large as 250 acres (100 hectares). A dominant male's range may overlap with those of up to nine females. Adult males travel widely at night during the breeding season (October to February), fighting with rival males and mating with receptive females. They also call to advertise their presence and scent-mark tree trunks using a gland on their sternum.

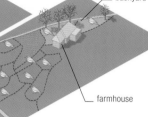

Phascolarctos cinereus

⬦ Up to 31 in (78 cm)

◉ Native to eucalyptus forests of eastern Australia. Introduced to western Australia and nearby islands.

▢ Woolly marsupial with gray-brown fur on back, white chin and chest, and long tufts of white hair on ears. Males are generally larger than females.

≫ 191

UP A GUM TREE
Koalas feed on the leaves of around 30 species of eucalyptus. Their opposable digits and curved claws help them grip branches.

CASE STUDY
SELECTIVE LOGGING

A study in New South Wales has shown that carefully managed logging can minimize the effect on koalas' home ranges. About a quarter of the white cypress pines, a tree that is used as a daytime shelter by the koala, were removed from a forest during the study, but the koala's main food trees, three species of eucalyptus, were deliberately left untouched. The koalas were unaffected by the loss of the trees.

TOOTH AND CLAW
Tigers are generally solitary, so when a stranger is encountered on another's territory a fight usually ensues. They are powerful animals with an impressive weaponry of sharp teeth and claws.

Cat fight

Tiger

Both male and female tigers maintain territories. These need to have dense vegetation for cover, a source of water, and plenty of prey. Also, a territory usually contains several dens where the tiger can rest and where females give birth to and rear their cubs. Territories of male tigers are up to three times larger than females' territories, and male and female ranges overlap. A male tends to retain exclusive breeding rights to the females in his territory as long as he can defend them from invaders. To minimize the risk of conflict, tigers leave signs that an area is occupied by scent-marking their territories with urine and feces or leaving scratch marks on trees. They are also quick to colonize ranges that have been vacated by another tiger dying. If a male takes over another's territory, he may kill any offspring he finds before mating with the resident females. Humans threaten tiger populations by poaching, fragmenting their habitats, and reducing the density of their prey.

MALE AMUR TIGER HUNTING
Tigers hunt by stealth, approaching potential prey (which includes deer, buffaloes, and wild pigs) silently in a crouching position, before launching an ambush. They kill by breaking the animals' necks or by suffocation.

FEMALE BENGAL TIGER SCENT-MARKING
Tigers spray urine mixed with a musky scent from an anal gland onto trees and rocks to mark their territories. Females increase their rate of spraying just before they are ready to mate.

Panthera tigris

⬌ 6½–12¼ ft (2–3.7 m)

◐ Forest in northeast China, Korea, Russia, northern India, and Nepal.

▭ Orange-red coat with black stripes and paler underside. Strong shoulders and limbs with broad paws and long, retractable claws.

≫ 375

1,411 The estimated number of tigers remaining in the wild in India.

▶ **VARIATION IN HOME RANGE SIZE AND PREY DENSITY**

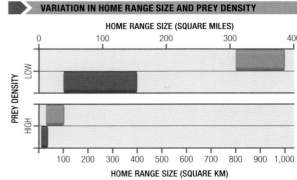

HOME RANGE SIZE (SQUARE MILES)

HOME RANGE SIZE (SQUARE KM)

PREY DENSITY — LOW / HIGH

In areas of low prey density, such as eastern Russia, tigers have large home ranges. By contrast, where prey density is high, as in Chitwan National Park, Nepal, home ranges are small.

KEY
- Females
- Males

Treetop territory
Brown-throated three-toed sloth

Brown-throated three-toed sloths spend most of their time high in the canopy of rain forest trees, feeding on leaves, sleeping, and resting. They typically live 66–98 ft (20–30 m) off the ground and transfer from one tree to another by using overlapping branches and climbing plants such as lianas. Sloths move slowly, hanging upside down from their long limbs, which are tipped with three hooklike claws. They also metabolize their food slowly and have relatively small muscle mass, so they are not able to generate much of their own body heat. Consequently, they seek or stay out of the sun during the day to adjust their body temperature as required. Brown-throated three-toed sloths are usually solitary and occupy a range of less than 5 acres (2 hectares). When ready to mate, females attract males into their territories by a screaming call. They have one baby a year, which they carry around on their chests until their offspring is able to be independent.

Bradypus variegatus

- 16½–31 in (42–80 cm)
- Lowland rain forest in Central and South America.
- Shaggy, coarse, brown-gray coat, often tinged green with algae. Brown throat, dark brown forehead, and stripes on either side of the eyes.
- >> 311

DESCENDING TO THE GROUND
The brown-throated three-toed sloth moves to the forest floor about once a week to defecate in a small hole that it digs with its tail. Sloths move awkwardly on the ground, but, if necessary, they can swim across rivers or areas of flooded forest.

Making their mark
Garnett's galago

Garnett's galago, also known as Garnett's greater bush baby, is a nocturnal primate that eats fruit, gum, and insects. It is generally solitary, although it may encounter other animals when feeding and females may sleep with their offspring. Like many other bush babies, Garnett's galago has a habit of washing its hands and feet with urine. It is not clear whether this behavior is concerned with scent-marking territory, or if it improves the animal's grip when leaping from tree to tree. Dominant males mark trees more often than females and subordinate males, by rubbing branches with a gland on their chest or with their urogenital region. Garnett's galagos also communicate by sound, by vocalizing and by rubbing their feet against a surface to make a noise.

Otolemur garnettii

- 10½ in (27 cm)
- Coastal, riverine, and highland forests of East Africa, from Somalia to Tanzania (including offshore islands).
- Coat color varies according to subspecies, from reddish to gray-brown, sometimes with greenish tones.

NIGHT VISION
Galagos have huge, light-sensitive eyes that enable them to see in the dark. Their large ears can move independently of one another, to help them detect noises made by insect prey.

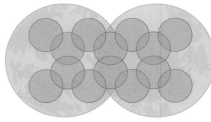

KEY
- Breeding males
- Breeding females

OVERLAPPING HOME RANGES
The home ranges of dominant male galagos overlap with those of several dominant females and their young. Interactions in these areas are generally friendly. Transient males may not have a specific home range.

large, rounded ears

conspicuous, spherical eyes

TAKING THE WATERS
Each day between 40 and 100 forest elephants visit the Dzanga Bai in the Central African Republic. Forest elephant herds gather at bais (swampy forest clearings) to dig for and eat mineral salts contained in the soil and to drink the mineral-rich water.

Town and country

Red fox

The red fox is a very adaptable carnivore that lives in many different habitats across its extensive range. In recent decades, it has become an increasingly common fixture in urban areas, where it exists in close proximity to humans. Foxes form small social groups consisting of a male (known as a dog fox), several females (vixens), and their dependent young (cubs). Each group's territory contains a den, or earth, where the females give birth to and rear their cubs. Well-trodden pathways connect the earth to other dens, hunting grounds, and food caches. Fox home ranges vary in size from 25 to 12,350 acres (10–5,000 hectares) depending on habitat quality. Territories are smaller and less stable in urban than in rural areas, probably because the urban environment changes more rapidly than the countryside.

Vulpes vulpes

 18–35 in (46–90 cm)

Wide variety of habitats in the Northern Hemisphere, including forest, tundra, desert, farmland, and towns.

Three color forms exist: one has a bright orange-red coat with black legs and a whitish underside; the second varies from silver to black; the third is a mixture.

EASY PICKINGS
Foxes frequently scavenge from trash cans in urban areas. They may also be fed by humans putting food out in their yards. In some areas, 50 percent of a fox's diet may be from human sources, and these foxes will have smaller territories.

DOG FOXES FIGHTING
Foxes mark their territories with urine and scent. When a male ignores these warnings and enters a rival's area, a fight may ensue, during which the foxes rear up and attempt to push one another over.

Trunk roads

Forest elephant

African forest elephants live in small family groups of between five and eight individuals deep in the forests of the Congo Basin. The dense vegetation makes these animals difficult to study, but satellite radio tracking indicates their home ranges could cover approximately 1,243 square miles (2,000 square km). An elephant may travel ⅔–9¼ miles (1–15 km) a day, feeding on grasses and leaves in the dry season and fruit in the wet season. Forest elephants visit watering holes daily, not only for water but also for soil containing minerals, such as calcium, potassium, and magnesium, which they need to stay healthy. In 2001, genetic analysis of the DNA of poached elephant ivory revealed that the African forest elephant might actually be a species distinct from the African savanna elephant, rather than a subspecies of it.

Generations of forest elephants have created a **network of trails** throughout the forest, linking fruit trees.

Loxodonta cyclotis

 8¼ ft (2.5 m) (male); 7 ft (2.1 m) (female)

Equatorial forests of Central and West Africa, in particular the Congo Basin.

Smaller than African savanna elephant with rounded ears, straight tusks with pink tinge, dark skin, and long, narrow jaw.

FOLLOWING THE TRAIL
Forest elephants move along three main types of "highway": boulevards, which allow them to travel rapidly between distant, favored areas such as forest clearings; foraging paths through medium-density forests with plenty of food; and alleys around the clearings.

Migration

Migration is the periodic movement of animals to and from different areas, usually along well-defined routes. In long-lived species, individuals make repeated annual migrations throughout their lives once they are sexually mature. In short-lived species, such as the monarch butterfly, which produce several generations within a season, the migration is undertaken by a succession of different individuals as the butterflies breed along the route.

Why migrate?

Many animals migrate to find the best location in which to lay eggs or rear young. This is often related to the need to avoid the lack of seasonal of food in one area and exploit an abundance of food elsewhere. Such movements are usually in response to predictable changes in the environment, for example, the different seasons in temperate latitudes, where weather conditions vary from harsh to favorable, and the wet and dry seasons in the tropics.

RECORD MIGRATIONS

Record	Animal	Distance
Longest round trip	Sooty shearwater	40,400 miles (65,000 km)
Longest nonstop flight	Bar-tailed godwit	7,200 miles (11,570 km)
Highest journey	Bar-headed goose	33,380 ft (10,175 m)
Longest aquatic journey	Gray whale	12,400 miles (20,000 km)
Largest land migration	Blue wildebeest	1.3 million
Largest air migration	Desert locust	69 billion

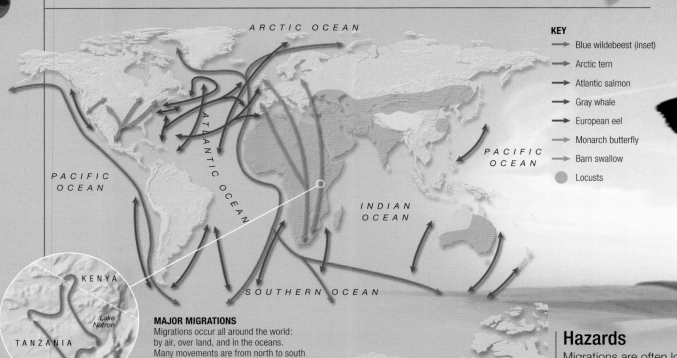

KEY
→ Blue wildebeest (inset)
→ Arctic tern
→ Atlantic salmon
→ Gray whale
→ European eel
→ Monarch butterfly
→ Barn swallow
● Locusts

MAJOR MIGRATIONS
Migrations occur all around the world: by air, over land, and in the oceans. Many movements are from north to south and back again with the changing seasons. Locust migrations are occasional and cover broad areas in search of food.

Partial and full migrants

In some species all individuals migrate (full migrants), while in others some remain resident in parts of the range (partial migrants). Whether or not an animal migrates can depend on local climate. For example, in Finland most European robins migrate south to escape the harsh winter, whereas in the British Isles, where winters are milder, most robins remain all year round. Migration can also depend on the stage an animal has reached in its life cycle. An immature American or European eel, for example, has no need to migrate to breeding grounds; it will make the journey from inland waterways to the Sargasso Sea when it is ready to reproduce (see p.152). Migration may also depend on an animal's circumstances. Older, more experienced Eurasian blackbirds in possession of a territory remain resident while younger, less experienced birds migrate.

LEAPFROG MIGRATIONS
Fox sparrows migrate along the western seaboard of North America. Populations that breed in Alaska and Canada migrate south in fall to overwinter in the US, leapfrogging populations with shorter migrations and those that do not migrate at all.

KEY
● Population A
● Population B
● Population C
● Population D

Hazards

Migrations are often long and hazardous journeys. Some birds choose to travel over land even though it is a longer journey, while others go over the sea by the shortest route, where there are fewer predators and they can often benefit from tailwinds. But birds migrating over open sea risk winds blowing them off course (resulting in birds stopping in places they are not normally seen) or storms forcing them to land on water. There may be increased risk of predation at the end of the trip: in fall, the Eleonora's falcon preys on exhausted songbirds that have flown over the Mediterranean to North Africa. Migrating over land can have its hazards, too, such as crossing inhospitable places like deserts.

ZEBRA CROSSING
During their annual migration, Burchell's zebras must risk crossing the crocodile-infested waters of the Mara River in Kenya's Masai Mara game reserve.

Triggers and preparation

Triggers to migrate include lengthening days as spring approaches, increased reproductive hormones and fat deposits, and growing restlessness. Many animals have an innate, near-annual rhythm that tells them when to migrate. Once in good condition, favorable weather may be the final trigger to move. Physiological changes are often necessary before migration. Birds' heart, flight, and skeletal muscles enlarge, while other organs may diminish in size. Fishes moving between fresh and saltwater display changes in their levels of salt tolerance, while amphibians that move between terrestrial and aquatic habitats alter the permeability of their skin.

NORMAL BODY FAT **READY TO MIGRATE**

LAYING DOWN BODY FAT
Birds that cross deserts or open oceans cannot guarantee regular food during migration. They deposit fat in their bodies as fuel for their flight. Small birds can double their weight before leaving.

Navigation

Animals that migrate use various cues to help them navigate. Compass cues indicate direction and might include the sun, stars, or the Earth's magnetic field (see p.131). Visual cues or landmarks, such as coastlines and mountain ranges, are used by animals to pilot their way toward their goal. Distinctive odors are also used to home in on breeding or roosting sites. True navigation relies on a mental map to determine position relative to a destination. In some species, young birds migrating for the first time travel with adults in flocks, but in many the adults leave first and the young follow later. They are born with the information for the distance and direction of their journey.

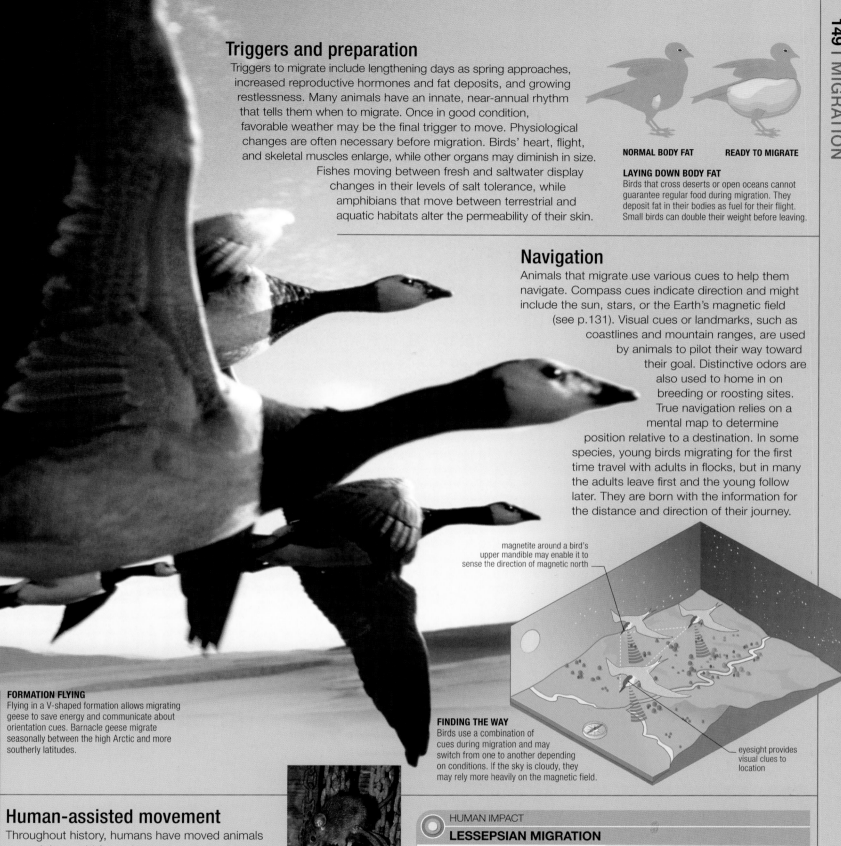

magnetite around a bird's upper mandible may enable it to sense the direction of magnetic north

FINDING THE WAY
Birds use a combination of cues during migration and may switch from one to another depending on conditions. If the sky is cloudy, they may rely more heavily on the magnetic field.

eyesight provides visual clues to location

FORMATION FLYING
Flying in a V-shaped formation allows migrating geese to save energy and communicate about orientation cues. Barnacle geese migrate seasonally between the high Arctic and more southerly latitudes.

Human-assisted movement

Throughout history, humans have moved animals around the world for various purposes, sometimes with disastrous consequences. Goats were introduced to many oceanic islands to provide food for passing ships. In many cases, they have since caused significant environmental damage by stripping the land bare of vegetation. People have also taken animals, such as cats, to new places as pets, where they then kill the local fauna. And many species have been introduced in an effort to control others. For example, cane toads were imported to Australia to eat pests of sugar cane, but instead they eat almost anything else (see p.284).

ILLEGAL IMMIGRANT
The black rat has colonized much of the world by "stowing away" onboard ships. Other invasive species have been transported in the water in ships' ballast tanks or attached to the hulls.

HUMAN IMPACT

LESSEPSIAN MIGRATION

The opening of the Suez Canal in 1869 connected the northern end of the Red Sea to the Mediterranean Sea. For a long time, part of the canal, the Bitter Lakes, was so salty that few animals could survive in it. However, over time the salinity has gradually decreased and Red Sea species have been able to travel northward into the eastern Mediterranean. This movement is known as Lessepsian migration after the engineer of the Suez Canal, Ferdinand de Lesseps. At least 300 species are known to have made this human-assisted migration.

Ocean bound

Red crab

For most of the year, the red crabs on Christmas Island reside in burrows in the rain forest floor, feeding on leaf litter, but as the monsoon rains start in November, tens of millions of these vibrant crustaceans start marching toward the coast. Their trip takes about a week; on arrival, males dig burrows in the beach terraces where they mate with females (the burrows protect the crabs and their eggs from heat, dehydration, and predators). The male crabs leave soon after to trek back inland, but the females stay at the coast for two weeks while their eggs develop. Then, at the turn of the high tide in the last quarter of the moon, the females release their eggs, up to 100,000 each, into the sea.

Gecarcoidea natalis
- 4½ in (12 cm)
- Forests of Christmas Island and the Cocos Islands, Indian Ocean.
- Bright red crab with broad, rounded carapace. Males are usually larger than females.

47 million The number of red crabs that migrate from the forests of Christmas Island down to the sea to spawn each year.

AT THE SHORE
Once they reach the beach, the crabs head straight into the ocean to replenish the water and salts lost during their journey.

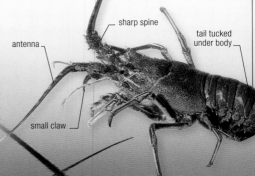
CRABS CROSS HERE

Across the sea floor

Spiny lobster

In late October and early November, regimented lines of spiny lobsters make their way across the sandy bottom of the Caribbean Sea. The migrations are thought to be triggered by fall storms that make the shallow waters cooler and more turbulent. The lobsters walk mainly at night and take shelter in crevices or in stationary groups in the open during the day. They take several days to travel 18–31 miles (30–50 km) to reach the edge of the deep ocean channels, where they spread out along the less disturbed reefs on the ocean fringe. Females spawn in this deeper water in spring and early summer, before returning to the shallows. Once the eggs have hatched, the larval lobsters drift on the ocean currents, eventually being brought back to the Caribbean Sea, where they mature.

Panulirus argus
- 23½ in (60 cm)
- Coral reefs and sea-grass beds in the Atlantic Ocean, Caribbean Sea, and Gulf of Mexico.
- Brown-gray lobster with yellow spots on the segmented abdomen.

DEFENSE POSITION
The spiny lobster is protected from most predators by the sharp spines on its exoskeleton, but if attacked it tucks its tail under its body.

sharp spine
tail tucked under body
antenna
small claw

SINGLE FILE
Each lobster uses its antennae and front legs to keep in touch with the abdomen and tail fan of the lobster in front. This "in line" behavior may be a defense against predators and also reduces drag.

Anax junius
- 2¾–3¼ in (7–8 cm)
- Still and slow-moving freshwater in North and South America, the Caribbean Islands, and Asia.
- Dragonfly with distinctive green thorax and two pairs of large, transparent wings.

North and south

Green darner

Each spring, a new generation of green darner dragonflies migrates from the southern United States to the north and to Canada, where they spend the summer breeding and feeding on mosquitoes. Approaching cold fronts in fall trigger the next generation of dragonflies to return south, sometimes covering as much as 87 miles (140 km) in a day. On arrival, the dragonflies breed and their offspring overwinter as nymphs, then metamorphose into adults in spring to start the cycle again. In this way, successive generations of offspring migrate first north then south, then north again. The migrating dragonflies are a temporary food source for kestrels.

Searching for food

Peach–potato aphid

As its name suggests, the peach–potato aphid moves between different host plants as an aid to its survival. In fall, adult aphids mate and lay eggs on peach and related trees such as apricot and plum. The eggs remain dormant until spring, when they hatch into nymphs that feed on the trees' flowers, leaves, and stems. Winged forms of the aphid leave in search of new food on a wide variety of summer vegetable crops including potatoes. The female aphids breed fast, giving birth to live young by parthenogenesis (see p.328). In fall, the aphids return to the peach trees. The peach–potato aphid is a major pest as a carrier of plant viruses.

Myzus persicae
- Up to 1/16 in (2 mm) (wingless form)
- Worldwide, on peach trees during fall, winter, and spring and various crop plants in summer.
- Winged adults have pale green-yellow abdomens with black heads and thoraxes. Wingless adults are more variable in color.

MONARCHS IN MEXICO
Suitable conditions for overwintering monarch butterflies in Mexico occur only in a relatively small area in the state of Michoacán. The fir trees are festooned with the orange and black butterflies from November to March.

Mass migration

Monarch butterfly

One of the most conspicuous of all insect migrations is that of monarch butterflies in North America. In fall, they move south to avoid the cold temperatures of more northerly parts of the continent. They overwinter in milder climates in a state of reproductive diapause, meaning they do not breed during this time. In spring, these striking butterflies move north in search of their food plant, milkweed (plants of the genus *Asclepias*, which produce milky sap). As they move, females lay eggs and die, and the new generations continue the journey. By the time they have reached the most northerly parts of their range, the butterflies will be second-, third-, or even fourth-generation descendants of those that left the south. Monarch butterfly migration appears to be triggered by changes in day length and temperature, and there must be a genetic component to the migration that allows flight routes to be inherited by offspring, since no individual butterfly ever makes the journey twice. The overwintering populations of monarch butterflies in Mexico are threatened by destruction of their forest refuges for lumber; intact forest is vital to maintain the microclimate needed for the butterflies' survival. Gaps in the forest cover can leave the butterflies susceptible to cold and rain. Several sanctuaries have been established for the protection of monarch butterflies.

Danaus plexippus

↔ Wingspan 3¼–4½ in (8.5–12 cm)

◑ Native to open habitats and forests in North America. Also found in Australasia and parts of Europe.

▭ Adults have orange wings with black borders and veins and some white markings. Caterpillars are striped.

KEY

⬤ Summer range

⬤ Spring range

⬤ Winter range

→ Northerly migration routes

MIGRATION ROUTES
Monarch butterflies that overwinter in coastal California spend the summer inland, to the west of the Rocky Mountains. Those that winter in the highlands of Mexico travel via Texas to northern states east of the Rockies, although some butterflies have been tracked flying to states to the west. The distance between summer and winter ranges can be as much as 3,000 miles (4,800 km).

CANADA

Northern limit of milkweed

Great Lakes

Rocky Mountains

UNITED STATES OF AMERICA

MEXICO

0 ___ 500km
0 ___ 500 miles

Occasional migration

Painted lady

The painted lady is a sporadic migrant: in some years, streams of butterflies head north from their winter ranges in the deserts of North Africa, southwest US, and Mexico; in other years, very few butterflies are seen. The mass migrations are precipitated by rains in arid areas that cause an abundance of food plants for the butterflies and a consequential boom in their population. Particularly spectacular migrations tend to occur in El Niño years. When their food supply is exhausted, the butterflies travel north in search of further food, across the sea if necessary, reaching northern Europe and the northern US by midsummer. The butterflies are aided on their travels by southerly winds.

Vanessa cardui

- Wingspan 2–3 in (5–7.5 cm)
- Meadows, hillsides, and marsh habitats worldwide, except for Antarctica.
- Butterfly with orange and black upper wings with white spots on pointed black tips of the forewings.

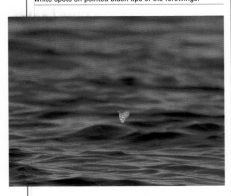

Moving in convoy

Boree moth

Caterpillars of the boree moth have voracious appetites, which compel them to keep moving. Having stripped bare the tree they were living on, they have no choice but to venture forth in search of a new food source. As each caterpillar walks, it extrudes a trail of silk, which is faithfully followed by its siblings, creating the illusion of one incredibly long, hairy caterpillar snaking across the ground. The caterpillars nest communally in their food tree in a ball, surrounded by silk and shed hairs, which has given rise to their alternative name of the bag-shelter moth.

Ochrogaster lunifer

- 1½ in (4 cm) (mature caterpillar); 1½ in (4 cm) (moth wingspan)
- Acacia and eucalyptus trees in Australia.
- Caterpillar is gray and hairy with a brown head. Adult moth is dark gray or brown with a pale dot in the center of the forewing.

Riding currents

Blue shark

During the course of a year, blue sharks in the North Atlantic Ocean undertake a clockwise migration, riding a series of ocean currents called the North Atlantic Gyre. The Gulf Stream takes the animals up the coast of North America, then they follow the North Atlantic Current across to European shores. The Canary Current carries them to North African waters, from where the North Equatorial Current delivers them back to the north coast of South America and the Caribbean. The longest distance so far recorded from a recaptured tagged shark is 4,250 miles (6,840 km) from Ireland to Venezuela, but journeys of around 1,900 miles (3,000 km) are common. The majority of transatlantic sharks are female. They mate in the western North Atlantic and give birth to their pups in the waters off Spain and Portugal and in the Mediterranean Sea.

Prionace glauca

- Up to 13 ft (4 m)
- Tropical, subtropical, and temperate waters worldwide.
- Long-snouted fish with long pectoral fins. Dark indigo-blue upper side shades to white underneath. Weighs up to 440 lb (200 kg).

CASE STUDY
TRACKING SHARKS

Since the early 1960s, blue sharks have been tagged to provide information on their movements. Anglers and commercial fishermen are encouraged to take part in the program, applying identification tags to sharks they have caught, either intentionally or accidentally, before they are released. The tags are attached to the shark's dorsal fin or implanted in the muscle of its back. If the shark is recaptured, scientists can start to draw a map of its migratory journeys. More recently, satellite tags have allowed the sharks' travels to be mapped without the need for their recapture.

ON THE MOVE
The migrations of the Atlantic population of blue sharks have been the most extensively studied, but the Pacific population has been found to migrate long distances too. There is also a population in the Indian Ocean.

Seeking freshwater

European sea sturgeon

The European sea sturgeon is anadromous, spending much of its early life at sea and returning to the river of its birth when sexually mature. Females lay up to 6 million sticky eggs in shallow water, on gravely riverbeds. After hatching, juveniles make their way downstream, becoming acclimatized to the increasing salinity as they near the sea. The European sea sturgeon was previously abundant around Europe, but it is now one of the most endangered fish as a result of over-exploitation for its eggs (which are eaten as the delicacy caviar), the deteriorating quality of its freshwater spawning grounds, and obstacles to migration, such as hydroelectricity projects. This sturgeon is now thought to breed in only one river basin in France, and a captive breeding program has been established.

Acipenser sturio

- Up to 16½ ft (5 m)
- Coastal waters of northeastern Atlantic, Mediterranean, and Black Sea, and adjacent rivers.
- Olive-black upper body with white underside. Five rows of scutes.

Return journey

European eel

Unlike the European sea sturgeon, the European eel spends most of its life in freshwater but returns to saltwater to breed, a behavior known as catadromy. Having started life in the ocean, young eels (elvers) arrive at estuaries and travel inland along rivers. The eels remain upstream for more than ten years, feeding and maturing. In July each year, adult eels return to the sea, sometimes crossing wet grass to reach a different watercourse. These eels develop larger eyes to see in the ocean depths and a silver coloration below that helps conceal them from predators.

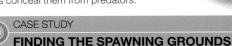

Anguilla anguilla

- Up to 4¼ ft (1.3 m)
- Sargassum (seaweed) beds of the western Atlantic, coasts of the northeastern Atlantic, and adjacent rivers.
- Long, narrow-bodied fish with continuous dorsal, anal, and tail fin. Dark scales on top and yellow below.

YOUNG AND OLD
The European eel progresses through various stages. The first-stage larva is called a leptocephalus (left). It then becomes a glass eel, an elver, and a yellow eel, before becoming a fully mature adult (silver eel, below).

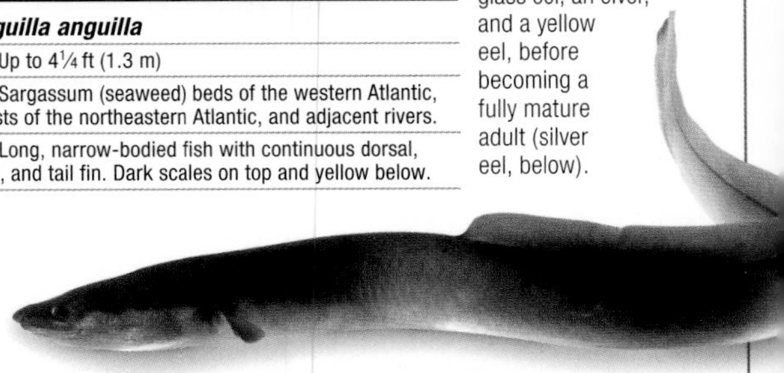

CASE STUDY
FINDING THE SPAWNING GROUNDS

From 1904 to 1922, Danish biologist Johannes Schmidt led expeditions in the Mediterranean Sea and the North Atlantic to find the spawning grounds of the European eel. He recorded the length of larval eels caught in various locations, eventually catching the smallest, ⅜ in (1 cm) long, in the Sargasso Sea. In the western Sargasso, Schmidt also found the breeding grounds of the American eel (Anguilla rostrata), a related species that matures in the rivers of the eastern United States. The larvae drift on ocean currents to reach coastal waters, the American eel larvae exiting the current before the European eels.

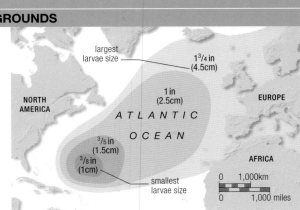

largest larvae size — 1¾ in (4.5cm)

NORTH AMERICA

1 in (2.5cm)

EUROPE

ATLANTIC OCEAN

⅗ in (1.5cm)

⅜ in (1cm) — smallest larvae size

AFRICA

0   1,000km
0   1,000 miles

Heading upstream
Chum salmon

Like the European sea sturgeon, salmon are anadromous, meaning that they live mostly in the sea but return to freshwater to breed. Chum are one of five species of salmon that frequent the North Pacific Ocean and the rivers that border it in countries including Canada, Japan, Korea, and the United States. After spending between one and three years at sea, chum salmon travel inland as far as 2,000 miles (3,200 km) up the Yukon River through Alaska into Canada. The annual "salmon run" occurs during fall, with spawning taking place between November and January. Around two weeks later, the adults die, contributing valuable nutrients to the ecosystem. Their eggs remain protected in the gravel riverbed over winter and hatch in early spring. The fry stay in the river for a year or more before traveling downstream to the sea between March and July.

Oncorhynchus keta

↔ Up to 3 ft 3 in (1 m)

◆ Temperate and cold waters of North Pacific and adjacent rivers.

📖 Silver bluish green salmon. Spawning males develop darker markings with vertical bars of olive and grayish red on their sides.

MIGRATION HAZARD
Along their way upstream, migrating salmon must contend with a variety of dangers, not least hungry grizzly bears that gather at waterfalls and may wait for hours to catch a flying meal.

LEAPING FALLS
It is hard work returning to the spawning grounds. Salmon must jump up waterfalls and rapids, propelling themselves forward against the flow of water with their strong muscles and flicking tails.

HUMAN IMPACT
PARASITIC LICE

Salmon is a popular food fish, which has prompted a boom in commercial salmon farming. However, the industry is threatening wild salmon populations by exposing them to parasites. Sea lice are crustaceans that occur naturally on the salmon's skin, but the raising of thousands of adult fish in close proximity in pens causes parasite numbers to rise far beyond normal levels found in the wild, lowering the health of the fish. Young wild salmon migrating downstream from their spawning grounds pass the salmon farms on their way to the ocean and become infested with parasites as they go.

SPAWNING GROUNDS
By the time they reach the spawning grounds, these sockeye salmon (*Oncorhynchus nerka*) have developed distinctive coloration, with a red upper body and green head. The males have hooked snouts.

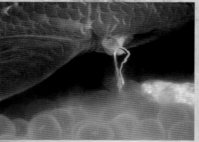

FERTILIZING EGGS
Female salmon lay between 2,000 and 6,000 eggs in shallow depressions called rudds. Males then release sperm over the eggs before the females cover them with gravel for protection.

NEXT GENERATION
Recently hatched salmon are known as alevins. They remain in the rudd for around 12 weeks, until the yolk sac attached to their belly is used up and they have to emerge to feed themselves.

Back to the birth pool
Yellow-spotted salamander

Yellow-spotted salamanders hibernate in woodland, beneath leaf litter or underground; with the first thaws of snow, they migrate to their breeding pools. This can be as early as December to February in southern parts of their range or as late as March to April in the north. They return to the pool in which they were born, which is usually less than 650 ft (200 m) from their hibernation areas. After breeding, the adults leave the eggs to develop into larvae, which may overwinter in the pools in their larval form or metamorphose into adults and leave the pools that year. Occasionally, these salamanders will lay their eggs beneath the ice of a frozen pool.

Ambystoma maculatum
- 4½–10 in (11–25 cm)
- Moist mature woodland in North America.
- Stocky, dark gray, black, or brown salamander with two rows of bright yellow spots along the sides of its body.

Dangerous journey
European common toad

Like salamanders, European common toads attempt to migrate back to the pond in which they were born in order to breed. The migration begins in fall but is interrupted by a period of hibernation in midwinter, when the toads hole up underground to wait until the cold weather has passed. They resume their journey in spring, and it is then that large numbers of toads are frequently killed while crossing streets built on their traditional migration routes. Those toads lucky enough to reach the breeding ponds mate in a frenzy between March and June, before returning to their home range, which may be anything between 180 and 5,250 ft (55 and 1,600 m) away from the pond.

Bufo bufo
- Up to 7 in (18 cm)
- Terrestrial and wetland habitats throughout most of Europe.
- Broad, squat-bodied toad with warty olive green-brown skin. Exudes a distasteful secretion to ward off predators.
- 284, 370

AVOIDING TRAFFIC
Tunnels or underpasses built beneath roads close to breeding ponds can help reduce toad mortality from collisions with cars. Other measures include warning signs and people carrying the toads across in buckets.

Long-distance swim
Leatherback turtle

This giant of the ocean makes lengthy annual migrations. Using ocean currents to help it on its way, the leatherback turtle feeds in the rich, temperate waters of the northern and southern Atlantic and Pacific oceans in spring and summer, but it returns to more tropical climates to find beaches on which to lay its eggs. Although only females venture onto land, males also migrate, coming close to shore to mate with the females. Satellite tagging has revealed extensive migrations: one record-setting leatherback was tracked swimming 12,774 miles (20,557 km), from a beach in Indonesia across the Pacific to the west coast of the US and part of the way back again. Leatherbacks are prone to eating plastic refuse, mistaking it for jellyfish, and can choke to death as a result. They are also sometimes caught in fishing nets.

Dermochelys coriacea
- 5¼–7 ft (1.6–2.1 m)
- Temperate, subtropical, and tropical waters worldwide.
- Largest of the marine turtles, with relatively long front flippers.

OPEN OCEAN
With a span of up to 9 ft (2.7 m), leatherback turtles have the longest front flippers relative to their size of any turtle. They usually cruise at around 1¼ miles (2 km) per hour.

CASE STUDY
SATELLITE TRACKING

Scientists increasingly use satellite tags to track the movements of leatherback turtles in the world's oceans. The tags are mounted on harnesses that are designed to disintegrate gradually and fall off the turtle. They are usually fixed to the females once they have finished nesting and to males that are accidentally caught at sea by fishermen. For up to two years, a tag can relay information about a turtle's whereabouts via satellite to a computer. In addition to location information, the tag transmits data such as dive depth and duration, which give clues about behavior such as foraging.

MISSION ACCOMPLISHED
Female leatherback turtles lay an average of 110 eggs per clutch in a hole in soft sand that they dig with their flippers. The young hatch after 60 to 70 days and rush headlong to the sea.

LANDFALL
The females pull themselves onto gently sloping, sandy, tropical beaches to lay their eggs above the high-tide line. Most species of turtle return to the beach of their birth and the leatherback is no exception, although they may visit another beach in the same general vicinity.

Peak performance

Bar-headed goose

Bar-headed geese reach extreme high altitudes during their migration over the peaks of the Himalayas. The birds are supremely adapted to the demands of their trip: their wings have a large surface area relative to the bird's weight to provide extra lift; their blood hemoglobin absorbs oxygen faster than that of other birds; and their downy feathers keep them warm by trapping body heat generated by flying. Bar-headed geese are capable of traveling more than 1,000 miles (1,600 km) each day and can fly at speeds of 50 mph (80 kph). Annual migration allows the geese to avoid severe winter storms on the high plateaus of Central Asia, where they breed in the summer, and summer monsoon rains on the Indian subcontinent.

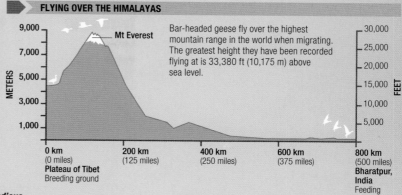

FLYING OVER THE HIMALAYAS

Bar-headed geese fly over the highest mountain range in the world when migrating. The greatest height they have been recorded flying at is 33,380 ft (10,175 m) above sea level.

Chart axis labels: 9,000 / 7,000 / 5,000 / 3,000 / 1,000 METERS; 30,000 / 25,000 / 20,000 / 15,000 / 10,000 / 5,000 FEET; Mt Everest

0 km (0 miles) Plateau of Tibet Breeding ground; 200 km (125 miles); 400 km (250 miles); 600 km (375 miles); 800 km (500 miles) Bharatpur, India Feeding ground

Anser indicus

- 28–32 in (70–82 cm)
- Mountain lakes and wetlands in Central Asia.
- Pale gray-bodied goose with orange legs and bill. Two distinctive black bars on the head give it its name.

WINTER QUARTERS
Bar-headed geese spend the winter in wetlands in India, northern Myanmar, and Pakistan, feeding on grasses and cereal crops such as barley, rice, and wheat.

BREEDING GROUNDS
In summer, bar-headed geese live at high altitudes, on the Tibetan Plateau in Tibet, Qinghai in China, and Ladakh in Kashmir. The geese, such as the ones on the water in this photograph, congregate at mountain lakes to breed and feed on short grass.

Roaming the ocean

Wandering albatross

This albatross spends most of its life at sea, soaring above the waves or resting on the surface. It ventures thousands of miles across the Southern Hemisphere from its breeding islands close to the Antarctic Circle, occasionally crossing the equator or circumnavigating Antarctica in its search for food. One bird was tracked traveling a staggering 3,700 miles (6,000 km) in just 12 days. Wandering albatrosses nest on a few islands covered in tussock grass between November and July. Males and females take turns incubating the egg and caring for their single chick while the other feeds at sea.

Diomedea exulans

- 3½–4½ ft (1.1–1.4 m)
- Open ocean and remote oceanic islands of the Southern Ocean.
- Adults have white bodies, with white and black wings. The large, pink hooked bill has tubular nostrils.

FLYING SOLO
Young albatrosses take up to ten years to reach maturity and during that time may hardly ever make landfall. They often accompany fishing vessels, feeding on discarded fish.

9.8ft The wingspan of the wandering albatross, which is greater than that of any other flying bird.

LONG-LINE FISHING

It is estimated that 100,000 albatrosses drown each year on longlines baited for bluefin tuna. The lines, which are pulled behind fishing boats, can be up to 80 miles (130 km) long and carry as many as 10,000 hooks. The birds try to catch the bait while it is close to the surface, become hooked, and are dragged underwater as the lines sink. International conservation efforts advocate the use of measures by fishermen to help prevent these deaths.

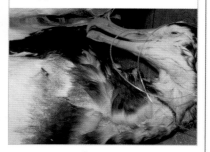

COMMUNAL FEEDING GROUNDS
Bar-tailed godwits (seen here in a mixed flock with other shorebirds) frequent estuaries in the winter. They use their long, sensitive bills to probe for crustaceans, mollusks, and worms in the mud.

CASE STUDY
E7, THE RECORD SETTER

In 2007, biologists fastened satellite transmitters to 13 bar-tailed godwits on their feeding grounds in New Zealand. They were about to witness the longest-ever nonstop flights made by a bird. A female, nicknamed E7, left the mouth of the Piako River on March 17 and flew 6,340 miles (10,219 km) nonstop to Yalu Jiang, China, arriving on March 24. She spent five weeks there before leaving on May 1 and traveling to Alaska, stopping occasionally en route. E7 arrived at her breeding grounds at Manokinak on the Yukon–Kuskokwim Delta on May 15, where she stayed until July 17, before moving to another site in the delta. On August 29, she departed and smashed her own record by flying nonstop to New Zealand, a distance of 7,200 miles (11,570 km), in just over 8 days.

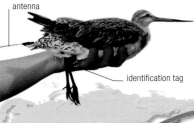

antenna

identification tag

ALASKA

CHINA

1—15 May
4,500 miles
(7,237 km)

P A C I F I C
O C E A N

17—24 March
6,340 miles
(10,219 km)

29 August—7 September
7,200 miles
(11,570 km)

NEW ZEALAND

Longest nonstop flight
Bar-tailed godwit

This large wading bird is a long-distance globe-trotter, capable of flying nonstop from breeding ranges in the Arctic regions of Europe, Asia, and western Alaska across the equator to feeding grounds in South Africa, Australia, and New Zealand. During the Northern Hemisphere summer, bar-tailed godwits are resident on the coastal tundra of the far north, where they lay between two and four eggs in cup-shaped nests in the grass. After raising their young, the birds fly to "refueling stations," such as estuaries, to feed and bulk up their bodies before flying south to the Southern Hemisphere. As the Southern Hemisphere winter approaches, the birds molt into their russet-colored breeding plumage and put on weight in advance of their northward migration. Some bar-tailed godwits overwinter in Europe, where they are closer to their breeding grounds and require less energy to get there. Although their feeding rate is the same as birds that migrate from Africa, they spend less time feeding before they begin their journey.

Limosa lapponica

◀▶ 14½–16 in (37–41 cm)

◉ Arctic coastal tundra and sandy intertidal areas in South Africa, Australia, and New Zealand.

▥ Neck, breast, and belly are brick-red in summer, changing to off-white in winter.

FATTENED UP FOR FLYING
The bar-tailed godwit lays down huge fat reserves (up to 55 percent of its body mass) before embarking on its epic nonstop journeys. Its digestive tract shrinks in size to make room for the extra fuel.

Learning the route
Whooping crane

The young of many water birds follow their parents on their first migration in order to learn the route. Naturally occurring whooping cranes migrate 2,500 miles (4,000 km) between a single summer breeding area in Wood Buffalo National Park, Canada, and a single wintering site in Aransas National Wildlife Refuge, Texas. The birds' reliance on just two sites prompted conservationists to establish other populations in Florida and Wisconsin, and to assist birds in their migration (see panel, right).

Grus americana
- 4¼ ft (1.3 m)
- Open, grassy plains and marshland in northern Canada and Texas, Florida, and Wisconsin.
- Mainly white with black primary feathers and red and black markings on the head. Long neck and legs.

RARE BIRDS
In 1941, the migratory flock of whooping cranes numbered just 15 birds. In 2007, there were 73 mating pairs in Wood Buffalo National Park, 53 resident birds in Florida, and 52 birds in Wisconsin.

 HUMAN IMPACT
OPERATION MIGRATION

In 2001, conservationists hatched a plan to reintroduce whooping cranes to Wisconsin. To teach the hand-raised birds the migration route from Wisconsin to Florida the cranes were "imprinted" on an ultralight aircraft. The birds were played the noise of the aircraft's engine while still inside the egg and soon after hatching were introduced to the plane. Their first flights were taken following the aircraft down the runway and they eventually followed it 1,250 miles (2,010 km) across seven states to Florida.

Following the sun
Barn swallow

Barn swallows breed throughout the Northern Hemisphere in summer but travel south to sunnier climes in South America, Africa, southern Asia, and northern Australia for the northern winter. They migrate during the day, feeding on insects caught on the wing. In contrast to some migratory birds, they do not put on much weight before the journey. This makes them vulnerable to starvation when crossing large areas with little food such as the Sahara Desert. They are also at risk from storms and exhaustion. Barn swallows can cover up to 200 miles (320 km) per day when migrating.

STREAMLINED FLIER
With its long, pointed wings and elongated tail streamers, the barn swallow is well-designed for long-distance flying.

Hirundo rustica
- 7 in (18 cm)
- Open grassland, meadows, and farmland habitats worldwide except Australia and Antarctica.
- Off-white underparts, metallic blue above with a red-brown throat and forehead.

TAKING A BREAK
Barn swallows migrate in large flocks and frequently stop to rest on structures such as telegraph wires. Flocks gather in premigratory roosts in late summer and early fall before embarking on their southerly journey.

Vertical migration
Long-tailed sylph

Several species of hummingbird show altitudinal migration, moving up and down mountainsides in search of nectar-producing flowers. The long-tailed sylph frequents forests in the Andes at altitudes of between 3,300 to 9,800 ft (1,000 to 3,000 m). Hummingbirds require an abundance of energy-rich nectar. They may move to higher altitudes for a period of weeks or months when the flowers come into bloom; alternatively, they may travel each day from lower elevations. Hummingbirds play an important role as pollinators in the ecosystem.

KEEPING WATCH
Once they have found a good nectar source, hummingbirds (especially males) may defend it from intruders. They keep a close watch from a nearby perch on an exposed branch.

Aglaiocercus kingi
- 4–7½ in (10–19 cm)
- Subtropical and tropical moist montane forest in Bolivia, Colombia, Ecuador, Peru, and Venezuela.
- Bright iridescent blue and green feathers. Tail is longer than body.

Population pressure
Norway lemming

Norway lemmings migrate sporadically every few years when their populations explode. In a typical year, the rodents live in tunnels beneath the snow in winter, moving to higher or lower ground in spring. There they live on mountain meadows or in forests, continuing to breed before returning in fall to the alpine zone. In years with a mild winter, an early spring, and a late fall, food is abundant, reproduction is fast, and survival of litters is high, resulting in a summer soaring of lemming numbers. Lemmings are often wrongly said to commit mass suicide by jumping from cliffs. Population pressure can trigger mass migration, usually away from the meadows toward the forests. Obstacles in their path, such as boulders, rivers, cliffs, or ravines, may force the lemmings into a "bottleneck," causing them to panic and take reckless flight.

Lemmus lemmus
- 4–5 in (10–13 cm)
- Tundra, mountain meadows, and alpine and boreal forests of Scandinavia and Russia.
- Rounded, brown and black rodent with a short tail. Flattened claw on the first digit of the front feet aids digging in snow.

RIVER CROSSING
Caribou frequently cross lakes and rivers while migrating. They are strong swimmers, and their thick, air-filled coats help them stay buoyant and warm in the icy water. Both sexes have antlers, but they are larger and more branched in males. These caribou are crossing the Kobuk River in Alaska.

Endurance test

Caribou

Caribou undertake one of the most arduous annual migrations of any terrestrial mammal. Herds may number thousands of animals and complete a 3,100-mile (5,000-km) round trip, visiting spring calving areas and summer and winter feeding grounds. They are forced to move on by the seasonal availability of the tundra plants on which they feed. In summer, the herds take refuge from flies and mosquitoes in windy coastal areas; in winter, they move into subarctic boreal forests, where snow cover is less than on the open tundra. Caribou herds have been recorded running as fast as 50 mph (80 kph) while migrating. Groups are largest during the spring migration and smaller during fall, when mating occurs. Caribou are also called reindeer, particularly in Europe and Asia, where many are partially domesticated and are tamer than wild animals. Reindeer from herds in Eurasia have been introduced to North America, where they may mix with the native caribou.

Rangifer tarandus

↔ 5–2½ ft (1.5–2.3 m)

◉ Arctic tundra and boreal forests of the US, Canada, Asia, and northern Europe.

⬚ Coat is brown in summer and gray in winter, and rump is white.

DIGGING FOR FOOD
Norwegian reindeer grazing on lichens and other plants beneath the snow. The reindeers' broad hooves act like snowshoes to help them walk on the snow and to dig beneath it.

NEW LIFE
A female caribou tends to her minutes-old twin calves in Canada's Northwest Territories. Twins are rare; most females have only one calf each year. Births take place in May or June on inland calving grounds.

WOLF KILL
Although young caribou can run soon after birth, large numbers of calves succumb to predators such as gray wolves, which track the migrating herds and stalk the birthing grounds looking for easy prey.

HUMAN IMPACT

LIVING WITH REINDEER

Native peoples of the Arctic and subarctic have a close association with reindeer, relying on them for food, skins, and transportation. These people live a nomadic life, moving with the semidomesticated herds that are making their way between the coast and inland areas. Reindeer are rarely bred in captivity, but they have been tamed for milk production and to pull sleighs. Here, a Nenet herder leads her reindeer across snow-covered pastures in Siberia. Reindeer herding is also an important part of Sami culture in northern Scandinavia (Lapland). Native peoples in North America and Greenland have a long history of hunting wild caribou for their meat and hides.

A home for all seasons

Little brown bat

Like many other bats living in temperate zones, little brown bats migrate between several different roosts throughout the year. On emerging from hibernation in spring, they travel to summer roost sites, often in buildings, where the females give birth to a single pup between May and July. In fall, bats transfer to hibernation sites, where they spend winter in a state of torpor. This behavior helps them survive a time of year when few insects are available to eat.

Myotis lucifugus

⬌ 2¼–4 in (6–10 cm)

⊙ Forested areas of North America, from southern Alaska and Canada to the highlands of Mexico.

📖 Small, light to dark brown-colored bat with a plain nose and relatively short ears.

FLYING TO HIBERNATE
Migrations to winter sites need not always be toward warm areas. Little brown bats may fly north, sometimes up to 310 miles (500 km), to spend winter in a cave or disused mine.

dark brown to black wings

plain nose

African odyssey

Straw-colored fruit bat

As their name suggests, these African bats feed on fruit—and they undertake quite a journey to find enough of it to fulfill their requirements. The bats follow the annual rains north through sub-Saharan Africa before returning south at the end of the rainy season. Their extensive migration takes them hundreds of miles. Along the way, they spend the day in large, noisy colonies in tree roosts. At night, they leave their roosts and venture forth to find fruit, spreading out to feed. The vast population of straw-colored fruit bats plays a vital role in pollinating and dispersing the seeds of many economically important plants, including lumber trees such as iroko, a valuable hardwood, and cash crops such as cashew nuts, mangoes, and figs.

Eidolon helvum

⬌ 5½–8½ in (14–22 cm)

⊙ Forest and savanna in sub-Saharan Africa, the southern Arabian Peninsula, and Madagascar.

📖 Dull brown or gray bat with straw-colored fur on its neck and back. Large eyes and long, narrow wings.

TIMELY ARRIVAL
Every November, between 5 and 10 million fruit bats descend on Kansaka National Park in Zambia. Their arrival coincides with a boom of fruit in the park. It is estimated that the bats eat 5,000 tons of fruit each night.

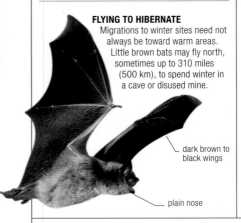

Ocean voyagers

Humpback whale

Many of the great whales make extraordinary journeys through the world's oceans in search of food and safe places to give birth, and humpback whales are no exception. The high-latitude oceans provide rich feeding grounds during each hemisphere's summer, and here the whales gorge themselves to store up energy for their long migration and the months that follow. In the Northern Hemisphere, humpback whales feed more often on fish, whereas those in the Southern Hemisphere eat mainly krill. As winter approaches, humpback whales move toward the Equator on a journey of 3,100 miles (5,000 km) across the open ocean in search of warm, sheltered waters, where the females give birth and mating takes place. During this time, adults survive by metabolizing layers of fatty blubber beneath the skin, and the calves drink their mothers' rich milk. Eventually, they must return to polar waters to feed. The population of humpback whales in the northern Indian Ocean may be resident all year (see panel, below).

Megaptera novaeangliae

⬌ 46–59 ft (14–18 m)

⊙ Open oceans worldwide, except extreme north and south.

📖 Predominantly black whale with white undersides to the long narrow flippers. Scalloped edge to fluke.

» 246

LOOKING FOR LANDMARKS?
When spy-hopping, a whale lifts its head vertically out of the water while rotating to look around. It may be checking for landmarks while migrating.

FIGHTING OVER A FEMALE
Male escorts accompany female whales in the breeding grounds, warding off competitors with assertive behavior such as tail-slapping. They may also sing complex songs to attract females.

CASE STUDY

MIGRATION ROUTES

Northern Hemisphere humpbacks spend the summer in feeding grounds in the northern Atlantic and Pacific oceans. In winter, they migrate south to breed in warmer waters around the Caribbean, West Africa, Japan, Hawaii, and Mexico. Southern Hemisphere humpbacks follow the same pattern, spending the summer feeding in the rich, cold waters of the Southern Ocean off Antarctica and migrating north to overwinter in the warm waters of Australia, the Pacific islands, southern Africa, or South America.

ATLANTIC OCEAN

INDIAN OCEAN

PACIFIC OCEAN

ATLANTIC OCEAN

KEY
- Major feeding areas (summer)
- Major breeding areas (winter)
- ➝ Possible migration
- ➝ Main migration

TREKKING ACROSS THE PLAINS
As they cross the Serengeti Plain in Tanzania, white-bearded wildebeest throw up clouds of red dust from their hooves. Not all wildebeest are migratory; smaller herds may remain resident throughout the year.

KEEPING UP WITH MOTHER
Wildebeest calves are born in the middle of the herd and within days can keep up with the adults when running. This helps them avoid becoming prey during the migration.

Mass movement

Blue wildebeest

Each year, around 1.3 million white-bearded wildebeest (one of five subspecies of the blue wildebeest) undertake a spectacular migration on the plains and savanna grasslands of East Africa (see map, right). Their herds are further swelled by hundreds of thousands of other ungulate species, including Thomson's gazelles, zebras, and elands. The animals are compelled to move on in search of fresh food, water, and minerals, such as phosphorus, that are important to their health. It is deficiency in this mineral that is thought to spur the herds to leave their dry-season ranges just before the onset of the rainy season and head south to the short-grass plains. Along the way, the wildebeest have to contend with predators, including lions and hyenas on the plains and crocodiles in the rivers.

Connochaetes taurinus

⬌ 6¼–7 ft (1.9–2.1 m)

◉ Plains and savanna grasslands in East Africa, from the Equator south to the tip of South Africa.

▭ Large antelope with slate gray to brown coat and black face, mane, and tail. Curved horns resemble those of a cow.

CIRCULAR MIGRATION ROUTE
White-bearded wildebeest follow a clockwise migration around the Serengeti Plain. Soon after calving in the southeastern plains during the wet season (January and February), the herds head northwest, toward Lake Victoria. By June, they have reached the transitional pastures. The herds then turn north toward the Masai Mara, where they spend the dry season (July to October) before returning south in November to complete the circle.

MOTHER AND CALF ON THE MOVE
A female humpback whale makes the return journey to polar waters with her young calf. The calf is weaned at about 11 months but may stay with its mother for more than a year.

Animal architects

Animals produce some of the most impressive architecture on Earth. Their building methods vary from simply fetching and dropping materials to more advanced construction techniques, including interlocking, weaving, or gluing materials together to ensure they stay in place. Some animals make their nests out of pliable substances such as mud, while others spin structures from silk, or dig burrows in the ground. Social animals build large structures relative to their body size by working as a team.

Why build?

Animals build structures for a variety of functions. Many live in their constructions for only a short time; for example, caddis fly larvae build themselves a protective case from grains of sand or other materials, and some frogs excavate shelters to help them stay moist during drought. Animals often build structures for raising young, as in the case of birds' nests and mammals' burrows. Social insects, such as ants, termites, bees, and wasps, construct elaborate nests to house entire colonies. Some animals build structures to capture prey or store food, while others communicate using architecture—for example, bowerbirds build courtship "stages."

WINTER DEN
Female polar bears dig dens under the snow to provide a safe, warm environment during the winter when they give birth to their cubs. They suckle them for several months before emerging into the spring sunshine.

Building behavior

Animals may be genetically programmed to build in a certain way without an image of the end goal and its function, or they may display a degree of ingenuity and flexibility. For example, a beaver can adapt the shape of its dam according to local conditions. Building usually involves relatively simple, repetitive behaviors, and most animals select or make standardized materials for their constructions. For example, caddis fly larvae reject sand grains that are either too small or too large for their cases, and martins choose just the right consistency of mud for their nests. Most animals use their feet or mouthparts to manipulate building materials; their level of specialization depends on whether they are used for other functions as well, such as feeding.

CONVERGENT EVOLUTION
Both weaver ants (right) and tailorbirds (above) use silk to stitch leaves together to make their nests. Weaver ants use silk extruded from their own larvae, while tailorbirds make use of the silk from spiders' webs. They may also use plant fiber or even stolen household thread. These similar sewing behaviors have evolved independently of one another in unrelated species.

CASE STUDY
LEARNING BUILDING SKILLS

To find out how the ability of adult male village weavers to build nests was affected by their experience when young, researchers gave some fledgling males fresh green building materials to handle (control group), but other fledglings received none (experimental group). When a year old, the experimental males were unable to weave a single strip in the first week that they were given reed grass. After three weeks of practice, their success rate at weaving was still only 26 percent, whereas the experienced control group achieved a rate of 62 percent.

KEY

Experimental

Control

BIRD GROUP

0   10   20   30   40   50   60   70   80   90   100

SUCCESS RATE AFTER 3 WEEKS' PRACTICE (PERCENT)

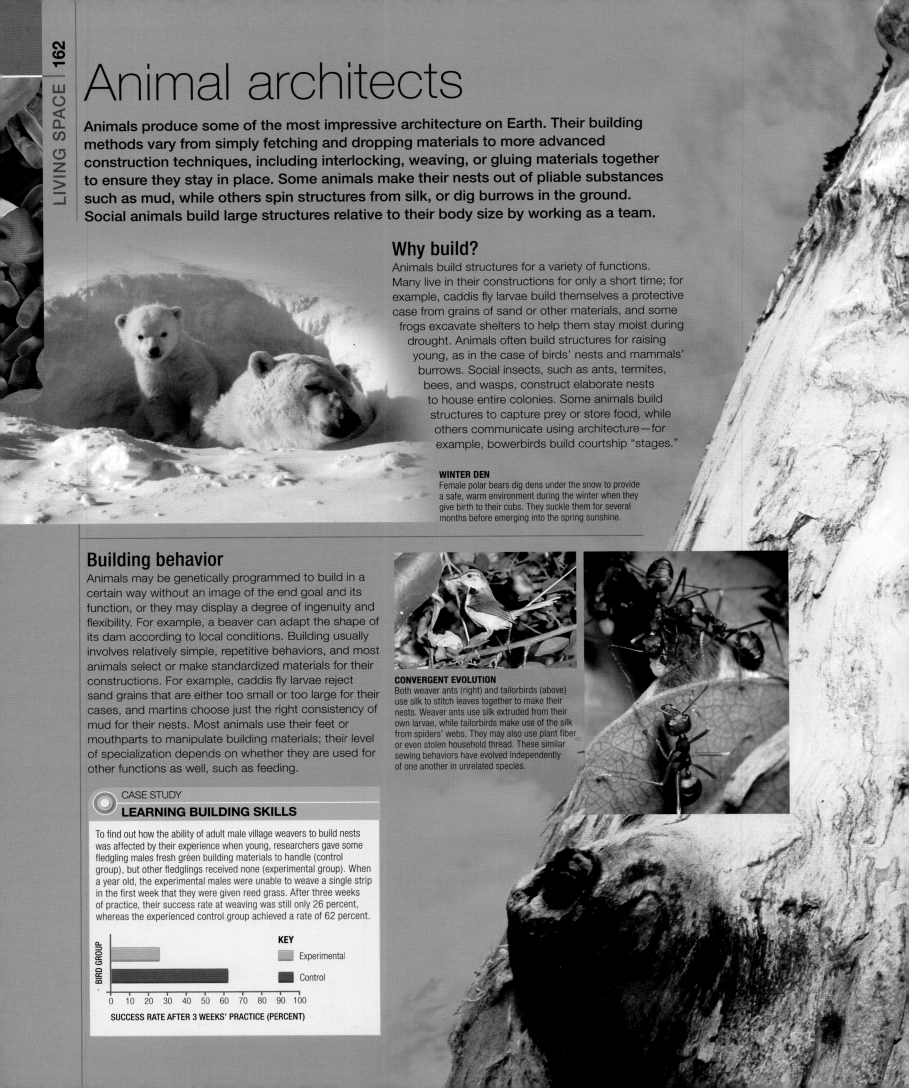

CAVITY NESTER
A pair of northern flickers takes between one and two weeks to excavate a cavity in a tree, where they lay their eggs and rear their chicks. Abandoned flicker nests create homes for other cavity nesters.

Building materials

The natural world provides numerous organic and mineral building materials, such as grasses for weaver nests and trees for beaver lodges, sand and pebbles for many fish nests, and the earth itself for burrows. Some materials require little in the way of processing, but others need to be manipulated or mixed with other substances, such as saliva or water, before being used for building. Many animals secrete building materials, such as silk, mucus, or wax, from glands in their bodies. Some use materials derived from others in their constructions, for example many birds collect soft feathers or fur to line their nests, whereas others find spider silk with which to build them. Animals can be very choosy about the materials they use in their architecture, selecting particular colors, for example.

⬤ MATERIALS AND STRUCTURES

PROVIDED BY THE ENVIRONMENT
Paper wasps chew fibers from dead wood to make a paper pulp with which they construct their intricate chambered nest, which is resistant to water. Male featherfin cichlids pile sand into a nest that also serves as an arena for displaying to prospective mates. Mute swans collect reeds and other bankside vegetation to build their nests.

PAPER WASP

FEATHERFIN CICHLID

MUTE SWAN

PROVIDED BY THE ANIMAL
Silkmoth caterpillars spin a cocoon of silk around themselves for pupation. Spiders also use silk, but for building webs. Termites mix saliva with mud to construct the walls of their termite mounds. Cave swiftlets also use spittle to build their nests. Other animal-derived materials include beeswax and mucus, which is used by some frogs for foam nests.

TERMITE

CALLETA SILKMOTH

PROVIDED BY ANOTHER ANIMAL
Hermit crabs take over the empty shells of marine mollusks, including the edible periwinkle. As the crab grows, it moves into progressively larger shells. Many animals live in cavities that were created by another species; for example, the elf owl nests in old woodpecker holes in the stems of cacti. Increasingly, humans provide homes for wildlife, such as a bird house for a colony of purple martins.

HERMIT CRAB

ELF OWL

PURPLE MARTIN

Stone walls

Hard corals

The world's most impressive underwater constructions are built by colonies of tiny invertebrates. Anthozoan coral polyps, most measuring only a few millimeters across, secrete skeletons of aragonite—a form of calcium carbonate—as they grow. Over time, the skeletons build up into structures known as coral reefs. Coral reefs are typically found in shallow, clear water around tropical

CORAL REEF
Corals take different forms according to how the polyps grow and secrete their skeleton. Over time, reefs erode and are compacted to form limestone.

coasts or on top of sea mounts (the summits of underwater volcanoes). This is because corals require abundant sunlight for their symbiotic algae, zooxanthellae, to be able to photosynthesize and provide them with nutrients. Corals grow asexually by budding or division (see p.328). In addition, corals may reproduce sexually (see p.333). The resulting larvae eventually settle on the ocean floor and grow into new polyps.

1,240 miles The length of the Great Barrier Reef, the world's largest reef system

(see p.328)
(see p.333)

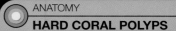

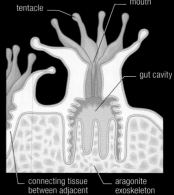

ANATOMY
HARD CORAL POLYPS

Each polyp sits in a cuplike exoskeleton of aragonite. Adjacent polyps are linked to one another by connective tissue. Tentacles surround the central mouth, through which food is taken in and waste is ejected. The mouth leads to the gut cavity. The tentacles bear stinging cells called nematocysts, which are used to paralyze or kill prey.

tentacle — mouth

gut cavity

connecting tissue between adjacent polyps — aragonite exoskeleton

VISIBLE FROM SPACE
The 3,000 or so individual reefs and 900 islands that compose the Great Barrier Reef can be seen by satellite. The reef is located in the Coral Sea, off the coast of Queensland, Australia.

Delicate case

Paper nautilus

The female paper nautilus (or knobby argonaut) secretes a paper-thin calcareous shell that serves as a shelter for the animal and a brood chamber for its eggs. The paper nautilus is actually a type of octopus, only distantly related to the true *Nautilus* species, and its shell lacks the gas-filled chambers found in *Nautilus* shells. The paper nautilus's egg case is usually 4½–6 in (12–15 cm) long but may reach more than 10 in (25 cm). It is secreted by the web between a pair of the animal's eight arms and is enlarged along the outer edge as the paper nautilus grows.

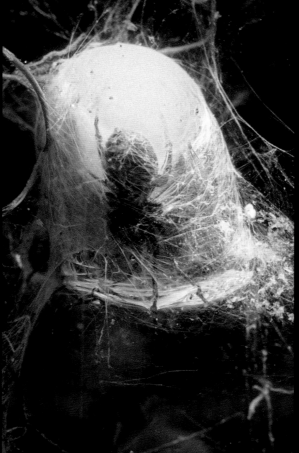

Argonauta nodosa
↔ 4–12 in/10–30 cm (female), 1¼–1½ in/3–4 cm (male)
⊙ Surface waters of Southern Hemisphere oceans, from the Indo-Pacific to the east coast of South America.
▭ Octopus with tentacles covered with suckers. Chromatophores in the skin allow it to change color from red to silver. Only females possess a shell.

Diving bell

Water spider

The water spider is able to spend its whole life beneath the water's surface, thanks to its own supply of air. It spins a web that is anchored to underwater vegetation, and then fills it by returning repeatedly from the surface with air bubbles. This "diving bell" serves as a place to breathe, hide from predators, consume prey, and breed. Male water spiders build their diving bells adjacent to those of females and break through to the adjacent bell when ready to mate. The female creates a silken cocoon around 30–70 eggs at the top of her diving bell. Water spiders may seal their bell when hibernating and build a separate bell elsewhere in which to shed their skin.

SILKEN RETREAT
The water spider rarely needs to replenish the air supply in its diving bell, because oxygen diffuses in and carbon dioxide diffuses out.

Argyroneta aquatica
↔ ¼–½ in (0.8–1.5 cm)
⊙ Ponds, streams, ditches, and shallow lakes in northern and central Europe and northern Asia.
▭ Brown-gray above water; takes on a silvery sheen underwater because air bubbles are trapped against the body.

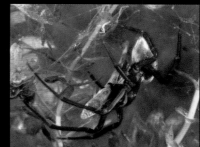

HUNTING UNDERWATER
Water spiders wait for prey, such as insects and small fish, to get close to their underwater lair. They swim out and subdue their prey with venomous jaws, before returning to their diving bell to eat it.

Complex web

Black and yellow garden spider

The black and yellow garden spider is one of several species of orb-web spiders, which weave relatively large, circular webs that are suspended vertically to catch prey. The black and yellow garden spider spins a web that is up to 2 ft (60 cm) in diameter and positioned 2–8 ft (60–240 cm) above the ground. Orb-web spiders have three claws on each foot, to help them handle the threads while spinning. Silk is extruded from several spinnerets on the underside of the spider's abdomen. The spinnerets are served by different glands that produce silk of different types and thicknesses. For example, sticky thread is used for prey-catching parts of the web. Orb-web spiders typically consume much of their web each evening and rebuild it anew for the next day.

Argiope aurantia

⬌ ³⁄₈–1¼ in/9–28 mm (female); ³⁄₁₆–³⁄₈ in/ 5–9 mm (male)
☀ Sunny habitats, from southern Canada, through the US, Mexico, and Central America south to Costa Rica.
📖 Oval abdomen bears striking yellow markings on black. Black legs with red or yellow near the body.

30 The number of minutes it takes most orb-web spiders to build an entire web.

CONSTRUCTING AN ORB WEB
First, the spider connects two structures with a strand of silk forming a bridge line or primary thread. Then it begins the web by constructing scaffolding lines, which connect the structure to its support. Next, the spider makes a frame of threads radiating from a central hub. Then it attaches a temporary spiral to the radial threads. Finally, the web is completed by the spider spinning close spirals of sticky thread.

ORB WEB
The spider sits and waits on its web for an insect to become trapped. The central, strengthened part of the web is called the stabilimentum.

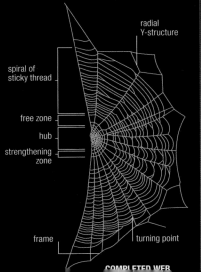

radial Y-structure
spiral of sticky thread
free zone
hub
strengthening zone
frame
turning point
COMPLETED WEB

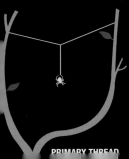

PRIMARY THREAD

SCAFFOLDING LINES

CENTRAL HUB

TEMPORARY SPIRAL

Multipurpose tower block
African mound-building termites

For such small insects, termites construct incredibly large and elaborate structures in which to live. A mature termite mound may be home to 3–5 million individual termites. Inside, there is a complex network of chambers, passageways, and ventilation channels that extend above and below ground level. The mound has specific areas designated for waste, for storing and growing food, and for egg laying and larval development. The queen termite resides in a royal chamber, built to surround her pulsating, egg-producing abdomen. Worker termites tend to her, removing the eggs as she lays them to nursery chambers, where they develop. The queen termite secretes a pheromone from her body, which stimulates the workers to build pillars, arches, and eventually walls around her to create the royal chamber. Pheromone deposits may also help direct the construction of walls and passageways within the termite mound.

Macrotermes species

📏 Up to 1¼ in (3 cm)

🌐 Savanna in Africa and Southeast Asia.

📖 Worker termites are usually pale brown to white and are blind and wingless. Reproductive forms are often darker and have compound eyes and two pairs of wings.

TOWER BLOCK

Macrotermes termite mounds can reach heights of 20–23 ft (6–7 m). In dry areas, vertical shafts are excavated to reach the water table, which can be as much as 150 ft (45 m) below the ground.

AIR-CONDITIONING SYSTEM

Termite mounds have an ingenious, built-in ventilation system: variations in pressure or temperature cause air to circulate, cooling and freshening the colony. Wind, passing over openings on top of the mound, decreases the air pressure, drawing clean air into openings at the mound's base and through its passageways.

warm, stale air exits ventilation shaft

cool, fresh air enters mound

fungus garden

royal cell

living chambers and nursery areas

FUNGUS GARDEN

Many termites cultivate fungal fruiting bodies on which they and their nymphs feed. The fungi thrive on the cellulose contained in chewed plant matter supplied by the termites.

Paper houses
Common wasp

Common wasps are social insects that build nests out of paper to house their colonies. Only the queen wasps (the sole egg layers) survive the winter to found a new colony in spring. They select a suitable site for the nest, either underground in an abandoned animal burrow or in a sheltered location, such as a garden shed. There they begin to construct a nest from chewed wood either from nearby trees or wood. The wood pulp dries into paper, a remarkably strong yet light building material. Once complete, the nest typically has a number of horizontal layers of cells that open downward. These house the eggs and developing larvae of the colony. Surrounding these brood cells are a series of spiral chambers, which provide strength to the nest as well as trapping air for insulation.

Vespa vulgaris
 ³⁄₈–¹⁄₂ in (1–1.5 cm) (worker); ¹⁄₂–³⁄₄ in (1.5–2 cm) (queen)

Nests underground or in buildings near yards, woodland, and meadows in Europe, Asia, North Africa, and North America.

Wasp with black and yellow markings, a distinct waist between the thorax and abdomen, and two pairs of wings. The sting is on the tip of the abdomen.

NATURAL CALLIPERS
Common wasps use their jaws to chew wood and place it in position on the nest, then they use their mouthparts to work the pulp to the required thickness. The jaws of wasps that use paper to build their nests are shorter and broader than those of wasps that build with mud.

EARLY STAGES
A single queen starts by constructing a stalk from which the nest is suspended. She then begins to add cells, laying a single egg into each one. When fully grown, the workers complete the nest.

CURVED WALLS
As the colony grows, the workers gradually demolish the innermost walls of the nest and build new ones around the outside. A completed nest can house 5,000–10,000 wasps.

Wax combs
Honey bee

Honey bee colonies live in beehives formed from several layers of honeycomb. The honeycomb's cells are used to house the colony's developing brood and to store food in the form of pollen and honey. Worker bees build the comb out of wax, which is secreted from glands in their abdomen and manipulated with their mouthparts. Workers produce different cells according to their intended purpose. Cells for the larvae of drones (whose only duty is to mate with the queen) are larger than those for worker larvae; and those that will contain future queens are even bigger, oval in shape, and are arranged vertically rather than horizontally.

Apis mellifera
¹⁄₂–1 in (1.5–2.5 cm)

Worldwide. Some subspecies are native to Europe, Africa, Middle East, and Asia. Introduced to North and South America.

Hairy, yellow-brown body. In workers, the ovipositor is modified to form a sting.

>> 185, 424–25, 463

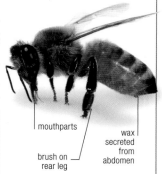

mouthparts

brush on rear leg

wax secreted from abdomen

WORKER BEE

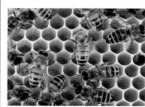

HONEYCOMB
Honeycomb consists of sheets of regular, six-sided cells. When a cell is filled with mature honey, or when a larva is ready to pupate, each individual cell is capped with a wax lid. Wild bee colonies (right) live in hollow trees or rock cavities.

Leaf nests
Weaver ants

Weaver ants, also called green or tree ants, use living leaves to construct their nests in the tops of trees. The nests provide shelter for the workers and developing young. A single colony of weaver ants can consist of 100,000–500,000 individuals and may have up to 150 different nests in 12 or more trees. One of the colony's nests will contain several egg-producing queen ants. This nest is characterized by having more ant trails connecting with it than any other. Workers travel along these trails to distribute eggs to other nests. At the edge of the colony's territory there are barrack nests, where older worker ants live and defend the boundary. Weaver ants are voracious predators of pests that damage fruit crops, such as citrus fruits, mangoes, and cashews. Fruit growers therefore introduce weaver ant colonies into their plantations and install bamboo bridges between trees to help the ants move around. The ants reduce the need for chemical insecticides.

CHAIN GANG
When an ant finds two leaves with sufficient flexibility to form a nest, chains of its fellow worker ants line up and straddle both leaves, pulling their edges close. They hold them there while other workers "stick" the leaves together.

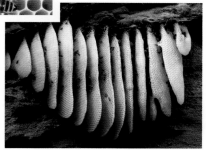

GLUE TUBES
Adult weaver ants use sticky silk extruded by the larvae to join leaves together when nest building. Unlike other ant species, the larvae do not use their silk to create cocoons.

GREEN HOUSE
Once several leaves have been glued into place, the nest is complete. Worker ants move in with some of the colony's eggs, which they tend through the larval and pupa stages to adulthood.

Oecophylla species
About ¹⁄₄ in (6 mm)

Trees in tropical forests of Africa, Asia, and Australia.

Relatively large, red-brown ants. Distinct separation between head, thorax, and abdomen. Six legs attached to the thoracic region. Antennae have 12 segments.

150 The number of nests that may be found in a mature colony of weaver ants

Second-hand homes

Shell-brooding cichlid

The shell-brooding cichlid uses empty snail shells as nurseries for incubating its eggs. The female cichlids are attracted to nests of shells collected by the much larger males. Larges males have an advantage over smaller males in territorial disputes and when competing for shells. Conversely, it is an advantage for females to be small, so they can fit deep inside the snail shells, where they lay their eggs and remain for up to two weeks to brood them until the hatchlings are ready to leave. There are also some medium-sized males that will sneak into a resident male's territory, where as many as 14 females may be nesting in different shells, in an attempt to mate with the females. Another tactic is employed by dwarf males, which are small enough to enter a shell to fertilize the female's eggs.

Neolamprologus callipterus

- 4½ in (12 cm) (male); 1¾ in (4.5 cm) (female)
- Fresh water of Lake Tanganyika, central eastern Africa.
- Gray-brown fish with elongated dorsal fin. Males are much bigger than females (sometimes up to 27 times larger).

SHELL COLLECTORS
Male cichlids collect empty snail shells and carry them back to a nesting area, which they attempt to defend from intruders. The largest males tend to have more shells and consequently attract more females than smaller males.

Foam nursery

Gray foam-nest frog

The gray foam-nest frog breeds during a brief window of time in the rainy season, when seasonal pools are available. A mating pair finds a location on a branch in a tree overhanging a pool. There, the male begins to create a nest by whipping fluid (a secretion produced by the female) into a foamy substance with his long legs and webbed feet. The pair may be joined by single males that take part in the nest building; in addition, these males release sperm as the female deposits her eggs into the foam. On average, the nests of the gray foam-nest frog contain approximately 850 eggs, which take around 3½ days to hatch into tadpoles at a temperature of 77° F (25° C). The tadpoles live in the foam for another two days before emerging simultaneously and dropping into the pool below.

Chiromantis xerampelina

- 1¾–3 in (4.5–7.5 cm) (male); 2¼–3½ in (6–9 cm) (female)
- Subtropical and tropical forest, savanna, shrubland, and grassland in central and southern East Africa.
- Gray-brown mottled frog with large eyes.

WHIPPING UP A NEST
The female lays her eggs into the foam whipped up by the males (top). The outer layer of the foam hardens into a nest around a moist interior. Oxygen diffuses through the foam, enabling the tadpoles to breathe until they drop into a pool of water (above).

Animal shelter

Gopher tortoise

The gopher tortoise uses its strong, stout forelegs and wide, flat claws to dig burrows, about 15 ft (4.6 m) long and 6½ ft (2 m) deep, in sandy, well-drained soil. A tortoise may have several active and inactive burrows within its territory, retreating underground to avoid predators and the midday sun as well as to sleep at night and hibernate. A total of 302 invertebrate and 60 vertebrate species have been recorded as using gopher tortoise burrows for shelter, including frogs, lizards, snakes, and rats.

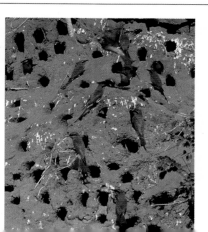

Gopherus polyphemus

- 10 in (25 cm)
- Sandy ridges, sand dunes, and longleaf pine forests in the southeastern US.
- Tortoise with a brown-gray upper shell, dull yellow-tan undershell, and gray-brown soft parts.

Solid structure

Hamerkop

Also known as the hammerhead, the hamerkop builds the largest roofed nest of any bird. The nest is built in a fork between tree branches. First, a platform is made out of sticks, and then the sides are built up into a deep basin. Next, a domed roof of sticks and mud is added. The small entrance is usually located at the side near the base, as a precaution against predators. Both the entrance tunnel and the nest chamber are lined with mud. The nest can reach 6½ ft (2 m) high and wide and may take up to six weeks to build. When complete, it can support the weight of a grown man on its roof. The whole structure is decorated with unusual objects such as feathers, snakeskin, bones, and even man-made items. A pair of hamerkops may build several nests within their territory, but use only one. Other birds, such as eagle owls and Egyptian geese, often move into the spare nests.

Scopus umbretta

- 18½–22 in (47–56 cm)
- Freshwater wetland habitats in sub-Saharan Africa, Madagascar, and southwestern Arabian Peninsula.
- Medium-sized wading bird related to pelicans. Brown in color with a strong bill and large, shaggy crest at the back of the head.

TEAM WORK
Hamerkops mate for life, and a pair labors for about fours hours a day to build their massive nest. When it is finished, the female lays between three and nine brown eggs in the nest chamber.

Sandbank burrows

Carmine bee-eater

Carmine bee-eaters excavate horizontal burrows in vertical sandbanks along rivers. Their colonies may contain thousands of individuals, often divided into smaller groups known as clans. When starting to excavate a nest burrow, a bird flies repeatedly at the bank beak first, until it makes a slight depression onto which it can cling. It then uses its bill and feet to dig a narrow tunnel measuring 3¼–6½ ft (1–2 m) in length. Two of the carmine bee-eater's toes are fused at the base, making them perfect for using as a shovel. Immature birds without a mate may help their parents dig a new tunnel.

Merops nubicus

- 10½ in (27 cm)
- Lowland river valleys, floodplains, and riverine forests in sub-equatorial Africa.
- Colorful bird with a bright orange-red back, pink-red chest, blue-green crown, and blue undertail. The southern subspecies has a pink-red throat, the northern subspecies a blue-green throat.

High-rise living

White stork

The white stork builds one of the largest nests of all bird species. A pair mates for life and tends to return to the same nest site every year, adding a new layer of sticks and earth to the huge nesting platform that was used the previous year. Both males and females take part in building the nest, although the male collects most of the materials. In addition to sticks, he may select rags and paper discarded by humans. Birds that remain faithful to their nest sites tend to have a lower risk of breeding failure than pairs that start anew elsewhere. White storks also help boost the survival of their eggs and chicks by bringing fresh cattle dung to the nest to help keep it warm.

Ciconia ciconia

■ 3¼–4 ft (1–1.2 m)

◆ Breeds in Europe, northwest Africa, and southwest Asia; winters in tropical to southern Africa and the Indian subcontinent. Inhabits open farmland close to marshy wetland feeding areas.

▭ Large wading bird. Predominantly white with black flight feathers on its wings and a red bill and legs.

SAFE FROM PREDATORS

At Los Berruecos in Spain's Extremadura region, white storks nest out of harm's way on the top of dramatic granite boulders.

MAN-MADE ROOST

White storks often build their nests on the roofs of buildings, such as churches or towers. Because of their close association with human habitation, storks have long been considered a symbol of good luck and are also the fabled deliverers of new babies to people. In many parts of Europe, people construct lofty platforms to encourage the birds to nest. Nests on buildings tend to last longer than those in trees because buildings can better withstand the nest's weight; one nest taken down from a cathedral weighed more than three-quarters of a ton.

Tree house

Pileated woodpecker

The pileated woodpecker uses its strong bill to excavate large nest cavities in trees, typically 14¾–80 ft (4.5–24 m) above the ground. It may excavate a new nest each year or it may reuse an existing hole for several years. The trees used for nests vary according to region, but include aspen, western larch, ponderosa pine, and Douglas fir. They are often dead and already hollow, making them easier to drill into than living, solid trees. The nests frequently face east or south, to benefit from the warmth of the sun. Other birds, such as American kestrels, wood ducks, and screech owls, may use old pileated woodpecker holes for nesting once they have been vacated. Pileated woodpeckers also chip away at trees to uncover food in the form of carpenter ants and beetle larvae that live in the wood. They pick these up with their sticky, barbed tongues. Woodpeckers' feet are adapted for walking up vertical tree trunks by having two toes that point backward.

SPITTING SAWDUST

Both sexes assist with building the nest cavity, which is lined with wood chippings. Between three and five eggs are laid and incubated alternately by each parent.

Dryocopus pileatus

■ 16½ in (42 cm)

◆ Coniferous and deciduous forests of North America, particularly southern Canada and the eastern US.

▭ Large woodpecker with predominantly black body and brilliant red head crest. Males have a red moustache extending backward from the bill.

SHOCK ABSORBERS

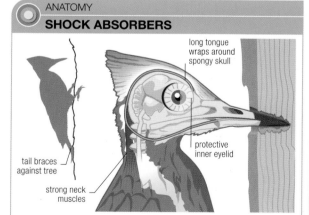

long tongue wraps around spongy skull

protective inner eyelid

tail braces against tree

strong neck muscles

Woodpeckers hammer trees 20 times a second at a speed of 15 mph (24 kph). They have several adaptations to allow their bodies to deal with the shock of hitting such a hard substance so fast and furiously: the chisel-shaped bill is anchored to the skull by a thick bone to prevent jarring; the skull is relatively thick and formed of spongy bone that acts as a cushion for the brain; the muscles behind their bills and in their necks contract just prior to the impact to help absorb the pounding and transmit the shock through the whole body to protect the head; and a third inner eyelid closes to restrain the eyeball and shield the eye from flying splinters.

COMPETING FOR FEMALES
A male southern masked weaver displays by flapping his wings beneath his finished nest (bottom left). A rival male has only just started his nest (center), but he may yet be successful, because females prefer fresh green nests to older brown ones.

Woven globes

Southern masked weaver

The southern masked weaver bends, knots, and stitches pliable grasses into a globe-shaped nest suspended from a tree branch. Groups of male southern masked weavers build their nests in the same tree, selecting positions at the ends of twigs as protection from tree-climbing predators, such as snakes. Once the initial hoop of woven grass is in place, the weaver starts to construct the nesting chamber. The length of the bird's reach determines the size of the spherical chamber, and a porchlike entrance is added once the nesting chamber is complete. When a female moves in, she lines the nest with soft grasses and feathers before laying a clutch of about five eggs.

Male weavers prefer to select fresh green vegetation for their nests. Young leaves are more flexible than older ones and can be woven more easily. Also, the females prefer nests made from newer materials. Weavers use a complex array of fastenings, including spiral binding and knots such as the half hitch, overhand, and slipknot. Birds that are experienced in handling fresh green building materials are better able to construct their woven nests than those without similar experience. Male weaver birds can fly a total distance of 230 miles (370 km) to collect materials when building their nests.

Nest weaving has evolved independently at least twice in birds—once among the weaver birds of Europe, Asia, and Africa, and a second time among the orioles, oropendolas, and caciques (both are New World blackbirds) of North and South America. In the case of the weaver birds, it is the males that construct the nests, whereas the female oropendolas and caciques do most of the nest building.

>>01　　　　>>02　　　　>>03

WORK IN PROGRESS
>>01 The male southern masked weaver begins making its nest by selecting a thin branch from which the nest will hang.　>>02 Next, it constructs a vertical ring or hoop of woven grass strips.　>>03 It continues to add to the hoop by winding and knotting more strips with its bill.

Ploceus velatus

- 4½–5½ in (11–14 cm)
- Southern African shrubland, savanna, grassland, open woodland, inland wetland, and semi-desert.
- Female is greenish yellow; male in breeding coloration has a black face, throat, and beak, a bright yellow crown and chest, a greenish yellow back, and a red eye.

230 miles The total distance traveled by male weaver birds to collect fresh plant material when nest building.

SIMILAR SPECIES
There are around 60 species of weaver birds in the genus *Ploceus* and all share similar traits. To collect nest material, male weavers, for instance the village weaver (*P. cucullatus,* above), land near the base of a leaf, cut into it, and fly off with a long, thin strip. Female weavers, such as the little weaver (*P. luteolus,* right), inspect a potential mate's nest before deciding whether to stay and breed.

Decorated stage

Vogelkop bowerbird

Male Vogelkop bowerbirds build elaborate display stages out of sticks in order to attract mates. Their constructions are large and impressive, built on the ground, and measuring up to 6 ft (1.8 m) across and 4 ft (1.2 m) high. Populations of Vogelkop bowerbirds differ in their bower design and taste for decoration. For example, in the Arfak mountains, they tend to build huts with arched entrances, which they adorn with brightly colored flowers and fruits; while in the Fakfak mountains, they construct tall spires or maypoles and decorate them with relatively drab decorations, such as snail shells, nuts, and fungi.

Amblyornis inornata

⬌ 10 in (25 cm)

⊙ Mountain habitats of the Vogelkop Peninsula of Irian Jaya, Indonesia.

📖 Plain, olive-brown bird.

GROWING FAMILY
Between 6 and 12 eggs are laid in the cosy nest. Once the chicks have hatched, both parents work hard to provide their growing brood with insects. Relatives, whose own breeding attempts have failed, sometimes help.

Expandable home

Long-tailed tit

The long-tailed tit builds a globe-shaped nest out of spiders' webs, mosses, lichens, and feathers. Usually placed in shrubs, such as gorse, bramble, blackthorn, or hawthorn, the nest is held together by the small, rough leaves of the mosses, which hook onto the loops of the stretchy spider silk. As the brood grows, the nest expands to accommodate them. The outside of the nest is covered with silvery lichens and white spider cocoons, both of which provide camouflage by reflecting light off the exterior. The nest is lined inside with a soft, warm layer of 2,000 or more feathers, which can comprise about 40 percent of the nest's mass. Long-tailed tits adjust the thickness of the insulating feather layer in their nest according to prevailing environmental conditions, the most important being ambient temperature.

Aegithalos caudatus

⬌ 5–6 in (13–15 cm)

⊙ Deciduous woodland, hedgerows, and scrub in Europe and Asia.

📖 Small songbird, black and brown above, off-white below, with a white crown on the top of the head.

Mud nest

House martin

House martins build a deep, cup-shaped nest of mud underneath the eaves of buildings. Successive layers of mud are built up and the nest is lined with soft materials, including grass and hair. A narrow entrance hole at the top allows the house martins in but prevents other larger birds, such as sparrows, from entering and occupying the nest. Relatives of the house martin, such as other martins and swallows, show an interesting spectrum of nest-building activities. Their ancestors were burrowers, a behavior that is still followed by bank swallows. Others, such as the purple martin and tree swallow, make use of existing cavities. Barn and cliff swallows both construct nests from mud like the house martin, but the barn swallow's nest is a relatively shallow cup perched on top of a beam, while the cliff swallow sculpts a spherical nest with a projecting entrance tunnel.

Delichon urbica

⬌ 5 in (13 cm)

⊙ Open habitats in Europe, North Africa, and temperate Asia in the Northern Hemisphere summer. Overwinters in similar habitats in sub-Saharan Africa and tropical Asia.

📖 Blue-black head, back, and tail, and a white rump and underparts. Shallow fork to the tail.

BUILDING WITH MUD
House martins gather pellets of mud in their bills from nearby ponds, streams, and puddles before adding them to the nest. Both sexes participate in nest building, and several breeding pairs may construct their nests close together.

Thatched roof

Sociable weaver

Sociable weavers live communally in groups of up to 500 birds in the avian equivalent of an apartment block. The huge nests resemble haystacks placed in the branches of acacia trees. The birds work year-round to maintain their nests because since the thick, thatched roofs provide protection from the cold winter nights and hot summer days that are typical of the desert. There may be up to 300 openings in the underside of the nest, each leading to a tunnel that terminates in a chamber. Sociable weavers share these chambers with other birds, such as the South African pygmy falcon, chats, finches, and lovebirds, while vultures, owls, and eagles may build their nests on the roof.

Philetairus socius

⬌ 5½ in (14 cm)

⊙ Open savanna grassland and thorn scrubland in northern South Africa and southern Namibia.

📖 A buff-brown bird with buff-white underparts and a black chin.

BUILDING MATERIAL
Weavers use various materials when building their nests. The initial structure consists of large twigs and stems, into which grasses are poked; sharp spikes of straw deter predators from the entrances, and the chambers are lined with soft fur and cotton.

Hydro engineering

North American beaver

North American beavers are masters at controlling water through construction. In order to have sufficiently deep ponds in which to build their homes, known as lodges, they first build dams to control the flow of water and raise its level. The largest beaver dam so far discovered was at Three Forks in Montana; it measured 2,130 ft (650 m) long, 13 ft (4 m) high, and was 23 ft (7 m) thick at the base. In addition to dams, beavers construct canals from favored feeding areas, along which they float food back to the lodge. Beavers can have a positive effect on the ecology and movement of water in their environment. Their dams can help control soil erosion and flooding, while their ponds provide valuable wetland habitats for other wildlife. However, their activities can also be harmful. They may cause flooding, for example if they block drains beneath roads, and there may also be economic damage to tree crops.

The ponds and lodges help protect beavers against predators such as wolves, lynx, and bears. They also provide shelter from the cold in winter. When the ponds freeze over, the beavers remain in their lodges or move freely under the ice.

CHISELING AWAY
Beavers have strong skulls and large teeth, perfect for cutting through tree trunks and eating the bark and cambium (the soft layer immediately beneath the bark). Their teeth continue growing throughout their lives, but are worn down by gnawing.

Castor canadensis

◧ 35–46 in (90–117 cm)

◐ Wetland, streams, and rivers in North America, except far north of Canada and parts of southern US and Mexico.

▭ Large rodent with a waterproof brown-black coat, short, rounded ears, and a broad, flat, scaly tail.

BEAVER LODGE
A beaver lodge may be located on an island behind the dam, on the edge of the pond, or on the shore of a lake. Some beavers excavate burrows rather than build a lodge.

POND AND DAM
The shape of a beaver dam is determined by the speed of water flow. In slow water the dam is straight, but in faster rivers it is curved in order to make it stronger.

roof of lodge covered with piles of sticks and sealed with mud

sleeping chamber above water, where mother beaver nurses her kits

underwater passage

beaver packs mud to seal dam

food cache of stored wood for winter eating

heavy stones brace dam

MAINTENANCE WORK
Beavers are quick to rebuild their dams if they become damaged. They drag tree trunks by their teeth and carry mud and stones in their forepaws.

House of straw

Eurasian harvest mouse

Pregnant female Eurasian harvest mice weave spherical nests in which to give birth and raise their young. The nests are typically built 12–51 in (30–130 cm) above the ground, attached to the stalks of reeds, cereal crops, and grasses. The mouse usually builds at night—first, she shreds grass leaves with her teeth, then she weaves the strands into a hollow ball that measures approximately 4 in (10 cm) in diameter. More grasses are threaded into the structure to build up several layers, and the finished nest is lined with a soft bed of shredded leaves and grass. The nest may have several entrances, but the female keeps these closed throughout the first week after she gives birth. Litters usually consist of five or six young.

Micromys minutus

◄► 2–3¼ in (5–8 cm)

◉ Reed beds, hay meadows, cereal crops, and grassy hedgerows in Europe (except most of Scandinavia) and northern Asia.

◻ Small mouse with a blunt nose, short, rounded ears, and a prehensile tail. Golden reddish brown fur with a white underside.

STAYING ALERT
Their mounds afford the prairie dogs a good view of the surrounding prairie. They maintain a lookout for potential predators, which may include coyotes, bobcats, eagles, and hawks. If they spot a predator approaching, they give an alarm call and dive underground.

Underground town

Black-tailed prairie dog

Colonies of black-tailed prairie dogs live in extensive underground burrow systems called towns. Towns are divided into wards, and the wards into coteries. Each coterie is home to several closely related females, an unrelated adult male, and their offspring. A coterie may have as many as 50 or 60 entrances into the burrow system. The burrows are on average 16½–33 ft (5–10 m) long and 6½–9¾ ft (2–3 m) beneath the ground. Some entrances are surrounded by a mound of earth 3¼ ft (1 m) high, resembling the rim of a volcanic crater. The mound helps ventilate the burrow system by altering the air flow over it, causing fresh air to be drawn through the tunnels. Its steep sides also help protect the animals from predators and flash flooding. Other entrances have a shallower, domed mound, and some have no mound at all.

Cynomys ludovicianus

◄► 14–17 in (35–43 cm)

◉ Dry, open, short- to mid-grass prairies from central Texas to southern Canada.

◻ Rodent with brownish red coat and white underbelly. Tail has a black tip. Body hairs have white tips in summer and black tips in winter. Small eyes and ears.

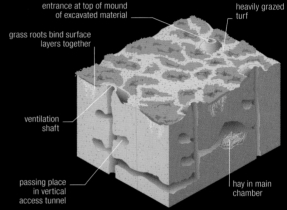

entrance at top of mound of excavated material
heavily grazed turf
grass roots bind surface layers together
ventilation shaft
passing place in vertical access tunnel
hay in main chamber

400 million The largest number of animals ever found in a single prairie dog town, in Texas.

BURROW SYSTEM
Black-tailed prairie dogs spend time underground in their burrow systems at night, in the heat of the day in summer, and during inclement weather in winter.

Night nest

Chimpanzee

Most nights, chimpanzees build a new nest in which to sleep. Their beds are usually high up in trees, 33–66 ft (10–20 m) off the ground, safely out of the reach of predators, with females nesting higher than males. They use tree branches and leaves to construct a round platform measuring between 24–31 in (60–80 cm) in diameter. Nest building can take as little as one to five minutes, depending on the experience of the builder. Chimpanzees generally sleep for about 12 hours each night and also rest in nests during the day, between bouts of foraging. In addition, they may retreat to bed if they are ill or injured. Infants sleep with their mothers until a new sibling arrives, at which point they start to build their own nests, often practicing their technique on the ground. Biologists can use the number of fresh nests in trees to estimate the number of chimpanzees in an area, while the noise of construction can also reveal their location. Gorillas and orangutans construct arboreal nests similar to those of chimpanzees, although gorillas also nest on the ground.

Pan troglodytes

◄► 29–37 in (73–95 cm)

◉ Gallery forest, rain forest, and woodland savanna across equatorial Africa.

◻ Ape with black hair, sometimes tinged with gray or brown. Infants have white tail tuft and face which darkens with age.

≫ 247, 454, 460, 465, 480–481

MAKING THE BED
First, the chimpanzee pulls several thick branches together and presses them down to make a stable platform. It then weaves thinner branches and twigs around the edge and uses broken twigs and leaves to provide padding for the center of the bed.

LAZING AROUND
The daytime nests of chimpanzees may be old rather than freshly built and are frequently in the same tree in which the animals have been feeding. They are often lower down than nighttime nests.

Honduran white bat

The Honduran white bat lives in rain forests containing plenty of *Heliconia* plants, and it uses their long, broad leaves to make tents under which it roosts. The bat nibbles through the veins on either side of the leaf midrib, causing the leaf to fold down to form an inverted V-shape. Each tent may be inhabited by between one and 12 bats, usually a single male and his harem of females. A colony of bats may have several tents scattered throughout its area of forest. The bats use the tents during protection from the elements, such as the sun and rain, and from predators, which include opossums and snakes. The green light filtering through the leaf onto the white fur of the bat makes them almost indistinguishable from their shelter. They are so confident in their camouflage that the bats will take flight only if they detect movement on the main stem of their *Heliconia* plant.

Ectophylla alba
- 1½–2 in (4–5 cm)
- Rain forest in lowland Central America, including parts of Honduras, Nicaragua, Costa Rica, and Panama.
- Small white bat with black wing membranes and yellow-orange facial features, including a triangular nose-leaf.

Ringed seal

All seals require access to the water's surface in order to breathe. When openings in the sea ice start to freeze over in the fall, ringed seals create breathing holes through the ice, using the claws of their front flippers, so that they can pop up for air. In the spring, females excavate lairs or caves out of snow that has accumulated in drifts above their breathing hole, a behavior that is unique among seals. Here, they give birth to a single pup and nurse it for about 40 days. The lair helps the pup survive the biting cold and offers some protection from predators. However, polar bears can detect the snow caves by their scent and sometimes break through the ceiling. An adult seal stands a chance of escape by diving into the water through its breathing hole, but if the pup is still too young to swim it becomes easy prey. Ringed seals often have more than one lair, with adjacent lairs up to 2¾ miles (4.5 km) apart.

BREATHING HOLE
Ringed seals maintain breathing holes in a layer of ice up to 6½ ft (2 m) thick by digging with their strong claws.

Phoca hispida
- 2½–5¼ ft (0.8–1.6 m)
- Ice floes, landfast ice, and open water in the Arctic Ocean, northern North Pacific, northern North Atlantic, Baltic Sea, Bering Sea, and Sea of Okhotsk.
- Predominantly gray seal with whitish rings on its back, a small head, and a short snout.

Earthworks

European mole

European moles spend most of their lives underground. They are able to dig about 66 ft (20 m) of tunnels each day, throwing up characteristic mounds of discarded soil as they excavate, much to the chagrin of gardeners attempting to achieve the "perfect lawn." A single mole's tunnel system may cover an area up to ⅓ mile (0.5 km) across. They are solitary and territorial, behaving aggressively to their neighbors and taking over their tunnels if they leave or die. During the breeding season, between March and May, male moles may extend their burrows in search of mates. Females give birth to between two and seven young underground, where they remain for about five weeks before striking out overland to establish their own territories.

WORM TRAP
Moles immobilize earthworms that drop into their tunnel systems by delivering a bite to the head. Earthworms can sense the vibrations of a digging mole and will endeavor to get out of the way.

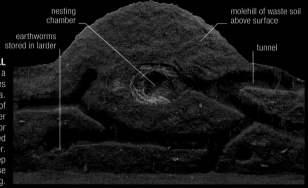

nesting chamber

molehill of waste soil above surface

earthworms stored in larder

tunnel

UNDER THE HILL
A fresh molehill is a sure sign that moles are present in an area. Beneath, a network of shallow and deeper tunnels leads to one or more nest chambers filled with dry plant matter. This is where moles sleep and where females raise their young.

Talpa europaea
- 4½–6½ in (11–16 cm)
- Rich, deep soils beneath arable fields, deciduous woodland, and permanent pasture in temperate Europe.
- Cylindrical body covered with black velvety fur and a bare nose with sensitive whiskers.

ANATOMY

DIGGING TOOL

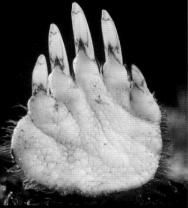

The mole's front paws are shaped like shovels, with five strong claws. They are permanently turned out in a perfect position for pushing soil aside. Moles also have other features that help them in their burrowing lifestyle—their tiny eyes are almost completely covered by fur, their nostrils open to the side rather than the front, and they have no external ears that might otherwise get filled with earth.

HUNTING AND FEEDING

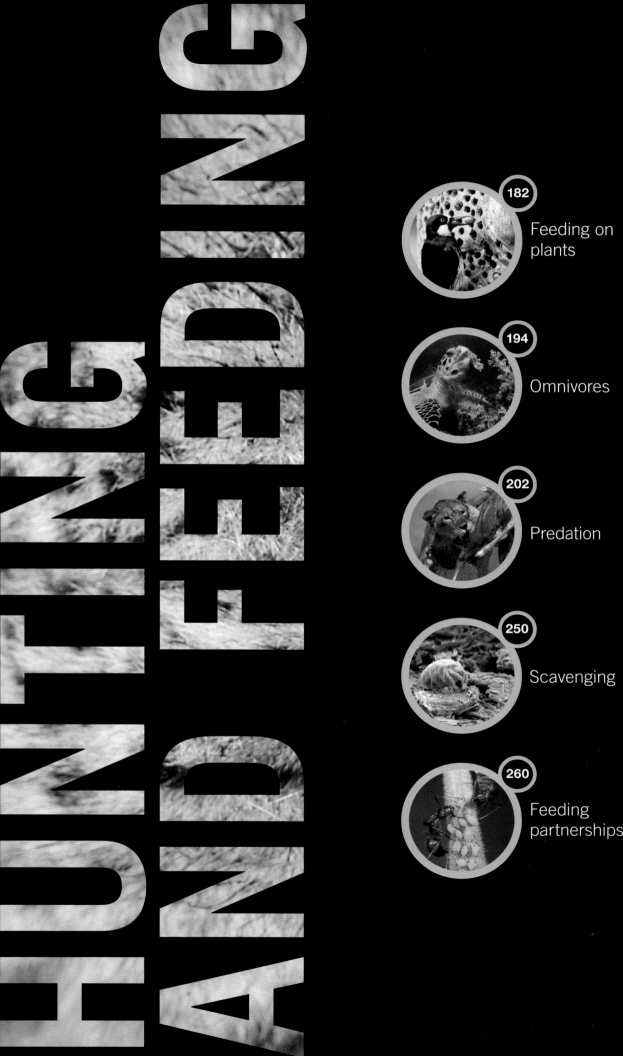

HUNTING AND FEEDING

Feeding is a fundamental need of almost all animals because they require food to provide energy for the various internal chemical processes essential for life. Even though the details of how food is obtained and what food is eaten may vary between animals, the basic processes involved are common to all of them. They must locate food, capture or gather it, process it (by chewing, for example), ingest it, and digest it. To achieve this, a range of feeding behaviors has evolved.

KEYSTONE SPECIES
The starfish *Pisaster ochraceus* feeds on herbivores and so controls biodiversity of rocky shores.

Hunger

The physiological motivation to eat—to replenish spent reserves, maintain a positive energy balance, or fatten up for an event such as migration or hibernation—is controlled by a part of the brain called the hypothalamus and by fluctuating levels of hormones. But there are also other motivations that drive animals to feed. Some may become conditioned to feed at a particular time of day or in response to a particular sight, smell, or taste. In some cases, simply coming across food is sufficient motivation to feed, particularly if food is scarce. For many social species, seeing group mates feeding is enough to stimulate feeding. In such situations, an animal may eat more food than it would if were it alone, and it is more likely to eat a novel food if others are eating it.

CHOOSY BEARS
Bears are more selective when food is abundant, choosing to eat only the most energy-rich parts of the fishes they catch. Quality is less important than quantity when food is scarce, and whole fishes are eaten.

Carnivores, herbivores, and omnivores

Animals can be classified according to their diet. Carnivores feed on other animals. To do so they must be able to locate, kill, and eat their prey, and so many have specialized prey-detection mechanisms, well-developed weapons, and exhibit specialized feeding behaviors, such as stalking and ambushing. Some carnivores feed on species far larger than themselves and so must cooperate with one another to bring down prey. Herbivores feed on plants, and many specialize in a particular part of the plant, such as fruits or leaves. Like carnivores, herbivores require special feeding adaptations, such as grinding teeth to chew tough plant material. Omnivores, scavengers, and detritivores (which feed on decaying organic matter) are generalists; they eat a wide variety of foodstuffs and therefore often (but not always) lack highly specialized feeding adaptations. Instead, they require behavioral and anatomical flexibility to locate, process, and utilize a wide variety of foods.

DUNG EATER
The dung of herbivores is an important component of the diet of this Egyptian vulture. The dung is rich in carotenoids, which give the facial skin of the bird its distinctive yellow color.

Food chains and webs

Feeding is essentially the transfer of energy from one organism, the prey, to another, the predator. The energy in an ecosystem originates from organisms that harness energy from the sun (plants) or from chemical reactions (deep-sea bacteria). These primary producers are eaten by primary consumers, which may in turn be eaten by other consumers. In this way energy is transferred through "chains" of organisms. Each step in the chain is called a trophic level. Typically, the bottom of a chain (primary producers) consists of a large number of organisms, whereas the top (apex predators) consists of fewer, often larger, individuals. Chains are components of more complex food webs involving many species and many levels.

SECONDARY CONSUMER

PRIMARY CONSUMER

PRIMARY PRODUCER

FOOD CHAIN
Relatively few very large blue whales (secondary consumers) rely on billions of krill (primary consumers), which in turn depend on a massive amount of phytoplankton (primary producers).

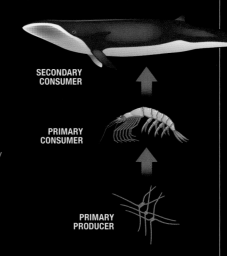

| PRIMARY PRODUCERS | PRIMARY CONSUMERS | SECONDARY CONSUMERS | TERTIARY CONSUMERS | QUATERNARY CONSUMERS |

phytoplankton / krill / baleen whales / birds / protozoans / carnivorous zooplankton / penguins / seals / pelagic fishes / squid / decomposer bacteria / copepods / seaweed / decomposer invertebrates / detritus on sea floor / demersal fishes / small toothed whales / orcas

FOOD WEB
The Antarctic Ocean food web may seem complex, but it is actually less complicated than the food webs of many other ecosystems. Like all food webs, it is delicately balanced and is vulnerable to disruption, from climate change or overexploitation, for example. Disruption of one link in the web might affect the entire web and could even lead to ecosystem collapse.

CACHING FOOD
When a kill is too large to eat in a single meal, or if it is to dangerous to eat it where it fell, solitary hunting carnivores like this leopard will often store the carcass and return to it later.

Competition and cooperation

Food resources are not infinite, so individuals and populations have to compete to secure their share. In some situations, one animal will be dominant with respect to another and may be able to monopolize a food source because of this heightened status. Or by defending a feeding territory, an individual or group may be able to secure for itself all that it needs. But when food is distributed across too large an area or numbers of competitors are very high, territoriality may not be an effective strategy. Species can coexist and minimize competition by each occupying a particular niche in the environment. For example, they might feed on slightly different foods or feed at different times or in different places.

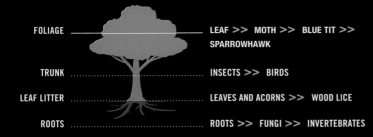

FOLIAGE	LEAF >> MOTH >> BLUE TIT >> SPARROWHAWK
TRUNK	INSECTS >> BIRDS
LEAF LITTER	LEAVES AND ACORNS >> WOOD LICE
ROOTS	ROOTS >> FUNGI >> INVERTEBRATES

DETRITUS FEEDERS
Detritivores, like wood lice, feed on detritus such as decaying wood, leaves, and other plant material. In this way they assist in the recycling of plant material back into the soil.

OAK TREE NICHES
An oak tree is a complex habitat that provides various niches for specialist decomposers, herbivores, omnivores, and carnivores. These, in turn, are linked in several food chains.

HUNTING PARTNERS
Coyotes catch small mammals startled by digging badgers and are more successful when hunting with badgers than when hunting alone.

On the other hand, individuals may need the help of others of their species to be successful. Cooperation may increase the chance that a territory can be defended and also that food will be found, either because a group can search a larger area or through direct communication about the location of food. Cooperation may also allow animals to catch prey that they cannot catch alone or allow a group to manage a resource for mutual benefit.

Foraging strategies

Carnivores and herbivores eat different foods but the basic principles of feeding are common to all species. They need to find food, process it, and eat it. They need to make sure that they get the particular food they need when they need it, and to do so they need to maximize the efficiency of their foraging. So just as a bear usually selects only the most nutritious salmon, a goose usually grazes only the best-quality grass. Another herbivore, the surgeon fish, is restricted to a low-quality diet of algae so it simply eats a lot to obtain enough energy. Foraging strategies also need to be flexible, and animals need to learn what foods they can and cannot eat.

Optimal foragers

Animals are not indiscriminate in their feeding behavior. Instead, they optimize efficiency through a trade-off between the costs of finding and processing food, and the benefit of the energy gained from the food. For example, small marine iguanas restrict themselves to low-quality food found between the high- and low-water lines because the extra energy they would get if they fed on better-quality food from beyond the low-water line is less than the energy costs involved in diving to reach it. Shore crabs show a similar behavior when feeding on mussels (see below). Even sessile fan worms feed optimally, balancing the energy spent opening and closing their fans against the amount of food in a current of water.

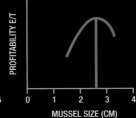

BREAKING SHELLS
Ravens drop shells to open them. They fly only as high as necessary for the drop to break the shell.

HUNGER
A physiological motivation to feed

OTHERS ARE FEEDING
A social motivation to feed

SEARCH FOR FOOD
Some animals actively hunt for food; some collect it from their surroundings; and some remember previous locations of food

FIND FOOD

IS IT SAFE TO EAT THIS FOOD?
Some animals avoid eating food that has made them ill in the past or will not eat new types of food they have not eaten previously

IS IT SAFE TO EAT HERE?
Animals vary in their feeding behavior in response to the risk of predation or of having food stolen from them by competitors

SHOULD THE FOOD BE SHARED?
If food is abundant, animals may share it with others. However, if food is scarce, they may eat a small amount and cache the remainder

IS IT POSSIBLE TO DO BETTER?
Animals are optimal foragers and do not always eat the first food available if better-quality food can be obtained easily and safely

FORAGING DECISION TREE
Foraging strategies are, in effect, a series of decisions in which finding, choosing, processing, and eating involve a series of behavioral choices.

EAT

MUSSEL ENERGY
When feeding on mussels, shore crabs preferentially select mussels ¾–1 in (2–2.5 cm) long because they give the highest energy profit, taking into account their calorific value (E) and the time spent opening them (T).

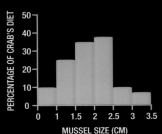

PERCENTAGE OF CRAB'S DIET

MUSSEL SIZE (CM)

PROFITABILITY E/T

MUSSEL SIZE (CM)

Feeding on plants

Plant material is available as a potential food source in nearly all of the environments of the world. Plants turn the energy of the sun into food—a process know as autotrophy—that is usable by animals and underpins almost all food chains. Therefore, the eating of plants is fundamentally important to ecosystems.

Plants as food

Some animals specialize in eating one kind of plant, or even one part of one kind of plant, while others generalize, consuming a range of plants. Grazers eat grasses—and are often anatomically specialized for this—while browsers consume plants selectively. Granivores and frugivores eat seeds and fruits respectively, and ultraspecialists like hummingbirds drink nectar from flowers. Nectar is energy-rich, as are fruits, while seeds are rich in proteins and oils. Leaves and grasses are not very nutritious, meaning animals often have to consume large amounts of them. Plants are not passive in this relationship: some deter predators with toxins or spines, while others encourage them for the purposes of seeds pollination or dispersal, for example.

molariform teeth

ELEPHANT SKELETON
Elephants have large, ridged molariform teeth, arranged on a conveyor; as the front teeth wear out, those behind them slide forward, taking their place.

Hummingbirds are hovering nectivores, with long beaks and tongues for drinking nectar from flowers.

Koalas are leaf eaters with a diet composed almost entirely of eucalyptus leaves.

Furniture beetles are domestic pests. They burrow into damp lumber, where their larvae eat the wood.

Wild mustangs are grazers, using their incisor teeth to clip the short grasses that make up 80–90 percent of their diet.

TOXIC LEAVES

As a defense against being eaten, the leaves of many plant species are laced with toxic chemicals. Some caterpillars that feed on these toxic leaves disable the plant's defenses by severing leaf veins to slow the flow of the poison. Others excrete the toxins they eat and some, like the Monarch butterfly caterpillar (left), use them for their own defense.

TYPES OF PLANT FOOD

When thinking of plants as food, there is a tendency to picture animals grazing grasses. Plants, however, are more than just green matter, and animals have adapted to prey upon almost every part of the plant. Insects, birds, and mammals consume nectar and pollen, and a wide variety of animals eat flowers, fruits, and seeds. Species such as pigs dig up plant roots and tubers, and in desperation browsers will chew twigs and bark. Termites and the larvae of wood-boring beetles have evolved the ability to digest cellulose, which allows them to eat wood.

GERENUKS FEEDING ON ACACIA

Gerenuks are unique among browsing antelopes, as they stand fully erect on their hind legs while leaning against a tree with their front legs while feeding. They can reach heights of more than 8¼ ft (2.5 m).

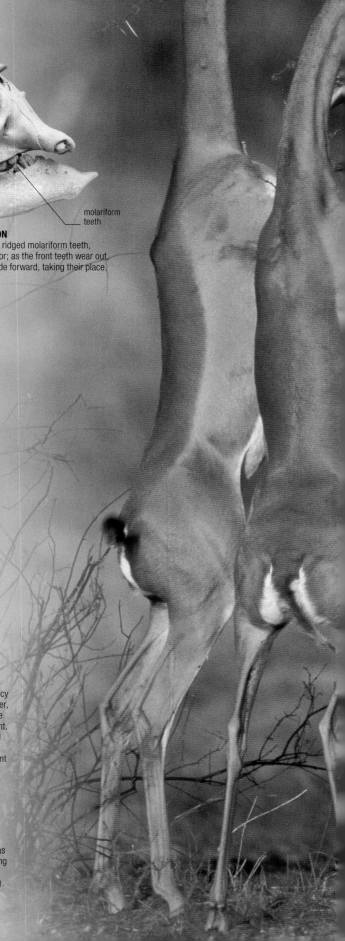

Managing crops

Some foods become available in a glut, with availability far outstripping demand. When the food is perishable, animals recruit others to share the supply. If the food can be stored, animals may benefit from managing it. Some birds, for example, store seeds and nuts in fall to prevent winter food shortages. Other animals manage quality rather than quantity. Some grazers struggle to digest grasses, but new grass is slightly more digestable, so some species crop and rotate patches of grass, ensuring a fresh supply.

SCATTERED PANTRY
During the fall months, a jay will store 4,500–11,000 acorns, each in a different site. Remarkably, it will retrieve them many months later as food for its nestlings.

ROTATING HARVEST
In winter, brants move as a flock from one feeding field to the next. They coordinate their movements to ensure that they do not return to individual fields too soon.

Brants wait for a period of **4 days** before they return to feed on land that they have heavily grazed.

Mutual benefit

Some plants benefit from being food. Many flowers are pollinated by animals moving between blooms as they eat nectar and pollen. Some seeds have a tough coating that requires them to be digested before they will germinate, and many seeds have far higher germination rates if they have passed through the gut of an animal. Also, animals can carry the seeds a long distance from the parent plant.

AFRICAN ELEPHANT DUNG
Large seeds pass through an elephant's gut and are deposited to germinate in a pile of dung. Elephants disperse the seeds of many tree species, including some with no other known dispersal mechanism.

Plant defenses

While some plants do benefit from their relationships with herbivores, most attempt to resist predatory animals. They defend themselves with toxins and spines, or have a growth form that makes feeding difficult. Animals can adapt to plant defenses—some eat an antidote to plant toxins, some develop immunity to them, and some utilize the poisons for defense. Some herbivores have evolved to reach past spines, some have harder teeth to grind tough plants, and some, like the chimpanzee, use tools to crack open tough nuts.

GIRAFFE
The 20 in (50 cm) long tongue of the giraffe snakes between thorns to pick small clumps of leaves. Giraffe saliva is thick, coating spines eaten accidentally so that they can be safely swallowed.

Scouring ice

Antarctic sea urchin

All sea urchins are typically grazers. Crawling across the sea floor, they use their powerful jaws, which consist of five downward-pointing, chalky, bladelike teeth, to bite and scrape at food. The Antarctic sea urchin scrapes food from the seabed and directly from sea ice, feeding upon a film of diatoms and on clumps of red algae. Unlike other urchins, this species also consumes the feces of Weddell seals. Urchins are able to use their numerous tube feet to gather up material that has been stirred up in the water.

Sterechinus neumayeri

- ↔ Up to 2¾ in (7 cm)
- 🌊 Shallow waters of the Southern Ocean.
- 📖 Small, variable in color, ranging from greenish gray to red or purple–violet. Long spines extend from its round shell.

GROUP GRAZING
Groups of Antarctic sea urchins congregate at diatom mats, where they graze on these microscopic algae.

ANATOMY
ARISTOTLE'S LANTERN

Echinoderms such as sea urchins have an elaborate apparatus for feeding called Aristotle's Lantern. It is made up of 50 skeletal elements that are largely internal, with only the tips of the five downward-pointing calcium carbonate teeth, arranged in a downward-pointing cone, protruding. In the center, a fleshy substance serves as a tongue. Sixty powerful muscles work together to push the cone outward and to open and close the jaws.

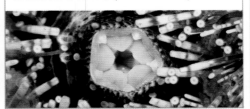

Voracious swarming

Desert locust

During times of drought, the desert locust is a solitary, drab, well-camouflaged insect. However, when the desert rains finally fall it undergoes something of a transformation in both appearance and behavior, becoming both brightly colored and highly gregarious. So dramatic is this transformation that the two forms were long thought to be distinct species. Rain triggers voracious feeding among the insects, causing them to lay down body

reserves and mate. Newly hatched locusts do not fly. These hoppers, as they are known, form larger and larger swarms, molting, growing, and eating the equivalent of their own body mass each day as they consume everything green in their path.

Locusts are indiscriminate feeders, eating leaves, stems, shoots, fruits, and seeds of both noncrop and crop plants, and they can cause devastation to the rural economies of the countries they afflict. During their fifth and final molt, the hoppers develop wings, and swarms of tens of millions of individuals take to the air, traveling up to 125 miles (200 km) per day in search of fresh habitats in which to continue to feed and breed. If this coincides with a dry period, the emerging nymphs will revert to the solitary form.

PLAGUE PROPORTIONS
A swarm of locusts can cover up to 463 square miles (1,200 square km) and will indiscriminately consume leaves, stems, shoots, fruit, and seeds of any plants in their path.

Locusta migratoria

- ↔ Up to 3¼ in (8 cm)
- 🌊 Desert in North Africa.
- 📖 Winged insect with short antennae and variable coloration depending upon life stage.

CROWDING TOGETHER
When grasshoppers crowd together, the physical contact stimulates production of pheromones, which in turn causes the insects to swarm.

69 billion The estimated number of locusts in a swarm that devastated parts of northwest Africa in 2004.

Probing proboscis

Cabbage white butterfly

Caterpillars of the cabbage white butterfly are typical folivores (leaf feeders). The female usually lays its eggs on the leaves of cabbages, cauliflower, or other similar plants. Once the eggs hatch, the green caterpillars feed on the flowers and leaves of their host plant. As a free-flying butterfly, the diet of the cabbage white changes, and it then becomes a nectivore (nectar feeder).

Capable of powerful flight, the butterfly searches for food plants across a wide area and locates them by their scent. Having landed on a suitable flower, it applies hydrostatic pressure to two specially elongated mouthparts that are usually held coiled beneath the head. Once straightened, these mouth parts zip together to form a drinking tube, the proboscis, which can be guided into the nectary of the flower to extract the sweet nectar.

PRECISION DRINKING
The proboscis of this butterfly dips repeatedly into the multiple nectaries of the flower, sipping sweet nectar from each of them.

Pieris brassicae

- ↔ 2–2½ in (5-6.5 cm) (wingspan)
- 🌊 Farmland, meadows, and parkland throughout Europe, North Africa, and Asia to the Himalayas.
- 📖 Small, strong-flying butterfly, with black spots on white forewings.

Processing pollen

Honey bee

This social insect uses sophisticated communication to find sources of food and builds elaborate structures to process it. Foraging worker bees visit up to 40 flowers per minute, collecting pollen and sucking up nectar to be stored in the honey sack, a specialized gut structure. Bees find food by sight and smell, but when a successful bee returns to the hive it communicates to other workers the location of nectar-rich flowers by means of the waggle dance (see p.463). The way in which the dancing bee moves communicates both the direction and distance of the flowers from the hive.

The colony is made up of sterile female workers, male drones, and a queen. In the hive, flower nectar is repeatedly swallowed and regurgitated by the workers until it becomes honey. Stored pollen and honey are then fed by workers to the developing larvae in their care. Some of the larvae are put into separate chambers, and fed royal jelly, a secretion from the feeding glands of the workers themselves. These individuals will develop to become future queens.

Apis mellifera

↔	½–1 in (1.5–2.5 cm)
◉	Thought to have originated in India, now one of the world's most widespread domesticated insects.
☐	Small honey-brown-colored body, with sparse hairs on its thorax and abdomen.

» 167, 424–25, 463

BEEKEEPING
Commercial beekeepers collect honey and take it away from their hives. Hives may also be moved between farms to maximize the pollination of crops.

HONEYCOMB
The hexagonal cells of a honeycomb serve as both a pantry in which to store honey and pollen, and a nursery in which the young bees are raised.

50,000 The number of bees in a typical domestic beehive.

HUMAN IMPACT

COLONY COLLAPSE DISORDER

In recent years beekeepers have reported the sudden disappearance of adult worker bees from colonies that appear otherwise to be doing well (they have plenty of stored honey and a developing brood). This phenomenon has been labeled colony collapse disorder, or CCD. The cause of CCD has yet to be determined, if in fact there is a single cause. Suggested causes include a resistant parasitic mite, *Varroa destructor*, climate change, the use of antibiotics, increased exposure to pesticides, and viral, bacterial, and fungal infections. However, the impact of CCD is clear: this is a problem on a global scale that is having a huge economic impact, not just in lost revenues from honey production but also because honey bees pollinate so many important crop plants.

POLLEN GATHERING
Bees collect pollen from the flowers they visit. This is stored in the pollen basket, easily visible as a yellow-orange ball on the hind legs. While nectar is gathered as an energy source, pollen is collected primarily for its protein and other nutrients, and is used as food for larvae.

LIVING LARDERS
Some honeypot ant workers (called repletes) have enlarged abdomens filled with nectar, which they regurgitate on demand for other members of the colony. The repletes are fed by other workers, which obtain food by gathering nectar from flowers, as well as "milking" aphids and scale insects for honeydew and preying on other invertebrates, such as termites.

Blue damselfish

The blue damselfish is a pugnacious herbivore that defends an exclusive feeding territory. The impact of the territorial damselfishes upon their coral reef habitats is so great that they are often referred to as being a keystone species. They feed selectively upon the most nutritious parts of algae and sea grasses, which may in turn benefit from the fishes' habit of voiding their waste within the territory. Through their selective grazing, damselfishes influence the growth of their favorite food plants and control the growth of algae; without this control, the algae would proliferate and suppress the growth of the underlying coral.

SURVEYING THE PLOT
A blue damselfish tends its crop of nutritious algae and defends it against competitors. Without the grazing action of damselfishes, the coral reefs would become overgrown with algae, which would inhibit their growth.

Chrysiptera cyanea

◆▶ Up to 3¼ in (8.5 cm)

◉ Coral reefs of western Indo-Pacific, to Micronesia and Samoa.

📖 Male is small and bright blue, with yellow lips and tail. Females and juveniles often have black spot at base of tail.

Powder blue surgeonfish

Living on a diet of algae, which has limited nutritional value, surgeonfishes, or tangs, consume large volumes of food and have an unusual range of gut symbionts (beneficial organisms) to aid with digestion. Surgeonfishes also have beaklike mouths that are equipped with a row of tiny, sharp teeth to scrape and bite at algal turfs and mats. This beaklike mouth allows them to nip food items from between obstacles, and their bite is so precise that they can pick off algae from coral without damaging it. When food is scarce, a surgeonfish will vigorously defend its territory, but if food is plentiful they will occasionally feed in schools with others of their species, and will even share a territory with a blue damselfish (see left). This strategy is advantageous because the smaller damselfish takes a relatively small share of the food but is an aggressive defender of the communal patch. Competition between surgeonfishes species is minimized because each species in a community has slightly different food preferences. For example, of the three species of surgeonfishes occurring together on Florida coral reefs, the blue tang prefers red algae, the ocean surgeonfishes prefer green algae, and the doctorfishes specializes in brown algae.

Acanthurus leucosternon

◆▶ Up to 10 in (25 cm)

◉ Coral reefs of the Indian Ocean and Indonesia.

📖 Oval, powder-blue body with prominent yellow dorsal fin, steep forehead, and black face.

GRAZING IN SCHOOLS
When food is plentiful, surgeonfishes may feed in schools. When food is scarce, they are solitary feeders and each individual will defend its territory against other surgeonfishes and other species.

STRETCHING TO EAT
On the drier Galapagos Islands the cacti tend to be taller and the tortoises have to rear up and stretch their necks to feed. The saddleback shape of the shell allows greater neck movement than the domed shells found in tortoises that live on wetter islands.

A FAVORED FOOD
On the wetter islands, tortoises migrate from one side to the other to take advantage of fresh, lush grass. They can also obtain most of the moisture they need from the dew on such vegetation.

Arboreal browser

Monkey-tailed skink

The monkey-tailed skink is herbivorous and uses chemical cues to identify edible leaves and flowers. It spends the daylight hours sheltering in the trunk of a hollow tree and emerges at night to feed, using its prehensile tail to climb through vegetation. The tail is crucial to the skinks' arboreal lifestyle to such an extent that, unlike most lizards, it is unable to shed it when attacked. Their young are live born rather than hatched from an egg, and ride on the back of their parent until they are able to climb themselves.

Grazing giant

Galapagos tortoise

Galapagos tortoises graze on the leaves and fruits of more than 50 species of plants. They prefer lush grass, but their toothless jaws are well adapted to cut and tear at all types of vegetable matter, including tough bromeliads, fallen fruits, and the fleshy but prickly pads of cacti. On the wetter islands, the tortoises drink water when it is available, but on the drier islands they obtain much of the liquid they need from their food and can also store fat within their large shells.

Geochelone nigra
- Up to 4½ ft (1.4 m)
- Galapagos Islands off the coast of Ecuador, South America.
- A giant brown tortoise.

Corucia zebrata
- Up to 30 in (75 cm)
- Tropical rain forests on the Solomon Islands.
- Long olive-green lizard with a prehensile tail. Four limbs with sharp claws and wedge-shaped head.

BUILT TO CLIMB
Monkey-tailed skinks use their long, grasping tails and claws with razor-sharp hooks to climb through the tropical rain forest in search of the edible leaves and flowers on which they feed.

Diving for seaweed

Marine iguana

Marine iguanas are traditionally portrayed as strong swimmers that dive to feed on beds of offshore seaweeds. In fact, only larger individuals—those above 4 lb (1.8 kg)—habitually dive to feed. Smaller individuals—those up to 2¾ lb (1.2 kg)—feed exclusively on the less lush seaweeds of the intertidal areas, restricting their feeding to the period of the day when the tide is out and the sea is relatively calm.

The constraints of the tide present difficulties to small iguanas, who have to limit their exposure to sea water so that their body temperatures do not fall too far—the sea around the Galapagos Islands is often chilly, with a 57–77° F (14–25° C) annual range. These animals must feed whenever the tide is out, but if this is shortly after dawn they risk being too cool and sluggish to feed, and if the tide falls shortly before dark, they may be chilled by splashing waves and not have sufficient daylight to reheat before nightfall. Small animals huddle together at night to conserve heat.

Underwater foragers do not face the same problems and typically bask each morning before concentrating their foraging time during the late morning and around noon. This allows plenty of time to bask and reheat during the early afternoon when the sun still heats the island rocks.

Smaller iguanas do not feed underwater because iguanas are actually relatively poor swimmers, and smaller animals are the poorest swimmers of all. They would

therefore take a long time to reach the beds of seaweed or algae, risk being dashed on the rocks by waves, and use up a lot of their energy. Smaller bodies cool faster than larger ones and therefore small iguanas would be restricted to short dives. So the limitations of their small size seem to restrict their feeding opportunities to the shore.

Amblyrhynchus cristatus
- 20 in–3¼ ft (50–100 cm)
- Galapagos Islands off the coast of South America.
- Black or dark gray-colored, large-headed lizard with a scaly appearance and dorsal crest. The long whippy tail is used for swimming.

INTERTIDAL FEEDER
Younger and smaller iguanas are unable to swim to underwater seaweed mats and so must graze in the intertidal area between the low- and high-water marks.

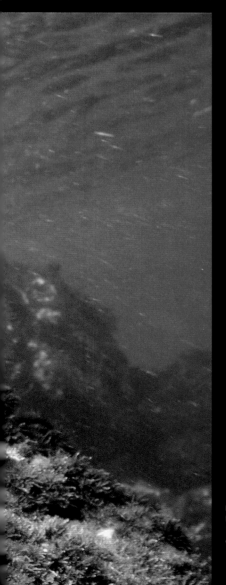

UNDERWATER FEEDING
Using their claws and powerful legs, large iguanas are able to resist the swell of the sea to tear at submerged algal mats and seaweed.

30 The number of minutes that marine iguanas can spend underwater while diving for food.

HEATING UP
By day, marine iguanas bask on sun-warmed rocks to raise their body temperatures. By night, they crowd together in groups to conserve heat.

Larder tree

Acorn woodpecker

As its name would suggest, the acorn woodpecker specializes in feeding on the acorns of oak trees, although it sometimes also feeds on insects and the fruits of other plants. Like other woodpeckers, it has a stiffened tail and two forward-and two backward-pointing toes on each foot to enable it to climb the trunks of trees, and a specially adapted bill and skull to allow it to drill into wood.

In many parts of their range, extended family groups of these birds may drill huge numbers of holes into the trunk of a larder tree, which they stuff full of acorns to serve as a winter food store. In other areas, they make use of natural crevices or even suitable cracks and holes in manmade structures. Groups of birds defend and use this larder as a common resource and may even breed communally, with one or more pairs of birds in a group breeding and being assisted by a number of nonbreeding birds. Although they are often sedentary birds, using the same larder for a number of years, acorn woodpeckers will move great distances if a failure of the local acorn crop occurs.

Melanerpes formicivorus

- 7½–9 in (19–23 cm)
- Oak woodland in the southwest US and Central America.
- Black with white breast and cheek patches and red crown and yellow throat.

ARRANGING ACORNS
Each acorn woodpecker in a flock works to defend the larder and to maintain the quality of the storage holes. It will regularly rearrange their acorns into smaller and smaller holes as they dry and shrink.

50,000
The number of acorns often stored by acorn woodpeckers in a single tree.

Plucking fruits

Toco toucan

Although massive in appearance, the prodigious bill of the toucan is surprisingly fragile and lightweight. It is composed of a hollow horny sheath over crisscrossing strengthening rods of bone, and can easily be broken. Toucans will forage for food on the forest floor, but they are essentially birds of the forest canopy, where their long bill enables them to reach out and pluck fruits from hard-to-reach branches.

A fruit held firmly in the tip of the bill can be maneuvered toward the throat by the bird's very long tongue, or it may be flicked back with a toss of the head and swallowed with a flourish. Wild toucans eat the fruits of more than 100 species of forest plant and are almost completely fruit eating, although they do eat insects as a source of protein during the breeding season.

Ramphastos toco

- 21–23½ in (53–60 cm)
- Lowland rain forest (below 5,500 ft/1,700 m) in northeast and central South America.
- Largest of the toucans, with a white breast and an enormous yellow bill with a red keel and a large dark spot at the end.

Hovering for nectar

Blue-chested hummingbird

The blue-chested hummingbird, like all hummingbirds, has special adaptations to its nectar-feeding lifestyle. The unique arrangement of the wing bones and joints enable these birds to hover almost motionless, and their extremely long bills and even longer tongues enable them to reach deep into flowers to collect the nectar that forms 90 percent of their diet. However, nectar lacks many essential nutrients and hummingbirds supplement their diets with insects. But to spend all of their time on the wing would be too energy expensive, so 85–90 percent of the time is spent sitting still.

Amazilia amabilis

- 3½ in (9 cm)
- Forested areas of Central America and northern South America.
- Small, bronzy green bird with glittering green crown, violet-blue chest, and long, pointed bill.

Gorging on berries
Bohemian waxwing

Although they occasionally eat insects, flowers, and sap, Bohemian waxwings are almost entirely dependent on fruits, and are one of very few temperate bird species that can be described as frugivorous (fruit-eating). Fruits tend to be abundant but seasonal and patchily distributed. For this reason, Bohemian waxwings are gregarious throughout the year, often breeding in loose colonies and forming large and widely ranging flocks during the nonbreeding season. Winter flocks of waxwings often come into close contact with humans, exploiting the fruits of ornamental garden shrubs and trees. Birds collect fruits while perched on a branch, often plucking them and swallowing them whole. When a bird cannot reach berries from a perch, it will briefly hover to pluck them on the wing. Most curiously, these social birds have been observed to perch next to one another along a branch and pass berries backward down the line from one bird to the next. Eating berries does, however, have risks. Waxwings that eat fermented fruits often succumb to intoxication, which can be fatal.

FORAGING IN FLOCKS
Bohemian waxings can strip a tree bare of fruit very quickly and travel significant distances between trees. In this way they are important in the dispersal of fruit seeds.

Bombycilla garrulus
- 5½–16½ in (14–17 cm)
- Forest in Europe, Asia, and North America.
- Gray-brown bird with distinctive crest and black mask. Red "wax" spots on the secondary wing feathers.

Secret store
Marsh tit

These avid food hoarders might hide up to a hundred seeds in a single morning, and thousands across a winter. Each seed is stored in a different place, and seeds are often some yards apart. Impressively, they have the ability to relocate and retrieve stored seeds days or weeks later. This strategy allows them to take advantage of food from sources that cannot be consumed at a single sitting, such as a sunflower head or a backyard birdfeeder. Not all tits have this ability; blue tits for example do not store food and have poor food-retrieval abilities. Comparisons of the brains of storing and nonstoring species have revealed that hoarders, such as the marsh tit, have a well developed hippocampal region, the area of the brain associated with spatial memory.

BIRDFEEDERS

Garden birdfeeders save the lives of millions of birds worldwide each year when there is a shortage of wild food. Feeding in this way can bring birds and humans closer together than ever before. Provision of food all year round has even changed the behavior of some species, and the list of regular garden birds continues to grow. However, birdfeeders increase the densities of birds in a relatively small area and therefore may increase the risk of disease transmission, so good feeder hygiene is absolutely essential.

ACROBATIC BIRD
The marsh tit, like all of the tits, is an accomplished acrobat and, if necessary, is able to hang upside down to collect seeds. After collecting the seeds, the marsh tit hides each one in a different location, which it remembers so that it can retrieve it later.

Parus palustris
- Up to 4½ in (12 cm)
- Widespread in wooded areas of Europe and Asia.
- Small, agile bird with brown or beige upper parts, buff-colored breast, and black cap.

Cone feeder
Red crossbill

Also known as the common crossbill, this bird feeds almost exclusively on the seeds of coniferous trees. The distinctive crossed bill enables it to pry open the tough cones of conifers before they ripen and open naturally. This gives these birds an advantage over other finches that share their forest habitat but which do not have a bill adapted to the task. Their resinous diet means that crossbills must often visit water to drink and clean their bills. By specializing in this way, crossbills are able to breed whenever the cone crop ripens, even if this is in the middle of winter.

Loxia curvirostra
- 5½–8 in (14–20 cm)
- Coniferous forests in the Northern Hemisphere, particularly Scandinavia and northern Britain.
- Large, stout finch, ranging in color from greenish yellow to brick-red, with characteristically crossed, pointed bill.

CLOSING AND OPENING
A crossbill feeds by poking its closed bill into a cone and then opening the bill's crossed tips. This pries open open the scale of the cone and enables the bird to extract the seed.

ANATOMY
ADAPTED BILL

Although crossed mandibles are a common feature of the bills of all crossbills, the particular size and shape of the bill varies between species and even between populations within a species. Each distinct bill form is an evolutionary adaptation to enable the birds to specialize in prying apart the scales of their preferred type of cone, whether it is spruce, pine, or larch.

longer upper bill

Exclusive diet
Koala

Although they occasionally browse other tree species, koalas feed almost exclusively on the fibrous leaves of eucalyptuses. Powerful forelimbs, opposable digits, and strong claws enable them to move with ease through trees to reach their food, which they nip off with sharp incisors. Their modified cheek teeth, a single premolar, and four molars with high crowns on each jaw, enable them to grind the leaves to a smooth paste. Eucalyptus leaves are low in protein, high in toxins, and difficult to digest, but the digestive system of the koala is specially adapted to meet this challenge. The toxins are deactivated and the paste is digested by bacterial fermentation in a greatly enlarged cecum, which, at about 6 ft 6 in (2 m) long, is the longest of any mammal.

WEANING BABY
After emerging from the pouch, a young koala eats small amounts of its mother's "pap," a specialized form of feces that is soft and runny. This introduces into the young's digestive system the bacteria it will need to digest eucalyptus itself. The pap is also a rich source of protein for the growing young koala.

Phascolarctos cinereus
- 28–31 in (72–78 cm)
- Eucalyptus forest and woodland in eastern Australia.
- Small, gray bearlike marsupial with characteristic pale ear tufts.

Flying frugivore

Great fruit-eating bat

Around one-third of the world's bat species are herbivores, feeding on fruits, leaves, pollen, and nectar. The great fruit-eating bat is an important pollinator and seed disperser for a wide range of plant species, some of which are economically important crops, for example mango, wild banana, and durian. Flowers and fruits are often locally superabundant, and vast flocks of bats may descend upon a fruiting tree attracted by one another's calls and by the smell of the ripe fruit. These flocks increase competition between bats and attract predators, so many bats use their teeth to tear off a fruit, which they carry away to consume in solitary safety.

Artibeus lituratus

⬌ 3½–4½ in (9–11 cm)

⦿ Caves or large trees in forested areas of southern Mexico through Central America, to southern Brazil, and northern Argentina.

📖 Large brownish gray bat with a distinctive white stripe above the eye.

A TASTE FOR FRUIT
Great fruit-eating bats are considered pests in some areas because of the devastating impact they can have upon crops.

Bamboo specialist

Giant panda

Classified as a bear, the panda may be presumed to be a carnivore or an omnivore rather than a herbivore, particularly given that its diet is known to include meat, fishes, eggs, tubers, and plant material. It also has bearlike teeth and a digestive system more typical of a carnivore.

However, 99 percent of a panda's diet is vegetarian and is composed of plants of just one type—bamboo. Having a carnivore's gut, the panda is not efficient at digesting cellulose (plant glucose). It is able to digest just 20 percent of the food it eats while a more typical mammalian herbivore might digest 80 percent. The most protein-rich leaves of the plant are eaten preferentially, and the bamboo is crushed and ground by powerful muscled jaws equipped with large flat molars, but even this processing does not make bamboo a high-quality foodstuff, and the animal needs to eat a lot of it. An adult panda can consume up to 88 lbs (40 kg) of bamboo per day and take 12–14 hours doing it.

Stands of bamboo are synchronous in their flowering, death, and regeneration, which means that pandas need to range across relatively large areas of forest supporting a range of bamboo species to ensure a sufficient supply of food. They feed mainly on the ground, but they are also excellent climbers and able to swim.

EXTRA DIGIT

At first glance, the giant panda paw appears to have an extra digit: five fingers and one thumb. This thumb, however, is actually an elongated wrist bone, the radial sesamoid, which is used by the panda as a pseudo-thumb. With it the panda is able to handle food with considerable dexterity, gripping bamboo shoots firmly in one hand, while biting leaves from them.

true digits have claws

thumb

Thumblike extension of wrist bone without claw

Ailuropoda melanoleuca

⬌ Up to 6¼ ft (1.9 m)

⦿ Temperate forest with a dense bamboo understory in southwest China.

📖 Long-haired, black and white bear.

BAMBOO BEAR
The giant panda is so closely associated with bamboo forests, and so reliant on bamboo, that it is known to local people as the bamboo bear.

Fruit and nectar eater

Kinkajou

Kinkajous rarely leave the forest canopy, and the bulk of their diet is forest fruit. They are particularly fond of the sweeter, more fleshy fruits, which they collect in a manner similar to monkeys; using dextrous hands to process their food while hanging onto the tree with their tail and feet. The muzzle of a kinkajou is less pointed than that of its close relative the racoon. This flatter face and extremely long tongue enables it to lap nectar from flowers. Kinkajous sleep during the day, and feed at night.

Potos flavus

⬌ 31in–5 ft (80–115 cm)

⦿ Tropical forests of Central and northern South America.

📖 Mammal with dense golden fur, and a superficial resemblance to both a monkey and a cat.

Night grazer

Hippopotamus

Given their bulk, hippopotamuses eat surprisingly little each day. Most of their time is spent wallowing in warm water, but they do not feed on aquatic plants. Each night they leave the water and venture out to feed almost exclusively on grasses, which are digested in their multichambered alimentary canal by the fermenting action of microorganisms.

Remarkably, hippopotamuses consume just 1.5 percent of their enormous body mass each day, which would indicate that their daytime wallowing and nocturnal grazing is particularly energy-efficient.

Hippopotamus amphibius

⬌ 10¾–11¼ ft (3.3–3.5 m)

⦿ Rivers and lakes in West, Central, East, and South Africa.

📖 Heavy body, gray-brown above, and pink below, with short legs. Eyes, ears, and nostrils are positioned at the top of the massive head.

GETTING A MOUTHFUL
Hippopotamuses have formidable teeth, but they use their thick lips to nip at vegetation. They have occasionally been recorded supplementing their diet by scavenging on the carcasses of dead animals.

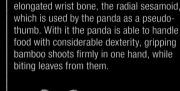

Chewing the cud
African buffalo

This buffalo has been described as one of the most successful grazers in Africa. It can be found in as diverse a range of habitats as swamp, forest, and grassland. It prefers taller grasses, using its long, almost prehensile tongue to pull at clumps of grasses that are then clipped by its wide incisors and grazed to a pulp by its broad molars. Through their grazing, herds of buffaloes modify their habitat in a way that makes it more suitable for other more selective grazers, and this promotes the growth of fresh food. As a result, herds of buffaloes may be quite mobile. They are able to avoid overheating by remaining inactive by day and feeding at night.

Syncerus caffer
- ⬌ 7¾–11¼ ft (2.4–3.4 m)
- ◉ Grassland and woodland in sub-Saharan Africa.
- 📖 Thick-set, heavily built member of the cow family, with a reddish brown coat and a pair of large upward-curving horns with a large central boss.

SUPER GRAZER
One of the most successful of the grazing vertebrates, the African buffalo prefers lush grass but will graze coarse grass and herbs when this is scarce.

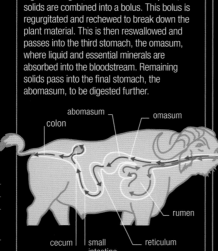

ANATOMY
FOUR STOMACHS

The stomachs of ruminants (mammals that chew the cud) have four chambers. Food passes into the rumen and reticulum, where digestion begins, fermentation takes place, and solids are combined into a bolus. This bolus is regurgitated and rechewed to break down the plant material. This is then reswallowed and passes into the third stomach, the omasum, where liquid and essential minerals are absorbed into the bloodstream. Remaining solids pass into the final stomach, the abomasum, to be digested further.

- abomasum
- colon
- omasum
- rumen
- cecum
- small intestine
- reticulum

→ passage of food (first time)   → passage of food (second time)

Grazing the ocean floor
Dugong

The only strictly marine mammalian herbivore, the dugong, or sea cow, slowly meanders through the sea-grass beds that are common in shallow, sandy-bottomed waters. As they rip out clumps of sea grass, they leave behind trails of bare sand and uprooted plants. This encourages regeneration of the sea grass, promoting the nutritious new growth that they favor. By repeatedly re-cropping the sea grass, they maintain the quality of their food.

Dugong dugon
- ⬌ 8¼–13 ft (2.5–4 m)
- ◉ Shallow tropical waters of the Indo–Pacific region.
- 📖 Long gray-green mammal with a broad head and crescent-shaped tail.

DIGGING DEEPER
Dugongs graze sandy-bottomed waters and dig for rhizomes using their flexible, thick upper lip.

Reaching the heights
Giraffe

The extraordinarily long neck of the giraffe is an evolutionary adaptation that enables it to compete with the many smaller herbivores of the crowded savanna ecosystem. Giraffes' extreme height enables them to reach above their competitors and to selectively browse the best parts of the tallest trees. They feed on the fruits, flowers, and fresh shoots of 40–60 different tree species, including mimosa, commiphora (myrrh), and the spiny acacia.

Giraffes are able to nip leaves from between the long thorns of acacia because their long muzzles, flexible lips, and long, dextrous, tongues can reach deep within clumps of tree branches and because their lips and tongue are protected from the thorns by thick, horny bumps called papillae.

An adult giraffe consumes up to 77 lbs (35 kg) of food each day, and to ensure access to a sufficient quantity and quality, roams widely. In lean times, giraffes eat dried leaves, twigs, and even tree spines. In common with other ruminants (see panel, left), they first chew and swallow their food, then regurgitate and rechew it several times prior to complete digestion. Uniquely, they are able to ruminate while walking, an adaptation which perfectly suits their nomadic lifestyle.

Giraffa camelopardalis
- ⬌ 12½–15½ ft (3.8–4.7 m)
- ◉ Savanna, grassland, and open woodland in sub-Saharan Africa.
- 📖 Large, long-legged and long-necked hoofed mammal with a patchwork sandy-colored and brown coat.

OVERCOMING A PRICKLY PROBLEM
Thick, leathery lips and a very long tongue enable the giraffe to selectively browse tender leaves from around the sharp spines of acacia trees.

Omnivores

Omnivores eat a wide variety of foodstuffs, often mixing vegetable and animal material. They respond quickly to changes in the availability of food and take advantage of new food sources. Their breadth of diet enables them to survive in situations where specialists would struggle.

Feeding patterns

Although generalist feeders may seem to be indiscriminate in their food selection, most species do discriminate, choosing to eat less tough leaves, for example. Filter-feeding mollusks ingest all small solids in their feeding current, but have an internal mechanism for separating food from nonfood.

Many omnivores appear to specialize at a particular point in their annual cycle—some populations of brown bear, for example, mainly eat moths in the late summer—so variations are noticeable in omnivore diets over long time periods.

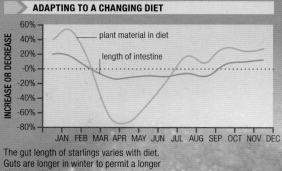

ALL-DAY FEEDING
Chimpanzees feed all day, starting early and eating almost everything in reach. As the day goes on, they become more selective, choosing the ripest fruits and most succulent leaves. Presumably, when satisfied, they can afford to be more discerning.

ADAPTING TO A CHANGING DIET

Chart: INCREASE OR DECREASE (y-axis: 60%, 40%, 20%, -0%, -20%, -40%, -60%, -80%; x-axis: JAN FEB MAR APR MAY JUN JUL AUG SEP OCT NOV DEC)
— plant material in diet
— length of intestine

The gut length of starlings varies with diet. Guts are longer in winter to permit a longer digestion time for the plant material, which is hard to digest, that forms the bulk of their diet at this time.

Feeding behavior

As generalists, omnivores tend to lack physical adaptations for feeding, and their anatomy often combines that of carnivores and herbivores. Omnivore teeth, a mixture of carnivore and herbivore teeth, are a good example of this. Omnivores do exhibit behavioral adaptations, such as an ability to manipulate and process a variety of foods, and they are often good problem solvers—several omnivores have learned to open trash cans. There are drawbacks to having a relatively indiscriminate diet. Animals feeding on seasonal foods often suffer nutritional imbalances, but they are physiologically adapted to withstand them.

FEAR OF THE NEW
Rats are highly neophobic, showing a strong reluctance to eat unknown foods. This behavior may have evolved to protect them against accidental poisoning.

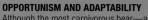

OPPORTUNISM AND ADAPTABILITY
Although the most carnivorous bear—and dependant upon the fat of marine mammals for much of its energy—the polar bear is a highly adaptable opportunist omnivore, and in times of need will eat berries, kelp, and trash.

SEARCHING FOR FOOD
Using its powerful and sensitive snout, the wild boar searches inquisitively for buried food. It will dig up roots and tubers, eat plants, kill small animals, and even scavenge carcasses.

FILTER FEEDING
Baleen whales, such as this Southern right whale, feed by swimming open mouthed through water containing zooplankton, and other small pelagic animals. Water enters the front of the mouth and then passes out of the sides, through baleen sieves.

CONSPICUOUS CROWN
This peacock worm has
extended its feathery,
banded tentacles into
the water to feed.

Fan feeder
Peacock worm

The peacock worm lives in a muddy tube that extends from the
seabed. It constructs the tube itself, secreting mucus and binding
it with sand and mud. To feed, the worm comes to the mouth of
its tube, extending fans of finely divided featherlike tentacles
into the water. The worm waves its tentacles to trap material
suspended in the seawater, including grains of sediment
and plankton. It sorts its catch using the tiny hairlike
structures (cilia) that cover its tentacles. Edible particles
are transported toward the mouth to be eaten, while
larger, inedible particles are added to the tube that
surrounds the worm. If threatened, the worm will
quickly disappear into the safety of its tube.

Sabella pavonina

◄► Up to 12 in (30 cm)

⊙ Mud and sand in shallow water
around the shores of Europe.

📖 Slender worm inhabiting muddy tube;
featherlike feeding appendages give it
flowerlike appearance.

RISING UP
By adding material
to their tubes as
they filter the sea
water around them,
peacock worms are
able to increase
their height.

Picking up a scent
Northern lobster

During its larval stage, the northern lobster, or American lobster,
is an opportunist carnivore, feeding on plankton. As it matures,
this crustacean becomes a generalist omnivore. It will scavenge
if necessary but prefers to hunt for its food, which includes
crabs, mollusks, bristleworms, echinoderms, and sometimes
other lobsters. Usually a nocturnal hunter, it locates its prey by
detecting scents in the water. The lobster's long antennae
and shorter antennules are incredibly sensitive and allow it to
discriminate between the odors of different prey. It has many
mouthparts, with differing functions, which include holding food
or passing it to the lobster's jaws, where food is crushed and
ingested. Thriving in cold, shallow waters, the northern
lobster is fiercely territorial, occupying burrows and
crevices on the seafloor.

Homarus americanus

◄► 8–24 in (20–60 cm)

⊙ In crevices in ocean water along the
North Atlantic coasts of Canada and the US.

📖 Long blue and red crustacean with a
massive pair of front claws.

TOOLS FOR THE JOB
The northern lobster has two
massive front claws. One is used for
crushing and breaking the shells of
its prey, while the other has a sharp
cutting edge for tearing at flesh.

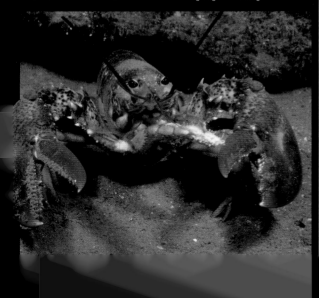

Predatory pollen lover
Soldier beetles

Both the gray-brown larvae and vividly
colored adult soldier beetles are voracious
carnivores. Adult females lay eggs in soil.
As they develop, the wormlike larvae
spend most of their time among leaf
litter, where they prey upon
ground-dwelling
invertebrates, including
snails and slugs.

Soldier beetles are
important predators of
caterpillars, aphids, and
other insects. Adult soldier
beetles congregate on the flowers
of herbaceous plants, particularly
pollen and nectar-rich species such as
goldenrod and umbillifers, where they mate
and prey on other visiting insects. While
inhabiting the flowers, the beetles become
omnivores, supplementing their diet with
pollen and nectar.

Soldier beetles are named for their
coloration, which resembles a military
uniform. The bright colors are a warning
to predators that the beetles taste
unpleasant. These insects have flexible
wing covers, giving them their alternate
name of leatherwings, and a long body
that, unlike those of other beetles, is soft.

Family Cantharidae

◄► Up to ¾ in (2 cm)

⊙ Herbaceous vegetation in sunny positions worldwide.

📖 Slender, elongate beetles with parallel elytra
(forewings) and distinctive red, yellow, and black
coloration. Head has curved jaws and slender antennae.

WELCOME ARRIVAL
Colorful soldier beetles are welcomed by
gardeners, since they are predators of
aphids and caterpillars, which are
perceived as pests.

Lethal teeth

Piranhas

Piranhas have a reputation for being fearsome predators. Their typically sharp, slicing teeth, which interlock when their mouths are closed, and their protruding lower jaws make them efficient biters. Piranhas also have a keen sense of smell, which is used to locate food even in the murky waters of flooded rivers. They usually prey on fishes and invertebrates that are smaller than themselves, but they occasionally feed in a frenzied pack, and also sometimes kill and eat larger animals, such as capybaras, horses, and even humans. However, there is a less fierce side to these fish. During flooding, piranhas move out into inundated areas and feed on decaying vegetation and the seeds and fruits of forest plants. The pacus, those piranha species that specialize to a greater extent on fruits and seeds, tend to have flatter, thicker teeth more suited to crushing seeds than to biting flesh.

Serrasalmus species

▣ Up to 13 in (33 cm)

◉ Rivers of South America east of the Andes.

▣ A somewhat round, laterally flattened silver fish with contrasting dark fins and belly. Both jaws have a single row of sharp, interlocking teeth used for puncturing and shearing.

RAZOR SHARP
A large mouth and interlocking, razor-sharp teeth enable this piranha to tear chunks of flesh from larger animals and even humans.

STRIPPING FRUIT
The sharp biting teeth of piranhas are perfect for stripping the flesh from forest fruits. Some species have thicker crushing teeth to break up the seeds inside.

Coral crunching

Bullethead parrotfish

Like all parrotfishes, the bullethead parrotfish is best described as an omnivorous herbivore. Parrotfishes' main food is marine algae, which they graze from coral reefs, thereby preventing algae from smothering the coral. However, parrotfishes also eat living and dead coral. They do this to gain access to micro-algae that colonize dead coral and to the symbiotic zooxanthella (micro-algae) of living coral. To enable them to bite hard coral, the relatively small teeth of parrotfishes are fused into beaklike plates. These wear quickly and so grow constantly. To crush the coral they have additional pharyngeal teeth in their throats. As a result of their feeding, they are considered a major erosion force in reef systems, but the fine coral sand they excrete may help stabilize the reef.

Chlorurus sordidus

▣ Up to 16 in (40 cm)

◉ Shallow coral reefs of the Indo-Pacific region.

▣ Males are blue with yellow and orange markings and blue lips, Females are reddish brown with red lips.

CORAL CLEAN UP
Parrotfish erode dead coral by biting into it with their beaklike plates at rates of up to 78 bites per minute.

Filter feeding

Whale shark

This giant fish feeds on both planktonic plants and animals as well as smaller fish, crustaceans, and squids. Whale sharks migrate through the oceans of the world to exploit areas of rich feeding such as the Australian Ningaloo Reef. There, they congregate to feast on the plankton explosion associated with the mass spawning of corals.

Whale sharks are thought to be able to determine the best feeding areas by the use of olfactory cues. They usually feed by cruising slowly through food-rich waters, passing huge volumes of water in through their mouths and out through their gills, where food particles are trapped for swallowing. Whale sharks have also been seen using their mouths like a giant bucket, swimming upward through a dense patch of food to engulf it.

SIMILAR SPECIES
Whale sharks are not the only filter-feeding sharks. Basking sharks (left) and megamouth sharks (below) also have huge mouths and enormous gill arches. Such adaptations enable them to be efficient filter feeders.

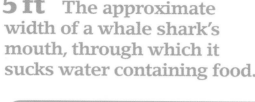

5 ft The approximate width of a whale shark's mouth, through which it sucks water containing food.

NO ESCAPE
The huge, gaping mouth of a whale shark scoops up a school of small fish. All the water the shark swallows will be pushed out through the gills, while the fish will be trapped by sievelike membranes.

Rhincodon typus
- ↔ 39–66 ft (12–20 m)
- ◐ Worldwide, in tropical and temperate waters.
- ▥ The world's largest fish, having a huge head and prominent ridges running along its gray and brown body which is patterned with white spots.

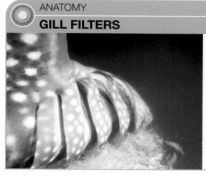

ANATOMY
GILL FILTERS

Whale and basking sharks, two of the three filter-feeding sharks, synchronize gulping in water and opening their gills. They also create suction to draw in water by expanding their buccal cavity (throat), or gulping air at the water surface. Water pumped through the gills passes through a sieve of bony projections termed gill rakers, which trap any potential food particles larger than ⅛ in (3 mm). Basking sharks shed their gill rakers in winter and grow a new set each spring, suggesting that they are seasonal feeders The third filter feeder, the megamouth shark, has softer gill rakers and may use its silvery palate and a luminescent stripe above its lips as a lure to prey.

Mixed diet

Brazilian tree frog

While the tadpoles of many species of frogs are omnivorous, feeding on vegetable material, carrion, invertebrates, and even cannibalizing one another,

BERRIES NOT BUGS
Fruit-eating frogs, only 1½ in (4 cm) long, are able to eat berries that are up to ½ in (1 cm) in diameter.

adult frogs are almost entirely carnivorous. However, the Brazilian tree frog is the exception. It rests in the pools of water that form within bromeliads during the day and forages by night, when it eats invertebrates, but its diet also includes the brightly colored fruits and seeds of a range of plants. The seeds of one of its preferred plants, *Anthurium harrisii* (an arum), are known to germinate when they have been defecated by the frog, so it is thought that this might be an important method of dispersal for this particular plant.

Xenohyla truncata
- ↔ Up to 1½ in (4 cm)
- ◐ Subtropical and tropical marshes of Brazil.
- ▥ Small brown tree frog.

HUMAN IMPACT
TURTLE TRADING

As critically endangered species, all marine turtles are listed by CITES (the Convention on International Trade in Endangered Species), and their trade, capture, and harassment is banned under international law. However, cessation of trade alone is unlikely to prevent the extinction of the hawksbill turtle—their nesting beaches (in some 60 countries) must also be protected. They are still illegally hunted for food and eggs, and the intricate patterning of their shell is particularly sought after for jewelery and decorative furniture.

Toxin tolerance

Hawksbill turtle

Hawksbill turtles feed among the shallow algal beds of inshore waters or around coral reefs. They consume a wide variety of foods, including seaweed, mollusks, crustaceans, and small fishes. Their strong, sharp beaks are used to bite off chunks of both soft and hard coral colonies. When feeding on jellyfishes, such as the deadly Portuguese man-of-war, turtles close their eyes as a defense against being stung. The bulk of their diet, however, consists of sponges, many of which are highly toxic and packed with siliceous structures, called spicules, that are as sharp as shards of glass. Neither defense appears to deter the turtle.

Eretmochelys imbricata
- ↔ 2–3ft 3 in (0.6–1 m)
- ◐ Shallow reefs and inshore areas of subtropical and tropical waters worldwide.
- ▥ The smallest marine turtle, recognized by its shell shape, with distinctive central ridge, serrated edge, and overlapping scutes.

Changing tastes
Bearded dragon

These lizards alter their feeding habits during their lives. Juvenile bearded dragons are largely insectivorous so they are considered carnivores. They hunt small insects on the ground and in trees, constantly turning their heads as they look for prey and, when they have spotted an insect, bursting into activity to chase and catch it. Between periods of hunting, the young lizards rest and bask, often in trees. As the lizards grow, their diet changes and they begin to cons material, including leaves, fruits, and flowers. These plant parts are bitten off by powerful jaws. Bearded dragons have rounded rather than pointed snouts, a typical shape among herbivorous lizards. The tongue also plays an important part in their feeding: it can be flicked out to taste a food to check if it is edible, and it can also be used to pick up fallen fruits and flowers.

Amphibolurus barbatus
- ◄► 10–12 in (25–30 cm)
- ⊙ Desert, scrubland, and forest in eastern Australia.
- ▥ Gray, brown, or black lizard with a short tail, heavy body and head. Yellow lining to the mouth and a beard of throat spines.

CAUGHT IN MID-FLIGHT
Adult bearded dragons still consume animal prey, but their larger size allows them to diversify, feeding on larger insects, like this one, smaller reptiles, and small mammals.

Ground feeding
Southern cassowary

Being flightless and too large to climb, the southern cassowary feeds on the ground, searching through the leaf litter to find fungi, snails, insects, and small animals, such as frogs, to eat. It sifts through the litter by scratching at it with its feet and turning it over with its bill, but it also uses the calcified cartilage casque that projects from the top of its head as a shovel.

CASQUE SIZE
Male southern cassowaries generally have larger casques than females, and the casques continue to grow as the birds age. The red and blue coloration of the skin on its neck indicates that it is at least three years old.

Casuarius casuarius
- ◄► Up to 5½ ft (1.7 m)
- ⊙ Dense tropical forest in New Guinea and Australia.
- ▥ Large, thick-legged bird with solid crest or casque, brown and black plumage, and striking red and blue skin on the neck and face.

Flexible feeder
African harrier-hawk

Palm nuts and other fruits are often eaten by the African harrier-hawk, or gymnogene, but it is also an accomplished hunter, and includes insects, small mammals such as rabbits, birds and their eggs, bats, and reptiles in its varied diet. A harrier-hawk will walk on the ground to search out food, or undertake low foraging flights over patches of short vegetation, pouncing on its prey. However, most often this species is observed clambering through trees and shrubs to forage using its wings, feet, and bill to steady itself as it climbs. The hawk's slender bill is used to probe beneath bark and in crevices to find insect larvae and small reptiles. There are also observations of the bird hanging upside down from a gray-headed social weaver's nest, and grabbing an adult bird in its bill as it exited the nest hole.

The most remarkable thing about the African harrier-hawk is its double-jointed ankles; the joints bend both forward and backward. The bird uses its long, flexible legs to reach at seemingly impossible angles in search of hidden prey. Using this technique, African harrier-hawks have been seen hanging from the nests of weaver birds and reaching deep inside them to find the eggs and young.

CAVITY EXPLORER
The combination of small head, long neck, slender bill, and long, flexible legs make the African harrier-hawk skilled at finding food in small holes and crevices.

Polyboroides typus
- ◄► 24–26 in (60–66 cm)
- ⊙ Forest, woodland, and grassland in sub-Saharan Africa.
- ▥ Medium-sized gray raptor with naked yellow face and long yellow legs.

Soil supplements

Red and green macaw

In common with some other herbivores, red and green macaws exhibit geophagy, literally, soil eating. Large flocks of red and green macaws (and other parrot species) congregate on the eroded faces of riverbanks and mud cliffs to socialize and sometimes to nest in crevices and cavities, but most commonly in order to eat the soil.

The macaw diet is composed largely of fruits, seeds, berries, and nuts. Using their keen eyesight to forage in the forest canopy, groups of red and green macaws locate food and dextrously pluck fruits from the trees. Using their feet and sharp, hooked bill they tear open the flesh so that they can get at the hard seed or nut within. The macaw's bill can generate an enormous biting force, making it able to crack even the hardest nuts.

In order to avoid competition with other forest herbivores, for example monkeys like the saki, macaws eat underripe fruits and plants that are chemically defended and generally unpalatable, or even toxic to other animals. It is possible that macaws eat soil to supplement the mineral content of their diet, but it has also been shown that by electing to eat the particular soil type found at clay licks, the birds are able to neutralize the toxins in their gut.

Ara chloropterus
- ↔ Up to 3 ft 3 in (1 m)
- ⊙ Tropical forest in eastern Central America and northeastern South America.
- ▭ Large red, blue, and green parrot with a naked white face striped with small red feathers.

48

The pressure, in pounds per square inch, that can be generated by a macaw's bill.

SELF-MEDICATION
Macaws regularly travel considerable distances to gather at favored clay licks and eat the soil. The soil may detoxify toxins from some of the plants in the macaws' diet, and soil eating may therefore be viewed as a form of self-medication.

Fruit and meat

Kea

Like all parrots, the kea eats fruits, nuts, and seeds, but unlike other parrots, it has a taste for meat. Some dig into the nesting burrows of sooty shearwaters to kill and eat their chicks. Others, living in the hills and mountains—sometimes above the snow line—scavenge the carcasses of dead sheep. In the past, keas were seen eating the fat from the backs of live sheep, as a result of which they were hunted almost to extinction.

Nestor notabilis
- ↔ 18 in (46 cm)
- ⊙ Wooded and alpine areas of New Zealand's South Island.
- ▭ Olive-green parrot with scarlet underwings.

ADAPTABLE TOOL
The kea's elongated bill is perfect for biting, tearing, and lifting a variety of prey and objects, even prying rubber parts from cars, a behavior that has given it a reputation as a vandal.

Seasonal food

Great bustard

Historically a bird of open grassland, the great bustard is well adapted to survive in the modern agricultural landscape, particularly in areas of cereal growing. However, its persecution by humans has reduced its population considerably. Young bustards are almost entirely insectivorous, but as they age, the birds include increasing amounts of vegetable material in their diet. They forage in open areas, meandering in loose flocks and picking at selected food items. The birds adapt their diets in response to fluctuations in food availability associated with seasonal agricultural practices and a habitat dominated by annual plants. In summer they consume more insects (particularly beetles and their larvae) and also take small vertebrates, such as frogs and mice; in spring, fall, and winter they are almost exclusively vegetarian, with a very varied plant diet, including cereal crops.

Otis tarda
- ↔ Up to 3½ ft (1.1 m)
- ⊙ Scattered populations are found across the grasslands of Europe and Asia.
- ▭ Robust reddish brown and gray bird. Breeding males grow moustachial whiskers 8 in (20 cm) long.

HEAVYWEIGHT COMPETITION
The world's heaviest flying birds, male great bustards congregate at leks (communal display sites) and compete for the attention of females.

HUMAN IMPACT

REINTRODUCTION IN BRITAIN

After an absence of almost 200 years, the great bustard might once again become a familiar bird in parts of Britain. A program of reintroduction using birds of Russian origin (genetically the most similar to historical UK populations) was started and in 2007 a released bird laid eggs, although unfortunately they did not hatch. Extensive surveys determined that in the release areas, insect numbers in the summer would feed the growing chicks, but it may be necessary to manage winter feeding areas alongside crops to ensure the birds' survival over winter.

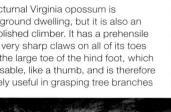

Unfussy eater

Virginia opossum

The nocturnal Virginia opossum is usually ground dwelling, but it is also an accomplished climber. It has a prehensile tail and very sharp claws on all of its toes except the large toe of the hind foot, which is opposable, like a thumb, and is therefore extremely useful in grasping tree branches while searching for food. With excellent night vision but poor distance vision, opossums are more likely to use touch and smell to locate food. The Virginia opossum eats a huge variety of food, from fruits, seeds, and plant material, to eggs, insects, and small vertebrates, including some reptiles, amphibians, and other mammals. It is even able to prey on poisonous snakes, having a higher resistance to snake venom than other mammals.

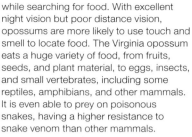

Didelphis virginiana

- 15–21½ in (38–55 cm)
- Forest, woodland, and farmland in Central America, the US, and southern states of Canada.
- Ratlike marsupial with silver-furred face and naked, prehensile tail.

CLEANING UP CARRION
Virginia opossums are extreme generalists and will eat almost anything. They are also opportunists and scavenge, taking advantage of carrion whenever they find it.

Shovel snout

White-nosed coati

A member of the racoon family, the white-nosed coati spends its days in a bustle of gregarious activity as it searches, often in groups, for food. It forages for its food, mostly on the ground and usually by digging and snuffling through the leaf litter, although it is also a skilled climber.

Coatis eat nuts, fruit, carrion, eggs, and small animals, such as insects and other invertebrates and small reptiles, which they sniff out with their excellent sense of smell and highly developed snout. The snout is shovel shaped and long, protruding beyond the lower jaw. It is muscular and flexible and can be pushed into crevices or under bark in the search for food. Coati teeth differ from those of most other mammalian carnivores, in that the molars are flattened for crushing and grinding, rather than for shearing flesh.

Nasua narica

- 2½–4¼ ft (0.8–1.3 m)
- Wooded areas of southeast Arizona, US, and Mexico, through Central America to Panama and northeast Colombia.
- Long-nosed, long-tailed, slender carnivore with a distinctive white muzzle and white face pattern.

FOND OF FRUIT
The white-nosed coati can climb to reach fruits and other arboreal foods, using its long tail to help it balance; however, this species is primarily a ground forager.

Tireless forager

Wild boar

To obtain the high levels of protein they need to survive, wild boars are generalist omnivores, using their snouts to locate and then dig out buried food. Their ability to find food in a wide range of habitats explains their global success. Ranging widely, and foraging from dawn to dusk, wild boars rest during the middle of the day and night. Plants, especially fruits and nuts, constitute 90 percent of their diet. The remaining 10 percent has been known to include insects, eggs, small vertebrates, carrion, and even refuse, their exact diet varying with the seasons.

Sus scrofa

- 3–3½ ft (0.9–1.1 m)
- Woodland in Europe, North Africa, and Asia.
- Typically porcine with large head and compact body, brown and black in color and sparsely bristled.
- ≫ 485

AN ADVENTUROUS PALATE
Young wild boars are even less particular about what they eat than their parents, which increases their chance of survival in an environment where food availability fluctuates.

HUMAN IMPACT

ACCIDENTAL REINTRODUCTION

Three hundred years ago, wild boars in Britain had been hunted to extinction, but in the 1990s they were again found in the wild. It is believed that some animals may have escaped or been released from the wild boar farms that were popular ventures at the time. Significant numbers were then found in many rural areas throughout southern and western England. While some view it as a welcome return, many farmers disagree, citing damage to crops and harassment of their cattle.

Huge appetite

Blue whale

Believed to be the largest animal ever to have lived, the blue whale is a filter feeder that migrates to the southern oceans each summer to feed mainly on krill (small shrimps), and also consume other crustaceans, squids, and small fishes associated with krill swarms. During the summer feeding season, a blue whale can consume up to 4.4 tons (4 tonnes) of krill every day. This allows the whales to lay down reserves of fat and oil, which will provide energy during the rest of the year when food is less abundant. A feeding whale opens its mouth, relaxes its throat, and takes in a vast volume of water and associated food. It then closes its mouth, tightens its throat, and uses its massive tongue to force the water out through huge baleen sieves that hang from its upper jaws. The krill are trapped against the inner surface of the baleen sieves and are then swallowed by the whale.

Blue whales can be found in oceans all over the world, although the three primary populations are in the North Atlantic, North Pacific, and the Southern Hemisphere. Typically living in groups of two or three animals, they mate and calve in tropical to temperate waters in the winter months and feed in polar waters in the summer.

Balaenoptera musculus

- 79–89 ft (24–27 m)
- May be found in all of the world's oceans, although absolute numbers are small.
- Mottled bluish gray; more slender in appearance than other whales.

2,204 lb The amount of food needed to fill up a blue whale's stomach.

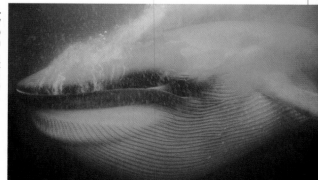

GETTING A MOUTHFUL
Krill undertake a daily migration between deep water and the ocean surface. To reach them, blue whales feed at depths of 330 ft (100 m) by day and close to the surface at night.

Occasional carnivore

Brown bear

Although they are often perceived as fearsome carnivores, brown bears are actually omnivores, with a diet that is at times composed largely of plant material. Their diet varies with the season and geographical location, but tends to include green vegetation, berries and fruits, roots and tubers, insects, and carrion. When they are available, bears will catch fishes, and they occasionally hunt mammalian prey, particularly newborn deer in spring. They have the well-developed canines of a typical carnivore, and extremely powerful jaws with which to kill prey and crush food. Their paws and strong forelimbs enable them to dig, and their sheer bulk means that they are able to defend carrion against predators such as wolves.

Ursus arctos

⬛ 5½–9¼ ft (1.7–2.8 m)

⬤ Upland forests and tundra regions in North America, northern Europe, and Asia.

▭ Large blonde, brown, or black bear with a wide face and prominent mid-shoulder hump.

≫ 413

BERRY TIME

Brown bears on the Alaskan tundra like to eat bright red, carbohydrate-rich bearberries (hence their name) when they appear in fall.

SHOOTS AND LEAVES

Belying their fearsome reputation, brown bears actually consume significant amounts of plant material, such as plant shoots in spring and fruits in fall.

CASE STUDY

PLANT EATERS AND MEAT EATERS

A study of brown bears in North America revealed that those which feed predominantly on meat and fish (mainly salmon), which are comparatively rich in nutrients, are significantly heavier than those whose diet consists mainly of plant material, which is relatively poor in nutrients: female plant-eating bears had an average weight of 209 lb (95 kg) compared to 474 lb (215 kg) for female meat eaters. In addition, female meat-eating brown bears had larger litters, on average, than plant eaters, and the population density of meat-eating bears tended to be higher. Factors other than diet may also affect bear population density, however—for example, human activities, such as logging and recreational activities.

PLANT-EATING
BEAR, 209 LB (95 KG)

MEAT-EATING
BEAR, 474 LB (215 KG)

FOOD SHARING

Brown bear cubs remain with their mothers until at least the second spring of their lives, and will learn how to hunt, forage, and fish. This mother bear is sharing the catch with her cub.

GONE FISHING

Brown bears exhibit a range of fishing techniques, from waiting and watching the water before pinning down a passing fish, to simply diving in and chasing their prey. When fishes are plentiful, a bear will choose the younger, more nutrient-rich fishes, sometimes only eating the most energy-rich parts, and discarding the remainder.

Predation

All organisms need energy to survive, and in order to obtain energy, most animals have to feed on living organisms, such as plants or other animals. Predators are animals that have evolved to hunt, capture, and feed on other living creatures. As their prey develops ways to avoid being caught, predators have to develop skills and behaviors that allow them to successfully find, catch, and kill their chosen food.

Feeding strategies

Many predators specialize on one species of prey or a few closely related species—the numbers of predators and prey being an important factor in regulating both populations. When prey is abundant, the population of predators tends to increase. This may continue until there is a shortage of prey, causing the numbers of predators to fall. Large fluctuations in predator and prey populations can occur due to factors such as disease and weather conditions. Some predators may take a number of species within the same size range, while others attack anything suitable they encounter in a particular type of habitat.

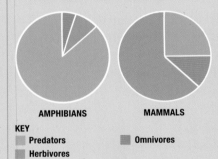

AMPHIBIANS   **MAMMALS**

KEY
■ Predators   ■ Omnivores
■ Herbivores

RATIO
Within an animal group there may be a range of feeding strategies—amphibians are mostly predatory, while most mammal species are herbivores. While many species are entirely carnivorous or herbivorous, there are some that are omnivorous (use both feeding strategies).

○ CANNIBALISM

Cannibalism, where an animal eats members of its own species, is widespread. Many species practice cannibalism because of factors such as overcrowding or food shortage. Female tiger sharks have two uteruses and in each, the largest of the developing embryos will eat any smaller embryos. Sexual cannibalism, observed in praying mantids and some spiders, is a special case where males are eaten during copulation. By eating young cubs, male lions taking over a pride bring the females into heat so that they can mate and produce their own litter. Sometimes cannibalism occurs when individuals are injured or die, as with the scavenging tadpoles shown here.

Speed

To avoid being eaten, an animal has a limited number of options. It can avoid detection by being camouflaged and still; it can protect itself mechanically with spines or armor, or chemically with a noxious odor or taste; or it can try to outrun a predator. In this case, the need for speed has generated an "arms race" over time, where hunting animals and their quarry evolve increasingly better morphological, physiological, and behavioral traits. Often predator and prey become very evenly matched and success or failure is often down to luck, surprise, or health.

⊳ HIGH-SPEED PREDATORS

kph	50	100	150	200
peregrine falcon				185kph
cheetah		112kph		
lion	80kph			
coyote	69kph			
black mamba 20kph				
sailfish		109kph		
shortfin mako shark	74kph			

mph	50	100

■ Air
■ Land
■ Water

The top speed attainable by predators depends to a large degree on the medium in which they operate. Stooping peregrines, the fastest of all predators, minimize wind resistance by being streamlined and are helped in acceleration by gravity. The high density of water restricts the speeds that can be achieved by aquatic predators.

CHEETAH
The cheetah is well adapted to hunting. Its lightweight skeleton, large muscle mass, and nonretractable claws give it good acceleration and a maximum speed of up to 70 mph (113 kph) over short distances.

Detecting prey

Predators have evolved a range of senses appropriate to their prey, the environment in which they live, and their hunting strategy. In aquatic habitats, some predatory species may simply wait for the water currents to bring food to them. Active predators need to look for food and can increase their chances of success by concentrating on areas where their prey is likely to congregate. For diurnal (day) predators, vision is likely to be the most important sense, and their eyes need to be forward facing to allow distance to be judged accurately. Nocturnal predators, such as owls, may have good hearing and eyesight. Subterranean predators may rely exclusively on touch—cave-dwelling whip-spiders feel for their prey in total darkness using long, slender front legs. Chemosensory organs that detect airborne odors or waterborne chemicals enable some predators to locate their prey at a distance.

Sharks have an incredible sense of smell and can detect certain molecules in the water at concentrations of only 1 part per 25 million.

○ PREDATORY SENSES

SIGHT
Eye structure differs between animal groups. Most arthropods have compound eyes made up of multiple light-gathering units, while vertebrates and cephalopods have camera-like eyes that use a single lens to focus light and form an image.

HEARING
Hearing is the ability to detect sound vibrations transmitted through air, water, or a solid medium. Hearing organs vary in complexity, from simple structures to the highly complex ears of mammals. A barn owl can locate prey through hearing alone.

SMELL
Smell is a chemoreceptive sense for detecting odors in air. Most mammals, especially carnivores, such as foxes, have a well-developed sense of smell for detecting prey. Animals give off odors for communication purposes.

TOUCH
Mechanoreception is found in a wide range of animals. It is highly developed in spiders (such as this tarantula), which use sensitive vibration receptors on their legs to detect the presence and movements of prey.

TEMPERATURE SENSING
The ability to visualize infrared radiation has evolved in snakes such as boas, pit vipers (shown here), and pythons. Temperature-sensing organs on the head allow these species to find warm-blooded prey in complete darkness.

ECHOLOCATION
Echolocation (biological sonar) has evolved in most bats, dolphins, porpoises, and other toothed whales. Echoes received from high-frequency calls are used to locate and identify prey.

Stealth

Many predators, whether they are active chasers or ambushers that lie in wait, rely heavily on stealth to be successful. Hunting of any kind expends huge amounts of energy, and failure may not only result in hunger but also seriously reduce the survival chances of the predator's young. Since it is likely that its prey has also evolved good vision, often with eyes located on the sides of the head to give a wide, nonoverlapping field of view, a predator needs to be able to approach its target without being detected itself. Prey species may feed in groups and large numbers of eyes mean that some can always keep watch, making life difficult for a predator. One adaptation that helps both predators and prey conceal themselves is camouflage. Coloring can allow an animal to blend in with the background and disruptive markings can help break up the body outline, which makes prey difficult to see but also helps predators get close enough to make a kill. To increase their chances, predators often make use of vegetation cover and move as noiselessly as possible, keeping low to the ground as they stalk.

SILK TRAPS
Spiders have developed the ability to produce silk and use it to trap insects. In many species, the snare takes the form of a characteristic web, spun across a gap in vegetation.

LURES
Several snakes have evolved lures to entice prey closer. Often the lure is wiggled around, its color contrasting strongly with the rest of the predator's body.

STALKING JAGUAR
Hunting in the dense rain forest of Central and South America, the jaguar takes a wide range of prey, including caimans, anaconda, peccaries, and capybaras. It has a very powerful bite, allowing it to crush skulls and shatter turtle shells.

○ OPPORTUNISM

Many predators are opportunists. Rather than targeting any particular species or type of prey, they simply move around their preferred habitat looking for suitable food. Hedgehogs forage on the ground and among leaf litter, where they find earthworms, insects and their larvae, slugs, and even small vertebrates.

LYING IN WAIT
A pack of wolves attack a group of musk oxen, who will attempt to form a defensive circle with their horns facing outward.

Cooperative hunting

In some species, cooperation enables members of a group to obtain more food than they would be able to by hunting alone. Cooperative hunting is more likely to arise if individuals are related to each other and is an important element in the evolution of social groups. Cooperative hunting has many benefits: it increases foraging success, affords better protection from rivals or enemies, allows larger, better-defended prey to be targeted, and reduces the risk of injury to individuals. In African hunting dogs, the size of the pack determines the size of the prey. Small packs will select impalas and small antelopes, while larger packs are able to kill species such as wildebeests. Cooperative hunting has been studied in vertebrates such as chimpanzees, dogs, lions, hyenas, orcas, porpoises, sharks, fishes, and birds. Among invertebrates, social insects such as army and driver ants are well known for this feeding strategy.

Weapons

Predators have evolved an array of weapons to seize and kill prey. The most common weapons among vertebrates are teeth and claws. Mammalian carnivores have enlarged canine teeth for killing, and their carnassial teeth mesh together to tear through flesh. The claws of carnivores are large and curved for catching and holding prey. Fish-eating species typically have a large number of sharp, pointed teeth for securing slippery prey. Birds that dive for fishes have sharp, pointed bills with backward-facing serrations for gripping. Birds of prey have large talons for holding prey and strong, hooked bills for tearing it apart. Invertebrates have a great variety of weapons, including venomous stingers.

venom duct

groove (or hollow fang) down which venom flows

teeth curve backward

venom gland

SNAKE SKULL

lower jaw (mandible)

temporal muscle

carnassial tooth

lower canine

masseter muscle

HYENA SKULL

CONTRASTING SKULLS
The hyena has a massive skull with relatively short jaws, giving it a powerful grip. In most mammalian carnivores, the carnassial teeth are sharp, shearing flesh before it is swallowed. In contrast, a snake's skull is delicate, and the loosely articulated, flexible jaws, open very wide. In vipers, killing is done using toxic venom injected into the prey by two fangs.

TALONS
Three forward-pointing talons and one backward-pointing talon ensure that this red-backed hawk gets a firm grip on its prey.

CLAWS
Scorpions combine claw strength and venom to subdue and kill prey. Although this fat-tailed scorpion has relatively slender claws, its potent venom allows it to easily overcome a small reptile.

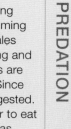

Killing techniques

Predators kill in various ways depending on the size and nature of each species. Dismemberment, strangulation, drowning, impaling, and poisoning are the main methods. Large carnivores, such as tigers, kill their prey as quickly as possible, avoiding personal injury or prey escape. Small prey is bitten on the back of the neck, breaking the spinal cord and severing the blood vessels. Death is often instantaneous. Larger animals are seized by the throat and held until they die of asphyxiation. Toxic salivary secretions have evolved in many animals, including snakes, spiders, jellyfish, and even some mollusks.

CLAM EATERS
Some species are not just eaten by one predator but by a whole range of predators, each using a different technique. Although they have tough, hinged shells and strong muscles to keep them shut, bivalve mollusks are a favorite food of many animals, including small sharks, walruses, squid, and many shorebirds.

The shore crab uses its strong claws to crack and pry open bivalves.

A moon snail drills a hole in the prey's shell, before injecting enzymes to dissolve the contents.

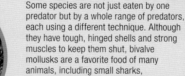

BIVALVE

American oystercatchers probe into mud and either pry or hammer shells open.

This common starfish pulls the shell open and everts its stomach inside.

Sea otters eat floating on their backs and often use rocks to bash open the shells.

Eating prey

Prey may be eaten in a number of ways depending on the predator. With very large predators consuming large numbers of small prey, such as baleen whales feeding on krill, there is no need for preprocessing and the food is simply swallowed. In contrast, snakes are adapted to eating prey as large as themselves. Since they cannot chew it, it is swallowed whole and digested. Most predators cut their food into pieces in order to eat the most nutritious parts. In other animals, such as starfish, digestion takes place outside the body.

DIGESTING FIRST
The mouthparts of many flies are adapted for sponging and licking. The house fly cannot eat solid food so has to liquefy it before it can be consumed. To do this it regurgitates part of its previous meal, as well as salivary enzymes, before feeding.

BEFORE DEATH
An assassin bug picks a weak spot in its prey's exoskeleton, such as the soft, flexible membranes between plates of cuticle. Its sharp mouthparts stab through the surface, injecting toxic, protein-dissolving enzymes. Once liquefied, the body is sucked up by the bug.

EATING WHOLE
Like all snakes, the eyelash viper cannot chew its food and swallows it whole. Once caught on the back-curved teeth, the prey is propelled slowly down the throat in a ratchetlike fashion.

PLAYING WITH FOOD
Young predators such as cats that play with their prey before killing it are thought to be practicing their hunting and prey-handling techniques. This polar bear is tossing a piece of meat into the air before consumption

SAVE FOR LATER
The red-backed shrike stores food it cannot eat immediately. It makes a larder by impaling items on thorns or wedging them in forked twigs. This behavior allows the bird to hoard prey when it is abundant, and to handle larger items such as small lizards.

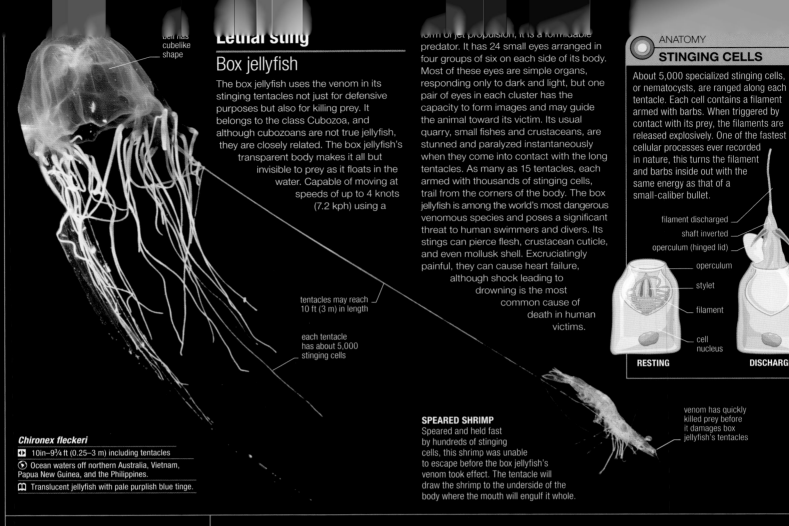

bell has cubelike shape

Lethal sting
Box jellyfish

The box jellyfish uses the venom in its stinging tentacles not just for defensive purposes but also for killing prey. It belongs to the class Cubozoa, and although cubozoans are not true jellyfish, they are closely related. The box jellyfish's transparent body makes it all but invisible to prey as it floats in the water. Capable of moving at speeds of up to 4 knots (7.2 kph) using a form of jet propulsion, it is a formidable predator. It has 24 small eyes arranged in four groups of six on each side of its body. Most of these eyes are simple organs, responding only to dark and light, but one pair of eyes in each cluster has the capacity to form images and may guide the animal toward its victim. Its usual quarry, small fishes and crustaceans, are stunned and paralyzed instantaneously when they come into contact with the long tentacles. As many as 15 tentacles, each armed with thousands of stinging cells, trail from the corners of the body. The box jellyfish is among the world's most dangerous venomous species and poses a significant threat to human swimmers and divers. Its stings can pierce flesh, crustacean cuticle, and even mollusk shell. Excruciatingly painful, they can cause heart failure, although shock leading to drowning is the most common cause of death in human victims.

tentacles may reach 10 ft (3 m) in length

each tentacle has about 5,000 stinging cells

SPEARED SHRIMP
Speared and held fast by hundreds of stinging cells, this shrimp was unable to escape before the box jellyfish's venom took effect. The tentacle will draw the shrimp to the underside of the body where the mouth will engulf it whole.

ANATOMY
STINGING CELLS

About 5,000 specialized stinging cells, or nematocysts, are ranged along each tentacle. Each cell contains a filament armed with barbs. When triggered by contact with its prey, the filaments are released explosively. One of the fastest cellular processes ever recorded in nature, this turns the filament and barbs inside out with the same energy as that of a small-caliber bullet.

filament discharged
shaft inverted
operculum (hinged lid)
operculum
stylet
filament
cell nucleus

RESTING   **DISCHARGED**

venom has quickly killed prey before it damages box jellyfish's tentacles

Chironex fleckeri
- 10in–9¾ ft (0.25–3 m) including tentacles
- Ocean waters off northern Australia, Vietnam, Papua New Guinea, and the Philippines.
- Translucent jellyfish with pale purplish blue tinge.

Glue guns
Velvet worm

This species of velvet worm emerges after dark to hunt the forest floor for crickets, termites, worms, and insect larvae. It uses its antennae to feel for prey, but has a pair of simple eyes and can aim its glue guns at objects up to 12 in (30 cm) away. The mucuslike glue, which is produced by the large slime glands that run along the length of its body, can make up a tenth of the weight of the animal. It is squirted from holes at the tip of a pair of modified legs called the oral papilla and once expelled hardens quickly. Once the prey is trapped, the velvet worm bites it and injects it with salivary enzymes. The velvet worm has curved jaws which it uses to bite off softened parts off the prey and suck up dissolved fluids. Consuming a large prey item may take all night.

Macroperipatus acacioi
- 4½ in (12 cm)
- Rain forest in Brazil.
- Soft-bodied and wormlike with small surface warts and numerous pairs of stumpy, unjointed legs.

Camouflaged hunter
Giant cuttlefish

The giant cuttlefish, the world's largest, stalks or ambushes its prey. Cuttlefish can change their color and skin texture to match their background since their skin contains up to 200 pigment cells called chromatophores per square millimeter. There are three types of chromatophores—yellow, red-orange, and brown-black—and below these, reflecting cells called iridophores provide shades of blue and green. Cuttlefish have excellent binocular vision and can judge distance well. Fishes and crustaceans are snared by two long tentacles covered in suction pads. Once brought to the mouth, the prey is bitten and toxic saliva injected. It is then ripped apart by a sharp, parrotlike beak.

DEADLY STRIKE
When prey is spotted, a giant cuttlefish turns toward it and, holding its arms together to guide it, launches its tentacles with deadly speed and accuracy.

Giant cuttlefish can **wiggle their tentacles** to lure prey

Sepia apama
- Up to 5 ft (1.5 m)
- Rocky ledges on reefs and among sea grass off the southern coast of Australia, including Tasmania.
- Soft elongate body with an internal bone and skirtlike fin. Eight arms and two much longer tentacles.
- » 342

Pinned down
Horned helmet shell

Also called the giant horned helmet shell or conch, this marine snail hunts and eats sea urchins. Males are smaller than females and have fewer, but larger and blunter knobs or horns. The front of the shell has an upturned groove called the siphonal notch along which a siphon lies and projects into the water. It is through this siphon that the snail "tastes" the water for the chemical scent trails left by wandering sea urchins and other types of echinoderms, their principal food. During the day, the horned helmet shell lies buried in shallow water with just the tips of its horns exposed, but when darkness falls

>>01   >>02   >>03   >>04

it moves out of its hiding place to hunt for food. Once it has closed in on its prey, it raised its body and pins down its victim using its large muscular foot. Despite its size and weight, it is unharmed by the urchin's sharp spines.

Cassis cornuta
- ◆ Up to 15½ in (40 cm)
- ◉ Indian Ocean from East Africa to Australia and Pacific Ocean east to Hawaii.
- ▥ Knobbed shell with peach-colored aperture. Males are larger than females.

STALKING A SEA URCHIN
>>01 The snail locates its prey by detecting its scent trail. >>02 It raises its body by flexing its foot. >>03 The snail moves over the urchin before pinning it down. >>04 It then secretes mucus to dissolve a hole in the urchin's shell. Using a toothed radula, or "tongue," it enlarges the hole through which it can extract the urchin's internal organs.

Poison dart
Cone shells

These sea snails hunt marine worms, other mollusks, and even fishes, paralyzing them with the venom from a poison gland that is injected by a harpoon-shaped dart. The venom is very fast acting, causing almost instant paralysis. Alerted by the smell of

prey nearby, the snail extends its proboscis, and when contact is made it fires a harpoon with explosive speed into the body of the prey. The victim remains attached so it can be drawn back into the proboscis, which expands to engulf it. Indigestible parts of the prey and the used harpoon are later expelled.

PROBOSCIS AND HARPOON
The snail's proboscis emerges from the opening at the end of its shell. Just behind its tip lies a hollow, barbed harpoon that it uses to impale its prey.

Family Conidae
- ◆ Up to 10 in (25 cm)
- ◉ Warm tropical seas worldwide.
- ▥ Brightly colored, roughly conical shell with an aperture running its full length.

spider hangs from foliage

sticky globule is swung toward prey

Ordgarius magnificus
- ◆ Legspan up to 1 in (2.5 cm)
- ◉ In eucalyptus trees and shrubby vegetation on the east coast of Queensland and New South Wales, Australia.
- ▥ Pale spider with very broad yellow or pink-spotted abdomen, and two distinctive dorsal bumps.

Deadly threads
Magnificent Bolas spider

This bolas spider is a specialist nocturnal predator of moths, sheltering in leaves tied together with silk during the day. Like all bolas spiders, it entices moths to their doom by producing an imitation of their sexual pheromone. It is thought that this chemical is contained in the sticky blobs of glue at the end of the catching thread. The spider aims and throws its sticky lure toward a passing moth and, if successful, pulls up the thread, bites the prey, and may eat it immediately or wrap it in silk for later consumption.

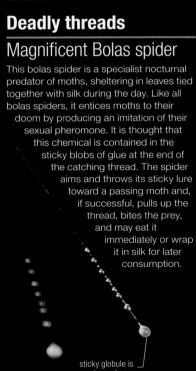

Casting a net
Rufous net-casting spider

This spider hides during the day and comes out after dark to catch nocturnal prey such as ants, crickets, beetles, and other spiders. It spins a small sheet of pale blue, elastic, fuzzy silk held in a silk framework and then holds the net open with its first two pairs of legs. Any passing insect is enveloped in the net.

LARGE EYES
The rufous net-casting spider is also known as the ogre-faced spider for the fact that two of its eyes are very large and forward facing. It has excellent vision and relies entirely on sight to detect prey.

Deinopis subrufa
- ◆ Legspan up to 5 in (13 cm)
- ◉ Wooded and garden habitats in southeast Australia and Tasmania.
- ▥ Long, slender abdomen is light gray or pinkish brown to dark brown. Slender sticklike legs.

Flower pouncer
White crab spider

These spiders hide in silken retreats spun between leaves, or sit in or beside flowers, camouflaged by a resemblance to flower parts or buds. Like most crab spiders, this is an ambush predator. At night it can catch moths, but during the day catches flies and even honey bees that visit whitish flowers such as daisies and jasmine. The spider seizes the insect, bites it behind the head, and holds it until it stops struggling.

Thomisus spectabilis
- ◆ Legspan up to 1½ in (3.5 cm)
- ◉ Among vegetation and flowers in Australia.
- ▥ Whitish abdomen and some dark markings. Grayish cephalothorax with pale banding on legs.

FISHING SPIDER

With its fangs sunk deep into its victim's flesh, a fishing spider begins to feed. As an adult, the leg span of this species can reach 4½ in (12 cm). It is widespread in northern South America, where it sits by pools in the rain forest, waiting for passing prey, which it seizes with its front legs before injecting a fast-acting toxin.

Silk pit

Funnel-web weavers

These spiders owe their common name to the shape of their webs. They typically make a flat, sheetlike structure with a funnel-shaped retreat in the middle or at one side of the web. They spend the day deep inside their protective retreat, emerging after dark to hunt. Sitting in wait at the entrance of their funnel, the spider rushes out to grab any suitable prey that walks across or flies onto the flat part of the web. After biting it and injecting it with a fast-acting venom, the funnel-web weaver takes the prey back to the safety of the retreat to eat it. Some species, called house spiders, make their webs inside houses and outbuildings, usually in dark corners and basements.

Family Agelenidae

Legspan up to 3¼ in (8 cm)

Among a wide range of vegetation or inside buildings worldwide.

Hairy bodies and long, hairy legs. Drab in color, but abdomens may have dark bars, chevrons, or spots.

Leaping for prey

Jumping spiders

Jumping spiders do not make a web to catch their food but stalk prey during the day and move within range before leaping to seize it. They have excellent binocular vision with the middle pair of front-facing eyes greatly enlarged. Not only is their eyesight extremely acute, but, unlike other spiders, they can move the back of their main eyes inside their head so that they can look from side to side without moving. When hunting, these spiders attach a safety thread to a fixed point.

SEIZING PREY
Jumping spiders can jump 50–60 times their own body length. Their legs extend not by muscular action but by having fluid forced rapidly into them.

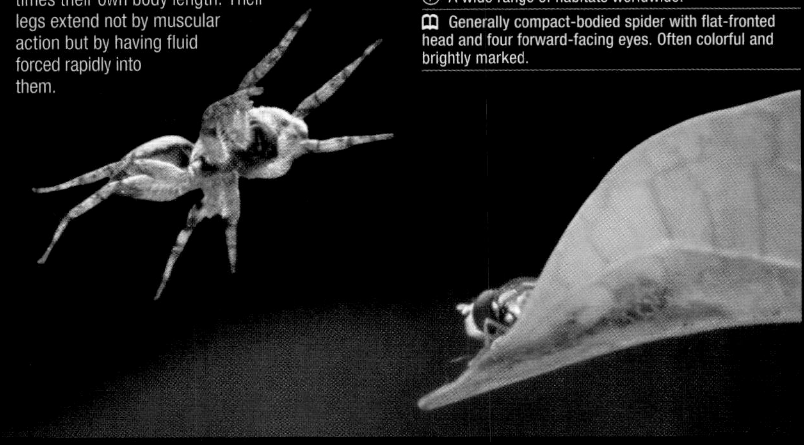

Family Salticidae

Legspan up to ⅝ in (1.8 cm)

A wide range of habitats worldwide.

Generally compact-bodied spider with flat-fronted head and four forward-facing eyes. Often colorful and brightly marked.

Decorated trap

Decoy spider

This decoy spider decorates its vertical orb web with conspicuous patterns of silk, called stabilimenta, which incorporate the remains of its prey, its own shed skins, and even plant and fungal material. Studies have shown that by decorating their webs decoy spiders may attract or intercept more prey, although the decorations may have other functions. It has been suggested that these obvious patterns may prevent birds and large insects from flying through the webs by accident, or that sitting at the center of its web, legs folded, the decoy spider is camouflaged from predators. It is also possible that the web debris advertises the success of a female spider to potential mates.

Cyclosa insulana

Legspan up to ¾ in (2 cm)

Forests and yards from the Mediterranean to Southeast Asia and northern Australia.

Drably-colored spider with a misshapen, knob-ended abdomen.

RAPID STRIKE
>>01 Using its acute vision and a specialized location technique, the mantis calculates the exact distance, speed, and direction required to snatch its prey. >>02 The front legs are fully extended before the tibiae are flexed around the prey in a vicelike grip. >>03 The mantis retracts its legs and brings its prey up to its mouth. The strike has lasted less than 100 milliseconds.

>>01 >>02 >>03

Climbing the walls

Giant centipede

These large centipedes are prone to drying out and typically forage away from sunlight, after dark. Their prey comprises insects, such as crickets and cockroaches, and vertebrates such as birds, lizards, and mice. They mainly feed on the ground among leaf litter and under stones, but are now known to be able to climb up the walls of caves, where they prey on roosting bats, which can be up to twice their own mass. Despite their considerable size, giant centipedes are extremely fast-moving and agile and can move with ease over rocks vertically and even upside down. The first pair of legs has been modified into stout, sharp claws that inject powerful venom from poison glands. The venom is usually injected near the head of their prey, where it works quickly, and while the prey struggles, the centipede wraps its other legs around it.

Scolopendra gigantea
- ↔ Up to 14 in (35 cm)
- ⊙ Forest in Central and South America
- ▭ Robust flattened bodies with reddish brown segments each with a pair of yellowish legs. Head has a pair of segmented antennae and strong mandibles.

SECURE GRIP
A bat retuning from a nocturnal foraging trip has been plucked out of the air at the entrance of a cave. Giant centipedes can hang from the ceiling or an overhang, maintaining a firm grip with at least five pairs of legs.

Extending mouth

Lesser emperor dragonfly nymph

As with all dragonflies, the nymphs of the lesser emperor dragonfly live in lakes and ponds among vegetation and bottom debris, where they hunt for prey which they catch using a concertina-like lower mouthparts (see panel, right). Their gills are located within the rectal chamber and, if required, water can be forced out at high speed for a jet-propelled escape from potential enemies.

Anax parthenope
- ↔ 2¾ in (7 cm)
- ⊙ Lakes and ponds in Europe and Asia.
- ▭ Greenish brown abdomen with broad blue bands at base, and pale greenish brown thorax.

SPECIALIZED MOUTHPARTS

The aquatic nymphs (or naiads) of dragonflies are highly predatory and have specialized mouthparts (mandibles) for catching prey. The mouth is long, hinged, and prehensile, with a pair of hooked palps, and folds back on itself. It can be shot forward using muscular action and hydraulic pressure in 25 milliseconds or less.

CALCULATED STRIKE
>>01 A passing fish has alerted this dragonfly nymph to its presence. The nymph watches it for a short distance.   >>02 When ready, the nymph launches itself upward and extends the lower mouthpart forward from underneath the head.   >>03 Impaled on either side by the sharp hooks on the palps, the fish is brought to the mandibles.

>>01   >>02   >>03

Sudden ambush

Common praying mantis

Like all other mantids, the common praying mantis has a highly specialized predatory lifestyle. A skilled ambusher, it remains motionless and relies on its cryptic green or brown coloration to avoid being seen. It has a distinctive triangular head that is very mobile and has a pair of large compound eyes, which face forward to provide it true binocular vision. It gauges distance to its prey by moving its head to measure the prey's apparent movement relative to its background. Known as binocular triangulation, this technique is widespread among vertebrates but much less common among invertebrates. There are many modifications of the mantis's body that make it a superb hunter. The first segment of the thorax, which carries the specialized front legs, is very long. Together with the elongated upper segment of the front legs, this gives the mantis a very broad reach. The front femur is greatly enlarged to house the muscles that operate the tibia, and has rows of sharp spines on its inner surface. The front tibia is also spined and folds back like a jackknife to mesh with the spines on the femur, making a formidable trap. The middle and hind pair of legs are used for walking and holding onto vegetation. The common praying mantis is mainly active during the day and eats a wide range of insects, spiders, and other arthropods. When prey is caught and subdued, the mantis uses its tough jaws to slice through tissue and chitin with equal ease.

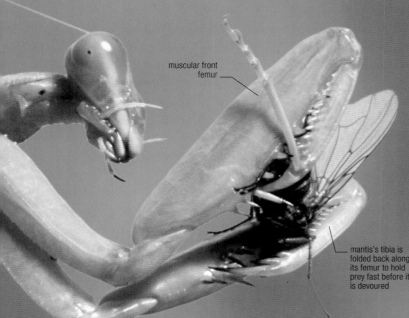

muscular front femur

mantis's tibia is folded back along its femur to hold prey fast before it is devoured

Mantis religiosa
- ↔ Up to 2¾ in (7 cm)
- ⊙ In all kinds of vegetation in Europe; introduced to North America.
- ▭ Elongate, green or brown insect with large, spiny front legs and distinctive triangular head.

HELD FAST
The prey is impaled and held by the front legs, so there is no need for venom, and a mantis eats its food alive. Generally the whole victim is eaten, leaving only fragments.

Aquatic assassin

Giant water bug nymphs

Giant water bugs are fierce predators both as adults and as nymphs. Nymphs have large bulging eyes and either lie in wait for prey to pass close enough to lunge forward and grab it with their specially modified front legs, or hunt actively using their middle and hind legs to swim. Once the prey is caught, the bug uses its sharp mouthparts to stab it, usually in the neck, and inject highly toxic saliva, which paralyzes the victim. Similar in composition to some snake venom, the toxin dissolves the prey's flesh so that the liquefied meal can then be sucked up by the bug. Although the larvae of aquatic insects form a large part of the diet of giant water bugs, surprisingly, they will also readily attack crayfish, tadpoles, frogs, fishes, and even small water birds, all prey that are much larger than themselves.

THROAT WOUND
This giant water bug nymph has successfully ambushed a frog by attacking it from below, injecting toxic venom, and keeping clear of the amphibian's powerful hind legs.

Family Belostomatidae
- Up to 6 in (15 cm)
- Freshwater streams and ponds worldwide, especially the Americas, southern Africa, and Southeast Asia.
- Streamlined body with strong grasping front legs.

> The saliva of giant water bug nymphs is similar to the venom of some snakes. It is **extremely toxic** and paralyzes the bugs' victims.

Surface predator

Common pondskater

These gregarious bugs are well adapted for catching small insects trapped by the film at the surface of fresh water. The front legs are short and used to grasp prey as the pondskater eats, while the middle and hind legs are very long, and splay out to support the insect on the water and propel it across the surface at great speed. Pondskaters are covered in dense, water-repellent hairs, and the front legs have ripple-sensitive hairs that enable them to detect and locate the movement of their prey.

Gerris lacustris
- ½ in (1.5 cm)
- On still or slow-moving water in Europe.
- Slender body, brownish above and silvery gray beneath, with long middle and hind legs.

Open jaws

Giant antlion larva

Giant antlion larvae bury themselves in coarse sand, with just the top of their heads and open jaws showing above the surface, while they wait for insects and other prey to ambush. Sensitive hairs and relatively good eyesight tell the antlion when to strike. Anchored deep in the sand, it can subdue large prey. The toothed, sickle-shaped jaws are two hollow tubes through which salivary enzymes can be injected into the prey to paralyze it and dissolve its internal organs. The resulting soup is then sucked back up and eaten. Some antlion larvae build special conical pits in loose sand. They then flick sand grains at passing insects to knock them down into the bottom of the pit where they are seized and eaten.

Palpares immensus
- 2 in (5 cm)
- Sandy areas among long grass in southern Africa.
- Fat-bodied with a slender neck and squarish head, which has very large jaws armed with sharp teeth.

CAPTURED
Once the toothed jaws of the antlion larva have snapped shut, crushing the prey's body, there is no escape. It will quickly be dragged under the surface and eaten.

Sticky snare

Fungus gnat larva

Often called glow worms, the larvae of this gnat live in a mucus tube supported by a loose scaffolding of silken threads. From this structure hang as many as 50 vertical threads coated in small beadlets of a sticky, gluelike substance. To attract flying insects such as mosquitoes, midges, mayflies, caddisflies, and even beetles to their sticky snares, the larvae produce a soft blue-green glow from the rear ends of their bodies. When an insect becomes trapped in the glue, the larva moves slowly along one of the horizontal parts of the web to the end of the thread and begins to reel the victim in.

GLOWING TRAP
The gnat larvae have to live in very sheltered locations as the slightest gust of wind would tangle the sticky beadlets on the threads together, making the trap useless.

Arachnocampa tasmaniensis
- Up to 1¼ in (3 cm)
- Caves, overhangs, and deep gullies in Tasmania.
- Soft-bodied, pale, maggotlike larva.

Bee killer

Asian giant hornet

Asian giant hornets hunt and kill a wide range of insect prey, including other hornets. Able to cover relatively long distances, the hornet carries its prey back to its nest, where it uses its strong jaws to butcher the victim. It is then fed to the developing hornet larvae. However, the adults do not feed on what they catch, but are instead fed by their own larvae, which regurgitate a rich mixture of amino acids for them to drink. When Asian giant hornets attack bee colonies, it is not the adult worker bees they carry off, but the soft-bodied bee larvae. Just a handful of hornets can decimate a bee colony in a short time, an attack for which the introduced commercial honey bee has no defense. However it has been discovered that Japanese populations of the Asian honey bee have evolved a unique thermal-execution technique to deal with such an attack. Hundreds of worker bees form a tight ball around the invaders, and the intense heat generated by their wing muscles literally burns the hornets to death (see p.313).

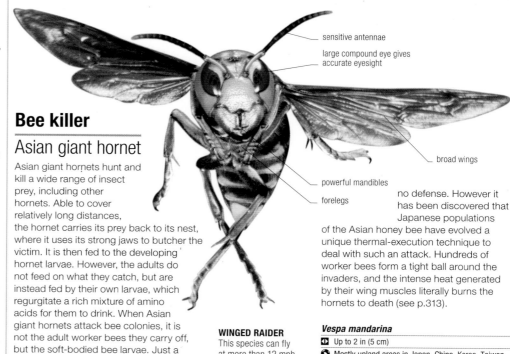

- sensitive antennae
- large compound eye gives accurate eyesight
- broad wings
- powerful mandibles
- forelegs

WINGED RAIDER
This species can fly at more than 12 mph (20 kph). In addition to powerful venom, it also has strong jaws.

Vespa mandarina
- Up to 2 in (5 cm)
- Mostly upland areas in Japan, China, Korea, Taiwan, India, and Nepal.
- Large-bodied hornet with broad orange head, dark thorax, and yellow and black banded abdomen.

Hairy trap

Allomerus ant

These ants have evolved a unique mechanism for capturing large prey that might otherwise escape them by jumping or flying away. First, they trim away some of the hairs of a host plant stem, leaving pillars of hairs. These are used to support a spongy platform that they make using regurgitated material combined with the trimmed hairs. The platform is disguised as a hairy stem and made with many small holes so that the ants can hide beneath. The construction is reinforced by a species of sooty mold that is controlled by the ants. Once the trap has been set, the ants hide below, with their jaws open, ready to catch any prey that passes along the stem.

Allomerus decemarticulatus
- ¹⁄₁₆ in (2 mm)
- Rain forest in South America.
- Yellowish orange, smooth-bodied ant.

FALSE FLOOR
The stem of the ant plant *Hirtella physophora* is covered by a secondary surface built entirely by the hiding ants.

SLOW DEATH
>>01 When large prey such as a grasshopper walks on the surface of the ants' trap, its legs are grabbed from below, and it is then gradually stretched like a victim on a medieval torture rack. >>02 Once immobilized, the grasshopper is stung. >>03 The prey is then carried along to the ants' home inside a leaf pouch, where it will be cut up and eaten.

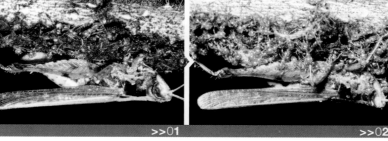

>>01   >>02   >>03

Super-sized raider

Marauder ants

In this species there is a great variation in size between different castes. The workers fall roughly into three sizes: very small workers, known as minor workers; major workers; and large ants known as supermajor workers, which may be several hundred times heavier than the smallest workers of the colony. This extreme range of worker sizes allows these ants to utilize a much larger range of prey and to defend themselves against attack.

In large numbers, marauder ants can even attack the nests of green turtles. Marauder ants go out on foraging raids for prey to feed to their developing larvae but tend to have more permanent nest arrangements than other raiding ants.

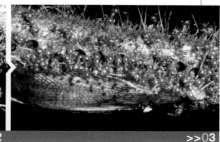

SUPER-SIZED ANT
Dwarfed by the supermajor worker, swarms of minor workers aid their much larger counterpart.

Pheidologeton affinis
- Up to ½ in (1 cm)
- Forest and grassland in Southeast Asia
- Shiny yellowish brown to brown head, thorax and abdomen, and yellowish legs.

Path of destruction

Driver ants

Also known as safari ants, these ants form colonies that can comprise many millions of individuals. They may stay in one place for anything from a week to several months. When local food supplies start to diminish, the ants move off in a large column, consuming anything they encounter. During this nomadic phase, the workers carry their developing brood in their jaws. Although insects and other invertebrates are their main prey, larger animals such as vertebrates can be overwhelmed and if unable to escape, will be hacked to pieces and eaten.

Dorylus species
- Up to 1 in (2.5 cm)
- Savanna and woodland in Africa and East Asia.
- Brown to black bodies with paler legs.

ON THE MOVE
Bigger soldier ants, which are armed with large, curved and toothed jaws, patrol the outside edges of the perpetually moving column and are constantly on guard for potential attackers.

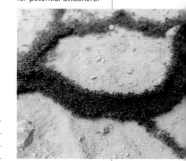

Attack from beneath
White shark

The white shark, a formidable predator also known as the great white, typically employs a lightning-fast strike from below to disable large prey. The blow can seriously incapacitate or even kill prey in an instant.

Despite its size, the white shark is effectively camouflaged by countershading. Its body is gray or bluish brown on top so that prey swimming near the surface find it hard to see the shark when looking down into the water beneath them. Similarly, the shark's underside is pale so that when its prey is below, the shark's silhouette against the sky is minimized.

When hunting, white sharks are able to maintain their body temperature, especially that of their brain, and use a range of senses—electroreception, scent, hearing, and vision—to locate prey. They will often have an exploratory bite to test if an item of prey is suitable. Juveniles usually eat rays, other sharks, and squid, but adults hunt seals, sea lions, dolphins, and some large fishes, such as tuna. Although this shark is a top predator, occasionally it will scavenge carrion such as whale carcasses.

FULL BREACH
The sheer force of its attack has carried this female white shark clear of the water. Having spiraled through the air, she re-enters the water with her prey still gripped in her mouth.

IMPACT FROM BELOW
>>01 This shark has stalked and attacked a seal from below, launching it out of the water. **>>02** Although the seal has avoided the shark's grasp, its body has taken the full force of the strike. **>>03** The injured seal falls back into the water. The shark may attack the seal repeatedly until it is weak enough to be eaten.

>>01   **>>02**   **>>03**

25 mph The speed reached by white sharks when they attack prey from below.

Carcharodon carcharias

- ⟷ Commonly up to 20 ft (6 m), but may be longer.
- ◐ Found mainly in coastal waters where prey is abundant. Worldwide in temperate waters.
- 🕮 Robust, torpedo-shaped body. Head has a conical snout and small, dark eyes. Pectoral and first dorsal fins are large, and two tail lobes are similar in size.

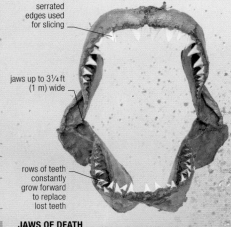

serrated edges used for slicing

jaws up to 3¼ ft (1 m) wide

rows of teeth constantly grow forward to replace lost teeth

JAWS OF DEATH
The large triangular teeth of the upper jaw have serrations on both sides and are used for slicing through flesh. The teeth of the lower jaw are much smaller and help secure prey.

◎ HUMAN IMPACT
ATTACKS ON PEOPLE

The recent decline in white shark populations reflects the fact that the losers in most shark–human encounters are the sharks. As humans spend more time in the sea, they inevitably encroach on the habitats of sharks, so this enforced interaction has also resulted in increased numbers of shark attacks. However, the prevalent perception that sharks—especially the white shark—are man-eaters is contradicted by the fact that a decreasing proportion of shark attacks has resulted in fatalities.

INCREASING SURVIVAL RATES
While the number of white shark attacks on humans increased during the 20th century, the proportion of fatalities dropped considerably, probably due to improved medical help.

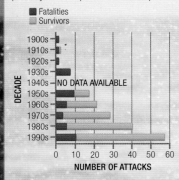

■ Fatalities
□ Survivors

DECADE	NO DATA AVAILABLE
1900s	
1910s	
1920s	
1930s	
1940s	NO DATA AVAILABLE
1950s	
1960s	
1970s	
1980s	
1990s	

0 10 20 30 40 50 60
NUMBER OF ATTACKS

Night hunting

Sand tiger sharks

Also known as the gray nurse shark or ragged-toothed shark, this large, slow-moving species feeds mainly on fishes, skates, and rays as well as large crustaceans and cephalopods. During the day, it typically hides in caves and reefs, sometimes swimming in small groups very close to the bottom. At dusk it moves into the open to hunt for food.

LOCATING PREY
Sand tiger sharks are often solitary, but when food is abundant they can feed together. Like all sharks, they have electroreceptive organs to locate prey.

Carcharias taurus
- Up to 10½ ft (3.2 m)
- Typically in shallow sandy areas and reefs, almost worldwide.
- Stout, grayish brown body with flattened head, conical snout and prominent teeth.

Electrical sensing

Scalloped hammerhead shark

Like other hammerheads, the scalloped hammerhead shark's most distinctive feature is its broad, flat head. The most likely explanation for this bizarre shape concerns the capture of its prey. All sharks have special sense organs, called the ampullae of Lorenzini, capable of detecting weak electrical fields emitted by other animals. These organs form a system of jelly-filled canals in the head and snout connected to the outside via small pores. In hammerhead sharks, the underside of the hammer is particularly well endowed with these organs, and the increase in area due to the shape of the head may help them detect bottom-living prey more effectively.

SENSE ORGANS
It is thought that sharks can detect electrical signals as low as 15-billionths of a volt from the movement of prey.

Sphyrna lewini
- Up to 13¾ ft (4.2 m)
- Warm temperate to tropical coastal waters worldwide.
- Brownish gray above and pale below. The hammer-shaped head has a wavy or scalloped front edge.

Hidden angler

Hairy frogfish

Also known as the striated or striped frogfish, the hairy frogfish is a stealth predator that lives on the seafloor hidden among rocks, weed, and coral. Concealed by highly effective camouflage, it draws prey toward it with a lure. Its coloration is very variable, and its body is covered with long and branching skin tufts that completely obscure the outline of the fish. The tubelike openings of the gills are hidden just below the pectoral fins, and to make their disguise even more effective they will hide among urchins and sponges, and in coral crevices.

The hairy frogfish's stalked lure is a modified dorsal spine that can be bent backward along the head when not being used to attract prey. The lure can even regrow if it gets damaged or bitten off. Frogfishes do not always need to use their lure, since they are so well camouflaged against the substrate that small fishes will sometimes even mistake them for a place to shelter.

SWIFT SNATCH
The speed of the frogfish's gape-and-snatch movement has been measured at an extraordinary 1/6,000th second, making it among the fastest known predatory movements of any vertebrate.

Antennarius striatus
- Up to 10 in (25 cm)
- All subtropical oceans, to depths of 33–656 ft (10–200 m).
- Variable coloration, often light yellow, orange, green, gray, or brown with black stripes or elongate blotches. Eyes have prominent radiating lines.

enlarged dorsal spine has appearance of weed

"bait" at end of stalk

ANGLING FOR PREY
Frogfishes sit absolutely motionless on the seabed, camouflaged against the substrate. This keeps them hidden from predators but also accentuates the movement of the lure, which they twitch to attract prey.

Water cannon

Banded archerfish

Although the banded archerfish catches aquatic prey such as shrimps and worms, it is best known for the unique way it catches prey out of water. The fish uses its mouth to squirt a narrow, powerful jet of water to knock insects from the vegetation above it. The head is narrow with the eyes close to the snout, giving it binocular vision. When the fish spots potential prey, it sticks its snout out of the water and presses its tongue onto a groove that runs along the roof of its mouth. By rapidly closing its gill covers, a stream of water is forced along the groove and out through the small aperture at the end. Adults are very accurate and can shoot a number of times in quick succession to dislodge prey, which is then swallowed, sometimes before it reaches the water. If prey is close to the water, the archerfish may jump out of the water to catch it.

Toxotes jaculatrix
- Up to 15½ in (40 cm)
- Mainly in mangrove swamps of Southeast Asia, India, Australia, and the western Pacific.
- Silver-bodied and laterally compressed with dark vertical bands.

apparent location of insect

angle of refraction

insect

REFRACTION ERROR
As light passes from air to water it bends or refracts. The archerfish is able to compensate for this refraction and shoot at the true location of its prey.

archerfish swims just below surface

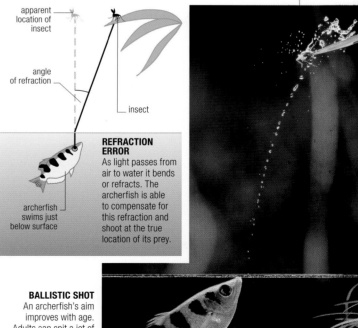

BALLISTIC SHOT
An archerfish's aim improves with age. Adults can spit a jet of water more than 6½ ft (2 m). They can also judge the size of the prey and therefore how much water is needed to knock it down.

EASY MEAL
Also known as the copper shark due to its color in sunlight, the bronze whaler shark can grow to over 9¾ ft (3 m) in length. It feeds on other sharks, squid, and bottom-living fishes but is often attracted by large schools of fishes, such as sardines on an annual run that takes place off the east coast of South Africa between May and July.

SCENTING PREY
Although their eyes are prominent, moray eels have relatively poor eyesight, and rely instead on a good sense of smell and sensory pores on the head to detect their prey.

Concealed weapon
Mosaic moray eel

Hiding in crevices and under rocky ledges, these thick-skinned, mucus-covered eels typically lie in wait for something to pass close enough to be seized. They mainly feed at night on fishes, crustaceans, and mollusks and move with a snakelike, sinuous motion powered by their long dorsal and anal fins. They sometimes feed during the day and have been observed to stalk their prey over short distances. The eel's head has a characteristic long snout with curved jaws, armed with many razor-sharp, needlelike teeth. A second set

of jaws (see panel, below) ensures that the eel can secure its prey even if it only gets a partial grip on it. Other bony fishes typically use suction to swallow prey; sudden expansion of the mouth cavity causes water to rush in, taking the prey along with it, but in moray eels, the head is relatively narrow so it would be difficult to ingest anything but small prey using this feeding technique.

Enchelycore ramosa
 Up to 5 ft (1.5 m)
⊙ On rocky reefs off southeast Australia, northern New Zealand, and the South Pacific.
▥ Snakelike, scaleless, yellowish gray body with a mosaic-like pattern.

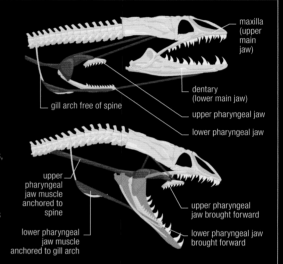

ANATOMY
EXTRA JAWS

Moray eels have a second set of jaws halfway down their throat called the pharyngeal jaws. Prey items are caught and held fast by the sharp teeth on the primary jaws, but because it is difficult to pull food in through the narrow mouth using suction (see above), another mechanism is needed. Contraction of special muscles brings the pharyngeal jaws into play in a mechanism unique to moray eels. These secondary jaws, also bearing large, back-curved teeth, move forward rapidly from well behind the skull to take up a position inside the mouth. Once the prey is secured, other muscles contract, pulling the pharyngeal jaws backward, and dragging the prey down into the esophagus.

maxilla (upper main jaw)
gill arch free of spine
dentary (lower main jaw)
upper pharyngeal jaw
lower pharyngeal jaw
upper pharyngeal jaw muscle anchored to spine
lower pharyngeal jaw muscle anchored to gill arch
upper pharyngeal jaw brought forward
lower pharyngeal jaw brought forward

Secret flashlight
Stoplight loosejaw

This fish's common name comes from the presence of red and green photophores (light-producing organs) on the sides of its head, which it uses to catch prey. The lower jaw is very long and armed with slender fangs that curve backward. To seize prey, the jaw can be pushed forward in front of the head, and once prey is snagged on the teeth, the jaw is retracted. There is no skin between the bones of the lower jaw, and the species can swallow prey almost as big as itself.

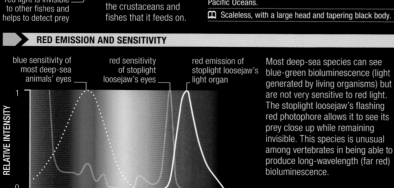

blue-green light used to attract prey
DEEP-SEA DEVIL
The stoplight loosejaw's striking appearance remains hidden from the crustaceans and fishes that it feeds on.

red light is invisible to other fishes and helps to detect prey

Malacosteus niger
 Up to 10 in (25 cm)
⊙ Deep areas of the Atlantic, Indian, and Pacific Oceans.
▥ Scaleless, with a large head and tapering black body.

RED EMISSION AND SENSITIVITY

blue sensitivity of most deep-sea animals' eyes
red sensitivity of stoplight loosejaw's eyes
red emission of stoplight loosejaw's light organ

RELATIVE INTENSITY

WAVELENGTH (NM)

Most deep-sea species can see blue-green bioluminescence (light generated by living organisms) but are not very sensitive to red light. The stoplight loosejaw's flashing red photophore allows it to see its prey close up while remaining invisible. This species is unusual among vertebrates in being able to produce long-wavelength (far red) bioluminescence.

NOCTURNAL FEEDER
These nocturnal fish hide during the day in dark crevices and under submerged wood. They have poor eyesight but have a special electrolocating system to move around in the darkness and find food.

Gnathonemus petersii
 Up to 14 in (35 cm)
⊙ In muddy, slow-moving rivers in West and Central Africa.
▥ Dark fish with rectangular, flattened body ending in a slender, forked tail.

Electric organs
Elephantnose fish

These fishes live in muddy and murky water and need a system other than eyesight to locate and determine the nature of nearby objects. They use a kind of radar by producing electrical discharges from a special organ made up of modified muscle cells near the tail. The discharges then generate a weak electrical field around the mucus-covered body of the fish. Obstacles, prey, or other fishes that come into range of the electric field alter its shape according to their own conductivity, and these changes are picked up by electroreceptors all over the body. These receptor cells are particularly abundant on

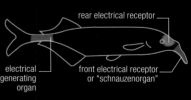

rear electrical receptor
electrical generating organ
front electrical receptor or "schnauzenorgan"

ELECTRIC ORGANS
The scientific name meaning "thread jaw" refers to the fingerlike sensory organ on the bottom jaw, which is used to feel for worms, insects, and crustaceans in the bottom sediment.

downward-curved snout or schnauzenorgan, which the fish also uses to probe the bottom. The brain of these fishes is enlarged to process the complex information coming from the electro-locating system, the ratio of brain to body

Fly catcher
Brown trout

Wild brown trout return from the sea to spawn in fresh water and while there eat a wide range of insects, worms, mollusks, crustaceans, and even smaller fishes and frogs. They feed from the bed of the stream, and when certain insect species are hatching and rising to the surface, the trout gorge themselves. They often rise out of the water to reach flying insects. Because of their varied feeding habits, anglers use lifelike models of a wide range of insects for fly fishing, where they try to mimic the appearance and behavior of the trout's natural food. Trout can be very selective in their feeding, and fishermen have to try to imitate what the trout are currently eating.

Salmo trutta
⬌ Up to 4½ ft (1.4 m)
◉ Rivers and streams of Europe and Asia, and the northeast Atlantic, but widely introduced elsewhere.
📖 Stocky body with olive green to silvery dorsal surface covered with darkish spots.

POWERFUL LEAP
Using its powerful tail to jump clear of the water a brown trout will sometimes try to catch fast-flying, agile prey such as damselflies.

Plankton pickers
Garden eels

Garden eels have good eyesight and rely mainly on this sense to catch zooplankton, other invertebrates, and even small fishes that drift past in the current. They live in colonies and typically remain in their burrows in the sand. Even when feeding, they only emerge partially, and always leave one-third of their body length buried below the surface. The burrow is coated on the inside by mucus secreted by a special gland in the eel's tail. This substance binds the sand grains together and prevents the burrow from collapsing. Also known as the Indian spaghetti eel, the garden eel is extremely wary of predators, and will retreat in an instant, sealing the entrance of the burrow with a plug of mucus until the danger has passed.

Gorgasia maculata
⬌ Up to 28 in (70 cm)
◉ Sandy shallows of the western Pacific Ocean, from the Maldives to the Solomon Islands and the Philippines.
📖 Pale and slender-bodied, ⅜ in (1 cm) wide.

DECEPTIVE APPEARANCE
Garden eels live gregariously in colonies known as eel gardens (hence their name), where they sway around like stalks of sea grass.

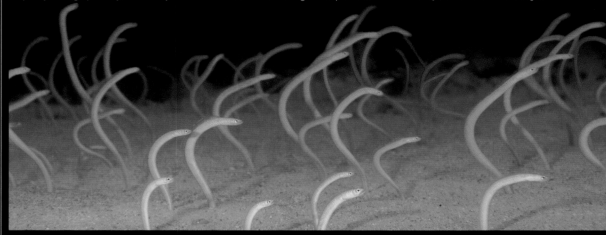

Side swipe
Atlantic sailfish

Sailfish feed on very fast-moving fishes such as mackerel and tuna, striking down or sideways at prey from behind using their long bill. Groups of sailfish can use their sails to herd schools of fish. One of them then scythes through the school, thrashing its bill from side to side to cripple and kill the fishes, which are eaten head first.

STREAMLINED FOR SPEED
The characteristic "sail" is the large first dorsal fin, which can run almost the entire length of the body. The sail is usually kept down and to the side but erected when the fish is threatened or excited.

Istiophorus albicans
⬌ Up to 9¾ ft (3 m).
◉ Caribbean Sea, extending across Atlantic Ocean to West Africa.
📖 Smoothly tapering blue body, with blackish blue fins. Elongated upper jaw forms a pointed bill.

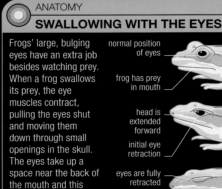

Pelophylax perezi
⬌ Up to 4 in (10 cm).
◉ Rivers and ponds in France and the Iberian Peninsula.
📖 Greenish, brown, or gray with mottled pattern with long pale dorsal stripe.

LONG REACH
The tongue of the Perez's frog has a sticky upper surface, and is attached toward the front of the mouth rather than at the rear. This, together with their ability to jump, gives the frogs a longer reach for capturing prey.

Unfolding tongue
Perez's frog

These frogs never venture very far from permanent bodies of water and typically sit at the water's edge on muddy banks or rocks to sunbathe and feed. The males have a pair of vocal sacs and call to attract mates. They can be active by day and night, and their diet consists primarily of insects, spiders, and other small invertebrates, which they catch using their sticky extendable tongues. When not in use, the tongue is folded backward toward the throat. A row of very small teeth in the upper jaw, as well as some small teeth in the roof of the mouth, hold prey in place before it is swallowed. The frogs in turn are eaten by owls and several species of aquatic birds. They are always ready to dive into the water and hide at the slightest sign of danger.

ANATOMY
SWALLOWING WITH THE EYES

Frogs' large, bulging eyes have an extra job besides watching prey. When a frog swallows its prey, the eye muscles contract, pulling the eyes shut and moving them down through small openings in the skull. The eyes take up a space near the back of the mouth and this action helps push the food down.

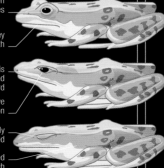

normal position of eyes

frog has prey in mouth

head is extended forward

initial eye retraction

eyes are fully retracted

prey is pushed toward stomach

AIDING DIGESTION
The komodo dragon's powerful legs and strong claws hold down prey as they tear of large chunks of flesh. To accelerate its digestive process a lizard will then bask in the sun.

Lethal bite

Komodo dragon

Although Komodo dragons also eat carrion, they will ambush other reptiles and small mammals, as well as goats and deer, usually administering a lethal bite (see panel, right). Swallowing can be a slow process, and so that the lizards do not asphyxiate while eating, a breathing tube under their tongue connects to the lungs. A loosely hinged lower jaw and an elastic stomach deal with meals that may be up to 75 percent of their own bodyweight.

Varanus komodoensis

⬛	6½–9¾ ft (2–3 m)
⬤	Grassland and lowland forest on the Indonesian islands of Komondo and Flores and others in between.
📖	Heavy bodied, grayish brown with darker markings, very long tail and long yellow forked tongue.

» 373

⊙ ANATOMY
DEADLY SALIVA

The mouth and teeth of Komodo dragons are home to more than 50 species of pathogenic bacteria. Animals that are bitten and manage to escape will usually die from the effects of blood poisoning. This may work to the lizard's advantage since it is able to detect the smell of a dead animal up to 6 miles (10 km) away. The bite of other monitor lizards is also slightly venomous, causing swelling and pain for many hours.

River ambush

Nile crocodile

Young Nile crocodiles eat insects and other invertebrates, and as they grow, will take larger prey such as reptiles, amphibians, and birds. Their ability to rest motionless in the water with just the eyes and the tip of the nostrils showing allows them to get very close to unwary prey before they launch an attack. On land, they are rather slow moving, but can swing their legs underneath the body for a faster gait. In the water, they are incredibly swift, using their powerful body and tail to propel themselves forward at bursts of up to 18 mph (30 kph). Adults usually eat fish, but will lie in wait for animals to come down to the water's edge to drink. Sometimes they gather in numbers at river crossings where groups of migrating species such as wildebeest have to run a deadly gauntlet. Since they cannot use their teeth to cut through meat, crocodiles spin themselves around in the water to tear meat from the carcass —although this is known as the death roll, the prey is usually dead already. Nile crocodiles can go for long periods without eating but when food is available they can consume up to half their own body weight at a single meal.

Crocodylus niloticus

⬛	Up to 20 ft (6 m)
⬤	Waterways throughout Africa and western Madagascar.
📖	Large and squat, short splayed legs and long tail. Back dark with tough scales, underside yellowish and softer.

» 401, 476

19ft The length of some Nile crocodiles, the largest freshwater crocodiles

FEEDING FRENZY
A group of hungry Nile crocodiles converge on a zebra victim before ripping it apart.

POWERFUL JAWS
With a huge gape and formidable bite, a Nile crocodile can hold onto large prey such as zebras, buffaloes, or wildebeest and drags them into the water to drown.

Tongue lure
Alligator snapping turtle

This turtle lies in the water with its hooked jaws held wide open. The inside of its mouth, like the rest of the head, is drably colored and patterned to blend in with its background except for the tip of its tongue, which is long and reddish. The turtle wiggles its tongue around, imitating the movement of a worm to lure fishes close enough that it can snap its jaws shut on top of them. In addition to eating fishes, snakes, amphibians, and even other turtles, this species will also readily eat carrion if given the opportunity.

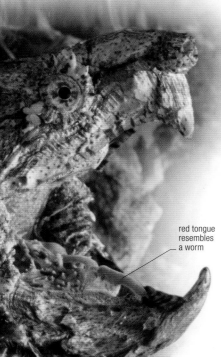

red tongue resembles a worm

WELL CAMOUFLAGED
Even the outline of the turtle's eyes is broken up by radiating lines, so the only conspicuous thing is its red tongue.

Macroclemys temminckii
- Up to 26 in (65 cm)
- Lakes and rivers in southern North America.
- Brown turtle with hooked jaws and shell with spiked plates.

READY TO STRIKE
Vivid green coloring with blue, yellow, and white flecks give superb camouflage, while enlarged front teeth enable the snake to grasp its prey securely.

large eye with vertical pupil

temperature-sensing pit

Most toxic
Inland taipan

Small mammals such as mice and rats form this snake's prey, and it will also steal their burrows. It gives several bites in quick succession, and the venom is so fast acting that the prey is limp and paralyzed almost the instant it is bitten. The inland taipan is the most toxic land snake in the world. The venom is many hundreds of times more toxic than that of a diamondback rattlesnake and 50 times more toxic than that of the Indian cobra. A bite can prove fatal to a human unless antivenin is available.

BLACK HEAD
Having a dark head allows the snake to warm up rapidly up in the morning sunshine by simply poking its head out of its burrow.

Oxyuranus microlepidotus
- Up to 6½ ft (2 m)
- Arid scrub and grassland in central Australia.
- A glossy, grayish brown snake with irregular dark markings.

Sensing blood
Green tree python

This snake is a nonvenomous constrictor that lives mainly in the tree canopy and eats small mammals, such as rodents and bats, as well as reptiles and birds. It rests curled in loops over horizontal branches looking out from the middle of the draped coils. Prey is usually caught by the snake holding onto a branch with the rear part of its body while it strikes with its head. The snake has special temperature-sensing pits along the margins of the lower jaw that enable it to detect the presence of warm-blooded prey. The pits detect radiant heat and allow the snake to track and catch prey even in total darkness. Once prey is caught, the snake wraps several coils of its body around it and tightens its grip every time its victim exhales, suffocating it in the process.

Morelia viridis
- Up to 6½ ft (2 m)
- Rain forests in New Guinea, Queensland Australia, and some islands in Indonesia.
- Bright green snake with a broken pale stripe along the back.

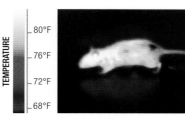

IMAGING PREY IN INFARED
Seen through a thermal imaging camera, a rodent stands out clearly from the cool background. Prey may seem just as obvious to the green tree python.

Spawn hunting
Northern cat-eyed snake

Known as a cat-eyed snake because of its slightly protruding golden-brown eyes with catlike vertical pupils, this species will eat adult tree frogs, toads, and lizards if it gets the chance, but prefers to eat frogspawn and young tadpoles. The viperlike head has grooved fangs at the back of the mouth, and the venom it injects is only mildly toxic. Cat-eyed snakes hunt at dusk and after dark around ponds, forest pools, and streams where frogs are mating and laying eggs. Although they do hunt on the ground, in forested areas they will climb among the branches of trees to look for tree frogs. Attracted by the frogs' nocturnal mating calls, the snake silently slithers among the foliage to feast on masses of their spawn. These snakes are not very abundant; however, to compensate for this, mated female cat-eyed snakes can store sperm for several years.

FROGSPAWN FEAST
A northern cat-eyed snake, hunting in forest foliage, gorges itself on frogspawn, its preferred food. It frequents any lying water where frogs and lizards lay their eggs.

Leptodeira septentrionalis
- Up to 35 in (90 cm)
- Lives in forested areas in the southern US, Mexico, and Central America.
- Triangular head, dark bands on paler grayish brown, narrow body.

Death grip
Central American boa

The general background color and patterning of these solitary snakes serves as good camouflage against the forest floor and among trees. Boa constrictors eat rodents, bats, and other mammals as well as birds and lizards, and when fully grown can tackle capybaras, monkeys, and even wild pigs. To help them locate prey, there are some simple heat-sensitive scales on the head, and they have a good sense of smell. When catching bats, they hang from trees or cave entrances where the bats roost and snatch them out of the air as they fly past. The mouth has curved teeth to hold the prey as the body coils around it. Once the prey has been killed and swallowed whole, it may take several weeks for the snake to digest it completely.

Boa constrictor imperator
- Up to 14¾ ft (4.5 m)
- Forest, savanna, cultivated areas, and mangrove swamps in Central and South America.
- Stout-bodied snake with flattened head and dark markings.

DEADLY COILS
Boa constrictors are nonvenomous and kill by asphyxiating their prey, squeezing them slowly to death in their powerful coils.

TELESCOPIC TONGUE
The tongue of a panther chameleon is extended by a unique system that catapults it toward prey at speeds in excess of 16½ ft (5 m) per second. The sticky end wraps around the prey, and the tongue is retracted into the mouth.

Flexible jaws
Common egg-eater snake

These snakes live in forests and wooded areas populated by nesting birds. A good sense of smell allows them to detect whether or not an egg is rotten before they try to eat it. A highly flexible neck enables them to take even large eggs into their mouths whole, before the shell is broken by teethlike projections from the spinal bones. The snake then swallows the liquid contents and regurgitates the fragments of broken shell. Egg-eating snakes can fast for long periods. When food is plentiful, they gorge themselves and their metabolic rate increases, as does the diameter of the liver and small intestine. When threatened, the common egg-eater snake can generate a loud hissing noise by repeatedly coiling and uncoiling its body, which rubs its lateral scales together. They will also strike out open-mouthed, even though they have no teeth to attack with.

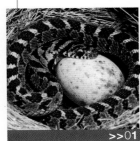

>>01   >>02   >>03

Dasypeltis scabra

↔ Up to 3 ft 3 in (1 m)

◉ Forest and woodland in sub-Saharan Africa.

▢ Slender snake with grayish brown body and rough scales.

SWALLOWED WHOLE
>>01 By dislocating its jaw, the snake begins to consume an egg that is much larger than its head.   >>02 Once it has taken the egg into its throat, the snake begins to close its mouth around it.   >>03 Muscular contractions press bony projections of the spine on to the egg to break it. The snake then swallows the contents.

Flightless forager
Stewart Island brown kiwi

This bird is a subspecies of the Tokoeka, a New Zealand kiwi. Like other kiwis, the Stewart Island brown kiwi is flightless and well adapted to terrestrial living and foraging. It has large, powerful legs with claws to scrape and dig, and, unusually for a bird, foot pads that enable it to move around silently on the forest floor as it probes for food. Kiwis are the only birds to have nostrils at the end of their bills, and they use these to smell for prey among vegetation and below the ground. Because they are so well adapted to living and hunting on the ground, kiwis have been described as honorary mammals.

PROBING BILL
After sunset the kiwi hunts for snails, spiders, and insects. It uses its keen sense of smell and hearing to locate prey underground.

Apteryx australis lawryi

↔ Up to 15½ in (40 cm)

◉ In forest and coastal scrub, only on Stewart Island off southern New Zealand.

▢ Rounded, wingless bird, with long, slender bill and light brown mottled plumage.

LOOKING FOR MOVEMENT
A secretary bird stamps on the ground with its large, stout-toed feet to flush prey out of hiding.

This large eagle occupies the same **ecological niche** as the bald eagle in North America.

Dive bombing
Peregrine falcon

Peregrine falcons have extremely acute vision and power dive at high speed from above their prey. Typically a peregrine will come out of its dive just behind the prey, aiming to hit the wings of the victim rather than risk injury with a direct body hit. If the impact does not kill the bird, it will break the bird's neck with its sharp, hooked bill. Its diet mainly comprises pigeons, doves, waterfowl, and gamebirds, as well as reptiles and small mammals.

Falco peregrinus

↔ Up to 21½ in (55 cm)

◉ Worldwide, but absent from New Zealand, high mountains, deserts, and polar regions.

▢ Bluish to dark gray, white face with dark stripe.

Stamping for prey
Secretary bird

This large bird feeds on snakes such as adders and even cobras, but will also consume lizards, amphibians, rodents, young birds, bird eggs, and insects. Small animals are eaten directly, but larger prey is stamped to death before being consumed. Dangerous prey such as snakes are first stunned by being stamped on, then killed by being pecked behind the neck. Small creatures are eaten whole, while larger prey are pinned to the ground and pulled apart.

long, powerful legs used for striking and pursuing prey

Sagittarius serpentarius

↔ Up to 4½ ft (1.4 m)

◉ Open grassland in sub-Saharan Africa.

▢ Light gray plumage and black flight feathers, with black feathers at back of head, and long legs.

Surface paddling
White-vented storm-petrel

Despite its small size, this bird is quite a strong flier, and feeds from the surface of the ocean, fluttering with rapid, almost batlike, wing beats above the surface of the water. As it does this, it paddles its yellow webbed feet up and down on the water while it looks for planktonic organisms, such as crustaceans and small fishes, to eat. The white-vented storm petrel lives most of its life over open water, only coming to land to breed. It often nests in hollows or lava tubes but the presence of introduced rats has threatened its populations.

FLUTTERING HUNTER
The common name of this small bird refers to the patch of white plumage at the base of the tail, that extends round to the underside.

Oceanites gracilis

↔ 6 in (15 cm)

◉ Waters off Chile and Peru, and around the Galapagos Islands.

▢ Mainly black with longish, slender dark legs. Nostrils fused into a single tube on top of the bill.

Snatching fish

White-tailed sea eagle

One of the most distinctive features of birds of prey is the way they often kill with their feet. The white-tailed sea eagle feeds mostly on fishes, small mammals, and other birds, such as ducks. When hunting for fishes, it sits in a good perch and scans the water using its excellent eyesight before swooping down to seize fishes swimming near the surface with its large, hooked talons. The bottoms of its feet have sharp outgrowths to help keep a firm hold of the slippery prey. The eagle takes food back to its nest or perch, where it holds it down and rips it apart using its large, vulturelike bill. Preferring open coastal locations over inland sites, the territory of a white-tailed sea eagle may be more than 50 miles (80 km) across if prey is not very abundant.

Each adult bird needs to consume around 18 oz (0.5 kg) of prey each day, but can survive short lean periods. Although they are superb hunters, these eagles will sometimes take carrion, searching the shore for dead fish, or stealing prey from other predators such as otters and ospreys. In some areas, these eagles may compete with golden eagles for rabbits and hares.

After a spectacular aerial courtship, which involves the birds cartwheeling through the air with their talons locked together, pairs of eagles bond for life and build a large nest, or eyrie, of twigs and sticks in a tree or on a sheltered rocky cliff. Females usually lay one or two eggs, and the young are fed for three months. The mortality rate is high with 60–70 percent of the young birds failing to survive their first winter.

Haliaeetus albicilla
- Up to 35 in (90 cm)
- Coastal areas, but also inland wetlands, rivers, and lakes, in Europe and Asia.
- Large eagle with brownish body, white tail, and yellow, hooked bill.

SURFACE SWOOP
Swooping low over the water on its powerful broad wings, a white-tailed sea eagle can pluck fish from the surface without getting itself wet.

long wing tips

Feet first

Osprey

Since their diet consists entirely of fishes, ospreys are also known as fish eagles. They have several special adaptations for catching fishes up to 4½ lb (2 kg) in weight. Their toes are of equal length, and the outer toe is reversible, allowing the bird to have two toes hooked into either side of a fish's body. Not only do the feet have sharp talons to hold slippery fishes, they also have barbed foot pads to increase their grip. Their hunting technique consists of flying high above the water to spot fishes below, then, after hovering for a second or two, diving down to enter the water talons-first with outstretched legs. Ospreys will enter water to a depth of more than 3 feet (nearly a meter) to catch fishes.

> Ospreys can **close their nostrils** to keep water out of their nasal passages when diving.

CARRYING THE CATCH
Sometimes ospreys have difficulty getting airborne from the water. Once in flight they carry the fish headfirst to reduce wind resistance.

Pandion haliaetus
- 26 in (65 cm)
- Anywhere there is open water and plenty of fishes, worldwide except Antarctica.
- Brown upper body and wings, white underside.

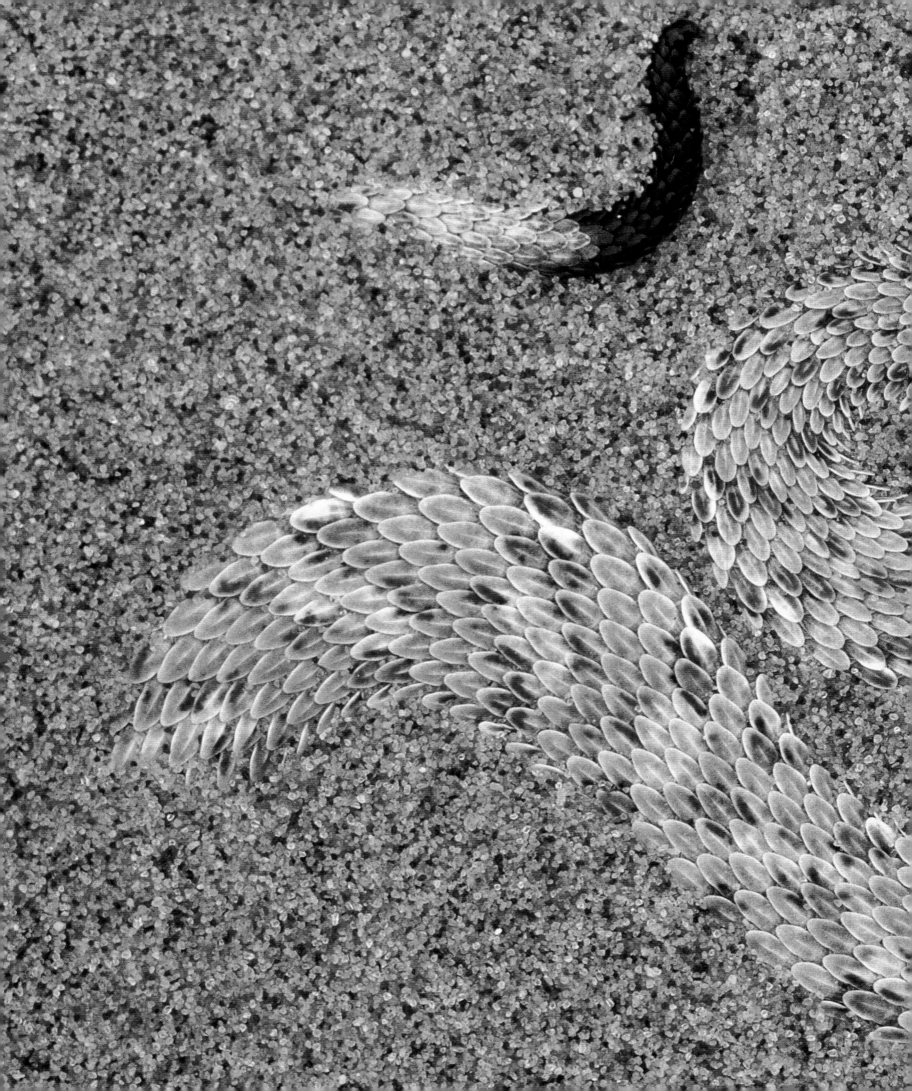

Tail lure
Peringuey's desert adder

This species, also known as the Namib desert sidewinding or sand adder, hunts by burying itself in the sand with just its tail and eyes—located on the top if its head—showing, making good use of its excellent camouflage coloring. The end of the tail is exposed and this, especially in very dark-tailed examples of the species, is used as a lure. The prey—attracted by the movement and grublike appearance of the tail—is grabbed and injected with venom. This subdues the prey, which is then swallowed whole. Favorite prey of this snake include desert lizards and geckoes. As an adaptation to living on shifting desert dunes, and even to climbing steep inclines, Peringuey's desert adder moves by a process known as sidewinding. The body is moved in a series of lateral movements, leaving sinuous marks that are characteristic of the species. Living in very dry conditions, such as the almost rain-free Namib desert, the snake gets most of the water it needs to survive from its prey, particularly lizards, which have a high water content. However, it also draws a supply of fluid from the condensation that settles on its body.

Bitis peringueyi

◀▶ 10–12 in (25–30 cm)

⊙ Coastal sands in Angola and Namibia.

📖 Body pale brown, orange, or sandy, with gray-brown spots, and paler underside. Eyes on top of flattened head. Tail typically brown.

KEEPING COOL
Peringuey's desert adder buries itself in sand (far left and above) to keep cool and conserve moisture as well as to conceal itself from prey.

TAKING THE BAIT
A desert lizard has fallen for the snake's appetizing-looking tail lure and is in the process of being swallowed whole.

Snakes have **rectangular scales** on the underside of their body, the edges of which **provide traction** like tread on a tire.

ANATOMY
SIDEWINDER MOVEMENT

Sidewinding is a variation of the more typical undulating motion that snakes use to move around, and is seen especially in species that live on loose sand in deserts or slippery mudflats where there are no firm objects such as rocks against which the snake can push. By throwing its body into a series of lateral loops, the snake moves sideways with most of its body clear of the surface at any time. This allows it to move over very hot sand, leaving behind a series of J- or S-shaped tracks.

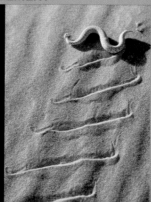

RAPTOR PAIR
Group members cooperate when catching and sharing food and defending their breeding territory from predators such as ravens, great horned owls and coyotes. Harris's hawks are not fast fliers but have excellent vision and hearing.

Group hunting
Harris's hawk

This hawk's usual prey are small mammals such as ground squirrels and wood rats, birds, and reptiles, but by hunting together in groups of up to six individuals, it is able to take prey as large as jackrabbits, hares, or large gamebirds. When prey is spotted, the hawks land and scare the victim from its hiding place by force of numbers. One of the group then captures and kills it. A small number of a hunting group may also take turns to fly ahead to scan for prey. Group hunting, which is very unusual among raptors, may be an adaptation to the scrubby terrain in which they live. These social groupings are formed with a breeding alpha female and male, subordinate beta adults, and gamma birds of either sex, usually juveniles.

ENERGY MAINTENANCE

ENERGY (kcal per hawk per day)

energy maintenance threshold

GROUP SIZE

For Harris's hawk the benefits of group hunting are considerable. It has been observed that by hunting in groups each individual bird can obtain a much larger amount of food energy per day compared to hunting alone or as one of a pair. Groups of five or more were able to maintain a sufficient energy level for survival.

Parabuteo unicinctus
- Up to 30 in (75 cm)
- Semi-desert, open woodland, and scrubland in Central and South America, and southern North America.
- Brown plumage, reddish shoulders, white tail tip.

Sensitive eyes
Common kestrel

The diet of common kestrels consists mainly of small mammals, such as voles and mice, but they will also catch small birds. It might seem that the kestrel would have a difficult task catching small, fast-moving prey but they have evolved a special hunting ability. The eyes of kestrels are sensitive to ultraviolet light, and they use the fact that rodent urine reflects ultraviolet light to find their prey. Voles, mice, and other rodents habitually mark their trails with urine and feces, so kestrels are able to scan large areas of habitat for their prey while they hover. By locating densely populated areas, they increase their chance of success by concentrating their attentions where the chances of a kill are highest. When prey is spotted, kestrels hover before quickly diving to the ground to seize it with their talons.

eye sensitive to UV light

Falco tinnunculus
- 12–15 in (30–38 cm)
- Moorland, meadow, farmland, and urban areas in Europe, Asia, and Africa.
- Males are smaller and grayer than the reddish brown females. Tail has dark bar accentuated by white tip.

FIXED POSITION
Often seen hovering above roadsides and farmland, kestrels can maintain a fixed position, even in blustery conditions.

Mob rule
Great white pelican

These large birds catch fish in their bill pouches while swimming on the surface of water. They often fish cooperatively in groups, attracted by large numbers of fish. Several individuals or larger flocks of pelicans form a line or a semicircle and drive the fish into shallower water where they can be collected easily. The pouch below the lower jaw of the bird extends back to the throat and is very elastic, being able to hold more than 20 pints of water. Fish are swallowed whole by the pelican holding its head upright. After squeezing out the excess water, it lets the entire catch slip down its throat.

Pelecanus onocrotalus
- Up to 6 ft (1.8 m)
- Lakes and wetlands in southern Europe and Asia, Africa.
- White plumage, yellow legs and pouch, bluish bill.

FEEDING FRENZY
A group of great white pelicans have corraled a number of small fishes into shallow water and have begun to scoop them up, filling their pouches.

Plunge diving
Cape gannet

These birds use a plunge-diving technique from as high as 98 ft (30 m) above the surface to catch schooling fishes such as sardines and anchovies. When suitable fishes are spotted, the gannets start a dive from a height determined by the depth of the school. Just before they hit the water, the gannets pull their wings back and close to the body, to form a streamlined, arrowhead shape. Having entered the water, they can chase prey using their large webbed feet and wings for propulsion. The sharp bill has fine, toothlike, backward-pointing serrations for holding on to slippery fishes. After a dive, they then return to the surface using their natural buoyancy, and typically swallow their prey before they take to the air again. These foraging trips may last many hours, with the birds first feeding and then resting on the surface to digest food for themselves, then catching more fish and returning to their nesting site to feed their chicks by regurgitation.

Morus capensis
- Up to 3 ft 1 in (95 cm)
- Coastal islands off southern Africa.
- White plumage with black tail and wing feathers. Head and neck feathers are golden yellow, with distinctive black stripe down the middle of throat.
>> 271

19ft The distance below the ocean surface that Cape gannets may reach when diving for fishes.

ON THE SARDINE RUN
Cape gannets are attracted to a spectacular annual migration event that takes place between May and July off the east coast of South Africa, in which schools of sardines many miles long pass through the waters.

Probing mud

Eurasian oystercatcher

BURIED PREY
Oystercathers have a strong bill for stabbing and probing into sand or silt for shellfish.

These distinctive waders hunt for shellfish such as cockles and mussels, though not oysters, and will also feed on limpets, marine worms, and crabs. Each bird uses its own individual technique to open shellfish. Some birds hammer the shells rather than prying them apart. Young birds tend to learn the technique their parents used. Oystercatchers feed gregariously except when breeding, when some move inland to rivers and lakes to find worms.

Haematopus ostralegus

- Up to 17½ in (45 cm)
- Estuaries, sandbanks and mudflats in Europe and Asia.
- Stocky bird with black and white plumage, an orange bill, red eyes, and pinkish legs.

ANATOMY

DIFFERING FEEDING STRATEGIES

The competitive exculsion principle states that no two species share the same feeding niche. Wading birds have different sizes and shapes of bills to deal with the great variety of animals living buried in sand and silt. Long-billed species can reach deeply buried prey, such as lugworms, whereas shorter-billed species can only penetrate to a depth of an inch or two (a few centimeters). In this way, several species can coexist, feeding in the same area, since they do not compete with each other for the same foodstuff.

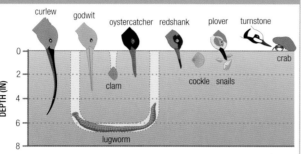

curlew godwit oystercatcher redshank plover turnstone

crab

DEPTH (IN)

clam cockle snails

lugworm

Loaded bill

Atlantic puffin

Puffins dive into the sea from the air or from the sea's surface and can swim more than 200 ft (60 m) underwater using their wings for propulsion and their webbed feet as rudders. They catch small fishes, especially sand eels, and crustaceans and mollusks, which they swallow unless they are feeding young, in which case they are taken back to the burrow. Usually the fishes are lined up in the puffin's bill facing alternately head, then tail, so that more can be carried than if they were all facing the same way.

PROPERLY PACKED
Puffins use their tongue to hold fishes against a small spine in the roof of their mouth. This means that they can open their bills to add more fishes.

Fratercula arctica

- 10 in (25 cm)
- Coasts of Norway, northern Russia, British Isles, Iceland, Brittany, Greenland, and from Labrador to the northeastern US.
- Stocky bird with large, parrotlike bill, orangish legs, black and white plumage.

≫ 434

Parasol technique

Black heron

Sometimes called the black egret, the black heron is also known as the umbrella bird for its unique fishing technique, variously called shading, mantling, or canopy feeding. When hunting, the bird stands in the water, flicks its wings open, and holds them both in front of its body to form an elegant parasol-like shelter over the surface of the water. Small fishes are then attracted to the shade cast by the feathery shelter, since this is where they might expect to find some protection from predators. By creating shade, the bird also greatly reduces the glare from the sun so that it can bend its neck to see the fishes in the water below more easily. Black herons will often feed near spoonbills, which stir up the mud with their long bills. Disturbed fishes will then generally flee to the nearest available shelter, which might be provided by a submerged log, or more unfortunately for them, a heron's spread wings. Black herons also stalk aquatic insects and amphibians, and follow seasonal rains to find food.

CREATING A CANOPY
When the heron is using its shading technique, the front of its wings meet and the tips of the wing feathers dip into the water all around the bird.

Egretta ardesiaca

- Up to 26 in (65 cm)
- Wetlands, lagoons, and lake margins in sub-Saharan Africa and Madagascar.
- Long neck and legs, black or dark slate gray plumage, and yellow feet.

Stealth attack

Great gray owl

The great gray owl is a stealthy predator, hunting in silence, mostly after dark. In open areas such as forest clearings, it generally adopts a sit-and-wait strategy, listening for the movement of prey from a perch, but it also flies close to the ground in search of food. Small mammals form most of its diet with voles being the most important food in many regions. Other prey includes mice, squirrels, rabbits, moles, and weasels.

Strix nebulosa

◧ Up to 33 in (85 cm)

◐ Boreal forest and taiga in North America, Canada, northern Europe, and Asia.

▢ Large facial disk with yellow eyes. Gray plumage.

DISH FACE

The great gray owl's large, concave facial disk acts like a radar dish to focus the sounds of moving prey onto its asymmetrically placed ears. It has very acute hearing and can even detect small mammals moving through tunnels under more than 12 in (30 cm) of snow. The owl will then crash through the snow layer to seize the prey in its talons. Indigestible parts are later regurgitated as a dense, grayish black pellet.

STRIKING BIRD
The great gray owl is an impressive bird with long, broad wings and distinctive markings. A white "mustache" under the facial disk is broken by a black "bow-tie."

Sting extraction

European bee-eater

These colorful birds eat large insects such as dragonflies, large flies, and butterflies, but are best known for eating stinging insects such as bees, wasps, and hornets, which they catch in midair. Several bee-eaters perch together where prey is plentiful and keep watch. When an insect is spotted, they fly to intercept it and return to the perch. If the prey is a bee or wasp, a bee-eater strikes it against a hard surface again and again to disable it or remove the sting and also squeezes it in its bill to try to empty the venom sac. After this, it eats the prey or feeds it to its young. In a single day, a bee-eater may consume more than 200 bees.

Merops apiaster

◧ Up to 12 in (30 cm)

◐ Open countryside and near rivers in southern Europe, north Africa, and parts of Asia.

▢ Slender, colorful bird. Dark eye stripe, yellowish throat, brown upper, and bluish green underparts.

bill used to squeeze
out venom

SQUEEZING VENOM
The bee-eater hunts for prey in open arid or semiarid habitats and catches insects in mid-air before returning to a perch.

Mid-air capture

Spotted flycatcher

Perching in a characteristically upright and alert manner, the spotted flycatcher keeps a lookout for insects that fly past. From its vantage point, it flies on short hunting sorties, returning to the same spot to eat what it has caught. This species feeds on a very wide range of insect prey in addition to flies, including beetles, bugs, moths, butterflies, and even dragonflies.

CAUGHT IN MID-FLIGHT
The bright coloration of this butterfly might advertise its distastefulness to another predator, but it has not saved it from a spotted flycatcher.

Muscicapa striata

◧ Up to 5½ in (14 cm)

◐ Deciduous woodland and hedgerows in Europe and Asia.

▢ Gray-brown with longish wings and tail, creamy breast with faint streaks, streaked head, and black legs.

Butcher bird

Red-backed shrike

Red-backed shrikes, like flycatchers (see left), choose prominent perches, including man-made objects such as posts and telephone wires, that give them a good view of the surrounding habitat. They then wait for passing prey, which can be caught in flight or on the ground. When there is an excess of food, the birds store their victims by impaling them on plant thorns for a short period of time. These "larders" are typically located in bushes or trees, but sometimes the birds use artificial structures such as barbed wire. Prey includes insects, reptiles, and small mammals such as shrews. Smaller items are eaten whole, but larger prey are impaled or wedged securely before being pulled apart by the shrike's stout, hook-tipped bill.

Lanius collurio

◧ Up to 7 in (18 cm)

◐ Heathland and scrub in Europe and western Asia.

▢ Males have gray head with broad, black stripe or mask, reddish back. Females duller and a little smaller.

BUTCHER'S HOOKS
Impaling their victims allows red-backed shrikes to feed on larger prey, such as mammals or lizards, over time.

>>01 >>02 >>03 >>04

PLUNGE-DIVING FOR PREY
>>01 With pinpoint accuracy and lightning speed, a common kingfisher dives toward its prey. >>02 Just before it hits the water it spreads its tail feathers and opens its wings to slow down. >>03 The bird opens its bill slightly as it enters the water, and its momentum carries it just far enough to catch the fish. >>04 The kingfisher lifts its catch clear of the water before returning to its perch.

Lightning strike

Common kingfisher

Also known as the Eurasian kingfisher, this species feeds entirely on aquatic animals. Individual birds have a number of perches along a riverbank. From these vantage points, which may be up to 2½ ft (2 m) above the surface, the bird will look for movements in the water below. When it spots prey, it either dives into the water or hovers momentarily, with its bill pointing downward, as it gathers a final accurate fix on its victim. The problem of refraction (the change in the direction of light as it travels from water to air) is minimized by the bird's sharp eyesight and vertical dive. As it enters the water, the kingfisher's bill opens slightly; its eyes are protected from damage by a membrane. As it makes contact with the prey, the bird shuts its bill around it. Once at the surface, insects, crustaceans, and small fishes are swallowed immediately, but large fishes are beaten against the kingfisher's perch before being swallowed head first. It is important that large fishes are killed before being swallowed to avoid the bird being damaged internally by moving fins or scales.

SWIFT CATCH
Having caught a fish by the middle of its body, a kingfisher begins its return to the surface, carried partly by its natural buoyancy and partly propelled by wing action.

Alcedo atthis

Up to 7 in (18 cm)

Near clear ponds, lakes, streams, and rivers in Europe, Africa, and Asia.

Bright metallic blue above and brownish below. Short wings, short tail, and long, pointed beak.

Kingfishers' eyes have filters that reduce glare and reflection from the water's surface.

A PENGUIN'S LAST MOMENTS
This fleeting glimpse of a leopard seal's head may be the last thing a penguin sees, although in many cases the bird will never know what hit it. By being such fast, agile swimmers, leopard seals can take their prey totally by surprise.

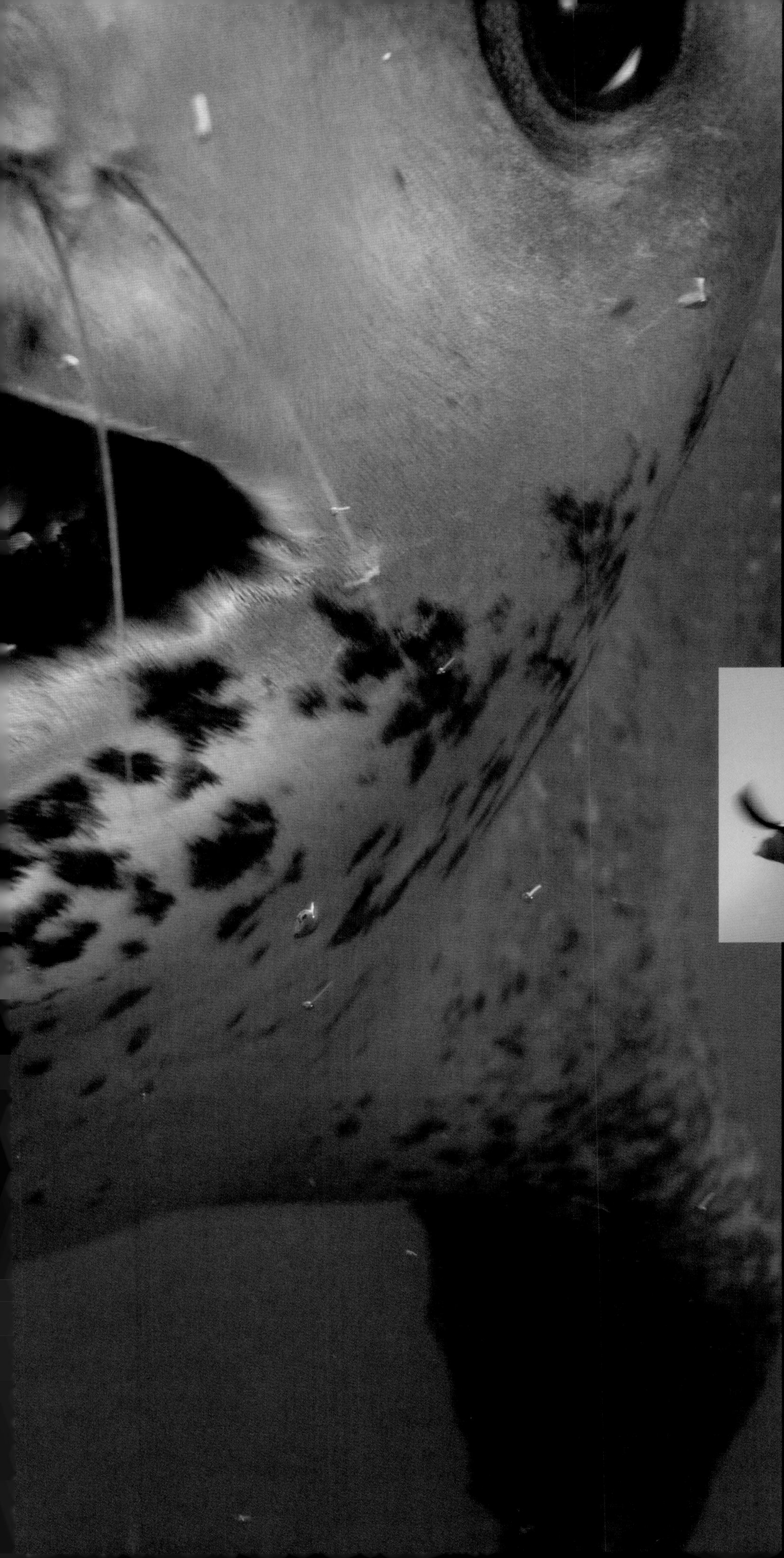

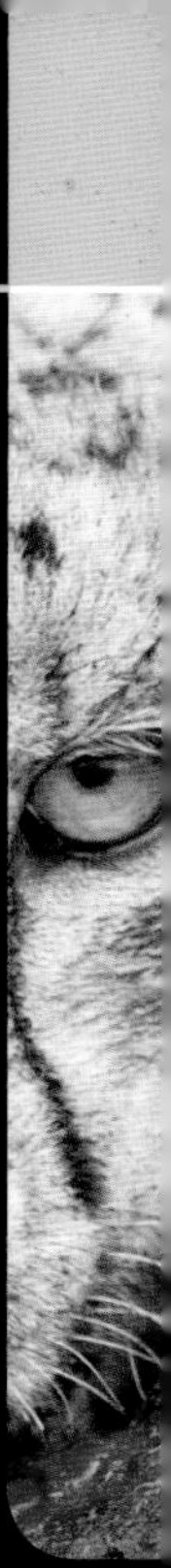

Underwater ambush

Leopard seal

Leopard seals are keystone predators in the Antarctic marine ecosystem. This means that their presence is essential to the stability of the food chain. They fill the same ecological niche that polar bears occupy in the Arctic, and orcas are their only natural predators. Leopard seals are cumbersome on land and, as a result, hunt only in the water, feeding on a wide variety of prey. When young, the seals eat krill, squid, and fishes, but when they become adult they tackle larger prey, such as penguins, and smaller seals, such as crabeater seals and fur seals. These very agile hunters have excellent eyesight and a good sense of smell.

In summer, they hunt around pack ice, keeping close to the shoreline. They lie in wait, partially submerged, to look out for penguins on the ice floes and ambush them when they dive into the water. Their dark back and pale underside makes them hard to detect from above or below, and since they can swim faster than the fastest penguin they do not need to dive deeply to find prey. Their powerful hind flippers are used in a side-to-side motion to propel them, and their long front flippers allow them to change direction very quickly.

In a typical ambush attack, a leopard seal seizes a penguin by its hind legs from behind and thrashes it around until it dies. Seabirds resting on the surface are not safe either, since leopard seals sometimes take them too.

Hydrurga leptonyx

- 9¾–11½ ft (3–3.5 m)
- Ocean water in Antarctica.
- Large seal with streamlined and muscular body. Silvery dark-gray back, pale underside, pale throat with dark spots.

TORN APART
The leopard seal's torpedo-shaped body enables it to propel itself through the water at great speed and surprise its prey. Once it has caught a penguin in its jaws, the seal shakes it vigorously to tear off chunks of flesh.

ANATOMY

RIPPING AND SIEVING

The leopard seal has pointed front teeth and long canines that curve backward, features that are well adapted for holding firmly onto prey. The molars, which are also sharp, can mesh together, allowing them to act as sieves to strain krill from the seawater. Unlike its terrestrial namesake, the leopard seal does not have carnassial teeth—that is, the teeth do not fit very closely against each other in a way that could slice and cut cleanly through meat. Instead, to break up its prey into manageable pieces, a leopard seal thrashes its victim around violently in the water and beats it against the surface of the water.

HUGE JAW
The skull of a leopard seal is long and almost reptilian in shape. The loosely hinged lower jaw, which can open very wide, is powered by muscles attached over a large area of the skull.

sharply pointed front teeth

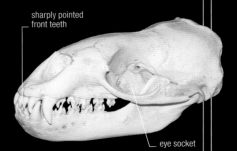

eye socket

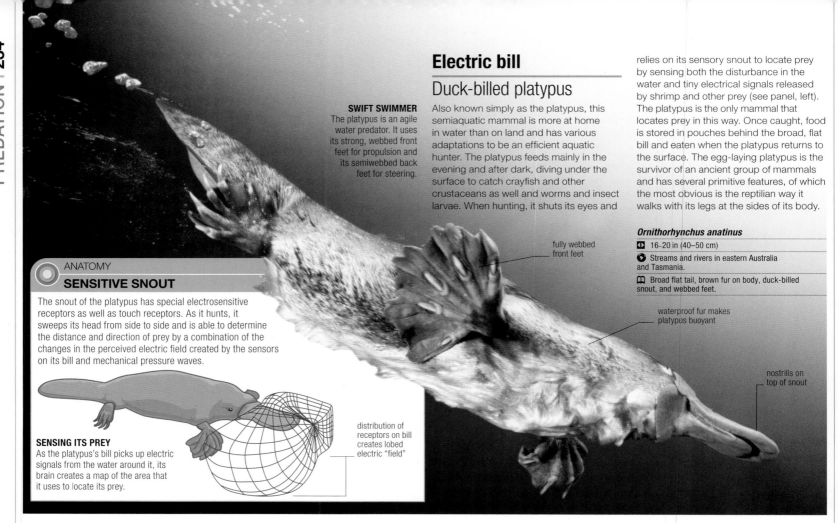

SWIFT SWIMMER
The platypus is an agile water predator. It uses its strong, webbed front feet for propulsion and its semiwebbed back feet for steering.

Electric bill
Duck-billed platypus

Also known simply as the platypus, this semiaquatic mammal is more at home in water than on land and has various adaptations to be an efficient aquatic hunter. The platypus feeds mainly in the evening and after dark, diving under the surface to catch crayfish and other crustaceans as well and worms and insect larvae. When hunting, it shuts its eyes and relies on its sensory snout to locate prey by sensing both the disturbance in the water and tiny electrical signals released by shrimp and other prey (see panel, left). The platypus is the only mammal that locates prey in this way. Once caught, food is stored in pouches behind the broad, flat bill and eaten when the platypus returns to the surface. The egg-laying platypus is the survivor of an ancient group of mammals and has several primitive features, of which the most obvious is the reptilian way it walks with its legs at the sides of its body.

Ornithorhynchus anatinus

↔ 16–20 in (40–50 cm)

◑ Streams and rivers in eastern Australia and Tasmania.

▭ Broad flat tail, brown fur on body, duck-billed snout, and webbed feet.

fully webbed front feet

waterproof fur makes platypus buoyant

nostrills on top of snout

ANATOMY

SENSITIVE SNOUT

The snout of the platypus has special electrosensitive receptors as well as touch receptors. As it hunts, it sweeps its head from side to side and is able to determine the distance and direction of prey by a combination of the changes in the perceived electric field created by the sensors on its bill and mechanical pressure waves.

SENSING ITS PREY
As the platypus's bill picks up electric signals from the water around it, its brain creates a map of the area that it uses to locate its prey.

distribution of receptors on bill creates lobed electric "field"

Sharp claws
Giant anteater

Giant anteaters are specialist predators of termites and ants and may consume tens of thousands of these small but nutritious insects every day. They are solitary animals, and although their eyesight and hearing are not well developed they have a superb sense of smell. The feet have five digits, but the middle three digits on the front legs are equipped with huge, curved claws for breaking open termite nests. This strength is necessary because the nests, which are made of soil mixed with termite saliva, are baked in the sun and become extremely hard.

Having long, curved claws requires the anteater to walk on its knuckles. In addition to breaking open termite nests, it also searches for insects under tree bark. It uses its long tongue to scoop out the insects, and although it has no teeth it crushes the prey against padlike growths inside its mouth before swallowing. Typically, an anteater will eat as many worker ants or termites as it can before the bites or stings of the soldiers become too irritating and it has to move on.

PROBING FOR TERMITES
The anteater's skull lacks teeth but accommodates an extraordinarily long tongue to probe deep inside ant or termite colonies. Coated in sticky saliva to trap insects, it can be flicked in and out twice a second.

Myrmecophaga tridactyla

↔ Up to 6½ ft (2 m)

◑ Savanna and forest in Central and South America.

▭ Grayish brown coat with black and white diagonal markings on shoulders. Long snout and tail, clawed feet.

Underground detection
Grant's golden mole

Although completely blind, Grant's golden moles have extremely sensitive hearing and can detect the slightest vibration in the sand. This ability to detect tiny seismic waves allows them to locate burrowing beetles, ants, grasshoppers, and spiders.

Well adapted to digging, Grant's golden mole has a small leathery nose and stout, strong shoulders and front legs. In addition, the front claws are curved and concave and used as tiny shovels when digging, while the hind feet are webbed for scooping and shifting soil backward.

Golden moles are actually more closely **related to aardvarks, hyraxes, and elephants** than the European mole.

Eremitalpa granti

↔ Up to 3½ in (9 cm)

◑ Coastal dunes and desert in southern Africa.

▭ Dumpy, slightly flattened body with yellowish gray, soft fur with silvery gray sheen.

SAND BURROWER
A Grant's golden mole has made a conspicuous ridge by burrowing just under the surface of the sand. At night it may forage for food on the surface but during the hottest part of the day it will burrow up to 20 in (50 cm) down.

Out of reach

Leopard

After a successful kill, leopards usually drag their prey up a tree and find a safe horizontal branch in which to rest. From here the meal can more easily be defended from other predators and scavengers such as hyenas. However, although they are good climbers, leopards cannot descend from tree branches head first, so they have to scramble down backward, turning to jump as they reach the ground. Leopards stalk their prey stealthily and have excellent hearing and eyesight, allowing them to hunt after dark as well as during the day.

Leopards' prey includes impalas, antelopes, duikers, and bushbucks, but they will also tackle species as big as elands. They also eat monkeys, rodents, birds, fishes, and reptiles. Once caught, the leopard's victim is quickly despatched with an asphyxiating bite to the throat.

CONSUMED AT LEISURE
Using their great strength and powerful neck muscles, leopards can drag prey up to nearly three times their own weight up trees.

Panthera pardus
- Up to 6¼ ft (1.9 m)
- Savanna in sub-Saharan Africa and parts of south Asia.
- Yellowish to cream fur with dark, rosette markings.

CLOSING IN
A perfectly timed swipe to the rear quarters will bring this gazelle down. Before it can recover, the cheetah will bite its throat to finish it off.

Swift pursuit

Cheetah

The cheetah has many adaptations that allow it to reach speeds in excess of 70 mph (113 kph) and accelerate from 40 mph (0–64 kph) in just three strides. Its spine is very flexible, and when the animal is galloping it is alternately flexed and straightened, allowing the powerful hind legs to achieve an even longer effective stride. The cheetah's face is short and flat with the eyes positioned to give good binocular vision. The eyes also have an image stabilization system to keep the prey in sharp focus when running. A black line down the face under each eye acts like an antiglare device.

The cheetah's nasal passages are large, as are the lungs, and the body has a low skeleton-to-muscle-mass ratio, with lighter bones and longer legs than other cats. The long tail acts as a rudder and allows the cheetah to achieve extremely tight turns when pursuing agile prey. Its shortish, relatively blunt claws are nonretractable, giving it permanent grip on the soil at high speeds much like spiked running shoes. Closing in on prey such as a fleeing impala, a cheetah can put on an extra burst of speed over a couple of hundred yards.

60 The average time in seconds it takes for the cheetah, the world's fastest land animal, to close in on its prey.

Acinonyx jubatus
- Up to 5 ft (1.5 m)
- Open grassland in East and southwest Africa.
- Lean cat with relatively small head and yellowish fur with small black spots.
- 414–15

Adaptable predator

Arctic fox

Arctic foxes hunt and eat animals such as lemmings and Arctic hares in the warmer months. In the winter, when prey is scarce, not only will they attack young seals in their dens and find fishes, but they will also scavenge carrion left by larger predators such as polar bears.

The key to the success of these hardy animals is that they are very adaptable and can survive by eating birds' eggs and even plant material such as berries if they are available. On the shoreline, they will feed on dead fishes or seals that have been washed ashore and may also eat shellfish and sea urchins from time to time. In winter blizzards, Arctic foxes dig dens in deep snow and can survive in extremely cold conditions of -58° F (-50° C), protected by their thick fur and, if the feeding has been good, a layer of body fat. A counter-current heat-exchange system in the legs ensures that blood returning to the body from the feet is warmed up. This means that, although the feet must survive at a lower temperature than the rest of the body, heat is not lost from the core of the body.

Alopex lagopus
- Up to 21½ in (55 cm)
- Arctic tundra in North America, Europe, and Asia.
- Compact body with short legs and snout, bushy tail.
- 308–309

ANATOMY

SEASONAL COATS

The coat of the Arctic fox changes from its brownish gray in summer, to blend well with the color of rocks and low-growing plants, to pure white in winter, providing very effective camouflage against the bright, snowy background. In addition, the fur grows much thicker in winter, to insulate the fox against the bitter cold of the Arctic tundra. When resting, the fox covers its face with its bushy tail.

The Arctic fox has **fur on the bottom of its feet** to enable it to walk on ice.

>>01   >>02   >>03

POUNCING ON PREY
>>01 To locate prey hidden under the snow, the Arctic fox listens intently for the sounds of burrowing or movement. It rears up in the air with its eyes focused on a spot on the snow above its victim.   >>02 At the peak of its leap, the fox extends its front legs and rotates its body forward.   >>03 The fox plunges head-first toward the ground and thrusts its front paws through the snow into its victim's tunnel or lair beneath.

STEALTHY APPROACH
To catch fleet-footed prey, lions stay very low to the ground using natural cover to get as close to the target as they can. In this way they can start to run before the prey has managed to spot them. This technique gives the lion the edge it needs before the prey can reach its top speed and escape.

Family hunting

Lion

When it comes to hunting prey, lions are adept at teamwork. Lionesses are lighter and quicker than males and do the vast majority of the hunting. Pride members hunt cooperatively and by doing so can take much larger prey than they would be able to tackle on their own. Although males may be large enough to attack buffaloes, single lions are seldom able to take on really large species such as elephants or male giraffes. Cooperation brings easier kills and carry less risk of injury, and also that ensure that enough food will be available for every member of the pride.

Hunting techniques vary. Typically one lioness will spook a prey animal or chase it, at speeds of up to 40 mph (70 kph), toward other members of the pride lying in wait. Sometimes the pride will surround a herd of prey and try to pick off a lone, young, or weak individual. Once the pride has made a kill, cooperation ensures that it keeps possession of its prize—a single lion would have great difficulty against a pack of hyenas intent on taking over the kill.

Cooperative hunting is made possible because lions form close social groupings lasting many years. A pride of lions comprises a number of related adult females and their young. The young raised by the pride may suckle from a number of females as well as their own mother. Adult males tend to live alone or in small groups called coalitions. When they take over a pride, the males, one of which will be dominant, are responsible for marking the boundaries of the pride's territory or area, which may be anything from a few tens to a few hundreds of square miles, defending it against threats, and, of course, mating with the females.

Apart from their large size and formidable teeth, lions have other attributes that make them efficient predators. They have excellent binocular vision, which allows them to judge distance very accurately, and their eyes are capable of working at low light levels, making night hunting possible. They use their strong, sharp retractable claws for grasping and grounding prey, before killing it with a neck-breaking bite or by asphyxiation. Although lions are top predators, they also scavenge from carcasses when the need arises and steal prey from hyenas.

ANATOMY
POWERFUL JAWS AND TEETH

The lion's skull and teeth are adapted for killing and eating sizeable animals such as zebras, wildebeests, elands, and kudus. The long, daggerlike canines and large jaw muscles ensure a strong grip and an efficient killing bite, usually to the neck. The pointed and sharp-edged premolars and molars, called carnassial teeth, in the upper and lower jaws work together like the blades of shears, slicing through flesh. The lower jaw only moves up and down so lions swallow chunks of flesh and do not chew.

upper incisor
upper carnassial
upper canine
lower carnassial
lower canine
lower incisor

Panthera leo

⬅➡ 5½–7¼ ft (1.7–2.2 m)

⊙ Parkland and open savanna in sub-Saharan Africa. A few hundred Asiatic lions (subspecies *Panthera leo persica*) live in the Gir Forest in Gujarat, northwest India.

📖 Coat color varies from creamy tan to brown. End of tail has dark tuft of hair. Males typically have thick mane that may be dark in color.

» 413, 446

>>01   >>02   >>03   >>04

AMBUSH AT A WATER HOLE

>>01 After a short chase, a lioness has caught up with a fleeing greater kudu. Sometimes lions will lash out with a front paw to trip the prey but usually use a burst of speed to jump at the hindquarters.   >>02 The lioness leaps onto the kudu's back, using her sharp claws to dig into the hide.

>>03 As the kudu stumbles under the weight, the lioness is able to maneuver herself up toward the neck of the stricken beast, where she opens her huge jaws to more than 10 in (25 cm) and delivers the fatal bite.   >>04 The animal is dead within a few seconds, and soon after the other members of the pride gather to share the meal.

Adult male lions typically eat 95 lb (43 kg) of fresh meat in a single sitting. They usually gorge themselves once every three or four days.

⯈ HUNTING SUCCESS

Research has shown that, apart from the number of lions cooperating and the type of prey, other factors can greatly affect hunting success. The brightness of the moon has a marked effect, success being much higher on moonless nights, especially in open habitats. The moon has less of an effect when lions are hunting in wooded areas. Habitat features are also important, with long grass cover bringing significantly greater success than short grass.

MOON VISIBILITY

% OF HUNTING SUCCESS

50
40
30
20
10
0

high and clear
low or obscured

GRASS HEIGHT

short
medium
long

NIGHT HUNTERS

Although lions will hunt at other times, they prefer the cover of darkness. Moonlight reflected by the back of their eyes gives away the presence of a large pride of lions waiting to start a foray.

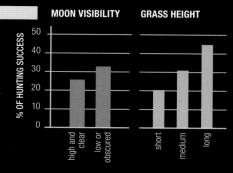

PACK HUNTING
An attack by a pack of African wild dogs reaches a climax: surrounded by the snarling pack and already injured, this lone warthog is going to need a lot of luck if it is going to escape. The dogs have to be careful since the warthog's sharp tusks could inflict a potentially lethal wound but, as always, there is safety in numbers.

Cooperative hunting

African wild dog

Like most members of the dog family, African wild dogs, or painted hunting dogs, live in groups tied together by intense social bonds. These bonds are an effective advantage in the hunt, since the dogs cooperate as a pack, running down and overpowering their prey in a long-distance chase. Strategically, their hunting is not cunning or stealthy. Relying on their excellent vision during the cool of early morning or late afternoon, they approach prey such as wildebeests, impalas, or zebras in full view. Surprise is unnecessary since they have the stamina to chase their prey until it is exhausted. The quarry is often able to gallop faster than the wild dogs' top speed of 37 mph (60 kph), but will eventually be chased down over distances of up to 3½ miles (6 km). The hunting pack keeps in touch constantly with high-pitched, yapping contact calls. During the chase, the dogs spread out to head off any sideways escape attempts. Zigzagging evasion movements of the prey, which would confound a lone hunter such as a cheetah, are ineffective against a pack of wild dogs. As the exhausted prey slows down, the dogs surround it and usually target its soft underbelly, disemboweling it. Hunts generally have a very high success rate with more than three out of four resulting in a kill. Hunting dogs have a very powerful bite and their large molars and premolars allow them to crush bone. When they have eaten, food is regurgitated to older dogs, pups, and other members of the pack that did not take part in the hunt.

Lycaon pictus

- Up to 5 ft (1.5 m)
- Savanna and lightly wooded parkland in sub-Saharan Africa.
- Slim bodied with long legs. Irregular patterning of white, yellow, and dark fur. Large, rounded ears.

HUNTING GROUNDS

The home range of African wild dogs varies with the size of the pack and the availability of prey, but can often be more than 620 square miles (1,000 square km).

lead dogs · **pack of dogs** · **pack fans out** · **impala herd** · **some impala escape** · **lead dogs chase isolated impala** · **one dog maintains direction and anticipates impala's direction change** · **some dogs pursue on flanks** · **flanking pursuers cut off impala's escape** · **lead dogs catch impala and others arrive at kill**

SCOURING THE SAVANNA

A typical African wild dog hunt is an endurance chase. While a whole impala herd might be targeted, the eventual victim will be the impala that falls behind, due to age or sickness. Evasive maneuvers are usually useless, as sideways escape is prevented by the flanking dogs, and the impala's erratic flightpath can be predicted and headed off by dogs bringing up the rear.

THE KILL

Separated from its herd and exhausted after a long chase, a red lechwe has been seized from behind by two lead dogs.

THE FEAST

In Botswana's Okavango Delta, a pack of hunting dogs have caught their favorite prey—an impala. They feast while vultures wait to scavenge whatever is left over.

Western pipistrelle

This common species of bat starts to forage in the early evening, well before dusk, and may also be seen flying after dawn. Using echolocation (see panel, below) to source its prey, the western pipistrelle feeds on a wide range of soft-bodied insects such as moths, flies, caddis flies, and small beetles. The exact nature of its diet changes over the course of a year, and the bat will feed on any species that is locally abundant or swarming nearby. It flies above the ground. The smallest bat species in the US, the western pipistrelle is sometimes mistaken for a large moth. Since it is a weak flier, it usually hunts in calm conditions. By day, it roosts singly or in small groups in caves and crevices. Although it lives in arid habitats, roosting sites tend to be near any available water because this usually provides a good source of hatching aquatic insects.

large, widely spaced ears

sound emitted via nose as well as mouth

Pipistrellus hesperus
◧ Up to 2¾ in (7 cm)
⊙ Desert and scrubby grassland in North America and Mexico.
▥ Pale yellow to brownish gray fur; black facial mask.

THE HUNT
A western pipistrelle closes in on a small moth. The bat can consume prey equal to 20 percent of its body weight in a single night.

▶ ATTACK SEQUENCE

In addition to making calls for communication and other reasons, bats emit ultrasound for hunting prey. This species produces its echolocation calls in the frequency range 53–90 Khz, with the highest energy being produced at around 62 Khz. Each frequency modulated note has a duration of between 4 and 5 milliseconds.

1 SEARCH PHASE To conserve energy, calls are produced, in the form of a series of "notes," at a rate of less than 20 per second.

2 APPROACH PHASE When prey is detected, the bat increases the rate of calls to get a more accurate location.

3 TERMINAL PHASE Call rate may increase to 200 times per second.

Sound detection

Greater horseshoe bat

This species of bat has a number of different hunting techniques and catches medium- to large-sized insects such as cockchafers, dung beetles, and large moths. Sometimes they will perch and fly out in pursuit of passing insects, while at other times they will attack prey from above or glean insects from the surface of foliage. When hunting, the greater horseshoe bat flies low and slowly, using an echolocation call with a constant frequency of 70–84 Khz. Leaving its roost at sunset, it typically forages while flying over open pasture, farmland, and in parkland—often next to water where prey can be abundant. When large prey has been captured, it is taken back to a convenient perch to be consumed. Like some other bats, this species may make use of doppler-detection calls. To do this, a bat must emit a long note with a constant frequency. If the bat and the prey are moving relative to each other at the same distance, there will be no change in the frequency of the perceived echo. If the prey is flying toward the bat, the frequency will appear to increase; but if the prey is moving away from the bat, the frequency of the reflected sound will appear to drop. This is exactly the same as when a vehicle with a loud siren passes a stationary listener—the pitch of the siren appears to increase as the vehicle approaches and decrease as it passes.

Rhinolophus ferrumequinum
◧ Up to 3 in (7.5 cm)
⊙ Open woodland, farmland, and parkland in Europe and parts of Asia.
▥ Horseshoe-shaped flap of skin around the nose, leaf-shaped, pointy ears, and light brown, fluffy fur, with paler fur on belly.

CASE STUDY
RECOGNIZING ECHOES

Bats emit a series of ultrasound squeaks, which are reflected by prey in different ways according to the size, shape, texture, and frequency of wing beats. From this a bat can determine the location, speed, and nature of its prey. The echo a bat receives from a delicate crane fly, for instance, will sound very different to that of a large, hard-bodied maybug. The motion pattern of flying insects provides a hunting bat with additional information. As the insect's wings move up and down, at one point they will be perpendicular to the direction of the sound transmitted by the bat, causing a brief increase in the level of the sound energy reflected, known as a "glint."

CRANE FLY
83

MAYBUG
83

FREQUENCY (KHZ)

FLYING PREY
A greater horseshoe bat makes a final turn toward its prey, which it will seize in its jaws. From the reflected sound waves received, the bat already has a good idea of what it is about to eat.

NIGHT FISHING
The fishing bat uses ultrasonic calls to detect activity on the surface of the water. It has long hind legs with large talonlike claws that act as fishing gaffs. The bat rakes its claws through the water to snatch fishes from beneath the surface. Its catch is transferred to its mouth, chewed, and stored in extendable cheek pouches as it continues to hunt.

Feeding on frogs
Frog-eating bat

Also known as the fringe-lipped bat from the numerous fleshy outgrowths on its lips and chin, this species is a specialist predator of frogs although it will also feed on other small vertebrates and insects. The bat uses the mating calls of male frogs to locate its prey, and is both able to tell if a frog is too big to deal with and to differentiate between edible and poisonous species. The bat's ears are especially sensitive to the relatively low frequencies of the frogs' choruses, and some frogs keep quiet when frog-eating bats are foraging.

Trachops cirrhosus
- Up to 4 in (10 cm)
- Lowland forest in Central and South America.
- Reddish brown fur and large ears. Chin and lips have pink, fleshy warts.

Rounding up
Long-beaked common dolphin

The main prey of these fast-swimming dolphins are fish and squids, and in some parts of the world pods of long-beaked common dolphins hunt schooling fish cooperatively. Members of a pod swim around schooling fish, herding them into a tight ball before individuals take turns plowing through the fishes, attacking and eating them as they go.

Long-beaked common dolphins are very social, communicating with each other by sonar clicks and traveling in pods numbering anything from less than a dozen to many hundreds of individuals. The long-beaked species is similar in appearance to the short-beaked common dolphin, and for a long time the two were considered to be one species. Besides having longer beaks, they are slightly longer and more slender than the short-beaked species.

FEEDING CIRCLE
These long-beaked dolphins have taken control of a fish school. While some of them dart in to feed, others will keep circling.

Delphinus capensis
- Up to 8¼ ft (2.5 m)
- Coastal waters of the Atlantic, Pacific, and Indian oceans.
- Back and flippers dark brownish or black; creamy white underside with pale markings along sides.

The jaws of a long-beaked common dolphin can have more than 200 teeth for gripping slippery fishes and squids.

SURE GRIP
Although the Amazon river dolphin swims quite slowly, its neck is also extremely flexible, allowing it to turn its head at almost right angles to its body as it looks for food. It has no dorsal fin, but has large flippers and tail flukes, which are an adaptation for swimming in shallow water or flooded forest.

River hunter
Amazon river dolphin

The largest of the freshwater dolphins, the Amazon river dolphin, or boto, has a number of adaptations for finding food in murky, slow-moving waters. Although it has good eyesight and hearing, it is able to echolocate prey and has a number of stiff, sensory hairs along the front of its beak that help it feel among the sediment and debris on the bottom of the river. The beak has peglike teeth at the front to seize prey, such as crustaceans and fishes and flatter, molar teeth farther back to crush and grind the food.

Inia geoffrensis
- Up to 8½ ft (2.6 m)
- Slow-moving waters in the Amazon and Orinoco river basins of South America.
- Pink or gray dolphin with long snout but no dorsal fin.

Versatile predator
Orca

The orca, or killer whale, is the largest dolphin species in the world. Intelligent and social animals, orcas often travel in large, maternally based family groups called pods and communicate with each other with a range of whistling and clicking calls. There are physical, behavioral, and genetic differences between populations of orcas, and it is not certain exactly how many subspecies or even species there are. Five distinct orca types have been identified, some of which feed on a range of fishes, sharks, cephalopods, and turtles, while others attack seals, sea lions, and even whales. Feeding behavior depends on the type of orca and its prey. Orcas that follow migrating herring schools may feed singly or work in a group to corral fishes into a tight ball, slapping it with their powerful tail flukes to stun or kill as many as they can. Orcas that hunt marine mammals may kill their prey by ramming it, hitting it with their tails, or tossing it into the air. When hunting

whales, members of a pod usually select a calf or a weak adult. By chasing and tiring it out, they separate it from the rest of the group and drown it by not allowing it to resurface for air. In shallow water, orcas may almost beach themselves to feed on seals, elephant seals, and sea lions.

ACROBATICS
Orcas are able to reach speeds of 35 mph (56 kph). When traveling quickly, they jump out of the water. This behavior is known as porpoising.

Orcinus orca

- Up to 8m (26ft)
- Coastal and offshore waters in oceans worldwide from polar regions to the tropics.
- Black bodies with white undersides, flanks, and a white patch behind the eye. Males have a large triangular dorsal fin, while female's is shorter and more curved.

CASE STUDY

WAVE HUNTING

Orcas have a unique cooperative hunting technique for capturing seals resting on small ice floes. "Wave-hunting" begins with a number of orcas looking for likely targets by holding their heads out of the water, a behavior known as spy-hopping. Several orcas will then swim together toward and under the floe to create a large wave to wash over the ice and carry the seal into the water. To ensure that the seal is dislodged, some orcas may deliberately nudge the floe from the side. At the other side of the floe, another orca waits to eat the seal when it is finally knocked off. While wave-hunting, adult orcas can be accompanied by juvenile individuals, which learn how to perform this technique by example. When fully trained, the juveniles will take part in the hunt themselves. This complex behavior relies upon communication and coordination to be effective.

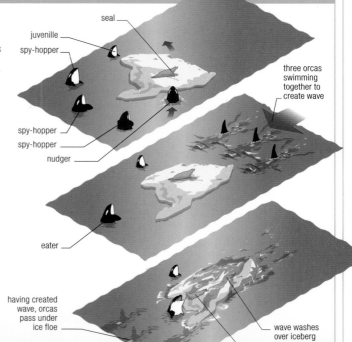

seal
juvenille
spy-hopper
three orcas swimming together to create wave
spy-hopper
spy-hopper
nudger
eater
having created wave, orcas pass under ice floe
wave washes over iceberg
seal washed toward waiting orca

SPY-HOPPING
A spy-hopping orca has spotted a lone seal on an ice floe and others may join it to try to knock it into the sea.

BEACH ATTACK
This orca has almost beached itself by rushing into the shallows to catch seals. Mother orcas teach their young how to carry out this risky maneuver.

CORRALING A SCHOOL
Here a fish-eating orca is corraling a school of fish. It flashes its white underside at them then slaps the fish ball with its tail flukes.

Bubble-netting

Humpback whale

Humpback whales strain food from surface water using up to 400 bristly baleen plates located on either side of the mouth. When the mouth is closed, water is squeezed out through the baleen plates, trapping food. Different humpback whale populations have different feeding habits. North Atlantic pods feed mainly on fishes, such as herring, sand lance, salmon, and mackerel, but those in southern oceans also feed on krill. Humpback whales use a number of feeding techniques, ranging from hitting fishes with the pectoral fins or tail flukes, to swimming through schools, swallowing fish as they go. A more complicated approach, called the ring of foam technique, involves the whale slapping the surface of the water with its tail as it swims in a circle around a school of fish. The whale then dives down and swims up through the ring of foam, swallowing fish that have gathered in the center. A vertical extension of this technique, and the most impressive feeding method practiced by humpback whales, is known as bubble-netting. Here a single whale, or several acting cooperatively, dive down and then swim up toward the surface while exhaling continuously. The rising air forms a curtain, or if the whales swim in a wide circle, a complete cylinder of bubbles, inside which the fishes become trapped. The whales then swim up through the concentrated school, swallowing thousands of fishes. Besides confusing and herding the fishes, bubble-netting may also make the whales less visible to their prey.

THROAT PLEATS
Deep throat pleats, running from the front of the head to halfway down the underside of the body, allow humpback whales to accommodate large volumes of water containing food.

CASE STUDY
LEARNING TO LOBTAIL-FEED

Humpback whales may produce variations of existing feeding techniques, which are then learned by other whales. In one such case, an Atlantic population of humpbacks initiated the bubble net technique using a lobtailing behavior in which one whale slaps the surface of the water with its tail. This tail slap may act as a marker for the whales as they rise from below or may temporarily stun the prey.

LEARNING
In less than a decade, lobtailing spread and was practiced by more than half the Atlantic humpback whale population.

KEY
■ observations
···· best model

RISING BUBBLES
Bubble nets are formed when a whale swims in a set pattern underwater while slowly exhaling. When cooperating with other whales, there is a division of labor. Some make the bubbles, others herd the fishes from below.

whale lobtailing
whale then dives down
waiting whale
first whale creating bubble-net
fish in a ball
waiting whale
path taken by whale
bubble-net beginning
whale swims up in a helix pattern

NET SHAPES
The shape of the nets, which may take the form of sheets, semicircles or cylinders, are revealed when the bubbles break the surface.

WHALE GROUP
A group of humpback whales has surfaced inside a ring of bubbles to swallow trapped fishes. Bubble nets created by groups of whales may have diameters of up to 98 ft (30 m).

Megaptera novaeangliae
◀▶ 49–66 ft (5–20 m), females larger than males

◆ Oceans and seas worldwide. Whales migrate thousands of miles, from summer feeding grounds in polar waters, to equatorial waters in winter to breed.

▭ Blue-black back with paler underside. Head and lower jaw covered with knobs called tubercles. Long white pectoral fins, and broad, wavy-edged tail flukes.

RESISTANT TEETH
In addition to catching prey in water, the Eurasian water shrew also hunts on land for earthworms and beetle grubs. It has red-tipped teeth due to the presence of metallic deposits in the enamel, which are thought to increase their resistance to wear.

Venomous bite

Eurasian water shrew

Eurasian water shrews rest in burrows during the day, emerging at night to feed on aquatic invertebrates, such as freshwater shrimp, caddis flies, and the larvae of other insects, although they may also feed on small newts, frogs, and fish. Because they have a high metabolic rate, they need to consume about half their own body weight every day in order to survive. When diving underwater, their thick, oily fur traps air, giving them a silvery appearance. Unlike other shrews, the Eurasian water shrew has a mildly toxic saliva, which may aid prey capture. They are solitary animals and hold territories, marked out with the secretions of scent glands.

Neomys fodiens

- Up to 4 in (10 cm)
- Europe and parts of Asia: semiaquatic, living on banks of streams and rivers, ponds, and marshland, but also in woodland, grassland, scrub, and hedgerows.
- Dense, black, velvety fur above and whitish yellow fur below. Head with long snout and small eyes and ears.

Probing bark

Aye-aye

The aye-aye sleeps during the day and forages in the forest canopy at night. Although it eats nuts, fruits, seeds, and fungi, it is best known for finding insect grubs buried deep in wood. Aye-ayes have excellent hearing and tap on the surface of wood to locate hollow cavities beneath bark. They then chew a hole in the wood using their long incisor teeth before using their bony, elongated, double-jointed, middle fingers to pry insect larvae from inside. They also use their middle fingers to tear at fruits, extracting the nutritious pulp.

LARVAE SEEKER
These elusive primates are the ecological equivalent of a woodpecker. Larvae of woodboring insects, such as the longhorn beetle, make up an important component of their diet.

Daubentonia madagascariensis

- Up to 16 in (40 cm)
- Rain forest in Madagascar, seasonally dry forest, and cultivated plantation.
- Dark brown, gray, or black fur with scattered white hairs. Short snout, and large hairless ears.

Sensitive nose

Star-nosed mole

This mole's most distinguishing characteristic is a circle of 22 pink, fleshy tentacles at the end of a hairless snout. These tentacles are in constant rapid motion and are covered with thousands of sensory receptors. They are used to identify food solely by touch, and a large portion of the mole's brain deals with processing this detailed tactile information. The star organ is vertically symmetrical with 11 tentacles varying from $\frac{1}{16}$–$\frac{3}{16}$ in (1–4 mm) in length on each side. On contact, the lower tentacles, which are the shortest and most sensitive, assess the nature of the food. The diet consists mainly of invertebrates, such as earthworms, encountered when tunneling, but also freshwater insects, crustaceans, snails, and small fishes encountered while swimming.

Condylura cristata

- 7–7½ in (18–19 cm)
- Eastern North America, in a wide variety of habitats with wet soil, including forest, meadow, marshland, and the margins of streams, lakes, and ponds.
- Stocky, cylindrical body with dense, blackish brown, waterproof fur, large clawed front feet, and a thick tail.

SENSORY COMPENSATION
Although the star-nosed mole is virtually blind, only able to differentiate light and dark, the incredibly sensitive nasal organ allows it to detect, identify, and consume small prey in a fraction of a second.

COOPERATIVE HUNTING
In parts of Africa where there is continuous canopy cover, chimpanzees must cooperate to catch prey such as the western red colobus monkey. Communication and coordination between members of the group are essential.

Blocker
To prevent the monkey from escaping, blocker chimpanzees track it

Ambusher
An ambusher seizes the monkey, before biting and beating it to death.

Chaser
To keep the prey moving forward in the desired direction, it is chased from behind by several chimpanzees.

Colobus monkey
Because of the thick canopy cover, there is nowhere the monkey can climb where it cannot be followed.

Driver
When all the members of the hunting party are in place, the driver chimpanzee surprises the prey and the chase begins.

Blocker

Chaser

Planned assault

Chimpanzee

Chimpanzees are largely omnivorous, their diet consisting mainly of fruits, leaves, nuts, and roots, as well as insects and bird eggs. They may also hunt larger vertebrates, such as bush pigs and colobus monkeys, usually targeting young individuals. These hunts require advance planning, learning from observation of others, and trial and error. Cannibalism between chimpanzee groups is known to take place. Chimpanzees are intelligent, highly social primates. They move on the ground using a form of quadrupedal locomotion called knuckle walking, while their long front limbs and strong hands also allow them to swing from branches in the forest canopy. Their thumbs are short but opposable, permitting a precision grip and delicate manipulation of food and other objects. The chimpanzee is the only animal, except for humans, to make tools specifically for hunting. They have been seen breaking branches from trees, which they strip of bark and sharpen to spear bushbabies as they sleep. Sticks are also used as hammers, thrown as weapons, or used to probe termite and ant colonies.

Pan troglodytes

- Up to 5¼ ft (1.6 m) tall (standing height)
- Tropical forests and wet savanna in west and central Africa.
- Coarse, dark brown, or blackish body hair. The face, digits, palms, and soles of the feet are hairless. The face is dark or mottled with a prominent brow ridge.

SUCCESSFUL HUNTING
A successful hunt means that there is enough meat to go around. Males tend to eat more meat than females, who usually get their protein from insects.

Scavenging

Scavengers are animals that feed on the decaying remains of other living things. While some animals feed exclusively this way, others turn to scavenging if their food is in short supply when conditions are harsh.

Recycling nutrients and energy

When plants and animals die, large amounts of nutrients are locked in their bodies. These valuable energy-producing resources become available to scavengers, who do not waste them. Human activity has greatly increased the opportunities for some scavengers. The growth of cities, the extensive raising of livestock, and the availability of roadkill provide scavenging species with rich pickings.

VITAL SOIL CONDITIONERS
Earthworms primarily consume decaying plant material. Their feeding activities maintain soil structure and fertility.

FEEDING ON SMALL CARRION
The carcasses of small mammals and birds attract larger scavengers such as foxes and crows as well as burying beetles, which conceal carrion in the ground in order to feed their young.

EVOLVED FOR SCAVENGING
The black and white plumage of Marabou storks has inspired the name "undertaker bird." These scavengers have featherless heads and necks—special adaptations for reaching inside carcasses to feed.

Decomposers

Once scavengers have consumed the accessible portions of the carrion, the rest, including indigestible parts (such as bones, hair, and feathers, as well as excrement) is broken down by decomposing organisms such as fungi and bacteria. Decomposers are vital in the food chain. Their activities convert leftover organic matter into carbon dioxide and essential nutrients such as nitrogen and phosphorus, in forms that can be easily absorbed by photosynthesizing algae and plants—the primary producers in the food chain. In this way, nutrients are returned to the system. Ecosystems depend on the maintenance of such biochemical cycles.

FOOD CHAIN

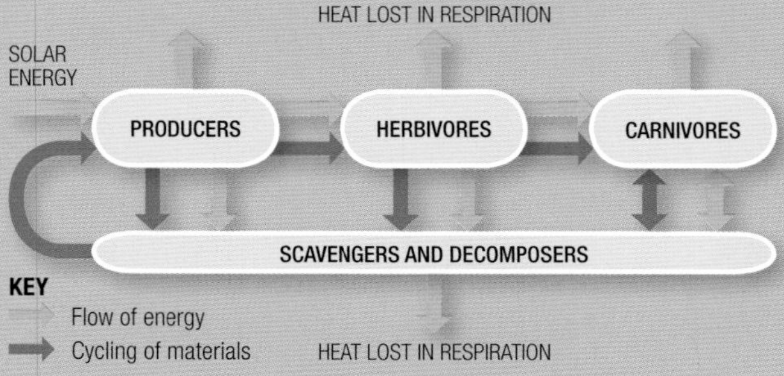

HEAT LOST IN RESPIRATION

SOLAR ENERGY

PRODUCERS → HERBIVORES → CARNIVORES

SCAVENGERS AND DECOMPOSERS

KEY
→ Flow of energy
→ Cycling of materials

HEAT LOST IN RESPIRATION

CYCLE OF LIFE
When an organism dies, be it carnivore, herbivore, or plant, scavengers take what they need before the decomposers get to work. In this way, nutrients are recycled and returned to the food chain.

Benefits of scavenging

Scavengers consume the leftovers of predators or the bodies of animals that have died by accident, from disease, or from other natural causes. Freshly dead animals are just as nutritious as live ones, and one advantage of being a scavenger is that it is easier and safer than being a predator. A scavenger doesn't have to tackle the defenses against predation that the dead animal may have had, such as biting, kicking, jumping, or running, or chemical defenses such as repugnant odors, unpalatable secretions, or poisons.

WOOD LOUSE
Wood lice eat dead plant, fungal, and animal matter. Their feeding activities and feces return nutrients to the soil, especially in woodland.

MAGGOTS
Blow flies lay their eggs on dead animals. Their larvae feed by producing enzymes that liquefy the tissues of the carrion into a rich soup.

Soil conditioning
Common earthworm

Earthworms play an important ecological role in conditioning soil (Charles Darwin drew attention to their important part in the history of the world). Worms pull leaf litter and other decaying matter from the surface of the soil down into their burrows where it breaks down and is then eaten. Worm casts (their excrement) are rich in nutrients essential for microorganisms and plants.

MADE FOR BURROWING
Each body segment bears eight short, bristlelike hairs that grip the sides of burrows as the earthworm moves. The tail can be flattened to anchor the worm as it retracts the front of its body.

Lumbricus terrestris
- Up to 10 in (25 cm) (extended body)
- In soil, especially in grassland, in Europe, but widely introduced elsewhere.
- Long, cylindrical, segmented body, reddish brown above, yellowish below.
- **»** 368, 445

27 tons The combined weight of common earthworms that can be present in just 2.5 acres (1 hectare) of land.

Grasping food
Horseshoe crab

Horseshoe crabs are generalized scavengers that move along the seabed and dig across its surface to find food. Their broad diet mainly consists of snails, marine worms, decaying seaweed, and algae. Horseshoe crabs have six pairs of limbs, the first five of which have pincers. These are used to grasp food as the animal moves along, and pass it to the mouth, which is situated between the legs. The feeding activities of these scavengers aerate the surface of the seabed.

Limulus polyphemus
- Up to 24 in (60 cm)
- Muddy or sandy bays and estuaries along eastern coast of North America.
- Greenish olive to brown, tough horseshoe-shaped body with three regions (head, abdomen, spikelike tail), six pairs of jointed limbs.

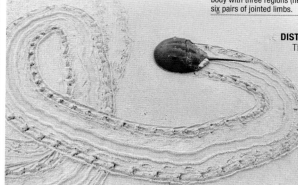

DISTINCTIVE SHELL
The horseshoe crabs is actually more closely related to spiders and scorpions than to other true crabs. The front part of its body, the prosoma, is covered by a tough, horseshoe-shaped shell or carapace.

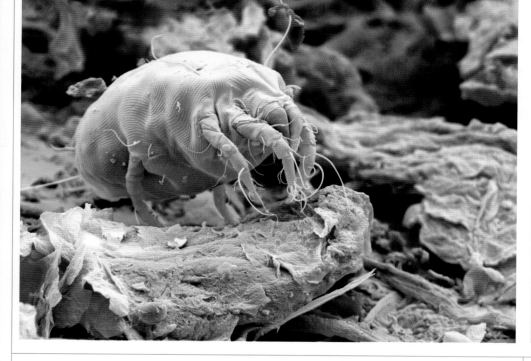

Skin scavenger
Dust mite

Humans shed up to 1/16 oz (2g) of skin flakes each day. Dust mites feed on these as well as hair fragments and fibers that accumulate inside homes. They cannot tolerate dry conditions or sunlight, but can be abundant in sheltered, humid areas such as mattresses, pillows, or other bedding. They secrete digestive enzymes onto a particle of organic matter to break it down before ingesting it into a very basic gut, and eat the same food particles several times over to extract the full food value. Dust mites produce as many as 25 minute particles of fecal matter per day.

Dermatophagoides pteronyssinus
- Less than 1/32 in (0.4 mm)
- Humid microhabitats such as nests and human dwellings, nearly worldwide.
- Round body, pale or whitish, eight pairs of legs.

HUMAN IMPACT
ALLERGIC REACTIONS

The dust mite is a common trigger of allergic symptoms in humans. It reproduces very quickly, given the right conditions, and many thousands of mites have been found in just 1/32 oz (1 g) of house dust. The shed bodies of dead mites, as well as the many thousands of fecal pellets they produce in their lifetimes, contain a number of allergens that can trigger and exacerbate conditions such as eczema and dermatitis. Inhaled dust-mite allergens cause asthma and hay-fever-like symptoms in millions of people worldwide.

Sifting sand
Sand bubbler crab

These small crabs live in vertical burrows in the sand near the high-water mark. When the tide is out, they dig toward the surface. On emerging, they clear sand out of the burrow, smooth the area around the entrance, then begin to feed. The crab uses its front claws to scrape a trench in the surface of the moist sand, moving in a straight line away from its burrow. Using a claw, it scoops sand into its mouth, where it is sifted to remove organic matter, which is eaten. During this process, the sand is manipulated into a small ball. The crab places this ball beside the trench and continues. After a while, the crab returns to the burrow and begins to dig another trench, working in a different direction.

Scopimera inflata
- Up to 1/2 in (1.5 cm)
- Sheltered sandy beaches along eastern and northern coasts of Australia.
- Grayish brown, small, bubble-shaped body. Insides of claws reddish, outsides pale. Blue mouthparts.

MAKING SAND BALLS
Sand bubbler crabs leave intricate patterns of balls of compressed sand around their burrows as they feed. The number of balls is an indication of how long the tide has been out.

Rotten diet
Flat-backed millipedes

These slow-moving millipedes feed almost exclusively on decaying leaves and other rotting plant material using their mandibles to bite and crush the food they find. Their distinctive flattened shape and the sideways expansions of the upper surface of the body (the dorsal surface) allow flat-backed millipedes to force their way through leaf litter and other moist, dark microhabitats such as compost heaps, rotten wood, and tree stumps.

Polydesmida species
- 1 1/4–5 in (3–13 cm)
- Variety of habitats, especially woodland leaf litter, worldwide.
- Long, flattened, with around 20 body segments. Body segments flat-topped often with lateral projections.

Periplaneta americana

Up to 1½ in (4 cm)

Widespread in tropical and subtropical regions; indoors in warm temperate regions.

Reddish brown, oval-shaped, flattened body; large wings extend beyond abdomen.

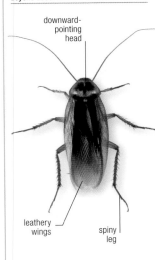

downward-pointing head

leathery wings

spiny leg

World traveler

American cockroach

American cockroaches originated in Africa but have traveled on the ships of traders to become widely established in much of the world. They feed on a broad range of plant and animal material and tend to forage for food after dark using long, sensitive antennae to feel their way around. Fast moving and very agile, they are able to move about 50 body lengths in a second, and their flattened bodies allow them to squeeze through small cracks. Although they have wings, they do not fly readily except in very hot conditions. These natural scavengers are serious pests when they invade food-processing factories, kitchens, and other places where they can find warmth, shelter, and food. Around houses they are found in cellars, drainage systems, and sewers.

LABORATORY TESTING
Because of its large size and ease of culturing, the cockroach has been used extensively by scientists for research, including insecticide testing.

Feces foraging

Dung beetles

These beetles feed and raise their young on animal feces. Competition for dung is intense—one pat of elephant dung can attract 4,000 beetles in 30 minutes. The female constructs a large ball, and the male rolls it away to bury it. Underground, the female smears the dung ball with soil and her own excrement. Once it has aged for a while, she divides it into smaller balls, lays an egg in each, and stays to care for her brood.

Scarabaeus species

Up to 1½ in (4 cm)

Savanna in southern and East Africa.

Stout-bodied beetle; front of head shovel-shaped with toothlike projections. Wing cases have purplish violet sheen.

THE BIG PUSH
Dung beetles can roll balls of dung as large as 2 in (5 cm) across, and are able to move dung balls that weigh 50 times or more their own body weight.

 HUMAN IMPACT

HELPING FARMERS

Dung beetles are important recyclers in natural and agricultural habitats. Their activities can clear vast quantities of dung in a relatively short time, return valuable nutrients to the soil, and maintain good soil structure and aeration. If beetles are not present, the recycling process is retarded and nitrogen, essential for plant growth, is lost to the system. Over time, pastures and arable land can become seriously degraded. In addition, any uncleared dung provides a breeding ground for disease-carrying and nuisance flies that can have an adverse effect on humans and domestic livestock.

>>01   >>02   >>03   >>04

Grave diggers

Burying beetles

These beetles bury the carcasses of small birds and mammals as a food source for their larvae. When a dead animal is found, a mating pair excavate the soil beneath the carcass so it caves in, burying the dead animal. The beetles then remove the fur or feathers, using these to line the burial chamber. The female lays her eggs in the soil close to the chamber, and the hatched larvae move in to feed. Competition for a found carcass can be intense, with several pairs of beetles fighting over it for control.

INSIDE THE BURIAL CHAMBER
>>01 Burying beetles have large antennae that detect the presence of a dead animal from some distance. >>02 When a carcass is located, it is buried to safeguard it from other scavengers and flies. >>03 The brood develops inside the burial chamber, eating the carcass. >>04 The parents also eat the flesh and regurgitate liquids for their young to eat.

Nicrophorus species

Up to 1¼ in (3 cm)

Widespread in a range of habitats.

Stocky, slightly flattened body, black or black and red patterned; wing cases shortened, exposing some of the abdomen.

Tied in knots

Japanese hagfish

Like other hagfish, this scavenger feeds inside the bodies of dead (or sometimes live) fishes, by entering through the mouth, anus, or gills. It can tie its body in a knot, which it moves along the length of the body. It uses this skill to brace itself against a predator to force an escape or to pull its head away from a carcass, helping the mouthparts tear off a portion of flesh.

Eptatretus burgeri

Up to 24 in (60 cm)

Inshore temperate waters of northwestern Pacific.

Long, slime-covered, finless body with flattened tail. White line along its back.

Scavenging in schools

Sawtooth barracuda

Occasionally, sawtooth barracudas are seen alone, but more typically they are found in groups of several hundred individuals. They swim on the seaward side of reefs and employ a sit-and-wait ambush strategy when hunting for food. They can swim very fast over short distances to intercept their prey (which are usually fishes from a number of school-forming species).

Sawtooth barracudas have a large gape and sharp, pointed teeth of different sizes. Although they are voracious predators, they also scavenge if the opportunity arises. Large predators such as sharks often leave rich pickings behind after a kill that sawtooth barracudas will clean up. They have been known to follow scuba divers, and it is thought that they mistake them for large predators, and keep close to them in order to scavenge.

Sawtooth barracudas are caught for food, but eating even a small amount of their relative the great barracuda can result in ciguatera poisoning, caused by toxins accumulated in their food.

SCHOOL ACTIVITY
Also known as the chevron barracuda because of its distinctive body markings, the sawtooth barracuda is most active after dark but can be seen swimming in relatively large schools during the day.

Sphyraena putnamae

Up to 3¼ ft (1 m)

Outside reefs and lagoons in western Pacific, coastal northern Australia, Indian Ocean to East African coast.

Grayish green fish, with dark chevron markings. Large head with strong jaws; lower jaw juts out.

Detritus digger

Red mullet

This bottom-dwelling species is found in small schools at depths of up to 330 ft (100 m). It prefers soft-bottomed areas where there is an abundance of invertebrate life. The sensory barbels under its chin (used to locate prey such as mollusks, worms, and crustaceans buried in sediment) are very mobile and, when not in use, can be folded back into a groove under the body.

Mullus surmuletus

Up to 16 in (40 cm)

Muddy and sandy bottomed inshore waters of Mediterranean Sea, eastern North Atlantic, Black Sea.

Reddish with darker red line along midline and yellowish stripes below. Pair of long barbels below mouth.

Ocean trash can
Tiger shark

The tiger shark is an efficient scavenger, following traces of blood or carrion for long distances in the water. It is also a highly skilled hunter. It has good eyesight (even in murky water), electrosensory pits called ampullae of Lorenzini, which enable it to detect small muscle movements of prey in darkness, and an excellent sense of smell. It is very maneuverable and can turn quickly from side to side. When hunting, a tiger shark uses its long fins to generate lift as it swims through water, and the long tail fin can generate enough power for bursts of speed up to 18½ mph (30 kph) per hour. This shark preys on a wide range of vertebrate species ranging from fishes, smaller sharks, porpoises, seals, turtles, and birds. It also eats invertebrates such as squid, horseshoe crabs, and conches. It is the second most dangerous shark to humans after the white shark (see p.214), although it does not eat human flesh.

The tiger shark's apparent disregard for the food value of the items it eats has earned it the name of "the garbage can with fins." Stomachs of tiger sharks have been found to contain many indigestible man-made and waste items, such as bits of tire, wire, and tin cans.

ANATOMY
UNIQUE TEETH

The teeth of tiger sharks have a distinctive cockscomblike outline. They are notched and finely serrated on both sides. The shape may have evolved to allow the shark to cut through the shells of large mollusks and turtles as well as flesh and bone. When biting, the snout rises and the lower jaw opens to give a large gape. The lower jaw then lifts and the upper jaw moves forward as the mouth closes. The upper jaw then retracts—this action helps the shark cut chunks out of its prey. In its lifetime, a shark may replace many thousands of teeth as new ones grow forward constantly, displacing the functional teeth at the front of the jaws.

Galeocerdo cuvier

⬍ Up to 25 ft (7.5 m)

◐ Inshore or open ocean in tropical, subtropical, and warm temperate waters worldwide.

▥ Blunt, broad head, streamlined body, large upper tail lobe. Bluish green with tigerlike stripes above, whitish or yellowish below.

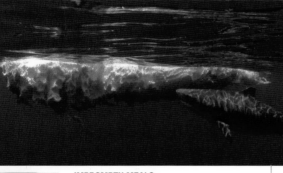

IMPROMPTU MEALS
A tiger shark bites voraciously into the carcass of a marlin (left) found in Australian waters, and another feeds on the carcass of a sperm whale (above) in the waters off Hawaii.

Adaptable scavenger
Jungle crow

Although primarily a countryside species, the jungle crow has done well in urban areas. It has broad feeding habits and will eat almost any live or dead animal or vegetable food. It scavenges at carrion as well as household waste. The bird's success is due to its ability to adapt to new environments and novel foods. These crows have even been seen to place walnuts on roads and wait for cars to run over them before eating the kernels, a tool-using ability seen in many crow species (see p.478).

Corvus macrorhynchos

⬍ Up to 24 in (60 cm)

◐ India to northeastern and Southeast Asia. Woodland, yards, and cultivated areas with some trees.

▥ Dark gray plumage except black tail, wings, face, and throat. Heavy bill.

Fatal attraction
Black-browed albatross

Long-line fishing and trawling are responsible for killing many of these impressive birds. Once a common albatross species, the black-browed albatross is now endangered. It feeds on fishes as well as octopuses and squid. But it is the attraction to floating carrion that has led it to fall victim to modern fishing practices. Albatrosses dive to catch baited hooks and become caught themselves. By using bird-scaring devices and setting lines only after dark, fishermen are able to reduce the slaughter. After feeding at sea for long periods, ranging over vast distances, they return to land to breed.

A FREE LUNCH
Fishing boats that are at sea for long periods throw large quantities of fish offal and bycatch overboard. Here, a large number of black-browed albatrosses gather behind a trawler to feed.

Thalassarche melanophrys

⬍ 31–37 in (80–95 cm)

◐ Islands and open waters of the Southern Ocean.

▥ Black-and-white plumage with orange bill, white head with characteristic dark stripe above eyes. Long narrow wings.

≫ 142, 403

REMAINS OF THE DAY
Using its claws to hold its food, a Eurasian griffon stands over what is left of a dismembered carcass. This species eats only carrion, and it is thought that it softens any tough meat with blows of its large, strong bill.

Carrion feeder

Eurasian griffon

As soon as temperatures rise in the morning, Eurasian griffons take to the skies in the mountainous regions in which they live and, using rising air currents, soar high above the ground. They remain on the wing, often in groups, for many hours and can cover great distances as they scan the terrain below for promising objects to investigate. Their diet consists entirely of fresh carrion, although they will resort to rotting meat if no other food is available.

Eurasian griffons have a weak sense of smell and rely on the highly visible activities of other animals feeding at a carcass. When something attracts them, they descend rapidly and, depending on the number and nature of the other scavengers present, may either wait their turn or take over the situation. Since they have relatively small heads and bills, they generally need another (usually mammal) scavenger to have ripped open the hide of a freshly killed animal before they can feed. After eating, Eurasian griffons like to wash their feathers in fresh water before resting in the sun.

Gyps fulvus

◁▷ Up to 3½ ft (1.1 m)

⊙ Southern Europe, North Africa, and Asia. Mountainous and open regions, grassland, and shrubland.

⊞ White head with white neck ruff and strong hooked bill, pale brown body plumage, broad wings with dark flight feathers.

LOUNGING TOGETHER
These social vultures share nest sites and also feed and rest together in small colonies of up to 20 pairs of birds.

8 hours The average amount of time per day that Eurasian griffons spend in flight searching for food.

SIMILAR SPECIES
Like the Eurasian griffon and the African white-backed vulture (below), the turkey vulture (left) from the Americas has a bald head; feathers would become clogged with blood when the bird puts its head inside a carcass.

COMPETITIVE SCAVENGERS
Hyenas are the most abundant carnivores in Africa and obtain food by both hunting and scavenging. They are often one of many different scavengers to find a carcass. Sometimes, ferocious fighting breaks out when competing scavengers congregate around potential food. This spotted hyena is trying to hold off a pack of African wild dogs.

No waste
Tasmanian devil

The largest carnivorous marsupial in the world, this nocturnal creature eats a wide range of dead and live foods including small mammals, birds, reptiles, insects, and amphibians. It has excellent hearing, sensitive whiskers, and a good sense of smell, enabling it to find carrion in the dark. It is an efficient scavenger, and also hunts prey up to the size of wallabies. Its large head, powerful jaws, and sharp teeth allow it to tear through flesh and splinter bone, leaving nothing behind.

CARCASS COMPETITION
The Tasmanian devil is a solitary scavenger. The smell of a large carcass may attract several devils, and loud screeching and aggressive displays are used to establish dominance without risking injury.

Sarcophilus harrisii
- 2½–3½ ft (0.75–1.1 m)
- Variety of habitats, especially forest and meadow, in Tasmania, Australia.
- Stocky muscular body, broad head, tail half the length of body. Black fur, white patches on chest and rump.

Urban opportunist
Common raccoon

Active by day and night, common raccoons lead an omnivorous lifestyle and have good hearing and night vision. In addition to live food, they will also eat fresh roadkill and other carrion. In suburban areas, they have become able scavengers. Their front paws are very sensitive, allowing them to select, manipulate, and examine small items of food before eating them. Their varied diet includes insects, crustaceans, mollusks, fishes, small mammals, and birds as well as fruits, seeds, and other plant material.

Procyon lotor
- 26–39 in (65–100 cm)
- Grassland, woodland, and suburban habitats in North and Central America, from southern Canada to Panama.
- Fur gray to black with distinctive black "bandit mask" patches around eyes; bushy tail with faint dark rings.
- » 363

NIMBLE FORAGERS
Common raccoons can be pests in suburban areas because they scavenge around garbage dumps. They are agile climbers and use their slender front paws to open simple fastenings and remove trashcan lids as they forage for food.

Bone crusher
Spotted hyena

Also known as the laughing hyena after its characteristic vocalizations that sound like human laughter, this species is often thought of as a scavenger but it is, in fact, also the most common predator in sub-Saharan Africa. Mostly solitary hunters, hyenas increase their success rate and tackle much larger species (such as wildebeests and zebras) if they hunt in groups. They often chase prey for long distances without tiring until eventually, their quarry becomes exhausted and is pulled to the ground. Hyenas and lions compete for food and often fight over it. Sometimes hyenas steal the remains of kills from lions, but in some cases, the reverse happens.

SUPEREFFICIENT DIGESTION
Hyenas can consume up to a third of their own body weight in one meal. They can crush and eat bones, even those of elephants, and can digest just about every part of their prey.

Crocuta crocuta
- Up to 6¼ ft (1.9 m)
- Sub-Saharan Africa, mostly in savanna.
- Light gray, cream, or reddish brown with dark spots. Heavy head and neck, black muzzle, mane hair slopes forward, front legs longer than hind legs.

Natural scavengers
Polar bear

The main prey of polar bears are ringed seals and sometimes bearded seals, but they will eat anything they can kill, such as young walruses and whales, fishes, seabirds, and caribous. To hunt, they most often sit very still by a hole in the ice where seals surface to breathe. When a seal appears, the bear strikes the seal with a front paw and drags it out onto the ice before biting its head. On the surface of the ice, polar bears rely on their superb camouflage to stalk resting seals. They creep up as close as they can and, when they get within range, can run at about 30 mph (45 kph). Even so, only a few hunts are successful, so scavenging is important.

Carcasses of whales or walruses on the seashore, or caribous or musk oxen on land, provide an important source of food. Polar bears have an excellent sense of smell and can detect a carcass from great distances. As natural scavengers, they will investigate novel items, which can lead to problems near human settlements in the Arctic where some have suffered serious internal injury due to eating man-made materials.

A LUCKY FIND
A gray whale carcass on the coast of northern Alaska attracts a number of polar bears. The retreat of sea ice in the summer can leave bears stranded on land and unable to reach seals, their preferred prey. Scavenging is the only option if this occurs.

Ursus maritimus
- Up to 8¼ ft (2.5 m)
- Sea ice and coastal areas throughout Arctic (circumpolar).
- Thick white or cream colored. Relatively narrow head with long muzzle and neck; small ears and tail, strong legs with very broad feet.
- ›› 406

The intestines of polar bears are adapted to **digest the fats of marine mammals.** Growing bears eat the meat while adults eat mainly seal blubber.

Not all feeding relationships involve one animal killing and eating another. Often they are a partnership from which two individuals derive mutual benefits. Sometimes the benefit to one animal has no discernable effect upon the other, but in many cases, although the preyed-upon animal does not die to provide food, it does suffer and may die as an indirect result of the relationship.

Symbiosis

Symbiotic relationships are long-lasting associations between members of two species. In obligate symbioses, one of the species involved cannot survive without the other. For example, the ant *Acropyga sauteri* and the mealybug *Pseudociccidae rhizoecinae* are entirely dependant upon one another. The bug needs the ants' nest as a place to live, and the ants rely upon the bugs for food. Other forms of symbiosis are facultative, meaning that although both parties can survive alone, at least one of them would suffer from independence. Some symbioses, such as that of the bug and the ant, clearly benefit both of the animals involved, but others are more exploitative and one animal suffers at the other's expense. Infestations of parasites are a good example of this. Parasitic relationships also show the intimate nature of some symbioses, with one animal living inside, or on the other. In other cases, the two animals share a common home. Some partners come together for a short period, when one needs the other to clean it of ticks and dead skin, for example.

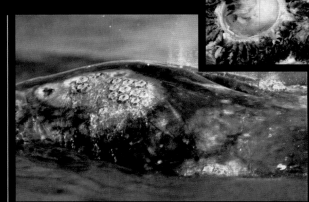

BARNACLES AND WHALE LICE
In an example of phoretic commensalism, whales carry barnacles through food-rich water. Whales suffer, however, from carrying parasitic whale lice. These in turn are the food of several species of fishes, with whom the whales enjoy a mutualism.

PARASITE ← **PARASITISM** **HOST** [+ / −]

PARTNER 1 ← **COMMENSALISM** **PARTNER 2** [+]

PARTNER 1 ← **MUTUALISM** **PARTNER 2** [+ / +]

TYPES OF SYMBIOSIS
Symbiosis is usually characterized according to whether one or both of the animals involved gains from the relationship. For example, in a mutualistic partnership, both parties benefit.

Commensalism

It is easy to show that an organism benefits or suffers as a result of its relationship with a member of another species, but it can be surprisingly difficult to prove that a relationship has no effect at all. Many relationships defined as commensalisms involve phoresy—the transportation of one animal as the passenger of another. The larvae of some midge species, for example, attach themselves to the scales of Amazonian catfishes. They are transported by these fishes to better feeding areas than they would be able to reach on their own, and hosts are unaffected by their presence. White-fronted terns follow hunting pods of Hector's dolphins to quickly find fishes during the birds' breeding season, an example of facultative commensalism.

Parasitism

Parasites live at the expense of their hosts. They feed directly from them and in some cases live out part, or all of their life cycle, in or on them. A host animal may die as an indirect result of a parasitic infection, but it is unusual for a parasite to kill its host directly. They are usually far smaller than their hosts and reproduce at a far faster rate. In many cases, parasites and their hosts have coevolved to the extent that some parasites have only one host. Parasites may live their entire life associated with a single host, or have a complex life cycle involving a number of host species. The feeding apparatus and behavior of parasites is usually highly specialized.

EATING THE INSIDES
Pearl fish live inside sea cucumbers, feasting upon their gonads. The fish enters by reversing into the host's anus. It can twist around to defecate through this without leaving home.

○ ANATOMY
REPLACEMENT TONGUE

Cymothoa exigua is a crustacean parasite of the spotted rose-snapper. This 1¼–1½ in (3–4 cm) long parasite sneaks into the snapper's mouth via the gills and attaches itself to the tongue. It feeds on the fish's blood, diverting it from the tongue into its own mouth via six claws on its first three pairs of legs. Eventually, starved of blood, the tongue withers away. The crustacean attaches itself to the tongue stump and incredibly becomes a functioning tongue substitute. At this stage, the parasite reduces the amount of blood it takes from the host and switches its diet to include food particles in the mouth of the fish. The fish is able to carry on feeding as usual, suffering only in that it is forced to share its meals with this unusual parasite.

BLOOD SUCKING
The piercing mouthparts of a female mosquito act like a serrated syringe, and her saliva promotes blood flow from her host.

INFESTATIONS
Ticks, like those on this hedgehog, are blood sucking parasites that are very hard to remove. Severe infestations can reduce a host's vigor.

Mutualism is a symbiotic relationship that benefits both of the animals involved. In many cases, one animal cleans another, eating parasites and cleaning wounds. In other cases, such as the pollination of flowering plants, the reproduction of one organism relies on the feeding behavior of another. Ants feed off the honeydew of aphids, but offer them protection in return. Termites and their gut bacteria could be said to be another example of mutualism; without the bacteria, the termites would not be able to digest wood.

FEEDING AND FERTILIZING
Honey bees visit flowers to collect pollen and nectar to take back to their hives. As they move between flowers, they transfer pollen from one plant to another, thereby ensuring fertilization.

DENTAL HYGIENE
Some partnerships appear risky. These cleaner shrimps are literally in the jaws of death, but the coral grouper they are cleaning suppresses its motivation to feed while cleaning is in progress.

Space invader

Beef tapeworm

Beef tapeworms attach themselves to the intestinal wall of their host and absorb predigested food directly from its gut. Eventually, the host cannot eat enough to sustain both itself and the parasite and loses weight. The beef tapeworm, also known as the unarmed tapeworm, infects cattle and, occasionally, humans who eat undercooked, contaminated beef.

Taenia saginata
↔ 16½–56 ft (5–17 m)
⊙ Worldwide.
📖 Elongate intestinal parasite with characteristic four-suckered scolex (head).
≫ 382

Blood sucker

Asian tiger leech

Leeches are segmented worms found in marine, freshwater, and wetter terrestrial habitats. Some of them are predators, feeding on a range of small invertebrates, such as snails, insect larvae, and worms. The most familiar leeches however, are hemophagic parasites, which suck blood directly from living hosts. Leeches in the genus *Haemadispa*, incuding the Asian tiger leech, are all bloodsuckers. Leeches attach to their host by means of biting jaws or a sucking proboscis. They maintain the flow of blood by secreting a long-lasting anticoagulant into the wound. Once full, they simply fall away and digest their meal.

Haemadispa picta
↔ Up to ¾ in (2 cm)
⊙ Tropical forests in mainland and Southeast Asia.
📖 Brown and orange striped body and a distincive, prominent head.

WAITING FOR DINNER
This Asian tiger leech waits on a leaf for a passing animal on which to feed. It detects its host by sensing movement with its 10 eye-spots and by sensing the carbon dioxide its host breathes out.

Stinging gloves

Boxer crab and anemone

Crabs and anemones often associate with each other for mutual benefit. Some crabs carry anemones around on their backs, and hermit crabs encourage anemones to live on the surface of the shells they inhabit—in both cases, the anemone provides protection for the crab. When a crab molts or changes its shell, it has to shed the anemone in the process, becoming vulnerable while it is exposed. To minimize the danger, the boxer crab carries a pair of anemones in its modified, claw-bearing legs (chelipeds). If the crab is disturbed, it waves its anemone "boxing gloves" at potential predators, presenting the stinging tentacles as a defensive weapon. When the crab molts, it puts the anemones down and can then quickly pick them up again if required. Since its claws are often full, this scavenging crab has adapted to use small claws on its first pair of walking legs to tear food into bite-sized pieces. The anemone also benefits from this relationship. The boxer crab is a messy eater and stirs up food particles, which the anemone can collect and eat.

MOPPING UP FOOD
Boxer crabs use their anemone "gloves" as mops to wipe up scattered food particles. They pick and eat some of the food off the anemone, then they leave the rest for the anemone to finish off.

Spreading disease

Sheep tick

The sheep tick feeds directly on the blood of its host and in the process may be the vector of a number of diseases, including louping-ill in sheep and Lyme disease in humans. It attaches itself to its host by means of the backward-pointing spikes of its harpoonlike mouthparts (known as a hypostome). Ticks can feed on blood for up to two weeks before falling from the host and laying thousands of eggs, after which they die.

FULL OF FOOD
Engorged ticks swell as they fill with the blood of the host; females can increase in size by 200 percent. When they have had enough blood they will drop off.

HEAT SEEKERS
Unable to jump or fly, hungry ticks wait in the vegetation for a host to pass by, then they drop onto the animal as it passes. The ticks are attracted to both the body heat and respired carbon dioxide of their hosts.

Ixodes ricinus

↔	¹⁄₁₆–³⁄₁₆ in (2–4 mm)
◐	Scrubby vegetation in woods and meadows throughout temperate regions worldwide.
🔲	Small, black-legged tick with variable black, gray, or brown body.

Feather feeders

Bird lice

Bird lice are ectoparasites, living on the bodies of birds and among their feathers. Their mouthparts are modified for biting and chewing, and they feed primarily on the bird's skin and feathers. Some species consume blood, which they obtain either by biting through the skin of the bird or by drinking at scratches that result when the birds attempt to rid themselves of the lice's irritating presence. Lice move between hosts in communal roosts and young birds that are brooded by their infested parents. Most birds have lice, and they are not necessarily detrimental in the long-term, but severe infestations can damage the health and reduce the vigor of the host.

FEATHERED VICTIM
Lice cling to the feathers of birds to resist their attempts to remove them. To deter lice, some birds fill their nests with pungent plant material.

Family Philopteridae

↔	¹⁄₁₆–³⁄₁₆ in (1–5 mm)
◐	On birds, worldwide.
🔲	Small, wingless insect with broad head and flattened body.

Buried alive

Tarantula hawk wasp

The male tarantula hawk is a wasp that feeds on the flowers of milkweed and other plants, while the female drinks nectar and eats rotting fruits, which often intoxicates them to the point of being unable to fly. But when it comes to raising their young, these wasps are fearsome parasites of tarantula spiders. Female hawk wasps track down spiders using scent and tend to attack spiders resident in a burrow, which usually means females during the breeding season or both sexes at other times. Breeding male spiders are often ignored by tarantula hawk wasps because they do not feed themselves while searching for mates and therefore become emaciated. When a tarantula hawk wasp locates its prey, an intense fight often takes place, until eventually it manages to penetrate the spider's guard and sting it. The wasp's powerful poison does not kill its victim, it only paralyzes it. Once subdued, the spider is then dragged either into its own burrow or into a burrow

SUBDUING THE MEAL
Having found a victim, the giant tarantula hawk wasp thrusts with its stinger to inject a powerful venom that paralyzes its prey.

FINAL JOURNEY
Having subdued its prey, the tarantula hawk drags the unfortunate spider into a burrow that will soon become a sealed tomb.

prepared by the wasp as a nest chamber. In the burrow, the female lays a single egg on the spider and leaves, sealing the burrow behind it. If the egg fails to hatch, the spider may recover. However, if the egg hatches, the spider's fate is sealed: the larval wasp feeds on the still-living spider, sucking its juices until it eventually dies, then the larva consumes the remains of its host, leaving the vital organs until last as a means of keeping the meal fresh.

Pepsis heros

↔	Up to 2 in (5 cm)
◐	Arid areas of the southern US and Central and South America.
🔲	Blue-black body and rust-colored wings. Females' sting is particularly long, up to ¹⁄₄ in (7 mm).

Farming aphids

Carpenter ants and aphids

Many species of ants, including carpenter ants, have a mutualistic relationship with aphids. Rather than eating the aphids, ants tend small groups of them, stroking the aphids' bodies with their legs and antennae to stimulate them to produce a drop of sugar-rich honeydew. After taking honeydew from a number of aphids, and storing it in its abdomen, an ant returns to its nest, where it regurgitates the honeydew to feed to its siblings. The aphids also benefit from this relationship because the ants protect them from potential predators, such as ladybug beetles, aphidlions, and lacewings, and transfer them from wilted to healthy plants. Carpenter ants are omnivores, eating insects, fruits, and other plant material. They use their powerful biting jaws to hollow out nests in wood. If the wood is part of a building these insects can become serious pests, although contrary to popular perception the ants don't actually eat the wood, because they are unable to digest cellulose. Scout ants locate food by day and lay down pheromone trails that are followed by foraging parties under the cover of darkness.

98yd The approximate distance worker carpenter ants are willing to travel from a nest in search of food.

PROTECTING THE FLOCK
Ants effectively farm their aphid charges, herding them, "milking" them for their honeydew, and offering protection.

OPPORTUNISTIC SCAVENGERS
Sally-lightfoot crabs are scavengers that feed primarily on algae uncovered by the retreating tide, but they are happy to eat almost anything, including dead animals. They have been observed picking over the bodies of basking marine iguanas. The lizards presumably tolerate this behavior because the crabs are picking off dead skin and ectoparasites.

Boring fish

Sea lamprey

The sea lamprey attaches to its prey, which consists of other fishes, dead or living, by means of its suckerlike mouth and secretes an anticoagulant into the wound to promote blood flow. Once satiated, the boring fish simply detaches and falls away, leaving its victim with a horrific gaping wound that is slow to heal and susceptible to infection. Host fishes often die as a result of this form of parasitism. Sea lampreys hatch in rivers where, as larvae, they remain for a number of years in a muddy burrow to filter feed. After they have undergone metamorphosis, and assumed a free-swimming juvenile form, these jawless parasitic fishes leave the rivers and migrate to the sea. Following a second metamorphosis, the adult fishes eventually return to rivers to breed.

RINGS OF TEETH

Lampreys attach to their prey by suction, clamping themselves to the skin of their host with the sucking lips of their oral disk. The disk is filled with concentric rings of inward-pointing horny teeth, which become progressively larger the closer to the center of the disk they are. Using these teeth, lampreys rasp a gaping hole in tissues of their unfortunate prey, and feed on their victim until they have had enough, after which they detach and swim away.

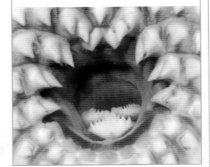

SEA LAMPREY
The superficially eel-like sea lamprey has a small head with relatively huge, flexible lips, which make ideal suction pads. The lamprey's gills open through a series of holes behind the eyes.

SUCTION POWER
Once attached to a host, a sea lamprey is almost impossible to detach. Here, a lamprey is being carried upstream by a migrating salmon. Incredibly, the host fish is still able to leap despite the extra drag caused by the parasite.

Petromyzon marinus

⬌	Up to 4 ft (1.2 m)
🌐	Coastal seas of North Atlantic and rivers draining into it.
📖	Superficially eel-like, lacking jaws and with gills that open through holes rather than slits.

Flesh eater

Cookie-cutter shark

The cookie-cutter shark is a nocturnal predator thought to use bioluminescent lamps on its belly to lure its prey within striking distance. These lamps give off patches of an eerie greenish light that may resemble small fishes. It is known to eat squid and small fishes, but is most notorious as a parasite of larger prey. Just as would-be predators, such as larger fishes, cetaceans, and other species of shark, are about to strike at what they think is a smaller fish, the cookie-cutter turns on them and bites ferociously. First, it sinks the large, razor-sharp, triangular teeth of its bottom jaw into its hapless victim, then it uses its strong lips to latch onto its prey like a suction pad. Finally, it spins to tear out a circular plug of flesh, a pulling action

Isistius brasiliensis

⬌	Up to 22 in (56 cm)
🌐	Tropical waters worldwide, from the surface to 11,480 ft (3,500 m) deep.
📖	Small, cigar-shaped shark.

WOUNDED DOLPHIN
This dolphin bears the telltale wound that is certain proof of an unpleasant encounter with a cookie-cutter shark.

aided by the momentum of its fleeing victim. The cookie-shaped wounds inflicted by this shark give the cookie-cutter its name.

LETHAL GRIN
The lips of the cookie-cutter shark form a suction seal around the mouth. The teeth are small in the upper jaw and large and triangular in the lower jaw.

Hitching a ride

Live sharksucker

The live sharksucker, also known as a remora, is a relatively poor swimmer and prefers to hitch a ride from larger species of fishes (including sharks), whales, dolphins, manatees, and even turtles. The sharksucker benefits from being carried

because it saves energy. Breathing is also easier, because a sharksucker at rest uses energy to pump water across its gills, whereas one being carried is held in a current and does not need to. Meanwhile, the host expends extra swimming energy when carrying a sharksucker. Some sharksucker species feed on the scraps of food left by their feeding hosts; the sharksuckers that attach themselves to

manatees are copraphagic, with a taste for the feces of their hosts. Such relationships are probably examples of parasitism or commensalism, because the host fish does not benefit in any way. However, some sharksucker species do enjoy a more mutually beneficial relationship with their hosts, cleaning their skin and gills and picking off parasitic copepods.

Echeneis naucrates

⬌	Exceeds 3 ft 3 in (1 m)
🌐	Tropical, subtropical, and temperate waters worldwide
📖	Streamlined fish with distinctive suction plate on its head and neck.

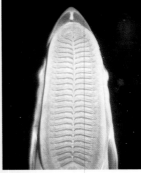

SUCTION DISK
Unlike other fishes, which use their mouths for attachment, the dorsal fin of the live sharksucker has evolved to become a serrated cartilaginous suction plate on the top of the head and neck. Disk muscles raise and lower the serrations to create suction.

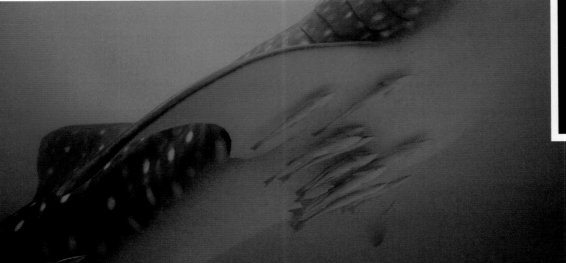

HOLDING ON
A large host, such as this whale shark, is able to support a large number of sharksuckers, each imposing a drag cost upon their host, slowing it down. The energetic leaps and splashes of the spinner dolphin are thought to be a behavior developed in part to dislodge sharksuckers.

Chemical trails
Candiru

This tiny parasitic catfish is hemophagic, feeding on the blood of other fishes. Candirus live in burrows on sandy riverbeds, where they wait for potential prey to come along. When hungry, they follow chemical cues in water expelled from the gills of their victims and insert themselves under their gill plates. Fierce spines behind the head puncture the surface of the gill and enable the parasite to attach to its host. The spines release blood, which the candiru sucks up; once it has gorged itself, it falls away.

HUMAN IMPACT

FEARED FISH

Candirus are infamous for their ability to parasitize humans by entering the urethra of unfortunate bathers. It has been suggested thst the candiru locates its victim by following a trail of urine in the water to the genitalia, but this has not been well documented. Once there, they have to eat their way through the mucosal lining of the body to feast on the blood of their victim. Removal of the fish is excruciatingly painful and difficult due to the opening of the umbrella of backward-pointing spines behind the fish's head. Drastic remedies, such as surgical removal of the fish or even penile amputation, have been reported.

Vandellia cirrhosa
- Exceeds 6 in (15 cm)
- Muddy and sandy beds of the rivers of the Amazon and Orinoco basins.
- Eel-shaped, translucent fish.

Cleaning stations
Bluestreak cleaner wrasse

When the external parasite load of a reef fish becomes unbearable, it will visit the "cleaning station" of the bluestreak cleaner wrasse. The cleaners perform a dance to advertise their services to their "clients," which often wait patiently, even lining up with other fishes. If they become impatient, they may adopt a pose that signals their desire to be cleaned to draw attention to themselves. The bluestreak cleaner wrasse picks over the bodies of its clients, nipping off parasites at the rate of about five per visit and consuming dead skin and mucus. In this role, cleaners are essential to the health of the reef and its fishes. Some cleaners may be tempted to cheat—taking a bite out of the larger fish—but they risk losing the client's business in the future.

Labroides dimidiatus
- Up to 5½ in (14 cm)
- Reefs of the Indo-Pacific, Red Sea, and East Africa.
- Slender fish with black stripe along its bluish yellow body and blue dorsal fin.

DANGEROUS GAME
Bluestreak cleaner wrasse have recently been shown to react to their predators, including this tiger grouper, more quickly and to spend longer cleaning them, the opposite of what might have been expected.

Stealing the catch
Galapagos penguin

As in the case of its close relatives, the Galapagos penguin is a carnivore, preferring to feed on small fishes, including the sardines, anchovies, and pilchards that abound in the cold waters around the Galapagos Islands. These penguins often feed alongside pelicans, which retain bigger prey in their throat pouches, allowing smaller fishes to escape—these are subsequently snapped up by the waiting penguins. Recently, however, penguins have been seen to abuse this harmonious relationship by stealing the larger fishes directly from pelicans' pouches. The Galapagos penguin also actively hunts its prey: propelled by stout, flipperlike wings, it pursues its victims through the water at great speed. Because the eyes of a penguin are situated above its bill, this bird usually attacks its prey from below, grabbing fishes and then holding them in its short, stout bill. Flocks of penguins often feed together, driving schools of confused fish toward one another and breaking up larger schools so as to more easily target their catch.

SMASH AND GRAB
Galapagos penguins nip greedily at the bulging pouch of a pelican, hoping to steal a fish rather than hunting for their own.

Spheniscus mendiculus
- 14 in (35 cm)
- Endemic to the Galapagos Islands.
- Small penguin with two black bands across its white breast.

Mugging for a meal

Grey heron

The grey heron is an opportunistic carnivore that eats whatever prey it comes across. Its cosmopolitan diet commonly includes fishes, amphibians, crustaceans, reptiles, insects, mammals, and small birds. It stalks its prey with deliberate strides or stands motionless in ambush and jabs with its strong, sharp bill and long, powerful neck. Small prey is swallowed immediately with a toss of the head, while larger items are clubbed or stabbed to death and swallowed whole, usually head first to smooth their passage. Often feeding in the company of others, herons are accomplished kleptoparasites: individuals and groups will attack and steal from other birds, usually other herons. Observations suggest that adult birds are more successful as both hunters and robbers than younger individuals.

Ardea cinerea

- 35–39 in (90–98 cm)
- Wetlands in Europe, Asia, and sub-Saharan Africa.
- Tall, gray bird with white belly and black crest.
- >> 452

ROBBING FROM THE FLOCK
Herons are ruthless flock mates, stealing from one another with a brutality that is as shocking as it is effective.

ATTACK!
Breeding skuas defend their nests vigorously and will attack all comers, including humans. They repeatedly dive at their target, pecking with their daggerlike bill.

DEFENDING THE NEST
Skuas that patrol breeding colonies will eat eggs and kill unattended chicks. By breeding in colonies, birds like this gentoo penguin (right) may be able to work together to fend off attacks by skuas.

In-flight piracy
Great skua

Skuas are carnivores and scavengers that feed on a wide range of foodstuffs, including invertebrates, fishes, birds, and carrion. Great skuas will catch their own prey if they have to, and have been known to kill and eat smaller seabirds, such as puffins and guillemots, but as skilled kleptoparasites they prefer to steal from other birds. These pirates of the sky patrol seabird colonies and harass birds returning to their nests with food. The skuas pull at the wings and tails of the other birds, causing them to stall in flight, and they peck at their heads and bodies. When the persecution becomes unbearable, the other birds drop their catch, which is snapped up by the skuas. Of course, the skuas will steal from one another too, and a prize may change hands several times before it is eaten.

Stercorarius skua

◀▶ Up to 24 in (60 cm)

⊙ Breeds in colonies in Iceland, Norway, Faroe Islands, and Scotland; winters throughout northeast Atlantic.

▢ Large brown gull-like bird with distinctive white wing panels.

A taste for blood
Yellow-billed oxpecker and African buffalo

Like a number of species of insectivorous birds, the yellow-billed oxpecker feeds in association with herds of grazing and browsing mammals, possibly because the herds disturb insects as they move and their dung attracts swarms of flies. But the oxpecker–herbivore relationship is an intimate one. Oxpeckers spend most of their day perching on a mammal host—for example, a buffalo, rhinoceros, giraffe, or elephant—and spend almost 70 percent of their time feeding there, either alone or in the company of flock mates. This relationship is often described as a mutualism, which means both parties benefit. The benefit to the bird is that it has a moving larder, and the host benefits because the bird cleans it. Oxpeckers feed on ticks and other irritating parasites that their host cannot scratch off, feeding particularly around the eyes, ears, and anus. Recently, however, it has been discovered that there is a more sinister side to this relationship. The birds do eat huge numbers of ticks, but it seems that their taste is for the blood that is inside the engorged tick rather than for the actual tick itself. Oxpeckers have been observed using their bills to scissor open their host's wounds and drink their blood. By keeping wounds open, the birds expose their hosts to the risk of infection and parasite infestation.

OPEN WOUND
Oxpeckers use a particular scissoring bill action to maintain the flow of blood from open wounds in the skin of their host.

13,000
The approximate number of ticks one oxpecker can consume in one day.

◉ HUMAN IMPACT
EXTINCTION

The yellow-billed oxpecker is described as common throughout its range by the IUCN (International Union for the Conservation of Nature). However, even though it is not considered at risk, its populations are declining. In the late 1800s, overhunting of wild herbivores, decimation of cattle by rinderpest, and an increase in pesticide use significantly reduced the availability of food for oxpeckers in South Africa and they became extinct in that country until recolonization occurred in recent times. This is a salutary lesson: even a common species can disappear quickly.

PEST CONTROL
An oxpecker can remove between 600 and 1,200 ticks from a host, in this case a buffalo, in a single day, concentrating on the areas around the eyes and ears that are difficult for the host to reach.

Tick picking

Española mockingbird

The four species of mockingbirds endemic to the Galapagos Islands are omnivores, and it has been said that they will eat almost anything, a fact to which tourists visiting the islands will testify. The española mockingbird has the most varied diet of all, using its long beak to pierce birds' eggs and eating insects, carrion, plant material, and the feces of other species. They have even been seen picking scraps and drops of saliva from between the teeth of seals. Española mockingbirds have a taste for blood; they feast on seal placenta and eat blood-congealed sand. They will also peck at other animals' wounds, keeping them open and vulnerable to infection. Their attentions are tolerated by marine and land iguanas, with which they have a mutualistic relationship, because they provide a valuable cleaning service, removing ticks and dead skin. To encourage cleaning, the iguanas raise themselves up to allow the birds to access ticks on their difficult-to-reach underparts.

Mimus macdonaldi

⬌	Up to 12 in (30 cm)
⬤	Endemic to Española, Galapagos Islands.
📖	Distinctive long tail and legs and long, downward-curving beak.

WORKING PARTNERSHIP
Española mockingbirds and marine iguanas enjoy a mutually advantageous relationship. The reptile raises its tail to allow the bird access to ticks in the region of its cloaca.

Following the leaders

Cape gannet and dolphins

Cape gannets feed primarily in flocks on anchovies and sardines, which they catch with spectacular plunge-dives, lunging from mid-air to seize individual fishes with their daggerlike beaks. They are strong fliers and will travel great distances to find schools of fish, often in the company of dolphins. The dolphins are the leaders in this partnership. They guide the gannets to their prey and then force the fishes to the surface in dense "bait-balls" several yards in diameter. As both dolphins and birds plunge repeatedly into the ball to take their fill, air bubbles produced by the plunging birds probably help concentrate the fishes within the killing zone, making it easier to catch them.

THE RACE IS ON
Cape gannets follow a pod of long-beaked common dolphins as they pursue a school of sardines off the coast of South Africa. Both species follow the annual migration of the sardines.

Young gannets have just 10 days in which to learn to feed; they leave their nests with a 10-day reserve of fat.

FEEDING FRENZY
Cape gannets leave trails of bubbles as they plunge-dive to feast on a sardine bait-ball that has been formed by a pod of long-beaked common dolphins.

Exploiting the pack

Common raven and gray wolf

Ravens depend on carrion as a food source; indeed, they have even learned to fly toward gunshots in order to scavenge the carrion left by a hunter. However, their main source of carrion is the prey of wolves. Ravens follow wolf packs and scavenge at their kills. Such is the competition between them that the size of wolf packs may even have evolved in response to it: a pair of wolves will lose on average 37 percent of a kill to the ravens attracted to it, but a pack of six will lose just 17 percent because they are better able to chase the ravens away. The relationship between ravens and wolves is not entirely one-sided, however. Ravens often find carrion that has been killed by animals other than wolves—if this is the carcass of a large animal, such as a deer or moose, their beaks cannot tear into it and so the ravens yell to attract other ravens for assistance. When this occurs, wolves in the vicinity also hear the calls, follow the sight of gathering birds, and so are led to the carcass. The wolves are able to open the body with their sharp teeth, and so by working with the ravens they are able to share the spoils.

Ravens hide surpluses of food and are capable of finding these stores after considerable lapses in time.

COMPETITION FOR THE KILL
As many as 50 ravens may be attracted to a kill. This gray wolf in Minnesota is unlikely to be able to chase the birds away from its deer kill without some help.

Blood letting

Common vampire bat

Vampire bats locate their prey (usually horses and cattle) by listening for the sounds of their breathing. The wounds that a bat inflicts on its prey when biting into its flesh will cause the victim to bleed freely for more than the 20 minutes that it takes the bat to drink its fill. In that time, a bat may consume 50 percent of its body mass. Flying animals are at risk if they gain too much weight, but these bats are able to process their meal quickly, successfully avoiding weight gain by converting nutrient-poor blood plasma to a stream of dilute urine within minutes of starting a meal.

ANATOMY
STOPPING CLOTTING

The saliva of a vampire bat contains two important classes of chemical compounds that assist it in feeding. The first are anesthetics, numbing the pain receptors of their prey so that they do not feel the bite. The second are anti-coagulants that maintain the flow of blood from a wound by preventing blood clotting. One of the anticoagulants, draculin, has shown early promise in human medicine.

LAPPING UP
Although popular culture would have us believe otherwise, vampires do not suck blood from the neck of their victims. Instead, they use their cheek teeth to shear hair away before using razor-sharp incisors to cut into the skin. They then lick the flowing blood from the wound with a rapid flicking of their tongue.

Desmodus rotundus

- Up to 3½ in (9 cm)
- Forest and farmland in Mexico, Central, and South America.
- Small, flat-nosed brown bat with large incisors.

Feeding the troop

Banded mongoose and warthog

Parasites such as ticks are a real problem for mammals that move through the densely vegetated savanna and forests of Africa. Tick levels and transmission rates are high generally and may be higher still among species such as the warthog that make use of burrows. To rid themselves of parasites, warthogs roll in mud or on baked earth, but they can dislodge only some of the parasites in this way and their stocky bodies make it difficult to reach all of the affected parts of their skin. However, the banded mongoose can be very useful in removing the warthogs' remaining ticks. Mongooses are largely insectivorous, but they will consume a wide range of foods, including ticks. Warthogs may allow troops of mongooses to pick the ticks from their bodies, providing the whole troop with a meal, but it can be risky for the mongooses, because warthogs have been known to kill and eat their pups in the process.

A GOOD SCRATCH
This large group of banded mongooses will quickly pick the blood-filled ticks from the skin of this warthog, reaching all of the places it cannot reach itself.

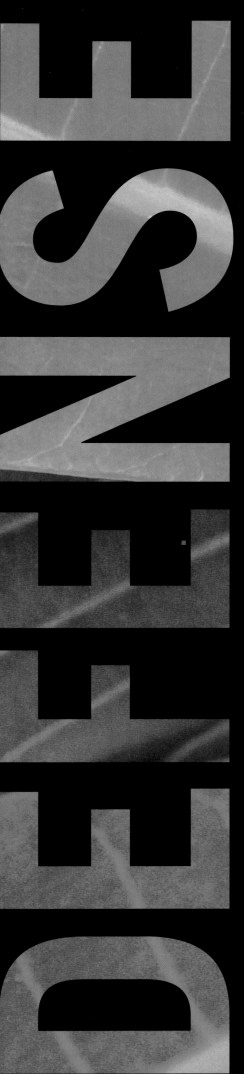

DEFENSE

DEFENSIVE ARMOR
Slow-moving animals often rely on physical
defenses for protection when out in the open.
Thorns, spines, and bristles are a common defense
in reptiles, such as this thorny devil, echinoderms,
and insects, which all have naturally hard skins.

DEFENSE

Animals need to defend themselves from attack by predators. Humans rarely have to worry about this, but for the majority of animals, especially those lower down in the food chain, defense is an everyday necessity. All animals must eat, and to do so often means coming out into the open to forage or hunt. The pressure to survive has resulted in a wide array of defense mechanisms, involving both behavior and body design.

Evading predators

The easiest method of defense is to avoid contact with predators. Hiding in a nest, burrow, or dense vegetation is a good way to achieve this. Small, nocturnal mammals emerge under cover of darkness, when predators that hunt by sight are at a disadvantage. Using smell, they can easily forage for food. In the ocean, sediment plains are dotted with numerous burrows where fishes, crabs, and shrimps live in safety, rarely leaving their shelters. Running, swimming, or flying away is another device for evading attack. Many animals living out in the open can outmaneuver their predators if they see them soon enough. Poisonous animals can stay put, their color often warning predators not to touch them.

HIDING
Many ground-nesting seabirds raise their young in deep burrows, where they are safe from aerial predators such as gulls.

The sheer size of the blue whale ensures that it deters most predators, except for humans—it can reach lengths of 90 ft (30 m).

Confusing predators

If a predator does not recognize an animal as prey, it will ignore it. The ability to look and behave like something else, either animate or inanimate, helps some animals survive. A huge range of techniques have evolved throughout the animal kingdom, all aimed at preventing predators from spying their prey. If the prey is spotted, then confusion becomes the aim. Camouflage enables animals to merge into the background, so that they are difficult for a predator to spot. The physical shape and color imposed on an animal by its camouflage is only part of the story. If an animal does not behave in the

PLAYING DEAD
Animals as varied as weevils (shown here) and opossums use the technique of pretending to be dead. In this way, they fool their enemies into leaving them alone.

CAMOUFLAGE
Disguised against the seabed, flatfishes move in short bursts and then remain still after partly covering themselves with sand.

right way, its disguise will be ineffective. Keeping still is often important. The animal must rest in a place where it matches its surroundings, or be able to change its camouflage to suit. Some parasites exploit this by altering the behavior of their host, so that it moves to a conspicuous position where it will be eaten by the animal that forms the next host for the parasite. Other animals confuse predators by pretending to be larger than they really are, or by imitating something dangerous or unpleasant. Some insects and amphibians use various strategies at different stages of their life cycle. A caterpillar may resemble a bird dropping, whereas the butterfly adult has false eyes on its wings.

false
eye-spot

SHOCK TACTIC
False eye-spots are part of the camouflage of butterflies, butterflyfishes, and even frogs. In order to startle or confuse a predator, the animal must behave in a certain way, normally by suddenly revealing the eye-spots.

Stand and fight

Animals with good physical defenses in the form of weapons can fight their enemies. Predators cannot afford to use too much energy or be injured when capturing their prey and will often give up on a difficult target. Small animals with no obvious weapons may still be successful in deflecting a predator away from their nests or young. Birds are especially good at this, because they can fly up and escape if the predator gets too close. Similarly, small fishes such as clownfish will try to drive larger fishes—and even divers—away from their home, as long as they have somewhere safe to take refuge if necessary.

STANDING FIRM
The ability to move quickly out of harm's way allows small animals to stand up to larger ones in order to defend their nest site or territory. This water dikkop can move much faster than a crocodile.

Weapons and threats

Predators have evolved a fearsome array of teeth, claws, and venom to help them catch and eat their prey, and for their own defense. In response, prey animals have evolved defense weapons, physical and chemical armor, and complex behavioral strategies for evading their enemies. Many animals try to avoid an attack in the first place by warning off would-be predators.

Weapons

Carnivorous and scavenging animals are naturally equipped with weapons such as teeth and claws that can also be used for defense. Peaceful herbivores need extra protection, and many have armored heads equipped with horns, antlers, or spikes. In mammals, these are usually specialized teeth, such as the tusks of elephants, or are made from the horny material that comprises nails and hooves. Dolphins simply use their tough snout as a battering ram to defend themselves against sharks. In contrast, hoofed mammals often lash out with their hind legs, and tropical surgeonfishes protect themselves with knifelike spines on either side of the tail. Some fishes even employ electric weapons to stun and deter their predators.

⦿ TYPES OF WEAPON

HOOVES AND LIMBS
Hard hooves and feet, designed for running fast, also make excellent blunt weapons with which to kick a predator, or even a rival in the case of zebras. Ostriches have powerful leg muscles and feet that can dismember a lion. Mantis shrimps use their claws to punch with a force that can break bones and are so fast that the victim does not have time to react.

CLAWS
Strong claws are used to dig burrows or root out food, but are just as effective when used to protect young, such as bear cubs, against predators. Large predators, such as tigers, use their claws primarily to bring down prey, but may need to defend their territories and young from rivals of their own species. When not in use, all cats can sheath their claws.

PROJECTILES
Other than humans, only a few primates are known to pick up and throw objects at their enemies. However, many animals, such as the fireworm (left), have irritant hairs or loose spines that break off in the mouths or limbs of predators that try to attack them. These can then be regrown. Some tarantulas can spray irritant hairs like a rain of miniature arrows.

VENOMOUS SPINES
Many marine animals live sedentary lives on the seabed and are protected by venomous spines. These are generally used for defense and are only brought into play if the animal is attacked or trodden on. Venomous fishes such as weeverfishes (left) and stonefishes have sharp spines in their dorsal and pectoral fins that act like hypodermic needles.

TEETH AND FANGS
While most animals capable of biting will do so in self-defense, some have modified teeth or jaws that make formidable weapons. Some snakes use hollow fangs to inject venom, and blue-ringed octopuses do the same using a beaklike structure in the mouth. Working together, even small ants can drive a predator away from their nest by repeatedly biting it.

Armor

Armor is widely used by slow-moving animals, such as tortoises, that are unable to escape from fast predators. In the oceans, many animals are completely immobile and physical protection is essential for their survival. Reptiles and bony fishes already have protective scales, and many species from these groups have developed their scales into body armor. However, this is often at the expense of mobility—boxfishes, for example, are well protected but are clumsy swimmers. Crustaceans and mollusks have external shells, which can be reinforced to make protective boxes. The oceans provide them with minerals to build up their shells, but this is less easy in mineral-deficient freshwater.

EXTERNAL SKELETON
Many crustaceans are well protected by their hard external armor, but become vulnerable whenever they shed their shell to allow for growth. The animal must hide during these periods.

limpet shell

MOBILE HOMES
Limpets and other marine snails can rapidly retreat inside their shells, clamping down or shutting the door when danger threatens.

protective carapace

PROTECTIVE BOX
A heavy suit of armor is an effective defense, but severely limits movement. This tortoise would be helpless against fire or flood.

Survival strategies

Animals with no armor or weapons need either an effective means of escape or a way of intimidating and deterring their predators. Poison, stings, or bristles are good defenses, and have been adopted by many otherwise defenseless amphibians and insects. This only works for individual animals if their predators learn to avoid eating them. Bright warning colors—usually yellow, red, or orange against a contrasting dark background—can be seen easily by vertebrates with color vision, and are used by animals as diverse as shield bugs, poison frogs, and sea snakes. Unusual behavior is also an effective survival strategy. Pretending to be dead, for example, will put off predators that are used to hunting live prey.

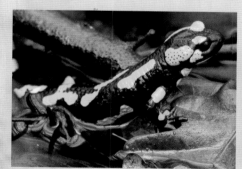

Amphibians that are toxic or distasteful often exhibit striking colorations. Predators soon learn to avoid these warning signs.

Feigning death is a tactic used by the Virginia opossum when it is threatened by a predator.

With nowhere else to hide, open-water fishes often leap above the surface to escape aquatic predators.

Against all odds, small animals will sometimes stand up to larger ones, especially when protecting their young.

DEFENSIVE WEAPON
Although potentially deadly, rhinoceroses, such as this black rhinoceros, only use their horns to protect themselves and their young from predators, and their territories from rivals. Many herbivores live and graze in the open, and so need to be able to defend themselves, or run fast and escape their predators.

Hiding away
Tubastrea coral

During the day the long, orange polyps of this cup coral retract inside their hard skeletons so that they are safe from the multitude of day-active fishes, many of which would eat coral polyps given the chance. After dark, the polyps' tentacles stretch out to feed on plankton.

Tubastrea faulkneri

- ⊞ Colony reaches about 5 in (13 cm) across
- ◐ Coral reefs off Australia and in Indo-Pacific.
- ⬚ Hard coral that forms low, tufted colony of separate cylindrical corallites.

Swift retreat
Christmas tree worm

The combination of lightning-fast reactions and a stonelike outer case enable this marine worm to survive attack by predators. Only its twin spirals of feeding tentacles, resembling miniature Christmas trees, are visible to the outside world. The rest of the worm is hidden inside a tough tube made of calcium carbonate, which the animal secretes around its body. For extra protection, it embeds itself in the head of a large coral. The Christmas tree worm is extremely sensitive to water vibrations and shadows, and if approached it withdraws almost instantaneously into its tube. When the danger has passed, the worm slowly extends its tentacles once more and resumes feeding. The color of the tentacles is variable: a single coral head may be peppered with yellow, blue, purple, red, orange, and brown individuals. Related fan worms and feather duster worms also build their parchment tubes in coral and rock crevices for protection.

Spirobranchus giganteus

- ⊞ About ¾ in (2 cm) (visible part)
- ◐ Inside corals in shallow tropical waters worldwide.
- ⬚ Colorful tube worm with twin whorls of tentacles on the head; secretes calcium carbonate tube around body.

OPEN TUBE
With its tentacles extended, the worm can collect plankton and organic matter from the water. The tentacles are also used to extract oxygen from the water.

CLOSED TUBE
When the worm retreats into its tube, the entrance is neatly plugged by its operculum (a lidlike structure). This one is not quite closed.

Limb regeneration
Starfish

If a starfish loses one or more arms to a predator, the missing appendages simply grow back. Most species of starfish have this amazing ability. A few starfish go a stage further—if their body is torn apart, a single arm can regenerate the entire central disk as well as the other arms. Usually the arm needs to include part of the disk to do this. During the initial stage of this process, the starfish is called a "comet form."

Fromia species

- ⊞ About 3¼–4 in (8–10 cm) in diameter
- ◐ Coral reefs in Indo-Pacific.
- ⬚ Relatively small, five-armed starfish; usually red or orange coloration, with paler tubercles on arms.

— original arm

COMET FORM
This regenerating starfish has grown five new arms instead of four. They will eventually grow to the same size as the surviving arm.

Sticky tentacles
Leopard sea cucumber

A predator grasping this apparently succulent animal is in for a surprise. Sea cucumbers are sluggish relatives of sea urchins. They lack urchins' sharp spines but are far from defenseless. If threatened, a sea cucumber ejects a mass of sticky tentacles called Cuvierian tubules out of its anus. Once in the water the tubules, part of the respiratory apparatus, lengthen, writhe around, and deter the attacker—or even entangle it completely.

Bohadschia argus

- ⊞ Up to 12 in (30 cm)
- ◐ Shallow water reefs and rubble areas in Indo-Pacific.
- ⬚ Fat sea cucumber with distinctive yellow "eye-spots."

REAR ASSAULT
These ejected tubules will eventually break down and disintegrate. The cucumber grows new ones internally and repairs its ruptured rectum.

anus

Cuvierian tubule

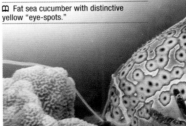

Rapid escape
Queen scallop

Queen scallops use a form of jet propulsion to escape their enemies. These bivalve mollusks spend much of their lives resting half-buried on the sea-bed, opening their shells to filter feed, so are vulnerable to attack by starfish. However, they can make a rapid exit by jetting off forward in a series of erratic jerks. When disturbed, a scallop uses its strong adductor muscle to open and shut its shell rapidly, expelling a stream of water with

The jet-propelled escape of a scallop is less effective in warmer waters.

great force. The scallop can detect movement and light using hundreds of simple eyes around the edge of its mantle (outer layer of skin), but sometimes does not respond until the starfish touches it.

Aequipecten opercularis

- ⊞ Up to 3½ in (9 cm)
- ◐ On sediment in northeast Atlantic, from Norway south to Canary Isles, and Mediterranean.
- ⬚ Bivalve mollusk with its two convex shell valves decorated by thick, radiating ridges.

SPEEDING TO SAFETY
At the last moment this scallop has swum up and away from a spiny starfish. Later it falls back down to the sea-bed.

Spiny deterrent

Venus comb murex

A starfish or any other predator that wanted to eat a Venus comb murex would have great difficulty getting anywhere near the shell entrance. Similarly, even fishes with strong jaws would have trouble crushing the shell of this marine snail, and after its death the ferociously spiny shell remains a hazard to unwary bare-footed bathers. However, some scientists speculate that the real function of the spines is not defense but to support the animal when it is moving over soft sediment.

SPIKY PROCESSION
The muscular foot and head tentacles of this murex are visible through its shell spines as it creeps forward (from left to right).

Murex pecten
- Up to 5 in (13 cm)
- Muddy sea-beds in Indo-Pacific.
- Marine snail with very long, straight siphonal canal and long shell spines.

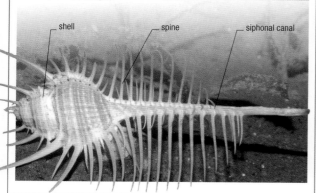

shell · spine · siphonal canal

Flashing blue

Blue-ringed octopus

The blue rings on this small octopus warn of its deadly nature. When the octopus is agitated, these markings pulse a vivid and iridescent blue, but when it is resting the blue is more subdued. The animal's saliva contains deadly venom to subdue or kill its prey, but is equally effective against potential predators—those that survive soon learn to leave the octopus alone. There are three or four similar species in the same genus, all called blue-ringed octopus, and all are venomous.

15 The number of minutes it takes a blue-ringed octopus bite to kill an adult human.

Hapalochlaena species
- 4–9½ in (10–24 cm)
- Shallow reefs, rocky areas, and coasts in tropical west Pacific and Indian Ocean.
- Small octopus with distinctive blue rings on body and tentacles.

Cloud of ink

Day octopus

The day octopus is most unusual among octopuses in that, as its name suggests, it is active during the day. When it comes out of its hiding places to hunt, it usually sidles along with precise movements, using its arms. If frightened, it uses a very different method. An individual attacked by a predator discharges a jet of water and shoots off backward with its arms trailing. At the same time, it releases a cloud of dark ink and changes color. The predator is either distracted by the ink cloud or enveloped in it, and the octopus can swim away behind it. Squid have a similar escape response but also use jet propulsion for normal swimming. In both

SIMILAR SPECIES
The giant Pacific octopus, shown here moving rapidly away from the camera, has few predators but may still release a cloud of ink if threatened.

Octopus cyanea
- Body 6½ in (16 cm); arms about 31 in (80 cm)
- Shallow reefs in Indo-Pacific, from eastern Africa to Hawaiian Islands.
- Large, long-armed octopus; usually brown, but able to produce a wide variety of color changes and skin texture changes for camouflage.

octopuses and squid, water is sucked into the mantle cavity and squirted out of a tubelike funnel when the mantle contracts. This is normally a rather gentle movement linked with respiration.

Octopus ink, made in a special sac and released into the funnel, is a concentrated

form of melanin, the pigment that colors and protects human skin. Other chemicals in the ink temporarily dull a predator's sense of smell and irritate its eyes. Some deep-sea squid release a burst of luminous material to dazzle their predators in the dark ocean depths.

1,000 The number of times one day octopus was seen to change its skin patterns during a seven-hour period.

VANISHING ACT
This day octopus is seen leaving a trail of black ink as it jets away over a shallow reef in Hawaii. Day octopuses often excavate their own lairs in reefs or the rubble around them.

Venom injection

European hornet

Like other wasps, the European hornet is protected by a powerful sting. It is the largest European social wasp, with a sting big enough to deter predatory lizards and birds. The sting is also used as a weapon to kill other insects for food. For humans, a single sting is usually painful but not harmful. However, a hornet killed near its nest releases alarm pheromones to summon other hornets, which can result in multiple stings. The sting of the Asian giant hornet can be lethal to humans.

Vespa crabro

◧ ¾–1½ in (2–3.5 cm)

⊙ Woodland in Europe and temperate Asia, from Britain east to Japan; introduced to North America.

▭ Large social wasp with dark thorax and yellow and black abdomen.

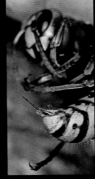

SMOOTH STING
This hornet is being held so that its sting is visible. The sting has no barbs, so it can be withdrawn and used again many times.

Hair spray

Tarantula spiders

Although these large spiders deliver a venomous bite, it is used to subdue prey and seldom to defend themselves. The primary defense for many tarantulas is the ability to release a spray of irritant hairs known as urticating hairs. These grow on the spider's abdomen, which is known as the opisthosoma. The hairs come off easily and a spider releases them by rubbing its legs over the opisthosoma. The hairs have barbs and can be mildly to intensely irritating, depending on where

Family Theraphosidae

◧ Legspan up to 11 in (28 cm)

⊙ In trees and ground burrows worldwide, especially in subtropical and tropical regions.

▭ Very large, hairy spiders. Coloration ranges from brown to black, with pink, red, brown, or black markings.

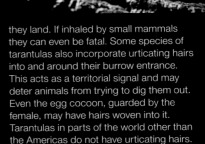

they land. If inhaled by small mammals they can even be fatal. Some species of tarantulas also incorporate urticating hairs into and around their burrow entrance. This acts as a territorial signal and may deter animals from trying to dig them out. Even the egg cocoon, guarded by the female, may have hairs woven into it. Tarantulas in parts of the world other than the Americas do not have urticating hairs.

DEFENSIVE SPRAY
A large bird-eating spider in the genus *Pamphobeteus* uses its legs to flick a hail of tiny barbed hairs at an attacker. The irritant hairs are extremely unpleasant.

Fighting stance

Sydney funnel-web spider

This spider is one of the most dangerous in the world. When disturbed, it rears up to intimidate its tormentor and glistening drops of venom appear on its large fangs. If molested, it will bite repeatedly and can slice through a fingernail. Holding on tightly to its enemy, the spider injects a venom containing atraxotoxin, a poison that attacks the nervous system. Primates (including humans) are very sensitive to the venom, which can kill in just 15 minutes. Strangely, common domestic pets such as cats and rabbits are barely affected. Most incidents of humans being bitten occur in summer and fall, when the male spiders leave their burrows and wander in search of females to mate with.

Atrax robustus

◧ Body ¾ in (2–4 cm); legspan 2¼–2¾ in (6–7 cm)

⊙ In silk-lined, funnel-shaped burrows in damp forests and yards in Australia, mainly near Sydney.

▭ Large, glossy black spider with massive fangs and hairy legs and abdomen.

POISED TO STRIKE
This funnel-web spider is standing its ground, with its palps and front legs raised and its fangs held up and forward, ready to strike. If provoked further, the spider will bite.

Sting in the tail

Fat-tailed scorpion

A scorpion's sting is effectively its second line of defense, the first being to run away and hide. If cornered, a fat-tailed scorpion will raise its tail up into the classic curved posture ready to strike with its pointed sting. This species and others in its genus are among the most venomous, injecting a neurotoxin that is sometimes fatal in humans. It catches its prey with its strong claws, and may also use the sting to subdue larger prey.

Androctonus crassicauda

◧ Up to 3¼ in (8 cm)

⊙ Under stones and debris and in walls in arid areas of Turkey and Middle East.

▭ Olive-brown to black body with very wide, thick tail.

metasoma (tail)

sting

chela (claw)

Keeping watch

Snapping shrimps and shrimp gobies

The relationship between snapping shrimps and shrimp gobies provides a rare example of cooperative defense. These species must work together to survive. The shrimp digs a burrow as a shelter, working like a tiny bulldozer. It has poor eyesight and, engrossed in its work, relies on the shrimp goby to keep watch. The shrimp communicates with the goby using its long tentacles, and can tell from the fish's tail movements when danger threatens.

PROTECTIVE PARTNERSHIP
Pictured here are the shrimp *Alpheus randalli* and the shrimp goby *Amblyeleotris yanoi*, in Indonesia.

Mutual defense

Leach's hermit crab

Hermit crabs live in empty mollusk shells, which they use to protect their soft abdomen. Leach's hermit crab gains extra protection by living in association with the cloak anemone, *Adamsia carciniopados*. The anemone wraps its wide base around the crab's shell and body, hanging its own body and tentacles downward. If a predator attacks, the anemone discharges

AT EASE
The anemone's red-spotted base envelops the hermit crab's body and its shell home. The anemone grows at the same rate as the crab, so the pair never need to part.

Pagarus prideauxi

◧ About 2¾ in (7 cm)

⊙ Shallow sediment in northeast Atlantic, from Norway to Mediterranean and Cape Verde Islands.

▭ Small, crablike crustacean with a soft abdomen, pair of claws, and walking legs.

stinging threads called acontia. In return for this protective role, the anemone can eat the remains of the crab's meals. The anemone grows as the hermit crab does, so the crab never has to perform the risky maneuver of finding a larger shell home.

UNDER ATTACK
The anemone has fired its stinging threads in defense. Its soft body is tucked safely under the hermit crab's legs.

African foam grasshopper

This small African grasshopper defends itself against predators by secreting foul-tasting yellow foam. The secretion, derived from the insect's blood, is turned to foam by mixing it with air taken in through the spiracles (breathing holes) on the thorax. The foam's unpleasant active ingredient comes from plants eaten by the grasshopper. Although this grasshopper is not brightly colored, the yellow color of the foam probably acts as a warning that this species is not good to eat. It belongs to a family called gaudy grasshoppers, because many are very brightly colored.

African bombardier beetle

When under attack, this beetle gains time by spraying a potent cocktail of boiling chemicals from its rear end. Ants, one of the beetle's chief enemies, are small and mobile and can bite it almost anywhere. However, the beetle can aim its potentially lethal spray like the nozzle of an aerosol can. The chemicals react and heat up as they are mixed, just before spraying, and released oxygen acts as a propellant. The beetle gets drenched in the process, but scientists have not yet established how it is able to survive.

AIMING THE SPRAY
The beetle aims its spray with great accuracy, directing it with reflectors that move. It can hit targets all around its body.

CHEMICAL REACTION

This scanning electron micrograph shows the slit through which the beetle sprays its deterrent. The spray is made from two sets of chemicals stored in separate glands. Hydroquinones and hydrogen peroxide from one gland are mixed with enzymes from the other. The enzymes release oxygen from the hydrogen peroxide and this in turn oxidizes the hydroquinones, making them active.

Stenaptinus insignis
◄► ⅜–¾ in (1–2 cm)
⊙ On the ground in tropical areas of Africa.
📖 Small ground beetle with shiny, ridged, yellow and black wing covers. Shieldlike deflector near tip of abdomen used to control direction of spray.

Sinking escape
Leopard catshark

When danger threatens, leopard catsharks have an unusual response—they bury their heads in their fins. If a catshark feels threatened when swimming in the open, it curls around, covers its eyes and snout with its tail, and sinks rapidly down to the seabed. This behavior not only protects the catshark's vulnerable head but is also confusing to a predator. With its eyes hidden and its shape changed, it no longer looks like a fish and is effectively pretending to be dead. Unlike many sharks, catsharks are very flexible and when lying on the seabed will readily whip around and bite if grabbed by the tail. Their escape strategy may have evolved from this ability. Catsharks are slow swimmers, and vulnerable to faster-swimming predators such as larger sharks and seals. The patterning on their backs helps camouflage them when they are resting but is of less help when hunting.

Poroderma pantherinum
◄► Up to 33 in (85 cm)
⊙ Rocky reefs and kelp forests on and close to seabed off coast of South Africa.
📖 Small catshark with long nasal barbels and variable markings on its back.

South Africa's shallow rocky reefs are the only place in the world where leopard catsharks can be found.

PLUNGING TO SAFETY
Curled up into a ball, this catshark nearly dropped straight down onto the photographer below. The species is sometimes called the shy shark because of this behavior. Its leopardlike spots are not visible from the underside.

Airborne escape

Atlantic flying fish

In warmer parts of the Atlantic Ocean, sailors are often treated to the sight of flying fishes skimming the waves in front of their boat. Vibrations from boats and ships scare the fish into thinking that they are being chased by a large predator such as a dolphin or tuna, and this triggers their defensive maneuver. With powerful beats of its tail, a flying fish launches itself into the air, spreads its large pectoral fins wide, and glides for many yards before dropping back into the sea. It will sometimes perform a series of leaps and glides to be sure that the predator is left confused as to where its prey has gone.

During its "flight," the fish maintains momentum by vibrating the long lower half of its tail from side to side in the water below, leaving ripples on the surface.

Cheilopogon melanurus

- 🔼 Up to 12½ in (32 cm)
- ⬤ Warm coastal surface waters in Atlantic Ocean.
- 📖 Long, silvery fish with very long, winglike pectoral fins.

SIMILAR SPECIES
The four-winged flying fish (right) uses both its pectoral and pelvic fins in flight. This is a juvenile and has not yet developed the adult blue color. The so-called flying gurnard (above) cannot fly but instead may use its greatly enlarged, colorful pectoral fins to startle predators when lying on the seabed.

37mph The estimated gliding speed achieved by an Atlantic flying fish.

ADAPTATIONS FOR FLIGHT
The pectoral fins of the Atlantic flying fish are almost as long as its body, and expand and stiffen while in the air. The fish's powerful tail fin may sweep from side to side in the water up to 50 times a second.

Warning spines

Common lionfish

In contrast to the reef stonefish (see p.308), to which it is closely related, the common lionfish is protected not by camouflage but by vivid warning colors. Its fins and body are boldy striped in contrasting shades of red and white to indicate that it is best left alone. Its pectoral and dorsal fins are highly modified, consisting of long, venomous spines. These can inflict a very painful sting, though this is generally not life threatening to humans. Emerging at dusk, the lionfish will often stand its ground in the face of large predators and divers alike. The fish swims slowly, confident of its spiny protection. Its pectoral fins have the secondary function of helping corral fish against the reef to be snapped up.

MOBILE SPINES
The poisonous fin spines of the common lionfish are individually mobile and so can be directed at a predator to avert the attack.

Pterois volitans

- 🔼 Up to 15 in (38 cm)
- ⬤ Tropical waters of eastern Indian Ocean and western Pacific.
- 📖 Large, bony head, ornate head tentacles, and long individual fin spines.

Rapid inflation

Black-spotted porcupinefish

When a black-spotted porcupinefish is attacked, it sucks water into its expandable stomach, erects its spines, and turns itself into a prickly ball several times its original size. Few predators will tackle it in this state. As soon as the danger has passed, the water is regurgitated and the fish deflates back down to its normal size and shape. Although this is a very effective defense, these fishes prefer to hide during the day and are often found in holes and under rocky overhangs. Inflation uses up energy and it is better to avoid confrontation. When caught, they will often inflate at the surface, gulping in air instead of water. There are about 20 species of porcupinefishes, variously called porcupinefishes, balloonfishes, and burrfishes, which share the same defense mechanisms. The closely related pufferfishes have a further deterrent—a lethal poison in their internal organs, called tetrodotoxin. Porcupinefish eggs float in the plankton, and the young fish develop their spines 10 days after hatching. When small, they fall prey to many pelagic fish.

The porcupinefish's stomach expands to nearly 100 times its original size when it is threatened.

Diodon hystrix
- Up to 35 in (90 cm)
- Coral reefs in tropical and subtropical Atlantic, Pacific, and Indian oceans.
- Chunky fish with flexible, prickly skin, teeth fused into a beak, and large eyes.

BEFORE AND AFTER EXPANSION
When a possible threat presents itself, a black-spotted porcupinefish will hover quietly with its spines laid flat (below). It will only inflate (right) as a last resort. With its stomach full of water and all its spines erect, the fish now resembles a spiky soccer ball and can hardly move.

spines lie flat

long, sharp spines erect

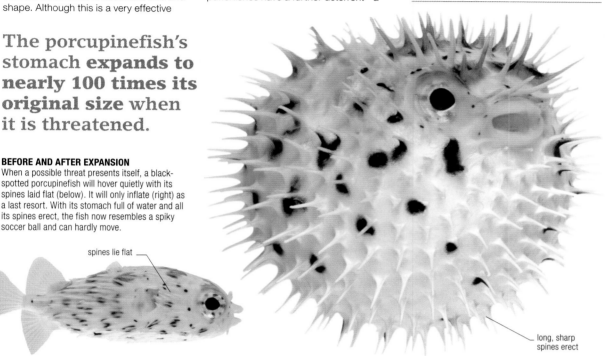

EXPANDING STOMACH

The stomach of porcupinefishes has evolved into a water reservoir, and is no longer used for digestion. Instead, food is absorbed in the intestine. The lining of the porcupinefish stomach is highly folded, but as the fish sucks in water the folds stretch out like the pleats in a skirt to accommodate its huge load. The rest of the fish's body organs are pushed upward against the vertebral column, which itself curves dramatically into a bow shape. The two-layered skin has a thin, elastic outer layer and a thicker, pleated inner layer. When the pleats are stretched out, the skin is stiff enough to hold the spines rigid, and the porcupinefish takes on its unpalatable bristling appearance.

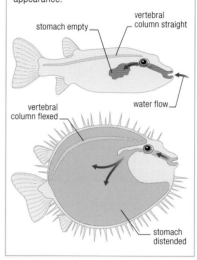

stomach empty / vertebral column straight / water flow / vertebral column flexed / stomach distended

Mucus tent

Bleeker's parrotfish

Many coral reef fish, including Bleeker's parrotfish, sleep tucked away in coral and rock crevices to avoid nocturnal predators. But this species greatly improves its chances of escaping detection by making itself a sleeping bag of slime. At night the parrotfish finds a suitable crevice and envelops itself in a cocoon of mucus. It can take half an hour to secrete the mucus from special glands in its opercular cavity, the protective chamber containing the gills. On contact with the water, the mucus swells and becomes gelatinous. Many night predators hunt by smell, and the cocoon stops them from detecting the parrotfish scent. Crustaceans hunting by touch are also deterred. Some other species of parrotfish dive under sand at night, but risk being unearthed by dolphins using echolocation to detect prey.

SLIMY COVERING
Safe in its mucus cocoon at night, this Bleeker's parrotfish seems to be unaware of the gray-faced moray eel next to it, although the one seen here is too small to harm the parrotfish.

Chlorurus bleekeri
- Up to 20 in (50 cm)
- Coral reefs in eastern Indian Ocean and western Pacific.
- Colorful fish with tough, fused teeth like a bird's bill.

Protective partnership

False clown anemonefish

A false clown anemonefish will spend its entire life in or close to a giant stinging anemone, even sleeping on the central body section of its anemone at night. Few predators risk reaching into the anemone's tentacles to attack the anemonefish. Other fish of a similar size would be stung and devoured by the anemone, but the anemonefish is protected by an invisible cloak of slime. The anemone is unaware the fish is there. In return, the anemonefish keeps its home clean and drives away butterflyfish, which feed on anemone tentacles.

Amphiprion ocellaris
- 3½–4½ in (9–11 cm)
- In giant anemones in eastern Indian Ocean and western Pacific.
- Small orange fish with three white bars, the central one bulging forward.

SAFE QUARTERS
An anemonefish keeps watch from the safety of its tentacled home, ready to wriggle farther in if danger threatens.

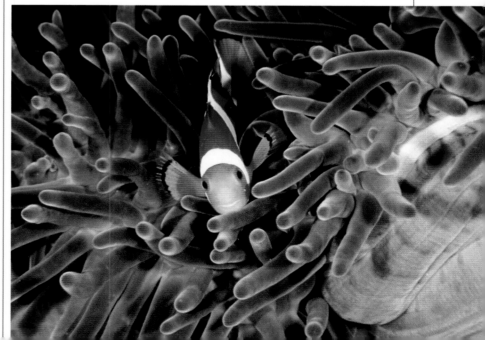

Warning marks
Fire salamander

The bold markings of this salamander are a warning that it is poisonous. Bulbous parotoid glands behind the eyes produce neurotoxins that cause hyperventilation and muscle spasm in vertebrates. The salamander can actively spray a predator from these glands to deter an attack. Toxins are also exuded onto its skin from rows of glands along its back.

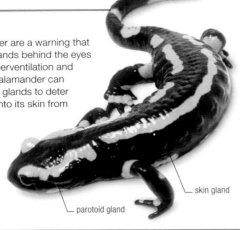

skin gland

parotoid gland

Salamandra salamandra
- Up to 10 in (25 cm)
- Woodland with ponds and streams in western, central, and southern Europe.
- Large, stout salamander with variable yellow markings.
- **》 372**

Hard to handle
Crocodile salamander

The crocodile salamander's defense is to be very difficult to handle. Except during the breeding season, it is secretive and spends most of its time hidden under leaf litter or in vegetation. If it does encounter a predator, it flattens its body, curls up, and raises its head and tail to deter its attacker. If this does not work and the salamander is picked up, it is likely to be dropped again because it has sharp spines along both flanks. These are the tips of its long ribs, which stick out of its skin at the end of lumpy warts. Unfortunately, this does not deter humans—the species is endangered by collection for the pet trade.

Echinotriton andersoni
- 5–6½ in (13–16 cm)
- Damp forest, grassland, and marshes in Japan; believed extinct elsewhere.
- Stout, flattened salamander with sharp spines along sides of body; resembles a miniature crocodile.

>>01

>>02

>>03

>>04

Flipping over
Yellow-bellied toad

The small size of this toad makes it especially vulnerable to predators such as birds and snakes. Often it manages to avoid being seen by simply squatting down and keeping still. Its brown, warty back helps it blend in, particularly in muddy areas. But if this does not work and a predator sees through its camouflage, the toad has another line of defense. Like many other toads, it secretes toxic, foul-tasting chemicals through its skin. The fiery coloration on its belly is an advertisement that it tastes unpleasant,

and when threatened the toad shows it off through a series of defensive postures called the unken reflex, an example of stereotyped behavior. First the toad flattens its body, then it arches up into a bent-back position and raises its legs to reveal as much color as possible. If necessary, it rolls right over onto its back to display the full splendor of its bright orange belly. In this position a predator might not even recognize the toad as a food item and will clearly see its warning coloration.

Bombina orientalis
- 1½–2¼ in (3.5–5.5 cm)
- Well-vegetated habitats in hills and mountains of central and southern Europe.
- Small toad with dark back and yellow belly with large dark spots.

STOP, DROP, ARCH, AND ROLL
>>01 On realizing that it has been seen by a potential predator, the yellow-bellied toad's first reaction is to stop still.   >>02 Next, it drops down and flattens its body as much as possible against the ground.   >>03 The toad quickly raises its head and arches its back to expose its bright underbelly, while lifting up its legs, which are also patterned on the underside.   >>04 Because the toad remains threatened, it now rolls over onto its back with its legs tucked in, exposing its brightly colored belly.

Deadly secretion
Cane toad

This huge amphibian protects itself by exuding a highly toxic secretion onto its skin from parotoid glands behind its eyes. When threatened, the toad turns so that the glands face the attacker since the toxin can be sprayed a short distance. In its native countries, predators have adapted to tolerate the toxin to some extent, but in Australia and Hawaii many pet dogs have died after picking toads up and humans have become ill.

SLIMY POISON
The white secretion on the shoulders of this toad is a heart poison that can kill its enemies.

Rhinella marina
- Up to 9 in (23 cm)
- Native to terrestrial habitats in Central and South America; introduced to Australia and the US.
- A large toad, with a heavy, squat body and short legs.

HUMAN IMPACT
INTRODUCED PEST

The cane toad was introduced into Australia in 1935 in order to control beetle pests in sugarcane plantations. It ignored the pests but was happy to eat almost anything else. The toad is itself now a serious pest, has spread widely in Queensland and further afield, and occurs in enormous numbers in some areas. It has a significant adverse effect on endemic wildlife.

Inflated posture
European common toad

A rapid getaway is not an option for this toad, which is rather a sluggish amphibian, although it can run for short distances and will sometimes jump. So if it encounters a fast-moving predator, it tries to intimidate its enemy by pretending to be much larger than it really is. When confronted, the toad raises itself up as high as possible on its legs and gulps in air to puff itself up.

DEFENSIVE STANDOFF
Confronted by a grass snake, one of its main predators, this common toad has inflated its body to make itself look bigger and has taken up a typical defensive posture.

Bufo bufo
- Up to 6 in (15 cm)
- Wide variety of habitats in Europe, but absent from Ireland.
- Largest European toad, with very warty skin and large parotoid gland behind eye. Skin color ranges from green or brown to brick red.
- **》 154, 370–371**

Family Dendrobatidae

⬛ ³/₈–2 in (1–5 cm)

◉ Rain forest in Central America and northern South America.

📖 About 170 species of small, colorful frogs with pointed snouts and suction-pad toes.

≫ 336, 345

Toxic skin

Poison frogs

Almost all poison frogs (also known as poison dart frogs) are vividly colored to advertise their extreme toxicity and unpleasant taste. They have evolved their highly poisonous skin secretions because many of their predators, especially snakes and spiders, are resistant to mild toxins. Different types of toxins are produced by different groups of poison frogs. The most toxic species will hunt for their insect prey out in the open during the day, confident that predators will heed their warning coloration. Some of the least toxic poison frogs have become mimics, with similar colors to the most poisonous species, and tend to be left alone too. All poison frogs are very agile, so their final line of defense is to leap out of harm's way.

POISONOUS TOUCH
The vivid orange-red skin on the back of this splash-backed poison frog (*Dendrobates galactonotus*) is a clear indication of its toxicity. Most predators will keep well away.

RAINBOW COLORS
Poison frogs exhibit an astonishing variety of aposematic (warning) colors and patterns, even within the same species. Pictured are *Dendrobates tinctorius* (above) and a black-spotted red form of *Oophaga pumilio* (left).

◉ HUMAN IMPACT

DIET-DEPENDENT POISON

Native Indian tribes in Colombia use the deadly secretions from poison frogs to tip their blowpipe darts. One species, the golden poison frog (right), is preferred because it has the most potent poison of all. A single frog contains enough poison to kill 10 people, and simply rubbing a blowpipe dart over the frog's back will tip the weapon with sufficient poison to kill a monkey. The frogs obtain their poison, batrachtoxin, from eating certain species of beetle. In New Guinea, batrachtoxin has been found in the feathers of birds that eat beetles, and this behavior may yet be discovered in other species too.

Backward glance

Four-eyed frog

Turning your back on your enemy may seem a foolish thing to do but this is how the four-eyed frog scares off would-be predators. On the rear of its body there are two large, round black markings. When the frog is squatting down, these are hidden by its thighs, but if it raises itself up on its hind legs, a predator is faced with what looks like a pair of staring eyes. Defensive "eye-spots" are also found in a heronlike bird called the sunbittern (see p.297), but are more common in insects than among vertebrates.

Eupemphix nattereri

- 1¼–1½ in (3–4 cm)
- Grassland and wetland in Brazil, Paraguay, and Bolivia.
- Small frog with a fat body, short legs, and two large eye-spots on rear.

FALSE GLARE
As well as exposing its huge false eyes, this frog has puffed itself up to reinforce the illusion that it is a formidable animal.

ACTIVE FORAGING
A box turtle is a sitting target when in the open, but extends its head out of its shell to check for danger.

Terrapene carolina

- 4–8½ in (10–21 cm)
- In moist forest and wet grassland in eastern half of the US.
- Terrestrial turtle with a high, domed, brown and yellow shell.

Trap door

Eastern box turtle

The slow-moving box turtle spends most of its life out in the open, searching for slugs, earthworms, and mushrooms, so is highly visible to predators. It has evolved a suit of armor for protection. Its tough, heavy shell has a domed upper part called the carapace and a flattened underside known as the plastron. When danger threatens, the turtle quickly pulls its head, neck, and feet back inside its shell. The plastron has a movable hinge, which enables it to close tightly against the carapace to hide the head and limbs.

TIGHT SEAL
When the turtle retreats in its shell, its plastron shuts like a trap door.

Tail shedding

African blue-tailed skink

If a predator finds an African blue-tailed skink, it will probably try to grab the lizard by its tail, attracted by the bright blue color. A few seconds later, the predator will be left with just a writhing tail, while the skink has scuttled away to safety. The skink purposely sheds its tail by a process called autotomy, as a distraction strategy to help it escape. The tail regrows but will be shorter and, in most cases, the same color as the rest of the body. This means that tail shedding is a last-ditch resort for the skink. Similar species of skink occur in the New World, and tail shedding is also found in other lizards.

Trachylepis quinquetaeniata

- Up to 10 in (25 cm)
- Widespread in moist, shaded habitats in Africa.
- Shiny lizard with a cylindrical body and long blue tail.

DECOY TAIL
The shed tail thrashes around for some time to distract the predator from the skink.

FRACTURE POINTS

A skink's tail snaps at a predetermined point. The break occurs as the skink contracts muscles at one of several weak fracture points between the tail vertebrae, or in some species in the middle of a vertebra. Other muscles contract around the severed tail artery to minimize bleeding. When the tail regrows, the new part is strengthened by a cartilage rod.

scaly skin   fracture point   blood vessel   tail vertebra

Shooting blood

Texas horned lizard

The unappetizing, toadlike appearance and sharp spines of this American lizard will themselves deter its more timid predators. However, if it is approached by a sufficiently determined attacker, this lizard can squirt a stream of blood at its enemy from a pore near the corner of each eye. The blood contains a foul-tasting chemical that is guaranteed to repel most wolves, coyotes, and domestic dogs and can be squirted for up to 5 ft (1.5 m). Due to pressure from human collectors, this unique lizard is now a threatened species.

BLOODY DEFENSE
The Texas horned lizard can squirt up to a third of the blood in its body without suffering any adverse effects. However, it has a limited ability to aim the stream of blood at its tormentor.

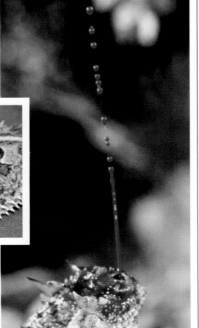

Phrynosoma cornutum

- 2¼–7 in (6–18 cm)
- Open, dry areas and grassland throughout central parts of the southern US.
- Squat, flat-bodied lizard with large head spines and prickly side scales.

HORNY HEAD
The horned lizard's mottled camouflage is its first line of defense, while the large "crown of thorns" on its head make it a tricky meal for most predators.

Nose to tail

Armadillo lizard

Like its mammalian namesake, the armadillo lizard rolls up into a ball when it feels threatened. It holds onto its tail with its strong jaws and is almost impossible to unravel. Its body, legs, and tail are covered in rows of tough, square scales with spiny edges that spring up as it curls around. When in this position, the lizard does not even look like a living animal and is usually left alone. The lizard's elaborate defense mechanism allows it to safely lead a sluggish lifestyle in open terrain.

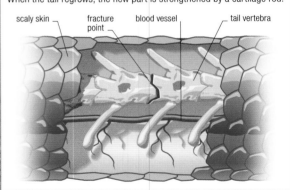

erect spine

Cordylus cataphractus

- 6½–10 in (16–25 cm)
- Dry scrub and rocky desert areas in southern Africa.
- Brown lizard with heavy armor of tough scales and spines.

RING OF SPINES
By rolling into a spiny ball, the armadillo lizard is able to protect its soft underparts and deter predators such as birds of prey.

Sudden launch

Flying lizard

Like many of their relatives, these forest-dwelling lizards spend much of their time clinging to tree trunks and keeping perfectly still. Their cryptic coloration makes them difficult to spot, and they rely on this camouflage and their agility in climbing trees for protection. However, the lizards can also turn head down, launch themselves into the air, and glide to another tree. Large, loose flaps of skin on each side of the body extend out as temporary wings, supported by the animals' long ribs. The ribs can move and be stretched out sideways. Strong claws help the lizards to land safely up to 26 ft (8 m) away.

Gliding is frequently used to move from tree to tree and is not just an escape system. However, male flying lizards are territorial and prefer to remain in one of the trees they have claimed as their small patch of forest. There will usually be at least one female, and possibly two or three, in each of his trees.

Draco volans

- 8–12 in (20–30 cm)
- Tropical forest in southern India and Southeast Asia, including Borneo and Philippines.
- Thin lizard with a long tail, winglike flaps, and a dewlap under the chin (used for display).

BRIGHT WINGS
The beautiful scarlet coloration of the flying lizard's "wings" normally remains hidden to avoid attracting the attention of predators. It is only revealed in flight and when the male is displaying to one of his females.

Venomous spray

Mozambique spitting cobra

Cobras are highly venomous snakes, and the Mozambique spitting cobra is especially threatening because of its ability to discharge venom over a distance of up to 9¾ft (3 m). The snake raises itself off the ground and flattens its neck to appear larger, then takes careful aim at a predator's head, especially the eyes. The venom is highly toxic but the cobra rarely bites, most predators being warned off by its aggressive posture and spitting prowess. It is, however, very nervous and due to its volatile temperament is considered one of the most dangerous snakes in Africa. Its bite is potentially fatal but effective first-aid treatment is usually successful. If the cobra is continually molested it will often play dead, in the hope that its tormentor will lose interest.

> **Spitting cobra venom is a potent nerve poison, but the snake itself is immune.**

DEADLY AIM
A Mozambique spitting cobra can rear up to at least one-third of its length and so can easily spit into the eyes of most predators. The venom can cause severe damage and may even result in blindness.

Naja mossambica

- 35–54 in (0.9–1.4 m)
- Savanna, woodland, and clearings in southeast Africa.
- Slender brown to gray snake with a narrow hood that can be erected.

Warning sound

Western diamondback rattlesnake

The loud rattling noise made by a rattlesnake when threatened is one of the most famous warning sounds in nature. Usually a western diamondback rattlesnake will stand its ground rather than slither away. Expending energy on an unnecessary strike is counterproductive, and so the snake warns of its presence by rattling the specially adapted tip of its tail. It will also lift its head up and stare at the intruder to look as intimidating as possible. If the warning is heeded and the snake is left alone, it normally then retreats to a safer hiding place. A rattlesnake bite is potentially fatal to humans but the snake attacks people only in self-defense. It uses its venom to kill birds and rodents for food.

Crotalus atrox

- 33–84 in (0.85–2.1 m)
- Dry rocky and desert habitats in the southwest US and Mexico.
- Large, thick snake with a distinct triangular head and a pattern of dark diamonds on its back.

ANATOMY
RATTLE RINGS

A rattlesnake's rattle consists of a series of hollow, interlocking rings made from modified scales, each one overlapping the next. When the tail is shaken, the rings rattle against each other, making the characteristic noise. The size and sound of the rattle increase with the age of the snake because a new rattle segment is added at each molt.

youngest scales are at base of tail

DOUBLE WARNING
Both the posture and the erect, shaking rattle of this diamondback rattlesnake warn that the snake will strike if approached too closely.

Walking on water

Sailfin lizards

The sailfin lizards of Southeast Asia live along rain forest riverbanks and are almost as much at home in water as out of it. They settle on branches overhanging water, both at night and during the day when basking. When disturbed, for example by a predator such as a snake, they instantly drop off their perches and run or swim away over the water.

Small insects, such as pond skaters, are well known for their ability to glide across water, using the surface tension to support themselves, but it would seem impossible for a relatively bulky vertebrate to do the same. This is, of course, true, but although sailfin lizards cannot truly be said to walk on water, they can nevertheless sprint over the surface for a short distance to escape from predators. They must run fast and slap their feet down hard to create an upward force. Somewhat like a person riding a bicycle, they will fall unless they maintain their forward momentum. They are good swimmers, too, aided by their flattened tails. Male sailfin lizards have a high crest of skin along the base of the tail; the crest is kept flat while the animal is running but erected during territorial displays. The "sail" may also be used to help catch the sun, so the lizard can warm up in the early morning and after swimming.

The sailfin lizards are the largest members of the Agamidae family. They share their remarkable ability to run on water with several other lizards, including

Hydrosaurus species

- Up to 35 in (90 cm)
- Forests of Indonesia, Borneo, Philippines, and Papua New Guinea.
- Medium-sized lizards with a small head, rounded body, long legs, and large feet.

the basilisks of the genus _Basiliscus_, which live in Central and South America. Basilisk lizards never stray far from water (like sailfin lizards, they settle on branches overhanging water). Young ones can run farther over the water than adults, but often they simply swim away. They can stay underwater for several minutes—unconfirmed reports say two hours—sufficient time for a predator to lose interest. Their predators are numerous and include raptors, snakes, larger lizards, and even fishes when they are in the water.

RUNNING ON WATER
Basilisk lizards, sometimes known as Jesus lizards, are well adapted for escaping from their enemies over water. They have unusually large hind feet, and each toe is edged with skin flaps. These are kept folded when the lizard runs on land but are unfurled when it runs over water. Pictured here are the striped basilisk (above) and plumed basilisk (left).

CASE STUDY

THE MECHANICS OF WALKING ON WATER

High-speed photography of the plumed basilisk lizard in laboratory tanks has shown that each stride over the water has three phases. During the "slap," the lizard's foot goes straight down, displacing water and creating a pocket of air around the foot; the upward force generated by the slap is enough to keep the lizard's body above the surface while it kicks its leg backward. This is the

"stroke," which gives forward momentum. Finally comes the "recovery" phase, when the foot is pulled up and out of the water ready for the next step. As long as it runs fast enough, the lizard stays upright by pushing sideways with its feet when necessary. This basilisk is able to reach speeds of up to 6 mph (10 kph) when running on water; juvenile lizards can cover greater distances before sinking.

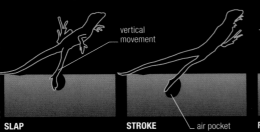

vertical movement

SLAP   STROKE   air pocket   RECOVERY   flat foot

SPRINT TO SAFETY
Looking like an Olympic sprinter, this sailfin lizard leaves a trail of water droplets as it races over the water surface. Here, the action has been captured in a studio, but in the wild a lizard fleeing from a predator would eventually run out of momentum, drop into the water, and swim the rest of the way.

FEIGNING DEATH
This grass snake has turned on its back, opened its mouth, and allowed its tongue to hang out in an effort to convince its tormentor that it is dead.

— limp tongue

Playing dead

Grass snake

A grass snake will sometimes play dead if it feels threatened or is cornered by an enemy. Predators such as birds of prey, used to catching live victims, may then ignore the snake entirely or be startled if it suddenly comes to life again. If an animal does pick up the snake, it releases a foul-smelling liquid from its cloacal gland. The grass snake is shy and nonvenomous, and rarely bites, but under pressure, it may hiss and feign a strike with its mouth closed.

Natrix natrix

- Up to 4 ft (1.2 m); rarely up to 6½ ft (2 m)
- Damp places, woods, fields, and yards throughout Europe.
- Brown or greenish snake with a yellow collar edged with black behind the head.

» 357

Leg power

Ostrich

Ostrich legs and feet are designed for speed, and this bird comfortably outruns most predators. When alarmed, it can sprint at 19 mph (30 kph) and even produce brief spurts of up to 45 mph (70 kph). Its top speed is only just short of the cheetah's, the fastest land animal of all (see p.235). If an ostrich is caught, it kicks out with its legs and can deliver a blow powerful enough to kill or badly injure its pursuer. The ostrich will also use posture to intimidate a rival or a predator. Its wings, useless for flying, are spread out and the feathers fluffed up, and the bird hisses loudly.

Intimidating pose

Common crane

By spreading its broad wings, the common crane makes itself seem more intimidating in the face of a predator. This threat display is usually seen during the breeding season, when the adults have eggs and chicks to protect. Cranes are also well known for their dancing display, which involves spectacular leaps, head bowing, and foot stamping. Normally part of courtship, this behavior is sometimes used as a threat.

Grus grus

- 4 ft (1.2 m)
- Wetland in Europe, Asia, and northern Africa.
- Tall, elegant wading bird with a long, pointed bill and long, bushy tail.

WINGS SPREAD
Faced by a red fox, this crane has spread its wings wide to keep the carnivore away from its nest.

DEADLY KICK
The massive leg muscles that give ostriches such a powerful kick are visible in this photograph of two rival males running at full speed. In contrast to hoofed animals, ostriches can only kick forward.

Struthio camelus

- Height 5½–9¼ ft (1.7–2.8 m)
- Savanna, scub, grassland, and semidesert in parts of Africa; introduced to Australia.
- Huge flightless bird with long, bare legs and a very long neck.

LIZARD INTRUDER
This monitor lizard is distracted by the threat display of a water dikkop, a mainly nocturnal bird that has been stirred into action to save its nest on the riverbank. Monitor lizards prefer to steal eggs from unattended nests, and this means the dikkop has a good chance of repelling its larger enemy.

Shock tactics

Sunbittern

This normally secretive bird of swampy forests and wetlands uses visual shock tactics to startle would-be predators. The sunbittern is difficult to spot when quietly hunting fish and frogs with its wings folded. It creeps slowly along the water's edge, where its subdued plumage of gray patterned with black and brown helps it blend in with the shadows. But the bird has a surprise hidden on the flight feathers of its wings. If it is tackled by a predator, especially when nesting, the sunbittern opens its wings to reveal a pair of false eyes. The eye-spots are red and black on a yellow background, creating a dramatic impact. Confronted by a supposedly huge animal with glaring eyes, most predators retreat. Eye-spots are uncommon in birds, but are also found in the four-eyed frog (see p.292) and many insects.

Eurypyga helias

- 17½ in (45 cm)
- Well-vegetated riverbanks, ponds, and wooded streams in Central and South America.
- Heronlike bird with a long neck, long, straight bill, and nonwebbed feet.

ALARMING PLUMAGE
A sunbittern displays the colorful false eyes on its fully spread wings in an attempt to protect its nesting site. This stunning display is also used in courtship.

Sticky defense

Red-cockaded woodpecker

Most woodpeckers nest in holes in trees, where their eggs and young are safe from many predators. However, their nest holes remain vulnerable to attacks by snakes, which can easily slither inside. To defeat marauding tree snakes, the red-cockaded woodpecker has developed a form of defensive behavior that puts its nest out of bounds. It drills small holes beside the entrance to its nest so that treacly sap exudes from the bark and congeals around the hole. Sometimes the woodpecker also strips away bark, leaving a smooth surface that is difficult for snakes to grip.

Red-cockaded woodpeckers are social birds that live in small family groups or clans. The main nesting pair in the group benefits from help by nonbreeding birds (usually young males from earlier broods), which means there are more individuals able to keep watch for predators.

> The red-cockaded woodpecker nests only in living pine trees. The resin clings to a snake's scales and inhibits its climb.

Picoides borealis

- 8–9 in (20–23 cm)
- Mature, open pine forest in the southeast US; often in fire-burned clearings.
- Small, black and white woodpecker, with a barred back and black speckles on breast.

NEST PROTECTION
Mounds of adhesive paste formed by exuded tree resin can be seen caked around the nest hole of this red-cockaded woodpecker.

Living dangerously

Water dikkop

Choosing a nest site on a riverbank close to that of a Nile crocodile might seem unwise, but this is exactly what a wading bird called the water dikkop is suspected of doing. The usual explanation for this behavior is that the bird gains added protection for its nest, because the female crocodile will aggressively chase away any potential nest thieves, such as lizards, that get too close to her stretch of bank. The water dikkop is a nocturnal bird. It keeps quiet and hides during the day, but at night it calls loudly and its alarm calls are believed to alert its crocodile companion to the approach of predators. When threatened, the bird also lowers its head, opens its wings, and runs toward the attacker. Scientists have questioned whether the water dikkop's choice of nest site is a deliberate defensive strategy or simply the result of chance, since dikkops and crocodiles both need sandy banks to nest and might end up as neighbors anyway. However, there are other cases of birds nesting near dangerous animals—for example, in Central and South America oropendolas hang their stockinglike nests from branches beside wasp or bee nests for protection.

Burhinus vermiculatus

- 15½ in (40 cm)
- Lakes, rivers, and wetland, especially with sandy banks, throughout southern Africa.
- Wading bird with long legs, very large eyes, and a thick, heavy bill.

TOUGH SCALES
Up close, pangolin scales look somewhat like the surface of a mature pine cone. The scales can be raised so that their sharp edges point outward, making it more difficult for a predator to penetrate the armor.

overlapping scales

scales cover legs

Armor plating

Cape pangolin

While most mammals are covered in fur or hair, the Cape pangolin is sheathed in a protective layer of close-fitting overlapping scales, although its soft belly has hairs. Its scales extend over its head almost to the end of its snout and the entire length of its tail and legs. The pangolin lives on the ground and digs a burrow where it can rest and give birth. If threatened, it runs for its burrow, but if it cannot get there in time, it curls up into a large, scaly ball that is virtually impossible to unroll. Hyenas are among the very few predators able to penetrate these defenses because they have bone-crunching jaws, and full-grown adults can bite through the scales, especially of a young pangolin. As a last resort, a cornered pangolin may rear up and squirt a foul liquid at its attacker, using special glands at the rear of its body.

Manis temminckii
- 16–28 in (40–70 cm)
- Open forests and grassland in central and southern Africa.
- Long, scaly mammal with tapering body, pointed snout, strong claws, and long tongue for eating ants.

Ball of scales

Brazilian three-banded armadillo

Armadillos are famous for being able to roll their heavily armored body into a tight, impenetrable ball—a highly effective form of defense. In fact, only two of the world's 20 species of armadillo, the Brazilian and southern three-banded armadillos, can do this. The other species have defensive armor as a deterrent, but if attacked they still prefer to flee to cover or quickly dig a burrow to get out of danger. Three-banded armadillos are different—by rolling into a ball and completely encasing themselves in their own shell, they can safely stay out in the open to confront the threat. Armadillo armor consists of bony, interlocking plates that form a rigid case over the shoulders and hips. In between are rows of plates alternating with thick skin, which open out like an accordion so that the animal has some flexibility. Armadillos belong to the order Cingulata, meaning "belted animals."

Tolypeutes tricinctus
- 12–14½ in (30–37 cm)
- Wooded savanna and dry, open country in central and northeast Brazil.
- Compact mammal with very thick, leathery shell segmented into a rear plate, front plate, and three movable bands. Strong claws and stout tail.

ROLLING INTO A BALL
>>01 A captive Brazilian three-banded armadillo walks across the ground, showing its distinctive shuffling gait, low to the ground with few soft parts of its body exposed.   >>02 As the animal starts to roll up, its tough skin stretches out between three bands of bony plates in the middle of its back.   >>03 The armadillo tucks in its head and limbs, and its hip and shoulder plates meet.   >>04 Finally the armadillo's armored head and tail join, completing its transformation into a scaly ball.

>>01

>>02

>>03

>>04

Flesh-piercing quills

Cape porcupine

Porcupines normally carry their quills lying flat along the back, but if danger threatens they erect a prickly defense of sharp, stout quills and longer spines. With their defenses up, they look much larger and more threatening. If a predator, such as a hyena, lion, or leopard, is brave or inexperienced enough to corner a porcupine, it is likely to receive a face full of spines as the porcupine runs backward into it. The nasty wounds may get infected, so a porcupine strike can prove fatal. To warn its opponent not to attack, the porcupine shakes hollow tail spines to produce a snakelike rattle.

Hystrix africaeaustralis
- About 20 in (50 cm)
- Variety of vegetated habitats in Africa, especially south of Sahara in rocky hills.
- Large rodent covered in coarse hairs, with spines and quills on rear half of body and along flanks.

erectile quills

stiff body hairs

SPINY RODENT
Porcupines have a spiny defense that is unique among rodents. The quills are shed easily, but contrary to the widely held belief, porcupines cannot flick them in the face of their enemies.

Hot tail

California ground squirrel

If caught out in the open by a rattlesnake, one of its main predators, this ground squirrel raises its bushy tail and shakes it like a flag. But first the squirrel pumps more blood into the tail to warm it up by several degrees. Rattlesnakes hunt by detecting infrared radiation (heat), using special pits in their face. The sudden rush of extra heat makes the squirrel seem larger and more intimidating to the snake.

Spermophilus beecheyi

- Body 12–20 in (30–50 cm); tail 5–9 in (13–23 cm)
- On ground and in burrows in most habitats in the western US.
- Stocky brown squirrel with a pale underside and white ring around the eye.

WARNING IN THE TAIL
The California ground squirrel tries to ward off snakes by throwing earth and tail waving. If all else fails, it uses a rush of blood to warm its tail—an unusual form of thermal defense that seems to be effective against rattlesnakes.

Gliding from danger

Spotted giant flying squirrel

Most tree-living squirrels can leap from tree to tree in dense forest, but this giant flying squirrel has taken the ability a step further. When it launches itself from a tree, it stretches its front and rear legs out wide, which pulls a membrane of loose skin taut between them. This unfurled gliding surface enables it to sail to another tree lower down.

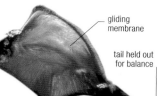

gliding membrane

tail held out for balance

Petaurista elegans

- 12–17½ in (30–45 cm)
- Tall lowland forest in Southeast Asia.
- Large, red-brown squirrel with whitish spots on back and a gliding membrane between front and back legs.

GLIDE ACTION
The squirrel can adjust its glide angle and direction by shifting its front legs, much as free-fall parachutists use their arms.

Toxic saliva

Slow loris

If a mother slow loris has to leave her baby alone, she first licks it, covering its fur with saliva. The saliva is harmless but the mother mixes it with foul smelling toxic secretions from a gland on the inside of her elbow. This unpleasant smell probably helps deter predators. A bite from a slow loris is especially nasty since a special tooth comb in the lower jaw helps transfer saliva.

Nycticebus coucang

- 12–15 in (30–38 cm)
- Rain forests in Indonesia and Southeast Asia.
- Small tree-living primate with huge eyes and nimble, gripping toes. Short, thick fur in a range of colors.

ESCAPE PLUNGE
Unable to leap away, this mother and baby slow loris are far from defenseless. If their pungent odor does not deter a predator, the mother will simply drop out of the tree onto lower branches or into the undergrowth, with her infant clinging on.

Chest beating

Mountain gorilla

The dominant male of each gorilla group, known as a silverback for his silvery gray mantle, has to protect his family from the threat of wandering male rivals or humans, the only predator of adult gorillas. He mainly deals with such threats by intimidating his opponents with an aggressive display, tearing wildly at the surrounding vegetation and beating his chest. This is combined with a terrifying series of loud hoots ending in a roar, and usually averts a violent encounter.

Gorilla beringei beringei

- 4¼–6¼ ft (1.3–1.9 m)
- Montane forest on borders of Rwanda, Uganda, and Democratic Republic of the Congo.
- Largest and strongest of all primates; silverback has massive head with bony ridge on top.

POWERFUL DISPLAY
Standing up on his hind legs, and beating his chest, this silverback is showing his opponent how large and powerful he is. If the intruder does not leave, he may charge and knock the intruder over.

DANGEROUS GAME
The defense put up by these Cape porcupines may not be sufficient against this young Kalahari lion. He will eventually learn to flip a porcupine over to expose its soft underside and kill it.

Prickly ball

European hedgehog

If a fox or another predator tries to pick up a hedgehog, it rolls up into a prickly ball with its head and legs tucked firmly into its soft underbelly. About 5,000 sharp, hollow spines cover its entire back. Each one is replaced roughly once a year as it gets damaged or wears out, ensuring that the hedgehog stays protected.

Erinaceus europaeus

- 8–12 in (20–30 cm)
- In woodland, yards, and grassland throughout Europe; introduced to New Zealand.
- Small oval-bodied mammal with short legs, pointed snout, and prickly back.

UP AND OVER
When erect, hedgehog spines are extremely sharp and strong, offering good protection from attack. Even so, if a predator manages to turn a hedgehog over (above), it may be able to reach the hedgehog's soft, vulnerable belly and kill it.

Hostile posture

Serval

Only a little larger than a pet cat, the serval does not have the advantage of impressive strength or size, and so, like a domestic tabby, it must rely on posture to dissuade potential predators from attacking. If cornered, this small, slim cat raises its hackles, arches its back, flattens its ears, raises and fluffs its tail, and spits and snarls. If this does not work, the serval may make slashing movements with its forepaws to encourage its aggressor to back off. The serval lives alone, marking out a hunting territory of several square miles by spraying urine, leaving piles of feces in prominent locations, and rubbing its scent glands against bushes and rocks. Other servals read these signs and stay away, with the result that individuals rarely meet outside the breeding season. In this way dangerous fights between servals are avoided.

Felis serval

- 28–39 in (70–100 cm)
- Widespread but uncommon in open habitats of sub-Saharan Africa.
- Slender cat with long legs, narrow head, large ears, and spotted coat.

SPITTING RAGE
This serval has adopted a defensive posture and is hissing and snarling. The small size of this hunter means that it could itself easily be attacked by a larger cat or hyena.

Offensive odor

Striped skunk

Being relatively small, a skunk might seem a straightforward target to a young and inexperienced predator. However, the bold black and white stripes of this solitary animal warn that it is extremely unpleasant to deal with. If approached too closely, it squirts a noxious-smelling fluid from glands on either side of the anus, with great accuracy, for a distance of up to 13 ft (4 m). The skunk gives advance warning of its intent by pattering its front feet and lifting up its conspicuous white tail, but if these gestures are ignored it will quickly spray its attacker.

Mephitis mephitis

- Body 13–17½ in (33–45 cm); tail 7–10 in (18–25 cm)
- Widespread throughout much of Canada and the US.
- Small, ground-living mammal with black and white body stripes and bushy white tail.

STINK BOMB
One spray from a skunk's anal glands is usually sufficient to teach a predator to leave it alone next time. Here, an inquisitive red fox cub advances closer than its more experienced parents.

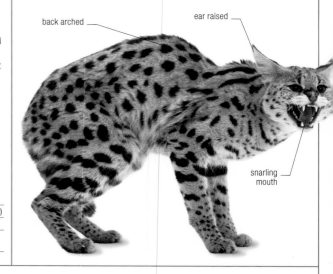

back arched

ear raised

snarling mouth

Tough hide

Indian rhinoceros

With its huge size, tough, layered skin, and curved horn, the Indian rhinoceros has few natural predators. Tigers will attack young rhinoceroses, but heavy folds of skin at the shoulder joints, flanks, and neck give armor-plated protection from smaller predators. The thick skin also helps protect individuals during occasional aggressive interactions between males. In spite of its ungainly bulk, an Indian rhinoceros can charge fast and furiously, and rival males will clash horns. Large adults are quite capable of killing an unwary tiger or a person. They have poor eyesight and may not notice a predator approaching upwind, but their hearing is excellent. Keeping their protective skin in good condition is essential, and these rhinoceroses spend the hottest parts of the day wallowing in shallow pools. This

Rhinoceros unicornis

- Up to 13 ft (4 m)
- Tall swampy grass and forest areas close to rivers in northern India, Nepal, and Pakistan.
- Dark gray rhinoceros with one short horn and tough knobbly skin.

keeps the skin supple and offers relief from biting insects, as well as preventing sunburn. In deeper water, these animals are excellent swimmers. Mostly, Indian rhinoceroses lead solitary lives, but loose groups form at favorite wallows. Unless numbers are high, newcomers to the wallow are usually tolerated after an exchange of grunts.

Unfortunately, neither its hide nor its horn are any protection against guns, and people are the Indian rhinoceros's main enemy. In Nepal, rhinoceros populations are protected by armed rangers, but poaching and illegal trading still go on, encouraged by the high price fetched for the animal's horn. The rhinoceroses are also disliked by farmers since they trample and feed on crops. Habitat loss has driven them to search for food in cultivated areas.

THICK SKIN
The legs and buttocks of this Indian rhinoceros are protected by thick skin, which is covered in large, hard tubercles. Heavy folds of skin hang down like a protective skirt, and even the tail is armored.

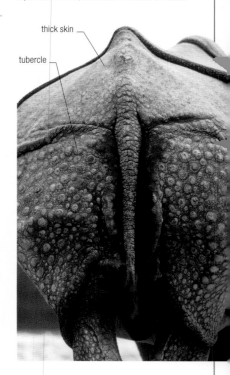

thick skin

tubercle

RARE BREEDING
The Indian rhinoceros is critically endangered in the wild. This baby, closely following its mother, was born in San Diego Zoo in 2006, as part of an endangered species breeding program. Females have only one baby about every three years.

Angry charge
African elephant

The sight of a charging African elephant moving at full speed is terrifying, although in healthy elephant societies (see panel, right) it is a rare spectacle. Elephants are by nature peaceful, living and traveling in family groups led by a mature female. Their size alone deters most predators, and young elephants are closely guarded by the extended family. However, a close approach by a pack of lions, or even unwary tourists, may not be tolerated, especially by a mother protecting her baby. When enraged, an elephant will face its tormentor, raise its head and tusks, and bring its huge ears forward and out. If this threat display does not work, the elephant

CHARGING BULL
Disturbed while cooling off in a water hole, this bull elephant has brought his ears forward and is swinging his trunk to appear as large and intimidating as possible.

Loxodonta africana
 13–16½ ft (4–5 m)
Open grassland, scrub, woodland, and occasionally desert, in Africa south of the Sahara.
Largest living land animal, with large ears, mobile trunk, and curved ivory tusks.

may charge, holding its trunk high and trumpeting loudly. Usually, the elephant stops or turns aside, but if very distressed it will gore and trample anything in its path. Bull elephants live on their own or in young bachelor groups and can be dangerous when in musth. A bull in musth has high levels of reproductive hormones, especially testosterone, in his blood, which makes him aggressive and more likely to charge.

HUMAN IMPACT
FRACTURED FAMILIES

Decades of poaching for the ivory trade, culling, and habitat loss seem to be having a destabilizing effect on elephant society in some areas. Unprovoked attacks by elephants on crops, people, and even other wildlife such as rhinoceroses, were once rare but appear to be on the increase. This "elephant rage" may result from long-term stress. The death of a mature female, or matriarch, often leaves her group floundering, while orphaned elephants (right) have no mother from which to learn. Careful management is required if elephants and growing human populations are to coexist.

Camouflage and deception

Camouflage and deception are mainly used by animals whose predators employ good eyesight to spot their prey. This survival strategy is especially common in insects, small mammals, and reptiles preyed on by sharp-eyed birds, and in seabed fishes that are hunted by larger fishes. Predators may also use camouflage when stalking prey. Camouflage is ineffective against predators that use smell or echolocation to track down their prey.

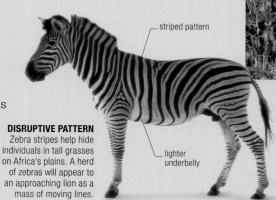

STALKING AID
Dappled with sunlight, a Bengal tiger hunting in long grass is so well disguised by its stripes that it can stalk unsuspecting prey to within a few yards.

Types of camouflage

Camouflage is achieved through the color, pattern, and texture of the outer covering of an animal. At its simplest, the animal matches the background color of its habitat, and can hide by remaining completely still. Disruptive patterning, for example stripes, breaks up the shape of the animal, so the predator sees patches of color that do not appear to relate to its prey. In open water, fishes and aquatic mammals use countershading. Their dark backs and pale bellies merge with their surroundings, whether viewed from above or below.

striped pattern

lighter underbelly

DISRUPTIVE PATTERN
Zebra stripes help hide individuals in tall grasses on Africa's plains. A herd of zebras will appear to an approaching lion as a mass of moving lines.

Permanent camouflage

Permanent camouflage is most effective in animals that remain in the same habitat most or all of the time. Extreme examples of this are animals that use other animals as a living home, often feeding on their hosts as well. In tropical oceans, sea fans and sea whips are host to a wide variety of small mollusks, shrimps, and fishes that live on their branches and are colored, patterned, and even shaped like their hosts. Pygmy seahorses (see p.305) and spindle cowries are just two sea-fan inhabitants that are covered in tubercles resembling the polyps or feeding heads of their living home. Their disguise is so good that many of these creatures have only been discovered after scientists have collected the sea-fans on which they were living. Many leaf-eating insects adopt a similar strategy.

HOME FROM HOME
This allied cowrie closely resembles its sea-fan home in shape, color, and texture. It remains well hidden as it feeds on its host.

closed wings are leaf-shaped

brown color matches that of a dead leaf

DISAPPEARING TRICK
With closed wings, this Indian leafwing butterfly resembles a brown leaf. The upper surfaces of its wings are bright orange.

Camouflage on demand

Animals that move frequently need a flexible system of camouflage. This is often provided by an ability to change color and sometimes texture to suit the animal's surroundings and is best developed in cephalopods, such as the common octopus, crustaceans, lizards, and fishes. The animal's skin contains layers of cells called chromatophores, which are filled with colored pigment. The pigment can be dispersed or concentrated to vary the skin tone. Cuttlefish, for example, display almost instantaneous color changes, which are controlled by the nervous system. In contrast, the slow color change seen in isopods, such as the isopod *Idotea*, is controlled by hormones.

COMING OUT OF HIDING
>>01 This Parson's chameleon is mostly green in color and blends in well against its background. >>02 The chameleon now has a reddish hue. Along with camouflage, changes in color and pattern are used to attract mates and to intimidate territorial rivals.

>>01

>>02

SLEEPING SAFELY

The mottled coloration of this great gray owl (also known as the dark wood-owl or Lapland owl) renders it virtually invisible against the rough gray and brown bark of the coniferous tree on which it is perching. When hunting, this owl will often use a tree branch to sit and wait, scanning the ground for small rodent prey. It hunts through forests across northern North America, Europe, and Asia, usually early in the morning and in the late afternoon, but also at night. The great gray owl is one of the largest owls in the world and it has few enemies. Even so, its camouflage allows it to doze in safety during the day, hidden from predators such as martens and wolverines, which will readily snatch inexperienced and clumsy juveniles.

WELL HIDDEN
This green crested lizard is colored to match its leafy home in the canopy of a Southeast Asian rain forest, hiding it from predatory arboreal snakes. Its camouflage also allows the lizard to stalk unsuspecting grasshoppers, its favorite prey.

Community camouflage

Sometimes, different species adopt the same camouflage to suit a specific environment. For example, floating rafts of Sargassum seaweed support a whole community of animals that drift along with the weed in the Atlantic Ocean. Within the confines of their seaweed home, kept afloat by numerous gas-filled bladders, the animal residents must live, mate, feed, and avoid being eaten. There are no holes to hide in and no rocks to slip underneath, so most of the inhabitants are camouflaged to resemble the seaweed in color and shape. As a result, animals as varied as prawns, crabs, and fishes all wear the same colors, and are mostly yellow and brown. The speckled color and slow movements of a filefish, for instance, help it blend in as it hunts for worms. Irregular seaweedlike skin flaps on the body and fins of the Sargassum fish make an excellent disguise.

A swimming crab scavenges for scraps. Even its eyes look like small Sargassum seaweed bladders.

A golden seahorse sways in the water with the seaweed, clinging on with its prehensile tail.

Mimicry

An edible species living alongside a similar looking poisonous or distasteful species can gain protection by mimicry. Animals as diverse as insects, snakes, and coral reef fishes have evolved this type of behavior, which is known as Batesian mimicry. For the harmless species to benefit, it must live in the same habitat and have the same predators as the poisonous species. Predators that have learned to avoid the poisonous species will also avoid the edible mimic. Many insects make full use of this type of mimicry. Palatable caterpillars and butterflies mimic poisonous species, while many harmless fly species resemble stinging wasps and bees. In most cases of Batesian mimicry, the model is far more common than the mimic. Too many mimics might result in predators learning by trial and error that the mimic is not poisonous after all. Another form of mimicry is Müllerian mimicry, in which several inedible species evolve to resemble each other. Over time, predators learn to avoid the patterns these animals exhibit.

imitation markings

IMITATED
The large tiger is a poisonous butterfly that lives in rain forests in Central and South America. Birds rarely make the mistake of eating it since they quickly learn that it tastes nasty. This protects the butterfly when it is feeding out in the open.

IMITATOR
The pattern of the butterfly *Papilio zagreus* is sufficiently similar to the large tiger butterfly for birds to avoid it, even though it is perfectly edible. This mimicry allows the harmless butterfly to feed in safety.

SEA FAN COVER
This delicate spider crab from the Red Sea is holding a piece of broken sea fan to conceal its telltale outline. The sea fan is dead and will not attach to the crab, but when it falls off it is likely to be replaced by other material.

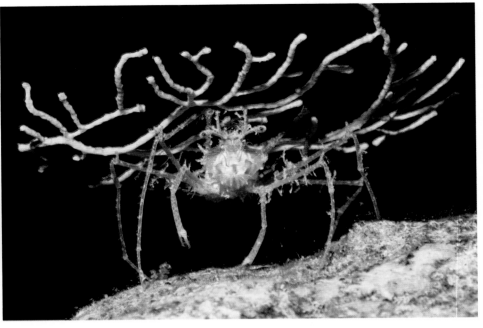

COLORFUL CLOAK
A jacket of red sponge covers the shell of this Indo-Pacific decorator crab, which moves slowly to aid its deception.

Masters of disguise
Spider crabs

Spider crabs are slow moving and have weak pincers so they make easy pickings for predatory fish. To protect themselves, many of the smaller species gather tiny anemones or loose pieces of seaweed, sponge, or other living material and attach these to their shell as camouflage. The material is hooked onto spines and hairs like Velcro, and in some cases it may grow and flourish on the shell, providing a highly effective living disguise. This defensive behavior is found in species of spider crab worldwide, but is especially prevalent on coral reefs where predatory fishes abound. Crab species that exhibit this behavior are often called decorator crabs.

Family Majidae
- ⬛ ⁵⁄₁₆–20 in (0.8–50 cm)
- ◈ Worldwide, except in polar oceans and seas.
- ▭ Oval or pear-shaped, spine-covered body with long, slender legs and small claws.

Tree imitators
Katydids

Katydids are also known as bush crickets. Like the true crickets (to which they are related), katydids sing to establish their territories and attract mates. Male katydids sing by stridulation—rubbing special areas of their forewings over one another. Females recognize the unique song made by males of their own species. However, the katydids' courtship system carries a risk because the sound can also attract the attention of predators, including birds, snakes, and small mammals. As a defense, most katydids are therefore colored green or brown to

Family Tettigoniidae
- ⬛ Up to about 13 cm (5 in) long
- ◈ Most species tropical, but family occurs in lush vegetation worldwide.
- ▭ Stout-bodied insect with vertical head, long antennae, biting jaws, and long legs; wings fold flat along body.

INVISIBLE CLOAK
Even at close range this lichen-mimic katydid from Sabah, Borneo, is very difficult to spot. The color and texture of its body and wing covers exactly match the lichen-covered tree trunk.

match the vegetation on which they live. Many have also evolved specialized camouflage. Depending on where they live and feed, different species imitate lichen, bark, twigs, or leaves. They are not adept fliers, and so if a predator approaches they prefer to stop singing, remain still, and rely on their camouflage for protection. Some return to the same branch or twig after foraging and chew out depressions to help mold themselves to their background.

Male common true katydids sing with distinctive regional dialects.

Twig impersonation
Giant stick insect

Also known as walking sticks, these huge insects bear a remarkable resemblance to twigs and are extremely hard to spot, even from up close. They depend on good camouflage since they move awkwardly and cannot easily fly away from danger—the females in particular have very small wings. Some related species have no wings at all. Giant stick insects are expert at keeping still and position themselves to look like just another twig of the plant on which they are feeding. By swaying from side to side, they give the illusion of plant stems moving in a gentle breeze. Like most stick insects, the female of this species lays fertile eggs without mating (parthenogenesis) and so does not even have to move to find a mate.

Phasma gigas
- ⬛ Up to 7½ in (19 cm)
- ◈ Trees and bushes in Papua New Guinea.
- ▭ Long, thin insect with long legs and small wings.

LICHEN MIMIC
As long as it remains still, this lichen-mimic katydid can remain hidden. It lives in the humid cloud forests of Ecuador's mountains, where lichens abound.

FOREST STICK
A stick insect hangs motionless under a branch in a Madagascan forest. Its hooklike feet help it to cling on tightly. If attacked, the insect may drop limply to the ground like a broken twig.

Leaf mimics

Leaf insects

These insects belong to the same group as stick insects (see opposite), but have flattened bodies designed to look like leaves and are much rarer. The true camouflage experts are the tropical phyllid leaf insects in the family Phyllidae. Each leg is flattened sideways to make it look like a small leaf or leaf segment and the abdomen is expanded. The disguise may be completed by false

WINGLESS FEMALE
A female phyllid leaf insect crawls over a leaf. Her body is massively flattened but she lacks wings and cannot fly away from her enemies. By contrast, male phyllids have fully functional wings.

midribs, veins, or disease spots and holes. The phyllids also have small eyes and short antennae to avoid giving themselves away. If their disguise fails, some phyllids can produce sounds by rubbing thickened segments of their antennae together to scare their attacker.

Family Phyllidae
- 1¼–4½ in (3–11 cm) long
- Well-vegetated areas in Mauritius, Seychelles, Southeast Asia, and Australasia.
- Brown or green insects with flat, wide abdomens, extended leg segments, and veined forewings covering transparent hindwings.

SPIKY CAMOUFLAGE
There is a huge range of body shapes in leaf insects. Pictured here is a well disguised leaf insect from the tropical family Heteronemidae.

CASE STUDY
INSECT FOSSIL

In 2006, an almost complete fossil of a leaf insect was unearthed in dried out lake deposits in Messel, Germany—the first one ever found. Dating techniques applied to the fossil suggest that it is about 47 million years old. Named *Eophyllium messelensis*, it closely resembles modern-day leaf insects, showing that leaf mimicry must be a very successful survival strategy. Leaf insects live in tropical areas, and this fossil provides further evidence that the western European climate was at one point much warmer than it is today.

False thorns

Thorn bugs

Female thorn bugs have greatly enlarged, unusually shaped thoraxes that make them perfect plant mimics. They spends their lives sucking sap from trees, especially fruit trees and ornamental varieties. Such a lifestyle might be expected to leave them vulnerable to attack, but thorn bugs in fact have few predators due to their thorny camouflage and unpleasant taste. The

nymphs hatch from eggs laid under tree bark, stay in a group, and are guarded by the mother. Their disguise is not as effective as the adults', so protection is vital. If a predatory insect approaches, the nymphs vibrate in unison, and this warning signal soon passes to the mother. Safe in her armor, she fans her wings and kicks out with her hind legs to deter the attacker.

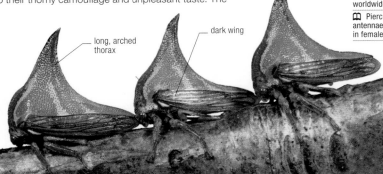

long, arched thorax

dark wing

Family Membracidae
- 3/16–½ in (0.5–1.5 cm)
- Forest, orchards, and yards worldwide, mainly in warmer regions.
- Piercing mouthparts and short antennae; thorax large and thorn-shaped in female.

LINE OF THORNS
Neatly lined up along a twig, these three female thorn bugs in Costa Rica closely resemble sharp thorns. Male thorn bugs have quite a different disguise and resemble flat-topped twigs.

Fake snake

Spicebush swallowtail butterfly

To avoid being eaten by birds, the caterpillar of this swallowtail butterfly has several lines of defense. It uses silk to fold a leaf in half to make a daytime shelter, emerging only at night to feed and molt. But if its shelter is pulled apart, the larva turns to shock tactics to frighten away its attacker. Raising its swollen front end and tucking its head down suddenly gives it the appearance of a green snake or tree frog, confusing its enemy.

Papilio troilus
- About 2¼ in (6 cm) (caterpillar)
- On spicebush and similar aromatic plants in eastern North America (from southern Canada south to Florida and Texas).
- Mature caterpillar is green with false eye-spots, and each segment has six blue dots edged in black; young caterpillar resembles a bird dropping.

MATURE LARVA
This head-on view shows the caterpillar's false eye-spots, which have two smaller white spots that give the illusion of reflections in rounded eyes.

COLOR CHANGE

>>01 When hiding, the broadclub cuttlefish takes on the appearance of the surrounding coral, with many small papillae that resemble coral fragments. However, as this rapidly taken sequence of photographs demonstrates, this large species of cuttlefish is able to transform its appearance completely in a short space of time.   >>02 In this photograph, the cuttlefish has positioned itself close to a sponge with similar coloration and texture.   >>03 The cuttlefish moves and suddenly changes color. It is now vivid yellow, probably in response to the perceived threat of the photographer's flash.   >>04 With its two small front arms raised in a defensive posture, the cuttlefish warily assesses the photographer.

>>01

>>02

>>03

>>04

Rapid transformation

Broadclub cuttlefish

This large cuttlefish is well known for its amazing ability to change color instantaneously. It can also modify the texture of its skin, which may start completely smooth but quickly becomes covered in little bumps and tall projections called papillae. This double ability provides the cuttlefish with excellent camouflage in a wide range of marine habitats. When the cuttlefish is among seaweed it will also hold its tentacles up and crinkle the edges to resemble the plants' waving fronds.

The broadclub cuttlefish can perform sudden, unexpected alterations in color to confuse and startle a potential predator. Different color patterns are also used to communicate intentions during courtship and territorial defense—for example, a striped zebra pattern is commonly worn when males challenge each other. When hunting, broadclub cuttlefish put on a light show of rapidly changing colors that may mesmerize shrimps and other prey while keeping their own predators at bay. These kaleidoscopic visual displays are controlled by layers of specialized pigment cells, known as chromatophores (see panel, below), in the cuttlefish's skin. Those nearest the surface contain yellow pigments, those in the middle layer are orange and red, and the deepest ones appear brown to black. By rapidly expanding and contracting the chromatophores under nervous control, the cuttlefish can produce a huge variety of skin patterns. The deep skin layers also contain iridophores, special cells that reflect light and modify the color.

BACKGROUND MATCH
Chromatophores are also found in cuttlefish's close relatives, octopuses and squid. This day octopus has changed color to blend in with the background coral. It can achieve a good match in an instant due to the complex layers of chromatophores in its skin.

Sepia latimanus

◄► Up to 19½ in (50 cm)

◉ Shallow reefs and rocky areas throughout Indian Ocean and tropical western Pacific.

▥ Cephalopod mollusk with flat, oval body, internal shell, eight arms, and two long feeding tentacles.

IRIDESCENCE
The intense luminous coloration of this tiny bobtail squid is caused by cells in the lower layer of the squid's skin, called iridophores, which reflect polarized light.

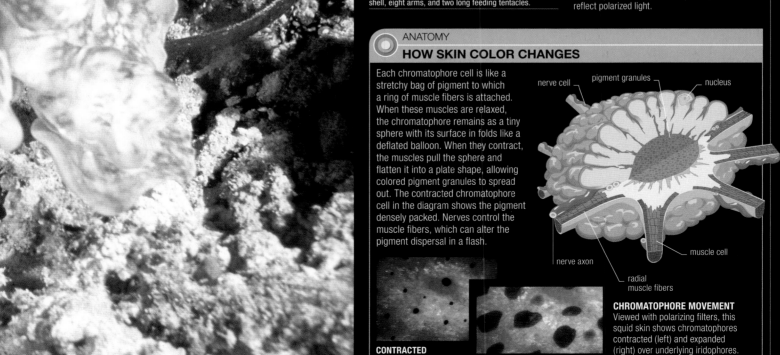

ANATOMY

HOW SKIN COLOR CHANGES

Each chromatophore cell is like a stretchy bag of pigment to which a ring of muscle fibers is attached. When these muscles are relaxed, the chromatophore remains as a tiny sphere with its surface in folds like a deflated balloon. When they contract, the muscles pull the sphere and flatten it into a plate shape, allowing colored pigment granules to spread out. The contracted chromatophore cell in the diagram shows the pigment densely packed. Nerves control the muscle fibers, which can alter the pigment dispersal in a flash.

nerve cell — pigment granules — nucleus

muscle cell

nerve axon

radial muscle fibers

CONTRACTED

EXPANDED

CHROMATOPHORE MOVEMENT
Viewed with polarizing filters, this squid skin shows chromatophores contracted (left) and expanded (right) over underlying iridophores.

LEAFY DISGUISE
Resting on a forest floor, this large saturniid moth is almost invisible, thanks to its very effective camouflage. Its brown color matches that of the dead leaves, while dark patches on its wings mimic holes chewed out of the leaves by other insects. By remaining completely still during the daytime, the moth avoids detection by predators.

False colors

Clearwing moths

Camouflage is not effective for active insects such as clearwing moths, which feed on nectar, juice, and other plant liquids and need to move around constantly between food sources, making them highly visible. Instead many species gain protection by a resemblance to stinging or unpalatable insects, especially hornets, wasps, and bees. This is an example of Batesian mimicry and is found in many different groups of animals. Predators that recognize these insects by their contrasting black and yellow stripes will avoid them.

Synanthedon species

- ⬌ ³⁄₈–1¼ in (1–3 cm)
- ◑ Trees and bushes in Europe and North America.
- ▭ Yellow and black stripes on body, narrow transparent wings, and simple antennae.

SERPENT MIMIC
One of several eels that mimic venomous sea snakes, the banded snake eel is a common sight on coral reefs in the Indian Ocean. Its long dorsal fin is scarcely visible, completing the disguise.

FALSE STRIPES
Clearwing moths that mimic wasps and bees have no need to hide and so can be active in daytime. They often rest in the open, confident in the protection afforded by their coloration.

Double deception

Banded snake eel

The banded or harlequin snake eel resembles a highly venomous species of sea snake, *Laticauda colubrina*, but is a true sheep in wolf's clothing as it is neither a snake nor is it venomous. This deception means that the harmless fish can hunt over shallow sand flats and through sea-grass beds during daytime in relative safety, although even so it tends to emerge mainly at night and often hides by burrowing in sand. It has poor eyesight and tracks down small fishes and crustaceans by smell, often probing holes and crevices. The effectiveness of the snake eel's mimicry is not known for certain—its range extends northwest into the Red Sea, where there are no native sea snakes.

Myrichthys colubrinus

- ⬌ Up to 3¼ ft (1 m)
- ◑ Reefs and sea-grass beds in tropical Indo-Pacific region.
- ▭ Snakelike eel with pointed snout and tail and inconspicuous long dorsal fin.

Almost invisible

Glass catfish

The glass catfish, or ghost fish, almost entirely transparent, looks like a swimming skeleton. This provides excellent camouflage, even in crystal-clear water, and seen from head-on the flattened fish merges into the background so effectively that it is virtually impossible to spot. Its transparency is a result of thin skin, oily flesh, and a lack of pigmentation. The glass catfish clusters in groups, with the fish lining up at an oblique angle to the water surface so that they are less visible. Like all catfishes, they have sensory barbels around the mouth to help detect prey, mainly aquatic insects and smaller fishes.

Kryptopterus bicirrhis

- ⬌ 2¾–6 in (7–15 cm)
- ◑ Rivers, streams, and floodplains in Southeast Asia.
- ▭ Long-bodied fish with thin, transparent skin, flattish head, and wide mouth.

TRANSPARENT FISH
A glass catfish is remarkably difficult to see—even when these fish gather in large schools, they are almost invisible. After death the fish loses much of its transparency, becoming milky white in color.

Blending in

Reef stonefish

This seabed resident has perhaps the best camouflage of any marine fish, enabling it to be an expert at ambushing prey. Its squat shape and knobby skin help it merge into its surroundings as it lies in wait for prey. To enhance its disguise, the reef stonefish remains motionless for hours or days at a time. Small tufts of seaweed may grow on its skin, and sediment settles on its back. A row of 12–14 venomous spines on the back of this fish gives it a defense of last resort against its own predators.

Synanceia verrucosa

- ⬌ Up to 16 in (40 cm)
- ◑ Tropical waters of Red Sea, Indian Ocean, and western Pacific.
- ▭ Stout, squat fish with very large head, upward-facing mouth, venomous spiny fins, and warty skin.

SIMILAR SPECIES
Closely related to stonefish, scorpionfish have a less deadly but nevertheless painful sting. If their camouflage fails, some species display the brightly colored inner side of their pectoral fins.

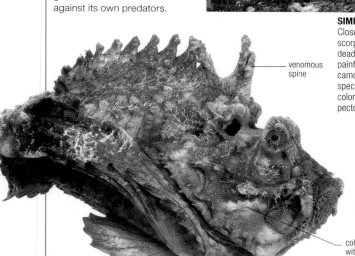

venomous spine

color of warty skin varies with background

LIVING ROCK
Due to its thickset head and rough, mottled skin the reef stonefish looks more like a rock on the seabed than a live fish.

Spine mimic

Razorfish

This relative of seahorses and pipefish is hidden from predators by a combination of its body shape and swimming style. It swims in synchronized groups in a vertical position, the fish seeming to glide sideways through the water. Each fish is enclosed in transparent bony plates that form a sharp ridge along the belly. Since the fish cannot flex their bodies, they swim using precise fin movements. This behavior helps disguise the fact that they are edible fish, especially when they group tightly together. A favorite hiding place is among the long spines of sea urchins, where they hang vertically. Here, the dark stripe along their body helps foster the illusion. Their prickly urchin shelter also helps to deter predators. Other hiding places include the branches of corals and sea whips.

FACING THE SEABED
A compact group of razorfish hovers over the seafloor. The fish swim head-down while searching for minute planktonic crustaceans with their long, tubular snouts.

Aeoliscus strigatus

- ⬌ Up to 6 in (15 cm)
- ◑ Reefs in tropical Indian Ocean and western Pacific.
- ▭ Highly elongated, laterally flattened fish with long black stripe along side of body.

Disappearing act
Pygmy seahorse

Together with stonefishes (see facing page), pygmy seahorses are serious contenders for best-camouflaged fishes in the ocean. These minuscule fish spend most of their life clinging onto the stems of *Muricella* sea fans with their prehensile (gripping) tail. A single large seafan is home to many seahorse pairs, and the fish have no need to leave their home at all. It therefore makes sense for them to be effectively invisible to the outside world. The fishes' blunt snouts and tubercles

CORAL LOOK-ALIKE
This pygmy seahorse was spotted by a sharp-eyed photographer off Mabul Island, East Sabah, Malaysia. The species also occurs in another color form, which is yellow with orange tubercles.

mimic the closed feeding polyps of the seafan and their bodies match the hosts' stem. In fact, the camouflage is so good that this species was discovered only after divers had collected a seafan and placed it in a tank to study. The seahorses have little need to move because they have tubular mouths for sucking up minute planktonic animals—the same food being caught by the polyps of their seafan host.

Hippocampus bargibanti
- 1 in (2.5 cm)
- Tropical waters of southwest Pacific.
- Long, rigid body protected by bony plates; angled head, tubular mouth, and prehensile tail.

SIMILAR SPECIES
An Australian relative of seahorses, the leafy seadragon scarcely looks like a fish. Its slow movements and loose, elaborate body tassels have evolved to mimic seaweeds and sea grasses.

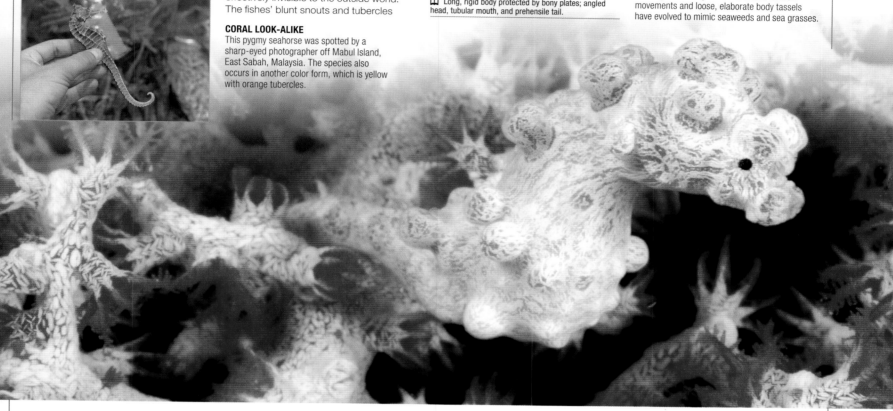

Hidden head
Longnose butterflyfish

Colorful butterflyfishes are perhaps the most obvious residents of coral reefs and attract the attention of predators, but their coloration also has the ability to confuse attackers. Many species, such as the longnose butterflyfish, have a patch of dark pigment hiding their real eye and a contrasting false eye-spot near their tail end. A predator, such as a grouper or shark, thinks that the tail is the head and attacks the wrong end, allowing the fish to dart away in the opposite direction.

Forcipiger flavissimus
- Up to 8½ in (22 cm)
- Coral reefs in Indo-Pacific.
- Brilliant yellow disk-shaped fish with long snout, small mouth, and dark eye-spot near tail.

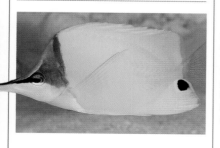

Toning down
Flounder

Flounder live out in the open on sand, mud, and gravel seabeds, where camouflage is essential to their survival. They half-bury themselves in the sediment to disguise their shape, and can lighten or darken their brownish skin color according to the type of surface on which they are lying. Their bright orange spots are a constant feature, but if the fish move into

an area of the seabed with many pale shell fragments, for example, they can fade their spots to a much paler yellow.

Related species of flatfishes that range over a wide variety of sediments have developed this ability further. In the laboratory, Mediterranean flounders can make a good attempt to match the

IMITATION SPINE
This partially buried flounder is well camouflaged but is also holding its pectoral fin vertically in the hope that, if spotted, it will be mistaken for the venomous spiny dorsal fin of a weever fish.

checkered squares or spots of an artificial background. Their color changes are, however, limited to the colors of their natural environment. Young flatfishes slowly develop chromatophores (pigment cells) in their skin after settling on the seabed, but only in the skin of the side facing upward. The result is that only the upper side of these fishes is colored.

BICOLORED
Pigmentation is restricted to the upper side of the flounder. Its underside is plain white and seldom, if ever, revealed.

Pleuronectes platessa
- Up to 3¼ ft (1 m)
- On sediment in northeast Atlantic Ocean, Arctic Ocean, Mediterranean, and Black Sea.
- Oval-shaped, right-eyed flatfish with long fins along both edges of body; upper side brown with orange spots.

Red for danger
Red salamander

The woodland habitat of this salamander is shared by birds of prey, raccoons, and skunks, all of which might be expected to prey on it. However, the salamander is similar in color to the young stage of the eastern newt, which is protected from predators by distasteful skin secretions. Any animal that has learned to leave eastern newts alone is likely to avoid eating red salamanders too.

Pseudotriton ruber
- 4–7 in (10–18 cm)
- Wooded areas near clean, cool streams in the eastern US.
- Stout, medium-sized red salamander with irregular black spots and blotches.

TOXIC MIMIC
The harmless red salamander (left) is a mimic of the juvenile eastern newt (below), which is protected by toxic skin secretions.

Hard to spot
Borneo horned frog

During the day, the Borneo horned frog stays motionless on the rain forest floor and relies on its camouflage to avoid detection. The "horns" and sharp ridges on its body break up its outline and look like the edges of leaves. The frog keeps still in the face of danger, only leaping away at the last second if spotted.

Rain forests are home to many other species of frog, most of which, like the Borneo horned frog, rest during the day and are protected by skin colors that closely match their habitat. Some frogs can alter their color to match their background. The main exceptions are poison frogs (see p.285), which have toxic skin and brilliant warning colors instead of camouflage.

GRAY TREE FROG
A resident of forests in the eastern US, the gray tree frog has a mottled coloring that blends well against lichen-covered bark.

DARWIN'S FROG
This frog has changed color to match its leaf perch. The froglet in the foreground has not yet developed this ability.

SOLOMON ISLAND LEAF FROG
This wide-mouthed frog lives in rain forests on the Solomon Islands and in New Guinea. It changes color between shades of yellow and brown.

BORNEO HORNED FROG
Thick creases on this frog's body mimic leaf edges, and the "horns" on its head cover its large eyes from above and behind. The eyes reflect light so they can easily give the frog's position away.

Megophrys nasuta
- Up to 4½ in (12 cm)
- Rain forest floors in Malay Peninsula, Borneo, and Sumatra.
- Brown frog with hornlike projections over the eyes and a long, pointed nose.

Deceptively clear
Glass frogs

The basic coloration of a glass frog is pale green, but because its skin is semitransparent, the color of the leaf on which it is sitting shows through, making it almost invisible. In the most transparent glass frog species, the internal organs can be seen as a dark blotch. The eyes are also visible, but since the frog's outline is so faint, these could be mistaken by a predator for marks on the leaf. Glass frogs are common in South America's humid forests, particularly montane cloud forests. They lay their eggs on leaves overhanging streams, and when the tadpoles hatch they drop into the water below to continue their development.

LEAFY MATCH
This glass frog has taken on the color of the leaf. Its eyes and internal organs can clearly be seen.

Hyalinobatrachium species
- ¾–1¼ in (2–3 cm)
- Trees in Central and South American forests.
- Small green frogs, similar to tree frogs but with eyes pointing forward and small finger pads.

Shielding the eyes
Eyelash viper

Often it is the eyes of an animal that reveal it to a predator. The eyelash viper has evolved modified scales above its eyes to avoid this problem. These scales look a lot like large eyelashes and are thought to break up the outline of the eyes so that a potential predator will not be able to tell which end of the snake is which. Since the viper is venomous, this is likely to be an efficient deterrent in most cases. The eyelash viper is a relatively small snake that occurs in a wide range of colors, from orange and red through to mossy green and mottled combinations of brown, green, and gray. It lives in trees, where its prehensile (gripping) tail helps it hold onto branches. An ambush predator, the viper is active at night and hunts small birds, rodents, tree frogs, and lizards, which it locates using a pair of heat-sensitive pits on its head.

Bothriechis schlegelii
- Up to 30 in (75 cm); usually much less
- Rain forest in Central and northern South America.
- Wide head with heat-sensitive pits on each side, "eyelashes," and vertical pupils.

MOTTLED FORM
This eyelash viper from Costa Rica is beautifully camouflaged in the dappled light of the forest.

modified, hornlike scales protrude over each eye

ORANGE FORM
The golden color form of the eyelash viper, known as the orapel, is relatively easy to spot. It is uncommon in the wild but a popular snake in captivity.

Bark blending
Mossy leaf-tailed gecko

Geckos are well known for their ability to cling to vertical surfaces and even hang upside down, but the mossy leaf-tailed gecko is a camouflage expert as well. It lives in the rain forests of eastern Madagascar, and spends the day resting head-down on tree trunks, venturing out in search of insect prey under the cover of darkness. Its camouflage, which mimics tree bark perfectly, is in subtle shades of gray and greenish brown.

The texture of this gecko's skin is the secret of its disappearing trick. The skin is covered with small knobs, fissures, and flaps that help break up the animal's outline. Even the surface of its eye, complete with a faint, indistinct pupil, resembles bark. The gecko also has an extra fold of loose skin around its head, body, and legs that forms a frilly "curtain." When threatened, the gecko flattens itself against a branch or tree trunk so that this skin splays out against the bark, thereby removing the telltale dark shadow that would otherwise catch a predator's attention.

KEEPING STILL
Having pressed itself tightly against a tree trunk, this gecko will not flinch unless prodded or grasped.

Uroplatus sikorae
- Up to 12 in (30 cm)
- Forest trees in eastern Madagascar.
- Large gecko with loose, folded skin, a wide, flat tail, and mottled, barklike coloration.

SIMILAR SPECIES
The flat tail for which leaf-tailed geckos are named is obvious in this image of a giant leaf-tailed gecko. The lizard's gaping mouth and erect tail are a response to being touched and are its final attempt to intimidate a potential predator.

WHITE OUT
The Arctic fox's thick white winter coat makes it almost invisible among the snow and ice of its northern home. Even its dark nose and eyes seem to match the scattered rocks. This disguise helps the fox when hunting and protects it from predators such as wolves and polar bears. In spring, as the snow melts, the fox will grow a lighter coat of gray or brown to match its changed surroundings.

FALL COLORS
Willow ptarmigans, such as this male photographed in Alaska in fall, blend in perfectly with tundra vegetation. Male willow ptarmigans are unique among the grouse family because they help with parental duties and defend their young.

Lagopus lagopus
- 15½–17 in (40–43 cm)
- Tundra, moorland, and open woodland with dwarf willow scrub in Alaska, Canada, northern Europe, and northern Asia.
- Stocky, chickenlike gamebird with feathered legs, feet, and toes; variable amount of white in plumage according to season.

WINTER COLORS
Several willow ptarmigans in winter plumage hunt for willow twigs and buds in the thick snow of the Canadian Arctic. During the winter, the birds form small flocks and favor sheltered locations such as thickets and lee slopes.

Seasonal plumage
Willow ptarmigan

Like many gamebirds, the willow ptarmigan or willow grouse lives and nests on the ground in open habitats, so camouflage is essential for its survival as it wanders in search of buds and insects. The feathers on its upperparts are barred with chestnut, black, and white, giving it a speckled appearance well matched to the willow scrub and moors that are its preferred home. Most willow ptarmigans stay in the same range all year, and therefore have to contend with deep snow for several months in winter. In their mottled brownish summer plumage, the birds would be very conspicuous against the blanket of white snow so, as winter approaches, they gradually molt into a pure white plumage. The populations in the British Isles, where the bird is known as the red grouse, do not change their plumage in this way because this far south the winters are milder and snow is less common.

CASE STUDY
LIGHT AND HORMONE LEVELS

The main factor controlling color change in the willow ptarmigan is day length, not temperature. To test this, captive birds were exposed to artificially long springlike days but kept at cold winter temperatures; they began molting into their colored plumage. An increase in daylight hours stimulates production of hormones that control molting. The white plumage develops when the hormone levels are at their lowest.

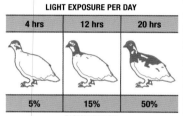

LIGHT EXPOSURE PER DAY

4 hrs	12 hrs	20 hrs
5%	15%	50%

PIGMENTATION

Charadrius semipalmatus
- 6–7½ in (15–19 cm)
- Breeds on stony beaches and flats in Canada and Alaska; winter range extends from US to South America.
- Small gray-brown wading bird with a white belly, black neck band, and short orange bill.

open wing is flapped while the other drags limply on the ground

DISTRACTION DISPLAY
Humans walking too close to a plover's nesting areas on pebbly beaches are often treated to its broken-wing display. The "injured" bird makes itself as obvious as possible, while its mate stays out of sight nearby.

Feigning injury
Semipalmated plover

Many ground-nesting birds, including several members of the plover family, use a distraction display to draw predators away from their eggs. This behavior is well known in the American semipalmated plover. During the nesting season, if a predator such as a fox comes dangerously close to the hidden nest of a pair of these plovers, the parent bird sitting on the eggs crouches down and stays perfectly still, while its mate moves away from the area and feigns a broken wing. This bird acts as a lure by walking away with one wing drooping and the other flapping furiously. The predator, sensing that the bird is in distress and would make an easy kill, starts to follow it. When the predator has been led far enough from the nest, the plover suddenly picks itself up and flies off, confusing the would-be attacker, which is left empty-handed.

SIMILAR SPECIES
All plovers nest on the ground. Their eggs, such as these belonging to the double banded plover of New Zealand, are extremely well camouflaged.

Ground cover
Nightjar

Camouflage is extremely important to nightjars, which are nocturnal birds that spend the daylight hours crouched on the ground, where they are vulnerable to predators. During the day, they rest on leaf and bark litter or among low vegetation. Their variegated feathers are finely barred and streaked with white, chestnut, black, and gray, enabling them to melt into the background, and the birds close their large eyes to slits to avoid giving themselves away. Nesting nightjars sit tight on their eggs on the bare ground, but if they are approached too closely will run and flutter noisily away at the last moment to draw attention from the eggs. Nightjars fly in search of moths and other insects at dusk and dawn, so they are scarcely more visible than during the day. Their silent, ghostlike flight, occasionally interrupted by a strange call similar to that of a cricket, is the basis for many folk stories and beliefs.

Caprimulgus europaeus
- About 11 in (28 cm)
- Breeds in meadow, scrub, and open woodland in northern and central Europe; winters in Africa.
- Small, hawklike bird with large eyes, a short, wide bill, short legs, and bark-colored plumage.

IMITATING BARK
Settled on its nest beside a rotting branch, this nightjar is almost invisible, although it has opened its dark eyes as the photographer approaches.

Branch impostor
Common potoo

During the day, the common potoo perches upright on a broken branch or tree stump, wings clasped firmly to its side, head held up, and its bright orange eyes shut. In this position, helped by its ability to stay statue-still, the bird looks just like an extension of the tree on which it is resting. Its subdued grayish brown plumage, speckled with shades of black and tan, helps the illusion. At night the potoo becomes active and may choose another perch from

which to dart out and catch large flying insects in its wide, net-shaped mouth. The common potoo also uses tree stumps for nesting, and lays its single egg in a hollow in the wood where it can be safely incubated by both parents.

WOOD PERCH
A common potoo clings motionless to its daytime roost in the cerrado (savanna woodland) of northeast Brazil. It is able to hold the stance for hours at a stretch.

Nyctibius griseus
- 13–15 in (33–38 cm)
- Tropical forest and grassland in Central and South America.
- Long, thin-bodied bird with a very large mouth, curved bill, large eyes, a long tail, and mottled brownish plumage.

Dappled disguise
Fallow deer

Female fallow deer give birth in woodland among dense undergrowth such as bracken. The single fawn (below) is left alone while the mother grazes some distance off so as not to attract predators to her baby. The fawn instinctively curls up in the thick vegetation, where its speckled coat provides good camouflage in dappled sunlight. So strong is this instinct that a young fawn will not move if approached. Adult fallow deer also have a spotted coat in summer, which helps conceal them as they wander through forest glades. However, they are less dependent on camouflage because they can run quickly.

Dama dama
- 4½–6¼ ft (1.4–1.9 m)
- Woodland and farmland in Europe; introduced to North America and Australasia.
- Medium-sized deer with a long black tail fringed with white and a white-spotted coat; breeding male has multi-tipped antlers.

Green cloak
Brown-throated three-toed sloth

A sloth spends virtually its entire life in tall rain-forest trees and moves through the forest canopy extremely slowly, spending up to 20 hours a day hanging upside down or propped in the fork of a branch. Most tree-living mammals are acrobatic climbers that can escape predators quickly. By contrast, the sloth's slow metabolism and sluggish lifestyle mean it cannot leap away to safety, and so it relies on being invisible instead. It has coarse, grayish brown fur that blends in with surrounding foliage, and

its slow, deliberate movements usually go unnoticed. During the rainy season, the sloth is even harder to spot because the high humidity causes green algae to spread across its back. If attacked, the sloth adopts an upright posture to lash out fiercely with its sharp claws.

ALGAE COAT
The green tinge to this sloth's fur is caused by a growth of algae, which do no harm to the animal and enhance its camouflage.

Bradypus variegatus
- 16½–31 in (42–80 cm)
- Lowland rain forest in Central and South America.
- Fat-bellied mammal with a shaggy coat and very long limbs ending in three toes with long curved claws.
- » 146

Ice white
Beluga

Adult belugas are completely white except for a dark edge along the tail and flukes (tail fins). This camouflage gives the whales reasonable protection against their main predators—orcas and polar bears—when traveling along the edge of pack ice and among shifting ice. However, when the pack ice is continuous, they must rely on surfacing at breathing holes. Here, despite their camouflage, they may be easy prey for polar bears in particular, which swipe out with their claws until the whales are too weak to dive again. Young belugas are dark gray or bluish gray, gradually becoming lighter as they grow.

REFLECTED LIGHT
Dancing light reflections help this beluga to blend in with the sea ice behind it. The species is a slow swimmer compared to other whales, making cryptic coloration a useful defense underwater.

BREATHING PARTY
Three belugas breathe at a hole in the ice. Surfacing is risky because predatory polar bears wait by these holes and the noisy expulsion of air might give the belugas away.

Delphinapterus leucas
- 13–16½ ft (4–5 m)
- Polar seas off the coast of Arctic Russia, Alaska, Canada, and Greenland.
- Medium-sized whale with a stout white body, bulging forehead, and no dorsal fin.

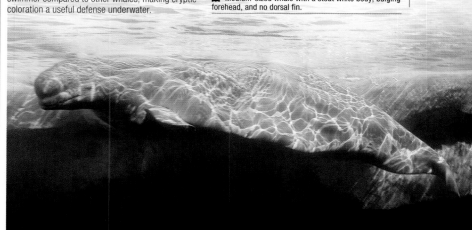

Group defense

Living in a group is advantageous for animals with little individual defense against predators in the open. Migrating birds, fishes, mammals, and some invertebrates frequently travel in large groups for protection. Animals also live in groups for reasons other than defense, such as reproduction, warmth, and foraging efficiently.

Safety in numbers

In many instances of group defense each individual is concerned only with its own survival. By living and traveling in a large group, an otherwise defenseless small migrating bird, fish, or wildebeest, reduces its chances of being attacked by predators. The bigger the group, the less risk a particular individual faces of being picked out by a predator. For highly intelligent social animals, such as dolphins and whales, living in an extended family provides active protection. Group members protect young or sick family members from shark attacks by surrounding them, before leaping and slapping the water to intimidate their tormentor. If the size of their group is not sufficient for protection, they may summon nearby dolphin groups using special calls. In these instances, individuals are protecting their family group, not just themselves as individuals.

ROCKHOPPER GROUP
Rockhopper penguins in the Falkland Islands run and dive into the sea en masse to avoid being picked off by hunting leopard seals.

INDIVIDUAL SURVIVAL
Wildebeests and zebras crossing a river during their annual migration pack close together, jostling for space at the center. Those on the edges of the group are more likely to be attacked by crocodiles or disturbed hippopotamuses.

SILVERY RETREAT
A school of silversides divides as a predator (a tarpon) tries to single out individuals. The split school may re-form behind the predator. Schools under attack often crowd closer together since individuals try to remain at the center.

ALARM CALL
Group-living pikas use loud calls to alert others in their colony to danger, before scurrying to the safety of their burrows.

Group communication

Flying, swimming, or running in huge groups requires instant responses between the individuals if the movement is to be coordinated and collisions avoided. Various senses are employed to achieve this. Group coordination is well developed in fishes, which use both vision and the lateral-line system (which detects vibrations) to maintain a nearest-neighbor distance of around 1–1.5 body lengths. This distance is standard throughout the school. Only those on the periphery can see a predator approach. As these fish change direction and speed, their neighbors detect this and follow suit, so the whole school reacts quickly and almost in unison. Sound is widely used among social animals, especially mammals, to warn others in their group of approaching danger.

Protective mound

Spiny spider crab

Like all crustaceans, spiny spider crabs must molt their hard outer shell at regular intervals to enable growth, and after molting they are soft and vulnerable to predators. During this dangerous time, these crabs gather together for protection, forming mounds on the sea floor. In summer, the crabs migrate to shallow water to breed, walking many miles from their deep-water winter feeding grounds. They form heaps on the seabed that contain up to 50,000 individuals. The only time a male can mate with a female is immediately after she has molted, before her new shell hardens. The vulnerable molting females are in the middle, surrounded by the hard-shelled males, which molt at different times.

TEMPORARY ARMOR
Sharp spines on this spider crab's shell make it a difficult mouthful for most predators much of the time, but the crab is briefly vulnerable to attack when molting.

Maja squinado

- Up to 8 in (20 cm); claws up to 17½ in (45 cm)
- Coastal waters from the UK south to Mediterranean and Cape Verde Islands.
- Pear-shaped crab with knobby, spiny shell and long claws and legs.

Deadly heat ball

Asiatic honey bee

Japanese populations of this small honey bee have a very unusual way of dealing with one of their enemies: the Asian giant hornet (see p.213). This fearsome 2 in- (5 cm-) long aerial predator is fond of both honey and bee larvae and has huge jaws, so only a concerted mass defense by the honey bees has any chance of success. They swarm all over the hornet and vibrate their wings to generate heat, raising the temperature inside the ball to a lethal 111° F (44° C), which cooks the predatory hornet.

In the wild, Asiatic honey bees nest in holes and crevices in trees and logs, and between rocks. Himalayan hill farmers keep colonies of the bees for their honeycombs.

Apis cerana

- ¼–½ in (0.7–1.5 cm)
- Flower-rich habitats in south and Southeast Asia, from sea level to 11,500 ft (3,500 m).
- Small, dark bee with hairy body and narrow yellow stripes on the abdomen.

CHEMICAL ALARM SIGNAL
If a worker honey bee spots a giant hornet close to the nest it releases pheromones to alert the other bees. A number of them will probably be killed before the invader succumbs to their heat ball.

COOKED ALIVE
Somewhere beneath this pile of bees is a giant hornet fighting for its life. The bees can survive a higher temperature than the hornet, so are able to cook it to death. They must kill the predator before it has time to release a pheromone to attract reinforcements from the hornet nest.

CASE STUDY

THERMAL EXECUTION

These photographs taken with a thermal imaging camera show how the temperature inside a scrum of honey bees rises as more and more bees join in and start to vibrate their flight muscles in their wings. High-temperature areas appear white, yellow, or red; cooler zones are blue, green, or purple. In the first two pictures, the central core temperature is rising rapidly to a peak of 104–111° F (40–44° C). In the third picture, the temperature has started to fall again, and in the fourth the ball has broken up and the bees are dispersing.

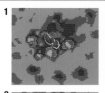

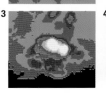
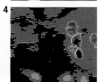

TEMPERATURE TOLERANCES
The body temperature of Asiatic honey bees, like most other invertebrates, is closely linked to air temperature. However, this species is adapted to survive extremes of weather, and can survive a maximum heat of 118–122° F, several degrees above that needed to kill a giant hornet.

105–111° F	97–98° F
104–105° F	95–97° F
102–104° F	93–95° F
100–102° F	91–93° F
98–100° F	89–91° F

Acid spray

Wood ant

These ants protect their nest from predators by swarming to its surface to squirt a jet of formic acid from their anal glands. A single ant's acid spray is unpleasant enough, but many ants firing together is a formidable defense. If a piece of fabric is dropped on top of the nest, it will soon be damp with spray and smell strongly of formic acid. Such a fierce attack is usually enough to deter a predator. Other glands in the ants' abdomens release alarm pheromones, summoning other workers. If this coordinated onslaught still does not deter a predator, the ants can also bite. Each colony may contain up to 300,000 workers, which build a huge mound of pine needles, twigs, and leaves over an extensive system of underground tunnels and chambers. The mound protects the nest and helps to keep the temperature constant. At night, the nest entrances are sealed and guarded.

MASS SPRAY
By squirting their defensive acid together, the wood ants in this colony produce a toxic mist several inches above the nest.

Formica rufa

- Worker ¼ in (6 mm); queen and male ⅜ in (1 cm)
- Sunny areas of open woodland, parkland, and meadow in Europe, North Africa, and Asia.
- Large, reddish brown ant with black abdomen and long antennae.

ANATOMY

FORMIC ACID STORE

Inside a wood ant's abdomen is a poison gland lined with cells that synthesize a watery solution of formic acid. This is passed along a duct into a reservoir where it is stored until needed. The acid is strong—at a concentration of up to 60 percent—so the reservoir is protected by a special lining. The ant fires the acid from an opening near the tip of its abdomen, which it can aim at an enemy. Alarm pheromones are released to alert other workers.

opening at tip of abdomen

legs braced

Crowd confusion

Striped catfish

Divers exploring coral reefs in the Indo-Pacific region frequently encounter strange ball-shaped objects hanging suspended in the water. These are compact schools of juvenile striped catfish, each containing about 100 individuals or more. The young catfish pack together for protection during the day, and the unrecognizable form of their schools may detract potential predators. At night the catfish hunt for crustaceans, mollusks, and worms on the seabed, using the four pairs of sensitive barbels around their mouth to locate prey hidden in the sand. They remain in a loose group, with those at the bottom of the school feeding while those at the top guard the school and wait their turn. Adult striped catfish live on their own or in small groups of up to about 20 fish, but are well protected by highly venomous spines located just in front of the first dorsal fin and in each of the pectoral fins. During the day, they often hide in crevices or under ledges on the reef.

Plotosus lineatus

◧ Up to 12½ in (32 cm)

⊚ Coastal reefs in Indian Ocean and western Pacific.

▥ Long, eel-like fish with mouth barbels, elongate fins along back and underside, and stripes along body.

DEFENSIVE BALL
A dense, writhing ball of striped catfish moves like a single large organism, making it difficult for would-be attackers to isolate individuals. The array of body stripes adds to the confusion.

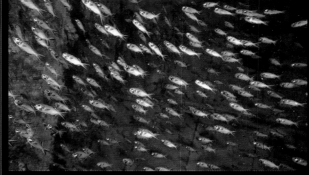

DAYTIME RETREAT
Flashlight fish conceal themselves by day (this school is hiding inside a shipwreck). At night they swim out into the open to feed, using bioluminescence to confuse their enemies.

Dazzling escape

Splitfin flashlight fish

Schools of these small fish use bewildering displays of pulsing light to outwit predatory fishes that might be tempted to eat them. The splitfin flashlight fish hide in caves and under overhangs of coral during the day, emerging at night to feed. Each fish has a glowing, light-producing organ under its eye, which it switches on and off as it swims along hunting for small floating zooplankton. The constantly blinking lights produced by a school confuse predators, which cannot pick out individuals from the crowd, and by turning all their lights off and changing direction, the fish can escape. On bright moonlit nights, this defense is less successful, so the flashlight fishes may not emerge from their hiding places.

Anomalops katoptron

◧ About 14 in (35 cm)

⊚ In tropical Indo-Pacific near caves and along steep outer walls of coral reefs, large form in deep water.

▥ Small, blunt-headed fish with a light-emitting organ under its large eye.

ANATOMY
BIOLUMINESCENCE

A flashlight fish employs bacterial symbionts to produce light. Its light-producing organs contain bioluminescent bacteria—that is, bacteria that glow continuously. They make this bluish light by oxidizing a compound called luciferin. The fish covers each organ with a flap of skin to control the flash frequency, at up to 50 flashes a minute.

On and off
These photographs of a small flashlight fish show it with its light-emitting organ covered (left) and uncovered (right).

Toxic taste

Western toad

Unlike most frog tadpoles, the tadpoles of this American toad have toxic skin. If an aquatic predator such as a fish or heron attacks them, it is unlikely to repeat the experience. Since the tadpoles are distasteful, it is advantageous for them to make themselves obvious to would-be attackers, rather than hide among water vegetation where they might be attacked by accident. The tadpoles achieve this by gathering in densely packed schools in the shallows of their pond or lake, where their massed black bodies stand out against the pale sand or mud bottom.

Bufo boreas

◧ 2¼–5 in (6–13 cm)

⊚ Throughout the western US. Tadpole in still, shallow fresh water; adult on land in burrows.

▥ Tadpole has jet-black body; adult has warty body with pale stripe down back.

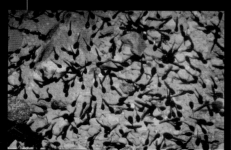

TADPOLE SOUP
Highly visible schools of toad tadpoles act as a warning to predators, which know from experience that the tadpoles are foul tasting.

Mob mentality

Carrion crow

Carrion crows frequently harrass birds of prey and other potential predators such as cats, snakes, foxes, and even humans. This behavior, known as mobbing, is a form of calculated preemptive attack in which several crows gang up to chase away the intruder. When a crow spots a bird of prey, it flies up and swoops down on it from above and behind, while making loud alarm calls to attract other crows. Soon the raptor finds itself being bullied by a crowd of hostile birds, some of which may even strike it with their bill or feet. This is often too much for the victim, which flies away to find somewhere quieter to hunt.

Group mobbing is a safe and effective method of removing a threat from an area, especially if there are vulnerable nestlings nearby. Young crows appear to learn, or refine, the mobbing habit by watching their parents. Many species of passerines (perching birds) also use mobbing to defend themselves—harrassing a roosting owl at its daytime perch, for example.

MOBBING RESPONSE
Although this pair of crows is under no threat from the Eurasian buzzard, which preys on rabbits and rodents, the crows' powerful urge to mob large predators is indiscriminate. It is triggered by the typical silhouette and flight style of birds of prey, rather than by identification of a particular species.

Corvus corone

◧ 18½–20½ in (47–52 cm)

⊚ Open country and urban areas; Europe and Asia.

▥ Large, all-black bird with a stout, curved bill and long primary feathers that resemble fingers in flight.

» 478

Mass distraction
Common starling

Having many eyes means that predators are quickly spotted, which is why common or European starlings are usually found in flocks, especially in winter. These highly gregarious birds feed together in fields, parks, and other areas of open ground, where they probe the earth for prey, such as spiders. Each bird in the flock can feed for longer and be less vigilant than when foraging on its own. At dusk, the flock streams back to a roosting site, usually in the woods or reed bed or on a building. Flocks may have a number of favorite roosts within an area. Often several different feeding flocks converge on the roost and merge into a single flock that may contain several hundred thousand birds, though such large flocks are increasingly rare. As the birds circle around the area, they form amazing shapes in the darkening sky. Flying in a flock protects the starlings from aerial hunters such as falcons and hawks, which cannot pick out an individual to strike and may be confused by the ever-changing shape of the flock. As the predator approaches, the flock may split, which confuses the predator further. The aerial gyrations of a starling flock coming into roost may last for half an hour or more. Once at the roost, the birds can huddle together for warmth. As dawn approaches, the starlings leave the roost in waves, forming new feeding flocks that move off to begin the day's foraging.

CASE STUDY
FLOCKING TECHNIQUES

When a lone hunter such as a falcon flies toward a starling flock, the birds pack together tightly, sometimes forming a ball. This makes it hard for the predator to pick out a particular bird, and also more dangerous for it to attack, because it risks injury by diving through the massed birds. How the starlings achieve such synchrony is not fully understood, but each bird must react to what its neighbours in the flock are doing, then adjust its speed and course accordingly. The effect of many such adjustments is that the flock moves as one. Falling darkness may increase the desire of each bird to head for the roost site, and to spot known landmarks, so that the flock eventually finds its way to the roost.

PREDATOR EVASION
This sequence of photographs shows how a flock of starlings responds to an attack by a peregrine falcon. When the falcon approaches, the flock bunches together, then splits into smaller flocks that move in different directions. This gives the falcon little time to mount an effective strike.

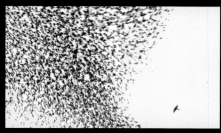

Sturnus vulgaris
- 7½–8½ in (19–22 cm)
- Wide variety of habitats throughout Europe, especially farmland and urban areas; introduced to North America, South Africa, Australia, and New Zealand.
- Small blackish bird with glossy, iridescent plumage that is speckled and spotted with white in winter.

TWILIGHT DISPLAY
As they fly in to roost, wave after wave of common starlings create complex, rapidly changing patterns in the evening sky. The flock protects individuals from predators. Starlings are social birds, and often coexist with humans in urban areas.

PROTECTING EACH OTHER
A school of round scad, or cigarfish, swirls around
a goliath grouper off the coast of Florida, US.
By surrounding the larger fish when it is swimming,
the round scad gain protection from predators,
such as trevally. Although the goliath grouper can
grow to 8¼ ft (2.5 m) long, it also benefits from
the cover provided by its smaller companions.

SOLAR GAIN
To get a better view sentries stand bolt upright, using their long tail to prop them up. In the early morning and evening, they prefer to face the sun, orienting their darker chest skin to absorb heat. A mask of black fur around their eyes cuts down glare so that they can look into the sun.

Sentry duty

Meerkat

Meerkats are second to none in their ability to use group living as a collective defense against predators. Close-knit colonies of 20–40 individuals share a large system of burrows in which they sleep and raise young. Each morning as the adults emerge, sentries are posted on mounds or bushes to watch for danger. The sentries stand up on their long hind legs, using their tails for balance, and scan their surroundings intently. They bark a shrill warning if they spot anything suspicious.

Usually only the colony's matriarch, or dominant female, is allowed to give birth, yet she must continue to lead foraging expeditions, so the subordinate females in the group play the role of helpful "aunts." They babysit the new pups and the older juveniles from the matriarch's previous litter and guard the colony throughout the day. Meanwhile, all of the other adults go out to hunt for food. Each individual in the foraging party takes a turn to be the lookout. If the alarm is given and the burrow is too far away, the meerkats dash for temporary bolt holes or stand nervously scanning the skies until the coast is clear.

Fear of big objects in the sky is probably instinctive in young meerkats, because they scatter if an aircraft passes overhead. They are also taught essential survival skills by their elder siblings, such as how to deal with scorpions and other dangerous prey.

Suricata suricatta

- 10–14 in (25–35 cm)
- Dry sandy plains and scrub in southern Africa.
- Small, slender mongoose with a thin, tapering, black-tipped tail and black eye patches.

» 438

GROUP OFFENSIVE
Meerkat clans are highly territorial and will make concerted mock attacks on any rival clan members that stray into their territory, a behavior that is known as mobbing.

CLOSE TO HOME
With several sentries on guard, the other meerkats in this group can afford to indulge in grooming and play. They will all vanish underground within just a couple of seconds if one of the sentries sounds the alarm.

104°F The temperature a meerkat sentry may have to endure out in the open during its guard duty.

ANATOMY

POWERFUL CLAWS

A meerkat has strong feet and claws suited to its burrowing lifestyle, and can shift its own weight in sand in a few seconds. Each foot has four toes equipped with ¾ in- (2 cm) long, nonretractable, curved claws, which act like shovels. The claws are slightly longer on the front feet. Meerkats can also close their small ears when digging to keep out flying sand. One study found that individual meerkats may dig as many 400 holes during half a day's foraging.

CREATING A DUST CLOUD
Meerkats dig fast and furiously in search of buried invertebrates and may even disappear from sight during their frantic hunt for food. Throwing up a sand cloud is also a good way of distracting predators.

Warning signal

European rabbit

When a group of European rabbits grazes out in the open, several will remain sitting up to keep an eye out for dangerous predators, such as the red fox or Eurasian buzzard. The sentries often use anthills and hummocks as lookout stations. If they see a predator, they thump the ground with their powerful hind feet as a warning signal to the others.

Oryctolagus cuniculus

- 14–15½ in (35–40 cm)
- Farmland, grassland, and open woodland in Europe; introduced to Australia.
- Long ears, brown fur, and a fluffy white tail.
- » 338

UNINTERRUPTED VIEW
These rabbits have grazed the area close to their warren to a low turf. This makes it easier to spot approaching predators.

Explosive exit

Mexican free-tailed bat

At nightfall millions of these bats stream out of their daytime roosts in Texas, US, and Mexico in one of the world's great natural spectacles. The largest roosts in caves contain up to 20 million bats, but even small colonies are home to thousands of individuals. From a distance, the massed bats resemble a smoke trail across the sky. The purpose of this dramatic, coordinated exit is to make it difficult for predators such as owls to pick off individual bats. Inside their roost, the bats are relatively safe from danger, although snakes sometimes pick off young and sick animals. Living in such enormous colonies has one disadvantage: the bats must forage farther from their roost to find enough insects for all of them to eat.

> HUMAN IMPACT
> ## PERSECUTION

Colonies of free-tailed bats are vulnerable to human interference. These bats can carry rabies, and, although the threat is small, numerous colonies have been destroyed as a result. Free-tails are sometimes demonized as "vampires," but in fact they eat only insects. The species is beneficial because it controls agricultural pests such as the cotton bollworm moth; a single colony of 20 million bats can consume 275 tons of insects every night.

DUSK EXODUS
On summer evenings, millions of free-tailed bats pour out of this cave in Texas. The swirling torrent of bats can take over an hour to pass and the sheer number of animals involved is sufficient to swamp potential predators. The entire Texan breeding population migrates to Mexico for the winter.

Tadarida brasiliensis

- About 3½ in (9 cm)
- Caves of the western and southern US, Mexico, Central America, Chile, and Argentina.
- Medium-sized bat with brown fur, large black ears, and a puckered nose.
- » 406

Gang warfare

Dwarf mongoose

Mongooses are renowned for killing and eating snakes, but it is only large, solitary species, such as the Indian mongoose, that do this. Dwarf mongooses are among the smallest members of the mongoose family and never attack snakes alone. What they lack in size they make up for in numbers, however. These mongooses live in groups of 12–15 family members led by a dominant female, and if a snake strays into their territory is repelled by a concerted group effort. A few mongooses hold the snake's attention with carefully timed rushes, staying just out of striking range, while the others try to edge into a position where one of them is able to dart in and nip the snake behind its head. The mongooses have sharp teeth, so can deliver a fatal bite.

Each dwarf mongoose group contains a single breeding pair and young of varying ages. The mongooses form a close-knit extended family unit, hunting together and taking turns to babysit their younger relatives. They roam through a territory that they defend from neighboring groups.

Helogale parvula

- 8–12 in (20–30 cm)
- Dry savanna, scrub, and semi-desert in central and southern Africa; often makes dens in termite mounds.
- Small, dark, slim-bodied mammal with a pointed muzzle, short legs, and a long, tapering tail.
- » 446

MASS ATTACK
Four dwarf mongooses surround an African puff adder, with their muzzles pointing to behavior the threat. If the dominant female has young nearby and the snake does not retreat, they will kill it to protect the group. Although venomous, the puff adder does not stand a chance against a coordinated group attack.

Solid defense

Musk ox

Adult musk oxen can weigh up to half a ton, and their huge size means that they have few natural predators. Their young, however, are very vulnerable, especially when newborn. Young musk oxen are often taken by gray wolves, but if the herd spots a wolf pack soon enough it has a chance to deploy an effective defensive strategy. The adults quickly gather into a circle of tightly packed animals, all facing outward, with the young hidden away in the middle. The hunting wolves meet a wall of tough heads and horns, and large bull oxen will also charge out of the ring, swiping their horns at the attackers. The defense is only broken if the wolves manage to get the oxen on the run.

Ovibos moschatus

- About 8¼ ft (2.5 m)
- Treeless tundra from Alaska east through northern Canada to Greenland.
- Huge hoofed mammal with downturned horns and a heavy bony plate across the head.

Leaps and bounds

Thomson's gazelle

Not only are these gazelles impressive sprinters, they also run in a special way to communicate with the rest of their herd and confuse their pursuer. As the gazelles race along they perform sudden bounding high leaps, a behavior known as pronking or stotting. The leaps alert other gazelles to the danger and startle the predator, usually a cheetah or lioness, which finds it harder to follow its prey. Another possibility is that the gazelles leap to demonstrate their fitness, in the hope that their enemy will give up the chase.

Gazella thomsoni

- 28–35 in (70–90 cm)
- Dry, grassy plains of East Africa, mainly in Kenya and Tanzania.
- Small, graceful antelope with a thick, dark streak across the flank and a white belly; male has long, pointed horns marked with about 20 rings.

ESCAPE MOVEMENT
During their initial flight from a predator, these gazelles may sprint at up to 50 mph (80 kph). They can maintain a speed of 37 mph (60 kph) for around 15–20 minutes.

Teamwork
African buffalo

Due to their massive bulk African buffaloes make intimidating opponents and are quite capable of goring a lion to death. However, they are vulnerable to attack by a pride of lions hunting together. They are also at risk from crocodiles, since they need to drink at least once a day. By living in large herds, sometimes several hundred strong, the buffaloes greatly reduce their chances of being attacked. A herd will often run from its enemies initially, moving at a surprising pace for such large animals, but the

buffaloes soon bunch together and turn to face the predators, with their calves safely behind them. The lions' strategy is to force the herd onto the run again, and then to single out young or sick animals that lag behind. In order to catch a buffalo, the lions must leap onto its back to bring it down. Even then, the herd will respond to distressed bellows from the victim and large adults might come running to its aid.

The largest buffalo herds, comprising mainly females and their young, are able to roam open savanna, traveling constantly in search of fresh grazing. In contrast, the males form smaller "bachelor" herds and keep to safer terrain with plenty of trees

and scrub to provide cover. Older, mature males are frequently driven away from the female herds and must fend for themselves. They wander alone, only joining the females during the breeding season from March to May. The bulls rely on their enormous size to deter lions, but as they get older are likely to be brought down if attacked.

35 mph   The top speed reached by a buffalo bull weighing three-quarters of a ton during a headlong charge.

Syncerus caffer
⬌ 6½–11½ ft (2–3.5 m)

◉ Grassy plains and open woodland within reach of water, in Africa south of the Sahara; a smaller subspecies occurs in equatorial forest in West and Central Africa.

▥ Large, heavily built hoofed mammal with muscular shoulders and huge hanging horns curled up at the ends.

REPELLING AN ATTACK
>>01 Confronted by a group of lions, this buffalo herd has packed together to form a defensive blockade.   >>02 The buffaloes stand their ground, keeping their calves behind a bristling wall of horns and hooves as the lions maneuver to locate a point of weakness. >>03 One of the lions rushes in to break the buffaloes' formation, but is immediately chased and harried by the lead animals in the herd. Most encounters like this end in stalemate, although the lions may try again later.

UNITED FRONT
A lioness turns to run as a buffalo herd squares up to her. If provoked, large buffaloes can toss lions aside with their horns, inflicting slashing wounds, so the cats are usually forced to retreat.

>>01

>>02

>>03

SEX AND REPRODUCTION

CLASPED TOGETHER
A male dragonfly uses special pincers at the tip of his abdomen to clasp a female around the neck while he holds onto the stalk of a plant. She curves her abdomen forward to receive his sperm.

SEX AND REPRODUCTION

Reproduction is a fundamental feature of all living things. All mammals, including humans, use sexual reproduction, in which offspring are produced by the fusion of special cells from two parents. Across the animal kingdom, however, there are many other ways of reproducing.

Ways of reproducing

There is great diversity in animal reproduction. At one extreme is asexual reproduction, in which parents use methods such as budding, to produce offspring that are genetically identical to themselves. At the opposite extreme, true sexual reproduction involves two genetically different parents, a male and a female, producing offspring that are genetically distinct from one another, and from their parents. In between these extremes, there is a variety of reproductive methods that produce varying amounts of genetic diversity among offspring. For example, hermaphrodites function as both males and females. Some hermaphrodites mate with themselves, producing less genetically diverse offspring than those that mate with a partner.

SEA SLUGS
Sea slugs are hermaphrodites, capable of producing both eggs and sperm. They reproduce in pairs, each one fertilizing its eggs with sperm from its partner.

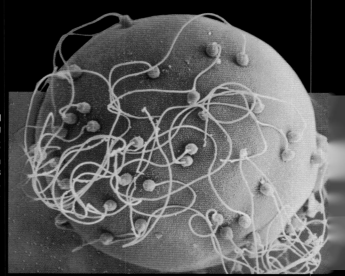

FERTILIZATION
Many sperm are seeking to enter this clam egg. In nearly all animals' eggs, a mechanism ensures that, as soon as one sperm has entered, another cannot do so.

Sexual reproduction

Sexual reproduction involves two essential features. First, special cells called gametes (eggs and sperm) are produced by a form of cell division called meiosis (see below), which results in each gamete being haploid—containing half the genetic complement of its parent. In meiosis, parental genes are "shuffled" so that each gamete contains a unique subset of parental genes. Second, each egg is fertilized by a sperm from a parent different from its mother, to form a zygote. The zygote is diploid, containing two alleles (copies) of each gene – one copy from its mother and one from its father. Eggs and sperm differ markedly in form and size; eggs tend to be large and immobile, containing the cellular material necessary to form the zygote, while sperm are much smaller, are very mobile, and are produced in much larger numbers.

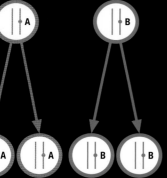
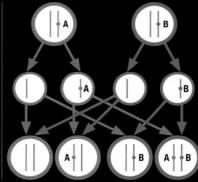

ASEXUAL   **SEXUAL**

ASEXUAL AND SEXUAL REPRODUCTION
Asexual reproduction produces offspring that are exact copies of their parents, carrying the same genes (A, B) as their parents. Sexual reproduction, involving gametes (see middle row) that each contain half the parent's genotype, produces genetically varied offspring carrying different combinations of their parents' genes.

MEIOSIS
Meiosis is the form of cell division by which gametes are made. Before parental cells divide, exchange of genetic material among chromosomes occurs, so each gamete has half of its parents' genes.

1 PREPARATION
Before meiosis starts to occur, chromosomes replicate in the cell nucleus to produce double chromosomes.

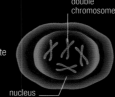

double chromosome

nucleus

4 TWO OFFSPRING
The separated cells each have one set of double chromosomes, of maternal and paternal pairs.

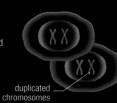

duplicated chromosomes

2 PAIRING
Chromosomes align in matching pairs and genetic material can now be exchanged between the pairs through crossing over.

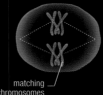

matching chromosomes

5 SECOND SEPARATION
As the cells separate again, the double chromosome splits, each half moving to one end of the dividing cell.

single chromosome

3 SEPARATION
The pairs of chromosomes separate, and a spindle pulls one of each pair to the ends of the cell as it splits.

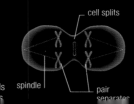

cell splits

spindle   pair separates

6 FOUR OFFSPRING
Four sex cells—with different genetic makeup from the parent cell and each other—are created.

nucleus

chromosome

REPRODUCTIVE DIVERSITY

PARTHENOGENESIS
This is a form of reproduction in which a female's eggs develop into offspring without being fertilized. In one form, eggs are produced by meiosis (see right), and develop into offspring that differ slightly from their mother, and one another.

SEQUENTIAL HERMAPHRODITISM
This involves animals that produce both eggs and sperm, but not at the same time. In protandrous hermaphrodites, sperm are produced when the animal is young, and eggs when it is older. In protogynous hermaphrodites, the reverse is true.

HERMAPHRODITISM
Animals that exhibit this behavior have male and female sex organs, and can produce eggs and sperm. Most do not fertilize their own eggs, but exchange sperm with a partner; exceptions include some parasites that are unlikely to meet a partner.

ASEXUAL AND SEXUAL COMBINATION
Some animals can reproduce asexually at certain times, and sexually at others. Typically, they reproduce asexually when their environment is stable, but switch to sexual reproduction when conditions deteriorate and become unpredictable.

Sexual evolution

Animals live in environments that are constantly changing, presenting each generation with fresh challenges. This means that, in order to maximize the chance that at least some of their young will survive, animals need to produce as many offspring as possible that differ both from themselves and from one another. Although genetic mutation can produce some variation in species that reproduce asexually, this is not enough in most circumstances and many animals need the capacity of sex to produce sufficient genetic diversity among their young.

Explaining reproductive diversity

The existence of diverse reproductive mechanisms is related to the fact that the environments in which animals live are variable, in both space and time. In a uniform or stable environment, animals that have survived to breed will thrive best if they reproduce themselves exactly, by asexual reproduction. In variable and unpredictable habitats, however, producing offspring that are genetically diverse, by sexual reproduction, increases the chances that some will survive.
Reproduction is like a lottery; asexual reproduction produces tickets that all have the same number, but, in sexual reproduction, each ticket has a different number.

SEX AND VIOLENCE
These two peaceful Caribbean cnemidophorus lizards (above) reproduce by parthenogenesis and exist only as females. Two male rival black grouse (right) fight for the possession of a small territory on which they can display to females.

The consequences of sex

A fundamental feature of sexual reproduction is that a very large number of tiny sperm compete to fertilize a limited number of large eggs. In many species, this is reflected in intense competition among males to mate with females. Males may compete violently, fighting one another, or they may compete to be attractive to females. The result is sexual dimorphism, in which males are commonly larger, and more brightly colored than females, or are equipped with weapons. In many animals, the female alone cares for the young, but there are a number of species in which the male also has a parental role, and a few where the male is the sole caregiver. In some species with male care, sex roles are reversed, and females compete for the opportunity to mate with males.

⊙ TEMPERATURE AND SEX

In many reptiles the sex of the offspring is influenced by the temperature at which the eggs develop. Turtle eggs incubated at low temperatures of less than about 84° F (30° C), are mostly male; eggs incubated at higher temperatures are mostly female (below, left). The reverse is true in lizards (below, right). In crocodilians, males develop from eggs incubated at intermediate temperatures of 73–90° F (23–32° C). Climate change could have serious consequences for these reptiles.

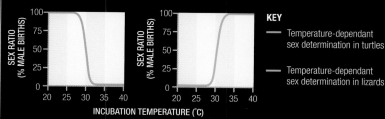

KEY
— Temperature-dependant sex determination in turtles
— Temperature-dependant sex determination in lizards

(y-axis, both graphs) SEX RATIO (% MALE BIRTHS) — 0, 25, 50, 75, 100
(x-axis, both graphs) 20 25 30 35 40
INCUBATION TEMPERATURE (°C)

Reproducing without a mate

There are a number of animals that reproduce without mating with another individual. In some species, all members are female and reproduce asexually through methods such as budding or division, while others are hermaphrodites and fertilize themselves.

Asexual reproduction

Asexual reproduction is common in plants, but it is relatively rare among animals. It involves the production of anatomic and genetic replicas—these offspring are called clones. Some animals, such as flatworms, can divide into two. Others, such as hydra (small freshwater predators), reproduce by budding—growing as a part of their mother's body, before detaching. Very few animals, however, rely solely on asexual reproduction. Cloning is only effective when conditions allow, but it does enable animals to build up very large populations in a short time. Most asexually reproducing animals switch to sexual reproduction when conditions are harsh or unpredictable.

ANEMONE BUDDING
Sea anemones grow from buds on their mother's body. Eventually, these buds detach and become independent.

TWO-HEADED WORM
Flatworms can reproduce by splitting in two, starting at the head. They separate, and form two new flatworms.

⦿ VIRGIN BIRTH

Some animals reproduce by a process called parthenogenesis, in which eggs develop without being fertilized by sperm. This tiny Komodo dragon was produced by a female who had not been kept with a male at Britain's Chester Zoo. This is the first time that parthenogenesis has been reported in this species, which is native to several islands in Indonesia. The capacity to reproduce in this way may have evolved to enable females to reproduce in isolation from males. However, it produces young with low genetic diversity that are less able to deal with disease and adverse conditions.

Hermaphrodites

Hermaphrodites are animals that produce both eggs and sperm. For these animals, every member of their species is a potential sexual partner. Being a hermaphrodite is often an adaptation for life where mating opportunities are rare. It is common among animals that live in isolation, such as parasites, and in sedentary or slow-moving animals. Most hermaphrodites use sexual reproduction when they can, exchanging sperm with a partner, but some fertilize their eggs with their own sperm if no partner is available. Animals such as snails mate with themselves only as a last resort, producing fewer young than when they reproduce sexually.

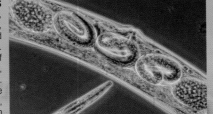

NEMATODE EGGS
This nematode worm, *Caenorhabditis elegans*, contains larvae developed from self-fertilized eggs. While a few members of the species are males, most are hermaphrodites. Those fertilized by a male produce up to 1,000 eggs, three times more than those that self-fertilize.

SCALE INSECT
Cottony cushion scale insects are serious pests of citrus trees. In most cases they are self-fertilizing hermaphrodites, but some males do occur.

CLONING APHIDS
Under good conditions in spring and early summer, aphids reproduce asexually, producing very large numbers of offspring that cause huge damage to crops and plants.

Budding potential

Hydra

This species (like other hydras) is a tiny animal that, in reproductive terms, enjoys the best of both worlds. When conditions are good and food is abundant, it reproduces asexually, by developing buds that grow into new individuals that detach from their parents and become independent individuals when fully formed. If conditions deteriorate in its pond—for example, if it starts to dry out or winter approaches—it grows ovaries and testes, which eject eggs and sperm into the water. These fuse to form a zygote (a fertilized cell) with a resistant covering that can survive until conditions improve.

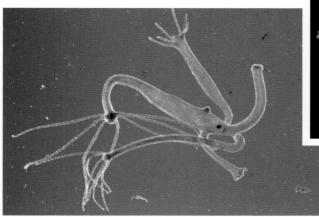

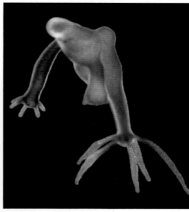

Hydra vulgaris

- ⬥ 1/16–3/4 in (1–20 mm)
- ◑ Attaches to vegetation in unpolluted freshwater ponds and rivers in the northern hemisphere.
- ▢ Long, thin, tubular body with foot at base; 5–12 tentacles around mouth; translucent light gray-brown to green.

BREAK AWAY
A hydra producing three offspring by budding (left); when fully formed the new hydras detach from their parent and become independent. Hydras are green or brown, depending on the kind of symbiotic algae living in their cells.

Breaking away

Red tree sponge

Like most sponges, the red tree sponge can reproduce both asexually and sexually depending on conditions. In asexual reproduction, part of the sponge, such as an arm, simply breaks off, drifts way, and settles elsewhere. Sponges are hermaphrodites and, at different times in their lives, produce both eggs and sperm. The eggs are usually kept within the body but sperm are emitted in dense clouds that look like smoke. Sperm are taken in by another sponge, whose eggs they fertilize to produce larvae.

Haliclona compressa

- ⬥ Up to 8 in (20 cm)
- ◑ Attached to rocks and coral reefs in the Caribbean Sea.
- ▢ Treelike body with cylindrical branches; ridged surface with bright orange or red coloring.

Colorful colonies

Jewel anenome

Jewel anemones reproduce asexually by simply dividing into two, resulting in a pair of genetically identical animals. The two small anemones can then go on to split again once they have grown. If conditions are good they can reproduce very quickly, building up vast numbers. These dense colonies cover rocky surfaces on the seashore or on underwater cliff faces. Jewel anemones are amazingly variable in color, ranging from pinks and greens, to reds and whites. Within this technicolor spectrum, each individual anemone itself has contrasting coloration—the tentacles tend to differ in hue to the body column, and the dozens of knobbed tentacle tips are often white. As individual anemones split and replicate themselves, distinct patches of color become visible within large colonies. The specatular displays that result are often described as resembling a "multicolored quilt."

PATCHWORK EFFECT
These distinct clusters of pink and green jewel anemones are groups of clones. Each patch of color is derived from an individual anemone.

Corynactis viridis

- ⬥ Diameter 3/8 in (10 mm); height 1/2 in (1.5 cm). Colonies can be several yards across.
- ◑ Attached to rocks above and below the low tide mark in western Europe, UK, and the Mediterranean Sea.
- ▢ Short, squat anemone with up to 100 tentacles with knobs at the end; variably and brightly colored green, pink, orange, red, and white.

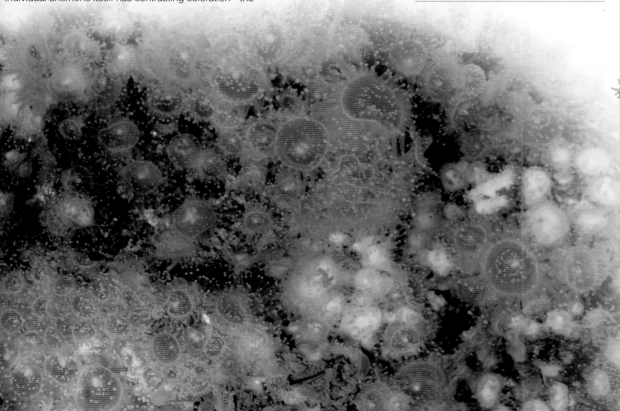

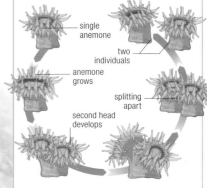

ANATOMY

SPLITTING UP

Jewel anemones divide in half vertically, in a process known as longitudinal fission. Division begins at the head, so that an individual has two mouths and two sets of tentacles. The body then splits in half downward, leaving two independent but genetically identical individuals. The splitting process can take from just five minutes to several hours.

- single anemone
- two individuals
- anemone grows
- splitting apart
- second head develops

IN THE PINK
A large colony of pink jewel anemones covering the face of a rock. Asexual reproduction enables anemones to colonize areas of good habitat fast.

From a distance

Giant clam

Because giant clams are immobile creatures, they cannot go in search of a mate. However, they are hermaphrodites, possessing both male and female sex organs, which solves the problem of reproduction. During midsummer, giant clams release both eggs and sperm into the water, but they try to avoid fertilizing their own eggs by discharging each at separate times; usually the sperm is released first. Also, they begin their sexually mature lives as males, developing female organs as they get older, so younger clams can only release sperm. When egg and sperm meet, they fertilize each other to form a veliger, a larva that swims in the open sea for some time before settling on a reef and developing into a clam. Genetic studies of giant clams on Australia's Great Barrier Reef show that clams living close together are no more closely related to one another than those living 620 miles (1,000 km) away, suggesting that sperm and eggs disperse widely on ocean currents before fusing into veligers. It has been estimated that veligers reach full sexual maturity at between three and seven years of age. While the giant clam usually fertilizes others of its own species, it is also thought capable of cross-fertilization with at least one other clam species.

Tridacna gigas

- ↔ Up to 5 ft (1.5 m)
- ◑ Coral reefs, embedded in sand or gravel within 66 ft (20 m) of surface in Indian and southwest Pacific oceans.
- 🐚 Bivalve shell, with mantle (fleshy siphonal tissue) that is brown, yellow, or green with iridescent blue or purple spots and wholly blue or purple in larger clams.

EGG RELEASE

This giant clam ejects a cloud of of eggs from its siphon directly into the water. Spawning of eggs and sperm can last up to 30 minutes with millions of eggs, and billions of sperm, being released and carried away on the current.

100 The number of years a giant clam is thought to live, though some may live as long as 200 years.

cloud of eggs erupts from exhalant siphon of clam.

ANATOMY

CLAM SIPHONS

Two siphons circulate water around a clam's body, allowing it to breathe, obtain food, and eliminate waste products. Inflowing water is pumped through the inhalant siphon, passed over the gills, and strained to remove food—microscopic plants (phytoplankton) and animals (zooplankton). After receiving carbon dioxide from the gills and other waste from the digestive tract, this same water is expelled through the exhalant siphon, which is also used to release sperm and eggs. Circulation is maintained by microscopic hairs called cilia located inside the clam.

Surviving without sex

Bdelloid rotifers

Rotifers are microscopic aquatic animals, many of which reproduce asexually when conditions are good, and resort to sexual reproduction when conditions deteriorate. One group, however, consisting of about 380 species, is entirely female and there is no evidence that they ever exist as males. These are the bdelloid rotifers, which first evolved about 80 million years ago. They produce eggs that require no fertilization—however, they are still able to produce genetically different offspring. Researchers have found two copies of a gene that helps bdelloid rotifers adapt and survive. The gene prompts the manufacture of proteins that protect the rotifer when its aquatic habitat dries out. One copy stops protein molecules from clumping together, while the other supports delicate cell membranes. This remarkable adaptation allows the bdelloid rotifer to stay alive even if it dessicates.

Order Bdelloida
- Microscopic
- Freshwater (common in ponds) and on mosses.
- Elongated, soft bodied, and leechlike, with corona of cilia, red eyes, and sensory antennae.

Cloned at birth

Aphid

Depending on the time of year, aphids use either sexual or asexual reproduction. In spring, eggs hatch into wingless females that each give birth to many young, by parthenogenesis, or development from unfertilized eggs. These young aphids, all of which are female, are born pregnant. Many generations of aphids are produced in this way while conditions are good. If their host plant begins to die, some of the females grow wings and fly, aided by the wind, to new host plants. As winter approaches, some female aphids develop into males. The males and females mate to produce eggs, which can survive the winter.

Family Aphididae
- Around 1/16 in (2 mm)
- Temperate regions of the world on plants, including trees and garden flowers.
- Tiny insects in a variety of colors, all with small heads and plump bodies.

BABY FACTORY
A female aphid gives birth to young that are genetically identical to herself, while continuing to feed on plant sap. Aphids reproduce prolifically and feed immediately, causing severe damage to plants.

Hermaphrodite fish

Mangrove killifish

The mangrove killifish is unique among vertebrates: it is a hermaphodite that fertilizes itself. It lives in mangrove swamps that frequently become so toxic that it has to escape to terrestrial refuges —one reason why it spends much of its life alone. Creating offspring without a partner is therefore a necessity, and the killifish does this by producing both eggs and sperm, which fuse within an organ called an ovotestis. The fertilized eggs are then deposited out of water, attached to plants and debris, and are dispersed widely by tides, wind, and rain.

COLORFUL LONER
The mangrove killifish's color varies according to its habitat. In muddy environments it is dark brown or green, in sandy places, pale yellow.

Kryptolebias marmoratus
- Up to 3 in (7.5 cm)
- Tropical regions with coastal mangrove swamps such as Brazil, Central America, Caribbean islands, and Florida.
- Long, slender body with dorsal and anal fins near tail. Color varies according to habitat, but all have black spot with yellow ring on base of tail.

CASE STUDY
FISH OUT OF WATER

The habitat of mangrove killifishes frequently dries out due to weather changes or can become toxic due to the formation of hydrogen sulfide. When this happens, the fishes escape by flipping and jumping over land. Remarkably, the structure of their gills and skin changes to allow them to breathe air, and they can survive for up to 10 weeks out of water. Some ride out the hostile spells by hiding in the burrows of blue land crabs; others wiggle into termite galleries in trees.

Adaptable female

Bonnethead shark

Also known as shovelheads, bonnethead sharks usually reproduce sexually, the female mating with a male and giving birth to between 8 and 12 young, called pups. In 2001, however, a female that had been kept on her own at a zoo in Nebraska gave birth to a single pup. DNA analysis showed that it was genetically identical to its mother, confirming that this was indeed a "virgin birth," the pup having developed by parthenogenesis from an unfertilized egg. This had not previously been observed in cartilaginous fishes. Bonnetheads are often found in large schools but, if a female is not able to find a male, it appears that she has a mechanism for producing young on her own.

A HEAD FOR SCENTS?
The function of the flattened head of the bonnethead is not known, but it may enhance the shark's sense of smell.

Sphyrna tiburo
- to 5 ft (1.5 m)
- Deep, warm water in the western Atlantic and eastern Pacific oceans.
- Slender shark with high first dorsal fin and flattened head with rounded front. Colors are brown, gray, or green above, paler or white below.

Whole eggs

Mourning gecko

Although some male mourning geckos have been reported, most populations consist entirely of females capable of producing eggs that will develop into young without being fertilized by sperm. This gives rise to offspring that are genetic clones of their mothers. Mourning geckos are communal breeders, with several females laying two eggs each in a nest in a tree cavity, a leaf axil, or under bark. Because every individual can reproduce, their numbers increase very rapidly, and they have successfully colonized many parts of the world, including northern Australia, where they have been introduced.

satiny brown skin

five toes

black spot with "W" or chevron markings on tail

PROLIFIC IMMIGRANTS
Like many other geckos, mourning geckos have successfully colonized oceanic islands, such as Hawaii. One reason for this may be that their eggs can survive immersion in sea water.

Lepidodactylus lugubris
- 2¾–3¾ in (7–9.5 cm)
- Wide variety of habitats, including buildings, in tropical Asia and Pacific islands, Central America, and Australia.
- Pale brown, satiny skin, with dark chevron or "W" markings on back and dark band along eye.

Finding a mate

For animals that live in long-term social groups, finding a mate is not difficult. Many animals, however, live solitary lives and have evolved ways to find mates, often over a great distance. In many insects and frogs, for example, males produce loud sounds that attract females.

Advertising for a mate

When attracting a mate, it is usually the male that has to produce sounds, visual signals, or odors that draw the attention of females, and some species expend a huge amount of energy doing so. Typically, they advertise in competition with other males of the same species, and the males that put most energy into their display are the most successful in attracting females. Advertising is dangerous, because a male's conspicuous signals may also be noticed by his enemies, such as predators or parasites. Some calling frogs, for example, are eaten by bats that home in on their calls.

Male mole crickets "sing" for females by rubbing their wings together in a burrow that amplifies the sound.

Male water lily frogs call to attract females to join them at breeding ponds.

Time and place

One way of finding a mate is for males and females to gather at a regular breeding site. Many amphibians, for example, return to the pond where they were born and continue to return there throughout their lives in order to breed. In some birds and mammals, mating occurs at traditional sites called "leks," where males fight over small display areas, and females choose which male to mate with; they base their choice on each male's appearance and the quality of his display.

HEADING TO A LEK
Gemsboks of southern Africa live most of their lives in herds. When it is time to breed, they head for traditional mating sites, or leks.

Staying together

Animals with long life spans can breed several times in their lives, and it is often advantageous to form long-term pair bonds. In a number of birds, pairs that breed together over several years improve their breeding success from year to year. Parrots and pigeons, for example, are renowned for their long-term monogamy, which can last many years. This is because, as well as developing individual breeding skills, stable pairs learn to complement one another. Australian sleepy lizards live solitary lives but, for up to 20 years, they seek out their regular partner in the breeding season. Pairs of animals that fail to breed successfully in their first year together often separate and find new partners the following year.

STAYING CLOSE
Like many bird species, ring-necked doves are monogamous, forming pair bonds that may last several years.

BABOON TROOP
Olive baboons live in troops of 15–150, consisting of a few males, several females, and their young. Males fight to establish dominance, and the more dominant males enjoy greater mating success.

● PARASITE MATING STRATEGIES

MASS EGG LAYING
Parasites that live inside their hosts have great difficulty finding a mate, as their host must become infected more than once by the same species of parasite before mating can occur.

HERMAPHRODITISM
If no mate is available, a simultaneous hermaphrodite parasite—one that is capable of producing both eggs and sperm—can simply mate with itself. This is a solution sometimes used by tapeworms.

MANIPULATION
Some parasites can manipulate the behavior of their host, making them more conspicuous to predators. This increases the chance of the parasite being passed to a new host.

PERMANENT COPULATION
Some protists, such as the species that causes the disease bilharzia, have another solution to the difficulty of finding a mate—male and female live attached to one another, in a state of permanent copulation.

Mass spawning
Hard corals

Hard corals are colonial organisms, consisting of many tiny individuals, called polyps, each of which lays down a calcareous "shell" to sit in. All individuals on the same reef synchronize their reproductive activity, shedding their sex cells into the water on the same day to produce large numbers of fertilized eggs; this precise timing is related to the lunar cycle. Eggs and sperm fuse in the water to form microscopic larvae, or planulae, that swim toward the surface of the sea, where they drift away from the parent colony. After a few days they sink to the seabed and, if they land on a suitable rock, start a new colony.

Lobophyllia species

⬛ ⅓– 6½ ft (0.1–2 m)

◗ Shallow, tropical regions of the Atlantic, Pacific, and Indian oceans.

📖 Colonies are flat and lobed with a surface of ridges and furrows, not unlike the surface of a human brain.

≫ 164

EGG AND SPERM RELEASE

≫01 Sperm is shed into the water by large numbers of individual polyps. ≫02 Shedding is coordinated, so that the sperm emerges in clouds. ≫03 The eggs, which are released on the same day, mingle with the sperm and external fertilization takes place.

>>01   >>02   >>03

Close relationship
Purple sea urchin

Purple sea urchins have no need to go in search of a mate, since they typically live close to one another in large colonies. Individuals mature at two years of age and breed between January and March. Males release sperm and females release eggs into the water, where they fuse to form tiny embryos; these fall back to the seafloor, where they settle and begin to grow. In general, adult urchins are sedentary but are able to move slowly to new places in search of food. They feed on fragments of algae that fall out of the kelp forest with which they are associated. They have the ability to scrape a depression in the rock, making themselves better protected against being displaced by waves.

Strongylocentrotus purpuratus

⬛ 2–4 in (5–10 cm)

◗ Low intertidal zones, with strong wave action, in association with kelp forest, on Pacific coast of North America, from Alaska to Mexico.

📖 Spherical body covered in long purple spines.

Fluorescent attraction
Ornate jumping spider

Male ornate jumping spiders have special scales on certain parts of their bodies that reflect ultraviolet light, enabling females to recognize males of their own species. Both sexes have cells in the retinas of their many eyes that are sensitive to ultraviolet light, but only the males have the light-reflecting scales. Males are very active in sunlight, displaying to both females and rival males with elaborate dances that involve waving their forelimbs and drumming their legs on

a leaf: these provide both visual and vibrational cues to potential mates and rivals. Males engage in frequent, often violent, interactions with other males, in order to defend their leaf. When a male detects a female, which is attracted to the male by its distinctive markings, it performs a courtship dance that leads to mating.

Cosmophasis umbratica

⬛ ¼ in (7 mm)

◗ Vegetation in sunny open woodland in Southeast Asia from India to Sumatra.

📖 Green and black with silvery white markings (male), or green, brown, white, and black (female).

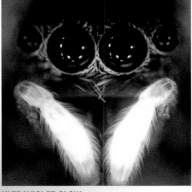

ULTRAVIOLET GLOW
Males reflect ultraviolet light in order to attract females; the light-reflecting scales are especially prominent on their forelegs.

MIDDAY ACTIVITY
Ornate jumping spiders are most active during late morning and early afternoon on plants that are exposed to sunlight.

Chirping call
Cicadas

Male cicadas attract females from far away by producing one of the loudest noises in the natural world. Unlike crickets and grasshoppers, which rub their wings, or wings and legs together to make a chirping sound, cicadas create a clicking noise using a pair of organs, called tymbals, on their abdomens. Tymbals are flat, circular structures that, like a metal tin lid, can be clicked in and out by the action of powerful muscles. The sound is amplified by air sacs that lie just beneath the tymbals. Close to the tymbals, the sound reaches an intensity of 120 decibels, which is painful to the human ear. Cicadas have a strange life history, living as nymphs under the ground for six or seven years and as adults for only a few weeks.

OUT IN THE OPEN
Cicadas are more often heard than seen. Most species are well camouflaged and sing from within vegetation.

Family Cicadidae

⬛ ¾–6 in (2–15 cm)

◗ Restricted to areas with trees or bushes; mainly tropical, but some species inhabit temperate regions.

📖 Prominent eyes, set wide apart on either side of head; squat body, roughly oval in shape. Wings are usually transparent, extend beyond apex of abdomen.

≫ 386–87

Blinking lights

Glow worms

Female glow worms attract males by producing bright green light at night. Glow worms are beetles but, while the male has a normal beetle life cycle and transforms from a larva into an adult capable of flight, the much larger female remains in the larval form and is unable to fly. The hindmost three segments of the female's body contain light-producing organs. These contain a layer of a protein called luciferin, which reacts chemically with the enzyme luciferase, water, and oxygen to produce light, but very little heat. The luciferin layer is backed by light-reflecting crystals and is covered by a transparent cuticle. A female is able to turn her light organs on and off by changing the flow of oxygen into them. She glows at night while sitting on a leaf or twig, and the male flies down to mate with her. Glow worm larvae

TREE DWELLER
This Douglas fir glow worm *(Pterotus obscuripennis)* is one of several species of glow worm found in North America, where they are more commonly known as fireflies. Glow worms are, in fact, neither worms nor flies, but beetles.

and adult females are predators of arthropods, including millipedes, whose formidable chemical defenses they are somehow able to overcome. Adult males have much larger eyes than females and live for a shorter period of time. In some species, both females and adult males have no mouths and so are unable to feed. Instead, they conserve as much energy as possible while searching for a mate and then die shortly after reproducing.

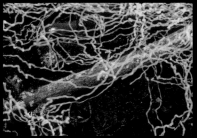

NIGHT LIGHTS
Two female common glow worms *(Lampyris noctiluca)* give out a soft glow (above), while the click beetle *(Pyrophorus noctilucus)* produces a green light trace (left).

Some tropical glow worms gather in large groups and synchronize their flashing displays. The exact reason for this behavior remains unknown.

Family Lampyridae

⬌ ¾ in (2 cm), female much larger than male

◉ Vegetation throughout temperate and tropical regions.

📖 Adult male glow worms are long-bodied beetles, with soft elytra (wing covers). Females retain grublike larval body form and lack wings.

Pattern of attraction

Purple emperor butterfly

The female emperor butterfly recognizes the male by its purple coloration, which is visible only from certain angles and light conditions. From June to August, males gather near the top of particular, large, prominent trees during the day. Females visit these trees to find a male, and mating can last for many hours. The female lays her eggs on willow trees, on which the caterpillars feed. Early in the day, both sexes are often seen on the ground, gathering essential salts from mud.

Apatura iris

⬌ 2¼–3¼ in (6–8.5 cm)

◉ Woodland in northern and western Europe and southeast England.

📖 Both sexes are dark brown with white markings; upper surfaces of male's wings have purple sheen.

UPPER SURFACE

UNDERSIDE

UP AND UNDER
The male purple emperor butterfly has a glorious sheen to the tops of his wings. The undersides are much less brightly colored.

Standing guard

Zebra wing butterfly

The male zebra wing butterfly seeks out virgin females and then guards them against rival males. When a male finds a female chrysalis, he defends it, waiting until the female is about to emerge. As soon as she appears, he mates with her. As a further device to ensure that he has exclusive mating rights over the female, he anoints her abdomen with a secretion that repels other males. The female lays the eggs on passion vines. Adults feed on nectar, individuals regularly patrolling a number of flowering plants. At night, they gather in communal roosts of up to 25 or 30 individuals.

Heliconius charitonius

⬌ 2¾–4 in (7–10 cm)

◉ Forests, among dense clumps of trees, and at forest edges in the southern US, northern Mexico, and Caribbean islands.

📖 Long, narrow wings in black with yellow stripes.

BEFORE AND AFTER
An initial phase male (top) swims above a terminal phase male on a reef. Only the terminal phase males have the blue head that gives this species its name.

Thalassoma bifasciatum
- Up to 10 in (25 cm)
- Coral and offshore reefs, sea-grass beds, and coastal bays in western Atlantic, Bermuda, Florida, Gulf of Mexico, northern South America, and the Caribbean.
- Long, thin body with pointed snout; color variable, depending on sex and age.

Changing sex

Bluehead wrasse

Bluehead wrasse are capable of undergoing a physical change that may include changing sex from female to male. Small female and male bluehead wrasse are said to be in the initial phase. The change turns them into terminal phase males (see panel, right). In groups of bluehead wrasse one terminal phase male, who may have started life as a female, does most of the mating. On smaller reefs, there are only a few terminal phase males, who defend territories that females visit; these males can mate with up to 100 females in one day. Initial phase males may fertilize some eggs by intruding when a terminal male mates and shedding their sperm on the eggs. On larger reefs, there are many terminal males and they are less territorial.

ANATOMY

BECOMING A SUPERMALE

Initial phase bluehead wrasse are yellow or white above a darker band, and white below. Terminal phase males are longer with different coloration, including a bright blue head. The aggressive behavior of the terminal phase males inhibits the transformation of the initial phase fishes, but as soon as the former die the change from initial phase male or female is triggered. This is linked to the sudden drop in stress and resulting surge in sexual hormones.

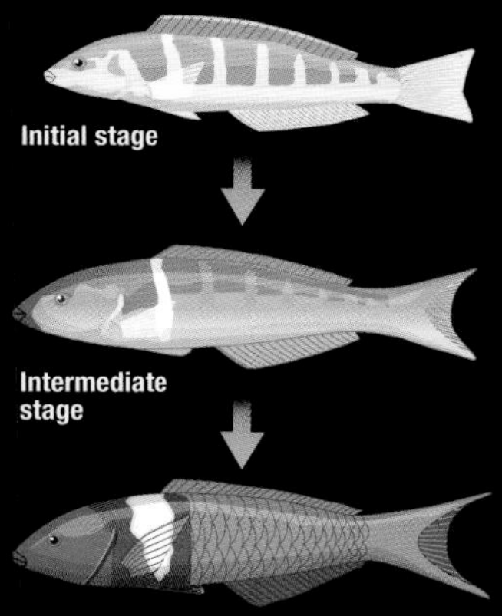

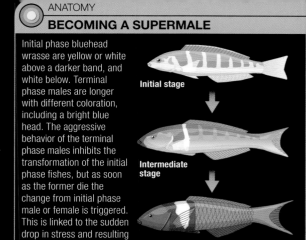

Perfect timing

California grunion

Precise timing is the key to reproductive success for California grunions. Mass spawning occurs four to eight times per year, during the spring and summer, and always at the highest tide in the monthly tidal cycle. The high tide seems to be the cue for males and females to gather and form a writhing mass at the water's edge. A female digs a burrow in the sand and deposits her eggs in it; a male then wraps himself around her and sheds his sperm onto the eggs. The eggs develop in the sand and, when the water reaches them at the next monthly high tide, they hatch and the young disperse into the ocean.

Leuresthes tenuis
- Up to 6 in (15 cm)
- West coast of US, south to Baja California, Mexico.
- Silvery with blue-green back.

LIFE'S A BEACH
The California grunion spawns at the water's edge at high tide, leaving its eggs to develop in the sand out of reach of marine predators.

Humming for a mate

Plainfin midshipman

Male plainfin midshipman fish invite females to visit their nests by producing a loud humming sound, interspersed with whistles, grunts, and growls. Mating happens at night, and when a female is close, the male uses the luminescent spots on the underside of his chin to display to her, lifting his head back to expose them. Males live in the intertidal zone; they burrow in mud during the day and emerge at night to feed and mate, sometimes leaving the water. Females spend most of their lives in deeper water, moving into the intertidal zone to breed. The male digs a nest next to a rock, on which the female lays her eggs. After spawning, the male guards the eggs and then the young, until they are large enough to fend for themselves.

Porichthys notatus
- Up to 15 in (38 cm)
- Intertidal zones of the Pacific coast of North America, from Alaska to Mexico.
- Toadlike face and purple or brown above, yellowish below, with numerous luminescent light organs.

NOISY NEIGHBOR
The sounds made by the male plainfin midshipman are so loud they can be heard above water. They can even keep humans awake at night.

Summer gathering

Short-tail stingray

Stingrays find their mates by gathering in large numbers at certain traditional sites in the summer breeding season. The female retains the fertilized eggs in her body and gives birth to fully formed young rays. While they are still inside their mother, these feed first on yolk and then, later, on a milklike fluid, containing mucus, fat, and proteins, which is secreted from her uterus. At birth they measure some 14 in (36 cm) across. The short-tail is the world's largest stingray, weighing up to 772lb (350 kg). Like most rays, it spends the majority of its time on or near the seabed, feeding on mollusks and crustaceans by crushing them with the hard, flattened teeth in its jaws. The spine on the tail can be up to 16 in (40 cm) long, contains poison, and is used in defense. A wound from a stingray spine can be fatal to humans but such wounds are rare.

Dasyatis brevicaudata
- Up to 14 ft (4.3 m)
- Coastal waters and estuaries around Australia, New Zealand, and South Africa.
- Dark gray or brown above, pale below; long whiplike tail with dorsal spine.

DRAWN TOGETHER
A large group of short-tail stingrays gathers off New Zealand's Poor Knight's Island to find a mate and breed. Outside the breeding season this species is usually solitary.

BOTTOM FEEDER
Stingrays find much of their food by electro-reception, picking up the tiny electrical impulses made by the muscles of their prey. This enables them to find animals hidden under seabed sand.

Two-part call

Coqui frog

Male coqui frogs produce a two-part advertisement call, which is made up of a low-pitched "co" and a high-pitched "qui"—hence the name "coqui." The ears of males are particularly sensitive to the low-frequency sound in the "co"; for them, it is a threat signal and it warns them to keep their distance. The ears of females are tuned to the higher frequency "qui," which is a mating call; females respond by approaching a calling male. Males call from leaves 3¼–6½ ft (1–2 m) above the ground. After mating, the fertilized eggs are deposited on the ground under leaves, and, unlike most frog species, develop into tiny frogs without experiencing a tadpole stage.

Eleutherodactylus coqui

- ↔ 1½–2¼ in (3.5–6 cm)
- ◐ Woodland; native to Puerto Rico and introduced to several other places, including Florida and Hawaii.
- 𝄐 Large eyes; brown or gray above, white or yellow below; large toe pads.

▶ CALL FREQUENCY

ATTRACTION AND THREAT
The call of the male coqui frog lasts for just over half a second, with a short gap between the "co" and the higher pitched "qui." Although we hear both parts of this call clearly, male coqui frogs can hardly hear the high-pitched "qui," whereas females are very sensitive to it.

FREQUENCY (KHZ) — 3.0, 3.0, 2.0, 1.0, 0

MILLISECONDS 0 100 200 300 400 500 600

Pneumatic trill

Great Plains toad

The Great Plains toad spends much of its life in an underground burrow, emerging only at night and after rain to feed. Heavy rainfall in spring and summer triggers mass migrations of toads to temporary pools, where large, noisy choruses can form. Breeding occurs over a few days. Larger males call from the pond edge, producing a prolonged, loud, metallic trill. Smaller males tend not to call but gather as "satellite" males (see panel, right) around the callers. Females are attracted to males that call most often.

Anaxyrus cognatus

- ↔ 1¾–4½ in (4.5–12 cm)
- ◐ Deserts and prairies in the central US, northern Mexico, and southern Canada.
- 𝄐 Plump body; color variable, usually brown or green, with large symmetrical dark blotches.

TRUE CALLING
Males have very large, sausage-shaped vocal sacs, representing a third of their overall size when fully inflated.

SILENT SNEAKERS

Calling male Great Plains toads both attract females and alert other males to their presence. By staying quiet, smaller males avoid conflict but also improve their chances of mating. They loiter near larger males, out of sight but within earshot. When females approach, drawn by the larger toad's calls, they intercept them and mate with them.

Favored location

Tiger salamander

The tiger salamander migrates at night to "traditional" breeding ponds after heavy rain. Males arrive a few days before females. Breeding populations can be very dense, making mating a competitive and sometimes chaotic business. The male courts a female by nudging her tail with his snout. When she responds, he deposits

Ambystoma tigrinum

- ↔ 3–6½ in (7.5–16 cm)
- ◐ Grassland and wooded ares near water in North America.
- 𝄐 Large, stocky salamander with rounded snout and small eyes. Color variable, most commonly black with yellowish markings.

a spermatophore, which she walks over and picks up. Males interfere with one another's mating attempts by depositing their spermatophores on top of those of their rivals. In some subspecies, eggs are laid in clumps; in others they are laid singly. The timing of breeding varies across their range; in northern areas, for example, the salamanders migrate in early spring as soon as the ice on their breeding ponds begins to melt.

FOREST HABITAT
When they are not breeding, tiger salamanders spend most of their time out of water, often in wooded areas. They are particularly active in wet weather.

ON THE MOVE
Tiger salamanders are found over a vast range and include a number of local variants, mostly classified as subspecies. This is the eastern tiger salamander, which is found in northern Minnesota.

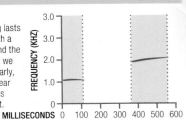

Following a trail

Adder

A few weeks after emerging from hibernation in the spring, male adders shed their skin and begin to move around their home range, looking for the odor trails left by females. When a male finds a trail, he follows it to locate the female. The male guards the female for several days, wrestling with rival males and seeing off any smaller individuals (larger males tend to be more successful). The "winner" then mates with the female several times, with each mating episode lasting around two hours. Because female adders only breed in alternate years, producing between three and 18 young in each litter, there are fewer of them, so there is fierce competition among males for females.

Vipera berus

- ↔ Up to 26 in (65 cm)
- ◐ Widespread in northern and western Europe, Russia, and Britain (absent from Ireland).
- 𝄐 Thick-bodied snake with a flat head; gray, green, or brown coloration with a dark zigzag stripe along back; some individuals may be entirely black.

THE BIG SWIM
Green turtles are powerful swimmers and can travel continuously for several weeks at a time. It is not known how they manage to navigate their way back to the same breeding site each season, but it is thought to be linked to the earth's magnetic forces.

Round trip

Green turtle

For green turtles, mating is just part of a huge journey across the ocean that they must undertake in order to breed. They live in one part of the ocean, but breed in another, sometimes making a round trip of 3,000 miles (4,800 km). Females breed at intervals of two or six years, so there are always more males than females in mating groups and males must compete to mate.

The female comes ashore at night, to the same beach where she was born, and lays up to 200 eggs in a deep burrow in the sand. The eggs hatch after two months, when the young make a hazardous journey down to the sea. Along the route, many are eaten by birds and other predators. The young feed on plankton and, being soft-shelled, are prey for fish. The few that survive mature at 10–24 years of age and they may live to be 100 years old. Green turtles are endangered, largely as a result of hunting by humans. From the 17th century, there was a steady trade of turtles from the Caribbean to London, to provide turtle soup. Even today, sea turtles continue to be captured for food and many are accidentally caught and killed in fishing nets. The most effective means of conserving green turtles in the wild is to protect the beaches where they lay their eggs so that they can continue to breed.

Chelonia mydas

- Up to 5 ft (1.5 m)
- Tropical and subtropical sea-grass beds and open water in Atlantic and Indo-Pacific oceans.
- Heart-shaped shell, in olive, brown, or black; paddlelike limbs; small head with a horny beak and no teeth.

SCRAMBLE FOR A MATE
Adult green turtles feed almost exclusively on sea grass and seaweed, which only grow in particular places in relatively shallow, coastal waters. Mating occurs around the feeding areas. Once pregnant, the females set off toward the beaches where they hatched decades earlier.

MEETING UP
Female green turtles gather in the shallows near a traditional nesting beach. Green turtles nest on sandy beaches in large numbers. By laying their eggs together over the same few nights, they maximize the chances of their young surviving, since the sheer number of hatchlings emerging together overwhelms predators.

CASE STUDY

TRACKING TURTLES

Green turtles can be tracked by tagging them with radio transmitters, the signals being picked up by satellites. Experiments have been done in which radio-tagged turtles approaching Ascension Island were displaced off course. Those displaced downwind easily found Ascension, but those displaced upwind took much longer to find it. This suggests that green turtles use wind-borne cues, possibly odors, to find their way back to the beach where they were born.

EPIC JOURNEY
Green turtles that live off the coast of Brazil make a 3,000 mile (4,800 km) trip to Ascension Island and back so they can breed safely.

Mating ground

Western capercaillie

Capercaillies find their mates at a traditional communal mating site called a lek during a long breeding season lasting through spring and summer. At the beginning of the season, males display from positions high up in trees, but later they move to the ground, each male defending a very small territory in which he displays. Male displays involve fanning the tail, jumping in the air, and producing a loud, complex call incorporating a variety of rattling, popping, and grinding sounds. Males defend their territories fiercely, not only against rival males, but also against dogs and humans.

MALE CAPERCAILLIE

SNOWY LEK
Male capercaillies pose and strut for the benefit of a female. Capercaillies are large birds, similar in size to a turkey.

Tetrao urogallus
- 2–3¼ ft (0.6–1 m)
- Coniferous forest in Asia and northern Europe, including Scotland.
- Male dark, gray, brown, and black with green sheen, female speckled brown; male much larger than female. Both sexes have red patch above eye.

Mate for life

Royal albatross

The royal albatross may live for up to 80 years and normally pairs for life. It reaches sexual maturity at 9–11 years of age, when it goes to one of a small number of breeding sites on offshore islands to find a mate. Pair formation involves an elaborate display in which the wings extend and the bill points skyward. A pair produces only one egg every two years. They usually stay together once the chick is independent, and return to the same nest each season. Being monogamous solves the problem of having to attract a new mate at the start of each breeding season.

Diomedea epomophora
- 3½–4 ft (1.1–1.2 m)
- Open ocean in the Southern Hemisphere.
- White with black-mottled wings and pink bill.

Changing plumage

White-winged fairy-wren

White-winged fairy wrens have a complex mating system, in which only a few males have bright blue plumage. They are cooperative breeders, with small territorial groups, in which a female feeds the young, assisted by helpers. In most of these groups, the males are brown, like the females, but in some he is bright blue; this "nuptial" plumage is not developed until a male is three years old. Among island sub-species, the males sometimes develop black coloration. The nuptial male is usually also the dominant male. Courtship may involve presenting the female with a petal as a gift. He nests with only one female and contributes to raising the resulting young. Cooperative breeding helps these birds raise larger clutches than individual pairs could alone.

BLACK AND BLUE
This sexually mature male white-winged fairy wren (left) has developed bright blue nuptial plumage. The female (above), in contrast, is brown.

Malurus leucopterus
- 4½ in (12 cm)
- Sparse, stunted vegetation in western Australia.
- White wings; female grayish brown above, white below with pale blue tail; male brown with pale blue tail; nuptial male bright blue with dark blue tail.

Prolific breeders

European rabbit

European rabbits are renowned for their breeding capabilities. Their living and breeding patterns vary with the nature of the soil. Where it is soft and easy to dig burrows, they tend to be dispersed over a large area, but if the soil is hard they use the same burrows for a long time and live in small colonies, called warrens. Males have larger home ranges than females and

Oryctolagus cuniculus
- 14–19½ in (35–50 cm)
- Now found in meadow, farmland, and woodland throughout the world, but originally from Europe.
- Gray-brown, paler below, with white fluffy tail.
- ≫ 320

ABUNDANT HERBIVORES
The capacity of rabbits to produce many young in a season means that populations rise rapidly, making them serious agricultural pests.

Rabbits have 100 million olfactory receptors while humans have only 5–6 million.

compete to mate with females as they become receptive, or ready to mate. Females can produce several litters, of five or six kittens, in a year. Males form a dominance hierarchy, with the most dominant male closely following and guarding a receptive female, seeing off rival males, until she is ready to mate. Both males and females have more than one mate, but the dominant male tends to attract the dominant female. While he fathers most of the young born in a group, other males may father around 16 percent.

READY TO MATE
When seeking out a mate, male rabbits use their powerful sense of smell to assess the reproductive condition of several females at a time. If a female is ready to breed the male rabbit will track her.

Scent and sound

Moose

Male moose produce long, moaning calls that can attract females from as far as 2 miles (3.2 km) away. They also produce a powerful smell and urinate around their wallow holes. Males compete for females and may fight, but often they avoid injury by assessing their relative size, the smaller male giving way to the larger. Mating occurs in September or October; a single calf, sometimes twins, is born eight months later. The young stay with the mother for a year. Otherwise moose live solitary lives, coming together only for mating. About 50 percent of young die in their first year; adults live for 8–12 years, with the longevity of males sometimes shortened by injuries sustained in fights. Unable to sweat to keep cool, moose are confined to areas where the temperature does not exceed 81° F (27° C).

Alces alces
- 8¼–10½ ft (2.5–3.2 m)
- Deciduous forest around the world at northern latitudes: northern North America and eastern Eurasia. Known as elk in Europe.
- Light brown-black, thick fur, long face, and prominent dewlap or "bell."
- >> 407

MEETING OF THE SEXES
Male moose are slightly larger than females and have large antlers, which can be up to 6½ ft (2 m) wide. The females don't have antlers.

MOOSE HAREM
Moose generally form simple breeding pairs, with one male and one female, which stay together for about a week. However, a male may attract several females, forming a harem. As with pairs, these are short-lived and females leave a few days after mating.

HEAVYWEIGHT CONTENDER
The male moose is a formidable animal. An adult male can be up to 7 ft (2.1 m) high at the shoulder and weigh over 1,100 lb (500 kg). Moose are the largest species of deer in the world.

Group attraction

Dugong

Highly social animals, dugongs used to occur in large herds. Their populations have been seriously depleted by humans and they are now seen either singly or in small social groups. Most dugongs display relatively simple breeding behavior. Both males and females reach sexual maturity at around nine years of age. When a female becomes sexually receptive, she attracts a group of three to ten males, who then jostle and fight to gain access to her. Mature males have small tusks, which may be used in these battles, although serious injuries are rare. A lekking breeding system (see panel, right) may have been much more widespread in the years before numbers of this species declined. Close relatives of manatees, dugongs are mammals and must breathe air. They dive for up to three minutes at a time to feed, using their muscular snouts to dislodge sea-grass plants, which they then eat whole.

Dugong dugon
- 8¼–13 ft (2.5–4 m)
- Shallow coastal waters of Indian Ocean, East Africa, Red Sea, northern Australia, and Pacific islands.
- Cream at birth, darkening to slate-gray; flukelike tail with concave rear edge; front flippers; prominent upper lip.
- >> 193

TRAVELING TOGETHER
A small group of dugongs swim over coral in search of sea-grass beds. Dugongs and their relatives manatees are commonly known as sea cows, due to their plant-eating habits. They are the world's only herbivorous marine mammals. Their preferred food ties them to coastal habitats.

DUGONG GROUPS LEKKING

In Shark Bay, off Western Australia, male dugongs hold small territories and display to attract females. The territories are temporary and defended against other males. When a female enters a male's territory, he performs various maneuvers to encourage her to mate. These include short swims across the seabed and turning belly up toward her.

Sexual rivalry

Like most other aspects of animal life, reproduction is a highly competitive business. Individuals have to compete for access to mates as well as for the resources, such as food and space, that are needed in order to procreate successfully. The fundamental differences between the sexes that result in sexual "dimorphism," or two distinct body shapes, also mean that, in most instances, it is males that vie with each other for females, yet there are several species in which females compete for males.

Male sexual rivalry

A female maximizes her reproductive success by producing, protecting, and feeding a limited number of young, as well as by ensuring that they are fathered by a high-quality male. Unless they help care for young, males maximize their success simply by mating with as many females as possible; as a result, they compete with one another for partners. Evolution thus favors greater male strength, large body size, and weapons such as horns, claws, and teeth for use in fighting. This is the reason that many males are larger and more heavily armed than females.

FIGHTING IT OUT
Two Madagascan short-horned chameleons grapple on a branch. Males have a short horn on the snout that is used when fighting over females.

Ritualized competition

Fighting takes it toll in terms of energy and time. It can also be fatal, especially when males possess dangerous weapons. Fortunately, natural selection has developed less costly and life-threatening methods of settling disputes in some species, usually based on signals or poses that indicate strength. Before resorting to violence, rival males often engage in postures and displays that reveal their true size to their opponent, providing an opportunity for the smaller animal to back down. With some animals, disputes are settled using entirely arbitrary criteria: for example, an individual claiming a preferred rock or sunny spot is recognized as the "owner" and is not attacked. This occurs when the benefits gained from the resource are low and the costs of fighting for it are high.

BLUE FOR A GIRL
An Australian satin bowerbird decorates a mating bower with blue objects that attract females. Blue items are rare, and so are often stolen from rivals' bowers.

A PLACE IN THE SUN
Male speckled wood butterflies claim spots of sunlight to which females are attracted. Sunspots are short-lived, so males do not waste time and energy contesting them.

⊙ CONFLICT AND COOPERATION

It is an evolutionary irony that, in some species, males can often attract females more effectively if they act together. The combined flashing displays of these male fireflies, for example, create an unmissable beacon for any females who happen to be in the vicinity. Of course, the presence of so many rival males in one place also means that, when the females do arrive, competition for the right to mate with them will be all the more intense. There is an additional risk: studies have shown that longer and brighter flashes among males — exactly what attracts females — also attract potential predators, so the line between sex and death is fine indeed.

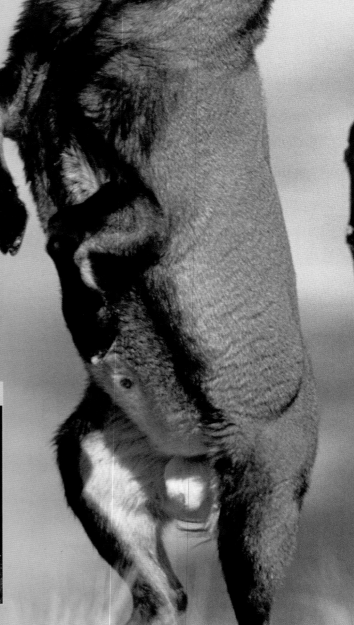

Female sexual rivalry

In a few animal species, the usual pattern of sex differences, or dimorphism, is reversed: females are noticeably larger and more powerful than males, and are therefore the ones who compete for mates. Large size in females usually evolves when larger females can produce more or bigger young than smaller females. Female competition for males is also associated with a situation in which males play a major role in feeding, raising, and protecting the young; male care then becomes a limited resource over which females will fight for possession. In some species, this results in polyandry—literally "several husbands"—in which a female has more than one mate. In moorhens, for example, females are like large, egg-laying machines: their clutches are often flooded or taken by predators and so must be replaced. They fight over the smaller males, who carry out all the duties of incubating the eggs and protecting the chicks once they have hatched. Some female moorhens even have two nests, each with its own male custodian.

FIGHTING MOORHENS
Two female moorhens lash out at one another in a battle over a male (right). Moorhens often produce two broods of young in a year, and the chicks from the first brood help to feed the chicks in the second brood (below).

MOUNTAIN-TOP DUEL
Two male Spanish ibexes battle for the possession of a group of females. Much larger than females, male ibexes have massive shoulders, thickened skulls, and huge horns. Fights are frequently very violent and can lead to serious injury or, occasionally, death.

Sexual tension

The reproductive interests of male and female animals sometimes conflict, resulting in patterns of behavior in which one partner acts in its own interests at the expense of those of its mate. One example of this is infanticide, when a male kills a female's young so that she can produce his own offspring more quickly. When a male lion takes over a pride of females, he kills any cubs still suckling from their mothers. Females do not come into heat until they have finished suckling their cubs, so killing these cubs means the females quickly come into season, ready to conceive young from the new male. Infanticide also occurs among primate species, including chimpanzees and baboons.

INFANTICIDE
A male lion (above) attacks a cub while its mother tries unsuccessfully to protect it. A female chimpanzee (left) threatens a male that is trying to kill her infant.

Battling broadside
Giant cuttlefish

Giant cuttlefish breed just once, dying shortly after an orgy of communal breeding. They migrate in large numbers to reefs off southern Australia, where males fight for the right to mate with females. They align themselves side by side, signaling their aggressiveness by changing color and fanning out their highly patterned arms in order to make themselves appear as large as possible. A smaller male will generally back down, but if two males of equal size meet they may attack each other with their arms and sharp beaks. Many cuttlefish bear scars from fierce battles, and some males may even lose tentacles.

Sepia apama

◄► 2½–5 ft (0.8–1.5 m)

⊙ Rocky reefs and seagrass beds in coastal waters around Southern Australia.

▥ Eight arms, two long tentacles; color variable.

SIDE STRIPES
Two rival males swim alongside each other in a threat display. They pulsate, creating a flashing effect with the stripes along their sides.

Pincer moves
Sally lightfoot crab

Sally lightfoot crabs use their chelipeds, or large pincers, in aggressive interactions with their rivals. Male sally lightfoot crabs have an enlarged right front pincer, which is held out from the body like a shield and brandished at an opponent. Disputes are usually resolved by a bout of mutual pincer waving, and only rarely does this escalate into a fight. They feed on algae and the carcasses of dead animals on the seashore. Young crabs are dark brown, camouflaging them among the rocks; adults are brightly colored and rely on their agility to avoid predators.

Grapsus grapsus

◄► 3¼ in (8 cm)

⊙ West coast of South America, Central America and Mexico; Galapagos Islands. Rocky shores, just above the water line.

▥ Brightly patterned, red, yellow, blue.

>> 270

Lashing out
Peacock mantis shrimp

Mantis shrimps have special appendages with which they can deliver one of the most powerful blows in the animal kingdom. Generally, this is used to break open the shells of their prey—snails, crustaceans, and bivalves—but they have been known to smash the glass of aquariums when held in captivity. In the wild, they live in U-shaped burrows in the sandy seabed. A female enters a male's burrow to breed and he guards her, lashing out at rivals with his powerful appendages.

LETHAL WEAPON

The claws of mantis shrimps are hinged structures, normally folded up against the body. The outer segment is club-shaped, and powerful muscles can flick it towards a rival or prey. This action is so fast that the water creates a vacuum in front of the club-head, which causes a shockwave.

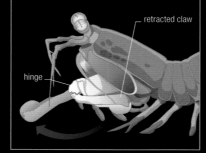

retracted claw

hinge

Odontodactylus scyllarus

◄► 6–7 in (15–18 cm)

⊙ Sandy and gravelly sea shore near reefs in Indian and Pacific oceans.

▥ Brightly colored and patterned, blue-green with leopard spots; bright red appendages.

Claw display
Kerengga ant-like jumper

This jumping spider gains protection from its enemies by resembling a kerengga, or weaver ant, both in appearance and the way it moves. The female resembles a single ant, the adult male an ant carrying a small ant. The "small ant" is in fact a pair of long chelicerae (claws) that make up a third of his total length. Males use their claws as swords when fighting over females and open them to reveal fangs. The claws are too clumsy to be of any use for feeding so males no longer eat once they are sexually mature.

Myrmarachne plataleoides

◄► ¼–⅜ in (6–12 mm)

⊙ Trees and bushes where there are weaver ant colonies in India, Sri Lanka, China, and southeast Asia.

▥ Dark brown and resembles a weaver ant. Male much larger than female.

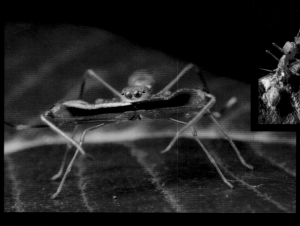

HEAD TO HEAD
When fighting, rival males face each other with their giant claws open, showing off their fangs. The victor is usually the male with the widest claw span.

MASS MATING
Mayfly swarms, such as this one over the Tisza River in Hungary, can be a spectacular sight. Nymphs all metamorphose at the same time and swarms can reach vast densities over short stretches of water.

Race to mate
Giant mayfly

Adult mayflies have the briefest of lives, during which they do not feed but devote all their efforts to breeding. They live for about a year as aquatic nymphs, buried in sediment at the bottom of lakes and rivers. Here they can reach population densities of around 500 individuals per square foot (more than 5,000 per square meter). They all metamorphose into adults at the same time, emerging from the water in vast swarms. As mayflies only survive for between one and three days after hatching out as adults, there is a desperate rush to mate. The male mayflies jostle with one another in competition for females before falling from from the air, their energy utterly spent. A female then deposits up to 8,000 eggs on the surface of the water.

Hexagenia limbata

◄► 1½–1¾ in (3.5–4.5 cm)

⊙ Large rivers and lakes in North America and Europe.

▥ Greenish yellow; two very long filaments at end of abdomen.

Body slam

Hercules beetle

Male hercules beetles have two long horns, which can be longer than the rest of body. The upper (thoracic) horn is fixed and has a hairy lower edge; the lower (cephalic) horn can be moved up and down so that the two horns act as pincers. Females differ in appearance to males, having a layer of reddish hairs on their wing cases and no horns. Hercules beetles are solitary but if males meet in the presence of a female they fight, engaging first in head-bobbing that produces a chirping sound. This may progress to a battle in which each male tries to grasp his rival between his horns and slam him to the ground. Wounds are common and the loser may be slashed in two.

Dynastes hercules

↔ ³⁄₁₆–½ in (0.5–1.5 cm)

⊙ Tropical rain forest in Central and South America and some Caribbean islands.

🗀 Yellow, green, or brown body with black spots; black head. Females may be larger than males, but look smaller because they lack horns.

SIMILAR SPECIES
Chaleosoma mollenkampi (left), from Borneo and other parts of Indonesia, has three horns, two above and one below. The European rhinoceros beetle, *Oryctes nasicornis* (above), has a single, backward curving horn.

A hercules beetle can lift an object **850 times** its own body weight, making it one of the strongest animals on earth.

Wide-eyed winners

Diopsid fly

These flies are also called stalk-eyed flies, because their eyes are on long stalks that protrude outward from the sides of their heads. Males with the longest eye-stalks are preferred by females and they usually win contests with shorter rivals that tend to have shorter eye-stalks. Males compete for prime positions at leks and meet each other face-to-face in contests so that they can compare the distance between their own eyes with that of their rival. The male with the shorter eye-stalk span generally backs down, avoiding what could be a costly fight that he is likely to lose.

Teleopsis dalmanni

↔ ¼–³⁄₈ in (6–9 mm)

⊙ Low-lying vegetation in humid places, such as on banks of streams or rivers, and in wetlands in Malaysia.

🗀 Yellow and brown with red eyes on long projections from side of head. Eye-stalks are much longer in males than in females.

STALK SPAN
A diopsid fly rests on vegetation near a river. Groups of flies meet in the morning near water at lekking sites to mate. Females cluster around males with the longest stalks. Males defend their positions in frequent displaying contests and the wide span between the fly's eyes is key to determining his success.

Fruit fight

Fig wasps

Fig wasps, of which there are about 650 species worldwide, live in a symbiotic relationship with fig trees. The wasps nest inside figs, their larvae feeding on the fleshy interior, and female wasps, which have wings, carry pollen from one fig to another. Males occur in two forms: winged and wingless. Wingless males never leave their home fig but dig a tunnel that enables winged males and females to reach the outside world. The wingless male fig wasps use their large, slicing jaws to engage in vicious fights with rivals for the right to breed with females that they encounter inside the fruit. In contrast, winged males lack jaws, do not fight, and mate with flying females outside the fig.

Family *Agaonidae*

↔ ¹⁄₁₆–⅛ in (1–3 mm)

⊙ Develops in fruit of fig trees, which are found throughout the tropics and in warmer temperate regions of southern Europe and Asia.

🗀 Minute wasps with small body and generally short antennae. Most have strong, metallic colors.

LEAVING HOME
These fig wasps are emerging from the fruit that provides them with shelter and sustenance. All fig wasps hatch inside the fruit, and males fight each other for the chance to mate with females. Males compete with wasps from other broods that may have hatched in the same fig.

Fighting flies

Stag fly

Male stag flies fight for the possession of sites where females will come to lay their eggs so that, when a female fly arrives, the winner is able to mate with her. Males have pronged, antlerlike projections on their heads and they use these to grapple with one another when fighting, locking their antlers together in a similar way to red deer stags (see p.351). At the same time, they extend their long legs, stretching them out as far as they can in order to make themselves appear as tall and threatening as possible to their rivals. Larger males have larger antlers and generally defeat smaller males, which tend to have small antlers (see panel, below). Contests between males over a female are usually resolved before mating begins, but rival males sometimes try to knock a mating male off the back of the female. Egg-laying sites are typically located on recently felled tree trunks that contain the rotting wood on which the larvae will feed. Once a male holds such a site, he releases a pheromone from a gland on his abdomen, which attracts females that are in a breeding condition and ready to lay their eggs. After mating, the male stays with the female, guarding her while she lays her eggs, and preventing other males from mating with her until she has finished.

Phytalmia cervicornis

⬌ ³/₈ in (1 cm)

⊙ Forests in Papua New Guinea.

▥ Very long legs; pronged projections on the head; reddish brown; eyes yellow and purple in males, yellow in female.

SIMILAR SPECIES
Two male goat flies *(Phytalmia mouldsi)* from Northern Australia (above) use their long legs as stilts and grapple with one another, their short, stout horns locked together. A male moose fly *(Phytalmia alcicornis)* from New Guinea (left) has broad, flat antlers, which can be so large and cumbersome that they become a hindrance.

ANATOMY

SIZE MATTERS

The relative size of two males' antlers determines which one will win a fight and thus earn the right to mate. Males vary in size, reflecting differences in their growth as larvae. The antlers of the smallest males are little more than stumps, as seen in the stag fly below, and these males have very low mating success. In many animals that have specialized weapons for combat, males try to avoid physical fights to reduce costs in terms of time, energy expenditure, and possible injury. Instead, they assess the size of each other's weapons and the male with the smaller weapons backs down.

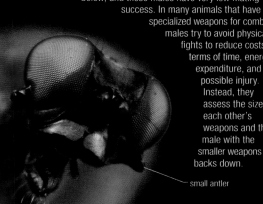

small antler

LOCKING HORNS
Two male stag flies grapple with one another for the right to claim a site where females will come to mate. Raising themselves up as high as they can on their long legs, they lock horns and seek to push one another over. Eventually, one will be pushed back and will give way to the victor.

Symphodus melops

◨ Up to 10 in (25 cm)

◉ Among seaweed just below tidal zone in Scandinavia and the British Isles.

▢ Male brown with greenish turquoise blotches on body and stripes on head; female reddish brown. Black spot on caudal peduncle.

In disguise
Corkwing wrasse

Large male corkwing wrasse construct nests using seaweed with females inspecting them as they build. If one seems a safe site, a visiting female lays its eggs there. The male then fertilizes these eggs and defends the nest until they hatch. Smaller adult males do not build nests, but become "sneakers." They mimic female coloration and behavior to dupe larger males and gain access to their nests. Once inside, they shed sperm on the eggs already laid, seeking to fertilize any that have not been fertilized by the nest's owner.

Breaking and entering
Bluegill sunfish

When it comes to fertilization, male bluegill sunfish take one of three roles: "parental" males, "sneaker" males, or "satellite" males, each with a different reproductive strategy. The parental male builds a nest. It finds a depression on the bed of a lake or stream and clears it of debris. It then grunts to attract a passing female. After courtship, in which they swim in circles and touch bellies, the female deposits eggs in the parental male's nest and he

IDEAL MATE
The nest-building "parental" male bluegill sunfish has sperm of a superior quality to the males that don't build nests, which is why female fish favor parental males with their eggs.

fertilizes them. The male then guards these eggs against predators and fans them to keep them well oxygenated. A female can lay up to 50,000 eggs, allocating batches of them to several different parental males, each of whom guards eggs from several females. Sneaker males dart into undefended nests, while satellite males mimic female appearance and behavior in order to gain access to nests. Both will shed their sperm once inside the nest, in an attempt to fertilize any unfertilized eggs.

Lepomis macrochirus

◨ 4–6 in (10–15 cm), occasionally up to 16 in (41 cm)

◉ Lakes and slow-moving rocky streams in the US and Canada.

▢ Small mouth, rounded, forked tail, olive-green above, yellow below, black spot on cheek, blue edges to gills.

Mouth to mouth
Red cichlid

The female red cichlid looks after up to 3,000 eggs in a nest inside a cave, while the male keeps guard outside. If there are confrontational interactions between the defending male and an interloper, they are normally resolved by means of a display of temporary bright colors, after which the smaller fish backs down. However, well-matched fishes of similar size and color engage in bouts of mouth wrestling.

Cichlasoma festae

◨ Up to 10 in (25 cm), female smaller than male

◉ Lakes and slow-moving rivers in South America.

▢ Female brown or green, mature male red or yellow, both with dark vertical stripes.

AGGRESSIVE LIP-LOCK
Also known as "red terrors," red cichlids are extremely aggressive fish. Here, two equally matched male rival cichlids have locked their mouths together in a trial of strength.

Butting in
Galapagos giant tortoise

Now highly endangered, these impressive creatures can live for over 100 years and reach maturity at 20–30 years. They spend their days moving between open areas during the cool part of the day and shady wooded areas when it is hot.

Galapagos giant tortoises mate during the rainy season, between January and June. Males use a variety of techniques to

establish their dominance and protect their mating rights, including raising their heads at rivals (see below) and shell butting, in which one male butts the shell of another in a show of aggression until one tortoise backs down. Mating itself is a lengthy process, and the underside of a male's shell is concave, which enables him to maintain a precarious grip on the back of the female during the slow task of mating. Once mating has taken place, females retire to dry areas of the island between June and December in order to nest.

Geochelone nigra

◨ Up to 4½ ft (1.4 m)

◉ Moves between open, dry grassland and vegetated areas with pools on Galapagos Islands (six subspecies— one on each of six islands).

▢ Dark ward shell, often covered in lichen. In some subspecies, front of shell behind neck arched.

≫ 189

HIGHER STATUS
Male Galapagos giant tortoises have an interesting method of establishing power. In a dispute, each tortoise raises its head as high as possible. The one that raises its head the highest gains dominance.

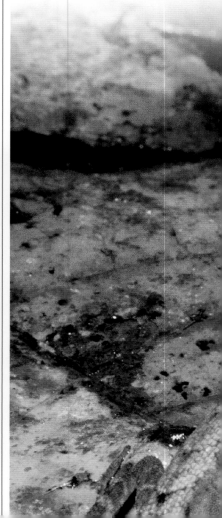

Wrestling match

Strawberry poison frog

Male strawberry poison frogs live only about 9¾ ft (3 m) apart from one another, and engage in prolonged bouts of wrestling in defense of their small mating territories. Active by day, they produce territorial calls in the morning and then, later in the day, change the nature of their call to one that attracts females. If a rival male enters into another's territory, the resident male increases its call rate as a warning to the intruder. If this fails to deter the rival, the two then grapple with each other, trying to force their opponent to the ground, until a winner emerges. The loser then vacates the territory, leaving the winner in possession. The bright coloration of poison frogs warns predators that they are toxic.

POWERFUL LEG PUSH
Strawberry poison frogs do battle chest-to-chest, each pushing down hard with strong back legs, trying to shove its opponent over.

Oophaga pumilio

↔ ½–1 in (1.5–2.5 cm)

◐ Rain forest, from sea level up to 3,165 ft (960 m) in Costa Rica, Nicaragua, Panama.

▥ Most commonly red body with black spots and blue, black, or purple hind legs.

A VICTOR EMERGES
When one male manages to force the other to the ground, the victor gains dominance over the loser and wins the contested territory.

20 minutes. The maximum length of time rival male strawberry poison frogs may wrestle each other.

WARNING SIGNAL
The brightly colored flap of loose skin hanging from the ground anole's neck acts as a flag of aggression, warning off rivals who challenge the male for its territory.

Hidden warning

Ground anole

This South American lizard feeds among leaf litter on the forest floor and is frequently found perched on tree trunks with its head pointing downward. Its pale and dull brownish green coloration affords it excellent camouflage in the gloom of the forest. However, when necessary, the male ground anole is able to produce a brilliant flash of color that makes it highly visible, both to potential mates and to rivals.

The dewlap is a flap of skin positioned under the ground anole's chin. It is the only brightly colored part of the lizard's body. Normally, it is folded away, but it can be unfolded and revealed to create a brilliant display. A special bone that is hinged at the base of the tongue is flicked outward and downward. This bone pushes out the dewlap to expose it. When defending its territory, the ground anole makes use of this colorful part of its body, displaying it to warn off other males that want to encroach on its territory. If the display fails to deter the rival, a fight ensues. The defender bobs his head, then rears up and proceeds to chase his rival. They then bite one another and use their long, muscular tails to lash each other, until in the end the weaker of the two males submits.

The colorful dewlap also serves another important function. Female ground anoles are attracted to the bright displays made by the territorial male. Different species of ground anole, otherwise very similar in appearance, have dewlaps of different colors, and the color helps the female identify males of her own species to mate with.

Norops humilis

↔ Up to 4½ in (11.5 cm), female slightly larger than male

◐ Lowland forest, especially common in abandoned cacao plantations in Costa Rica, Honduras, and Panama.

▥ Slender body, long tail, brown, adult male with red dewlap with yellow edge.

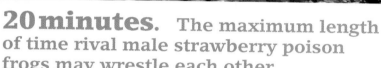

Writhing about

Speckled rattlesnake

Rattlesnakes have lethal weapons but avoid using them when fighting among themselves. They reserve their venom to kill prey and defend against enemies. However, males fight over access to females and engage in prolonged wrestling bouts lasting for over an hour, in which each attempts to pin his opponent's head against the ground. Mating occurs in spring, and females give birth to 3–11 young in late summer.

Crotalus mitchellii

- 24–30 in (62–77 cm)
- Arid scrub and desert in the southwest US and Mexico.
- Color variable: earth tones from brown to orange or pink, with dark speckled blotches along back and dark rings around tail.

Neck lock

Slow-worm

Male slow-worms are not territorial but frequently fight with rival males for the possession of females. They wrestle and bite each other around the head and neck, and older males often have many scars from previous fights. Females may also be scarred, since males grasp them firmly around the neck during mating, which lasts several hours. Fighting and mating occur in April, and females give birth to 6–12 live young in September or October. The exact timing of the birth depends on the average temperature during the summer. Young slow-worms are born later if the summer has been cold and, like their parents, go into hibernation during the winter months. Though they are often mistaken for snakes, slow-worms are in fact legless lizards.

Anguis fragilis

- 12–19½ in (30–50 cm)
- Well-vegetated, slightly damp habitats, including yards, in Europe.
- Snakelike shape; eyelid and external ear; very smooth skin; brown or gray, sometimes reddish or coppery in color. Females may have dark stripe on back.

Pecking contest

Mute swan

Among the heaviest of flying birds, a male mute swan can weigh as much as 26 lb (12 kg) and is a formidable opponent, both to rival males and to other animals, including humans, that approach his nest. Mute swans are monogamous, forming pairs in March or April. Males, known as cobs, and females, called pens, share in nest building, incubation of the eggs, and protection of the young. The cob, which is slightly larger, is particularly aggressive

in defending the territory, assuming a posture, called "busking," in which the neck is curved and the wings are arched over the back. If a rival is not deterred by this, a fight ensues in which they peck at each other and strike out with their wings. The nest, a large mound of vegetation built at the water's edge, is often used for several years. A pair normally produces five to seven young, called cygnets, but may produce up to 12. Pairs that breed successfully generally stay together for several years.

POWERFUL RIVALS

Fights between mute swans can be violent and occasionally end in death. Smaller birds are attacked if they stray too close to the nest.

Cygnus olor

- 4–5½ ft (1.2–1.7 m)
- Rivers, lakes, and reservoirs in Europe and Asia, naturalized in North America.
- Pure white plumage; orange bill with black knob at base, larger in male. Young (cygnets) gray-brown with black bill.

GETTING IN A FLAP

As soon as a rival swan enters a male's territory he charges across to confront it. By raising their bodies out of the water, each is able to judge the other's size, giving the smaller male a chance to back down and escape.

RUFFLED FEATHERS
Two independent male ruffs with darker coloring (left and right) display their breeding plumage along with a paler satellite male (center).

FEMALE CHOICE

The different strategies of male ruffs have evolved as a result of female choice. Females prefer to mate with males in busy parts of the lek. Therefore, independent males encourage satellite males to come close, by bowing. This increases the chances of a satellite male mating with a female attracted to an independent male's spot on the lek, but it also increases his chances.

satellite male | independent male

SATELLITE WELCOMED

female

INDEPENDENT MALE ATTRACTS FEMALE

SATELLITE CONCEDES DEFEAT

Dressing the part
Ruff

In the spring, ruffs gather at hereditary mating sites, called leks. The males display silently, jumping up and down and erecting the spectacular ruff and ear tufts around their heads. Males have three different mating strategies, each associated with a particular, genetically determined plumage pattern. Independent males have black or brown plumage and many defend small mating territories within the lek. Paler plumaged satellite males gather in groups around the independent males. A third group of males, whose plumage is intermediate between that of females and males, mimic female behavior and wander about the lek. A female, called a reeve, enters a lek and inspects the displaying males, before selecting one to mate with.

Philomachus pugnax
◀▶ 11½–12½ in (29–32 cm)

⬤ Marshes, lake shores, and estuaries in northern Europe, Scandinavia, Russia; migrates to Africa, Asia, western Europe in winter.

📖 Brown above, pale below. Males develop large erectile ruff around neck and ear tufts that may be black, brown or white in breeding season.

Holding court
Andean cock-of-the-rock

Male Andean cocks-of-the-rock display communally, competing to be the most attractive to females. Each male clears foliage from a small area on the forest floor, called a "court." When a female approaches a group of males, each male raises his fan-shaped crest and displays his brilliant orange plumage; they also hop up and down. A female moves among the males before choosing one, mating with him and then leaving the lek to go to a rocky area where she makes a nest. Once the mated female has left, the males wait for the next one to arrive and then display again. She often selects the same male as the female before her.

Rupicola peruvianus
◀▶ 8 in (20 cm)

⬤ Cliffs and rocky outcrops in tropical and subtropical rain forest in French Guiana, Guyana, and Surinam.

📖 Male brilliant orange with black and gray wings; female brown.

CHOOSING A MATE
The female Andean cock-of-the-rock (on the right in this image) is less brightly colored than the males. As with many birds it is she, rather than the male, who decides who to mate with.

BRIGHT AND BEAUTIFUL
The male Andean cock-of-the-rock stands out like a jewel in the shade near the rain-forest floor. His crest, raised here in display, is normally held flat against the top of his head.

CLEANING UP
A female dunnock (right) presents herself, ready to mate with a male. The male will attempt to remove a rival's sperm before fertilizing her himself.

Three's company
Dunnock

A female dunnock mates with more than one male during the breeding season—a mating pattern known as polyandry. Her two mates compete with one another to father as many of her young as possible, by mating with her frequently. Before mating, a male pecks at the female's cloaca, or reproductive opening, causing her to eject sperm left from previous matings. This increases the chance that his own sperm will fertilize her eggs rather than that of a rival. Both males provide paternal care for the young, and the amount of help each provides is related to the proportion of the young in the clutch he has fathered.

Prunella modularis
◀▶ 5½ in (14 cm)

⬤ Hedgerows, bushes, and coppices in Europe and Asia.

📖 Dark brown above, gray below; dark, thin bill.

Winning crest
Yellow-headed Amazon parrot

As in many parrots, both sexes of the yellow-headed Amazon parrot are brightly colored and they pair for life. During aggressive interactions, such as when competing for a mate, they raise their bright yellow crest as a sign of dominance—erecting the crest feathers makes the parrot look larger. They have a complex vocal repertoire, which they learn from other members of their local population, so that each population has its own vocal "tradition."

Amazona oratrix
◀▶ 15–17 in (38–43 cm)

⬤ Forest and mangroves in Belize, Honduras, Guatemala, and Mexico.

📖 Robust build, rounded wings, square tail. Bright green with yellow head and thighs and a red patch on the wings.

GOLDEN CROWN
The raised crest feathers of this yellow-headed Amazon parrot give the impression of increased size, especially in profile.

CLASH OF THE TITANS
Two bull elephant seals fighting. They roar loudly through their inflated noses, butt each other with bodies raised, and tear at the thick fat on the neck with their teeth. The resulting bloody wounds are usually superficial but can be fatal.

The **roar of the male elephant seal** can be heard **several miles** away.

Winner takes all

Northern elephant seal

Only a minority of male elephant seal males mate with females, and for those that do, success is short-lived. Between December and March, large breeding groups of seals gather on offshore islands. Males are much larger than females and fight violently to become "harem masters," giving them exclusive access to 10 or 12 females. Males vying for dominance will initially use visual and vocal displays to fend off any rivals, inflating their distinctive proboscises to emit incredibly loud roars. Should these displays fail to settle matters then physical combat ensues. Competing males rush at each other, rear their necks,

slap, butt, and bite in fierce clashes. The males' necks and shoulders develop thick, corrugated skin and a layer of protective fat to help minimize injury during these encounters. Despite this, severe injuries among males are common and may be fatal. Only one in ten males becomes a harem master and none holds the status for more than three years, whereas females may breed for ten years.

Mirounga angustirostris

- 9¾–16½ ft (3–5 m)
- Coastal waters of the Pacific Ocean; breed on offshore islands between Alaska and Mexico.
- Dark brown; male is darker. Male has huge, inflated proboscis.

» 405

CROWDED COLONIES
Almost reduced to extinction by hunters, northern elephant seals are now protected and numbers have soared. As a result, the few islands suitable for breeding have become very crowded.

PAYING THE PRICE
The violent lifestyle of males takes its toll, and some die as a result of fights. While females commonly live for 22 years, males rarely live for more than 17.

CASE STUDY
PUP MORTALITY

Elephant seals spend most of their time at sea, but must come ashore to give birth, to mate, and to molt. Mating takes place soon after the female has given birth, and the tiny pups are often crushed beneath the clumsy, lumbering adults, especially when they are fighting. As the population rises and breeding beaches become more crowded, mortality among pups becomes more common.

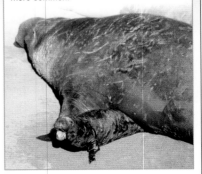

Locking horns

Red deer

During the fall rut, red deer stags compete to win a harem of hinds (female deer) with whom they mate exclusively. Older males are heavier with larger antlers; they proclaim the ownership of a territory, into which they herd their harem, by roaring. Harem holders are challenged by rivals, in a vocal contest. If this does not settle the dispute, the two stags go into a parallel walk, in which they walk side-by-side to assess each other's size. A closely matched pair will fight by charging at each other and locking antlers.

Cervus elaphus
- 5–6½ ft (1.5–2 m)
- Western Europe, Asia, northwest America, northwest Africa. Open woodland, plains, mountains, moorland.
- Reddish brown; male has mane on neck. Males grow antlers in August and shed from February to April.

ASSERTIVE CALL
With head thrown back and nostrils flared the roaring red deer stag signals his presence. The call is used to advertise his status, pronounce his territory, ward off rival males, and attract breeding females.

PARALLEL CLASH
Two bucks size each other up as they begin to fight, clashing their huge antlers. Some stags are injured or killed in such contests.

Kick in the teeth

Grant's zebra

Male Grant's zebras, like other zebra species, kick and bite viciously in defense of females. They live in small social groups containing a single stallion, several females, and their foals. Females remain in the group into which they were born for their whole life. Males leave when they become independent of their mother, living in bachelor groups until they are fully grown.

KICK IN THE TEETH
A Grant's zebra stallion uses his powerful hind legs to deliver a kick to a rival. Such blows can be deadly, capable of shattering the skulls of predators like hunting dogs.

Then they try to take over a group by challenging the stallion for possession of his harem, which may contain as many as 16 females. If food becomes patchily distributed, harem groups come together in large herds, which provides an opportunity for males to contest the possession of harems. Males use their sharp, chisel-shaped front teeth and hooves to fight, sometimes inflicting severe wounds on one another.

Equus burchelii boehmi
- 7¼–8¼ ft (2.2–2.5 m)
- Grassland and savannah in East Africa.
- Bold black and white stripes, vertical on the neck and body, horizontal on the rump.
- ≫ 465

Neck and neck

Reticulated giraffe

Young male giraffes establish dominance among one another with neck-wrestling contests that can last up to 30 minutes. These look friendly, but occasionally a male's neck may be broken. Giraffes live in loose social groups of up to 20 animals. Mature bulls roam among groups looking for females ready to mate. If challenged by another male, they fight by kicking and head butting.

STYLIZED COMBAT
These young male giraffes are engaged in a neck-wrestling contest. These are generally more of a ritual than violent clash. The winner may mount his opponent in a display of dominance.

Giraffa camelopardalis reticulata
- 15½–19 ft (4.7–5.7 m) tall
- Open woodland and wooded grassland in Northern Kenya, Somalia.
- Reddish brown with a pale reticulated pattern.
- ≫ 193, 395

Biting and butting

Bottlenose dolphin

Male bottlenose dolphins often have deep scars on their skin, suggesting that they fight one another for access to females. Dominant males bite, head butt, and scratch younger males with their teeth to establish sexual dominance. Acrobatic swimming displays are generally aimed at impressing females but they can also be used as a form of attack (see below).

Despite this rivalry, groups of males may cooperate in coercing females to breed. Coalitions of male bottlenose dolphins are known to have forced a female dolphin away from her pod by butting and body slamming her before taking it in turns to mate with her. They co-operate to fend off other male alliances who attempt to join in.

Tursiops truncatus
- 6¼–13 ft (1.9–4 m)
- In tropical and warm temperate open sea and coastal waters worldwide.
- Large beaked dolphin with pointed flippers, and sickle-shaped dorsal fin.
- ≫ 461

DIVE BOMBING
≫01 A male bottlenose dolphin leaps high out of the water, off the coast of Hawaii in the Pacific Ocean, and strikes another dolphin in the head with his fluke. A dolphin's tail is incredibly powerful since it is needed to propel the animal through the water. ≫02 The lower dolphin retaliates by rising up to strike the jumping dolphin with his rostrum, or beak.

ANATOMY

ARMORED SKULL

As they age, bull giraffes develop thickened deposits of bone on their foreheads. This layer gives vital protection to the brain, which could otherwise be damaged by the violent swinging and clubbing actions employed by competing bulls. A giraffe bull's brain can survive a swing of 11½ ft (3.5 m) and the impact of a blow that could knock a 1.6 ton (1,500 kg) rival off his feet. The bone is deposited at a rate of 2½ lb (1 kg) per year.

bony deposits

Courtship

Courtship involves interaction between males and females that culminates in mating. Ranging from the perfunctory to the very elaborate, successful courtship is about "getting it right"—mating with the right species and right sex, at the right time, and being in the right "mood," which means suppressing behavior incompatible with mating.

The right species

Mating with a member of another species is a serious mistake —an individual's reproductive potential can be wasted. In order to avoid this, males and females have evolved methods to send out signals that enable potential partners to distinguish them from members of other species. For example, male birds have species-specific color patterns and songs; male frogs have distinctive calls; and male and female mammals produce chemical scents called pheromones. Females have more to lose by making a mistake when choosing a partner; because they may have only one chance to reproduce, they need to be more discerning.

CALLING MALE
Male Verreaux's tree frogs call to attract females from perches on the banks of ponds. Their call differs to those of other nearby male frogs.

tasmaniensis
dumerili
signifera
verreauxi
ewingi
peroni
raniformis

FROG CALLS

DOMINANT FREQUENCIES
In some Australian ponds, male frogs of several species call for mates on the same nights. Species recognition is made easier for the female since males each have distinctive calls and call from particular places. The calls of species that are adjacent differ more than those that hold widely separated sites.

signifera
ewingi
verreauxi
tasmaniensis
raniformis
peroni
dumerili

FREQUENCY (KHZ)

4.0
3.0
2.0
1.0
0

0   100   200   300   400
TIME (MILLISECONDS)

Recognizing the opposite sex

Recognizing a member of the opposite sex is easy in species with sexual dimorphism, where one sex is markedly larger or more brightly colored than the other. Many species also have special signals, which can be visual, olfactory, or auditory, and signal which sex they are. Some male frogs are not good at sex recognition and clasp males as readily as females. A clasped male gives a "release call" that makes the other male let go. When sexual dimorphism is extreme, as in spiders, the male is in danger of becoming prey.

LITTLE AND LARGE
This tiny male black widow spider approaches a female with caution, signaling that he is a potential mate and not a meal.

Choosing a mate

Animals can improve their reproductive success by favoring certain partners over others. Many male fishes and amphibians select larger females, which produce more eggs. If males help care for the young, females prefer mates that are better at building a nest and defending it, or at feeding young. In species where males provide only sperm, a female's choice is often based on male appearance and behavior, which show that he has "good genes."

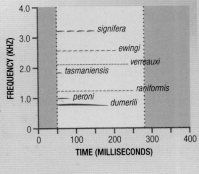

SIZE MATTERS
Female three-spine sticklebacks prefer males that are very aggressive in defending nests; males prefer fatter females.

SCENT OF A STRANGER
Mice discriminate among potential mates on the basis of their smell, preferring those that are not genetically closely related to them.

The right time

In many species, courtship behavior serves to synchronize the activities of males and females so that mating occurs at the best moment. Female mammals typically have a brief period when their eggs can be fertilized; courtship behavior both signals this and determines when it occurs by stimulating egg production. In colonial species, it is beneficial for individuals to lay eggs or produce young at the same time to lessen the risk of predation. The combined effect of many pairs displaying to their partners is to prompt such synchronization. In species with external fertilization (see p.366), precise coordination is needed to ensure that eggs or sperm are not lost before they can meet.

SMOOTH NEWT

Female smooth newts must signal to a male that they are ready to gather up his spermatophore (sperm packet) by touching his tail; if they do not, his sperm may be lost.

COURTSHIP DANCE

The courtship behavior of newts consists of a number of distinct phases. The male does not proceed from one phase to the next until the female has responded positively to the current phase by approaching him. Despite this, some spermatophores are missed by the female, so the later parts of the sequence are repeated.

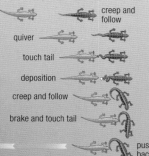

GIFT WRAPPED

A male European bee-eater presents a dragonfly that he has caught to a female. Courtship gifts like this serve two functions: they provide extra nourishment for the female as she develops her eggs, and they provide her with information about his potential as a provider for her young.

Persuasion

A function of some aspects of courtship behavior is to raise the sexual motivation of the partner and, at the same time, to suppress behavior that is incompatible with mating, such as aggression. This is especially true of animals that are solitary, such as polar bears, and for whom any other animal is normally an enemy. In social animals, such as baboons, all group members compete frequently for food and their natural aggression must be overcome for mating to occur. Being hard to persuade acts as a mechanism of mate choice for a female, since it ensures that she will mate only with males that can sustain a high level of courtship activity; such males are likely to have better genes.

LIFE AND DEATH

>>01 A male praying mantis has to persuade a female to mate with him, but not to eat him. However, this female bites off the male's head, taking it as a nuptial gift. >>02 The male has paid a high price for his chance to reproduce; a more cautious male might have survived.

>>01

>>02

Aerial acrobatics

Marmalade hoverfly

Marmalade hoverflies are accomplished flyers, a skill that the males exploit by hovering on the spot to display their fitness to females. True flies, such as this species of hoverfly, have just one pair of functional wings, instead of two like most flying insects. The second pair of wings are reduced to clublike structures that act as balancing organs, giving them superb control in flight. Each male hoverfly claims an aerial territory and hovers there for many minutes at a time, leaving his chosen point in space only to drive off airborne intruders, or dart after interested females and begin the mating process

Episyrphus balteatus

◀▶ 5/16–1/2 in (8–12 mm)

☉ Forest, grassland, and yards in Europe and northern Asia.

📖 Two-winged fly with large brown eyes and yellow legs. Flattened abdomen is boldly striped.

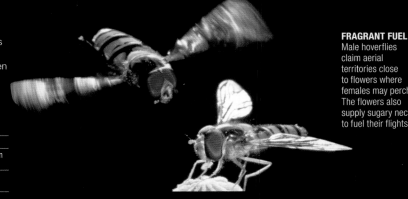

FRAGRANT FUEL
Male hoverflies claim aerial territories close to flowers where females may perch. The flowers also supply sugary nectar to fuel their flights.

Family Empididae

◀▶ 1/16–3/8 in (1–11 mm)

☉ On vegetation in lowland and damp habitats worldwide but mainly in Northern Hemishpere.

📖 Slender, dark gray-brown flies with small head, sturdy thorax, and long, hairy legs. Most species have elongated, downward-pointing proboscis.

Dance routine

Dance flies

These slender flies are named for their dancing courtship displays. Some species perform these while perched, the males using a ritual series of wing-flicks followed by a pedaling action of their front legs. If a male gets the dance right, the female responds in kind, and they mate. But if he is the wrong species of fly, with the wrong dance routine, the female may treat him as prey, and eat him.

Among most species of dance flies, the males "dance" in the air to draw attention to the nuptial gifts that they carry in their long legs. These are usually freshly killed insects such as other flies—including rival male dance flies of the same species. The gift-carrying males form dancing, airborne swarms to attract females, and when a male is approached by a female he passes her the insect in mid air and seizes her as she takes it. The linked pair then fly to a nearby perch, where the male supports the feeding female while he mates with her.

After mating, the male often retrieves his "gift" and flies back to the swarm to attract another female. He may use it several times, so it begins to look quite battered, but the females still take the bait.

> **CASE STUDY**
>
> ### EMPTY PROMISES
>
> Some male dance flies seduce females by presenting inedible gifts, saving the male the trouble of catching other insects. This female *Empis opaca* dance fly has been tempted by a ball of willow seed fluff that resembles an insect cocoon, and the male mates with her while she probes the fake offering. But careful observation has shown that many females see through the deception, and reject anything that is not clearly edible.

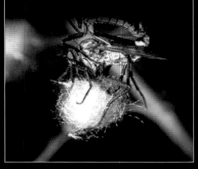

NUPTIAL GIFT
A male *Empis tessellata* dance fly mates with a female while she is sampling the plant bug that he has offered her. The male is supporting the weight of all three with his front legs.

Holding hands

Yellow scorpion

Courtship can be hazardous for a male scorpion. The female is larger, and although he is immune to her venom, she could easily overpower and eat him. After identifying himself with vibrating calls and distinctive scents, the male grasps the female's pincers with his own—partly to immobilize them, but also to guide her in a "dance" over the ground that ends with her taking up his sperm.

Buthus occitanus

◆ 4 in (10 cm)

◆ Desert and arid semi-desert regions of North Africa, the Middle East, and Southern Europe.

▭ Arachnid with two pincerlike pedipalps, jointed yellow body, and long tail ending in a sharp sting.

DEADLY DANCE
Tails entwined, a pair of yellow scorpions dance to and fro. As soon as the female picks up his sperm packet the male will beat a rapid retreat.

Chase and drop

Horn shark

Most fishes release large numbers of small eggs into the water, where they are fertilized by sperm released by the males—a process known as spawning. By contrast, sharks mate like land animals, with the male placing sperm in the female's body to fertilize her eggs internally. To achieve this, he must court the female to ensure her cooperation in the mating process. The male horn shark, for example, chases the female through the water until she is ready to accept his advances. They then sink to the seabed, where the male seizes the female and inserts one of his long "claspers"—modified pelvic fins—into her genital opening. He then pumps a mixture of seawater and sperm along a groove in the clasper, and into the female's oviduct. The whole procedure can last up to 40 minutes. A few weeks later, the female begins laying up to 24 fertilized eggs.

Heterodontus francisci

◆ 4 ft (1.2 m)

◆ Warm waters of the eastern Pacific, off California and Central America.

▭ Bottom-living shark with big, blunt head, a ridge over each eye, and two dorsal fins, each with a stout spine in front.

PINNED DOWN
Once the sharks have dropped to the sea floor, the male keeps a tight grip on the larger female's pectoral fin as he maneuvers his clasper into position.

Elaborate ritual

Pot-belly seahorse

Seahorses are bony fishes with armored bodies and prehensile tails, which they use to cling to seaweed as they feed. Almost uniquely, a female seahorse places her eggs in a pouch on the male's belly, where they develop until they are ready to hatch. One of the biggest species, the pot-belly seahorse, has an elaborate courtship ritual in which the male becomes more vividly colored and inflates his brood pouch with water. He swims toward a female with head tucked down and fins fluttering. If she is receptive, her own colors intensify and she adopts the same posture. The two then swim together, sometimes with their long tails entwined. This dance is rehearsed at dawn every day for three days or so until eventually, after a longer dance, the male urges the female to swim toward the surface with an upward gesture of his head. This elaborate routine is due to the long-term pair bond of the courting partners. Once at the surface, the female transfers 300 or more eggs to the male's pouch, injecting them through an opening at the front. He retains them for about four weeks until they hatch as tiny seahorses.

Hippocampus abdominalis

◆ 7–12 in (18–30 cm)

◆ Rocky reefs and sea-grass beds in coastal waters around southeast Australia and New Zealand.

▭ Large, mottled yellow to red seahorse with low crown, spines around eyes, deep-keeled body, and long tail. Male has prominent brood pouch on belly.

DANCING PARTNERS
As pot-belly seahorses dance together, their patterns intensify, with the paler colors becoming brighter to contrast with the dark spots on their bodies. Here the male is on the left, tilting his long snout to encourage the female to swim toward the surface.

SWOLLEN POUCH
When a male is ready to court a female, the brood pouch on his belly swells with water and changes color, turning white or pale yellow. This probably triggers an instinctive response in the female.

Lengthy dance

Banded pipefish

Slender, eel-like pipefishes swim together for hours in a protracted nuptial dance. Closely related to seahorses (see left), pipefishes have the same elongated snouts and bony, segmented body armor. The males also have the same reproductive role, retaining the females' eggs in a brood pouch beneath the body until they hatch. The banded pipefish is one of the most striking species, with its wasplike yellow and black bands and vivid red tail. Each male claims a territory in a favored patch of water, often in a tide pool or reef lagoon. In the early morning, a mature female that is ready to mate may enter the male's territory to attract his attention. The male then courts her, entwining his body with hers for two hours or more as they swim. Finally the female transfers her eggs to the male's brood pouch, where they are fertilized and start to develop into young pipefishes. The system ensures that the eggs are well protected, but once they are born the baby fish fend for themselves.

Doryrhamphus dactyliophorus

◆ 4–8 in (10–20 cm)

◆ Coastal waters and reefs in the tropical Indian and western Pacific oceans.

▭ Highly elongated fish, ringed with greenish yellow and black, and with a long, slender snout. Large oval red and white tail fin.

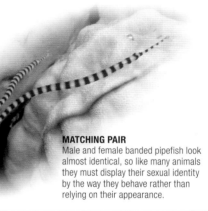

MATCHING PAIR
Male and female banded pipefish look almost identical, so like many animals they must display their sexual identity by the way they behave rather than relying on their appearance.

Lip locking

Gray angelfish

This elegant, slab-sided fish occurs on the coral reefs of the tropical Atlantic region, where it feeds mainly on sponges. It normally lives alone, but breeding pairs patrol a joint territory over deeper areas of reef, which they defend against other angelfishes. Having staked their claim, they perform a courtship display in which they may lock lips in an apparent kiss, before rising slowly, bringing their vents together and releasing their eggs and sperm into the water. They then separate and swim to the bottom, but repeat the procedure several times, releasing up to 75,000 eggs at each spawning.

Pomacanthus arcuatus

◆ 10–23½ in (25–60 cm)

◆ Coral reefs in Caribbean Sea, Gulf of Mexico, and tropical western Atlantic.

▭ Deep-bodied with gray head and pale mouth, dark-spotted gray body, bright yellow inside to pectoral fin, blue-gray band on tail, long tips on dorsal and anal fins.

TANDEM SWIMMING
A pair of gray angelfish cruises over a coral reef in tandem, ready to drive away any fish of the same species that may trespass on their chosen breeding territory.

Special delivery

Red-legged salamander

Like other amphibians, salamanders and newts must lay their eggs in water or very damp places. However, many salamanders mate on land, using a method that is quite unlike that of other vertebrates. The male's sperm is transferred to the female in a capsule called a spermatophore, which is placed on the ground for her to gather up. To ensure she collects the sperm package, most species have a complex courtship ritual. The male red-legged salamander releases an enticing pheromone that attracts the female. She then straddles his tail and he leads her in a circular "tail walk," stopping at intervals to anoint her snout with scent from a gland beneath his chin. Eventually he stops to deposit his spermatophore on the ground, before guiding her forward just far enough to take it into her oviduct.

Plethodon shermani

- 3¼–5 in (8–13 cm)
- Woodland in the eastern US.
- Sleek, slender salamander with long tail and large eyes; slimy skin mainly gray with red legs.

SEDUCTIVE SCENT
A red-legged salamander male turns to place a dab of scent on the female's snout during a tail-walk courtship in Nantahala National Forest, North Carolina, US. This species is one of the many lungless salamanders that absorb all their oxygen through their moist skin.

Triturus alpestris

- Up to 4½ in (12 cm)
- Mountainous regions of central Europe, to altitudes of 8,200 ft (2,500 m).
- Large-eyed, slender-bodied amphibian with short legs; brownish with dark spots and orange-red belly.
- » 401

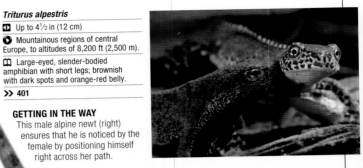

GETTING IN THE WAY
This male alpine newt (right) ensures that he is noticed by the female by positioning himself right across her path.

Demanding attention

Alpine newt

Newts have the same mating system as salamanders, but pursue their courtship underwater. Male European newts such as the alpine newt compete with each other for females, developing striking breeding colors and tall crests, and studies have shown that females tend to choose males with larger crests. A male alpine newt attempts to court a female by displaying his finery, commanding her attention by placing himself across the front of her. He releases a seductive pheromone into the water from a gland beneath his body, wafting it toward her with his tail, then deposits a soft-skinned spermatophore on the bottom where she can collect it.

Push-ups

Red-headed rock agama

Chameleons are not the only lizards that are able to change their skin color. The red-headed rock agama, or rainbow lizard, is named for the way a dominant male's head flushes bright orange-red or magenta during the breeding season, forming a dramatic contrast with his electric-blue body. He emphasizes the transformation by performing energetic push-ups with his forelegs to bob his glowing head up and down. This both discourages less brilliantly colored rivals and attracts females, for the vividness of the male's courtship colors are a measure of his health and vigor.

ARDENT GLOW
A male red-headed rock agama bobs his head at a female to show off his dazzling nuptial colors and persuade her to mate. These lizards often perform their courtship displays on bare rocks beneath the scorching African sun.

Friendly persuasion
Grass snake

Most snakes rely on scent to find a partner, using their forked tongues to pick up chemical signals that they analyze using an organ in the roof of the mouth. When a male grass snake locates a female, he follows her wherever she goes, and stimulates her by rubbing his chin along her back, flicking his tongue as he does so. If he is successful, they entwine their long bodies and mate.

SCALY CARESS
Much smaller than his partner, a male grass snake tries to persuade a female to mate by caressing her with his chin. She will eventually lay up to 40 eggs in a warm place.

Natrix natrix
- Up to 4 ft (1.2 m); rarely up to 6½ ft (2 m)
- Damp habitats, grassland, and meadow in Europe, Asia, and northwest Africa.
- Slender snake with oval head and round pupils, typically gray-green with yellow and black "collar."
- **» 290**

Biting embrace
Common snapping turtle

Notorious for its powerful bite, especially in its own defense, the snapping turtle is a strictly aquatic species that buries itself in the bottom mud of pools and streams to ambush its prey. It usually lives alone, but during the breeding season males and females come together for a rough courtship in which they bite each other and blow streams of bubbles. Eventually the male clambers on top of the female, gripping her shell with his claws. He curls his tail under her body until their vents meet, enabling him to fertilize her eggs.

Chelydra serpentina
- 8–18 in (20–46 cm)
- Muddy ponds, streams, and swamps in the US and southern Canada.
- Big-headed turtle with relatively small, smooth shell and long tail; usually tan to brown, sometimes black.

Color flush
Panther chameleon

Chameleons can contract or expand specialized color cells in their skin in order to change color rapidly. They use this ability to communicate with each other, and in many species, such as the panther chameleon, the males use sudden flushes of bright color during courtship. If receptive, a female will allow a male to fertilize her eggs, using one of two organs known as hemipenes. But if the female has already mated, she discourages the male by turning dark brown or black.

Furcifer pardalis
- 8–20in (20–50cm)
- Tropical forest and scrubland of Madagascar and surrounding islands.
- Large, deep-bodied lizard with prehensile tail and toes fused into two grasping hooks on each foot; very variable coloration.
- **» 222–23**

COOLING OFF
The red flush of a male rock agama is triggered by hormones and the heat of the sun. At dusk he reverts to a more discreet color scheme, making him less conspicuous to predators. Despite this, a dominant male retains his high status as defender of a family group and their joint territory.

Agama agama
- 8–10 in (20–25 cm)
- Rocky grassland in Central Africa.
- Long-tailed, flat-bodied lizard with triangular head; female brown with tan and buff spots; male blue-gray, turning bright red on head during courtship.

420 The number of different lizard species in the agama family.

Look to the skies

Blue-footed booby

Blue-footed boobies are ocean birds that breed in enormous coastal colonies, mainly on islands. The male selects a small nesting territory within the colony and parades around it, displaying to discourage rivals and advertising to females.

He spreads his wings, rotating them so their upper surfaces face forward, raises his tail, and positions his bill straight up in a posture known as "sky-pointing." He also performs a stately dance, lifting his big blue feet alternately to draw attention to their vivid color. If a female is suitably impressed by his performance, she will join him to form a pair. The two birds maintain their bond by continuing to display to each other using the same ritual postures. These rituals are performed before one bird leaves the nest to fly out to sea in search of food and are then repeated in greeting when the bird returns.

Sula nebouxii

- 30–33 in (76–84 cm)
- Breeds on eastern Pacific coasts and islands from Mexico to Peru, and Galapagos, feeding at sea.
- Large seabird with long, sharp bill, blue-gray face, white body, black wings, and bright blue webbed feet.

20,000
The number of pairs of blue-footed boobies that return to the volcanic Galapagos Islands to nest every year.

SKY-POINTING
The male booby's sky-pointing courtship display becomes part of a pair-bonding ritual that is performed by both birds.

FOOT-TAPPING DANCE
During its dancing display, a blue-footed booby raises each brightly colored foot in turn with a high-stepping flourish.

CASE STUDY
THE BLUER THE BETTER

Studies of breeding male blue-footed boobies have shown that those with the bluest feet have more breeding success, because females are more likely to choose them as partners. The females clearly find intensely blue feet attractive, but a deeper color may also be a measure of general fitness. Since young birds tend to inherit their fathers' assets, the feet of the whole population must be getting bluer.

Bearing gifts

Little tern

Courtship displays of male birds demonstrate that they are fit and healthy, and will pass on strong genes to their young. But for females, selecting a good provider can be just as important, because if her young are not fed well enough, they will starve.

The males of some species display their skills during courtship by offering potential mates gifts of food. A male little tern offers a freshly caught fish. This both proves that he can catch fish, and also provides the female with welcome extra nutrition at a time when she needs it to produce eggs. If she accepts, he will keep feeding her until she lays her clutch of two or three eggs. Little tern pairs usually stay together for life.

Sterna albifrons

- 8½–9½ in (22–24 cm)
- Nests on sand or pebbly beaches in eastern Atlantic, Mediterranean, Indian Ocean, and western Pacific and feeds at sea.
- Fine-billed, short-legged seabird with long, pointed wings and short, forked tail, white below, gray upperparts, and black cap.

FISHY OFFERING
Having caught a fish by plunge-diving into the water from the air, a male little tern offers it to his mate without even landing. Such a display is a practical demonstration of his fitness and fishing skill—both important qualifications in a father.

Seductive backslider

Red-capped manakin

In the lush forests of Costa Rica, vividly colored male red-capped manakins display on perches, competing against each other to attract females. Each performs a variety of rituals, including sliding backward along the perch with its head lowered and wings raised to reveal the bright yellow plumage on its legs. If this exhibition is good enough, the olive-green female will choose to mate with him. However, he takes no further part in raising her young. Instead, he continues to display, hoping to seduce more females.

Pipra mentalis

- 4 in (10 cm)
- Lowland tropical forest in Central America and northwestern South America.
- Female is small and olive-green; male is black with bright red head and yellow "thighs."

Flash of color

Red-winged blackbird

Dazzling courtship plumage can help a male bird win a mate, but it also makes him conspicuous to enemies. The red-winged blackbird avoids this by concealing his brilliant red shoulder patches beneath black plumage and flashing them only when he is defending a breeding territory and hoping to attract females.

Like the red-capped manakin (see left), this species is polygamous, with each successful male mating with many females. The females nest alone, so they are only interested in the male's fitness, as demonstrated by the vigor of his display.

Agelaius phoeniceus

- 7–7½ in (18–19 cm)
- Wetlands and farmland in North America and Central America.
- Male black overall, except for red, often yellow-fringed shoulder patches. Female streaky brown.

Weed dance

Great crested grebe

Some male birds court females by demonstrating their skill at building nests. The practical value of this is clear, but in many species the demonstration has been reduced to a ritual gift of nesting material.

Great crested grebes build their floating nests from water plants, and as part of their courtship, both male and female present each other with billfuls of waterweed or pondweed. This is the climax of a spectacular courtship ceremony that takes place on the lakes on which great crested grebes breed. The birds rear up out of the water, breast to breast, paddling rapidly, and swinging their heads from side to side. The balletic effect of this "weed dance" is enhanced by the head plumes of both sexes, which fan out to form flamboyant ruffs.

Other grebes have similar displays. The western grebe of North America engages in a dramatic "rushing" ceremony that involves both birds rising out of the water, and running across the lake surface side by side in a cloud of spray, their long necks arched in a graceful curve. Unlike many birds, male and female grebes of most species mirror each other's display in every detail and the sexes are difficult to tell apart.

Podiceps cristatus

- 18–20 in (46–51 cm)
- Lakes, rivers, lagoons, and coastal waters in Europe, Asia, Africa, Australia, and New Zealand.
- Long-necked, gray and white bird, adorned with chestnut and black head plumes in breeding season.

MUTUAL DISPLAY
Paddling furiously, a courting pair of great crested grebes dance together on a lake, each holding its offering of waterweed gathered from below the surface.

 CASE STUDY

THE DANCE EXPLAINED

The extraordinary courtship of the great crested grebe inspired some classic studies of animal behavior. In one of the earliest, published in 1914, the biologist Julian Huxley proposed that the displays had evolved from daily behavior patterns by a process of "ritualization." Huxley's work was built upon by K.E.L. Simmons, pictured below, whose *Studies on Great Crested Grebes* (1955) were widely read by birdwatchers and ornithologists.

WATER BALLET

>>01 In one of many variations of the weed dance, one bird may crouch in the water, while another dives and reappears with a billful of weed. **>>02** With powerful strokes of their lobed feet, the grebes push themselves up out of the water. **>>03** Breast to breast, they dance together on the surface, swiveling their heads from left to right. **>>04** The pair settle back down, but continue to shake and toss their heads to display their erected plumes.

>>01

>>02

>>03

>>04

Eye opener

Indian peafowl

Famous for its breathtaking plumage displays, the Indian peafowl is often regarded as an emblem of masculine finery. The female, or peahen, is well equipped for her maternal role with discreet, cryptic coloration, but the peacock is resplendent in deep violet-blue and iridescent green, with extended upper tail coverts adorned with vivid "eye-spots."

These extended coverts normally trail behind the bird, but in display he erects and spreads them to form a spectacular, rustling fan. He often backs toward any receptive female, swinging around to confront her with the magnificence of his display before taking several steps back and bowing.

If the peahen is impressed, she will join his harem of females, because, like most male birds with highly ornamented plumage, the peacock is polygamous. He takes no part in raising his young and being so conspicuous, would probably be a liability.

Pavo cristatus

- Male up to 7½ ft (2.3 m); female 34 in (86 cm)
- Forest and farmland in India, Pakistan, and Sri Lanka, and introduced worldwide.
- Ground-living pheasant; female mainly brown, green, and white; male has blue neck and breast, and long train of glossy green upper tail covert feathers.

CASE STUDY
MATING SUCCESS

The peacock is a classic example of "sexual selection" influencing evolution. Studies at Britain's Whipsnade Zoo have proved that peahens prefer to mate with the most impressive males displaying the largest number of eye-spots in their tails. Since the young inherit some of their fathers' genes, peacock tails have become more and more ornate. Yet the eye-spots are not merely ornamental. Other studies have shown that males with the biggest eye-spots tend to father bigger, healthier, more fit chicks that are more likely to survive—showing that the beauty of the peacock is more than skin deep.

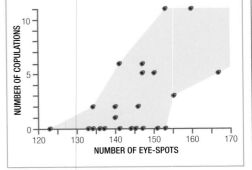

DRESSED TO IMPRESS
His tail fanned out in its full glory, a peacock displays to a group of peahens in Ranthambore National Park, India. The most magnificent males tend to be chosen by the majority of available females, so less favored males may not mate at all, leading to the extinction of their genetic line.

DAZZLING DISPLAY
The stunning display of the peacock is a familiar sight, thanks to its introduction as an ornamental bird to parks and gardens all over the world. Domesticated peafowl are very tame, but wild birds are shy and elusive.

Tree dancing

Raggiana bird-of-paradise

Few birds can match male birds-of-paradise for dazzling courtship displays. Their native tropical forests are rich in resources, so breeding females have little trouble finding food. They do not need help from the males, which are able to devote all their energies to displaying and trying to mate with as many females as possible.

Male raggiana birds-of-paradise display competitively, in groups that gather in traditional treetop display sites known as leks. They dance on perches to show off their glorious plumes, and by degrees they establish a hierarchy, with the most accomplished, energetic male occupying the best perch. This dominant male normally mates with most of the females that visit the lek, and it is likely that they choose him on the basis of his high status, rather than by judging the quality of his performance.

Paradisaea raggiana

- 13 in (33 cm)
- Tropical rain forest in eastern New Guinea.
- Female has buff crown and nape; male has yellow crown and nape, green throat, and long orange-red plumes.

FLAMBOYANT DISPLAY
The plumes of the male raggiana bird-of-paradise normally trail behind him (above), but he tosses them forward in a flamboyant display to impress a female (right).

On a roll

Giant panda

The giant panda has become an symbol of endangered wildlife because of its extreme rarity. Since it often refuses to breed in captivity, it was once thought to be reluctant to breed in the wild. However, when they are left to their own devices, male and and female pandas naturally live in overlapping ranges, and although they are generally solitary, they will find each other through scent-marking to engage in a brief courtship and mating period in spring. Males may compete for access to a female, who backs up to her chosen suitor with her tail raised to entice him. She may roll onto her back, squirm, and reach up to him with her forepaws. This usually encourages the male to mate, after which the female returns to her solitary life until her cub is born.

Ailuropoda melanoleuca
- Up to 6¼ ft (1.9 m)
- Cool, damp, mountain bamboo forest in central and western China.
- Bulky with typically bearlike build; white with black limbs, shoulders, ears, and eye patches.

>> 192

ROLLING AROUND
A captive female giant panda at the Wolong giant panda reserve in China rolls seductively on her back, inviting the watching male to mate with her.

HUMAN IMPACT
BREEDING GIANT PANDAS

The giant panda is threatened because its forest habitat in China has been reduced and fragmented by clearance for farming and lumber. But large tracts are now protected, and at sites such as Wolong giant panda reserve the animals are being bred in captivity and even hand raised, like this bottle-fed cub.

Thrill of the chase

Common raccoon

Encounters between male and female mammals often involve an element of aggression until the two settle their differences and sparring turns to courtship. Among common raccoons, which are highly social animals, these exchanges are marked by angry growls and bursts of chattering, as the animals chase through the undergrowth. Eventually they may mate, and females often form temporary relationships with males during the breeding season. These liaisons may involve up to four males, which appear to mate with as many females as possible—although the dominant or strongest males in any area generally mate with most of the females.

Procyon lotor
- 2–3¼ ft (65–100 cm)
- Forest, scrubland, and suburban areas in North and Central America, from southern Canada to Panama.
- Foxlike, with pointed muzzle; mainly gray with black mask across face, and bushy, black-ringed tail.

>> 258

Scent signals

Black rhinoceros

In common with most mammals, scent is vital to black rhinoceroses since they not only use it to locate food, mark territory, and identify both friends and enemies, but also to find breeding partners. A black rhinoceros has poor vision, but an excellent sense of smell, so it relies heavily on scent signals. When females come into season, they spray hormone-rich urine to attract males. The males often fight for the right to mate, and may inflict deadly injuries. The victors then proclaim their dominance by spraying urine, often charging back and forth in the process. This may give the male the confidence to approach a female, although she is likely to reject his initial advances. If successful, they will form a temporary bond before mating and parting.

Diceros bicornis
- 10 ft (3 m)
- Forest and wooded scrubland in sub-Saharan Africa.
- Massive browsing herbivore with thick, leathery, dark brown or dark gray skin, two horns on its snout, and pointed, prehensile upper lip.

TAKING COURAGE
A dominant male sprays to mark his territory (right), and to build confidence for a mating attempt that may be rejected by the female (below, on the right).

Singing swingers
Siamang

Many mammals use sound during courtship, but few are quite so vocal as the gibbons of Southeast Asia. These slender, agile, tree-living apes are famous for their loud, complex calls, which are often described as songs. Those of the siamang, the largest gibbon species, are given extra resonance and volume by a throat sac that inflates like a balloon, enabling their calls to carry for some distance through the forest.

Young gibbons of both sexes sing to attract mates, and although they keep moving through the forest to find partners, the process may take several years. Eventually they form long-term pair bonds and defend a joint territory. Most species advertise this with loud duets, in which the songs of the male and female are quite different. A male siamang screams, while a female gives a series of booms and barks. Siamang pairs call together, but in many other species the sexes sing alternately, with the female taking the longest, loudest solos. Their young may join in too, in a family chorus that echoes through the treetops.

GREAT CALL
Amplified by its inflated throat sac, the song of this siamang will be heard and noted by all its neighbors. It calls mainly in the morning, especially if it becomes aware of another siamang family group.

Symphalangus syndactylus
↔ 30–35 in (75–90 cm)
◆ Forest on Malay Peninsula and Sumatra.
▥ Long-armed ape with glossy black coat and pinkish gray throat sac.

STRENGTHENING BONDS

Some researchers believe that singing in a duet reinforces the pair bonds between mated siamangs. However, the duets are most frequently performed near the boundaries of their territory, when the pair sense the presence of neighboring groups that might trespass on their patch. By advertising the fact that they are in possession, they reduce the risk of a dangerous confrontation, while at the same time backing each other up and strengthening their relationship. So it seems likely that dueting is primarily territorial, but also helps maintain a bond that could be threatened by intruders.

SWIFT MOVEMENT
Gibbons are the only apes that habitually move through the forest canopy using their long, muscular arms. They can swing from branch to branch with astonishing speed and agility, and rarely make a false move.

Striking a pose

Blackbuck

Most hoofed grazing animals that live in open country associate in herds and do not form mated pairs. Rival males compete over females, and have evolved powerful bodies and horns for fighting or intimidating rivals.

A male blackbuck has long spiral horns that lock with those of rivals during clashes to reduce the risk of serious injury. He claims a territory by driving away other males—usually with threats rather than active fighting—and tries to monopolize a harem of females. The male displays to both

rivals and females using an imperious raised-head gesture with his horns lying horizontal, and may head off straying females to keep them within his territory for as long as possible. If a female comes into season, and is therefore ready to mate, the male can detect the hormone change from chemical signals in her urine. This triggers a lip-curling flehmen response that is common to most grazing animals, and which helps transfer the scent to a sensitive organ in the roof of the mouth. If the test is positive he will mate with the female, but then takes no further part in raising her young.

Antilope cervicapra

3¼–5 ft (1–1.5 m)

Open woodland to semi-desert in India and Bangladesh.

A long-legged gazelle with white underparts, eye patch, and chin; female is a pale fawn; bigger male is dark brown to black, with spirally twisted horns.

POSTURING
His upper lip curled back as he scents the hormones in a female's urine, a male blackbuck raises his head in a display of dominance.

CIRCLING
Alerted to the risk of losing a female to a rival, a male blackbuck circles around her to encourage her back to his territory.

Beach harem

California sea lion

Seals and sea lions must come ashore to give birth to their pups, and during this time the males take the opportunity to mate. Male California sea lions have the same breeding strategy as blackbucks (see left), attempting to control as many females as possible by claiming territories on the breeding beaches. They are much bigger than the females, and compete with rivals by actual and ritualized fighting. Throughout this time, they dare not leave their territories to feed. A male controls an average of 16 females, courting each with barks and head-shaking as he lumbers around her, nipping her shoulders and flanks. If the female is receptive, she responds by lying on her side, belly, or back and looking up at the male, encouraging him to mate with her.

Zalophus californianus

6–7 ft (1.8–2.1 m)

Breeds on Pacific shores of North and Central America, and the Galapagos Islands.

Sleek eared seal with long front flippers, and hind flippers that rotate forward to walk on land.

>> 485

A male California sea lion may go 27 days without food to defend his beach territory during the breeding season.

Gifted suitor

Amazon river dolphin

Most dolphins are marine animals—small toothed whales that hunt fishes and squid in the open oceans. A few dolphin species, however, live in the freshwaters of large rivers. These river dolphins have long, slender snouts, mobile necks, and small eyes, and they navigate and hunt in cloudy river waters mainly by echolocation.

The Amazon river dolphin, or boto, is usually solitary, living in the same stretch of river throughout the year, but in the rainy season the dolphins come together to breed. Rival males compete for access

to females, often biting each other aggressively, and many males bear the scars of combat.

Males initiate courtship by nibbling at the flippers or flukes of females, but some courtship displays involve the male picking up sticks, aquatic plants, or lumps of clay, and flourishing them at the females as if they were gifts, to impress them. These

males also tend to be more aggressive than average, and because of this, or their gift-carrying, they are the most successful in terms of the number of females they mate with, and the number of young they father.

Inia geoffrensis

Up to 8¾ ft (2.7 m)

Slow-moving waters in Amazon and Orinoco river systems in South America.

Long-snouted dolphin; dorsal fin reduced to ridged hump along back; gray coloring above, pale pink below.

>> 244

MAKING A SPLASH
>>01 A male Amazon river dolphin surfaces with a mass of waterweed gripped in his teeth.   >>02 He prepares to display to a female watching from nearby.   >>03 He tosses the weed around to create a splash, and to demonstrate his fitness.

>>01

>>02

>>03

BATTLE SCARS
Scarred by encounters with rival males, this Amazon river dolphin surfaces to display the pink skin that is unique to this species. Males tend to be pinker and larger than females, and it is likely that they are polygamous.

Mating

Mating behavior brings together sperm from the male and eggs from the female so that fertilization can occur. In some animals, fertilization is external, occurring outside the female's body; in others, it is internal, the sperm being introduced into the female's body, usually by means of a specialized sexual organ.

Internal fertilization

Internal fertilization is advantageous in many ways. It enables mating and egg laying to be separated in time and space, so that a female can lay her eggs at the optimum time, in a suitable place. For example, having mated, female newts lay their eggs one at a time, placing them around a pond and protecting each one by wrapping it in a leaf. It allows females to mate with several males before her eggs are fertilized, so that her young have diverse fathers, whose sperm must compete to fertilize her eggs. In mammals and many other animals, internal fertilization means that the young can develop inside the mother. Some animals use a sexual organ called a penis to transfer sperm, but many birds simply touch cloacae (genital openings), and many male amphibians transfer sperm in a capsule called a spermatophore.

During mating, a male dead leaf bush cricket passes sperm to the female in a spermatophore.

Female Alpine newts wrap each egg in a leaf to protect it from ultraviolet radiation.

SEASONAL SPAWNER
Reef-living Christmas tree worms are sedentary animals, so males and females cannot meet to mate. Eggs and sperm are shed into the water and carried away by currents, eventually meeting to form larvae.

External fertilization

External fertilization is often used by animals that cannot move around in search of a mate. It is most common in aquatic animals, where eggs and sperm are released into water. There is a risk when eggs are fertilized outside the body that some will fail to meet a sperm, so many species counter this by producing huge numbers of eggs and vast quantities of sperm. Among fishes and amphibians, external fertilization is sometimes associated with male parental care. This may be because, as the female lays the eggs before the male fertilizes them, he is left "holding the babies." For example, male sticklebacks and midwife toads provide care and protection for the developing eggs.

Hermaphrodites

Hermaphrodites (see p.325) are in a happy position— every individual of the same species they meet is a potential mate. Mating is often reciprocal, with each partner giving sperm to the other during the same mating act. Some slugs try to protect the paternity of their offspring by biting off their partner's penis after mating; a slug without a penis cannot provide sperm and so cannot attract another partner. Hermaphrodites are common in invertebrates.

HIGH MOUNT
A bull African elephant mounts a female. She is receptive for only a few days each year and only allows larger, dominant males to mount her.

SPERM SWAPPERS
Snails are hermaphrodites, and after an elaborate courtship, each snail inserts its long penis into the body of its partner to exchange sperm.

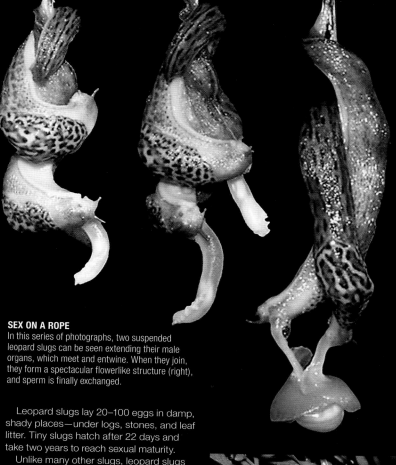

Suspended sex

Leopard slug

Like other slugs, leopard slugs are hermaphrodites—they possess both male and female sexual organs. But for leopard slugs, mating is a fascinatingly complex and prolonged process. Two slugs circle each other for up to two-and-a-half hours before they climb together to a secure place, often in a tree some distance above the ground. There they both secrete a thick "rope" of mucus upon which they slowly lower themselves, until the rope is about 3 ft 3 in (1 m) long. They entwine their bodies in a graceful midair dance as they move down along the mucus rope. Then each slug "everts" (extends by turning inside-out) its male sexual organ from the back of its head. These sleek, blue-white organs become longer and eventually meet and entwine. Then each slug inserts a sperm sac (spermatophore) into the body of its partner. After mating, the leopard slugs climb back up the rope and go their separate ways.

SEX ON A ROPE
In this series of photographs, two suspended leopard slugs can be seen extending their male organs, which meet and entwine. When they join, they form a spectacular flowerlike structure (right), and sperm is finally exchanged.

Leopard slugs lay 20–100 eggs in damp, shady places—under logs, stones, and leaf litter. Tiny slugs hatch after 22 days and take two years to reach sexual maturity.

Unlike many other slugs, leopard slugs eat fungi, decaying matter, some carrion, and even other slugs.

SIMILAR SPECIES
The leopard slug may have the most spectacular mating behavior, but others are equally interesting. The netted slugs above are joined by two inflated dart sacs, which may stimulate sex. The white mass between the mating black slugs (left) is sperm.

Limax maximus
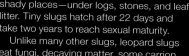 Up to 8 in (20 cm)

Near human habitation: gardens, yards, cellars; under logs, stones, vegetation. Native to Europe, introduced to North America, Asia, Africa, and Australasia.

Gray with dark spots or stripes, oval-shaped bumps on back, body flattened at rear.

Specialized tentacle

Giant Pacific octopus

In the male giant Pacific octopus, the third tentacle on the right is modified to enable him to fertilize the female. Within this tentacle, or hectocotylus arm, long strings of sperm (spermatophores), sometimes as long as 3 ft 3 in (1 m), are formed. During mating, the male inserts a spermatophore into a cavity in the female's body. After approximately a month, the female retires to a rocky den where she lays up to 100,000 eggs. Most cephalopods show little parental care, but the female giant Pacific octopus incubates her eggs diligently for seven months. During this time she neglects to feed herself in order to care intensively for her eggs, defending them against predators and siphoning water over them to keep them clean and well aerated. Once the eggs hatch and the tiny young leave the den, the mother dies.

Pacific giant octopuses are predators, feeding on shrimps, crabs, shellfish, and fish. They live for three to five years.

Enteroctopus dofleini
Up to about 30 ft (9 m) with 14 ft (4.3 m) arm span; female larger than male.

Coastal waters of northern Pacific Ocean to depths of 2,500 ft (750 m), from Japan to California.

Yellow, gray, or brown (color changes to camouflage against background); turns red when excited or angry.

>> 397

Sperm exchange

Nudibranch

Like all nudibranchs (bottom-dwelling sea slugs), *Nembrotha purpureolineatas* are hermaphrodites—they produce both eggs and sperm. They do not fertilize their own eggs, but come together in pairs to exchange sperm, just as their land-dwelling counterparts do. The genital orifice is situated on the right side of the body and, in order to mate, two individuals position themselves head to tail in a way that allows their right sides to touch. Nudibranch eggs are very noticeable to divers, due to their interesting forms and bright colors, and the fact that they are often laid in striking patterns, notably in spiral shapes.

The word nudibranch means "naked gills," referring to the fact that these colorful mollusks have soft bodies with no protective shells. Their bright coloration warns predators that they are not good to eat, and indeed, they are poisonous. The many species of nudibranch display a dazzling array of bright colors and bold color combinations that captivate divers.

Nembrotha purpureolineata
Up to 2 in (5 cm)

Coral reefs in tropical Pacific waters.

Creamy-white and brown body with purple-edged foot, red or orange tentacles and gills.

SPERM EXCHANGE
The male sexual organs of these mating *Nembrotha purpureolineata* touch and fit together in order to allow each sea slug to transfer sperm to the other.

Side by side

Common earthworm

For many hermaphrodites, mating involves two individuals exchanging sperm. On a mild, damp night, two worms come halfway out of their burrows, lie side by side with heads pointing in opposite directions, and secrete mucus to form a sheath that binds their bodies together. Their alignment allows a groove running along each body to come together with its counterpart, forming a tube for sperm to pass along. Mating takes up to four hours.

Lumbricus terrestris

↔ Up to 10 in (25 cm) (extended body)

◑ In soil, originally in Europe, now introduced to most parts of world.

📖 Pale brown, pink, or red, segmented body.

≫ 251, 445

Coiled up

Giant millipedes

In some giant millipedes, the female curls up into a tight ball when approached by a male, as if under attack. The male must make her uncoil to mate with her, and uses both persuasion and brute force. He stimulates her with glandular secretions and movements of his antennae, while using his strength to uncoil her body. Only strong males are able to force a female to uncoil. This is natural selection in action—only the strongest, most vigorous males produce offspring.

Superorder Juliformia

↔ Up to 12 in (30 cm)

◑ Leaf litter, topsoil, or bark of trees, in tropical and warm temperate zones.

📖 Long, cylindrical, segemented, reddish, dark brown or black body. Most species have 100–300 legs. Two segmented antennae.

MATING MILLIPEDES
When joined in mating, the male giant millipede coils his body tightly around the female.

Mating flights

Fire ants

Fire ants live in colonies with one or more queens, many males, fertile females (potential queens), and huge armies of sterile female workers. Mating occurs high up in the air during late spring or early summer. Fertile females and males partake in mass mating flights, after which the female seeks a suitable nesting site. Her wings come off, ready for her to change into a queen, then she buries herself and begins to lay eggs. She may live for several years, producing up to 1,500 eggs each day. The male dies soon after mating and becomes food for other ants and small birds.

Solenopsis species

↔ 1/16–1/4 in (1–6 mm)

◑ Underground, in dry to moist soil across diverse range of habitats, including fields, woodland, and open ground, worldwide.

📖 Dull yellowish red to copper brown or black, large head with curved jaws, segmented body with defined waist, light covering of fine hairs.

FIGHTING FOR A FEMALE
During a pause in a mating flight, these two male fire ants fight over the right to mate with a female. The winner will lose his life, as males die soon after mating.

Sperm replacement

Lesser red-eyed damselfly

In order to mate with a female, the male damselfly grasps her by the neck with the pincers at the end of his long abdomen, then carries her to a suitable spot on some vegetation. During mating, he keeps hold of the female and she curves her abdomen forward so that its tip engages with his genitalia. He then inserts his penis into her genital opening to first remove any sperm that may be left there from previous matings, before transferring his own sperm, contained in a spermatophore (sperm sack) to her. After mating, the pair fly off, in the same "tandem" position, to water. Here, the female lays her eggs on submerged plants. The male continues to hold her until she has finished.

LAYING EGGS
Two male lesser red-eyed damselflies hover above the water while holding these females on the surface. The females dip their long abdomens into the water to lay their eggs on plants just beneath the surface.

Erythromma viridulum

↔ 1 1/4 in (3 cm)

◑ In ponds, lakes, and ditches with floating vegetation in southern Europe and Africa; expanding into northern Europe.

📖 Black with iridescent blue markings, male slightly brighter than female; eyes red in male, brown in female.

IN TANDEM
The male (on the left) clasps the female firmly by the neck as she holds her genital opening to his genitalia, forming a mating "wheel."

Love bite
White-tipped reef shark

During mating, the male entwines his body around the female to position one of his pelvic fins in line with her genital opening. On the inner margin of each of the male's pelvic fins is a long clasper, an organ used to deposit sperm. One of these is inserted into the female, and to help maintain this mating position, the male uses his mouth to hold onto her pectoral fin or gill slits. Females commonly have scars in these areas.

Triaenodon obesus

⟷ Up to 6½ ft (2 m)

◉ Rests in caves and gullies around coral reefs by day, hunting in surrounding waters by night in the Pacific and Indian oceans and Red Sea.

▥ Long, slender body, brown-gray above, white below, with gray spots on flanks and white tips on dorsal fin and upper tail lobe.

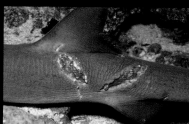

TWICE BITTEN
These scars on a female shark's flank (above) may have been caused during mating, because the male uses its teeth to hold the female in position (left). Females have thicker skin than males to allow for this, but sometimes, damage does occur.

ANATOMY
SPECIALIZED TOOL

The male damselfly has an elaborate penis that has evolved the ability to remove or push aside sperm from previous mating partners found in the female, thus increasing his own chances of fertilizing the largest proportion of her eggs. The penis is equipped with hooks or scrapers and covered with hairs that are used to remove the sperm. The part of the penis that is inserted into the female is called the aedeagus, and its structure varies between species. In some damselflies, it is used simply to push sperm from previous couplings to one side, in others, to remove it altogether. Some species insert liquid to wash sperm out.

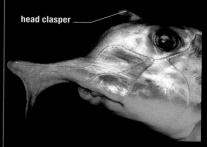

head clasper

Head lock
Ploughnose chimaera

Also known as elephant fishes or ghost sharks, ploughnose chimaeras are best known for the hoelike "nose" in front of the mouth, which they use to find food among sediment on the seabed. They live at depths of 660 ft (200 m) or more, but move into shallow, inshore waters in order to mate and lay eggs.

When mating, the male uses a special, spiny clasper on its head to grip the female in the right position. This retractable clasper is located in the center of the male's forehead, directly between the eyes, and looks like a small but menacing club, which is covered in thorn-shaped spines. Another pair of elongated claspers, which are also retractable, are positioned close to the pelvic fins. These are used to fasten onto the female and are inserted into her body to transfer sperm.

Callorhinchus milii

⟷ Up to 4 ft (1.2 m)

◉ Deep, temperate coastal waters of southwest Pacific, off southern Australia and along east coast of South Island, New Zealand.

▥ Silvery white on sides, blotched brown above, large pectoral fins, long tapering tail, large spine in front of first dorsal fin.

Sex slaves
Leafvent anglerfish

In the dark ocean depths, a slow-moving animal such as the leafvent anglerfish rarely encounters a potential mate. The male, who is much smaller than the female, makes the most of any such opportunity, attaching itself to the female's body permanently. Over time, its teeth, jaws, eyes, and nostrils degenerate until it is little more than a testis attached to the female. Because it feeds off the female, the fused male is often described as a parasite, but the relationship is mutually beneficial—the female has a constant supply of sperm for her eggs. As larvae, females and males are similar in size, but males become sexually mature when small, while in females, maturation is delayed until they are relatively large.

MALE ATTACHMENT
This female anglerfish has two males attached to her skin. Like many deep-sea animals, leafvent anglerfishes live in total darkness and are largely transparent – adult females have no skin pigmentation.

Multiple mates
Guppy

Also known as millions fish, guppies occur in huge numbers. Both sexes mate with several partners (females prefer the more brightly colored males). Having multiple partners benefits females—they produce more young with a greater chance of being larger, better at schooling, and more skilled at avoiding predators. Because they have genetically more diverse offspring, there is a higher chance that at least some will survive in their variable environment.

Poecilia reticulata

⟷ Male 1–1½ in (2.5–3.5 cm); female 1½–2¼ in (4–6 cm)

◉ Streams, ditches, pools in South America, West Indies (especially Trinidad); introduced to many parts of world.

▥ Female gray; male variable in color, with spots and patches of red, orange, yellow, black, and purple, and with large, fanlike tail.

Haplophryne mollis

⟷ Male 1¼ in (3 cm), female 8 in (20 cm)

◉ Deep in Atlantic, Pacific, and Indian oceans.

▥ Round, colorless body; large mouth with lure to help catch prey.

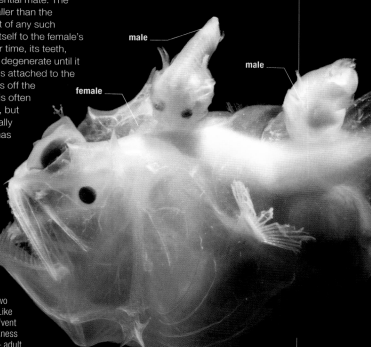

male

male

female

HOLDING ON
European common toads gather in vast numbers in spring to breed in ponds. Males greatly outnumber females and struggle with one another to cling onto them in a position called amplexus, the male on the female's back, grasping her with his strong forelimbs. The male holds on for several days until the female spawns, while trying to repel rivals.

Tail waving

Red-spotted newt

The breeding season for red-spotted newts occurs in late winter and early spring. When a male encounters a female, he waves his tail to attract her. The female, who is full of eggs waiting to be fertilized, responds by approaching him, but if she does not, the male leaps on her and clasps her around the neck with his muscular hind limbs. This allows him to keep waving his tail at her, and also to rub his cheek glands against her snout to expose her to an alluring pheromone. When she finally responds, he dismounts, moves away, and deposits a spermatophore (sperm sac), often at the bottom of a pond. The female follows him and picks it up in her genital opening, allowing the sperm to fertilize her eggs.

Notophthalmus viridescens

- 2¾–4 in (7–10 cm), female slightly larger than male
- Ponds, lakes, ditches, and slow-moving streams in the eastern US and southeast Canada.
- Green-brown with bright red spots. Male has deeper tail and larger hind limbs.

STRONG LEGS
During the breeding season, the hind limbs of the male red-spotted newt become enlarged. Their inside surfaces are covered in deeply textured patches that improve the male's grip on the female when mounting her.

Linking limbs

Fire salamander

When a potential mate is near, the male fire salamander nudges her with his snout, chases her, and sometimes bites her, until she submits to his advances. He then slips his body beneath hers, locking his forelimbs over hers, holding her in this unique mating position. He rubs glands on his snout onto the underside of her chin to stimulate her. When she responds, he deposits a sperm

sac on the ground, then flips his body and tail to one side so her genital opening falls onto it. The female retains fertilized eggs in her body until she gives birth to 8–70 larvae.

Salamandra salamandra

- Up to 10 in (25 cm), female slightly larger than male
- Cool, damp areas in forest or meadows, close to standing water, in western, central, and southern Europe and northwest Africa.
- Large, stout salamander. Black with yellow, orange, or red spots, blotches, or stripes, short tail.

>> 284

Hopping on

Natterjack toad

Unlike male common toads (see p.370), natterjack males ignore paired couples and look for a mate of their own. At night, they gather around ponds and call loudly, creating a chorus that can be heard by females up to 1½ miles (2 km) away. Females approach, and a male jumps on a female's back to mate. Only large males can call loudly for a long time, so small males cluster around them like satellites and attempt to mate with approaching females. Where natterjack populations are large, calling males attract so many satellites males that calling becomes an ineffective mating strategy. Males then abandon calling and go searching for females to mate with.

Epidalea calamita

- Up to 4 in (10 cm), female larger than male
- In open habitats where soil is sandy, in western and central Europe.
- Green or brown with yellow stripe on back, yellow or red bumps. Short limbs.

NUPTIAL PADS
The male has "nuptial pads" (hard areas of skin) on the forefingers, allowing him to grip the female firmly when he has mounted her.

Long embrace

European common frog

Common frogs spawn in the spring. When a male encounters a female, he clasps her in a strong embrace known as amplexus, pushing the horny pads on his thumbs firmly into her chest. Some pairs remain in amplexus for days, until the weather is warm enough for spawning. When it is, all mating pairs in the pond deposit their spawn simultaneously in the same place. Depending on her size, a female produces a clutch of 700–4,500 eggs. As soon as she does, the male sheds sperm to fertilize them, then releases the female.

Males typically outnumber females. A male that fails to find a mate may perform "clutch piracy"—he finds a fresh clutch of eggs, embraces it as he would a female, and sheds sperm onto it to fertilize any unfertilized eggs. Clutch piracy is highly successful. One study found that a single clutch contained a mixture of eggs fertilized by four males, including the male that was in amplexus with the female who produced the clutch.

WORTH THE WAIT
The male common frog rides on the female's back, clinging on and waiting for just this moment, when she releases a clutch of eggs. He then fertilizes them immediately.

COMMUNAL SPAWNING
This mating pair of common frogs is swimming in a sea of frogspawn that has been released simultaneously by all the females in the pond. Within this mass, the temperature is higher than elsewhere in the pond, allowing fertilized eggs to develop quickly.

Rana temporaria

- Up to 4½ in (11 cm), female larger than male
- All kinds of habitats with nearby water, in Europe and northwest Asia.
- Skin color variable, with black markings.

Gentle approach

Komodo dragon

Male Komodo dragons fight to establish territories where they are visited by females. If approached by a male, the female is initially hostile, repelling his advances aggressively with her teeth and claws. So he advances cautiously. He sniffs her to determine if she is ready to mate, then he lightly scratches her back and licks her, using this gentle contact to gain her trust. If she accepts him, he climbs onto her back and inserts one of a pair of male sexual organs into her genital opening. Sometimes, long-term pair bonds are formed between a female and male—an unusual pattern among reptiles. The female lays around 20 eggs, either in a burrow or in the deserted nest of a scrub fowl.

PINNED DOWN
Once he is certain that the female will submit to his amorous advances, the male Komodo dragon clasps hold of her firmly, then uses his powerful tail to lift up her tail, allowing him to mate with her.

Varanus komodoensis

↔	6½–9¾ ft (2–3 m)
◉	Grassland and lowland forest on Indonesian islands of Komodo and Flores and others in between.
▥	Heavy bodied lizard, grayish brown with darker markings, very long tail and long, yellow forked tongue.

≫ 220

≫ 220

HUMAN IMPACT
TERRITORY LOSS

Komodo dragons, the largest reptiles in the world, live only on a few small Indonesian islands. They are classified as a vulnerable species, largely due to habitat loss, both through natural events such as volcanic eruptions and as a result of human activity. And many are poached to supply an illegal trade in their skins. It is thought that only about 350 breeding females remain in the wild.

Tails entwined

Western whip snake

In early spring, western whip snakes are ready to mate very soon after they emerge from hibernation. Males begin to look for females, and travel from hibernation sites to their summer habitats to find them. Fast-moving and agile, these snakes may travel up to 2 miles (3 km) in this search, and fight with other males for access to females, each lashing at the other with its tail. The successful male then twists his tail around the female during copulation.

As with all snakes, the male has a pair of male sexual organs, which he inserts one at a time into the female's cloaca (the orifice leading to her reproductive organs). A few weeks later, in early to midsummer, the female lays 4–15 elongated eggs. The eggs hatch approximately six to eight weeks after being laid.

Hierophis viridiflavus

↔	Up to 5 ft (1.5 m)
◉	Dry, open, well-vegetated habitats in Europe, from France to Italy.
▥	Black with yellow markings, occasionally all black; small head.

Waiting game

Common garter snake

Common garter snakes hibernate in huge numbers in communal dens. Males emerge from hibernation first and wait at the den for the females to appear. The result is an orgy in which many males struggle to mate with each female. After mating, the male produces a secretion, which quickly hardens to form a mating plug in the female's genital opening, preventing other males from inseminating her. Once mating is over, the snakes disperse to their feeding areas, and females give birth later in the year to live young, usually 12–18 but occasionally more.

Thamnophis sirtalis

↔	18–44 in (46–130 cm)
◉	Grassland, scrubland chaparral, and forest, usually near water, in North America.
▥	Olive green to black with paler stripes.

≫ 446

≫ 446

MATING BALLS
Both common garter snakes (main picture) and their relatives, red-sided garter snakes (inset) form "mating balls" around females. As the females emerge from hibernation, up to 100 males surround each one, running their chins along her back and releasing pheromones to attract her. She will select just one of the males to mate with.

98 The maximum number of young ever recorded in a litter of common garter snakes.

Role reversal
Red-necked phalarope

These aquatic shorebirds spend most of their lives at sea and even mate in the water, coming back to the shore only to build nests in which they raise their young. Phalaropes are unusual among birds in the role reversal they display—the female is larger and more brightly colored than the male. She is also the aggressive partner and establishes a breeding territory, while the male alone incubates the eggs and feeds the young. Sometimes a female is polyandrous, which means she has two nests, cared for by two males.

WATER LOVERS
Unlike most other birds, red-necked phalaropes prefer to copulate in the water itself, out at sea, rather than on land or on a perch.

Phalaropus lobatus
- 8 in (20 cm), female larger than male
- Open seas around northern Europe, Canada, and Russia, breeding around lakes and pools in tundra.
- Long neck, sharp bill, gray above, white throat and underside, orange patch on neck.

Promiscuous bird
Aquatic warbler

Aquatic warblers are promiscuous—eggs in a female's clutch may be inseminated by as many as five males. To increase his chances of being the only father, a male mates with a female for as long as he can, sometimes for up to 30 minutes. By copulating for so long, he floods her with sperm, which can inseminate her seven or eight times in one coupling. Males have unusually large testes to allow for this.

Acrocephalus paludicola
- 5 in (13 cm)
- Dense vegetation around sedge marshes in central Europe and Russia.
- Pale with black and gold streaked back, two dark stripes on head.

Male attention
Northern goshawk

Goshawks are monogamous. The male is very attentive to the female while she is laying her eggs, rarely leaving her side and mating with her frequently—for each clutch of eggs, a pair will mate between 500 and 600 times. Diligent mate-guarding in this way reduces the chances of the female laying eggs that have been fathered by another male.

Accipiter gentilis
- 19–27 in (48–69 cm), female larger than male
- Broad-leaved and coniferous forest in North America, Europe, Asia.
- Gray-brown above, white and barred with gray below, white stripe above eye.

On the wing
Common swift

Fast and acrobatic fliers, common swifts spend their lives in the air. Unlike other birds, they even mate while flying, and their mating is one of the fastest couplings in the animal kingdom.

Typically, they mate early in the morning on sunny days, often in groups—they breed in colonies of about 30–40 pairs. Pairs stay together over successive breeding seasons, and male and female share in nest building (which is done using only materials caught in the air) and caring for the young, with each bird flying great distances to catch insect food on the wing. But while swifts are usually monogamous, they do occasionally mate with birds that are not their partners. Genetic studies of swift chicks have revealed that 4.5 percent are not the offspring of the mother's partner.

Apus apus
- 6½ in (16–17 cm)
- Europe, Asia, winters in Africa. Entirely aerial, nests in buildings and on cliffs.
- Black with whitish chin, narrow wings, short tail.

MID-AIR MATING
>>01 The male closes in on the female from behind. >>02 The female signals her readiness to mate by raising her wings, and the male approaches. >>03 The male moves himself into the mating position, directly above the female. >>04 The female raises her tail while the male lowers his, and the cloaca (the orifice that leads to the reproductive organs) of each bird meets the other's briefly. All this occurs while they are flying at high speed.

>>01   >>02   >>03   >>04

Fatal mating
Brown antechinus

The brown antechinus, or marsupial mouse, has a short and very stressful life. Normally solitary, brown antechinuses gather to breed in large communal nests when they are around 11 months old. Males and females form pairs, but the male has to work extremely hard to prevent other males from mating with his partner. He guards her and mates with her frequently but, despite his strenuous efforts, most litters—generally of around 4–12 young—are fathered by more than one male. The male brown antechinus puts so much effort into his mating activity that his immune system suffers and breaks down. He dies shortly after his one and only mating season. Many female antechinuses also die after their very first breeding effort, although some of them manage to live for as long as two or three years.

Antechinus stuartii
- 31–43½ in (80–120 cm)
- Forest with thick groundcover in eastern Australia.
- Pointed snout, large ears, long whiskers, short brown hair.

FREQUENT COUPLINGS
These brown antechinuses are mating inside a tree hollow. The male mates with his mate repeatedly in order to sire as many of her young as possible.

DYING YOUNG
This male brown antechinus has died at the end of his first breeding season, the result of stress induced by a highly competitive mating system.

Social sex

Bonobo

Bonobos use sex in a variety of social contexts—to resolve conflicts, as a greeting, as reconciliation after a fight, to soothe youngsters, and in exchange for gifts of food. Rather then being purely a means of reproducing, sex is part of everyday life for bonobos. Captive studies reveal that individuals of all ages and of the same or opposite sex mate with each other

and, although mating behavior occurs very frequently, females reproduce young every five to six years. The studies suggest that frequent sexual activity is instrumental in resolving power struggles, and that bonobos live in very peaceful societies, with few aggressive encounters. Bonobos are increasingly rare in the wild.

Pan paniscus
- 3 ft 3 in–4 ft (1–1.2 m)
- Humid forest in Democratic Republic of Congo.
- Black hair, black face, pink lips.

FACE TO FACE
Bonobos frequently mate face to face. This was thought to be unique, but gorillas have been observed in the same position.

> Bonobos are **highly sexually active** and mate in a variety of different sexual positions.

PAINFUL AFFAIR
During mating, a male tiger grasps the female by the scruff of her neck with his powerful teeth. His penis is barbed, which makes mating painful for the female.

Aggressive affair

Tiger

Tigers are solitary, nonsocial animals—the only bonds that exist are those between a mother and her cubs, a relationship that lasts for just 18 months. When ready to mate, a female signals the fact to males by roaring, moaning, and scent-marking. Once a male is attracted, the pair snarl at each other, separating several times before gaining one another's trust. The female then grooms the male, nuzzling and licking him, and rolls on the ground, waving her paws in the air, before lying on her belly and presenting herself to him. The male mounts her in a knees-bent position to avoid crushing her with his weight, then roars and bites her neck. The female jumps up, snarls, and swipes at him as he dismounts.

Panthera tigris
- 6½–12¼ ft (2–3.7 m)
- Wide range of habitats that provide good cover, water, and prey across Asia.
- Orange-red coat with black stripes and paler underside. Strong shoulders and limbs with broad paws and long, retractable claws.

>> 144–45

SIBERIAN TIGERS
These mating Siberian tigers are members of the largest subspecies of tigers and are adapted to a cold climate. They have a thick coat, are paler than other tigers, and have fewer stripes. Once widespread, they are now confined to two small areas in Russia.

HUMAN IMPACT
THE TIGER TRADE

Once inhabiting areas across a huge range in Asia, tigers are now confined to a few small, protected zones. The primary cause of their decline is loss of habitat, but they are also hunted for their skins, and for a variety of body parts that are used in traditional medicine and as aphrodisiacs.

BIRTH AND DEVELOPMENT

FIRST BREATH
A Nile crocodile takes a look at the outside world for the first time. Crocodile embryos develop within a toughened egg, nourished by yolk. In about three months, the embryo has grown from a single fertilized cell into a complex multicellular animal.

BIRTH AND DEVELOPMENT

Animal development is a lifelong process. Beginning at the point of fertilization, animals first grow and develop in a protected environment within their mother or inside an egg. After the event known as birth, young animals must learn and develop skills and behaviors required to support them throughout life.

The embryo

The development of the embryo is called embryogenesis. After fertilization, the zygote, or single cell, begins to divide rapidly, doubling in cell number with each division. Once around 100 cells exist, the embryo is known as a blastula, comprising an outer layer (the blastoderm), and an inner cavity filled with fluid (the blastocoel). The cells migrate to the inside of the blastula, forming different layers. At this point, the inside of the embryo starts to form, folding inward to create the mouth and anus. The internal organs then begin to develop.

STARFISH EMBRYO DEVELOPMENT
>>01 The fertilized single cell.   >>02 The cell rapidly divides, in a process known as cleavage. The stage shown has 8-cells.   >>03 The starfish blastula, showing the outer layer and inner cavity. >>04 Gastrulation occurs when the cells migrate within the blastula. Different cell layers form and the mouth and anus begin to take shape. >>05 The gut starts to form.   >>06 At this larval stage, the internal organs have begun to develop. >>07 The well-formed larva, viewed from the side.   >>08 A fully-formed young starfish.

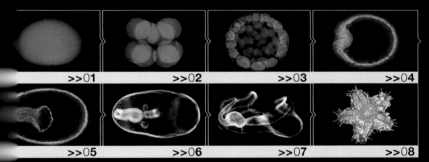

>>01	>>02	>>03	>>04
>>05	>>06	>>07	>>08

REPRODUCTIVE METHODS

OVIPARITY
Young develop inside eggs, nourished by yolk, with little or no development within the mother. Occurs in insects, amphibians, reptiles, fishes, and birds.

VIVIPARITY
Young develop inside the body of the mother, rather than within an egg. They are then delivered by live birth. Occurs in marsupials, for example.

OVOVIVIPARITY
Embryos grow inside eggs, which are retained within the female until they are about to hatch. Young feed on egg yolk. Often seen in sharks.

PLACENTAL MAMMALS
An advanced form of viviparity. Young develop inside the mother, nourished from her body via a placenta. The usual strategy among mammals.

Birth

Birth is the process by which an animal leaves its mother's body and enters the world. This typically refers to animals that undergo a live birth, in contrast to hatching, when animals emerge from an egg that develops outside the mother's body. Many animals carry their young within the uterus for a period of time before giving birth. This is known as the

LIVE BIRTH
A lemon shark gives birth in the Bahamas. Lemon sharks are viviparous, giving birth to 4–17 live young. Black and white sharksuckers swim close to pregnant females, waiting to eat the afterbirth.

MATE SUPERVISION
The male cuttlefish transfers sperm to the female in a package called a spermatophore. He then stands guard until she lays her eggs.

gestation phase, and its duration varies greatly between animals. Elephants, for example, have a very long gestation, carrying their offspring for 22 months prior to birth. To give birth, an animal goes through labor. This occurs by means of strong, rhythmic muscle contractions of the uterus, and, in mammals, is initiated by hormones. Across the animal kingdom, young animals emerge into the world at various stages—some are highly independent at birth, while others require extensive parental care for months or even years. The difference lies in the length of the gestation phase relative to the time taken for that animal to become fully independent. Precocial animals are relatively mature and mobile from the point of hatching or birth—these include many bird species, such as ducks. Conversely, altricial animals, for example rats, are born helpless. Their eyes are closed, they lack fur or feathers, and are dependent on their parents for an extended period of time.

Growing up

The process of animal development does not stop at birth. Many invertebrates and amphibians exhibit what is known as indirect development and, even after hatching, undergo radical changes in body form. During metamorphosis, these animals pass through various larval stages in order to change into their adult form. Direct development, in contrast, is when the young animal emerges as a miniature adult, although it may lack features such as hair, coloration, or sexual organs. This occurs in reptiles, birds, and mammals. Changes in body shape do still take place—sexual organs typically develop some time after birth—but essentially the juvenile resembles the adult form. Development is not just about physical form, however. Animals' brains develop throughout life, as they learn about the world around them, and form memories that are saved and drawn upon. While some behaviors may be instinctive—including courtship behavior, reproduction, and nest building—many behaviors have to be learned, and are the result of life experience and observation.

EARLY TRAINING
A cheetah cub accompanies its mother on a hunt in the Masai Mara, Kenya. By chasing small prey, such as this young Thomson's gazelle, under the watchful eye of its mother, the young cheetah is practicing the skills it will need to survive as an independent adult.

Life stories

An animal's life story can be described in terms of the different stages and transitions in its life cycle and development—for example, from juvenile to adult, along with associated morphological, physiological, ecological, and behavioral changes. Sometimes, as in the case of parasites and parasitoids (which kill their hosts), the life cycle of an animal is dependent on that of others.

Metamorphosis

Some young animals hatch, or are born as, miniature versions of the adult. In other species, juveniles bear little resemblance to the adults; they live in different habitats and display different behaviors. Their young must undergo metamorphosis (see p.386) for their bodies to change into the mature form. Butterflies, for example, transform from leaf-munching caterpillars into nectar-drinking, winged adults. Other animals, besides insects, change in form during their life cycle. Jellyfish begin life as planktonic larvae, which then come to rest on the seabed, before becoming free-swimming adults. Frogs and toads transform from aquatic tadpoles with gills and tails to terrestrial adults with lungs and limbs.

When ready to pupate, the caterpillar stops feeding. The caterpillar of the painted lady butterfly feeds on plants.

The caterpillar pupates inside a pupal case called a chrysalis, which is suspended from vegetation; in this case, the branch of a tree.

Painted lady butterflies change from egg to adult more rapidly in warmer climates.

FROM EGG TO BEETLE

Beetles undergo complete metamorphosis. After hatching from the egg, the larva, or grub, passes through several stages as it grows, before pupating. Although from the outside, there might appear to be little activity, inside the protective case of the pupa, the larval body structure is transforming into that of the adult beetle, which looks markedly different from the beetle grub.

EGG   EARLY STAGE LARVA   FINAL STAGE LARVA   PUPA   ADULT BEETLE

Parasitic life cycles

Parasites are dependent on one or more other species for the completion of their life cycle. Most live on (ectoparasites) or inside (endoparasites) the host animal, to which they cause varying degrees of harm. In the case of a parasitoid, it develops inside a host and usually causes death. In many parasitoids, such as parasitic wasps, it is the larval stage that is fatal to the host—the larva consumes its host from the inside. The adult, by contrast, is free-living. Some parasites have only one host and are said to have a direct life cycle; others have complex life cycles that require intermediate hosts for the larval stages, as well as primary hosts for the sexually reproductive adult stage. The eggs or larvae of many types of parasite can survive in the environment until they are able to infect a host.

EATEN ALIVE
Parasitoid phorid flies use their hooked ovipositors to place an egg into the head of a leafcutter ant. The fly's larva, or maggot, feeds on the host ant's body, eventually causing its death.

NEST INVASION
The common cuckoo is a brood parasite. The female lays her egg in the nest of a bird of another species, which then raises the chick as its own.

Early and late developers

Across the animal kingdom, newborn offspring require different levels of parental care and take varying lengths of time to reach maturity. Among mammals, marsupials have the shortest gestation periods, relative to body size. Their young are born early on in their development, and continue to grow in their mother's pouch. Placental mammals give birth at a comparatively later stage in their offspring's development. However, there remains a vast spectrum between those that can stand and move at birth and those that are born blind and naked. The former are "precocial," and require relatively little parental care; the latter are "altricial," and entirely reliant on their parents for some time before becoming independent.

HELPLESS YOUNG
Songbird chicks, like those of the American robin (left), are altricial. They stay in the nest after hatching and are cared for and fed by their parents for almost two weeks.

eyes open
down feathers

BORN FLUFFY
Domestic chicken chicks (right) are precocial and can walk immediately after hatching. They feed themselves, although their mother may lead them to acceptable food items, and broods them at night.

SELF-SUFFICIENT
Young marginated tortoises are nourished by their yolk sac for two weeks after hatching from their egg. During this time they stay underground, safely away from predators. There is no parental care.

yolk sac on underside

precocial tortoise

STANDING FOR SURVIVAL
>>01 Female wildebeest give birth to their calves in the center of the herd. Around 80 percent of the females calve during the same two or three week period. >>02 Newborn calves are very vulnerable to predators such as lions and hyenas, which follow the wildebeest migration. >>03 To have any chance of surviving, the calf must move with its mother. It is able to stand and run within minutes of being born.

CASE STUDY

BREEDING LIKE RABBITS

Some animals complete their life cycle very rapidly—they mature quickly and breed fast, but are often short-lived. Scientists refer to these animals as "r strategists," and the rabbit is a good example. Other animals, such as elephants, mature and breed slowly, and live longer. Such animals are known as "K strategists." Although r strategists are often selected for in unpredictable environments and K strategists in more stable ones, in reality, there is a continuum, and many animals display both r and K traits. Green turtles, for instance, are long-lived and slow to mature, but they produce a large number of offspring.

>>01   >>02   >>03

Unwelcome guest

Leucochloridium paradoxum fluke

The *Leucochloridium paradoxum* fluke is an endoparasite, living inside and feeding on the bodies of birds, including crows, jays, sparrows, and finches. Larval worms first infect an intermediate host, the amber snail, which unsuspectingly eats the worm's eggs when it feasts on bird droppings. The eggs hatch inside the snail into first-stage larvae called miracidia, which inhabit the snail's digestive tract. These grow into sporocysts, saclike structures containing cercariae, the next larval stage of the worm's life cycle. Normally, the snails would avoid exposed, sunlit areas, but when infected by larval flukes they are attracted to bright sunlight and tend to climb to the top of grasses. This makes them more visible to birds, the flatworm's final host. Once ingested by a bird, the larvae develop into adult worms in the bird's intestine.

AMBER SNAIL HOST
Brightly colored, banded sacs of flatworm larvae extend into the snail's tentacles, where they pulsate, attracting the attention of birds, which eat the snail and become infected by the parasite.

Leucochloridium paradoxum

- ↔ ⅙ in (1.5 mm)
- ◑ Europe and North Africa.
- 📖 Adult worm long, spiny, and flattened, with suckers that attach to the intestines of its final host.

Clear offspring

Garden snail

The offspring of garden snails are miniature, translucent versions of their parents. They hatch around two weeks after the eggs are laid in a hole in the ground. As the snail's body grows, so too does the shell, changing color at the same time. They take two years to reach maturity, with a shell diameter of ½–¾ in (1.5–2 cm) after one year and 1–1½ in (2.5–3.5 cm) after the second.

Helix aspersa

- ↔ Shell diameter 1–1½ in (2.5–3.5 cm)
- ◑ Moist habitats in woods, hedgerows, parks, and yards across western Europe, Mediterranean, North Africa, and Asia Minor.
- 📖 Adults have a muscular foot and a spherical shell, with bands of dark brown on a lighter brown-yellow base.

New armor

Slipper lobsters

Like other crustaceans, slipper lobsters have hard outer skeletons of chitin and calcium surrounding their bodies. This shell does not grow, so in order for the animal to increase in size it must shed its armor and grow it anew. In the larval stage they are planktonic and may molt a dozen times before settling on a reef or rocky sea bottom. Young lobsters molt several times each year, then less often as they get older. Before molting, they feed extensively, laying down fat reserves.
The lobster grows a soft new shell beneath the existing one, which cracks along lines of weakness to allow it to emerge. The lobster may eat its old shell to regain its valuable calcium content.

Family Scyllaridae

- ↔ Up to 12 in (30 cm)
- ◑ Wide distribution in warm oceans and seas, prevalent around the coast of Australia.
- 📖 Clawless crustacean, with antennae flattened into broad plates in front of the head.

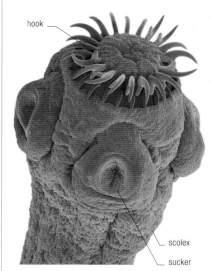

hook

scolex

sucker

Gut feeder

Tapeworms

There are around 5,000 species of tapeworm and all are parasitic. Adult worms live in the intestine of their final host, which is usually a vertebrate, such as a fish, pig, or human. The tapeworm uses the hooks and suckers on its scolex (head) to attach to the wall of the host's gut. These prevent the worm from being dislodged by bowel activity. There, it feeds on the gut contents, growing and producing reproductive segments full of eggs, which are shed with the host's feces. An intermediate host, often an invertebrate, then ingests the eggs and the cycle continues. Some worms need more than one intermediate host to complete their life cycle.

PARASITIC TAPEWORM
Tapeworms are covered in small projections called microtriches. These increase the surface area of the worm's body for absorption of nutrients from the host's gut.

Class Cestoda

- ↔ Variable (maximum recorded 59 ft/18 m)
- ◑ Worldwide, where hosts occur.
- 📖 Long and flat, with a small head and reproductive sections.

Changing shape

Moon jellyfish

Also known as the common jellyfish, the moon jellyfish is a relatively simple organism with a complex, multistage life cycle. It alternates between the free-swimming medusa (bell-shaped jellyfish) and the sedentary polyp forms. The polyps are general feeders, settling on the sea bed and using their tentacles to filter food from the water that flows past them. The adult jellyfish drift on the ocean currents and feed on copepods and phytoplankton that they trap using mucus and a fine fringe of stinging tentacles.

Aurelia aurita

- ↔ 2–15½ in (5–40 cm)
- ◑ Warm, tropical, coastal waters of the Indian, Atlantic, and Pacific oceans.
- 📖 Adult jellyfish is a colorless bell, through which four violet gonads are visible. The edge of the bell is fringed with tentacles.

MATURING INTO MEDUSAE
Free-swimming ephyra larvae bud off from the polyp, taking up to a year to mature into medusae or adult jellyfish.

POLYP STAGE

ANATOMY

JELLYFISH LIFE CYCLE

Adult jellyfish reproduce sexually: males release sperm through their mouths into the sea, where they enter the mouth of a female and fertilize eggs in the female's gonads. The resulting embryos move to the arms around the mouth to develop before being released into the plankton as planula larvae. Eventually, the planula settles on the sea bed to form a scyphistoma polyp, which reproduces asexually to produce more polyps. The scyphistoma buds to produce a strobila, or stack of immature ephyra larvae. As the stack grows, the ephyra farthest away from the base begin to mature and are released. These free-swimming ephyra larvae gradually mature into adult medusae, completing the life cycle.

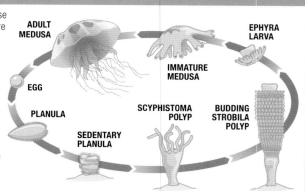

ADULT MEDUSA

EGG

PLANULA

SEDENTARY PLANULA

SCYPHISTOMA POLYP

IMMATURE MEDUSA

EPHYRA LARVA

BUDDING STROBILA POLYP

EMERGING ANEW
The slipper lobster's old shell fractures between the thorax and abdomen to allow the animal to pull itself out. The skin around the antennae, eyes, and gills remains intact. Depending on its size and age, a lobster may increase in weight by 6–24 percent after each molt.

Shedding skin

Emperor dragonfly

The emperor dragonfly is an insect that undergoes incomplete metamorphosis during its development to the adult form. Its eggs hatch into aquatic larvae called nymphs, which undergo a series of molts, shedding their brown skin as they grow. Each successive larval stage resembles the one before and is known as an instar. In total, the emperor dragonfly spends around a year in this aquatic nymph stage. The predatory larvae grow and molt quickly during summer, and in fall of the following year they molt into a final instar, which spends winter at the bottom of the pond or river in a state of diapause, or hibernation. Early the next summer, the final instar larva climbs out of the water and sheds its skin to emerge as a winged adult dragonfly. Adult dragonflies live for only a few weeks, hunting and becoming sexually mature before searching for

Anax imperator

- ↔ 3¼ in (8 cm)
- ⬡ Ponds and slow rivers in Europe, central Asia, North Africa, and Middle East.
- ▯ Adults of both sexes have a bright green thorax. Abdomen green with brown markings (female) or bright blue with a black line down the center (male).

FACIAL MASK
The aquatic nymphs of dragonflies are voracious predators. They lie in ambush before capturing prey such as tadpoles (as here) or small fish with a grasping lower mouthpart called the facial mask.

mates. Male dragonflies patrol stretches of water, defending them against other males, while welcoming females. Male and female dragonflies mate on the wing, the male clasping the female behind the head with his abdomen in a characteristic "wheel" mating posture. Sperm is transferred from the male's primary genitalia to a secondary or accessory organ and, from there, to the female. Once the female lays the eggs, the life cycle is complete.

EMERGENCE
When the nymph is ready to emerge, it climbs up a plant stem into the air and breaks out of its skin. After emerging, the dragonfly must wait for its wings to unfurl and harden before being able to fly.

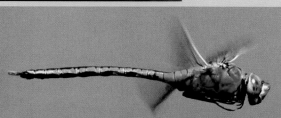

READY TO FLY
This male dragonfly is fully developed and hawking for prey over a pond. As an adult, it will spend nearly all of its time in the air, both hunting and looking for a suitable mate.

LAYING EGGS
Once they have mated, female dragonflies use an ovipositor at the end of their abdomen to lay their eggs on vegetation floating in the water. The eggs hatch into a new generation of aquatic nymphs.

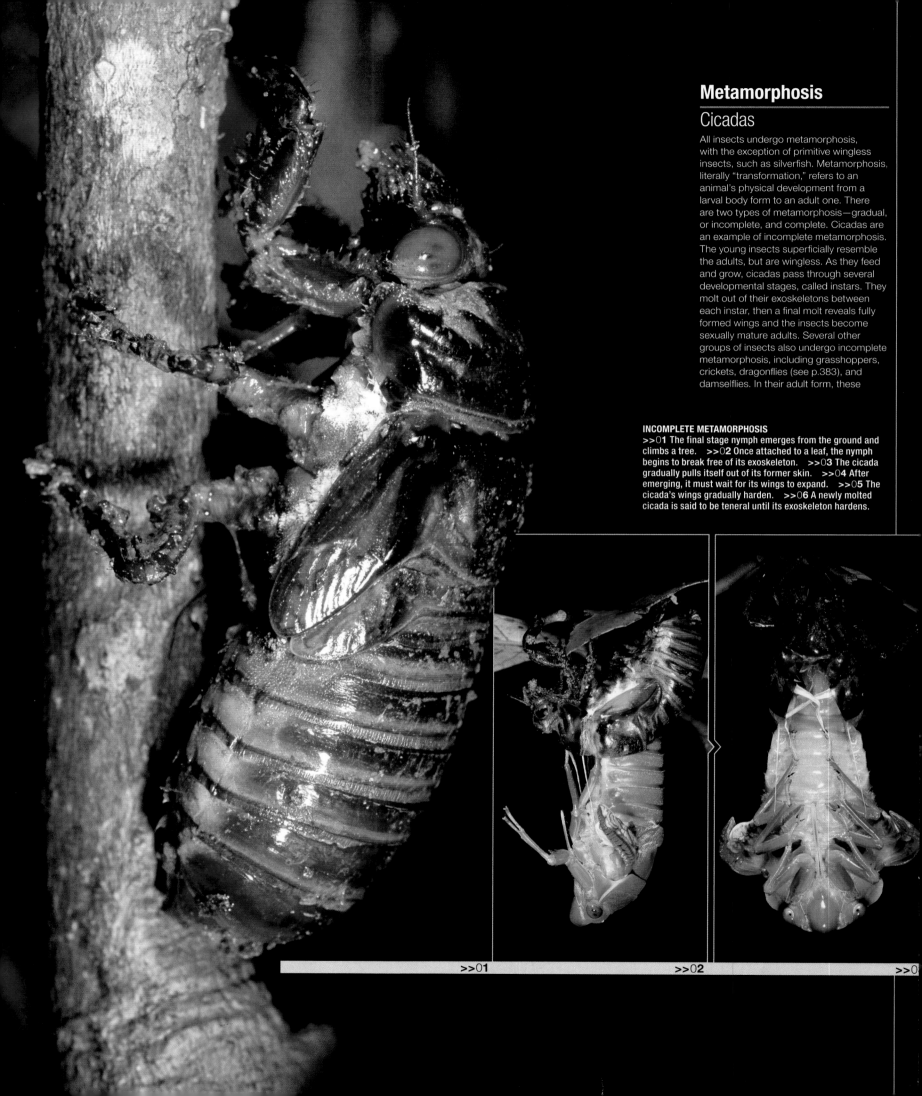

Metamorphosis
Cicadas

All insects undergo metamorphosis, with the exception of primitive wingless insects, such as silverfish. Metamorphosis, literally "transformation," refers to an animal's physical development from a larval body form to an adult one. There are two types of metamorphosis—gradual, or incomplete, and complete. Cicadas are an example of incomplete metamorphosis. The young insects superficially resemble the adults, but are wingless. As they feed and grow, cicadas pass through several developmental stages, called instars. They molt out of their exoskeletons between each instar, then a final molt reveals fully formed wings and the insects become sexually mature adults. Several other groups of insects also undergo incomplete metamorphosis, including grasshoppers, crickets, dragonflies (see p.383), and damselflies. In their adult form, these

INCOMPLETE METAMORPHOSIS
>>01 The final stage nymph emerges from the ground and climbs a tree.   >>02 Once attached to a leaf, the nymph begins to break free of its exoskeleton.   >>03 The cicada gradually pulls itself out of its former skin.   >>04 After emerging, it must wait for its wings to expand.   >>05 The cicada's wings gradually harden.   >>06 A newly molted cicada is said to be teneral until its exoskeleton hardens.

>>01   >>02   >>0

insects are sometimes called imagos, and the young are known as nymphs. Aquatic nymphs are referred to as naiads.

Insects that experience complete metamorphosis include beetles, butterflies (see p.380), bees, and flies. The changing form of their bodies during development is even more dramatic than in cicadas. Their larvae—variously called caterpillars, grubs, or maggots, according to the insect group to which they belong—also pass through several instars. They are often specialist feeders and may even be parasitic on other animals. Once they have finished feeding, the larvae pupate inside a cocoon or pupal case. During this time, they do not feed or move while their body undergoes a major transformation to the winged adult form.

Family Cicadidae

⬌ ¾–6 in (2–15 cm)

⊙ Woodland, worldwide except Antarctica.

▭ Wide-set eyes, short antennae, and large, transparent, heavily veined forewings. Various colors.

>> 333, 388

2,500 The number of species in the insect family Cicadidae.

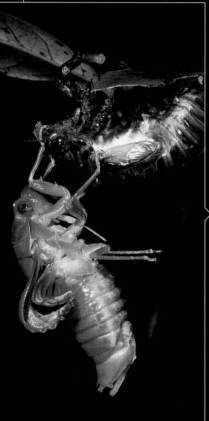

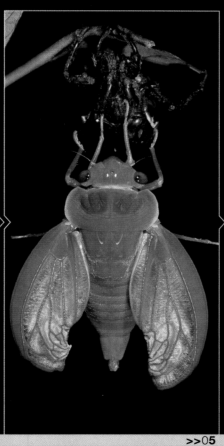

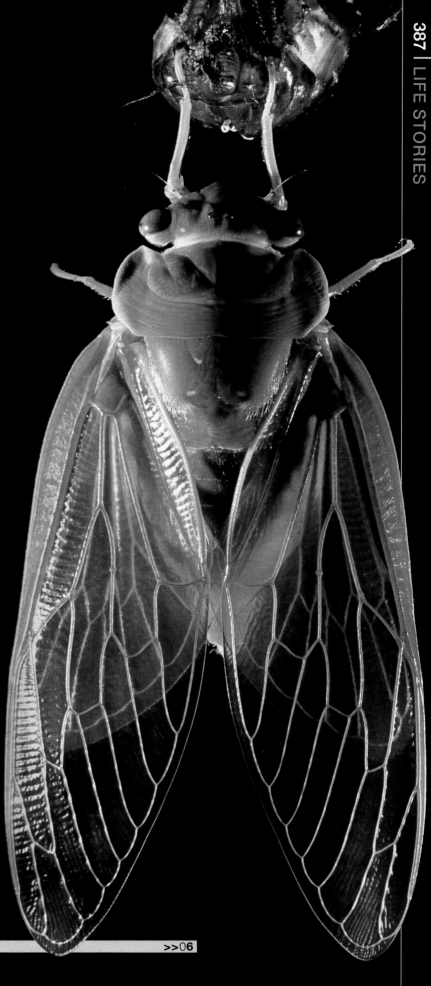

Mass emergence

Periodical cicadas

The periodical cicadas of North America are so-called because of their recurrent patterns of brood emergence. There are seven species, three with a 17-year life cycle and four with a 13-year life cycle, meaning that every 17 or 13 years respectively a brood emerges from eggs that were laid and hatched 17 or 13 years previously. The nymphs spend the intervening years underground, going through various stages of development and feeding on juices from tree roots. Adult males mature to make a deafening chorus of noise, which attracts the females.

Magicicada species

⬛ 1–1¼ in (2.5–3 cm)

◉ Deciduous forests in eastern US.

📖 Adults black and depending on the species may have yellow or orange stripes on their undersides. They have red eyes and translucent wings with orange veins.

FINAL MOLT Above ground, the final-stage nymph attaches itself to a tree and undergoes one final molt to become a winged adult. Initially, the adult is soft and pale, but it darkens as the exoskeleton hardens with age.

EMERGING NYMPH When ready, the final-stage nymph digs a small tunnel through the ground to reach the surface. Unlike the adults, nymphs do not possess wings.

STAGES OF DEVELOPMENT

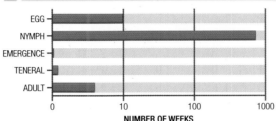

CICADA LIFE SPAN The total life span of the 17-year periodical cicada is 884 weeks. A massive 98 percent of this time is spent underground as a nymph. At the teneral stage, the cicada is soft and pale.

Safety line

Green lacewing

Green lacewing females each attach 400–500 eggs to leaves by thin silk threads. This keeps them out of the reach of insect predators, including their newly hatched siblings. Lacewing larvae are important predators of aphids, a crop pest, and they are widely used by horticulturalists as biological control agents.

Chrysoperla carnea

⬛ ½–¾ in (1.5–2 cm)

◉ Herbaceous vegetation across North America, Europe, North Africa, and Asia.

📖 Adults green with delicately veined, transparent wings. In winter, they become brown-red.

Dung incubator

Flightless dung beetle

Female flightless dung beetles select balls of buffalo dung in which to lay their eggs. They roll their ball up to 260 ft (80 m) away from the dung pat and bury it. Once a female has laid her eggs, she stays with the dung ball to tend her developing brood, for example by removing potentially harmful fungus from the ball's surface. Dung beetles take between 170 and 205 days to develop from an egg to a sexually mature adult.

Circellium bacchus

⬛ 1¼–2 in (3–5 cm)

◉ Scrub and thicket vegetation in the Eastern Cape Province, South Africa.

📖 Heavily armored, round, metallic-black beetle.

Big baby

Tsetse fly

After mating, tsetse fly females retain a single fertilized egg in their uterus. There it hatches into a larva, which is fed on secretions from a modified gland. The larva passes through three larval instars (stages) in five days; the female then deposits it on the ground, into which it burrows to pupate. Pregnant flies feed on the blood of other animals in order to sustain their offspring.

GIVING BIRTH At birth, the tsetse fly larva is large and ready to pupate. It breathes through black lobes at its rear end.

Glossina morsitans

⬛ ¼–½ in (7–14 mm)

◉ Savanna and woodland in Africa and Arabian Peninsula, south of the Tropic of Cancer.

📖 Brownish gray flying insect with specialized mouthparts for biting and drinking blood.

Body snatcher

Braconid wasps

Braconid wasp larvae are parasitoids—parasites that ultimately cause the death of their host. In this case, the hosts are the larvae of other insects, often beetle grubs, fly maggots, or caterpillars. A female wasp places its eggs inside the body of another animal, using her long ovipositor. The eggs hatch into larvae that feed on the host's fluids and internal organs. Viruses may help the wasp larvae to evade detection by disabling the host's immune system. Larvae of some species of braconid wasp remain within the host's body to pupate, while others cut round holes and emerge through the skin, pupating while still attached to the host or moving away to pupate elsewhere. There are 12,000 described species of braconid wasp.

COCOONED CATERPILLAR After the wasp larvae emerge from the body of their host, they wrap themselves in silk cocoons to undergo their final transformation to adult wasps.

Family Braconidae

⬛ Up to ½ in (1.5 cm)

◉ Worldwide.

📖 Most braconid wasps are relatively small and dark, with two pairs of transparent wings. Females have a long ovipositor for depositing eggs.

Food reserve

Spiny dogfish

Also known as the spurdog or piked dogfish, the spiny dogfish gives birth to a litter of 2–11 live pups after a lengthy gestation of 22–24 months. It is an ovoviviparous shark, meaning that the eggs are retained inside the female, enclosed within a thin, transparent shell called a candle, until the young are fully developed and ready to be born. Sharks show a broad range of reproductive strategies. The embryos of some species, for example the shortfin mako shark, feed inside the mother on her unfertilized eggs or by cannibalizing their siblings.

Squalus acanthias

- ↔ 2½–5 ft (0.8–1.5 m)
- ◐ Shallow and offshore temperate waters worldwide.
- 📖 Shark with two dorsal fins, each with a spine, a slate-gray to brown upper side, and a white belly.

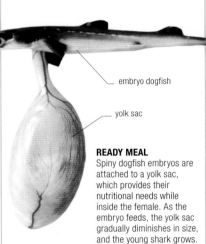

— embryo dogfish

— yolk sac

READY MEAL
Spiny dogfish embryos are attached to a yolk sac, which provides their nutritional needs while inside the female. As the embryo feeds, the yolk sac gradually diminishes in size, and the young shark grows.

Translucent home

Blotchy swell shark

The blotchy or Japanese swell shark is an egg-laying (oviparous) fish. After mating, the female produces two eggs, one from each oviduct, which become enclosed in egg cases or "mermaids' purses" as they pass through her reproductive tract. Each egg contains a single embryo and its food source, a sac of protein-rich yolk. The embryo undergoes most of its 12-month development detached from the mother's body, inside the egg case. During this time,

Cephaloscyllium umbratile

- ↔ 4 ft (1.2 m)
- ◐ Subtropical rocky reefs of the western Pacific Ocean from Japan to the South China Sea, possibly extending to Papua New Guinea.
- 📖 Fairly stout cat shark with blotches on its back. When threatened, inflates its body by taking in sea water in order to appear larger.

swell shark embryos are at risk from predatory snails, which use their horny radula ("tongue") to cut through the egg case. When the young shark is ready to emerge, it uses a double row of toothlike structures on its back to help break its way out of its egg case. Blotchy swell sharks

MERMAID'S PURSE
The embryos are held within a tough egg case that is anchored to seaweed or rocks using long tendrils. The light shining through this egg case reveals the yolk sac and embryo attached by the umbilical cord.

are at one end of the shark reproductive spectrum, with little or no embryonic development occurring within the mother. At the other end are sharks that form a very close link with their developing embryos. Some produce a sort of uterine milk called histrotroph to nourish their young, while others have a placenta through which nutrients can pass from the mother's blood to her developing offspring.

Face migration

Lemon sole

Adult lemon sole are bottom-dwelling (benthic) flatfish, but they do not emerge from the egg that way. Their planktonic eggs develop into pelagic larval fish, meaning they swim in open water. Gradually, the young fish start to swim on their sides, flatten out, and eventually settle on the seabed. In order to avoid having one eye looking at the sand, the lemon sole's left eye migrates around to the right side of its body. This new upper side of the body becomes elaborately pigmented, while the underside remains white. Lemon sole often partly bury themselves in the sandy substrate, so they are camouflaged and less visible to predators. When they swim, they do so close to the bottom, on their sides, and by flexing their body. Flatfish related to the lemon sole, such as brill, flounder, halibut, plaice, and turbot, all undergo the same process, although some species, such as the California halibut, are "sinistral," meaning that the right eye moves around to the left side of the body. The metamorphosis from upright to flatfish

is controlled by thyroid hormone, which also controls metamorphosis in amphibians. Other fish that live on the seabed may be flat, but from top to bottom, so they do not undergo this dramatic transformation to lie on their sides.

EYES TO THE RIGHT
Lemon sole are right-eyed, meaning that the left eye moves over to the right side of the fish's body (above). Some species, for example the summer flounder (*Paralichthys dentatus*), are left-eyed, and the right eye migrates to the left side of the body.

Microstomus kitt

- ↔ 8–28 in (20–70 cm)
- ◐ Stony and rocky seabeds of northeast Atlantic to a depth of 660–1,300 ft (200–400 m).
- 📖 Flatfish with small head and mouth. Speckled red-brown, pink, and orange dorsal surface with flecks of yellow and green. White underside.

> In some flatfish, unlike the lemon sole, the eye **migrates through the skull** rather than moving across the head.

ⓞ ANATOMY
TURNING HEADS

At 10 days old, the larval lemon sole swims upright and has a bilaterally symmetrical body and a relatively large skull, which will later become compressed as the face is distorted. Metamorphosis begins after 13 days: the left eye starts to migrate over the top of the head to the right side of the body. The transformation is complete after 35 days. Both eyes are on the right side, which is the adult lemon sole's upper surface and is now distinctly patterned.

TEN DAYS

THIRTEEN DAYS

THIRTY-FIVE DAYS

Surrogate mother

Bitterling

Bitterlings depend on a relationship with mussels for their reproduction. Before breeding, female bitterlings grow an egg-laying tube or ovipositor, 2–2¼ in (5–6 cm) long, behind their anus. The female hangs vertically in the water before inserting her ovipositor into a mussel, laying two or three eggs into the mussel's body cavity. The male bitterling then fertilizes the eggs by shedding his sperm into the flow of water being drawn into the shell by the mussel's siphon. When the baby bitterlings hatch they remain in the safety of the bivalve's shell for a period of three to four weeks, eventually emerging through the mussel's siphon. A female bitterling lays eggs several times over a number of weeks, so a mussel can contain young at various stages of development.

Rhodeus ocellatus

- 1½–3¼ in (4–8 cm)
- Inland waters, such as ponds, creeks, and reservoirs. Native to Taiwan; introduced in China and Japan.
- Silvery fish with rhomboid-shaped body. During the mating season, males become rosy red in color.

Color change

Emperor angelfish

Emperor angelfish undergo a spectacular transformation as they mature. Their coloration and patterning change so markedly that juveniles were first thought to belong to another species.

It is not known how the color change is mediated. The change may help immature angelfish avoid aggression from sexually mature adult angelfish, to which they might otherwise appear to pose a threat.

ADULT EMPEROR ANGELFISH

JUVENILE EMPEROR ANGELFISH

Pomacanthus imperator

- 15½ in (40 cm)
- Coral reefs of the Pacific and Indian oceans.
- Laterally compressed body, with a spine on the rear margin of the gill cover. Juveniles have concentric white circles on the body; adults have horizontal yellow stripes.

Total metamorphosis

European common frog

European common frogs, like most frogs, toads, and other amphibians, begin their lives as aquatic tadpoles, but later transform into terrestrial adults. Their metamorphosis is governed by a thyroid hormone. Some frogs, such as the common coqui, lack a tadpole stage, instead hatching from their eggs as tiny frogs. Tadpole metamorphosis is flexible, depending on environmental conditions. For example, low temperatures and low food supply slow growth rates and delay metamorphosis.

FROM WATER TO LAND
>>01 In spring, female common frogs lay batches of gelatinous eggs (frogspawn) in water.   >>02 Six days after fertilization, the eggs hatch into tiny tadpoles.
>>03 The tadpoles have tails and gills.   >>04 After 6–9 weeks, they develop hind legs, and their gills are replaced by lungs, so they must swim at the water's surface to breathe.   >>05 They then develop forelegs and their tails start to disappear.   >>06 Metamorphosis is complete. The frogs attain sexual maturity in 3 years.

Rana temporaria

- Up to 4½ in (11 cm)
- Damp habitats, ponds, and ditches of Europe and northwest Asia, except Portugal, much of Spain, Italy, and most of Greece.
- Adults have a broad head, short, tailless body, and long, powerful legs. Usually brown or gray.
- >> 372

TRANSFORMING TAIL
The tails of immature frogs (froglets) gradually disappear at the same time as other metamorphic changes are occurring.

Protective skin
Surinam toad

The tadpoles of the Surinam toad live within their mother's skin while they grow. During mating, the male toad grasps the female around her hind legs. The pair flips repeatedly in the water and each time the female releases up to 10 eggs that fall onto the male's belly, where they are fertilized. From there, they are transferred onto the female's back, where they sink into the skin, forming pockets, over the next few hours. In total, around 100 eggs are laid. The tadpoles hatch and complete their development within the mother's skin, which protects the eggs and tadpoles, keeping them safe from predators and ensuring they are kept moist. Even though they are not required for swimming, the tadpoles temporarily have tails. The tail helps each tadpole obtain sufficient oxygen by increasing its surface area of moist skin.

Pipa pipa
⬌ 4–6½ in (10–17 cm)

⬤ Ponds and swamps of South America and Trinidad.

📖 Flattened toad with a triangular head and tiny eyes. The front feet have long, unwebbed toes with star-shaped appendages; the hind feet have broadly webbed toes.

HATCHING TOADLETS
The fully formed young toads emerge from their mother's back after 12–20 weeks, usually when the female molts her skin.

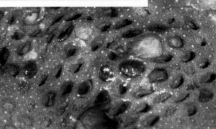

EGG PROTECTION
The eggs sink into honeycomb-like skin on the female's back and become encased in a cystlike structure covered with a horny lid.

Permanent juvenile
Axolotl

The axolotl is a type of salamander that never grows up. It is "neotenic" or "pedomorphic," meaning that it retains larval features into adulthood and sexual maturity. It is permanently aquatic and has feathery gills for extracting oxygen from the water. It also has juvenile skin and fins on its tail to help it swim. Axolotls become sexually mature at around one year of age. The male deposits a package of sperm or spermatophore on the lake bed via his cloaca, and the female then picks up the spermatophore to fertilize her eggs. Axolotls can transform into adult salamanders if they have hybridized with tiger salamanders or they can be induced to metamorphose by exposure to hormones or high iodine levels.

ALBINO AXOLOTL
Albinos are relatively common among captive axolotls. Wild axolotls tend to be a mottled brown-green color.

Ambystoma mexicanum
⬌ 8–17 in (20–43 cm)

⬤ Historically found in two lakes near Mexico City, one of which is no longer present. Endangered in the wild.

📖 Aquatic salamander with a larval body form, broad head, feathery gills, and tail fins.

Fatherly concern
Mallorcan midwife toad

All five species of midwife toad share a common behavior—it is the male toad rather than the female that cares for the eggs. During mating, the female lays her eggs, which are simultaneously fertilized by the male. He then winds them around his legs to protect them from predators. When they are ready to hatch, he lowers the eggs into a pool for the tadpoles to emerge. The Mallorcan midwife toad was believed to be extinct until a tiny population was discovered in 1980. A captive breeding program is helping the toad's recovery.

Alytes muletensis
⬌ 1½ in (4 cm)

⬤ Endemic to the Spanish island of Mallorca. Lives in small streams in limestone gorges.

📖 Relatively large head and eyes, long limbs, and golden brown skin with dark green to black blotches.

MALE CARERS
Male Mallorcan midwife toads carry their eggs in strings wrapped around their ankles, keeping them safe from attack. Mating occurs in May and June; the eggs are carried until they hatch into tadpoles.

CASE STUDY
PREDATOR EFFECT

Predatory viperine snakes (*Natrix maura*) were introduced to Mallorca around 2,000 years ago and pose a threat to midwife toads. Biologists have noticed differences in form between tadpoles that are exposed to these predators and those that are not. Tadpoles that share pools with one of these snakes tend to be leaner, with longer tails, narrower fins, and deeper tail muscles, allowing them to swim faster than tadpoles that do not coexist with a snake and tend to be fatter.

NONPREDATOR-EXPOSED TADPOLE

PREDATOR-EXPOSED TADPOLE

Live young
Viviparous lizard

Viviparous lizards give birth to live young enclosed in a thin egg membrane. They break out of the membrane within a day. The young lizards have residual yolk that provides them with nutrition during their first days of freedom, before they start catching invertebrate prey. Male viviparous lizards become sexually mature at around two and females at three years of age.

Lacerta vivipara
⬌ 5–6 in (13–15 cm)

⬤ Sunny, dry habitats including parks, moorland, meadows, and mountains in Europe and Asia.

📖 Brown lizard with dark markings, often bordered with white or yellow. Males are brighter below than females.

EGG-LAYING FEMALE
The female lays her eggs into a hole she has dug in the sand of a traditional nesting beach. When she has finished laying, she covers the eggs over and returns to the sea. The hatchling turtles emerge 40–75 days later.

Chelonia mydas
- Up to 5 ft (1.5 m)
- Tropical and subtropical seagrass beds and open water in Atlantic and Indo-Pacific oceans.
- Olive-brown sea turtle, named for the green tint of its fat and connective tissue rather than its skin.
- >> 337

Rapid egg production
Green turtle

A female green turtle may lay up to nine clutches of eggs in a single breeding season, each clutch numbering between 100 and 200 eggs. She may not breed again for several years. Many turtle nests are destroyed by scavengers, such as dogs, coatis, and vultures, and they are also threatened by man's activities. Hatchlings are vulnerable to seabirds and crabs on the beach and sharks and dolphins in the water. The high rate of egg production helps offset the high rate of mortality suffered by the eggs and hatchling turtles, ensuring that at least a few individuals survive to adulthood.

short, beaked head

paddlelike flippers

LATE BLOOMER
Green turtles are long-lived animals that may take up to 50 years to reach sexual maturity.

Attentive mother
Common pheasant

Common pheasants typically produce a clutch of 10–12 eggs, which are incubated by the female. The young are relatively well developed when they hatch and are ready to leave the nest immediately. They remain with their mother for 8–11 weeks before becoming independent.

Phasianus colchicus
- 21–35 in (53–89 cm)
- Woodland, farmland, scrub, and wetlands. Originally from Asia; naturalized throughout Europe, North America, Australia, New Zealand, and Hawaii.
- Male is rich golden brown with a bottle-green head and red wattle. Female is drab brown with rust and black markings.

Paternal instinct
Emperor penguin

The only penguin species to reproduce during the Antarctic winter, male emperor penguins withstand some of the harshest conditions on Earth while incubating their eggs. Most emperor penguin colonies breed on stable pack ice, selecting sheltered areas where walls of ice or icebergs offer some protection against the bitter wind.

Emperor penguins are ready to breed from around three years of age. After laying their single egg in May or June, female penguins leave for the ocean to feed and replenish the energy lost in egg production. The males are left to take care of the egg for over two months, during which they do not feed and they lose around a third of their body weight by metabolizing fat to keep warm. The females return from the sea when their eggs are about to hatch. They regurgitate fishes and squid for their new offspring and switch places with the male so that he can go to feed. Occasionally, the egg hatches before the female comes back and the male produces a protein-rich secretion to feed the chick for a few days. For the next 45–50 days after hatching, the parents take turns to go on foraging trips and care for their young chick. Initially they may have to walk 30–75 miles (50–120 km) to reach the open ocean at the edge of the pack ice, but as the Antarctic summer progresses and the ice melts, this distance gradually reduces. The young penguins remain in nurseries until they are 150 days old, when they leave the ice and head for the ocean.

CLOSE COLONY
Males huddle together to ride out the Antarctic winter. They may not see the sun for two months, temperatures can plunge to −49° F (−45° C), and blizzards may blow at up to 124 mph (200 kph).

ABANDONED EGG
Emperor penguin eggs weigh around 16 oz (450 g). Occasionally, eggs are dropped or are abandoned. An egg left in contact with the ice freezes in less than two minutes.

200,000 The estimated number of stable emperor penguin breeding pairs currently in Antarctica.

Tree climbing
Hoatzin

The hoatzin is a noisy bird that breeds in trees overhanging water, laying two to three eggs in a stick nest. If threatened, the nestlings throw themselves out of their nest into the water below. Young hoatzins have two claws on each wing that act as hooks to help them cling onto vegetation, and they use these to climb back up the tree once the threat has passed. Hoatzins are unusual in feeding entirely on leaves. They possess a greatly enlarged crop in their gut, where the leaves' digestion is aided by bacterial fermentation. The evolutionary history of the hoatzin is far from clear. They have been variously linked to gamebirds, cuckoos, and African turacos.

Opisthocomus hoazin

↔ 26 in (65 cm)

◐ Swamps, riverine forest, and mangroves in the Amazon Basin and Orinoco Delta in South America.

▥ Small head with blue face, maroon eyes, and a spiky, rust-colored crest. Body plumage is a combination of sooty brown, buff, and chestnut-brown.

HANGING ON
The wing claws are lost when the birds molt into their adult plumage and are able to fly up into the trees rather than climb up. Even as adults, hoatzins are poor fliers and tend to clamber around their arboreal habitat in a clumsy manner.

Decaying nest
Malleefowl

Male malleefowl build large mounds of decaying vegetation and sand in which the females lay their eggs. The males use their feet to scrape out a large depression, which they then fill with plenty of organic matter. They turn the vegetation over after rain to encourage decay, which generates heat; the mound is also warmed by the sun. The female lays her eggs at 5–17 day intervals. Clutch sizes are very variable but an average clutch will have between 15 and 20 eggs. These are layed in a chamber within the mound, which is then covered with a layer of sand. On hatching, the young mallee fowl dig their way out of the mound. They receive no parental care whatsoever and are able to fly and fend for themselves within a single day.

Leipoa ocellata

↔ 23½ in (60 cm)

◐ Semiarid scrub and low eucalyptus woodland in southern Australia.

▥ Well-camouflaged bird with mottled gray, brown, and black plumage, white underside, and large feet.

MALLEEFOWL MOUND
Males tend their mound religiously during incubation, maintaining its temperature at 92–93° F (33–34° C) by adding and removing layers of soil. They test the mound's temperature by probing it with their beaks.

Aptenodytes forsteri

↔ 3½ ft (1.1 m)

◐ Pack ice, coastal islands, and waters around Antarctica.

▥ Adult's back, head, and wing plumage black, ear patches and neck yellow fading into a white belly. Upper mandible of the bill black, lower mandible orange or pink.

⊙ ANATOMY
BROOD PATCH

The male emperor penguin incubates the egg on top of his feet, in contact with a bare fold of skin called the brood patch. This anatomical adaptation allows the adult penguin's body heat to reach the delicate egg more efficiently. The fold of skin extends down over the top of the egg to keep it warm and safe. The male incubates the egg like this for 65 days. Once it hatches, the chick also takes refuge beneath the brood patch until it is able to withstand the cold. Penguins have a thick blubber layer and densely packed feathers to keep them warm.

MARCH OF THE PENGUINS
Male emperor penguins can still walk with the egg incubating in the brood patch. Because their legs are set far back, penguins are efficient, graceful swimmers, but can look ungainly on land.

Protective pouch

Red-necked wallaby

The gestation period of a red-necked wallaby lasts just 30 days, after which the fetus is born when still fairly undeveloped. Within minutes of birth, it makes its way to a pouch on its mother's belly to continue its development. Soon after the birth, the female mates again. The resulting embryo remains in a suspended state called "embryonic diapause" for up to eight months. It is then born within 30 days of the first joey leaving the pouch. A female may therefore have a young-at-foot, which she continues to feed, a joey in the pouch, and an embryo *in utero* at the same time.

gray body

YOUNG-AT-FOOT
Wallabies continue to suckle until 12–17 months of age. After weaning, they feed mainly on grasses and herbs.

white belly

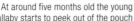

JOEY IN THE POUCH
At around five months old the young wallaby starts to peek out of the pouch and by six months it can hop in and out. At eight months, the joey is too large for the pouch but stays close to its mother.

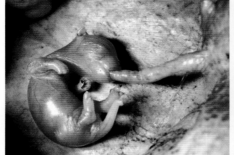

WALLABY SUCKLING
Newborn wallabies are about ½ in (1.5 cm) long. They crawl through their mother's fur to the pouch, where they latch on to one of four teats and suckle on their mother's milk for four months.

Macropus rufogriseus

◧ 28–41 in (70–105 cm)

◓ Coastal scrub, bush, and eucalyptus forest in eastern and southeastern Australia.

▥ Medium-sized wallaby with reddish coloration across the shoulders.

>> 412

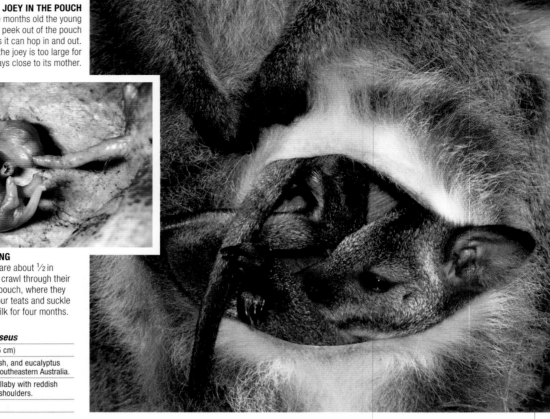

Egg-laying mammal

Short-beaked echidna

The short-beaked echidna is one of only five species of extant mammal that lays eggs. The others are three species of long-beaked echidna and the platypus. They are known collectively as monotremes, a reference to the single common opening

Tachyglossus aculeatus

◧ 12–17½ in (30–45 cm)

◓ Forest, deserts, and meadows in Australia; coastal and highland regions of southwestern New Guinea.

▥ Body is covered in cream and black spines interspersed with brown-black fur. The small head has a long snout and small eyes.

for the urinary, defecatory, and reproductive tracts. As in birds and reptiles, this opening is called the cloaca. After a period of gestation, during which the fertilized egg is nourished in the oviduct, female short-beaked echidnas lay a single egg into a specially developed pouch at the rear of their abdomen; the platypus lays up to three eggs in a burrow. The young echidna remains in the pouch for two to three months. Since the mother has no teats, the young suckles milk from a patch of skin on the mother's belly called the areola; this is also

STRONG DIGGER
All echidnas are adapted to digging, with short limbs and strong claws. As well as burrowing, they dig for ants and termites, using their sensitive snouts as a guide.

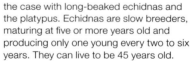

the case with long-beaked echidnas and the platypus. Echidnas are slow breeders, maturing at five or more years old and producing only one young every two to six years. They can live to be 45 years old.

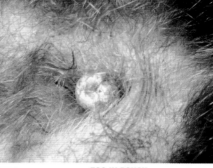

EGG IN POUCH
A leathery egg is laid directly into the female's pouch from the cloaca after 21–28 days of gestation. The young echidna uses its egg tooth to hatch around 10 days later.

YOUNG IN BURROW
When the young echidna, or puggle, becomes too big to remain in the pouch, the female leaves it in a burrow. She allows it to suckle until it is six months old. It reaches independence after one year.

Early hunters

American mink

American mink are opportunistic predators of prey as diverse as fishes, waterfowl, eggs, rodents, and rabbits. Young mink, called kittens or kits, are taught to hunt by their mothers at between seven and nine weeks of age. By 13–14 weeks they are independent and leave their place of birth, becoming sexually mature within a year. Their voracious appetites and habit of killing more prey than they can consume and stashing it for later has caused local declines in native wildlife in areas of Europe where mink have escaped from fur farms or have been introduced—the water vole is particularly threatened.

Mustela vison

◧ 12–21½ in (30–54 cm)

◓ Wooded areas and fields close to streams, rivers, and lakes. Native to North America but now established in Europe and South America.

▥ Long, slender body covered in glossy, well-waterproofed, brownish fur, often with a white patch under the chin. Short legs with partially webbed feet.

MINK LITTER
American mink make a nest or burrow in which to give birth to their litter of four to six kittens in spring. The young are weaned at around six weeks old.

Social clan

Badger

A badger sett or burrow is home to a social group or "clan" of up to 12 badgers, comprising a dominant breeding pair—the boar and sow—and their subordinate offspring. The boar and sow may mate any time between late winter and midsummer, but implantation of the resulting embryos is delayed for up to ten months. The embryos are eventually triggered to implant and continue their development according to changing day length and temperature. Around seven weeks after the implantation of the embryos, in February or March, between two and six blind young are born. They open their eyes at about one month of age and suckle for up to three months. Although they are independent and can disperse at seven to eight months of age, the females in particular often stay with their parents for longer.

Meles meles

⬌ 22–35 in (56–90 cm)

🜨 Across Europe and Asia. Setts located in woods and forests; badgers forage in adjacent fields.

📖 Stocky mustelid with a striking white-and-black-striped face, gray back, and black underside.

SOCIAL HOME

Each sett has a breeding chamber, lined with dried vegetation, where the cubs are born and remain until they are old enough to venture outside. They often spend time playing or grooming one another.

Close contact

Muskrat

Female muskrats build lodges or burrows in which to give birth to and care for their young. An underwater entrance leads to a nest that is situated above water level and lined with soft grasses. On average, a muskrat litter numbers six offspring, which are weaned at three to four weeks of age. Before they are able to thermoregulate and keep themselves warm, young muskrats huddle together to maintain their body temperature. In southern parts of their range, muskrats breed all year round, but in the north they typically breed between March and August.

Ondatra zibethicus

⬌ 16–24 in (41–62 cm)

🜨 Marshes, swamps, and wetlands in North America; introduced in Europe and Asia.

📖 Dense, dark brown fur. Relatively large head with small ears. Back feet slightly webbed for swimming. Long, hairless tail flattened from side to side.

Only child

Giraffe

Female giraffes usually have one offspring every 20–30 months. Gestation lasts around 15 months and the young are typically born between May and August. For the first week, the mother stands guard and feeds close to her resting baby during the day and suckles it at night. After three to four weeks, the pair will join the herd, where the young giraffe is cared for in a nursery with other young. Each female takes it in turns to watch the nursery while the other females feed. The young are fully weaned at between 12 and 16 months of age, but females do not breed until they are at least five and males at least seven years old. Giraffe herds contain animals of all ages, although males are generally less social than females.

7.9ft The length of an adult giraffe's neck; it contains seven elongated vertebrae.

It is illegal to kill giraffes in many African countries. However, they are poached for their hides, meat, and tails. The long, hair-tipped tails are made into fly swats, good-luck bracelets, and thread for sewing, and the hide is used to make buckets or shields. Hunting has not yet had a disastrous effect on giraffe populations, but it is a cause for concern. Many other animals are also poached for meat or other products, for example elephants for their ivory tusks and leopards for their fur.

NEWBORN GIRAFFE

Giraffes give birth while standing or walking. Within 20 minutes of birth, the newborn, which is up to 6½ ft (2 m) tall, is able to stand and suckle.

Giraffa camelopardalis

⬌ 15½–18 ft (4.7–5.5 m) tall

🜨 Savanna, grassland, and open woodland, particularly with acacia, in sub-Saharan Africa.

📖 Greatly elongated neck and long legs. Spotted brown and yellow coat. Both males and females have short horns on their heads.

» 193

Raising Young

Reproduction is a costly process. It takes time and resources, may influence an animal's chances of survival, and affect its future reproductive fitness. Parents must do whatever they can to maximize their offspring's chances of survival. Different animals approach the issue of caring for their young in a host of different ways.

CUB CARE
Male tigers play no role in raising their young. The female nurses them, teaches them to hunt, and remains with them for two years until they are independent. She can then reproduce again.

Parental care

Parental care is a behavioral strategy aimed at increasing the chances of a parent's offspring reaching adulthood. Not all animals care for their young (most egg layers, except birds, simply lay their eggs and leave), but there are many that do take an active role. This effort is costly—it takes time, is often risky, and detracts from an animal's ability to produce further offspring. A parent must decide whether to invest in its current offspring, or to save its investment for the future.

BIPARENTAL CARE
Frigate bird chicks fledge at around six months, yet their parents feed them for two years—the longest period of post-fledging care of any bird.

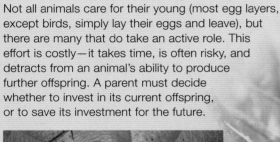

REPTILIAN CARE
Only around 3 percent of reptiles exhibit parental care. Viper mothers are one of the few groups that do look after their young, guarding the eggs or tiny snakes against predators.

Caregivers

Although it may be in all animals' interests for their offspring to receive parental care, different species have different approaches to raising their young. For species that use internal fertilization, the male cannot guarantee his paternity and often has more to gain by deserting the female and finding new mates. The female, in contrast, has little choice but to care for her fertilized eggs until the point of laying or birth. For species with external fertilization, such as fish, the reverse is often true. The female lays the eggs, which are then fertilized by the male. He must take responsibility if he wants to guarantee his paternity and ensure his eggs survive. Some species show joint or biparental care, while a few leave their young in the care of others.

KOALA CUDDLE
Koala joeys stay close to their mothers for one year, until they are weaned.

SAFETY IN NUMBERS
Dominant female goosanders commonly form nursery systems, which may include the offspring of other birds. Greater numbers help reduce the chances of their own young being taken by predators.

Length of care

How long a parent cares for its young is determined by several factors. Longer periods of care result in larger offspring with higher chances of survival. However, this level of investment decreases the number of broods a parent can produce in a lifetime, and may also place the parent at greater risk of predation. Hence there is some conflict between the benefits of care to the young and the cost to its parent. Some parents simply care for their young prior to birth, keeping the eggs safe until they hatch. Others remain with their young after birth, guarding their brood or feeding them until they can feed themselves. Prolonged periods of parental care occur in some mammals and birds—most commonly in long-lived, large-brained, social animals, which need time to grow and learn the skills necessary for survival.

FAMILY HERD
Elephants have large brains, live in complex social groups, and have long lifespans. When a new calf is born, the whole group helps to care for it and keep it safe.

Sticking close

Six-rayed starfish

Unlike many starfish, which release their eggs and sperm into the water and allow the eggs to develop without their care, this tiny starfish takes an active role in brooding its young. When a female six-rayed starfish is ready to spawn, she arches her body and stands on the tips of her arms to form a brood chamber. She then releases up to 1,500 large, yolky eggs (relatively few for a starfish), which she catches and holds beneath her body using her sticky tube feet. For around 40 days, the female incubates the embryos in this arched position, cleaning and tending them with her tube feet. The mass of embryos beneath her mouth means she cannot feed during this time. After the brooding time is up, the young starfish begin to move around on their own. At this point, the female resumes a flattened posture. She stays with her offspring, caring for them for another month until they are able to feed and are fully independent.

STANDING ON TIPTOES
When the female is ready to incubate, she searches for a safe location, such as the underside of a rock. She attaches herself using her tube feet.

Leptasterias hexactis
- ↔ Up to 2 in (5 cm)
- ◑ Rocky, intertidal zone of the northeast Pacific region, from California to Alaska.
- ▭ Tiny, six-limbed sea star with dark green, black, brown, red, or mottled coloration.

Maternal sacrifice

Giant Pacific octopus

Females of the giant Pacific octopus (the largest octopus in the world) make the ultimate sacrifice for their young. When they are ready to reproduce, they find a rocky den and lay up to 100,000 eggs. Over the next seven or more months, they carefully tend, clean, and aerate the eggs until they hatch. Females do not feed during this time and die shortly after the young emerge.

Enteroctopus dofleini
- ↔ 14¾–30 ft (4.5–9 m)
- ◑ On the continental shelf of the North Pacific, to depths of around 2,500 ft (750 m).
- ▭ Yellow, gray, brown, or mottled white, but capable of color change.

» 367

Double size

Gonatus onyx

For most of its life, the squid *Gonatus onyx* lives in relatively shallow water. However, when the female is ready to lay her eggs, she descends into water about 8,200 ft (2,500 m) deep, where there tend to be fewer predators. At this depth, she produces an enormous black mass of approximately 2,000–3,000 eggs. The egg ball is so big that it effectively doubles the body size of this tiny squid. It is suspended from hooks under the mother's arms. The female aerates the eggs using her tentacles, flushing water through and inflating the sac. She cares for them for six to nine months until they are ready to hatch.

MOTHER'S BURDEN
A female *Gonatus onyx* with a huge egg mass. This photograph was taken by a robotic submarine operated by the Monterey Bay Aquarium Research Institute.

Gonatus onyx
- ↔ Mantle 5½ in (14 cm)
- ◑ Abundant throughout the Atlantic and Pacific in mid- to deep waters.
- ▭ Also known as the clawed armhook squid; central suckers of the arms modified to form tiny hooks.

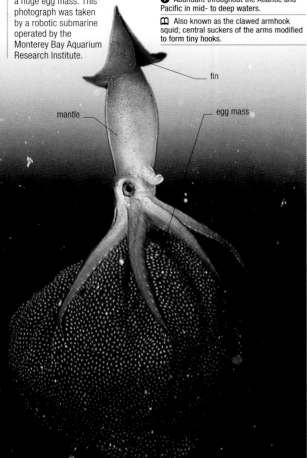

fin

mantle

egg mass

UNTANGLED WEB
This nursery web spider has built its protective, tentlike web on a young fern plant. The young spiders huddle together in a mass at the center of the web, while their mother keeps watch for predators.

Open-air nursery

Nursery web spider

The nursery web spider is named for the impressive structure it weaves in order to keep its immature young safe. Mating occurs in early spring. To avoid being attacked by the female and distract her attention while mating occurs, the male presents her with a gift of a wrapped insect. The female produces hundreds of eggs, which are held together in large white egg sacs. Initially, the female carries these in her jaws and pedipalps, or "feelers." When the eggs are about to hatch, she builds a tentlike nest and places the egg sacs within. Once the eggs hatch, they are contained inside the nest and the female stands guard outside, defending her young from predators for a week or more, until they can survive on their own. Although they are famous for their webs, these spiders do not weave traps during the rest of the year, preferring to hunt on foot and catch their prey using stealth.

Pisaura mirabilis
- ↔ Up to ½ in (1.5 cm)
- ◑ Widespread throughout Britain and northern Europe.
- ▭ Large wolf spider, gray or brown in color with pale stripe along abdomen.

Short-term care

Earwig

Earwig nests are built underground—a short tunnel with two chambers to house the brood of 50–90 shiny white eggs. The female tends and sorts her brood, carefully licking the eggs to prevent mold, and defending the nest against invasion or attack. Once the nymphs emerge, the female remains with them for another few weeks, providing them with food. Females cannot distinguish between their own eggs and those of other earwigs.

Forficula auricularia
- ↔ Up to ½ in (1.5 cm)
- ◑ Widespread throughout Europe.
- ▭ Reddish brown with a flattened body and a pair of pincers at the tip of the tail.

EGG-TENDING
Earwigs are subsocial insects, meaning that they do not cooperate to brood their young, but do have a level of parental care. Females sometimes unwittingly accept other females' eggs as their own.

FRESH MEAL
Caterpillar meals are paralyzed by the female, not killed, to prevent them rotting before the larvae have had their feed. Potter wasps get their name from the small, pot-shaped structures that they build as their nests.

wings

paralyzed caterpillar

nest made of sand and saliva

abdomen

Living larder
Potter wasps

Potter wasps are solitary wasps that live independently, without the social interactions seen in many other wasp species. A lone female seeks out a male to mate with before setting off to build a nest. Nests are usually based around a preexisting hole in a wall or rock, at the open end of which the female constructs a potlike cell. This is typically constructed from soil or chewed up leaves, held together with saliva and shaped like a small ball or vase with a single opening. The female wasp lays one or multiple eggs into individual brood cavities within the nest. Having laid each egg, she leaves the nest to collect food for her young to eat once they have hatched. The mother hunts

for caterpillars, which she paralyzes by stinging them. She transports the caterpillars back to her nest, holding them upside-down using her middle set of legs. As soon as the cell's brood chambers are lined with food, she seals the door, using

the same building materials to keep the cell watertight. After a few days, the larva hatches and emerges from its burrow to a welcoming larder full of fresh food. Once the nest is provisioned, the female wasp plays no further role in her offspring's care or development.

Eumeninae species

↔ Up to 1¼ in (3 cm)

◐ Widespread distribution, including Australia, North America, South America, Asia, Africa, and Europe.

▥ Medium to large, often thin-waisted with black and yellow or black and orange coloration. Also known as mason wasps.

Honey trap
Large blue butterfly

The caterpillar of the large blue butterfly brings the kiss of death to its unsuspecting hosts. Young caterpillars put themselves up for "adoption"—producing a sweet, honeylike substance from a gland at the rear of their bodies. This attracts the ant, *Myrmica sabuleti*, which "adopts" the caterpillar for its nectar, and takes it back to its nest. Once inside, the caterpillar acquires the red ant's scent, mimics the ant's sound, and readily provides honey for the nest. The unsuspecting ants are wooed by their visitor, and fail to notice the caterpillar busily feasting on their eggs and larvae.

caterpillar releases honeylike scent from its rear

ant pulls caterpillar to its nest

Maculinea arion

↔ ⅜ in (1 cm)

◐ Widespread throughout Europe; became extinct in the UK in 1979 but reintroduced in 1983.

▥ Adult butterfly blue with black outer margin to the wing. Caterpillar pinkish ocher with black head and tapering head and tail.

JUDAS KISS
The butterfly larva has succeeded in enticing an ant to carry it back to its nest; once in the ant's nest it will consume its offspring.

PIGGYBACK
Male water bugs can carry a load of up to 100 eggs, which are laid sequentially, the male and female copulating regularly between batches. In this way, the male can guarantee his paternity. These eggs are hatching.

Paternal care
Giant water bug

The male giant water bug literally piggybacks his offspring to success. The female water bug lays her eggs on the back of the male, who carries them around on his forewings, periodically exposing them to air to prevent fungal buildup. He may carry the brood for up to three weeks until they are ready to hatch and disperse. Mating may occur up to 30 times to produce each batch of eggs.

Diplonychus japonicus

↔ 1 in (2.5 cm)

◐ Streams and flooded rice-paddy fields of Japan.

▥ Broad, flat, aggressive beetle with sharp front legs for stabbing prey.

Maternal care
Parent bug

Insects that lay a single clutch are more likely to defend their eggs than those that have several clutches. Female parent bugs live up to their name by standing guard over their single clutch of offspring, fiercely defending them from parasites and predators. Some females may even work together—a simple form of social behavior. Females that work together tend to have better reproductive success than those that work alone.

Elasmucha grisea

↔ ¼ in (7 mm)

◐ Birch woodland throughout Europe.

▥ Brown, orange, or olive-green shield bug.

Pregnant father

Seahorses

In many fish species it is the male that cares for the young, but it is in the seahorse that the most extreme form of paternal care is observed. Male and female seahorses are monogamous, forming pair bonds that last for the whole breeding season. The bond between them is reinforced daily through courtship dances. Female seahorses lay their eggs into a special brood pouch inside the male's body. For the next two to four weeks, the young develop inside the male until they are ready to emerge. The male then goes through a form of labor—pumping and thrusting until the young seahorses are released.

GIVING BIRTH
The seahorse embryos grow inside the male's pouch until they can swim effectively. They emerge as miniature seahorses and are fully independent from birth.

Hippocampus species
- Up to 14 in (35 cm)
- Sea grass beds, around mangrove roots, and on coral reefs in shallow temperate and tropical seas.
- Head at right angles to otherwise upright body. Long tail hooks around substrate, vegetation, and other objects.
- » 305, 355

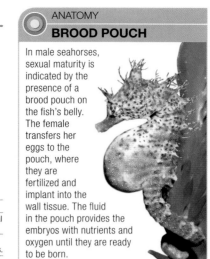

ANATOMY
BROOD POUCH

In male seahorses, sexual maturity is indicated by the presence of a brood pouch on the fish's belly. The female transfers her eggs to the pouch, where they are fertilized and implant into the wall tissue. The fluid in the pouch provides the embryos with nutrients and oxygen until they are ready to be born.

Mouth brooding

Jawfishes

Jawfishes are a common family of marine fishes, containing three genera, all of which share certain behavioral as well as physical traits. The most obvious physical characteristics are large, forward-facing eyes and a gaping mouth. Jawfishes use their mouths to dig their homes, for catching prey, and for threatening predators that venture too close to their territories. They also use them in a unique way during the breeding season. Males hover above females, flashing their body coloration as a signal that they are ready to spawn. Receptive females enter the male's burrow and deposit their eggs; they then leave, taking no other role in the care of their offspring. The male scoops the eggs into his mouth and broods them there until they hatch. He aerates the eggs by passing water over them. As they mature, the eggs become less sticky and start to break apart. He increases the amount he aerates them until, after 7–10 days, they are ready to hatch and disperse toward the water surface. From this point, the young jawfishes are fully independent.

ORAL INCUBATION
Jawfishes are aptly named for the method they use to brood and protect their offspring. This male *Opistognathus* species is keeping watch from his burrow with a mouthful of fertilized eggs.

Jawfishes live in burrows, which they excavate by filling their large mouths with sand.

Family Opistognathidae
- Up to 20 in (51 cm)
- Shallow reef areas of the Atlantic, Indian, and Pacific oceans.
- Elongate fishes with tapered bodies, forward-facing eyes, and large mouths.

DEFENDING THE BROOD
The scientific name of this fish loosely translates as "father living among the rocks." The eggs are laid upon rocky nest sites guarded by the males.

On duty
Sergeant major damselfish

Damselfish may be small, but they are among the boldest characters on coral reefs. Males defend nest sites (usually a rock or coral head), illustrating their dominance by turning near black in color and displaying aggressively to potential challengers. After a brief courtship, during which males and females chase each other, the female deposits up to 200,000 salmon-red eggs. The male defends and aerates the brood for around 160 hours, until the eggs hatch into tiny larvae and disperse.

Abudefduf saxatilis

◐ 9 in (23 cm)

◯ Coral reefs and rocky shores of tropical and subtropical waters; occurs only in Atlantic Ocean.

▥ Small, laterally compressed fish, silver with vertical black bars.

Sandy nest
Titan triggerfish

The titan triggerfish is the most formidable of all triggerfishes and can be quite an unnerving presence to an unsuspecting scuba diver. The female lays her eggs in a circle on a sandy depression, and the male guards them aggressively until the larvae hatch and disperse. His territory is typically in the shape of a cone rising vertically from the egg mass and widening toward the water surface. Naturally wary, titan triggerfish have strong teeth and will charge if they feel their nest is threatened.

Balistoides viridescens

◐ Up to 30 in (75 cm)

◯ Coral reefs of the Indo-Pacific region.

▥ Flattened body with two dorsal spines that can be erected in defense.

>> 140

AERATING THE BROOD
Male and female titan triggerfish take turns to care diligently for their eggs and keep predators at bay. This parent fish is gently aerating its eggs.

Water retention
African bullfrog

For much of the year, the African bullfrog lives in desert, which is dry for almost 10 months. To protect its moist skin from the harsh conditions, it hides in an underground burrow. In December or January, the rains finally arrive, forming puddles on the arid earth. The frogs soon emerge to spawn in these oases: females deposit their eggs, then leave the male to fend for the brood. With such a short-lived rainy season, the life cycle of the bullfrog must be rapid. The eggs hatch into tadpoles after just two days. But summer storms are sporadic, and the tadpoles' watery world soon dries out. The father, in addition to guarding his brood, must make sure the young stay moist. As one puddle dries, he searches out alternative areas, digging channels between the puddles and herding his young to safer ground. He watches over his offspring for around three weeks until they metamorphose.

4,000 The number of tadpoles in an African bullfrog brood. Males sometimes cannibalize their own young.

RESCUE MISSION
As the sun beats down on their nursery pool, shrinking it by the second, an African bullfrog male hurriedly bulldozes an escape channel through the claylike ground for his tadpoles. The new pool will provide temporary safety.

strong limbs for digging   moist skin

BIG BOY
The African bullfrog has a good sense of smell, sight, and hearing, useful in the breeding season when communicating with loud, roarlike calls.

Pyxicephalus adspersus

◐ 10 in (25 cm)

◯ Near waterways, rivers, and streams of Central, eastern, and southern Africa.

▥ One of the largest African frogs, with a well-rounded body and broad head.

RISKY RIDE
Although crocodiles have large teeth and extremely strong jaws, they lift their young offspring with remarkable care. The journey from their nest to the water's edge is one of the most perilous the youngsters have to make.

Guarding eggs
Four-toed salamander

The soft nest of the four-toed salamander usually consists of a mossy clump located above a pool of water. The female takes several hours to deposit her eggs. These have a sticky outer coating that is used to attach them to the surrounding sphagnum moss for protection. The female guards the eggs, while secretions from her skin help prevent them from acquiring any fungal infections. She remains with her clutch for several days, until just prior to hatching. When ready to hatch, the tiny larvae wiggle out of the nest and into the water below, assuming an independent existence.

SUNSHADE
Tiny leaves shield Alpine newt larvae from the damaging effects of the sun's ultraviolet rays.

Hemidactylium scutatum
- 2–4 in (5–10 cm)
- Wetland habitats close to mature forest, from Nova Scotia to Gulf of Mexico.
- Small, rusty brown or gray salamander with unique four-toed hind feet.

SOFT CUSHION
The four-toed salamander attaches its sticky eggs to moss, rotting logs, and leaf litter. If suitable nest material is limited, females may group together, sharing one site. The largest communal nest discovered contained over 1,000 eggs.

Individual wrapping
Alpine newt

Alpine newts live at high altitudes, where the atmosphere is thin and solar radiation levels are high. To protect their offspring from damaging ultraviolet light, female newts carefully wrap their larvae in leaves, forming tiny sunshades to shield them from harm. Many amphibians are sensitive to ultraviolet radiation. They can quickly suffer damage to their delicate skin, and exposure to the rays may cause death. This is particularly so during the egg and larval stages, before pigmentation has developed and when mobility is restricted.

Triturus alpestris
- Up to 4½ in (12 cm)
- Forested, mountainous regions of central Europe.
- Male has orange belly and blue-black or speckled upper side and small crest; female brownish beige.
- ≫ 356

Gentle touch
Nile crocodile

Although the Nile crocodile has a fierce reputation, it shows very gentle qualities when it comes to raising its young. The female crocodile lays a clutch of about 50 eggs near water, in a nesting chamber approximately 20 in (50 cm) deep in a sandy river bank. Once a female has found a suitable nesting site, she will revisit the same site every time she breeds. For the next three months, she guards the nest, defending it from flooding and scavengers such as the Nile monitor. Crocodile eggs have a tough shell, which makes hatching difficult. If a juvenile gets trapped, the mother lifts the egg into her mouth, softly rolling it in her teeth in order to crack the shell and release the offspring. Once the young crocodiles hatch, they call to their mother using tiny chirps. She carefully digs into the hole, lifts them out, and carries them to the water in her jaws. If threatened, the female lowers one or more young into her gular or throat pouch for protection. Hatchlings are about 12 in (30 cm) long at birth, and they stay with their mother for the first two years. Nile crocodiles tend to be solitary, and the young live in burrows to avoid suffering the extreme heat of their natural habitat.

Crocodylus niloticus
- 16½–20 ft (5–6 m)
- Waterways throughout tropical and southern Africa and Madagascar.
- Large, olive-green to brown body with black spots, netlike markings, toughened scales, and a powerful, muscular tail.
- ≫ 220, 476

GULAR POUCH
A crocodile has an elastic throat pouch that it uses to carry its young and hold prey. A flap of skin at the back prevents water from entering the lungs when feeding underwater.

≫01 ≫02 ≫0

PARENTAL CARE
≫01 The female Nile crocodile watches and stands guard as her offspring hatch out of their eggs and scramble up the bank toward her. ≫02 This young crocodile is struggling to break through the tough outer shell of its egg, so its mother assists, using her sharp teeth with amazing gentleness. ≫03 The female carries the hatchlings in her jaws as she swims, keeping them safe from predators. The head of a baby crocodile can be seen peering out from between its mother's teeth.

Termite protection

Monitor lizards

Monitor lizards typically inhabit savanna and other arid areas where temperatures can soar and the heat of the sun sucks moisture from any living thing. Breeding usually happens during the rainy season, however. Female monitor lizards often lay their eggs in old or active termite mounds. The benefit of this is that within the mound, environmental conditions are fairly constant. In addition, the termite inhabitants will actually repair and protect the mound (and the eggs within it) from marauding ants or predators. When the monitor hatchlings emerge, they dig themselves out of the mound and disperse into the bush. From this time on, the young lizards are fully independent.

Varanus species

- Up to 30 in (75 cm)
- Africa, India, China, and throughout Southeast Asia to Australia.
- Big, stout lizards with stocky limbs and strong claws for digging.

DESERT HOME
Hatchling savanna monitor lizards cling to the outside of the termite mound from which they have emerged. In desert conditions, these mounds provide a safe haven for eggs, with constant levels of temperature and humidity.

Maternity ward

Timber rattlesnake

The timber rattlesnake is a very venomous pit viper and one of North America's most dangerous snakes. Yet females of this species show maternal care of their young, and may even show kin cooperation,

preferring to cooperate with their sisters while caring for their young. Rattlesnakes mate in summer and fall and the sperm is stored until the following spring. Around seven live young are born in the following August. These remain with the mother for about seven to ten days after birth and may even follow her scent trail to find suitable dens in which to hibernate.

Crotalus horridus

- ◀▶ 5 ft (1.5 m)
- ⊙ Deciduous forest of the eastern US.
- 📖 Large, heavy-bodied snake with red stripe down back and black chevron cross-bands.

INTENSIVE CARE

Females do not feed during pregnancy or while caring for their offspring. They breed only every three to four years, but each litter contains up to 20 young. This female has quite a brood.

Male incubation

Emu

As the egg-laying period approaches, the male emu loses his appetite and begins to construct a nest using sticks and bark. The female lays the eggs and leaves. For the next eight weeks he sits on the nest, carefully turning the eggs around ten times per day. Once they hatch, he stays with the chicks for the next 18 months, teaching them to find food.

CRASH DIET

Male emus are such dedicated parents that they may lose a third of their body weight by not feeding while brooding their clutch of eggs.

Dromaius novaehollandiae

- ◀▶ 6½ ft (2 m) high
- ⊙ Common across mainland Australia.
- 📖 Large, flightless bird with long legs and soft brown feathers.

Penguin nursery

Rockhopper penguin

When it comes to breeding, rockhopper penguins like to do it en masse. Hundreds of thousands of pairs nest together on rocky slopes, with each pair returning to the same nesting area each year. Large numbers make it possible to always have someone on guard watching for predators. Rockhoppers lay two eggs, the first much smaller than the second. In most cases, only this second egg is raised. Incubation takes around 33 days, worked as shared shifts between males and females. Once the eggs hatch, the male cares for them while the female provides food. After 25 days, both parents join in the feeding runs, leaving their offspring in nurseries, under the vigilant gaze of the other adults present.

Eudyptes chrysocome

- ◀▶ 20 in (52 cm) high
- ⊙ Rocky shorelines of the Southern Ocean islands.
- 📖 Small penguin with red eyes and yellow head stripes that extend into plumes.

Back brooding

Eared grebe

Even before hatching, young eared grebes call to solicit care from their parents. Adult pairs build nests using mounds of leaves and aquatic plants. Into this, the female lays three to four creamy white eggs, which both parents take turns to incubate for around 22 days. One or two days before hatching, the embryo grebes begin to call to their parents, indicating when the

egg needs to be turned or cooled. Once they emerge, the chicks stay in the nest for two days before transferring to the back of one of the parent birds, where they are back-brooded. They stay in this floating nest for around ten days. During this time, the parents protect the chicks by shielding them with their wings.

Podiceps nigricollis

- ◀▶ 13½ in (34 cm)
- ⊙ Widespread waterbird found in every continent except Australia and Antarctica.
- 📖 Small black grebe with black head and yellow ear tufts.

UNDER THE WING

The small head of a chick is just visible poking out from under one of its parent's wings. Each parent can comfortably accommodate two chicks at a time.

Family home

Black-browed albatross

Black-browed albatrosses form long-lasting pair bonds, returning to the same partner and same nest site throughout their lives. They break this pattern only if a partner dies or if they "divorce." Divorce is a rare occurrence, happening only when a pair suffers repeated reproductive failure over consecutive years; the birds then look for other partners to improve their breeding success. Although adult albatrosses disperse to feed in the Southern Ocean over winter, they return to the same cliff-side spot every year in September. After an elaborate courtship ritual, which reaffirms a pair's bond, the female lays a single, large egg. Both parents incubate the egg, which hatches in December. The downy young grows rapidly, on a diet of krill and squid. It does not leave the nest until it is ready to fledge, about 17 weeks after hatching. The location of the colonies, on top of steep cliffs and hillsides, gives the birds a helping hand with takeoff and landing, since they can use updrafts to help lift their 8¼ ft (2.5 m) wingspans.

POT-SHAPED NEST

Black-browed albatross nests are constructed from mud and grass formed into a column about 12 in (30 cm) across and 17½ in (45 cm) tall. Adults pair for life, although their fidelity may be more to the nest site than to each other.

Thalassarche melanophris

- ◀▶ 31–37 in (80–95 cm)
- ⊙ Circumpolar, nesting on Sub-Antarctic islands.
- 📖 Large seabird with white belly and dark grey upper wings. Yellow to dark orange bill and distinctive dark brows above the eyes.

≫ 142, 253

CLINGING TIGHT
Orangutans are the largest tree-dwelling mammals, yet at birth they weigh just 3¼ lb (1.5 kg). Females carry their young continually for the first year, and even two-year-old juveniles will ride on their mother's back. They suckle from their mother for around four years, and remain with her until they are seven or eight years old, sleeping in her nest.

Fake baby

Common cuckoo

Cuckoos are brood parasites that lay their eggs in the nests of other birds, thereby avoiding any parental duties of their own. Dunnocks, pipits, and reed warblers are the usual hosts. The female cuckoo evicts one of the host bird's eggs and replaces it with one of her own. Cuckoo chicks are demanding and compete with their host's true offspring for nourishment.

GAPE OF DECEPTION
The tiny reed warbler (shown on the left) often falls victim to the cuckoo's sneaky tactics. The cuckoo chick monopolizes the nest with its frequent, rapid feeding demands. It pushes its step-siblings out of the nest and soon grows larger than its host.

Cuculus canorus
- 13–14 in (32–36 cm)
- Widespread summer migrant to Europe and Asia; winters in Africa.
- Slender body with gray head, back, and breast, white underparts, long tail, pointed wings, and stocky legs.

Tail rider

Tree pangolin

Pangolins are solitary animals, coming together only when both sexes are in breeding condition. Females give birth to a single young after a gestation period of 150 days. The newborn's scales are initially very soft, but harden after a few days. Pangolins have an unusual parental behavior—the juvenile is carried on the female's tail, piggyback style, until it is ready to wean at about three months old. It remains with the mother for another two months until it is prepared for full independence. If the baby is threatened, mother pangolins roll up around their young, forming a tight, protective ball with the offspring in the middle.

Manis tricuspis
- 14–23½ in (35–60 cm)
- Forests of western and central Africa.
- Small, brown scaly mammal with small head and long, prehensile tail.

Caravanning

Lesser white-toothed shrew

The lesser white-toothed shrew is a prolific breeder, producing four or five litters per year of one to six young each time. Babies wean at around 22 days. The female nests under logs or stones; if the nest is disturbed, she will move her young to safer ground. The young display "caravanning" behavior—forming a chain by grasping the tail of the animal in front.

Crocidura suaveolens
- 2–2¾ in (5–7 cm)
- Europe, Japan, and North Africa; absent in Britain except the Channel Islands and the Isles of Scilly.
- Tiny shrew, gray-brown in color with a pale underside.

IN CONVOY
Young shrews follow their mother to safety by forming a line and holding onto the tail of the animal in front with their teeth.

Warm nursery

Mexican free-tailed bat

Mexican free-tailed bats form the largest colonies of any mammal in the world. Different roosts are occupied at different times by the two sexes, depending on the breeding cycle and time of year. Maternity roosts can number many millions. In this dense mass of bats, the mother recognizes her offspring by its unique smell and piplike call. The young bats are weaned after five or six weeks. They join the adults in migrating from the summer roosts in Texas to the winter roosts in Mexico.

TIGHTLY PACKED COLONY
Female bats leave their young behind when they go out to forage. The close packing of baby bats helps them stay warm while the female is away.

Tadarida brasiliensis
- 3½ in (9 cm)
- Caves of western and the southern US, Mexico, Central America, Chile, and Argentina.
- Medium-sized bat with brown fur and distinctive tail that extends beyond the flight membranes.
>> 320

Protective mother

Polar bear

Polar bears are typically solitary, males and females coming together to mate for just a few days in late winter or early spring. Pregnant females overwinter in dens dug into the snow, within a few miles of the coastline, where they produce two or three tiny cubs. The cubs are born covered in fur, but with their eyes closed, and may weigh only 1¼ lb (600 g). The female remains in hibernation, nursing her cubs until April. By the time the young family emerges, the cubs may be 22–33 lb (10–15 kg) in weight. They stay with their mother for the next two or three years, during which time she provides for them, teaching them to hunt and protecting them from harm.

COLD COMFORT
Polar bears spend much of their time sleeping or roaming the ice in search of seals. Adults are good swimmers, but small cubs drown easily. For this reason, young families stay on solid ice.

Ursus maritimus
- 8¼ ft (2.5 m)
- Sea ice and coastal areas throughout Arctic regions (circumpolar).
- Large white or yellowish bear with stocky body and elongated neck.
>> 258

Mother's milk

Northern elephant seal

Despite being a marine mammal, the northern elephant seal returns to land to breed. Males and females haul out, or rest, on coastal beaches in December and January. Males defend harems and mate with many females. A female elephant seal typically delivers a single black pup, which she nurses for around four weeks while fasting herself. Her milk is very rich in fat, helping the pup gain weight quickly.

MILK SUPPLY
Female elephant seals usually nurse a single pup. Sometimes twins are born, or sneaky pups may nurse from females other than their mother.

Mirounga angustirostris

▪ 9¾–16½ ft (3–5 m)

◗ Coastal waters of the Pacific, from the Gulf of Alaska to Baja California.

▭ Large brown seal; male is darker and has huge, inflated proboscis.

» 350

10 lb The average weight gain by an elephant seal pup per day. The pup triples its birth weight in just four weeks.

Fishing lesson

Giant river otter

Giant river otters live in communal dens in the riverbank, centered around a dominant breeding pair. Females usually give birth in the dry season, bearing between one and five pups. All members of the family play a role in raising the young, teaching them to hunt by bringing them injured fish. This training begins at around three months and can be carried out by any adult. The young are weaned at nine months and may remain with the group for another two years before leaving to set up a group of their own.

Pteronura brasiliensis

▪ 5–6 ft (1.5–1.8 m)

◗ Rivers, lakes, and creeks of South America.

▭ Largest otter. Long, sinuous body with velvet brown fur and cream throat patch.

Keeping warm

Beluga whale

Beluga whales are an Arctic species, typically living in freezing waters along ice floes. In summer, females migrate to shallow bays and estuaries to deliver their single calf. The water in such areas is usually much warmer than the open sea.

As a result, the young do not waste energy on simply keeping warm, and can instead use it to grow and build up fat reserves. Beluga milk contains as much as 30 percent fat. Mothers suckle the young for up to 24 months, from nipples that are hidden in skin folds on the abdomen. The calf can swim independently from birth, but will often ride on its mother's back, or follow her slipstream, until it gains strength.

IMMATURE COLORATION
Belugas are social animals and usually travel in groups. The calves stand out with their gray skin, which changes to white as they mature.

Delphinapterus leucas

▪ 9¾–16½ ft (3–5 m)

◗ Arctic and subarctic marine areas.

▭ White with blunt head, tiny teeth, and no dorsal fin.

» 311

Fiercely protective

Moose

Moose are typically solitary animals, the only bonds being between a mother and her young. Mating occurs in September and October, with males fighting for access to mates. Females carry the young for around eight months before finding a quiet, secluded spot to give birth. They may deliver one calf, twins, or sometimes triplets. Young moose are gangly and weak and make easy targets for attack by bears or wolves, although females aggressively defend their young, rearing up on their hind legs or pounding potential predators with their hooves. Many choose to live near human civilization, where there are fewer wolves than in wilder places. Moose calf survival rates are very poor—in some areas, only 20 percent make it through the first year. Those that survive stay with the mother for a whole year, until she calves again the following breeding season.

FACING ATTACK
Bears and wolves are the biggest predators of young moose. The young quickly gain weight, and can swim and run within a few days of birth, but their chances of survival remain low.

Alces alces

▪ 8¼–10½ ft (2.5–3.2 m)

◗ Deciduous forest of North America, northern Europe, and Russia.

▭ Largest species of deer with giant antlers; brownish gray fur and wide hooves. Known as elk in Europe.

» 339

Babysitting

Banded mongoose

Banded mongoose females form strong bonds with other closely related females and work together as a group to raise their young. They reach sexual maturity at about nine months of age and usually produce litters of two to six offspring. Breeding females are assisted by helpers—usually those with fewer chances of reproducing themselves, but who support the group by acting as babysitters.

GROUP CARE
Babysitters often remain at the den, taking care of babies that are too young to go foraging.

Mungos mungo

▪ 21½–23½ in (55–60 cm)

◗ Grassland and woodland throughout central and eastern Africa.

▭ Small mongoose with black banding from the mid-back to base of the tail.

» 271

Play and learning

Learning is the way in which animals develop the knowledge and skills they need for survival. Young animals have much to learn about their environment—how to find food, avoid predators, and coexist in a group. It is a lifelong process—every animal must adapt its behavior as a result of individual experience.

Simple learning

Simple learning occurs when an animal's response to a repeated stimulus changes in the absence of any apparent reward. The major form of this is habituation, when an animal begins to ignore a stimulus following repeated exposure to it. For example, birds will initially be frightened of a scarecrow, but, over time, learn that it is harmless and stop responding to it. Habituation helps animals filter out unimportant information from their environment.

Associative and observational learning

Associative learning is when an animal's behavioral response becomes associated with a particular stimulus, by means of operant or classical conditioning. In operant conditioning, an animal learns the consequences (whether positive or negative) that result from an action, and therefore modifies its behavior to account for these. In cases of classical conditioning, a behavioral response is taught to be associated with a neutral stimulus—a process that is usually reinforced with a reward.

In the wild, many animals also learn by observation, watching the way in which others behave and using that knowledge to adapt their own behavior.

COPYCAT
Oystercatcher chicks watch their mother feeding. By copying her behavior, they learn to find food themselves.

VOICE RECOGNITION
Rockhopper penguin chicks and parents learn each other's calls so that they can find each other within their huge, riotous nurseries when the parent comes back from feeding.

MONKEYING AROUND
Young olive baboons play together on a branch. Social primates are some of the most playful animals. They have an extended juvenile phase, when they must learn about the environment and the social conventions of their group.

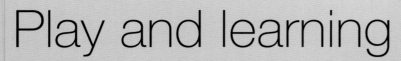

CASE STUDY
IMPRINTING

Very young chicks "imprint" on their parents by learning their distinctive call or visual shape. In hand-raising situations, chicks can be taught to imprint on physical objects instead. This common crane chick is feeding as though the object were its mother.

Play

Play is the name given to activities that have no obvious purpose, but may help to improve an animal's physical fitness, or help it practice skills such as hunting. It is most often seen in mammals and some birds, and is especially common in the young, which suggests a link with learning. Some animals play with inanimate objects, carrying them around or pouncing on them like prey. Others play with members of their family, engaging in play fighting or wrestling. Predators may also play with their prey. Play can be risky, exposing the animal to predation; it also consumes energy, so must somehow benefit an animal in terms of its future behavior.

Dolphins are extremely playful animals, often performing in spectacular group acrobatics.

Tiger cubs engage in practice fights, gaining the speed and agility they will need as territorial animals.

Panda cub play has no clear purpose, but seems to provide huge enjoyment.

Familiar voice
Wood duck

To avoid predators, this waterfowl nests in holes positioned high up in trees, 6½–60 ft (2–18 m) above the ground. The female lays a single egg each day until she has a clutch of 6–15 creamy white eggs. Once the clutch is complete, she begins to incubate her brood. At some point very early in the incubation period, she begins to call to the young inside the eggs. This imprints her voice upon the memories of the developing chicks. After 30 days of incubation the chicks hatch. Immediately, the female leaves the nest and flies to the ground where she begins to call to her brood. Driven by her voice, which they have already learned to recognize, the chicks climb to the opening of the nest and hurl themselves out of the cavity toward their mother who waits for them below. Wherever she goes, the young follow, drawn by the sound of her call.

This behavior is so strong that scientists have been able to imprint the sounds of human caregivers and even machines, such as cars, onto the memories of incubating wood ducks. The hatched chicks follow the person or object exactly as they would a mother duck.

Aix sponsa
- 17½ in (45 cm)
- Lakes and wooded swamps in eastern North America.
- Mid-sized duck. Male has iridescent green and purple head and crest. Female is dull gray.

EARLY DEVELOPERS
Wood ducks are "precocial," which means they are highly developed when hatched. On leaving the nest, right after hatching, some have been known to jump as much as 80 ft (25 m) to the ground without injury, before following their mother's call to water.

LEARNING FROM EXPERIENCE
A young blue-faced booby chick displays its fascination with a scarlet land crab that it has found lurking near its nest. This sense of natural curiosity will soon teach the young bird that crabs can deliver quite a pinch.

No fear
Blue-faced booby

Young animals learn through experience—in adventures inspired by curiosity and by testing their luck. Boobies get their name from the Spanish word "bobo" meaning "stupid fellow"—a reference to the comical expressions and gullible behavior that made them easy hunting targets for sailors in the past. They inhabit isolated islands with few predators, and so have not learned fearfulness. Their young retain an inherent sense of curiosity for their surroundings, which makes them entertaining and endearing to observe.

Sula dactylatra
- 31–35 in (80–90 cm)
- Tropical and subtropical islands in Pacific and Caribbean.
- White body with dark masked face, dark wings, and pointed black tail.

Learning the tune
Marsh warbler

Marsh warblers learn their own songs as well as mimicking the calls of other birds. They develop almost their full repertoire in the first year of life. Many young songbirds have to learn their songs. There is great variation, but the general form involves a sensitive phase, during which the birds memorize songs they hear, refining an built-in "auditory template," against which they try to match their songs. This practice period, or "subsong," is very variable and quiet. Next comes "plastic song," which is flexible, but louder and more normal, until finally it crystallizes into "full song."

INTERNATIONAL STUDENT
A marsh warbler embellishes its song by mimicking the calls of other birds (up to 84 different species), many of which are those of African species, learned in its African wintering grounds.

Acrocephalus palustris
- 5 in (13 cm)
- Low vegetation and thickets, usually near water; breeds in temperate Europe and western Asia, winters in southeast Africa.
- Medium-sized warbler with plain, brown-gray back and pale underparts.

Following footsteps
Ostrich

Ostriches live a nomadic life, roaming in groups of up to 50 birds. During the breeding season, males fight for a harem of two to seven females with which they mate. Females lay their eggs in communal nest pits scuffed out of the sand by the male bird. The male and alpha female take turns incubating the eggs. When the brood hatch out, the male is their chief caregiver. The tiny ostriches immediately learn to follow him, clustering around his feet as they try to keep up with the sometimes formidable stride of the group. The male shows them how to feed, and protects them from predators and the elements, using his wings to offer shelter.

FEELING BROODY
The male and alpha female of an ostrich group take responsibility for raising chicks, and are often seen surrounded by young birds. Sometimes they steal chicks from other birds to add to their own brood.

Struthio camelus
- Up to about 8¼ ft (2.5 m)
- African savanna.
- Tall flightless bird. Male has black fluffy feathers, female and chicks have drab coloration.
- 》 290, 430

CASE STUDY
NURSERY

Ostrich nurseries are made up of the chicks of many females, and cared for by one or more male birds. Several females from the neighborhood will deposit their large, white eggs in a communal nest, but only the alpha (first-paired) female will work with the male to incubate them, and she will often place her own eggs in optimum positions in the center of the nest. Once hatched, the brood of up to 40 young form nurseries. Having fought fiercely over mating, the male ostriches must cooperate to raise their young and teach them how to feed. When two males meet, their chicks instinctively group together to form a larger nursery.

SURF'S UP
A gentoo penguin surfs a wave as it returns to a beach in the Falkland Islands. Such frolics look like tremendous fun, but this behavior also serves a more serious purpose. By launching themselves from the water and landing far up the beach, penguins avoid being battered by waves or falling prey to predators that can lurk in the water beneath them.

Combat skills
Red-necked wallaby

Juvenile wallabies learn to fight from an early age. Fights between adults can be brutal, involving sparring with the long, clawed forepaws, or sitting back on the tail to kick the opponent with the hind legs. For juveniles, fighting is all about play and learning, and they are prepared to adjust their fighting skills in order to allow the play to continue for as long as possible. Evidence suggests that young males vary the strength of their play fights depending on the relative age of their opposition. When encounters involve a younger male, the older wallaby will handicap itself, by standing in a flat-footed way and pawing with less aggression than it would with a tougher rival. This aim of this is to prolong the encounter, providing more fun for all concerned.

Macropus rufogriseus
- 28–41 in (70–105 cm)
- Coastal scrub, bush, and eucalyptus forest in eastern and southeastern Australia.
- Medium-sized wallaby with reddish coloration across the shoulders, and distinctive black nose and paws.
- >> 394

PLAY FIGHTS
Through play, male wallabies develop fighting skills that allow them to challenge or maintain dominance within the group.

Chasing tails
Ring-tailed lemur

Ringed-tailed lemurs live in groups of about 20 in which females are dominant (power passes from an alpha female to her daughter) and social hierarchies are carefully observed. They have a strict breeding season, so all young are born around the same time. Within their first six weeks, baby lemurs start to socialize with others from their "playgroup," and chase each other, play-bite, and wrestle, as they learn about social relationships.

Lemur catta
- 15½–18 in (39–46 cm)
- Dry forest in southern and southwestern Madagascar.
- Brown-gray fur with reddish tinge, distinctive black and white-ringed tail.
- >> 434, 446

GAME PLAYING
Social rank is eventually established among young lemurs as they learn about hierarchies through games.

Snowball fight
Japanese macaque

Snow monkeys, or Japanese macaques, are the most northerly-living primates, except for humans, and many live in areas that are snow covered for at least a third of the year. They are famous for their bathing habits—many of them use hot thermal springs to keep warm. Others have learned to wash their food before eating—a skill developed by one bright female and passed on from generation to generation. But perhaps the most endearing learned behavior is making snowballs—young macaques carefully form clumps of snow using their hands and opposable thumbs before rolling them along the floor in play.

JUVENILE FROLICS
Wrestling may serve as practice for the time when males have to defend territories and fight for access to females.

SIMILAR SPECIES
Sumatran orangutans are more social than their Bornean counterparts. This baby is practicing the climbing skills it has learned from its mother. High up in the forest canopy, this is a perilous process.

Fun lovers
Bornean orangutan

The name orangutan is Malay for "man of the woods" and is appropriate to this creature's love of swinging around in the treetops. Agile climbers, Bornean orangutans use their long arms to carry them from branch to branch in search of fruit, nuts, and bark. In the wild, they are largely solitary animals. The main social contact occurs between a mother and her young. Newborns cling tightly to their mother's abdomen for the first year; they depend on their mothers for five years of life before becoming independent.

When artificially forced into groups (for rehabilitation purposes, for example), young orangutans are some of the most gregarious, fun-loving primates of all. Juvenile males and females engage in

hours of playful social activity, such as wrestling, tickling, chasing, rolling, and swinging. Wrestling tends to occur more often between males, where the two competitors push each other to the ground and tumble over each other. Chases are enjoyed by both males and females. As the young orangutans age, the time they spend in such activities declines and they have less and less interest in social activities.

Pongo pygmaeus
- 35in–3 ft 3 in (90–100 cm)
- Forest canopy in Borneo.
- Distinctive ape with long arms and coarse, orange-red coat.
- >> 404

SNOW MONKEY
Just like human children, Japanese macaque babies make and throw snowballs. It is not clear how they learned this behavior, yet whole groups of macaques engage in it as a social activity, seemingly just for fun.

Macaca fuscata
- 19½–26 in (50–65 cm)
- Subtropical to subarctic forest in Japan (excluding Hokkaido).
- Brown-gray fur with red face and hands, short tail.
- >> 478

Rough and tumble

Coyote

Like all dogs, coyotes are territorial animals that maintain strict dominance rankings within their packs, but they do take part in bouts of harmless social play throughout their lives, starting from just a few days after birth. When trying to engage one another in play, coyotes use subtle signals to show that their intentions are not aggressive. Play behavior in canids can appear very much like aggressive behavior,

40 miles The average distance a male pup travels after leaving its parents, in order to establish its own territory.

involving biting and shaking the head rapidly from side to side. When such behavior is punctuated by regular signals such as "bows" (where the rear legs stand, and the head and forelegs duck low to the floor), the coyote shows that it is only

looking for some rough and tumble. The "bow" signal states "I want to play—the actions I have made, and am about to make, are for fun." This same bowing behavior is seen in dogs and wolves, though their play fights are generally less

aggressive than those of young coyotes. To prolong social play with a weaker or younger individual, a strong coyote will refrain from biting as hard as it is able to, and will play less vigorously than its strength allows for.

Canis latrans

- ↔ 3ft 3in–5¼ ft (1–1.6 m)
- ⊙ Throughout much of North America.
- ▭ Wolflike, with grayish brown to yellowish fur and black-tipped tail.

» 460

EARLY LEARNING
Pups live in their dens until 6–10 weeks old. By the time they emerge, they have already learned many of the social signals used to communicate with the group.

Pouncing practice

Lion

For a young lion, learning to hunt is a basic requirement for survival, and begins early on in life. The cub has a lot to learn. Adult lions typically hunt in groups, stalking and tracking their chosen prey. Because they hunt in exposed spaces, lions must be able to coordinate their actions precisely and work well as a team. Lion cubs begin their training at around three months, chasing and stalking anything around them that moves. They are soon practicing "the kill" on half-dead or young gazelles, which

PLAYING HUNTER
Young lion cubs stalk their mothers' black-tassled tails before pouncing on them, practicing the skills they need to become successful hunters.

Panthera leo

- ↔ 5¼–8¼ ft (1.6–2.5 m)
- ⊙ Grassy plains and savanna in sub-Saharan Africa.
- ▭ Large, honey-colored cat; male has characteristic mane around head.

» 237, 437

the mother brings back to them. By the end of their first year, most cubs are able to join the pride in stalking and chasing prey and, after two years, they are proficient hunters in their own right.

Play fighting

Brown bear

Bear cubs spend much time play fighting and scrambling around with their siblings. Through such harmless fun, cubs practice fighting skills essential for survival in later life. In the wild, the biggest danger to cubs comes from other bears. If another bear threatens her young, a female bear quickly shoos her cubs up a nearby tree to escape attack, drawing on their climbing skills. Older bears can no longer climb, so must be able to fight to defend themselves and their territories. Social play fighting sometimes continues into adulthood.

Ursus arctos

- ↔ 5½–9¼ ft (1.7–2.8 m)
- ⊙ Forest and open landscapes in North America and Eurasia.
- ▭ Large bear with thick brown, blonde, or black furry coat.

» 201

PLAYMATES AND TOYS
Bear cubs will play with siblings, or even with animals of another species, and will also use inanimate objects in their play.

Forever young

North American river otter

Many animals play during their early years but abandon play behaviors in later life. North American river otters, like other otters, are unusual because their games continue beyond adolescence and throughout their adult lives. These playful creatures tumble and wrestle with one another and enjoy playing with inanimate objects. They like diving for rocks, rolling around, and playing "tag" or "follow the leader." Otters repeatedly "toboggan" down slopes, creating slides by following the same tracks each time (see panel, right). They seem to take enormous enjoyment in these capers and spend much time in play. The role of play in otter life and society is unclear. It may be a way of reinforcing social bonds within a group, practicing certain skills, such as hunting, or it could be a form of exercise. Otters are highly active and intelligent animals, so perhaps for them, play is simply a way of killing time in an engaging and entertaining manner.

19 yd The depth to which a river otter can dive. It can remain underwater for 8 minutes.

Lontra canadensis

- 35in–4¼ ft (0.9–1.3 m)
- Waterways and coastal areas in North America.
- Long streamlined body, short legs, thick, dark brown fur with paler underside. Feet are webbed, with claws.

CASE STUDY
TOBOGGANING

Observing river otters in the wild is fascinating. One of their most comical behaviors is "tobogganing." Otters of all ages will frequently slide down muddy banks or snow-caked slopes, sometimes finishing in the river below. They slide on their bellies, tucking their feet up to create a streamlined shape. The function of this particular behavior is not known—some researchers believe it is a form of locomotion, associated with travel but nothing more. Others see tobogganing as play behavior, undertaken for no reason other than the pure pleasure of the slide.

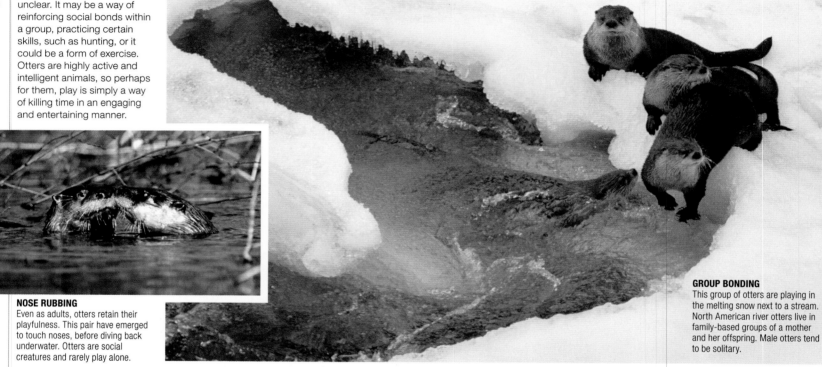

NOSE RUBBING
Even as adults, otters retain their playfulness. This pair have emerged to touch noses, before diving back underwater. Otters are social creatures and rarely play alone.

GROUP BONDING
This group of otters are playing in the melting snow next to a stream. North American river otters live in family-based groups of a mother and her offspring. Male otters tend to be solitary.

Group gymnastics

Dusky dolphin

Dusky dolphins are gregarious animals and regularly form large pods of up to 1,000 individuals. They are famous for their spectacular acrobatics. These agile swimmers are frequently observed leaping clear out of the water, twisting, turning, side slapping, back flipping, and creating a noisy, splashing display. The precise function of these behaviors within dolphin society is unclear. Some scientists believe they play a role in communication within the group (see p.461), signaling the presence of schools of fish to feed on. Others think they are associated with herding prey, an activity that dolphins perform as a coordinated group. Leaping out of the water to dive back in may be a way of dislodging parasites, or it could be nothing more than a form of play. Whatever the reason, dolphins seem to take great enjoyment from performing these magnificent gymnastics.

LEAPING FOR JOY
The dusky dolphin performs its acrobatics with unbounded enthusiasm throughout its 25-year lifespan.

Lagenorhynchus obscurus

- 6½–7 ft (2–2.1 m)
- Coastal areas in Southern Hemisphere: New Zealand, South Africa, South America.
- Smallish dolphin, blunt head, two white streaks across flanks.

Surfing for seals

Orca

For a whale, getting stranded on the shore can be fatal. Yet some killer whales, or orcas, intentionally beach themselves in the pursuit of land-living prey. In Patagonia, several orca pods have learned to surf waves onto beaches to grab unsuspecting seals from along the shoreline. Female orcas coax their young to follow in this dangerous game. To start with, the reluctant calves shadow their mothers, watching from the safety of the water. The females then push their offspring onto the beaches as a form of training.

Orcinus orca

- 16–26 ft (5–8 m)
- Common in all oceans and seas.
- Distinctive black and white whale with tall dorsal fin.

>> 244–45

Trunk training

African elephant

Knowledge is passed down through the generations in elephant families. Calves often play with adults, who teach them vital skills to equip them for life, such as how to make good use of one of their most important assets—the trunk. To a baby elephant, a trunk must be both a confusion and a delight. Until around five months, it often falls over its trunk and has little idea of its use or function. Trunks contain up to 40,000 muscles, and it takes observation of others and practice to learn how to control this versatile appendage.

SPLASHING AROUND
Young elephants particularly enjoy playing in water. This has the added benefit of helping to keep them cool.

DRINKING PRACTICE
Because it uses its mouth to drink its mother's milk, a young calf doesn't know how to use its trunk for drinking. Adults use the trunk to squirt water into their mouths, but babies lie down to drink through their lips. It is only by watching others in the herd that they learn what a trunk can do.

Loxodonta africana

↔ 18–24½ ft (5.5–7.5 m)

⬡ Broadleaf forest or savanna in East, South, and West Africa.

▢ Largest land mammal. Large ears, trunk with two lips at tip, both sexes have long tusks.

》 295, 439, 466–67

PLAY FIGHTING
Through play fights and learning to head butt opponents and solid objects, calves build strength in their muscles and develop their fighting skills.

Head butting

American bison

The bison's solid, muscular head and neck are used to shove or head butt opponents and win the favor of females. A bull with its head lowered is a menacing spectacle. Female bison and their young herd together, forming "playgroups" that allow calves to socialize with each other. After around two months, the calves start to develop their distinctive shoulder humps and horns, which they use in play fights, honing the skills that ultimately serve in the ruts adult males undertake during the breeding season.

Bison bison

↔ 9¾ ft (3 m)

⬡ National parks, some prairies, and woodland in North America.

▢ Large bovine mammal. Short curved horns, shaggy-coated muscular neck.

CASE STUDY

BUFFALO BILL

William "Buffalo Bill" Cody was a prolific bison hunter turned conservationist. When Europeans settled in North America, there were an estimated 60–90 million bison. By 1890, that number was just 1,000. Cody alone killed 4,280 in 18 months. He later helped establish a restricted hunting season. Today the population numbers 50,000.

ISLAND LIFE
These cape gannets *(Morus capensis)* have gathered in a guano-encrusted colony to breed. Both parents incubate their egg by wrapping their feet around it. The fluffy off-white chick stays in the colony until it fledges at about three months of age.

SOCIETY

Very few animals spend their entire lives in isolation from others, and some of the most spectacular displays of behavior occur when animals come together. Group living provides a host of advantages to an animal, but these benefits often come with challenges such as sharing resources and fitting in with social structures.

Solitary and group living

Some animals remain alone for most of their lives, except for during brief periods to mate or raise offspring. When food, water, or other environmental resources necessary for survival are scarce, or if an animal's predators and natural enemies are particularly good at finding grouped animals, it can pay to live alone. However, individual animals across many species form attachments with others (either within their own or with different species). The size of these groups can range immensely, from single pairs of long-term mating partners (in which the partnership is sustained long after the breeding season has finished) to vast colonies of thousands or even millions of individuals, within which each individual animal can face intense competition with its neighbors for space and resources.

Solitary predators such as ocelots rely on quiet stealth, and hunt alone.

Pairs of dikdiks defend sparse territories of scrub vegetation, which are only able to support a single breeding pair.

Tens of dolphins form pods and travel in fluid social groups, the membership of which can rapidly change.

Hundreds of baboons forage in highly social troops over vast areas of vegetation.

Thousands of penguins breed in dense colonies that are often situated in inaccessible, predator-free regions.

Millions of red-billed quelea, like several other species of bird, can form immense flocks that darken the sky.

Why animals are social

Because so many animals spend at least some of their life in social groups, social behavior must provide considerable advantages to group members. If there are greater benefits to be had than if an animal lived alone, social behavior will be favored by natural selection. Many studies have examined the advantages of living in groups, which differ from species to species, according to the animals' life histories. Most of these reasons focus around group-membership enhancing an individual animal's survival, either by reducing its risk of being preyed upon, or increasing its chances of successfully finding food. At the same time, group living confers reproductive advantages, both as a source of potential mates (and information about rivals) and as an extended child-care system.

REASONS TO BE SOCIAL

MOVEMENT
Traveling over long distances uses a lot of energy. Some birds and fish can take advantage of their traveling companions, riding their neighbor's slipstream to reduce their energy needs.

HUNTING AND FEEDING
Coordinated social hunting means that groups can capture prey that is difficult to catch alone. Having many pairs of eyes also means that poorly distributed food is more likely to be found.

DEFENSE
Social animals reduce the time they spend scanning for predators, since vigilance is shared among the group. The individual risk of predation is reduced as the group grows.

HEALTH BENEFITS
Although diseases can be caught from contact with others, forming groups also reduces health problems, for example it minimizes the attacks each group member receives from biting flies.

BREEDING
Many species collect together in groups for mating, where animals can both see and be seen by potential partners. Raising offspring is easier if others help with defense and food provision.

SAVING ENERGY
In cold environments, hard-won energy is constantly lost as heat. Many social animals huddle together at low temperatures, in order to insulate and share each other's body heat.

Group composition

The structure of groups differs vastly between species. In some, a group consists of a large mix of males and females of many different ages and ranks, while in others, all the members of a group will be of the same sex, age, or size. Exactly which individuals are found in a particular group changes over time. In some species, group membership is ephemeral, changing over the course of hours or days. Other species form groups that may be maintained for weeks or years, leading to intense prolonged relationships between the group members.

CONSTANT COMPANIONS
Social insects such as hornets divide up their breeding and colony duties to such an extent that it would be impossible for them to live in isolation from their nest mates.

LONE RANGER
Pumas are solitary, spending most of their lives alone. The meet briefly in order to breed.

Social status

The members of most social groups are not equal to each other. Instead, they operate systems in which high-ranking, dominant individuals have priority access to resources such as food, shelter, and mates, whereas low-ranking, subordinate individuals have fewer benefits. Possibly the best-known form of hierarchy is the "pecking order" seen in chickens. This involves unfamiliar birds fighting to assess which individual is dominant. The fights quickly lead to an established hierarchy, with each bird knowing its place. Once determined, there is little need for further aggression.

PECKING ORDER
If raised intensively, chickens will aggressively maintain hierarchies, whereas their junglefowl ancestors (right) live in peaceful groups, as birds quickly learn who is dominant.

Cooperation

The degree to which animals cooperate varies widely between species. It can be strongly dependent upon kinship, where helping close relations favors the survival of the cooperator's genes. The length of time group members stay together also plays a part, since this affects the likelihood of a favor being repaid by the recipient in the future. In some cooperatively breeding species, where group members are often closely related, division of labor is often seen, with different animals performing distinct roles within the group. This is particularly extreme in social insects and naked mole rats (right), where only a few individuals breed.

Queen (1) Produces and suckles young. Patrols tunnels and disciplines workers.

Breeding males (1–3) Harem males mate with queen but perform no other duties.

Soldiers (5–10) Act as sentries, defending colony from predators and invading mole rats.

Workers (50–200+) Dig tunnels, find food, tend to queen and pups in nursery.

Coalitions

Working alone means that none of the benefits gained have to be shared with others, but often single individuals don't have the power or stamina to gain or defend resources. In numerous socially living mammals, males can only breed if they control the access to harems of females, and the only way to gain this control is to fight incumbent males for it. This is difficult if there is a large imbalance of strength between the males, and one way around this is for males to form coalitions, in which several individuals gang up to attack the harem owner together. Other coalitions can form to defend territories and hunt difficult prey.

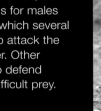

BACKING DOWN
This juvenile baboon (centre), is being disciplined by an older member of the troop. It is risky for youngsters to challenge dominant adults and they usually show submissive behaviour to avoid conflict.

Warfare

The increased strength that results from cooperation and the formation of coalitions means that groups can compete with others for access to resources. Launching attacks on neighbors is a good way to gain additional territory, and both good coordination and large group size confers distinct advantages to attacking groups. The ensuing battles are often short and violent. However, some species of sweat bee engage in extensive colonial wars, in which hundreds or thousands of individuals meet near potential nest sites and grapple with each other in fierce battles lasting for days.

SWEAT BEE

GROUP MEMORY
Female elephants tend to stay in the same social groups for their entire lives. This means that maintained information about migration routes and the location of water and foraging sites can be held by a group over long periods of time.

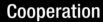

Standing firm

Mushroom coral

The vast structures of coral reefs are made up of millions of individual polyps, such as those of mushroom coral. Each one is an individual animal (although all the polyps in a head of coral are genetically identical). The solid structure of the reef is created by generations of polyps depositing layers of calcium carbonate, so only the outer surface of the coral heads harbor living polyps. Despite not being mobile, corals face extreme competition from each other. Mushroom coral grows relatively quickly and can take over space by shading slower corals, depriving them of food and light (some corals host photosynthesizing algae). Other species attack by squeezing out filaments that digest their neighbors' tissues, exposing the delicate skeleton.

Sarcophyton trocheliophorum

- Polyps less than ³⁄₁₆ in (5 mm), colonies up to 3 ft 3 in (1 m) wide
- Sheltered locations in reefs of Indian Ocean and Pacific.
- Smooth, leathery texture when polyps are retracted but looks furry with polyps expanded. Polyps have a fleshy stem and eight tentacles with feathery branches.

Some Hawaiian deep sea corals are known to be over 4,000 years old.

REEF BUILDERS
This reef contains soft mushroom and finger leather corals. Despite their name, some of the soft corals produce hard skeletal structures and are important reef builders.

PACKED TIGHT
Tiny individual polyps of mushroom coral are packed together to make up a colony. The polyps are called octocorals, for their eight tentacles.

Blood relations

Colonial sea squirt

A colonial sea squirt is made up of dozens of clones, which are all connected by a delicate fingerlike network of blood vessels. Blood is circulated by a heart that is able to pump in both directions. After attaching to rocks and other surfaces, the tadpolelike larvae of sea squirts rapidly lose many of the adaptations necessary for swimming, such as their tail and a spinelike structure called a notochord. They then begin to produce buds called zooids, which in turn produce further generations of zooids. As one zooid matures, its parent zooid will degrade and eventually be reabsorbed by the colony.

Didemnum molle

- ³⁄₈–³⁄₄ in (1–2 cm)
- Coastal water of northeast Australia (Queensland), the Phillipines, and southern Japan.
- Small dome-shaped colonial organism. Colors vary according to depth, from bright white to greenish gray or brown, with green interior, and dark pigmentation.

COLONY GROWTH
These colonial sea squirts have settled on a sponge. They harbor a symbiotic bacterium that produces nutrients from photosynthesis.

Close-knit family

Social spider

Despite their antisocial reputation, several species of spider display communal living. *Agelena consociata* will share a nest and web. This is often connected to nearby webs and individual spiders move freely throughout the groups of webs. Larger individuals construct the web and the structures necessary for trapping prey. All the spiders cooperate in capturing prey that falls into the sheets of silk, with up to 25 spiders required to subdue some of the larger items. Up to 40 spiders have been observed feeding simultaneously from the same item of prey.

WEB COMMUNITY
Social spiders weave large sheets of silk for prey to fall into. Within the sheets are many retreats that lead to one or more communal nests, concealing eggs or young spiderlings.

WAITING GAME
An *Agelena consociata* spider stands poised, ready to dart out and pounce on any prey that will fall into the dense silky sheeting of the web.

Agelena consociata

- ³⁄₁₆–³⁄₈ in (4–9 mm)
- Rain forest in Gabon, Africa.
- Small, brown spider with lighter colored strip running along back. Black, white, and brown stripes on legs.

HUDDLED MASSES
Outside their nest, honey bees are only
encountered in large numbers when they swarm
and hunt for a new place to live. The bees, gorged
on honey, carefully regulate swarm temperature,
and those on the outside of the swarm may be
much colder than those in the center.

Workers unite

Honey bee

A mature honey bee nest is formed of between 20,000 and 100,000 closely related female workers, which all share the nest's single queen as their mother. As a worker ages, she moves through a range of jobs. Her duties start inside the nest, where she cleans, tends to the queen and developing pupae, and builds the hive's waxy comb. She then moves on to riskier jobs outside the nest, such as defending against attack, and foraging.

Worker honey bees are vital pollinators in many environments, and collect sugar-rich nectar and protein-rich pollen from flowers in exchange for their pollination services. On returning to the nest, they are able to describe the location of good foraging sites to other foragers by performing a circular, buzzing "waggle dance" (see p.463) on the surface of the comb. This dance conveys detailed information about the distance to the site and its angle away from the nest.

Apis mellifera

- ⬌ ³⁄₈ in (1 cm) (worker), ¾ in (2 cm) (queen)
- Native to Africa, Europe, and Middle East. Domesticated worldwide.
- Yellow and black striped insect with moderately hairy body.

» 167, 185, 463

SWARMING

When a colony gets too crowded, the queen and half of the workers leave the nest and form a dense mass on a nearby tree. They then sit quietly while scouts search for a new nest site.

DRONE

The stingless male drones are solely involved with mating, which occurs away from the nest. Drones don't perform any useful duties within the nest, and they are vastly outnumbered by the workers.

WORKER

Most of the bees in a colony are female workers. They typically live for about six weeks, and perform a wide variety of different duties within the nest during that time. They are not able to reproduce.

QUEEN

Usually, a nest contains a single queen. When new queens are needed —if the colony gets too big or the queen too old—they are produced by feeding larvae laid in special comb cells exclusively with royal jelly.

CASE STUDY
DEMOCRATIC DECISION-MAKING

When a colony needs a new nest site, it sends hundreds of scouts out to look for suitable locations. Scouts hunt independently, and initially return with lots of possible options. If a scout finds a good site, it dances on the swarm's surface, pacing out the dimensions of the cavity to recruit other scouts to visit her find; where a stronger dance signals a better site. Over time, through comparison and disagreement, more scouts are recruited into favoring the best site available. When the number of scouts favoring one site reaches a critical threshold, they signal to the swarm and move it to the site that was chosen by a consensus vote.

Slave labor

Slave-making ant

At first sight, the nests of slave-making ants appear to be a harmonious mixture of different ant species. However, the extra species present are slaves held in thrall by the nest-owning ants. As well as hunting for food, scouts also look for the nests of these other species. When a suitable colony is found, platoons of raiding soldier ants are sent out to attack it. The raiders return home carrying stolen pupae, which are raised as slaves to work in the colony.

Formica sanguinea

◨ ¼ in (7 mm)

◉ Europe and temperate forest regions of Asia. Other closely related species are found in the Americas.

▥ Ant with red or black head, red thorax and legs, and a black abdomen.

CARRIED AWAY
Slave-making ants kidnap ants of other species, in this case the captive is a negro ant (*Formica fusca*).

Turf wars

Pavement ant

"Ant wars" can sometimes be seen in urban areas, where brown masses of fighters form on sidewalks. Swarms of hundreds or thousands of the small dark brown workers lock in combat for hours at a time, tumbling, biting, and pulling one another, while new recruits are guided to the melee along freshly laid odor trails. These are usually contests between adjacent colonies in the vicinity of their territorial boundaries (see p.140).

IN THE GRIP OF THE ENEMY
The ant in the center is being attacked by fighters from a rival nest. Despite the prolonged battles, only a tiny fraction of the workers that fight will be killed or seriously injured.

Tetramorium caespitum

◨ ¹⁄₁₆–³⁄₁₆ in (2–4 mm)

◉ Native to Europe, introduced throughout North and Central America.

▥ Small, dark brown ant with pale legs.

6½ The number of weeks the longest recorded battle raged between pavement ant colonies.

Eating together

Spotted eagle rays

Unlike other species of ray, spotted eagle rays may form large schools in open water during the nonbreeding season. Schools consist of hundreds of fishes and are often found swimming close to the surface. Small groups may splash and make agile leaps out of the water, possibly to help remove parasites. When foraging, eagle rays are often encountered swimming gracefully over the surface of reefs, sand, and mud. They enter estuaries and tidal rivers, where they hunt for live prey. Their taste for shellfish means that they are persecuted as a pest species.

Aetobatus narinari

◨ Wingspan 9¾ ft (3 m)

◉ Depths of up to 200 ft (60 m) in warm and temperate lagoons and coastal areas throughout the Atlantic, Indian, and Pacific oceans.

▥ Fish with flattened body, winglike fins, and long tail with spine at base. Top of body varies from dark blue to black with white spots. Underside white.

Segregated schools

Spiny dogfish

Like many other species of shark, spiny dogfish can form segregated groups depending upon their size, sex, and stage of development. Groups can be found containing only juveniles (of both sexes), immature females, mature males, or mature (and often pregnant) females. Mature females may split from males in order to conserve energy, as multiple copulations are expensive in terms of energy consumed, and females are able to store sperm for long periods of time. Sometimes very large schools can occur, as dogfish form dense aggregations at good feeding grounds.

Squalus acanthias

◨ Up to 5¼ ft (1.6 m)

◉ Cooler to warm temperate coastal shelf waters worldwide.

▥ Small, slender shark with slate-gray body, often with white spots and belly.

≫ 389

ROUND TRIP
After hatching in a river, young Atlantic salmon head out to the deep sea, where they form large schools. They mature for up to four years before returning to their home river to spawn.

Slipstream swimmers

Atlantic salmon

For a fish swimming in a school, it pays not to be at the front. A salmon swimming in the slipstream of another is pulled slightly by the drag generated by the fish ahead of it. This means that it needs to invest less energy in propelling itself forward, and can reduce the speed at which it beats its tail. Through the effort reducing benefits of schooling, salmon can swim for longer periods of time. By working as a group, with different fishes taking the lead, this effect can be improved. While it is costly for the individual in the lead it benefits the group as a whole.

Salmo salar

◨ 1¼–5 ft (40–150 cm)

◉ North Atlantic Ocean and some lakes in North America, Russia, and Scandinavia.

▥ Streamlined silvery fish with pointed head. Breeding adults darker red-brown. Males develop hooked jaws.

In the round

Sawtooth barracuda

Barracudas are often encountered in open water, swimming in large schools. These schools may take the shape of balls, spirals, or even doughnuts, where each individual barracuda curves in a large circle as it swims. Complicated group patterns like these are found in many animals that aggregate in large groups; when flocks of birds and schools of fish contain hundreds or thousands of members, the group appears to move as one, where every individual seems to change to a new agreed direction instantaneously. Rather than being directed by a few leading individuals, these complex patterns can come from each animal paying attention to its immediate neighbors. So, although a doughnut shape looks complicated to form and maintain, no group coordination is needed: all each barracuda needs to do is adjust its own speed and heading in response to the fish next to it.

Sphyraena putnamae

↔ 31–35 in (80–90 cm)

◐ Lagoons and reefs in tropical and subtropical regions of Pacific and Indian oceans.

▥ Elongated body with dark chevron markings along sides. Large mouth, with projecting bottom jaw.

>> 252

SYNCHRONIZED SWIMMING
These Indian mackerel are swimming with their mouths wide open to filter feed on plankton in the water. Mackerel swim in huge, closely coordinated schools, in which each fish positions itself with similarly sized fishes and synchronizes its movement with that of its neighbors. The entire school can appear to change direction simultaneously.

Nest protection

Spectacled caiman

During the breeding season, spectacled caimans construct large nests on riverbanks, piling a large mound of soil, wood, and leaf litter, in an area cleared of vegetation. Several different females may lay their eggs within this mound, which is then guarded by both males and females while the eggs are developing. Young caimans vocalize both before and after hatching. This could be to alert the attending parents, who provide assistance to the hatchlings in leaving their shells. Juveniles then stay in nurseries for over a year before they become independent. While in the nursery an adult caiman—not necessarily their parent—keeps a defensive eye on them.

Caiman crocodilus

6–6½ ft (1.8–2 m)

Forests and wetlands from southern Mexico to northern Argentina. Introduced to Florida and Cuba.

Dull olive-green, scaly skin. Bony ridge above eyes, giving it "spectacled" appearance.

Leaving together

Green iguana

Although they don't show parental care, female green iguanas often nest communally, which means that large numbers of hatchlings emerge together. Not only does this simultaneous hatching dilute the predation risk faced by individuals, but it also means that a communal effort can be made to dig out of the natal burrow—an arduous process that can take up to seven days. Once free, the juveniles then disperse to their future home ranges in the same groups they emerged with, and can be found sleeping together. Juveniles of this species are able to distinguish their relations. This may involve recognizing fecal scent or body odor.

BLENDING IN
The iguanas' green skin makes them inconspicuous in their favored surroundings. They are specialized leaf eaters and spend most of the day inactive.

Iguana iguana

4–5 ft (1.2–1.5 m)

Tropical rain forest in Central and Southern America and on Caribbean islands. Introduced to Florida.

Green lizard with large head and throat pouch, crest of long spines running along back, and long tail with black stripes. Large circular scale on lower jaw.

Shared nests

Ostrich

Although the nests defended by territorial male ostriches are incubated only by the guardian male and a single female, they can contain the eggs of up to 18 different females, sired by multiple fathers. Ostriches engage in a unique form of cooperative breeding, where females within a group may lay their eggs in a large number of different nests. However, a nest can only contain a finite amount of eggs. Although around 40 eggs are laid in a nest, only around 20 can be successfully incubated. Females are able to identify their own eggs and eject those laid by intruders. On hatching, chicks from multiple parents are cared for in nurseries.

Struthio camelus

Height 5½–8¾ ft (1.7–2.7 m)

Savanna regions of southern Africa.

Flightless bird with naked head and legs. Males have black plumage with white tail and wing tips. Females and young have brown plumage. The largest living bird.

≫ 290, 409

Vanishing act

Steller's eider

Outside of the breeding season, Steller's eiders group in lagoons and bays to forage. Large numbers of these sea-going ducks form rafts on the water surface. Eiders exhibit synchronized diving, in which an entire raft of ducks can suddenly vanish underwater. The eiders are preyed upon by birds such as bald eagles (*Halaieetus leucocephalus*) and gyrfalcons (*Falco rusticolus*), and cordinating their dives in this way may reduce the predation risk that the ducks experience. Lone ducks abandoned at the surface could stand out as targets to predators when the other ducks are underwater.

Polysticta stelleri

17–18½ in (43–47 cm)

Coasts of northern Japan, Arctic Norway, Russia, and Alaska.

Medium-sized marine duck. Male has white head with clownlike markings, a black collar and back, and yellow breast. Female is dark brown.

Pairing up

Black-legged kittiwake

Kittiwakes live in coastal colonies on rock faces and form monogamous pairs. Pairs of kittiwakes will usually stay together over a long period of time. However, "divorce" may occur when the members of a pair are unable to coordinate their incubation and brooding activities, when they are unsuccessful at raising offspring, or if one fails to return to the nest site. Forming long-term partnerships confers benefits to the members of a pair: those that stay together tend to lay eggs earlier in the season, and will successfully raise more chicks than birds that have only recently formed a pair.

Rissa tridactyla

15–16 in (38–41 cm)

Coastal areas in breeding season, winters out at sea. Found throughout North Atlantic and North Pacific.

Medium-sized seabird with yellow bill. Body white with black-tipped gray wings. Short legs are usually black.

Pecking order

Whooper swan

In the fall, whooper swans fly long distances down from their Arctic breeding grounds to southerly wintering sites. Membership of the groups found on these wintering sites can be very stable, and groups are generally made up of closely related birds. Both group size and kinship are important in forming social hierarchies: large family groups will dominate small families, and groups composed of relatives will have a higher social status than groups of unrelated individuals. Each year, the composition of the group changes slightly as older swans die, and young males mature. These young males have to fight, lunging and sparring for dominance within a group.

Cygnus cygnus

- 4½–6 ft (1.4–1.8 m)
- Large stretches of water, wetlands, and rivers throughout northern Europe and Asia.
- Large white bird with long, thin neck. Black bill with yellow triangular patches. Black legs.

Vast colonies

King penguin

During the breeding season, king penguins can form vast colonies on beaches and snow-free valleys near the sea. The colonies are segregated, and breeders tend to be separated from nonbreeders. Despite the potential pressure for space and resources, there is little antagonistic behavior seen within the colony. In a breeding pair, both parents incubate and brood the chick, which will take around nine months to fledge. As it gets older, the chick is left alone within the colony for long periods, while its parents forage for food.

600,000 The number of birds that can be contained in a king penguin colony.

Aptenodytes patagonicus

- 33–37 in (85–95 cm)
- Southern Indian Ocean (the Falklands, Macquarie Islands, Îles Crozet, Heard Island, and Marion Island).
- Penguin with white belly, silver-gray back, and black head. Orange patches on neck and over each ear.
- » 459

KING COLONY
This immense colony of breeding king penguins is interspersed with groups of unattended fluffy brown juveniles.

HUMAN IMPACT

SHRINKING RANGE

Penguin populations are in serious trouble. Most penguins rely on krill for much of their nutrition. Krill in turn rely on winter ice for breeding sites, and for the algae growing on the underside of the ice sheets. As a result of rising sea temperature, there is less krill to go around. Some penguins also need to haul out on pack ice to molt. If birds swim too far before they find solid ice, they drown.

DANCE TROUPE
For lesser flamingos, impressing a mate in front of your friends takes on a whole new dimension. Groups of tens to hundreds of birds gather and march back and forth in formation, raising and lowering their bills. During the peak of breeding, a lake may be filled with many dance convoys, all traveling in different directions than each other.

Flocking together

Terns

Most species of tern are highly gregarious birds, and can form flocks of tens or hundreds, often from a mixture of species, as in this mixed flock of yellow-billed royal terns (*Sterna maxima*) and black-billed sandwich terns (*Sterna sandvicensis*), right. Young terns remain with their parents for weeks or months after fledging, perfecting the difficult task of plunge-diving for fish. Some terns migrate with their parents and stay with them for much of the winter.

Although they sometimes hunt alone, terns often have a better success rate at finding food when they are in a flock—the birds usually catch more fish than if they are hunting alone. However, there is competition for the good fish within the flock, and on average each fish caught will be smaller than if the tern fed alone.

Sterna species

- ◨ 8–21½ in (20–54 cm)
- ◉ Near coastal and inland water worldwide.
- ▥ Slim, streamlined birds with long, pointed bills and predominantly white plumage. Some have black spots or patches on head, and trailing plumes over neck.

» 358

Land and sea

Atlantic puffin

Although they roost in noisy colonies on sea cliffs, nesting for Atlantic puffins means much more than sitting on a windy stone shelf. If they are unable to find a suitable hole beneath rocks, they will excavate one themselves, going 28–39 in (70–100 cm) deep into the cliff.

Away from the colony, puffins can often be seen offshore floating in raftlike formations. These rafts may be formed solely of puffins, but it is common to see them mixed with other birds (such as guillemots and shearwaters). Sometimes the rafts form single lines of birds, all facing in the same direction.

Fratercula arctica

- ◨ 10 in (25 cm)
- ◉ Coasts of Norway, northern Russia, British Isles, Iceland, Brittany, Greenland, and from Labrador down to the northeastern US.
- ▥ Black and white seabird with multicolored bill.

» 229

SITTING PRETTY
Puffins are unusual among cliff nesting seabirds because they prefer to nest on the ground during the summer, as above, rather than on rocky ledges.

Communal nests

Rook

Rooks are garrulous, intelligent, and highly social birds. From February onward, they build nests communally in large groups, called "rookeries," at the tops of trees. Within these noisy assemblages, breeding pairs defend a small area of space around their nest. Rookeries are remarkably stable from year to year, and rooks fight for ready-built nests at the beginning of the breeding season, since the existence of an old nest may be a good indicator of how well chicks will survive at the site.

Outside the nesting season, rooks from different colonies roost together. These roosts can consist of enormous numbers of resting rooks: at one Scottish roost 65,000 birds were recorded.

Corvus frugilegus

- ◨ 16–19½ in (41–49 cm)
- ◉ Open country or pasture with woods or clumps of trees across most of Europe, Middle East, and breeds as far east as Russia and China.
- ▥ Highly social black bird, with long bill and slight lilac tint to feathers.

Close neighbors

American cliff swallow

Breeding colonies of cliff swallows can consist of up to several hundred pairs of birds. They build gourd-shaped nests by cementing hundreds of small pellets of mud to the eaves of buildings, bridges, and other vertical structures. Nests may be reused from year to year, if they can be easily repaired. One advantage of living in such a close-knit colony is that if a swallow is having trouble finding food by itself, it can turn to its neighbors for help. All it has to do is identify a successful forager returning to the colony, and then follow it when it goes back out to find food. It is debatable whether successful foragers are intentionally leading others to good sites, but every colony member can benefit from the pooled information about food sources that is collected by successful birds.

Petrochelidon pyrrhonota

- ◨ 5 in (13 cm)
- ◉ Open farmland, towns, and mountainous areas. Breed throughout North America, migrating to southern South America in winter.
- ▥ Short-billed bird with steel-blue head and back, white forehead, orange-brown chest, and square-ended tail.

PACKED IN
In this colony of cliff swallow nests, each nest is a self-contained ball of dried mud, which is built up in layers and has one small entrance.

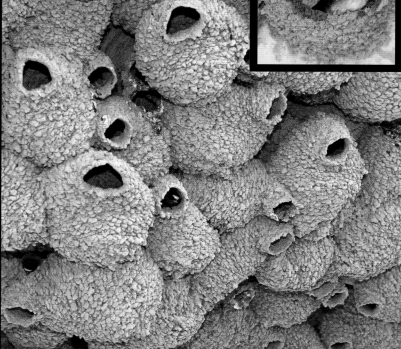

DRINKING UP
A flock of thousands of red-billed queleas quench their thirst en masse. The birds drink from the water's surface while still in flight.

Feeding frenzy
Red-billed quelea

Nesting colonies of this species of weaver bird can extend over hundreds of acres, and consist of millions of individuals, making it the most abundant bird in the world. It is also known as "locust bird." When a flock moves into fields of seed crops such as millet or sorghum, the birds will strip them bare, leading to severe countermeasures by farmers, who kill about 200 million queleas a year.

NEATLY PERCHED
The thin toes of queleas lock in position, allowing them to perch and even sleep on upright stalks. They roost in vast numbers.

Quelea quelea
- ◨ 5 in (12.5 cm)
- ⊙ Most non-rain-forest areas of sub-Saharan Africa.
- ▥ Small brown bird with red bill. In breeding season, female's bill turns yellow, male gains variably colored mask, crown, and breast.

Sharing warmth
Long-tailed bushtit

During the winter, noisy packs of dozens of these tiny birds are a common sight in North European woodlands as they pass through trees and bushes in messy waves. Nonmigratory, these birds manage to find enough food in harsh, cold environments. Being highly active in low temperatures means that high levels of energy are spent, but bushtits minimize the amount they lose as heat. In addition to having fluffy plumage, these birds huddle together in little groups during the night and periods of the day when they are not active. Forming a huddle means that birds retain heat, but the middle of the huddle is much warmer than the outside. During roost formation, birds will try to get into the center, and more subordinate individuals frequently end up stuck on the outside in the cold.

Aegithalos caudatus
- ◨ 5½ in (14 cm)
- ⊙ Throughout Europe and Asia.
- ▥ Tiny, fluffy-looking black and white bird with pink tinge to plumage and long, straight tail.

≫ 172

Cooperative colony
Naked mole-rat

Often compared to social insects such as ants and bees, naked mole-rats have a unique social system for a mammal. Living in colonies of about 75 individuals (going up to about 250 in larger colonies), reproduction is delegated to a single breeding female (commonly called the queen). The other members of the colony do not breed, instead they tend to the pups produced by the queen. This means that all the mole-rats in a colony are closely related to each other.

Tunnels provide extra living space for an expanding colony and are vital for accessing the edible parts of underground tubers and roots, which are the mole-rat's staple diet. Smaller workers excavate tunnels by chiseling at the walls with their teeth. Chains of mole-rats form to clear out the dirt produced by the digging, shoveling it along from one mole-rat to another, until it is finally kicked up and out of the tunnels into an expanding volcano-like pile by one of the larger workers.

CASE STUDY
KIDNAPPING

Some of the older, larger mole-rats in a colony act as soldiers. In addition to defending themselves against predators, mole-rats sometimes launch hostile takeovers on their neighbors, either occupying their excavated tunnels, or making off with younger pups. These kidnapped pups are raised as slaves, and grow up to tend to the needs of the queen and colony in a manner identical to that of the native workers.

Heterocephalus glaber
- ◨ 5½–7 in (14–18 cm)
- ⊙ Hot, dry regions of East Africa: Somalia, central Ethiopia, and northern and eastern Kenya.
- ▥ Pink, ratlike rodent. Hairless except for sensory whiskers.

NURSERY
This queen is suckling her young, which will also be tended to by the colony's workers. On average, a queen mole-rat gives birth to eight to ten pups per litter, producing over 500 pups over her lifetime.

1.2 The number of miles naked mole-rats travel above ground when dispersing to found a new colony.

EXCAVATION
A worker naked mole-rat gouges away at a tunnel wall with its enormous incisors.

Dominant females
Ring-tailed lemur

Primate societies often center on dominant males or breeding pairs, but male ring-tailed lemurs are submissive and females get first access to food and priority grooming. This total female dominance is seen only in a few other lemurs and in spotted hyenas. Although daughters normally stay with their mothers, they have to fight for their position within the female hierarchy.

Lemur catta

◀▶	17 in (43 cm)
◆	Forest in southwestern Madagascar.
🕮	Reddish gray primate with brown and white markings. Long black and white striped tail.

» 412, 446

Nocturnal group
Night monkeys

Night monkeys form groups of between two and six individuals, consisting of a breeding male and female, one or two infants and juveniles, and a subadult. The breeding pair are monogamous (although partners may change over seasons), and males provide care to the infants. Most species of night monkey are nocturnal, and the distance that a group ranges through a small, well-defended territory is strongly related to the amount of moonlight available.

Aotus species

◀▶	9½–14½ in (24–37 cm)
◆	Moist tropical forest from Panama southward to Bolivia, Paraguay, and northern Argentina.
🕮	Gray-brown, with yellow or orange fur on stomach and limbs. Three black stripes across crown of head.

Adoptive father
Barbary macaque

Male barbary macaques provide intensive paternal care. Fatherly duties include carrying, grooming, and playing with infants and babies. Males often focus their care on a single infant. However, there is often no genetic relationship between the male and the infant he is caring for. Nor does such attention mean that the male increases his chance of siring future offspring with the infant's mother. Males may instead carry infants as a tool for regulating interactions with other males, using familiarity with a baby as a means of forming coalitions.

Macaca sylvanus

◀▶	19½–28 in (50–70 cm)
◆	Forests in northern Africa, and a small population on Gibraltar.
🕮	Gray tailess primate with dark pink face. Males are much larger than females.

MACAQUE FAMILY
An adult female, juvenile, and newborn macaque huddle together. Like many other primates, the fur of the newborn is darker than that of the adults.

In 1980 there were about **20,000** barbary macaques in Africa. Today, there is **less than half** that number. The decline is due in part to **habitat loss** caused by logging.

Female solidarity
Olive baboon

Olive baboons live in closely knit troops of up to 150 predominantly female adults and juveniles. When males reach adulthood, they usually leave the troop that they were born into, spending time in several different troops during their lifetime, while females tend to stay within the same group for their entire life. Females within a troop are very closely related, and immediate relatives, including aunts and nieces as well as mothers and daughters, tend to stick together within the troop. Troop dominance hierarchies are very stable and are passed down. The daughters of a high-ranking dominant female inherit their mother's status; the youngest daughter inherits the highest rank, giving her priority access to food, and making her offspring more likely to survive. When not in breeding condition, females still associate with males, and can form long-lasting friendships, grooming, foraging, and traveling together, and defending each other against aggression from other troop members.

Papio anubis

◀▶	23½–29 in (60–74 cm)
◆	Widespread throughout equatorial Africa.
🕮	Highly social primate with greenish gray coat and long, pointed muzzle. Manes of males cover their head and shoulders.

» 454

BABOON TROOP
A maned male sitting next to a juvenile enjoys a moment's peace (bottom left), while the remainder of the troop rest in the clearing or forage on vegetation in the surrounding trees.

CASE STUDY
BABOON STRESS

Like humans, baboons live in social groups, and have leisure time to devote to social interactions. Hormonal responses that are normally generated by immediate dangers, such as predators, can be caused over longer periods by a dominant bully. So, like humans, baboons suffer from diseases linked to chronic stress. Grooming is one way of lowering stress levels.

Border patrol

Chimpanzee

Groups of chimpanzees occupy sharply defined territories, and the rare interactions between neighboring groups are often hostile. Border patrols, usually male coalitions, conduct violent coordinated attacks on neighbors, which can on occasion lead to death—although this is rare, since lethal attacks on members of the same species are uncommon.

BAD NEIGHBORS
Territorial competition is an important facet of chimpanzee social life. Males stay in their birth groups and may engage in warfare with neighbors.

However, violence can also occur within communities when younger males contend with the alpha male for dominance.

Pan troglodytes
- 29–37 in (73–95 cm)
- Forested habitats in equatorial Africa.
- Ape with black hair, sometimes tinged gray or brown.
- ≫ 174, 247, 454, 460, 465, 480–81, 482–83

≫ 174, 247, 454, 460, 465, 480–81, 482–83

≫ 455

CASE STUDY
CANNIBALISM

Raiding male chimpanzees are known to commit infanticide, and on several occasions they have been observed eating their victims. The reasons for infanticide and cannibalism are unclear, but they may cause the dead infant's mother to return to a breeding state more quickly. In a reserve at Gombe in Tanzania, an adult female and her daughter were also seen to steal and eat babies from females within their own community.

Top dog

Gray wolf

Pack-hunting animals such as gray wolves frequently impose a strict hierarchical order, with an alpha male and female dominating the other pack members. Successful coordination is required to bring down large prey, but once caught, the communal nature of the pack breaks down, and high-ranking individuals may get prime access to morsels from the carcass. Perhaps surprisingly, antagonism is rare among the wolves in the pack, since hierarchies are usually quite stable and are generally well established. A subordinate actively displays its position within the group by crouching in front of the dominant wolf with its ears laid back and tail wagging. Although submissive, the action appears to be friendly, since the subordinate will then push and lick at the muzzle of the dominant, and gently bite it.

GENTLY NUZZLED
A wolf is greeted with a friendly, licking behavior by another. This behavior is generally a display of submission and it is likely that the wolf being licked is the dominant member of the pair.

Canis lupus
- 4ft 3in–5 ft (1–2.5 m)
- Once found throughout North America and Eurasia. Now restricted to northerly parts of range.
- Large dog with bulky coat, colored various shades of red, black, brown, and white.
- ≫ 455

Gentlemen's agreement

Lion

When a male lion takes over a pride (group) of females, usually after a vicious battle with the previous incumbent male, his first act is to kill all the cubs. This brings the females into heat, and ensures that the male can then sire offspring of his own, whose survival depends on his ability to defend his position in the pride. This breeding strategy means that male lions are often at risk of severe injury, whether they control a pride or are trying to usurp a resident male. Some lions get around this risk by forming a coalition with other males. Although paternity is shared, forming a coalition means that the pride is better defended and increases cub survival.

DOUBLE STRENGTH
Male lions form coalitions of different sizes. Coalitions of two or three lions are often unrelated, but males in larger coalitions tend to be close kin.

PRIDE MOTHERS
Lions live in prides of 4–12 lionesses and their cubs. Lionesses frequently cooperate in hunting, which allows them to kill large, fast-moving prey

Panthera leo
- 5½–6¼ ft (1.7–1.9 m)
- Found in reserves in southern Africa, and the Gir Forest, India.
- Large, tawny-yellow cat with round ears and tail tuft. Males have mane of darker hair on head and shoulders.
- ≫ 236–37, 413, 446

≫ 236–37, 413, 446

Coastal colony

Steller's sea lion

Usually found on isolated rocky beaches, rookeries (colonies) of Steller's sea lions can be composed of hundreds of individuals. These sea lions normally return to the beach they were born on when they are ready to breed. At the start of the breeding season, the larger males haul themselves onto land and establish a territory to defend. Females arrive a few days later, and, after giving birth to a pup, usually mate with the male who "owns" the territory. This means that males have to constantly tend to their territory and vigorously defend it from potential usurpers. Consequently, males defending territories are unable to feed and instead rely on huge blubber reserves stored around their body for nutrition.

Eumetopias jubatus
- 7½–9¼ ft (2.3–2.8 m)
- Pacific coastal regions of the US, Canada, Russia, Japan, and China.
- Light brown seal with small ears. Males have coarse black manes and can be 2½ times the size of females.

BASKING SITE
Steller's sea lions form noisy rookeries at haul-out sites when they are resting and during the breeding season.

2 months The length of time male Steller's sea lions fast during the breeding season.

Communal den
Spotted hyena

Social hierarchies and the ability to fit in with the crowd are an important part of a spotted hyena's life from birth. These carnivores live in groups called clans, which are dominated by an alpha female and her relatives, and a pup's social position is inherited from its mother. Females give birth to pups in isolation, then two to six weeks later they transfer them to communal dens that are shared with several other mothers. Pups in shared dens sometimes attempt to suckle from females other than their mother, but the females are usually aware of such attempts and actively discourage any pups that are

trying to steal from them. The communal dens serve as a social hub for the clan, and nonbreeders will often drop by to check up on their clan mates. This means that the pups are integrated into the clan's social structure and know their place in the pecking order from a very early age.

SAFELY SURROUNDED
A cub peers inquisitively out from the safety offered by three of its clan members. Cubs continue to suckle until they are over a year old.

Crocuta crocuta
- 3 ft 3 in–5 ft (1–1.5 m)
- Desert fringe and savanna in central and southern Africa.
- Sandy yellow coat, covered with black spots. Distinguished by large neck and rounded ears.
- ≫ 258

Shared responsibility
Meerkat

These highly social carnivores live in societies where childcare is a shared responsibility. After birth, pups stay in the burrow they were born in for around three weeks, and are suckled by helpers (often young, unmated females), while their mothers forage for food. When the pups are old enough to leave the burrow, they stick with the foraging group and are fed small items of prey by helpers.

Suricata suricatta
- 10–14 in (25–35 cm)
- Dry open plains in southern Africa.
- Buff and silver mammal with dark-tipped, tapered tail. Broad head with black eye patches.
- ≫ 318–19

TEAM PLAYERS
A female meerkat suckles pups, which may or may not be her own (below). These social creatures also work together to defend the burrow (right).

Family herd
Mustang

Wild and feral horses like the mustangs found on North America's plains and deserts typically live in small, permanent family groups made up of one male (stallion), one to three females (mares), and their offspring. Unlike many other mammals, stallions tend to remain with the same mares over long periods of time. This long pair-bond may be a defensive

mechanism, since stallions will vigorously defend their harems against intruders and predators. Dispersal occurs when mature offspring of both sexes leave the group. Herds form when several family groups come together, and can contain hundreds of animals. Herding horses travel around together, and also graze or rest as a group. Herds can be temporary, but in some wild breeds, such as the Camargue horse found in southern France, family groups remain together permanently throughout the year.

2000 BCE The date that wild horses were first domesticated. Fewer than 33,000 wild mustangs remain in North America

Equus caballus
- 7 ft (2.1 m), with a huge amount of variation in domesticated breeds.
- Patchy distributions of feral horses throughout the world. Domesticated breeds found worldwide.
- Large hooved mammal. Variable color, ranging from black and dark brown to tan, gray, or white.

Girl group
Ring-tailed coati

The racoonlike coati is an agile arboreal forager, and has ankles that can face backward, enabling it to run up and down trees. Male coatis are generally solitary and tend to forage alone, but females live in small groups of five to ten individuals. When it is time to breed, females move away from the group, but rejoin later, along with their new infants.

Nasua nasua
- 2¼–4¼ ft (0.7–1.3 m)
- Rain forest regions of South America, as far south as northern Argentina.
- Dark brown mammal with long nose and narrow head with facial markings. Long brown tail with rings.

STAMPEDE
A herd of mustangs running through the desert in Wyoming. Much variation exists in coat color within wild populations.

Walking the line
Bactrian camel

Nearly extinct in the wild, bactrian camels have been widely domesticated. Their ability to cope with arid, desert conditions and extreme temperature differences allows them to inhabit regions inaccessible to other animals. Fat is stored in the two humps on the back and is used when food is unavailable. These adaptations allow camels to travel for long periods of time without food. During the mating season, numbers can reach over 100, but normally social family groups consist of up to 30 animals. When moving over large distances to find food, the members of a group form a linear traveling party, or "caravan," in which a dominant male acts as the leader.

Camelus bactrianus
- 9¾ ft (3 m)
- Restricted to three areas of desert in southern Mongolia and northwest China.
- Large ungulate with coarse beige coat and two large humps on back. Long face with split upper lip, sealable nostrils, and long eyelashes.

HUMAN IMPACT
TERRITORY LOSS

Critically endangered, the wild bactrian camel has been reduced to three small regions in central Asia. Its habitat has been lost to mining, industry, and nuclear testing. Every year, camels in protected regions are shot when they migrate into areas where they are in competition with livestock.

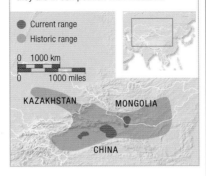

- Current range
- Historic range

0   1000 km
0   1000 miles

KAZAKHSTAN   MONGOLIA
CHINA

CAMEL CARAVAN
A small group of camels travels in a characteristic line along a ridge in the Gobi Desert. The camels sport thick fur to combat the cold.

Mothers and daughters
African elephant

Large herds containing hundreds or thousands of African elephants come together during times of drought, but more typically elephants collect in smaller family groups of around 10 or 20 related individuals. These small herds are matriarchal: an older dominant female controls the herd, and frequently remains in the position until her death, when her eldest daughter usually assumes the role of matriarch. Family groups may join together in loose herds, but the matriarch controls and vetoes group membership. At puberty, males are ejected from their herd and form separate small bachelor herds. Adult males will associate with female groups only to mate.

Loxodonta africana
- 13–16½ ft (4–5 m)
- Open grassland, scrub, woodland, and occasionally desert, in Africa south of the Sahara.
- Large mammal with gray wrinkled skin, trunk, and tusks. Distinguished from Asian elephant by larger ears.
- ≫ 295, 417, 466–67

Group greetings
Spinner dolphin

These gregarious dolphins are often found in pods (groups) containing hundreds of individuals. Pod membership is fluid, and changes regularly as smaller groups join and leave. When they are not resting, spinner dolphins are often very noisy, producing a huge range of whistles and clicks—individual dolphins may have signature whistles that enable them to be identified by others. When reuniting after long separations, spinner dolphins greet each other with lots of social interaction and vocalizations.

Stenella longirostris
- 5–11½ ft (1.5–3.5 m)
- Tropical and warm temperate waters of Atlantic, Pacific, and Indian oceans.
- Dolphin with distinct long beak and pointed flippers. Dark gray-black upper side, gray-tan side stripe, and pale under surface.

POD CASTING
Spinner dolphins produce a constant string of clicks and whistles as a form of social interaction. They also use the sounds to detect prey by echolocation.

COMMUNICATION

TEAM CALL
Like many animal signals, howling serves several functions, including declaring a pack's territory and strength, rallying pack members, and showing solidarity. When one wolf howls, the rest of the pack join in, at varying pitches, to create the impression of as large a pack as possible.

COMMUNICATION

A diversity of signals allow animals to communicate with their own species, enabling them to find mates, cooperate, and avoid conflict. The natural world is full of communication networks, from minute vibrations and electrical impulses, to cocktails of chemicals, colorful displays, and spectacular sounds.

FRIENDLY SIGNALS
Common between social animals, like these olive baboons, tactile signals are used by newborn infants to maintain maternal contact.

What is communication?

Communication involves the transfer of information between animals—usually of the same species—with specialized signals. These signals tend to have evolved from aspects of behavior, biology, or appearance that have become exaggerated, or "ritualized," to convey information. The leaping of a gazelle, for example, provides incidental information about its fitness and agility to a predator, but when the leaping is ritualized into a display of exaggerated movements, it becomes an active signal of fitness. This is not a fixed process, and some incidental aspects of appearance or behavior may be halfway to being formal signals. The diversity of signals reflects that of animals, their environments, and the information they need to convey.

Competition over mates, territory, or resources is another reason to communicate. Most aggressive signals actually reduce the need to fight. Showing off your size and strength by chest beating, like a silverback gorilla, can deter rivals, while marking territorial boundaries further reduces conflict. Those animals living in groups, however, tend to have the most complex communication. Close-knit groups often have signals that maintain cohesion, uphold social order, and enable cooperation, but even casual groups may have signals for danger, or to bring indiviuals together.

CHANNELS OF COMMUNICATION

CHEMICAL
Used across the animal kingdom, chemical signals are particularly popular among invertebrates. They are usually aimed at a general audience rather than a particular individual.

VIBRATION
Mainly used by arthropods but also by some vertebrates, vibration includes pressure waves that travel through wood or the ground, made by banging, tapping, or low-frequency infrasound.

VISUAL
Used by all groups of animals, visual communication is less developed in nocturnal and burrowing animals. It includes colors and markings, body language, and bioluminescence.

ELECTRIC
Known to be used by only two groups of fishes, electricity is only effective in water, over a very short range. Electrical discharge patterns are produced by a special electric organ.

ACOUSTIC
Used by arthropods and vertebrates, acoustic signals travel through air or water. They are made by a voice box, or by mechanical means, such as rubbing together body parts.

TACTILE
Used at close range before mating, or in social species that live close together, tactile messages are simple and usually friendly, and include tapping in insects and embracing in mammals.

Learning the language

The vast majority of animals instinctively produce and respond to signals given by their species: a male cricket raised in isolation still produces his mating chirp, and females that have never heard it before will respond. Scientists have even found the gene responsible for courtship behavior in the fruit fly *Drosophila melanogaster*. However, in some mammals and birds, learning is crucial to communication. Young songbirds typically go through stages before reaching full adult song, and it was recently discovered that adult male humpback whales change their songs regularly.

BABY BABBLING
Young pygmy marmosets produce a jumble of calls called the "babbling phase" before learning their vocabulary.

Why animals communicate

While the ways in which animals communicate are extremely diverse, the reasons for communication are fairly straightforward—finding a suitable mate, raising offspring, defending resources or a mate against rivals, and cooperation.The most fundamental of these is to find a mate of the right species, and a great many animals have their own courtship signals. These may be vocal, pheromonal, visual, tactile, acoustic, electric, or a combination of these. Some courtship signals, such as the bonding displays of many monogamous birds, offer information about the quality of a mate or cement long-term bonds. Parent–offspring signals, such as contact calls or begging, are used by animals with a long or intense period of parental care, particularly birds and mammals.

Talking a foreign language

Communication usually occurs within a species, but there are good reasons for interspecies communication. The most common examples of this are between prey and predators. In an attempt to avoid being eaten, some prey species signal to predators that they are dangerous, or extremely agile. Prey species also benefit from understanding and reacting to the alarm calls of others. An unusual example of interspecies communication is the honeyguide, singing to guide the honeybadger to beehives. The honeybadger opens the hive, and both eat the spoils.

AGGRESSIVE SIGNALS
Animals try to avoid physical fights and use signals to advertise their fighting ability. These rival common cranes make themselves appear as large as possible by opening their wings.

The poison frog *Atelopus varius's* bright colors are a warning to predators of its toxic qualities.

The rattlesnake produces a loud warning rattle by vibrating the modified scales at the tip of its tail.

The "stotting" display of the springbok tells predators that it is fit, healthy, and hard to catch.

Pheromones and smell

The word pheromone comes from Greek and means "carrier of excitement." Pheromones are chemicals released by animals that trigger a behavioral change or developmental reaction in another member of their species. In invertebrates, even tiny concentrations can produce dramatic effects, while the response of vertebrates is often more subtle.

SEA ANEMONE

An ancient language

Chemical signals were probably the earliest form of communication, and today the majority of animals communicate mostly or entirely this way (with the seeming exception of birds). Pheromones are the main form of invertebrate communication, and social insects such as termites coordinate their activities with complex chemical vocabularies. Arthropods use sensory hairs in the pits of their exoskeleton, or on their antennae, to detect pheromones, while vertebrates employ a vomeronasal organ, or an olfactory membrane.

POTENT APHRODISIAC
Female emperor moths produce a powerful attractant from a gland at the tip of their abdomen.

Types of pheromones

There are two main types of pheromone—primers and releasers. Primers produce a physiological change in the recipient: queen bees, for example, employ them to suppress the sexual development of workers. Releaser pheromones cause a behavioral response, and are of four main types—sex attractants, alarm signals, recruitment or aggregation signals, and marker or territorial pheromones. Once released, a pheromone has a physical existence apart from the animal that produced it, and can be carried huge distances by air currents, or deposited on the ground or a plant to be picked up later. Signals that need to carry long distances, act quickly, or switch on and off, like alarm pheromones, tend to be highly volatile and unstable. Those used for longer-term communication, such as territorial markers, are heavier, more stable compounds that may be active for days or weeks.

HONEY BEE QUEEN

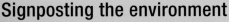
WEEVIL

PHEROMONE TYPES
Anthopleura elegantissima (top) uses a "releaser" pheromone as a warning to to retract vulnerable tentacles; honey bee queens (center) control workers with a "primer and releaser" system; and cabbage seed weevils (bottom) use "marker" pheromones.

SENSITIVE TO SCENT
Moths are very precise in detecting the composition of pheromones. The male ceanothus moth uses the thousands of hairlike sensilla on its antennae to detect tiny quantities of female sex attractant.

Signposting the environment

Many animals live in a landscape of smells, as prominent to them as signposts are to humans. Chemical messages are unique in that they can be left behind like a note or calling card, and are often used by animals that are widely dispersed, or need to defend a large area. Many ants leave odor trails to mark the route to a food source. These "trail pheromones" may only last minutes, because the information is only valid for a short time. Territorial markings, however, tend to be long-term and some, such as those of hyenas, can persist for weeks.

SCENT MARKING
Animals such as this female ring-tailed lemur—who marks her troop's territory with an anal gland—use specialized glands for scent marking. Other animals mark territory with urine or dung.

7 miles The distance a male emperor moth has been known to track the pheromone plume of a female.

CASE STUDY
MASS BROADCAST

Researchers decipher insect pheromones by separating out the constituent compounds and testing their effects. The "queen pheromone" of the honey bee allows a single queen to exert precise control over thousands of workers. It induces workers to release a pheromone that causes them to swarm around and protect her, as dramatically demonstrated by this human lure.

Alarm signal

Common earthworm

As it moves, an earthworm produces mucus that helps it slide through its burrow, and binds the soil of the burrow walls together to prevent them from caving in. If under attack, the worm secretes considerably more mucus, and adds an alarm pheromone to it. Other worms ignore normal mucus, but if they detect just a drop of mucus with this pheromone, they move away from the danger rapidly.

Lumbricus terrestris
- Up to 10 in (25 cm) (extended body)
- Soil in Europe; introduced across North America and western Asia.
- Reddish gray, made up of ringlike segments, with some tiny bristles.
- >> 251, 368

ATTRACTIVE TO SOME
Many predators seem to find worms covered in alarm mucus repugnant and spit them out, but some, such as perhaps this fire salamander and the red-sided garter snake, are actually attracted by it.

EXTRACTING ESSENTIAL OILS
This orchid bee is depositing a fatty substance onto an orchid to extract the scent oils—like the *enfleurage* methods once used by perfumers. In return, the flower is pollinated.

Perfume gift

Orchid bee

Apart from humans, orchid bees are the only animals known to blend fragrances into perfumes. Males collect scents from orchids, which they store in special leg pouches. They also collect ingredients from other flowers, fruits, tree sap resin, rotten wood, and even feces, to add depth and complexity to their scent. During courtship the male transfers this concoction to the base of its wings and hovers around the female, wafting it at her. It is believed that the female orchid bee finds a complex perfume most attractive.

Euglossa species
- 5/16–1 1/4 in (0.8–3 cm)
- Tropical and subtropical forest from New Mexico to Argentina.
- Brightly colored, many are metallic green, bronze, or blue-purple. In some, tongue is twice length of body.

Toxic love

Queen butterfly

Many butterflies use pheromones to attract mates, but this species has a particular refinement that enables the female to select the best father for her offspring. The queen butterfly feeds on plants that contain toxic alkaloids, such as milkweed. The male converts these toxins into a substance that he transfers to the female in courtship.

Danaus gilippus
- Wingspan 2 3/4–3 1/4 in (7–8 cm)
- Open sunny areas, including pastures, dunes, waterways in the Southern US, West Indies, Central and South America to Argentina.
- Orange or brown, black wing borders, white spots, black veins on front surface of hind wings.

The more poison the male has, the more attractive he is, because the female incorporates the substance into her eggs, protecting them against predators.

Chemical language

Weaver ant

The weaver ant has a highly sophisticated chemical communication system. For instance, foragers leave a trail pheromone to guide others to food and, if recruiting ants to fetch food, they touch them with their antennae, transferring the food's odor to persuade them to follow. If they encounter an intruder, foragers return for reinforcements and transfer an alarm pheromone to other ants, comprising four chemicals—the first commands "pay attention," the second says "look for the intruder," the third stimulates aggression, and the fourth sounds the attack.

Oecophylla longinoda
- Workers average 1/4 in (6 mm)
- Tropical forest and woodland in sub-Saharan Africa.
- Reddish brown, with well-developed eyes.
- >> 167

Chemical broadcast

Pine engraver beetle

The power of pheromones is all too evident in the damage wrought by engraver beetles and their relatives. Once a beetle has settled on a pine tree (usually one that is already stressed) it sends out a pheromone summoning others to come to the tree to eat and mate, which involves boring into the tree. New arrivals join in the chemical broadcast so that, with each successive wave of newcomers, the signal gets stronger, producing a mass attack that can overwhelm and kill even a healthy tree. The tree contributes to its own downfall—the pheromone is produced using chemical substances extracted from the tree itself.

Ips pini
- 1/16–1/4 in (2–6 mm)
- Pine forest in the southeastern, western, and northern US into Canada.
- Cylindrical body, reddish brown to black, often shiny, with concave back edge to elytra (modified forewings).

HUMAN IMPACT
TRAVELING INVASION

To prevent overcrowding, the pheromone broadcast by the engraver beetle has an upper limit, above which beetles are no longer attracted to the source. But they are still drawn to the area. They land on nearby trees and relaunch their offensive, leading to the death of entire clusters of trees.

Irresistible scent
Magnificent tree frog

The male sex pheromone of the magnificent tree frog was the first to be discovered in anurans. A substance called splendipherin reaches a peak during the breeding season. The female is immediately responsive to this compound, altering her posture, becoming more alert, and moving toward the source.

Litoria splendida

- 4¼ in (10.5 cm)
- Caves, rock crevices, close to human habitation; limited range in northwestern Australia.
- Olive to bright green back, pale underside, white or yellow patches.

UNDER MY SKIN
Male frogs are known to attract mates by calling, but the magnificent tree frog also attracts females with a chemical produced in glands at the front and rear of its head that is secreted through the skin.

Visible smell
Desert iguana

The strongest scents are volatile, which means they can change from liquid to vapor. But since these scents don't last in hot conditions, desert iguanas use "stable" scents to mark their territories. These last for days, but are not strong. However, iguanas' scent marks reflect ultraviolet light, which other iguanas can see clearly.

By investigating these, a desert iguana can tell who has been in its territory. Relatives, neighbors, and potential mates are tolerated, but the scents of strange males prompt an immediate aggressive reaction.

Dipsosaurus dorsalis

- 16 in (40 cm)
- Dry, sandy desert and scrubland, in rock crevices and creosote bush in the southwestern US, northwestern Mexico.
- Pale gray or tan to cream, pale brown netlike pattern on back, bands on tail.

MAKING A MARK
On the underside of each thigh the desert iguana has a row of pores that leave a twin trail of scent over the rocks and dirt wherever it goes, allowing this small animal to lay claim to a large territory.

Chemical masquerade
Red-sided garter snake

As many as 100 male red-sided garter snakes may descend upon one female in response to a pheromone she secretes, forming a writhing mass of bodies called a "mating ball." Each male tries to court the female by rubbing his chin along her back and positioning himself so he is ready to mate with her. At last one will succeed, mate, then mark the female with another pheromone to deter further suitors. Some males, however, have developed the ability to produce small amounts of the female pheromone. This distracts other males, who start to court these disguised males, enabling the masqueraders to get into an advantageous position and win the female. This highly successful deception allows them to achieve 70 percent of all matings.

Thamnophis sirtalis

- 15–36 in (38–91 cm)
- Grassland, scrubland, chaparral, forest, usually near water, in California, and across the US and into Canada.
- Slender, dark olive background color, red bars on sides, bold yellow stripes lengthwise along body.
- » 373

THE RACE FOR A MATE
On emerging from hibernation, there is intense competition between males, as the female red-sided garter snake will only mate with one male in a year.

Stink fights
Ring-tailed lemur

Scent-communication is important for ring-tailed lemurs, who use glandular secretions to both advertise status and mark territory. During the breeding season males in a group compete for access to females using scent as a weapon. The magnificent tail is smothered with scent from various glands and then arched high over the head and flicked at a rival male. The rival will frequently respond in kind, so that both males stand waving their tails at each other until one of them backs down.

TAIL PRIMING
Before a fight, a male lemur combs scent through its tail using a horny spur on the wrist, and wipes the tail across its body, impregnating it with pungent secretions from glands in the wrists and chest.

Lemur catta

- 15½–18 in (39–46 cm)
- Dry forest in south and southwestern Madagascar.
- Brown-gray fur with reddish tinge, dark triangular eye patch, black and white striped tail.
- » 412, 436

Social odors
Lion

Smell is used to reinforce bonds between members of a pride of lions and assert its claim to an area. Pride members nuzzle and rub against each other to exchange scents, and patrolling males regularly stop to spray bushes and prominent landmarks. Spray-marking an area is common after an aggressive encounter with other lions or when leaving a kill.

Panthera leo

- 5½–8¼ ft (1.7–2.5 m)
- Savanna plains and woodland in Sub-Saharan Africa, Gir Forest of northwest India.
- Short tawny fur with tail tuft. Male larger than female, with mane of variable color.
- » 236, 413

SENSING SEXUAL RECEPTIVITY
The male lion produces a spectacular grimace when sniffing a lioness in heat. Called the Flehmen response, this transfers hormonal information to an organ in the roof of the mouth, and is widely used in mammals to test the receptivity of females.

Team players
Dwarf mongoose

Mingling odors is a common way for groups of animals to maintain solidarity. The dwarf mongoose is intensely social, and both related and unrelated individuals in a pack help to raise the young of the alpha pair (usually the oldest male and female). Pack members jointly scent-mark objects in their home range, especially near the den, by rubbing an anal gland on a vertical surface, with an anal drag (often preceded by lifting a hind leg) on a horizontal surface, or by performing a handstand with treading motions to release scent into the air. They also anoint other members of the pack, including offspring, by rubbing them with anal and cheek-gland secretions to label them as part of the team.

Helogale parvula
⬌ 7–11 in (18–28 cm)
◐ Common in savanna, preferably with numerous termite mounds for refuge, in East and southern Africa.
▭ Smallest mongoose, thick brown fur with fine red or black hairs, small eyes and ears, long-clawed front feet.
≫ 320

Signposting the way
European otter

Otters leave piles of feces or "spraints" on prominent rocks and logs to advertise their territory and mark their possession of resources. Although solitary animals for the most part, the territories of males and females overlap and spraint marks allow them to build up a map of the movements of their neighbors. In the Shetland Islands and areas of northern Scotland, otters forage exclusively at sea but still need freshwater to drink. Here, piles of spraint are built up into highly noticeable signposts by generations of otters. One spraint station leads to another, so that otters newly returned to land are never far from a series of stations leading them to freshwater.

Lutra lutra
⬌ 21½–35 in (55–90 cm)
◐ Rivers, lakes, estuaries, and sheltered rocky coasts in Europe, Asia, and northern Africa.
▭ Carnivore with sleek brown fur, thick tapering tail, webbed feet.

SURPRISINGLY SWEET
Otter feces may contain fish scales and bones from their last meal, but are often described as smelling like newly mown hay or jasmine tea. With age, they fade in color but retain a sweet, musky scent.

Two-part message
Brown hyena

Brown hyenas live in clans of four to fourteen individuals who typically forage alone but share a communal den. They mark their huge home ranges by pasting grass stems with anal-pouch secretions, especially in the heart of their range. At one time, 20,000 pastings may be potent across a home range of 90–185 square miles (235–480 square kilometers). The brown hyena deposits two different secretions in turn, one above the other. A white pomade lasts for more than a month and probably functions to establish and maintain territorial rights. The second, a black watery secretion, fades within hours. It is likely that this is addressed to other clan members, telling them who has passed that way and how long ago, so that they can avoid foraging in areas that have already been covered.

FREQUENT PASTINGS
A hyena pauses two or three times per one-third a square mile (one square kilometer) to mark its territory with anal secretions.

Hyaena brunnea
⬌ 4¼ ft (1.3 m)
◐ Dry savanna and desert in southwest and southern Africa, including Skeleton Coast.
▭ Doglike, with broad muzzle, dark brown shaggy coat with straw-colored mantle, pointed ears, striped legs.

TWO-TONE PASTING
A hyena secretes a white territory-claiming paste, then a black one to communicate with other pack members.

Information depots
White rhinoceros

White rhinos are the most social of all rhinos. Females and their young associate in groups of up to 14 animals. Adult bulls, however, are solitary. The dominant bulls are territorial and regularly mark their territory by wiping their horns on bushes or on the ground, then scrape-marking with all four feet, and finally by spraying the spot three to five times with urine. Patrolling males urine-mark about ten times an hour. They also maintain 20–30 middens (dunghills), usually on the boundaries of their territory, where they always defecate, using slow, deliberate kicks before and after defecating to excavate and scatter the pile. Females, young rhinos, and nonterritorial males add their own deposits to the heap (without kicking), as though they are showing their allegiance. The piles become such conspicuous features of the landscape that other animals also use them as message stations, for posting their own scent messages.

Ceratotherium simum
⬌ 5½–6 ft (1.7–1.8 cm)
◐ Grassland with trees and water in southern and East Africa; once widespread, now in scattered populations.
▭ Slate gray to brown pleated skin, horned snout, wide square mouth, hump on neck.

Aquatic scent marks
West Indian manatee

Dispersed manatees may use underwater scent marks to pass on information. On arriving at the mouth of the Crystal river in Florida in October, some individuals rub up against prominent stones or submerged logs, rubbing with genitals, eyes, armpits, and chin—all spots where glandular secretions occur. They use the same sites each year and, if a rubbing post disappears, they find a new object nearby. Females rub more than males, perhaps to advertise their sexual receptivity to roaming males.

Trichechus manatus
⬌ 8¼–14¾ ft (2.5–4.5 m)
◐ Shallow coastal waters, estuaries, rivers, and lagoons in the southeastern US to northeastern South America and Caribbean.
▭ Large, streamlined marine mammal, with gray-brown skin which may harbor growths of algae.

Visual signals

Vivid patterns, elaborate ornaments, specialized postures, and facial expressions make bold and instant statements. For almost all creatures, visual signals are the fastest way of sending a message. But there are distinct disadvantages, too—they only work at close range and can sometimes draw unwanted attention.

Uniforms and badges

Distinctive colors and patterns identify animals to their own kind and to species they interact with, which is important when several related species live in the same habitat. The sexes of a species may look different, and traits that suggest vigor—an elaborate tail or impressive antlers—can become exaggerated as species evolve. Some markings act as badges of social status. The black bib of the sparrow is a status symbol. The larger the bib, the higher the rank.

PROFESSIONAL PERK
The blue of this wrasse is seen in other "cleaner fish." Predators identify the color with the fishes that rid them of parasites and dead tissue.

Body language

Some body language is universal. Animals make themselves appear as large as possible to seem more of a threat, and attract attention by waving arms or other appendages. When attracting a mate, postures help display desirable traits—the courtship dances of many birds display their plumage to full effect. Among social mammals in particular, postures or gestures can communicate much information, and larger monkeys and apes go a step further, using a range of facial expressions.

MALE MANDRILL
Surging hormones produce intense colors in this primate, indicating status. Facial expressions convey more immediate information.

Light shows

Some animals that live in the dark are bioluminescent (they emit light). An astonishing 80 percent of marine creatures emit light in order to find mates, avoid predators, lure food, and group together. Indeed, perhaps the most abundant vertebrate on Earth is a bioluminescent fish called the benttooth bristlemouth. Some tiny crustaceans are able to synchronize their flashes to produce breathtaking light shows.

SPARKLING LIGHTS
Among the most spectacular of underwater light shows is the spinning wheel of light produced by some jellyfish medusae, such as this *Thysanostoma loriferum*.

Intermittent signals

Some visual signals can be switched on and off to provide specific information. Many animals change their appearance when ready to breed, but sudden visual signals can be even more noticeable. Abruptly raising crown feathers, extending flaps of skin, swishing tails, or flashing colored patches can signal aggression, attract a mate, sound the alarm, or keep a group together.

INSTANT COLOR
Most of the time, the brightly colored flap of skin under the brown anole lizard's neck is folded away to avoid attracting attention from predators. But it can be displayed quickly whenever necessary.

SHAKE A LEG
To attract a female, this tufted male jumping spider waves his first pair of legs vigorously while swinging his abdomen from side to side.

Dancing for a partner
Jumping spiders

Male jumping spiders of the species *Maevia inclemens* come in two forms, each with its own distinctive courtship display. The tufted type begins his display ³⁄₈ in (9 mm) from the female and waves his legs in the air, while the gray type gets to within ¹⁄₈ in (3 mm) of a female before crouching low and sidling back and forth with his first two pairs of legs pointed forward in a triangular shape.

Jumping spiders have excellent vision and can see ultraviolet light. Males in many of the tropical species have brightly colored hair and hair tufts, often conspicuous in ultraviolet light, which are displayed as part of their elaborate courtship rituals.

Maevia inclemens
- ⬌ Male ³⁄₁₆–¹⁄₄ in (5–7 mm), female ¹⁄₄–³⁄₈ in (7–10 mm)
- ◐ Throughout the eastern and northern US.
- ▢ Male in two forms: tufted form with black body, white legs, three tufts on body; gray form with white stripe above eyes. Female brown with yellow stripe below eyes.
- ≫ 333

Giant claw
Porcelain fiddler crab

The male porcelain fiddler crab has a colossal claw that can weigh up to 40 percent of the crab's body weight. It is used both to intimidate other males and to wave at passing females in a bid to entice them into their burrows to mate. Competition is intense and males frequently cluster around a female. With her 360° vision, she has a wraparound view of waving claws to choose from. Both claw size and wave rate demonstrate vigor and attract females. Some crabs cheat—if a male loses his claw, he grows a flimsy fake which doesn't take much energy to wave but works well to impress females.

Uca annulipes
- ⬌ ³⁄₄–1¹⁄₄ in (2–3 cm)
- ◐ Intertidal mud flats, salt marshes, and mangroves in South and East Africa, Asia.
- ▢ Small reddish crab. Male with one normal and one greatly enlarged claw.

Light show
Ostracods

After dark these tiny crustaceans perform amazing light shows. They release a cocktail of chemicals from tiny nozzles that reacts with the oxygen in sea water to produce puffs of light. They use light as a means of protection, producing brilliant bomb clouds of light to startle predators. They also use it to communicate with each other. Males move rapidly through the water, painting dotted trails of blue light to attract females. Each species has its own light-show pattern—it may be very short or very long, and move upward, downward, laterally, or obliquely, much like patterns traced with a sparkler.

Cypridina species
- ⬌ Average ¹⁄₁₆ in (1 mm), up to 1¹⁄₄ in (3 cm)
- ◐ Marine, brackish, and fresh water worldwide.
- ▢ Tiny crustacean encased in clamlike carapace.

Flashing lights
Genji firefly

Fireflies are beetles that produce a glowing light that is used to flash messages in a way similar to Morse code. The yellowish light is produced by a chemical reaction involving proteins called luciferins, an enzyme catalyst, oxygen, and energy from food. After dark in summer, male genji fireflies fly and flash in a distinctive fashion to attract females. Other males are also drawn to these flashes and gradually synchronize their pattern to create swathes of pulsing light. Females follow these signals, emitting an irregular pattern of flashes of their own. On encountering a female, a male perches on a branch, changes his flash pattern and approaches her in order to mate.

Lucida cruciata
- ⬌ ³⁄₈–³⁄₄ in (1–2 cm)
- ◐ Along riverbanks and waterways in Japan.
- ▢ Black beetle.

Threat postures
Gray reef shark

Several species of shark use body language as a warning. When threatened, the gray reef shark produces exaggerated swimming movements, such as zigzagging, rolling, and spiraling up and down in the water, and also adopts an S-shaped posture, lifting its snout, arching its back, dropping the pectoral fins, and bending its body to one side. In intense displays a shark adopts an exaggerated posture and swims in a compressed S-shaped pattern or even in a figure of eight. The more intense the display, the more likely the shark will attack.

Carcharhinus amblyrhynchos
- ⬌ Up to 5¹⁄₂ ft (1.7 m)
- ◐ Coral reefs and atolls throughout Indo-Pacific Ocean, including Red Sea.
- ▢ Dark gray above, white underside. Some dark fin tips, black margin on tail fin.

GROUP FEEDING
Gray reef sharks are social creatures. They gather in groups on the edges of reefs where they feed on fishes, squid, and crustaceans. Although they are not endangered, their numbers have declined.

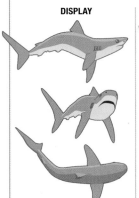

DISPLAY   **NORMAL SWIMMING**

CLEAR WARNING POSTURE
The left-hand column shows the gray reef shark's S-shaped warning posture, with nose up, fins down, and body bent to one side. The right-hand column shows the shark's normal posture.

Different uniforms

Butterflyfishes

When closely related species live in the same habitat, distinctive markings act as a uniform, making individuals conspicuous to their own kind. Butterflyfishes share the same basic body shape but have bold patterns in shades of blue, yellow, black, white, orange, and red. Identified on this reef (see right) are the pennant butterflyfish, with its long dorsal fin and stripes; the millet seed, with its yellow fin and black spot; and the chevron butterflyfish, with its pale body chevrons.

NOW YOU SEE ME...
Up close, markings help to identify species of butterflyfish, but at only 3 ft 3 in–6½ ft (1–2 m), they break up the outline of the fish to camouflage them.

Family Chaetodontidae
- ◧ 2¾–6 in (7–15 cm), with one species up to 9 in (23 cm)
- ◔ Coral reefs in all tropical waters, but largest number in western Pacific Ocean and Indian Ocean.
- ◫ Round, with compressed body and slightly convex forehead. Most species with brightly colored markings.

Handstand

Great crested newt

Like many newts and salamanders, the great crested newt uses both visual signals and pheromones to communicate. On encountering a female during the breeding season, the male performs a handstand while waving his tail in the air like a flag and wafting an attractive chemical substance toward her. If he is successful, this persuades the female to accept the sperm package that he drops on the floor of the pond at the end of his display. She picks it up in her cloaca (the chamber into which the genital tract opens) and, a few days later, starts to lay up to 300 eggs; using her hind legs, she carefully wraps each egg in a leaf in order to protect it.

Triturus cristatus
- ◧ Up to 6 in (15 cm)
- ◔ Pools and ponds across northern Europe, from Britain to Urals.
- ◫ Orange-yellow underneath with black blotches. Males with white or gray stripe along tail and jagged crest in breeding season.

LOOK AT ME
During this impressive handstand, the male shows off his crest and striped tail, which he waves to a potential mate.

Sign language

Panamanian golden frog

Although it calls like other frogs, this frog's native habitat is near noisy waterfalls, so it has developed a system of waving. When two males compete for territory or females, they each raise a bright yellow forearm and sometimes a foot, until one backs down. Males also wave away females that don't appear ready to mate, but allow fertile females to enter their territory unhindered. However, fertile females turn the tables and wave aggressively at males. If one approaches despite her warning, she mates with him, but does not if he is intimidated. So in this case, waving seems to be a way of testing the male's resolve.

Atelopus zeteki
- ◧ 14–19½ in (35–50 cm)
- ◔ Streams in rain forest and cloud forest in western-central Panama. Extinct in wild, few hundred in captivity.
- ◫ Bright golden-yellow with large black spots on back. Pointed snout.

THE LAST WAVE
The Panamanian golden frog is now extinct in the wild due to an outbreak of chytridiomycosis, a particularly virulent fungal disease that is sweeping through Panama.

Frilly display

Frilled lizard

During the breeding season, the male frilled lizard performs displays to claim territory. He lashes his tail against the bark of a tree to produce audible thumps, then raises his upper body in a push-up, following up with a series of partial erections of his magnificent frill. Such displays are performed most frequently in the morning and are not usually directed at any particular individual, but if another male doesn't take heed of the warnings and strays too close, a furious battle ensues. Prior to combat the males fan out their frills to the maximum and open their mouths, exposing a pink or yellow lining, before lunging at each other head-on, interlocking jaws.

Both sexes also employ the full frill display when cornered, or when handled by humans. One was reported displaying in response to a car traveling some 165 ft (50 m) away.

Chlamydosaurus kingii
- ◧ Up to 35 in (90 cm)
- ◔ Hot dry forest in northern Australia and southern Papua New Guinea.
- ◫ Uniformly bright golden-yellow with several large black spots on back. Pointed snout.

USING ITS ASSETS
Relative to its size, the frilled lizard has one of the largest visual displays of any animal. The huge flap of skin attached to its neck can be fanned out into a most dramatic Dracula–like collar some 12 in (30 cm) across.

Bowing and pointing

Northern gannet

These seabirds live in noisy, crowded colonies where nest sites are at a premium. Defense of nests can lead to vicious fights that may result in severe injury, such as the loss of an eye. But gannets manage to avoid many disputes using a range of ritualized visual signals. "Bowing," which is performed repeatedly, seems to be a significant signal of ownership. Standing in its nest, the gannet "bites" the ground at its feet, with wings slightly raised from its body and tail pointing upward. This develops into proper "bowing," with head inverted and bill to feet, and wings arched open. This conspicuous movement, accompanied by a loud call, seems to provide a way of reinforcing ownership of the nest without having to involve overt aggression.

Morus bassanus

- ◨ 35–39¾ in (89–102 cm)
- ◈ North Atlantic. Oceanic, often well offshore. Breeds on sea cliffs.
- ▢ Large white seabird with pointed tail, black wing tips, head tinged with orange buff.

WELCOME HOME
Northern gannet pairs greet each other by standing breast to breast with wings open and bills crossed, then indulge in mutual preening.

BICKERING
Nests of compacted grass, seaweed, and droppings are often reused year after year and are defended fiercely. Stretching forward with bill open, or ritualized sparring by jabbing bills at neighbors, are common.

CLAIMING TERRITORY
The bird to the right in this picture asserts its claim to its nest site by showing a mild form of "bowing" toward a neighboring pair.

Breeding pairs of gannets work together closely to raise their chicks, and negotiate parental duties using a clear visual dialogue. When one bird wants to leave the nest it signals its intention by "skypointing." Often both will do this simultaneously, but neither will leave until one shows willingness to stay by lowering its head. Only then will the other bird depart, safe in the knowledge that the nest remains protected. At the changing of the guard, the pair reassert ownership with "bowing" displays before settling down or bonding with breasts together and bills crossed.

TAKING TURNS
There is no argument here about who is staying and who is going. The bird with its bill pointing skyward will leave the nest to feed, while its partner tucks its head in and down, indicating it will stay and guard the nest.

Mixed messages

Grey heron

Grey herons build nests of sticks gathered by males and arranged by females. Even in a well-established pair, each is possessive of its personal space. Reunions at the nest can be tense, with birds adopting a range of hostile postures, such as the "arch neck" and "forward stretch," while raising their crests and body plumes, before settling down amicably.

Ardea cinerea

◨ 35 in–3ft 3 in (90–98 cm)

◉ Rivers, lakes, marshes, and estuaries in Europe, Asia, and sub-Sharan Africa, including Madagascar.

▢ Ash-gray above, whitish below. Adults have long daggerlike bill, and white head with black "eyebrow" ending in long slender plumes.

≫ 268

RUFFLED FEATHERS
In response to the male's "alighting display," the female (on the left) raises her plume and feathers, indicating readiness to defend her nest and chicks.

Feather raising

Palm cockatoo

These social birds use their crests in a range of visual displays. In territorial disputes they raise their crests while advancing toward an intruder with deliberate steps followed by rhythmic foot stomping. Males also raise their crests in courtship displays while enhancing the color of the bare reddish patch of skin on their cheeks and calling excitedly to a potential mate.

Probosciger aterrimus

◨ 19½–27 in (49–68 cm)

◉ Eucalyptus and savanna woodland in Queensland, Australia, New Guinea, and Indonesia.

▢ Large black parrot with naked red cheeks and black erectile crest.

BLUSHING CHEEKS
When agitated or excited, the shade of the red cheek patches deepens—a trait that makes this species unique among cockatoos.

Blowing the whistle

White-winged chough

These cooperative birds live in family groups of 4–20, comprising a single breeding pair and their offspring. To find food, the white-winged chough must search through leaf litter, and can only raise chicks if all members of the group assist in this arduous task. In return for helping to feed their siblings, juveniles pick up important skills and earn a chance to inherit the territory.

But when times are hard, hungry juveniles have been observed faking the gesture of giving food to chicks and eating it themselves later on. In order to keep all members of the group in line, a policing system has been developed, so that any bird caught cheating is publicly identified by being subjected to a spectacular "shaming" display, in which the whistle-blower puffs up its feathers, waves its tail slowly, and, at the same time, opens and closes its bill.

Corcorax melanorhamphos

◨ 19½–27 in (49–68 cm)

◉ Mostly on ground in wetter areas of open forest and woodland throughout eastern and southeastern Australia.

▢ Black, crowlike bird with red eyes and white wing patches visible in flight.

BOGGLING WITH INDIGNATION
The culmination of the white-winged chough's "shaming" display is "boggling," in which the eyes bulge out of their sockets. These two shocking scarlet orbs create a striking finale.

Crowning glory

Royal flycatcher

Usually inconspicuous in the forest, both sexes of the royal flycatcher have a concealed crest that can be raised into a magnificent fan-shaped crown, which is used in both courtship and aggressive encounters. When threatened, a bird may open its crest slowly and wave its head from side to side while opening its mouth. It has been suggested that the crown mimics a large gaping mouth, intensifying an aggressive message.

Onychorhynchus coronatus

◨ 6½–7 in (16.5–18 cm)

◉ Moist tropical and subtropical forest from Mexico to Brazil.

▢ Brown above with small spots on wing-coverts; greenish yellow below. Concealed erectile crest, red in males, yellow-orange in females.

REGAL DISPLAY
Spreading his scarlet diadem to the fullest, a male may try to impress a female by waving his head rapidly so that the feathers quiver.

Open mouthed

Blue tit

Blue tits raise broods of up to 10 chicks in cup-shaped nests, and both parents carry out the gargantuan task of feeding their young 100 food items (mostly caterpillars) each per day. In order to solicit food from their parents, nestlings perform vigorous postural displays, flapping their wings while calling loudly, and opening their bills to reveal brightly colored mouths. They beg more intensely when hungry, but also in competition with their nest mates. So, the larger the brood, the more insistently the nestlings beg, even if their harried parents provision them at the same rate. Such gaping displays are common among nestlings of many species of birds.

Parus caeruleus

◨ 4¼–4½ in (10.5–12 cm)

◉ Deciduous and mixed woodland and yards throughout Europe, Middle East, parts of Asia, and northwest Africa.

▢ Yellow underparts with blue wings, tail, and crown. Adults have white cheeks with thin black eyestripe.

HIGHLY VISIBLE
Research shows that nestling gapes reflect UV light, especially from the flanges (rims), creating contrast with their background for maximum visibility.

YAWN THREAT
A huge gape of 150° displays razor-sharp lower canines, used for fighting, that can be up to 19½ in (50 cm) long. This threat can be accompanied by water scooping, lunging, head shaking, rearing, roaring, and grunting.

Weapons on display
Hippopotamus

When foraging at night, hippos tend to be solitary, but when wallowing in water during the day, they spend time in herds comprising 15–20 individuals. These may be either bachelor males or territorial bulls with females and their young. Territorial bulls tolerate other bulls so long as they behave submissively, but hippos have a short fuse and can be highly aggressive, especially in the dry season when wallows dry up. Serious injuries are common. Ritualized threat displays, in which bulls throw back their heads and yawn widely, reduce instances of fighting. The slightest disturbance in a wallow can set off a wave of yawning and wheeze-honking.

Hippopotamus amphibius

↔ 10¾–11½ ft (3.3–3.45 m)

◐ Grassland and scrubland near wallows, lakes, and rivers in West, Central, East, and Southern Africa.

▥ Barrel-shaped, with short legs, and large head and muzzle; gray-brown to blue-black, with pinkish underside.

≫ 192

Follow the leader
Sun-tailed monkey

Primates' tails are designed to give them balance when leaping through the canopy or purchase while moving, but many species also use them to signal to other members of their group. Sun-tailed monkeys live in rain forest, traveling in troops of 5–15 individuals. Very little sunlight penetrates to the forest floor, so a bold signal is needed to keep the group together. This is provided by the white tail with its orange tip. The dominant male keeps his tail vertical, the orange tip flicking like a banner as he leads his group through the shadowy, dense undergrowth.

Cecopithecus solatus

◀▶ 19¹/₂–28 in (50–70 cm)

◉ Very limited distribution in lowland tropical rain forest in Gabon.

▥ Dark gray back, chestnut-orange saddle, white throat, and yellow-orange tipped tail. Male has blue scrotum.

Expressive gestures
Chimpanzee

Chimpanzees' bodies and faces act like billboards advertising their intentions. Because they live in multimale communities, males are constantly vying for power and access to females. Dramatic displays by high-ranking males help make them appear as large and as intimidating to other chimps as possible.

Chimpanzees reach out to each other with arm outstretched and palm upward in a gesture used to beg for food, ask for reassurance, appease a dominant individual, or in reconciliation. Equally, they may approach a dominant animal while bobbing and bowing in an exaggerated manner, or crouch down and present their backs in a pose similar to a female presenting before mating.

Pan troglodytes

◀▶ 29–37 in (73–95 cm)

◉ Gallery forest, rain forest, and woodland savanna across equatorial Africa. Once widespread, but now severely reduced.

▥ Ape with black hair, sometimes tinged with gray or brown, infants have white tail tufts. Faces darken with age.

≫ 174, 247, 460, 465, 480–81, 482–83

STRIKE A POSE
During conflicts, an adult male chimpanzee bristles his hair (called "pilorection") and may well stand on two legs while swaying back and forth and shaking a branch. He then follows this by crashing through the surrounding vegetation in a dramatic charging display, which may be accompanied by slapping the ground, dragging branches, and hurling rocks.

> Chimpanzee gestures are context based, **versatile, and voluntary.** Human language may have evolved from similar gestures.

POUT
The flexibility of chimps' lips allows for a range of facial expressions. A pout expresses anxiety, frustration, or distress, and is often used by infants.

FEAR GRIN
This important, nonthreatening signal given by a nervous individual can help diffuse an explosive situation, and may well be the origin of our smile.

PLAY FACE
This relaxed face is used in play, sometimes exaggerated by head shaking, especially when older individuals approach timid youngsters to play.

CLEAR INTENTIONS
This highly conspicuous lip flip is used in tense situations and conveys hostility. It can be a sign of fear but, when combined with an assertive stance, it acts as a warning.

Making a face
Gelada

Staring and flashing pale eyelids are ways in which many monkeys signal aggression. Male geladas also do a unique "lip flip" in uneasy encounters with other males. They defend harems of 3–20 females but may gather in herds of hundreds, so blatant signals are important. Both sexes have bare red skin on their chests. In females, this becomes swollen with bumps when they are sexually receptive.

Theropithecus gelada

◀▶ 19¹/₂–30 in (50–75 cm)

◉ Cliffs and high-plateau grassland in Ethiopia.

▥ Adult male much larger than female, with long, flowing mane. Both sexes have hourglass-shaped patch of red skin on chest, very pronounced in male.

Intimidation techniques
Olive baboon

Olive baboons live in troops of about 30–40 individuals of both sexes. Males move between troops, competing for dominance and acceptance from resident females. Yawning can be a sign of tension, but is usually aggressive, especially if accompanied by audible tooth grinding, which sounds like a knife being sharpened on a whetstone.

Papio anubis

◀▶ 21–33 in (53–85 cm)

◉ Semi-desert, scrubland, savanna, woodland, gallery forest, and rain forest across equatorial Africa.

▥ Brown-olive coat with dark face. Adult male much larger than female, with thick ruff of hair around neck.

≫ 436

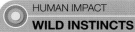

STATUS SIGNAL
The wolf to the left indicates his dominance by standing tall, with his tail and ears raised. The subordinate individual, to the right, cowers with tail tucked under and ears back in a clearly submissive posture.

Body language

Gray wolf

Members of a wolf pack work as a team to hunt, defend territory, and raise pups. There is a strict dominance hierarchy, centered around a single breeding pair, but a constant dialogue of body language largely prevents aggression. A raised tail and ears assert dominance, while lowering the tail is a sign of submission. Tails are such important communication devices that many members of the dog family, including jackals, foxes, and dingoes, have a black or white tail tip to make tail movements conspicuous.

If it feels challenged, a dominant wolf may raise its hackles and add a direct threat by drawing back its upper lips to expose powerful canines. To diffuse the tension, the subordinate responds by cowering, lowering its tail, and sometimes rolling over to expose its belly.

As with words, signals can be combined to produce many different and complex meanings. If it thinks an attack is imminent, a low-ranking wolf may give a mixture of signals: crouched with its tail low and ears flattened, but snarling and with the hair on its neck erect, indicating that it is submissive, but also willing to defend itself.

Canis lupus
- 3 ft 3 in–5 ft (1–1.5 m)
- Forest, taiga, tundra, desert, plains, and mountains in North America, Europe, Middle East, and Asia.
- Large dog with coat color from gray to tawny buff, but can also be white, red, or black; underside paler.
- >> 437

COMBINING SIGNALS
This snarl could indicate aggression, but if combined with signals such as a tucked-in tail and pinned-back ears, it expresses defensive submission.

HUMAN IMPACT
WILD INSTINCTS

Dogs retain much of their wolf ancestry and use many of the same signals. Despite centuries of domestication, many wolf-pup behaviors remain. The "play/prey bow," seen here, is an invitation to play and may have evolved from a crouched hunting posture. The dog raises its bottom and may wag its tail to signal friendly intention before pouncing.

Blowing balloons

Hooded seal

Male hooded seals compete for females during the breeding season with bizarre aggressive displays. In early adulthood, males develop an enlargement of the nasal cavity that hangs down in front of their upper lip. This is inflated to form a black "hood" (see below). The nostril lining can be blown out to form a red balloon (right).

Cystophora cristata
- 7¼–8¼ ft (2.2–2.5 m)
- Far North Atlantic Ocean, especially off Greenland. Breeds on heavy pack ice.
- Both sexes gray, with large black blotches and black heads. Adult males have "hoods."

RED SIGNAL
As a sign of aggression, the lining of one nostril is forced out through the opposite nostril, blowing up the nasal membrane like a red balloon that makes an attention grabbing "ping" sound when shaken.

Tail raising

White-tailed deer

Although scent plays a key role in communication between deer, many species also use visual signals. When fleeing from danger, white-tailed deer use their large white tails as a flag to warn the rest of the herd and keep it together, while simultaneously notifying the predator that it has been spotted. Males use a range of postures in hostile situations, such as standing on their hind legs and pawing with the forelegs, or presenting a broadside view of their bodies in order to appear as large as possible.

Odocoileus virginianus
- 5–6½ ft (1.5–2 m)
- Forested habitats of all kinds from southern Canada to northern South America.
- Reddish brown in summer, gray-brown in winter; throat, belly, and underside of tail white; male has antlers.

Sound

Since sound travels quickly, it is a highly effective and versatile way to communicate. Animals produce an amazing array of sounds for a wide variety of reasons, from the simple mating chirps of crickets to the defensive communal howls of coyotes, and the sophisticated vocabulary of chimpanzees to the minute alarm calls of ants. Sounds can carry simple or complex messages, over very short or incredibly long distances.

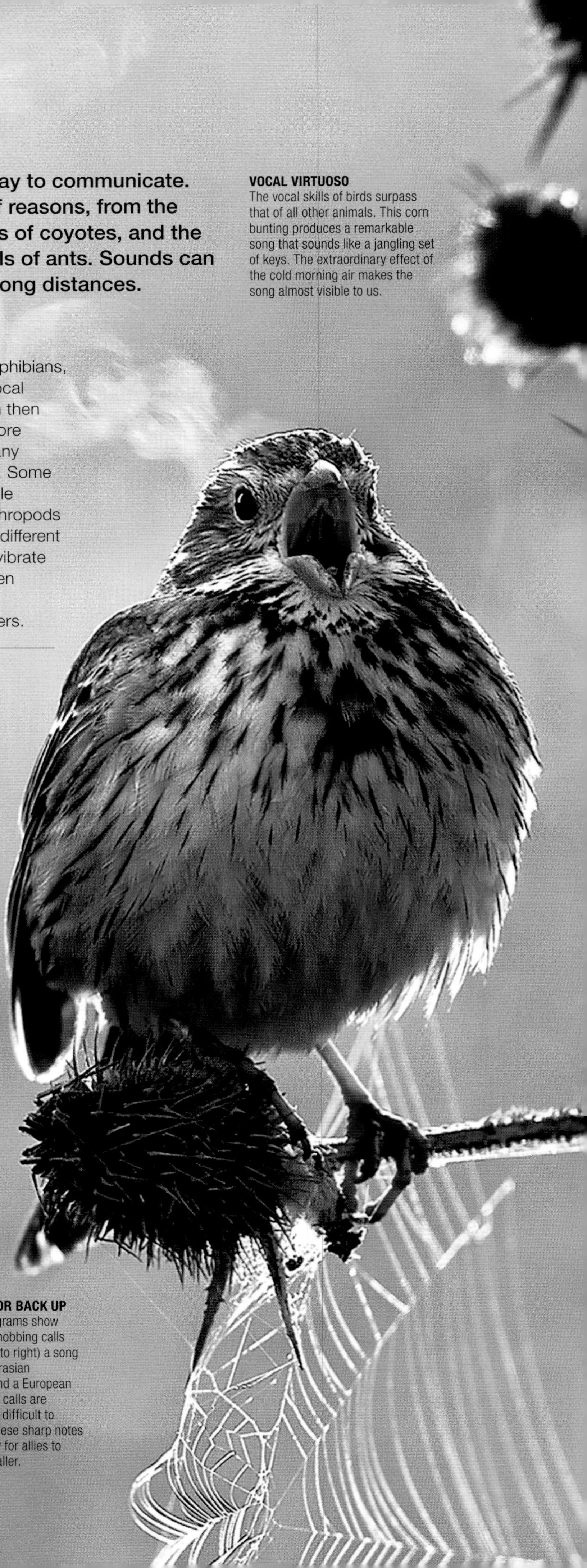

PROJECTING SOUND
Common chimpanzees (left) greet other members of the troop with individual "pant hoots." Male dainty green tree frogs (below) amplify their mating calls through their vocal sacs.

Making a noise

Audible displays are enormously diverse. Amphibians, reptiles, birds, and mammals can all make vocal sounds by expelling air from the lungs, which then passes a vibrating mechanism and one or more resonating chambers. However, there are many other ways in which animals generate sound. Some fishes expel air from their swim bladders, while others scrape parts of their gills together. Arthropods commonly use stridulation (rubbing together different body parts), and some snap membranes or vibrate their wings. Vertebrates that can vocalize often produce sounds by other means, such as drumming trees or snapping their wing feathers.

Sound and environment

Low-pitched sound travels farthest because it can pass through obstacles without being scattered. Forest animals, therefore, tend to have deeper calls, while animals in open environments have higher-pitched calls. Temperature and wind are also significant. At dawn, the air is cooler and there is less wind, so birdsong will carry up to 20 times farther than at noon. Liquids have a much higher density than gases, so sound travels four times faster in water than in the air, making effective long-distance communication possible.

SOFAR CHANNEL
The SOFAR (sound fixing and ranging) channel is a layer of the ocean where the speed of sound is slowest, due to the effect of lowering temperature and rising pressure. As sound waves are drawn to the area where they will travel the slowest, they are trapped in this channel and travel for hundreds of miles.

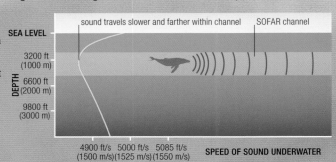

sound travels slower and farther within channel   SOFAR channel

SEA LEVEL

3200 ft (1000 m)

DEPTH

6600 ft (2000 m)

9800 ft (3000 m)

4900 ft/s   5000 ft/s   5085 ft/s
(1500 m/s)(1525 m/s)(1550 m/s)   **SPEED OF SOUND UNDERWATER**

Decoding signals

Vocal calls are designed to carry specific information. Low-pitched, short sounds often communicate simple, assertive messages. Calls that contain varied volume and pitch may encode more complex information, but don't carry as well. This is the reason that contact calls often start with an introduction of low notes to draw attention, like tapping a glass before a speech. Many animal alarm calls are quite similar. They tend to be short, high-pitched, and fade quickly, making them hard for a predator to locate.

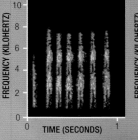
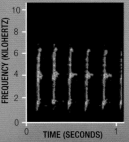
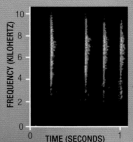

CALLING FOR BACK UP
These sonograms show the similar mobbing calls of (from left to right) a song thrush, a Eurasian blackbird, and a European robin. Alarm calls are purposefully difficult to locate but these sharp notes make it easy for allies to locate the caller.

FREQUENCY (KILOHERTZ)

10 8 6 4 2 0

TIME (SECONDS)

0   1

Hostile hissing

King baboon spider

The second largest of all African spiders, king baboons are impressively powerful hunters. They can tackle prey at least as large as themselves, including scorpions, other spiders, frogs, reptiles, and even the chicks of ground-nesting birds. They are aggressive and like several other large spiders, can produce a raspy hissing sound to warn off potential attackers. In an impressive display, they bare their fangs and rear up on their hind legs, then stridulate by rubbing the hairs on their front legs together. This motion produces an audible hiss, which the spider will continue to make until the threat has passed.

Citharischius crawshayi
- 4¹⁄₂–8 in (12–20 cm)
- Dry scrubland of eastern Central Africa.
- Large tarantula, covered in velvety brown-orange hairs. Females larger than males.

Country music

Common field grasshopper

Mature field grasshoppers appear in late June to July, sunning themselves in the morning before becoming active. Males attract females by "stridulating"—rubbing their legs against their forewings to produce chirps. The male field grasshopper produces a series of short, monotonous chirps repeated every two seconds. Rivals in the vicinity respond in order to maintain spacing, calling back and forth in a chorus. A tympanal membrane, located in the middle ear, detects the sound and is sensitive to changes in pulse rates, and durations, but not to the frequency. Different grasshopper species have different stridulation frequencies, but in each, the tympanum is probably tuned to one specific frequency, making them almost "deaf" to each other's songs.

Chorthippus brunneus
- ⁵⁄₈–1 in (1.8–2.4 cm)
- Widespread in dry grassy habitats throughout Europe, Asia and North Africa.
- Variable mix of pale brown and green. Mature males have orange-tipped abdomen.

LEG RUBBING
The inner side of the male's femur has small, peglike projections for the purpose of stridulating. The field grasshopper is distinctive as it has relatively few pegs compared to other species.

Love songs

Fruit fly

There are thousands of species of fruit fly, which share many similar characteristics. They are not social insects and only meet when attracted to the same food source, where they mate and lay eggs. A prelude to mating is a species-specific "song" produced by males. They make this sound by vibrating their wings. The power of this pulsed sound is so minute that a male has to be within ³⁄₁₆ in (5 mm) of a female for her to detect it. He sings by holding one wing out horizontally and vibrating it as he circles her, staying close to the featherlike receptors or "aristae" on her antennae. These are sensitive to the velocity of air particles and if the pattern of pulses is correct she will spread her wings to allow him to mount. Unlike most *Drosophila*, the males of this species possess distinctive, broadened heads. In addition to "singing," the males also engage in head-to-head combat to compete over females.

Drosophila heteroneura
- 3 in (6.5 cm)
- Endemic to Hawaii.
- Yellow-brown body; transverse rings on abdomen. Males have distinctive, broadened heads.

Courting cacophony

Oyster toadfish

These strange bottom dwellers produce a unique deep hum during the breeding season by contracting a sonic muscle against their swim bladder. This muscle can vibrate nearly 200 times a second, creating a sound so penetrating that it has been known to keep inhabitants of houseboats awake at night. After building a nest, often using decayed wood or old tin cans, males make their incredible foghorn sound. This attracts females, who swim into the nest to lay their large, adhesive eggs. They depart quickly, leaving the male to fertilize the eggs and care for the young.

Opsanus tau
- 12–15¹⁄₂ in (30–40 cm)
- Shallow, rocky waters along Atlantic coast of North America from the West Indies to Cape Cod.
- Large, flat head, fleshy flaps around mouth, and tapering yellow body. Possesses ability to change color to blend in with the ocean floor.

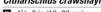

Dinner bell

Leaf-cutter ant

Most ant species are capable of producing high-pitched squeaks that are just audible to human ears. They do this by rubbing a scraper on their waist against ridges on the surface of their abdomen. Leaf-cutter ants cut and carry leaf fragments, which are used for cultivating fungus gardens, from which they feed. When the ants encounter a particularly desirable plant, they "sing" to call others in the vicinity. The more nutritious the leaf, the more intense the singing. If workers are trapped by a nest collapse, they can also squeak to summon help. Ants sense the sound through vibrations in their legs, but they may also be able to detect "nearfield" airborne sounds through the sense organs located on their antennae.

Atta cephalotes
- ³⁄₁₆–¹⁄₂ in (0.5–1.6 cm) (depending on caste)
- Forests throughout warmer regions of Central and South America.
- Brown to rusty-red; three pairs of spines, long legs.

HITCHING A RIDE
As the heavily-laden "mediae" (larger workers) carry leaf fragments back to the nest, they "sing" to attract tiny "minim" workers. These smaller workers hop on board the leaves, protecting the mediae from parasitic phorid flies.

Deep voice
American bullfrog

Many male frogs and toads produce loud croaks or "advertisement calls" during the breeding season, which serve a dual function of attracting females and intimidating other males. The dominant frequency of the call is related to a male's size and fighting ability and studies have shown that in many species, females prefer deep voices. Male American bullfrogs produce a particularly loud call, typically consisting of 3–6 vibrant bass croaks. The volume they are able to generate is due to their resonating external eardrums, which amplify their calls by up to 98 percent. Males gather around ponds and call in choruses, which attract both females and other males to the mating site. Since females are receptive only for brief periods of time, competition is intense.

Rana catesbeiana
◀▶ 3½–6 in (9–15 cm)

⊙ Streams, ponds, and swamps in Canada, US, and Mexico. Also introduced elsewhere.

▥ Green to brown above, pale yellow or white underside. Females larger than males.

VISIBLE VIBRATION
The deep call the bullfrog generates is similar to the bellow of a bull, hence its name. The reason for the loudness of the call is that the sound from the bullfrog's vocal chords is amplified by their large vocal sac (above), and then resonated by their eardrums. These eardrums visibly vibrate when the bullfrog calls (left).

Within a single vocalization, American bullfrogs will **extend the length of their call** by deliberately inserting a series of "stutters."

Natural amplification
Treehole frog

Treehole frogs are the only animals known to tune their calls to the acoustics of their surroundings. They breed in tree cavities in rain forests and when a male colonizes a new hole, he calls to attract a female. He emits a series of calls to "sample" the hole's acoustic properties, adjusting his pitch with each successive call to try to reach the resonant frequency of the cavity. The vocal range of individuals varies, as do the tree holes themselves, but when a male finds a hole that suits his voice, he increases his calling rate. The "resonance effect" amplifies his call by an extraordinary 10–15 decibels.

Metaphrynella sundana
◀▶ 1 in (2.5 cm)

⊙ Rain forests of Malaysia and Thailand.

▥ Mottled brown with broad snout.

Loud mouth
Tokay gecko

Most reptiles are either mute or can only produce extremely limited sounds, but geckos are a remarkable exception. This is probably because they are mostly active at night when visual signals are not that useful. Tokay geckos are solitary and particularly fierce in the defense of their territory. They are capable of producing an abrupt, loud bark, or *ga* sound during conflicts and may attack rivals and other species alike, inflicting a severe bite. During the breeding season in early spring, males can be heard regularly giving the distinctive "advertisement call" for which they are named. First they produce a series of rattles increasing in intensity and then a series of 4–11 bi-notes that sound like *to-kay*.

Gekko gecko
◀▶ 8–14 in (20–35 cm)

⊙ Mainland and islands of Southeast Asia and extreme southern China. Introduced elsewhere.

▥ Large gecko, big broad head and large jaws. Bright blue-gray color with orange spots.

GAPE DISPLAY
In addition to calling, male tokays use this "gape display" to intimidate rivals, showing an expanse of red tongue and black throat. Their bright colors may be the reason they are valued in Chinese medicine.

Blowing bubbles
North American ruddy duck

The male North American ruddy duck attracts a mate by blowing bubbles—or so it seems at first glance. In fact, he has an air sac concealed under his breast feathers, which are dense enough to trap the air between them. As part of his extraordinary display, the male starts beating a vigorous drumroll on his breast with his bill, which releases the air trapped by the feathers and produces a spurt of bubbles on the surface of the water in front of him. Females are attracted by the combination of the visual bubbling display, the slapping sound, and the croak of the male's air sac deflating.

Oxyura jamaicensis
◀▶ 14–15½ in (35–40 cm)

⊙ Marshy lakes and ponds throughout most of North America; also spread across much of Europe.

▥ Males rusty red with white face and blue bill; females mostly grayish brown.

Voice recognition
King penguin

King penguins huddle together in huge colonies for protection against the freezing blizzards of the subantarctic. Chicks learn the calls of their parents within the first month of their lives. Soon after this, the parents go to sea and bring food back for their young. On their return, parents and chicks are able to recognize each other's calls out of the thousands. Despite the cacophony, they can pick out familiar calls in the same way people can hear their name in a hub of conversation. This is known as the "cocktail-party" effect.

FINDING FAMILY
King penguin chicks face the challenge of locating their parents by recognizing and responding to their calls in a colony of tens of thousands.

CRACKING THE CODE

Researchers have conducted playback experiments and manipulated different parts of king penguin's calls in order to determine how they recognize each other. They found chicks responded only to the bass frequencies, which travel best through an intervening wall of bodies. Just the first quarter of a second of the parent's call is enough for recognition, and the parents continue to make the call every few seconds. It is only when the parent is around 36 ft (11 m) away that the chick will recognize and localize the call.

Aptenodytes patagonicus
- 35 in (90 cm)
- Breed on subantarctic islands and Falklands. Forage in Southern Ocean.
- Upper parts blue/gray-black, white belly, orange upper breast and ear patches.

>> 431

Mating boom
Eurasian bittern

During spring, male bitterns establish breeding territories by producing loud, low-frequency "booms" that carry farther than the calls of most other birds. Normally stealthy as they move through the reed beds hunting for frogs and other small vertebrates, in the breeding season males boldly advertise themselves to females and rival males with a series of two or three grunts followed by an audible intake of breath and then a deep *woomp* sound. This strangely muted sound, like a distant foghorn, can carry up to 3 miles (5 km) on a still night.

Botaurus stellaris
- 27–32 in (69–81 cm)
- Scattered across wetlands throughout Europe and Asia.
- Large buff-brown, heronlike bird with pointed head and bill and long legs.

Precise percussion
Red-naped sapsucker

Woodpeckers are unusual among birds because they employ something other than their syrinx (vocal organs) or wings as instruments to generate sound. Red-naped sapsuckers hammer their bills in split-second repetitions against trees to declare their territory. Dead trees are a vital resource for nesting, feeding, and roosting and by hammering on dead wood they advertise their presence. They also appear to pick their instruments carefully, drumming in locations that produce louder, longer-lasting sounds.

▶ SAPSUCKER SONOGRAM

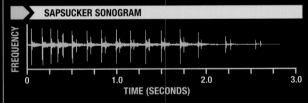

FREQUENCY

| 0 | 1.0 | 2.0 | 3.0 |

TIME (SECONDS)

Each species of woodpecker has its own drumming pattern. This sonogram is of a yellow-bellied sapsucker. Its sequence lasts 3–4 seconds and has a relatively slow tempo, with double beats that slow down during the last part of the drum.

Sphyrapicus nuchalis
- 7–8½ in (18–22 cm)
- Forested areas across northeast US, Canada, and Alaska.
- Black and white woodpecker, white wing patch, red crown. Male has red throat.

REVEALING SOUND
Recent sonographic research makes it possible to identify the sex and emotional state of this red-naped sapsucker from the way it drums.

Telling tales
Bare-faced go-away bird

These noisy, gregarious birds have earned their remarkable name from their distinctive alarm calls that sound a bit like the word *go-away*. The bare-faced go-away bird makes a bleating *go-ha* sound as well as a *ko-wo ko-wo* call, which is repeated by other members of the group. The white-bellied go-away bird has a penetrating *grr'waa grr'waa* call and the grey go-away bird makes a nasal *gwair* sound. From their vantage point in trees, go-away birds are able to see predators approaching before animals on the ground do, and many species have learned to pay heed to their alarm calls. This is often annoying to hunters, since their target is alerted long before the hunter gets close.

Corythaixoides personatus
- 19–20 in (48–51 cm)
- Common in savanna woodland in eastern and southern of Africa.
- Gray, or gray, white, and black turaco with crest and long, broad tail.

BARE-FACED CHEEK
The bare-faced go-away bird calls with a series of impulsive wild ringing chuckles, as well as a bleating *go-ha* when disturbed.

Wide repertoire
Great reed warbler

Male songbirds typically sing to defend territory and to attract a mate. Territorial songs, addressed to rival males, are simpler and carry farther, while songs used to attract females are more operatic. Female great reed warblers listen to the songs of many males before choosing one, opting for those with complex repertoires. The song is a loud, chattering *jit-jit-jit* with added whistles, and incorporates the calls of other birds. An extensive repertoire seems to indicate a healthy male and correlates both with the quality of his territory and the number of young produced.

VOCAL CASANOVA
This male will keep singing to attract females even after he has mated with one. Up to 40 percent of males have more than two females occupying their territory.

Acrocephalus arundinaceus
- 6½–8 in (16–20 cm)
- Breeds in reed beds throughout Europe and west Central Asia.
- Large warbler, brown-rust above, white throat and belly, conspicuous cream stripe above eye.

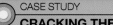

Air-raid siren

European robin

European robins are intensely territorial and both sexes sing with a series of short, high-pitched warbles. Defending their patch is important because they use a "perch and pounce" method of feeding, and any disturbance—from another robin or anyone else—is likely to send the bird's meal scuttling back into the undergrowth. In response to aerial predators, such as hawks, robins give pure-toned and high-pitched alarm calls that fade very quickly. These are perfectly tailored to be attention-grabbing while very difficult to locate.

SEASONAL SONG
The songs of the European male robin vary dramatically according to the season. Fall songs are soft and melodious, while spring songs are much more powerful, since they are intended to attract a mate.

Erithacus rubecula

⟷ 4½–5½ in (12–14 cm)

◆ Woodland, parks, yards, and farm hedgerows across Europe.

▭ Bright orange-red breast and face, gray-brown upperparts, and an off-white belly.

≫ 143

HUMAN IMPACT
SHEDDING LIGHT

Scientists used to believe that urban European robins sang more at night than their rural relatives because street lighting made them think it was dawn. Recent research suggests that noise rather than light makes the difference. Robins stand a better chance of getting their message across if their song is not drowned out by traffic.

Sophisticated alarms

Gunnison's prairie dog

Gunnison's prairie dogs have one of the most sophisticated alarm systems in the animal kingdom. These small rodents require different escape strategies to escape their many predators. Like vervet monkeys, they have alarm calls that refer to specific predators. A bark to warn of a human intrusion sends the whole coterie to their burrows; with a hawk-elicited bark, animals look up, but only those in the flight path bolt. A coyote-elicited bark makes them run to the lip of their burrows and watch the predator. Callers convey how urgent the threat is by increasing their barking rate in direct proportion to the predator's speed of approach.

FRIENDLY WARNING
Prairie dogs live in groups called "coteries." They warn each other of danger, but only some predators cause them to scurry into their tunnel networks.

Cynomys gunnisoni

⟷ 12–12½ in (30–32 cm)

◆ High mountain valleys and plateaus of southern Rocky Mountains in US, especially Four Corners area of Arizona, New Mexico, Colorado, and Utah.

▭ Yellowish buff rodent, pale underneath with white-tipped tail.

Dawn chorus

Venezuelan red howler monkey

The vocalizations of howler monkeys are among the loudest of any mammal thanks to a highly developed hyoid bone in their throats, which allows the various sounds to reverberate. At dawn every morning, they produce a chorus of calls that carry several miles through the rain forest. Howler monkeys don't maintain exclusive territories—they actually share their range with other troops. By announcing their presence at dawn and whenever they move, each troop informs their neighbors of their location and thereby avoids running into each other and competing over food.

Alouatta seniculus

⟷ 17½–28 in (45–70 cm)

◆ Wet and seasonal forest of northern South America.

▭ Thick reddish fur, wide, bearded jaw, and swollen-looking throat.

Wide vocabulary

Common chimpanzee

Chimpanzees' vocabulary may include at least 34 different vocalizations. When food is concentrated they gather in large groups, but much of the time they forage in small groups or alone. Every individual has a distinctive "pant hoot" and responds very differently to the pant hoots of others, depending on who they are and what they are up to. Different types of pant hoot are used in different contexts. For example, a pant hoot with a long wailing climax is associated with plentiful food. They also use a range of screams when threatened. To enlist support, abrupt *waa* barks are given during conflicts, a puzzled *huu* on encountering something strange, and a loud *wraaa* in response to danger, such as a leopard. One of the most socially significant vocalizations is the pant grunt. Low-ranking chimpanzees make these breathy grunts when approaching those of high rank. In a male leadership contest, one may scream or run away, but the battle is not over until formally conceded by deferential pant grunts.

CONTACT CALLS
Chimpanzees use pant hoots to maintain contact between dispersed members of a community. These vocalizations can travel several miles through the rain forest.

Pan troglodytes

⟷ 29–37 in (73–95 cm)

◆ Gallery forest, rain forest, and woodland savanna across equatorial Africa.

▭ Ape with black hair, sometimes tinged with gray or brown. Infants have white tail tuft and face that darkens with age.

≫ 174, 247, 437, 465, 480–81, 482–83

CASE STUDY
KNOCKING ON WOOD

Chimpanzees drum on the roots of large trees, pounding the buttress with their hands and feet. Adult males often drum and give deep roaring pant hoots while traveling, drumming on trees along their route to show their direction of travel. When trying to locate others, they may drum on the same tree several times, pausing in between to listen for a response.

≫ 01   ≫ 02   ≫ 03

PANT-HOOTING
≫01 A typical pant hoot starts with an introduction of low-pitched hoots. ≫02 This is followed by a buildup of deep-sounding pants that get progressively louder and higher in frequency. ≫03 This builds up to a climax of one to four high-pitched screamlike hoots. This is sometimes succeeded by a let down similar to the buildup, but in reverse. It is likely that the buildup functions as a sign-on, while the climax actually contains most of the information that needs to be conveyed.

Community voices

Mountain coyote

Coyotes live in packs of two to seven, but usually travel alone while foraging. Separated pack members will call back and forth to keep in touch. Bouts of calling almost always include both howls and a number of high-pitched barks. Long, pure-toned howls carry farther and provide more complex information, while abrupt barks are used for estimating each other's distance. A combination of the two calls allows them to closely coordinate their movements and cooperate in the defense of their territory. The latter is essential since incursions by other coyotes can result in the death of the breeding pair's pups. Mountain coyote voices are deeper in tone than those of their lowland coyote cousins and tend to be more voluminous.

Canis latrans
- 30–33 in (75–85 cm)
- Limited to Canada and the northwest US.
- Gray or grayish brown fur. Resembles a large, collielike dog; pointed ears and bushy tail.

>> 413

NIGHT CALLER
A coyote howl consists of a series of high-pitched yelps followed by a long siren wail, usually heard around dawn or dusk, but also through the night. The well-known barking chorus may sometimes be the work of only one coyote due to their ability to use different intonations.

The howl of a coyote reveals information about their identity, sex, and even their motivational state.

Signature whistles

Bottlenose dolphin

Bottlenose dolphins are highly social animals but do not live in stable groups; instead, they have a "fission-fusion" society in which group membership constantly changes. These dolphins are remarkable vocal learners and demonstrate faculties of cognition matched only by primates. To keep in touch with its group, or pod, each dolphin develops its own high-frequency signature whistle by the age of about two. However, they remain flexible and when males form an alliance, their individual whistles may gradually converge to produce a team call. In addition to signature whistles, researchers have identified a wide range of other whistles, 20 of which are commonly used. Flat-toned whistles are used when socializing, while "sine" whistles that rise and fall are used when traveling.

Tursiops truncatus
- 6¼–13 ft (1.9–4 m)
- Tropical and warm temperate seas worldwide.
- Streamlined aquatic mammal. Slate gray above, light gray below, beaklike snout.

>> 483

VARIETY PERFORMANCE
Bottlenose dolphins communicate with each other by using a wide range of squeaks and as many as 186 different whistles. They also use clicks to echolocate their prey.

Touch, vibration, electricity

The delicate vibrations traveling through a spider's web or the electrical exchanges of fishes living in murky waters, belong to sensory realms that we are only just beginning to probe thanks to advances in technology. Tactile signals, although familiar, are also not well understood because they are often hard to quantify.

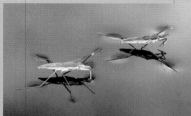

Touch

Touch is a very direct, immediate, and persuasive way of communicating: lionesses, for example, nip their cubs as a reprimand, and chimpanzees embrace to show solidarity. It is only effective, however, over a very short range, and so tends to be used by social species living in close proximity, by parents and offspring, or by animals coming together to mate. Insects, arachnids, and crustaceans all communicate with touch, but it is most developed among mammals and birds that have long periods of parental care. Various forms of tactile contact between parents and young have become "ritualized," and been adopted by adults as well. For example, adult wild dogs lick the faces of fellow pack members in a friendly signal derived from pups begging for food, while grooming among adult primates probably stems from mothers cleaning their offspring.

Vibration

Until recently, the number and variety of animals that broadcast messages using vibrations traveling through the ground, mud, vegetation, spiders' webs, or water has been uknown. The earliest land animals almost certainly felt vibrations in the ground long before they could hear airborne sounds. Technology, such as laser beams and geophones, can now detect minute vibrations and seismic signals, respectively.

DIVERSE MEDIA
Thorn bugs (top) send alarm signals as vibrations through plants. The golden mole (center) uses ground vibrations to communicate and catch prey. Male water striders (bottom) tap the water to attract mates.

SNIFFING OUT FOOD
This fox cub sniffs and licks its mother's mouth to sense what she may have eaten and persuade her to regurgitate it.

TURNING IT OFF AND ON
In the aba (*Gymarchus niloticus*) brief interruptions in an otherwise steady electrical discharge are a threat signal; longer breaks indicate submission.

Electricity

All animals produce a very faint electrical field around them created by minute currents that carry signals through the body, but as yet only fishes, monotremes, and a few amphibians are known to harness this. Most are aquatic, because water is a good conductor of electricity. Fishes sense their environment by picking up electrical signals with receptors along their lateral line, and a few, such as electric rays, use this as a weapon. However, as yet only the gymnotiforms of South America and the mormyrid fishes of Africa are known to use bursts of electrical discharge to communicate.

FELINE AFFECTION
Licking and grooming keep offspring clean, and have evolved to show affection between adults of many social mammals, such as these lions.

Vibrating web
Orb-web spider

The male orb-web spider courts the female by drumming on her web with his palps (pair of appendages near the mouth) and abdomen, or by inserting a "mating thread" into her web and jerking it. The frequency and rhythm of the signal identify him as the right species, and suppresses the female's hunting instincts, albeit temporarily, in order to mate with him.

Argiope bruennichi

- Male ³⁄₁₆ in (5 mm), females up to ¾ in (2 cm)
- Webs near ground in open grassy habitats in many parts of Europe.
- Yellow, black, and white stripes on abdomen. Creates zigzag pattern in web.

Head banging
Deathwatch beetle

Male deathwatch beetles tap out a courtship message with their heads and wait for the female to respond. The male moves toward the female, continuing the exchange until they locate each other. After mating, larvae hatch from eggs laid in the cracks of wood and spend two to ten years eating before emerging as adults. These beetles are named after the tapping sound heard in old wooden houses during the quiet of a death vigil.

Xestobium rufovillosum

- ¼ in (7 mm), larvae up to ³⁄₈ in (1 cm)
- Old trees and building lumber in damp areas in Europe, northern Asia (except China), and North America.
- Small brown beetle with yellowish scalelike hairs.

PICKING UP VIBES
Vibrations, produced by banging the front of their head, or "frons," against wood, travel through the substrate and are picked up by dense pads on the deathwatch beetle's feet.

BUSH TELEGRAPH
The southern green stink bug produces signals by sitting on a leaf or plant stem and vibrating its abdomen against the surface. These vibrations travel along the stem, radiating through the plant, into the roots, and across to other plants at speeds of 98–330 ft (30–100 m) per second.

Nezara viridula

- Up to ½ in (1.5 cm)
- Originally from Ethiopia, now widespread crop pest in Europe, Asia, Africa, North and South America.
- Green, shield-shaped body, five-segmented antennae.

Feeling the vibes
Southern green stink bug

In early summer, male southern green stink bugs, or shield bugs, produce wafts of pheromones to attract females, who fly toward the source. However, pinpointing the male's precise location is difficult, so when the female gets close, she lands on a leaf and starts to vibrate. An introductory pulse is followed by an intense burst over a narrow frequency range and then a burst over a broader range. After a five-second pause, she repeats the pattern. The vibrations travel through the plant and the male "listens" with his feet, stopping at junctions and straddling two stems to gauge the direction of the strongest signal. During the pauses in the female's call, he responds with a regular rhythm of five or so pulses of his own, which encourage her to continue singing until they find each other. If a female is not receptive to mating, she gives a low burst of vibrations and the male stops courting.

> **LASER VIBROMETRY**

The bug's vibrations are recorded by a vibrometer that detects deflections in a laser beam pointed at the plant. A computer transforms these into sonograms showing the exchange of "song."

FEMALE CALLING

MALE RESPONDING

Waggle dance
Honey bee

Bees share information about the location of flowers using one of the most exceptional forms of communication in the animal kingdom—the "waggle dance." Scouts return to the nest and inform their sisters of the distance to, and direction of, a rich patch of flowers. They do this by dancing up and down the vertical wall of the honeycomb.

The scout performs a "straight run" while waggling its body from side to side 15 times per second, and vibrating its wings. It then turns to the left, circles back to the starting point, performs another straight run, then turns to the right this time and circles back, repeating the pattern to create a figure-eight. The distance of the flowers is given by the duration of the straight run and the number of waggles—the farther away the flowers, the longer the straight run and the slower the tempo of the waggles. The direction of the flowers is given according to the angle of the straight run in relation to the sun's position. The bees do not have to see the sun since they can perceive polarized light, which tells them the sun's direction.

Apis mellifera

- ⅛–1 in (0.3-2.5 cm)
- Well-vegetated, flower-rich areas worldwide.
- Covered with dense golden-brown and black hair with striped abdomen
- » 167, 185, 424–25

GIVING DIRECTIONS
A vertical straight run by a scout represents flowers located in line with the sun. Those located at an angle to the right or left of the sun are disclosed by a corresponding angle to the right or left of vertical during the straight run.

the nectar source is at a -90° angle to the sun

SUN

the nectar source is at a 45° angle to the sun

NECTAR SOURCE

workers follow directions to nectar source

workers follow directions to nectar source

bee performs dance

NECTAR SOURCE

HIVE

bee performs dance

MAP DANCE
As the scout dances, appearing to reenact her journey in miniature, her sisters gather around her and follow her through her movements.

CASE STUDY
KARL VON FRISCH

Karl von Frisch won a Nobel Prize in 1973 for pioneering work on insect communication. He was the first to translate the waggle dance, a theory which, although greeted with scepticism at the time, has been proved to be accurate. But precisely how honey bees detect the scout's movements in the darkness of a hive remains something of a mystery. Recently, using a system of particle image velocimetry that can detect tiny air movements, researchers found that wing vibrations create jets of air that hit the followers at different angles depending on their position relative to the axis of the straight run, enabling them to "feel" the dance.

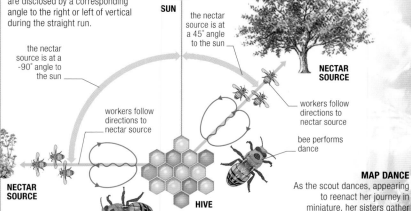

Tandem running
Shore ant

In addition to pheromones, many ants communicate using vibration and touch. The shore ant uses "tandem running" to lead a nest mate along an odor trail, from the nest to a newly discovered food source. As they go, the recruit frequently taps the front runner with its antennae to indicate that it is following. If it falls behind and the tapping stops, the leader adjusts its pace. It takes the leader much longer to get to the food in this way, and involves two-way feedback, suggesting that this may be a unique example of teaching in animals.

Temnothorax albipennis

↔ ⅛–³⁄₁₆ in (3–5 mm)

◆ Rock crevices, hollow nuts, and other fragile preformed cavities in coastal western Europe.

▥ Small orange-brown ant.

Fin rubbing
Blue gourami

The pecking order is well established within colonies of blue gourami and, at the beginning of the mating season, dominant males become increasingly aggressive, nipping and chasing subordinates. During courtship, spawning pairs also use tactile signals—the female typically directs one or more bites at the side of the male, triggering him to drop below her so that his dorsal fin touches her chest. He then starts rubbing back and forth until, finally, he clasps her and the pair spawn.

Trichogaster trichopterus

↔ 3½–6 in (9–15 cm)

◆ All kinds of fresh water, especially in densely vegetated areas. Native to Southeast Asia, introduced elsewhere.

▥ Variable color; anal fin extends beyond base of caudal fin.

Jamming frequencies
Ghost knifefishes

Ghost knifefishes live in loosely associated groups at the bottom of rivers and streams where they hunt at night for insect larvae and small crustaceans. They produce a weak electrical field and, in each group, one male advertises his dominance by giving out the highest rate of electrical discharge—900 pulses per second. The others have lower signaling rates and adjust them when passing each other to avoid causing interference. However, during a challenge, a rival will shift his frequency to match that of the dominant male, as though trying to jam his signal. The dominant male may zap his rival with a burst of high-frequency charge (up to 1000 hertz) but if the rival continues to imitate his frequency, the two males will fight, sometimes spending an entire night locked jaw to jaw.

ELECTRIC VISION

An organ in the fish's tail produces an electrical field. Sensors across the body pick up distortions in that field, allowing the fish to interpret its environment.

***Apteronotus* species**

↔ 7 in–4¼ ft (18–130 cm)

◆ Rivers and streams in Central and South America.

▥ Freshwater fish with small tail fin, small filament-like dorsal fin, very long anal fin.

Making waves
Alligator

Alligators are acutely sensitive to splashes and movement in the water, and use this attribute both to communicate and catch prey. This offers a tremendous advantage to an animal that inhabits murky water.

RIVER DANCE

The bull alligator raises its head and tail out of the water, waves the tail back and forth, inflates its throat, and emits a low-frequency sound so powerful, it makes the water dance along its back.

In early spring, male alligators establish breeding territories and warn away rivals using head slaps and bellows. The bellow consists of two parts. First, the bull vibrates, producing low-frequency "infrasound," which is followed by the audible bellow lasting three to four seconds. While an audible bellow can carry half a mile to the human ear, the vibration can travel even farther in still waters. It is thought that both the frequency and power of these inaudible signals are related to size, so that males can immediately assess their chances against a displaying rival.

Bellowing seems to alert other bulls and members of the opposite sex to the bellower's presence. During courtship, both the male and female bellow, as well as touch snouts, cough, and swim together—a complex ritual that can last for more than an hour before the pair eventually mate.

Alligator mississippiensis

↔ 9¾–16½ ft (3–5 m)

◆ Fresh, slightly brackish water swamps, lakes, rivers, in the southeastern US, especially Everglades in Florida.

▥ Armored body, huge jaws, muscular tail. Differs from crocodiles in having broad, rounded snout.

ANATOMY
VIBRATION SENSORS

The thousands of little black dots sprinkled across the alligator's face, especially around the jaws, are known as dome pressure receptors (DPRs). Disturbances of the water surface create pressure waves that are detected by highly sensitive DPRs, allowing the creature to sense potential prey and pick up vibrational signals from other alligators.

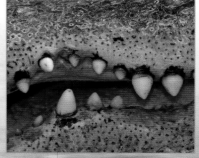

Preening feathers
Red-and-green macaw

Macaws live for about 30–40 years and usually pair for life. A close bond between partners appears to be essential in rearing young successfully—offspring stay with their parents, learning from them until they are three years old, despite being fully grown at six months. During large gatherings in fruit trees or at clay licks (riverbanks rich in minerals) families tend to stick together and, in between feeding, they cavort and play, regurgitate food for each other, and preen each other, all of which strengthen bonds.

EXPRESSING AFFECTION
Preening helps keep the feathers of the red and green macaw clean and free of parasites, but it also reinforces familial bonds. In fact, when parents stop preening their offspring it's a way of indicating to them that it's time for them to leave home.

Ara chloropterus
- Up to 35 in (90 cm)
- From Panama to Bolivia.
- Bright red breast and body, blue and green wings, blue and red tail. Bare white skin patch on face, red lines under eyes.

>> 199

Fancy footwork
Banner-tailed kangaroo rat

Banner-tailed kangaroo rats communicate by thumping out messages from their burrows using their enormous hind feet. Each individual advertises its territory with a unique foot-drumming pattern. Neighbors, who are often extended family members, recognize each others' signatures and respond with their own. If a stranger is heard, the foot drumming becomes increasingly vigorous, and they may even approach and challenge the intruder in a foot-drumming contest.

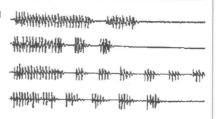

Dipodomys spectabilis
- 4–6 in (10–15 cm)
- Arid parts of New Mexico, south-central Arizona, and west Texas into Mexico.
- Buff-colored rodent with large hind feet, and a white-tipped tail.

BIG FOOT
The kangaroo rat has huge, four-toed hind feet that are almost half its body length. It drums with the tips of both hind feet, while balancing on its tail and fore feet.

> **KANGAROO RAT COMMUNICATION**

Foot drums are grouped into short bursts called foot rolls. Several of these form a sequence. These traces show the foot drumming signature of four rats. Each has a distinct number of foot rolls per sequence.

Staying close
Chimpanzee

Highly tactile, chimpanzees embrace, kiss, reach out with open palms for reassurance, or touch other chimps back to give it. Much of their time is spent on grooming, which plays a key role in communication (its function has been compared with that of human gossip). Grooming may occur in pairs or groups, and reveals a lot about the relationships between individuals. Low-ranking chimpanzees frequently groom those of higher rank to appease them or curry favor, and the dominant alpha male is often at the hub of a grooming group. Grooming is also a way in which males establish political coalitions—the alpha male may even groom allies to win support.

Pan troglodytes
- 29–37 in (73–95 cm)
- Gallery forest, rain forest, and woodland savanna across equatorial Africa.
- Ape with black hair, sometimes tinged gray or brown; white tail tuft and face of infants darken with age.

>> 174, 247, 437, 460, 480–81, 482–83

KISSING
On meeting, chimps sometimes kiss, and youngsters frequently embrace and carry infants around. Adults also embrace to show solidarity when excited or frightened, especially during conflicts.

FAMILY TIES
Infant chimpanzees are in close physical contact with their mothers for their first five years. A mother grooms her offspring during the early years, and older youngsters learn to return the favor.

CULTURAL DIFFERENCES
In Tanzania's Mahale Mountains, chimps like these use the "handclasp" when grooming in pairs, unlike their neighbors in Gombe, who rest an arm on a branch or hold it up when having an armpit groomed.

Back scratching
Burchell's zebra

Like horses, Burchell's zebras are nonterritorial; the one-male harems and bachelor herds coexist relatively peacefully. Closely related individuals engage in social grooming, during which two zebras nibble and scrape at the other's neck and back with their lips and incisors. Within the herd, mares and their foals and siblings groom most frequently, and low-ranking individuals groom higher-ranking members, which may help to appease aggression.

BACK TO FRONT
By standing nose to tail, zebras can groom each other's backs simultaneously and also keep a look out for danger in both directions.

Equus burchelli
- 7¼–8¼ ft (2.2–2.5 m)
- Grassland in eastern and southern Africa.
- Broad torso stripes. Southernmost subspecies have pale shadow stripes between flank stripes.

>> 351

CLOSE KINSHIP
Bonds between mothers and daughters are strong, but all females within a family group lavish physical attention on youngsters and may cross-suckle each other's infants. The matriarch, recognizable as the largest cow, is the central figure and is responsible for the welfare of the entire family.

Keeping in touch

African elephant

Related elephant females and their young live in close-knit families. When they grow beyond about 10 individuals they divide in two but remain close, and these "bond groups" often meet. Males leave the group at adolescence and travel in bachelor herds or alone, but join females when sexually active, or when large herds gather. Within this fluid society, relationships are complex and elephants use a wide vocabulary, including touch, to communicate.

At close quarters, touch is a very direct, immediate, and persuasive form of expression. A mother often reassures her young calf by embracing it with her trunk or rubbing it with her foot, steers it by gripping its tail and moving it ahead of her, or disciplines it with a slap. Courting elephants touch each other and entwine trunks, and related females reach out to greet each other, or rest their trunks amicably on each other.

Loxodonta africana

 13–16½ ft (4–5 m)

⬤ Open grassland, scrub, woodland, and occasionally desert, in Africa south of the Sahara.

📖 Largest living land animal, with large ears, mobile trunk, and curved ivory tusks. Larger ears than Asian elephant.

≫ 295, 417

GREETING CEREMONY
After even a short separation, related cows reach out their trunks as they meet. The lower-ranking cow puts its trunk in the other's mouth, like a calf sampling food from its mother's mouth.

LINK TO LIFE
Almost from birth, a calf uses its trunk to explore its environment through touch and smell, and to hang on to its mother when on the move. This ensures that it doesn't get separated from her and also lets its mother know that it is still with her.

LEAN ON ME
Family members seldom stray more than 130–165 ft (40–50 m) from each other. While resting or drinking, they often stand touching, leaning on each other or rubbing bodies, to reconfirm their close connections.

CASE STUDY

VIBRATIONS THROUGH THE FOOT

Elephants communicate over long distances with "infrasound." Females may be sexually receptive for only a few days every three to five years, and alert widely dispersed males with deep rumbles that carry more than 2 miles (3.25 km) in the air and generate seismic waves that may travel three times that distance through the ground. Elephant feet and trunks contain pressure-sensitive nerve endings that detect such infrasonic (inaudible) vibrations, and pick up other useful ground-borne, long-range information, such as the vibrations of a distant stampede.

INTELLIGENCE

LOST IN THOUGHT
It is hard to know what another human is thinking,
let alone another species. But this bonobo
(*Pan paniscus*), seemingly lost in thought, is likely
to be preoccupied with a fairly sophisticated
calculation given that she has a large brain and is
among our closest living relatives.

INTELLIGENCE

How do you define intelligence? One view is that it is the ability to solve problems. An animal's life is full of problems, such as finding food, escaping from predators, staying healthy, navigating the world around them, finding a mate, and raising young. The problem for us when we try to assess how smart animals are, is that it is hard to avoid believing that the most intelligent animals are those most similar to ourselves.

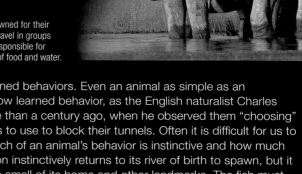

MEMORY FOR WATER
African elephants are renowned for their long-term memory. They travel in groups and the oldest female is responsible for remembering the location of food and water.

Importance of brain size

In general, the larger an animal's brain, the more intelligent the species. Other relevant factors include the overall size of the animal itself. For instance, the average human brain is 2 percent of its body weight. Yet, the brain of a sperm whale, which weighs around 172 lb (78 kg), is only 0.002 percent of its body weight. Another way to think about intelligence and brain size is to consider how many neurons there are in the brain and how many connections there are between them. The greater the number, the higher the level of intelligence. The size of the cortex, the outer, wrinkled, layer of the brain present in many animals, usually relates to social intelligence and in primates frequently corresponds with the intricacy of their relationships. Highly social animals have a higher ratio of cortex to brain.

BIOLOGICAL WIRING
Neurons are cells found in the brain and spinal cord that process and transmit information when electrically stimulated. Neurotransmitter chemicals transfer information across gaps between the neurons.

BRAIN SIZE
The brain consumes about 25 percent of the body's energy so that although there is an advantage in having a large brain, there is also a cost. Wolves are intelligent but not as smart as humans or monkeys; they have a smaller brain and fewer neuronal connections.

**HUMAN BRAIN
1,251 CUBIC CM**

**MONKEY BRAIN
100 CUBIC CM**

**WOLF BRAIN
75 CUBIC CM**

instinctive and learned behaviors. Even an animal as simple as an earthworm can show learned behavior, as the English naturalist Charles Darwin noted more than a century ago, when he observed them "choosing" what kind of leaves to use to block their tunnels. Often it is difficult for us to determine how much of an animal's behavior is instinctive and how much is learned. A salmon instinctively returns to its river of birth to spawn, but it must also learn the smell of its home and other landmarks. The fish must therefore also have a chemical memory and a built-in ability to navigate.

Types of learning

The ability to learn from experience is judged to be a key intelligence indicator. A number of species are capable of an important form of learning—category learning. This is the ability to categorize events or objects using rules. In the wild this ability makes sense: an animal needs to be able to categorize what is or isn't a predator and what is or isn't edible. It has been demonstrated through observation and experiments that animals learn in several different ways. Humans have used the aptitude of some animals to teach them skills either for entertainment or for work.

KNOW YOUR NEIGHBOR AND YOUR ENEMY
Sheep can recognize the faces of 50 other apparently identical sheep—a useful skill for a herd animal. Dolphins possess large brains, which allow them to learn novel behavior. They have been trained to guard ships and submarines and to attack suspected terrorist divers.

Instinct and learning

When assessing intelligence, it is necessary to distinguish between behavior that is innate, or instinctive, and that which is learned. Many animals have instinctive rules for complex behavior, which can appear intelligent. For instance, solitary wasps make a burrow for their young and catch and paralyze grubs for their larvae to feed on when they hatch. But if the wasp is prevented from carrying out any of these steps, it will continue regardless—an indicator of limited intelligence. Most animals show a balance between

INSTINCTIVE RETURN
Female Atlantic Ridley turtles (*Lepidochelys kempii*) instinctively return to the beach they were born on when it is time to lay their eggs.

⊙ DIFFERENT WAYS TO LEARN

HABITUATION
The animal learns to ignore frequent, unimportant stimuli that do not indicate a predator or food. For instance, rabbits may become used to or "habituated" to road traffic noise.

OBSERVATIONAL LEARNING
This is learning in which an animal watches another and adopts its behavior. Intelligent, social animals often learn by observing one another, or sometimes watching other species.

CONDITIONING
This occurs when natural behavior is linked to another event. A dog salivates when it sees meat. If a bell is rung at the same time, the dog may learn to salivate when it hears the bell.

TRIAL AND ERROR
This involves repeated attempts to solve a problem until successful. Chimpanzees may use a twig to fish for termites (observational learning), but figure out how long the twig should be by trial and error.

OPERANT CONDITIONING
This is used by humans to train animals by modifying their natural behavior. Such training often consists of rewarding desired behavior and/or punishing unwanted behavior.

SPONTANEOUS LEARNING
This occurs when an animal is able to figure out how to solve a problem without trial and error, watching other individuals, or by being taught. It is seen in humans but rarely in other species.

TIME FOR REFLECTION
Animals that can recognize themselves in a mirror are thought to have some form of self-awareness. This celebes crested macaque is examining its reflection in an old car side mirror.

ability in the wild. One of the animal kingdom's most expert tool users, the chimpanzee, fishes for insects with twigs and uses stone hammers and anvils to smash open palm nuts.

Problem solving

Most of an animal's problem-solving ability is focused on the search for food. A number of species, such as Clark's nutcracker, have the capacity to form mental maps. These birds store around 33,000 pine nuts across an area of 154 square miles (400 square km) during the fall. It's a prodigious feat to remember the location of all their hidden caches. Other species use mental maps to navigate immense distances—elephants in the Namibian desert frequently travel 44 miles (70 km) a day to find food and water. Another sophisticated type of problem solving is to use tools. Only a handful of species are able to do this. The carrion crow, one of the most accomplished tool users among birds, has been observed using tools in the laboratory, and tiny cameras attached to the birds have also recorded this

TOOL-USE CULTURE
A group of orangutans in Sumatra use tools such as sticks to ram holes in termite nests, flush out ants from their nests, or to poke honey from hives.

Culture and self-awareness

Once thought of as a uniquely human trait, some animal species seem to exhibit rudimentary cultural behavior: they can learn by copying one another so that a group will develop behavior that is passed on from one generation to another. This kind of culture may not be seen in other groups of the same species. For instance, orangutans in Sumatra are adept tool users and yet other populations of these apes do not use as many tools or else use tools for different purposes. Theory of mind, the ability to understand that another individual can think, was also thought to be exclusive to humans. But it is now known that some species can use deception, which requires a sophisticated understanding of another animal's thought processes. Others have a capacity for self-awareness: the test scientists use is whether they recognize themselves in a mirror.

CAPACITY FOR CONCEALMENT
Western scrub jays are able to deceive others. If they are seen hiding their food by other jays, they will hide it again. "Innocent" birds—those who have not stolen another bird's cache—will not do this.

COUNTING CORMORANTS
In China and Japan fishermen train cormorants to fish for them. The birds are allowed to eat every eighth fish and show their ability to count by refusing to dive until allowed their reward.

The western scrub jay stores food based on how hungry it might be the next day.

Sense of direction

Purple flatworm

Although they are primitive creatures, flatworms have a brain and nervous system, and are capable of learning. Experiments carried out in the 1920s revealed that flatworms can remember the location of buried food. They can even be trained to remember the route through a simple maze. In one experiment, flatworms were put into a double T-maze, a simple maze with a choice of turning left or right with food at one end. The worms remembered the route 90 percent of the time; a good adaptation for finding food, particularly for the purple flatworm, which lives in a natural coral maze in the wild.

Pseudoceros ferrugineus
- ³/₄ in (2 cm)
- Tropical coral reefs in the Red Sea, Indian and Pacific oceans, and off the coast of South Africa.
- Vivid fuschia-pink to deep red flat body, often with white flecks or dots; moves in undulating fashion.

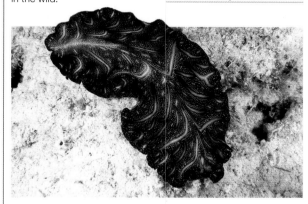

Light sensitive

Giant feather duster worm

These worms are distinguished by their mass of featherlike gills covered in eye-spots. They are sensitive to changes in light levels and will withdraw into their tube at the slightest change in background light levels or if there is any sudden movement in the surrounding area. This is an adaptive response—a shadow might indicate the approach of a predator. However, these animals can learn not to respond when light levels change in a regular and constant way, indicating that they can become habituated to nonthreatening changes in their environment.

Eudistylia polymorpha
- 10in (25cm)
- Tidal pools on the Pacific coast of North Ameria from Alaska to San Diego.
- Body encased in a tube; a plume of feather-like gills protrudes from the top.

Familiar smells

Garden snail

The garden snail is a common species in Europe. When this snail smells a new type of food, it sticks its tentacles straight up in the air and, as it starts feeding, it lowers them. When the animal smells this food on subsequent occasions, it immediately lowers its tentacles. In other words, snails learn to associate a smell with the notion that they will shortly be able to eat the food they have detected.

Helix aspersa
- Shell diameter 1–1¹/₂ in (2.5–4 cm)
- Native to Europe and parts of Asia; introduced to North, Central, and South America, South Africa, and Australasia.
- Pale yellow to dark brown shell with light and dark bands; gray, moist skin, four tentacles

Problem solving

Veined octopus

The veined octopus uses large shells found on the seabed to hide inside or creates a fortress with a number of smaller shells. It has also been known to hide inside coconut shells. If there is no shell available, this octopus has evolved the unusual trick of walking bipedally along the ocean floor. It uses the outer edges of two of its back arms, rolling the sucker edge along the ground as if tiptoeing backward, and wraps the other six arms tightly around its body. This disguises the shape of the octopus and helps it avoid predators. Octopuses are considered to be among the most intelligent of all invertebrates, able to distinguish shapes and patterns as well as solve simple problems. The veined octopus feeds predominantly on crabs; some species will look for lobster traps and pry out their hapless prey.

Octopus marginatus
- Head diameter 2 in (5 cm)
- Coastal waters around Sulawesi, Indonesia.
- Usually mottled gray or brown, rows of suckers on arms. Mouth with beaklike jaw.

PROTECTIVE SHELL
This veined octopus has made its own den inside a shell on the seabed. From the safety of its protective "walls," the octopus can lie in wait for its favored prey of small crabs and shrimps.

SIMILAR SPECIES
The mimic octopus (*Thaumoctopus mimicus*) can mimic other species by changing color and body shape. It seems to choose which species to mimic according to the threat it wants to deter.

CASE STUDY
BOTTLE OPENER

In laboratory experiments, common octopuses (*Octopus vulgaris*) have learned how to open jars to scoop out a shrimp or crab trapped inside. Part of their skill is due to their dexterity, but it is also a result of their distributed brain power: they have "mini brains", or ganglia, in each of their arms, which can operate independently of their brain to some extent.

Web of deceit

Fringed jumping spider

This species of jumping spider preys on other spiders. Camouflaged to look like leaf litter, it is even able to creep up on those spiders that have good eyesight. The fringed jumping spider's hunting technique also utilizes behavioral mimicry. It creates vibrations in another spider's web, imitating either the movements of an insect trapped in the web or a mating signal. When its intended prey approaches, the spider pounces. This species has excellent vision, but only over a small area. However, it is able to build up a picture of the entire scene by swiveling its eyes so that it can plot the best way to ambush its prey. For a small-brained creature (it has only 600,000 neurons—a cockroach has 1 million), the fringed jumping spider shows a remarkable capacity to plan ahead and develop new strategies to trick other spiders.

Portia fimbriata

- Leg span up to 3/8 in (1 cm)
- Tropical forests of Africa, Asia, Australia.
- Tufts of brown, white, and black hairs on legs and body giving appearance of detritus.

TRIAL AND ERROR
If it comes across the web of an unfamilar prey, the fringed jumping spider vibrates the silk randomly until it finds a signal that attracts its victim.

Six lateral eyes provide this spider with a 360° field of vision.

Swarm intelligence

Army ant

Army ants on the warpath can be an astonishing sight: up to 170,000 ants drive through the forest at 65 ft (20 m) per hour forming a column 49 ft (15 m) in length and 3¼–6½ ft (1–2 m) wide. With their ferocious bite and venomous sting, army ants are able to overpower any insect and small vertebrate they find in their path. Individual ants are not particularly intelligent, but the colony as a whole shows clever behavior, a phenomenon that scientists have dubbed "swarm intelligence." No ant general tells the colony when to start the raid or decides in which direction they should travel. Yet the raids are precisely timed and the swarm moves in what appears to be a highly disciplined manner. It seems that each ant responds to chemical markers left by other ants and makes a few, simple decisions on the direction it will take. Collectively these decisions make the colony function as a unit. Other ant species show similar collective intelligence.

Eciton burchelli

- ⅛–½in (3–12mm)
- Tropical forests of Central and South America.
- Golden to dull brown; long, spiderlike legs with tarsal hooks on the feet; soldiers have large heads.

SIMILAR SPECIES
The leafcutter ant (*Atta cephalotes*) of Central and South America has mastered a form of agriculture. These ants collect leaves to use as compost and grow a crop of fungi, harvesting the protein-rich fruiting bodies.

CASE STUDY
GOING THE DISTANCE

Desert ants (*Cataglyphis bicolor*) trek a long way in search of food, and are able to return to their nests using a direct route rather than retracing their outward path. The ants do this by orientating themselves according to the angle of the sun. However, they also need to judge the distance traveled. They do this by counting their footsteps. Researchers fit some ants with stilts, which increased their stride length and caused them to overshoot their target.

ARMY ON THE MOVE
Cooperation is the key to success for army ants. They will overcome virtually any obstacle in their path, for example, by forming bridges over gaps or plugging small holes with their bodies to help fellow ants across.

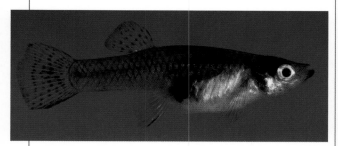

Counting fish

Mosquitofish

Many animals can tell whether one amount is larger than another and some fish species are able to discern whether one school is bigger than another. In the wild, this is a useful adaptive response since there is safety in numbers. However, mosquitofish have been shown to be able to distinguish the size of groups more accurately. Female mosquitofish prefer to be with the largest school and when researchers gave fish in an aquarium a choice of which group to join, they regularly chose a school of four fish in preference to one of three, and a school of three over one of two.

Gambusia holbrooki
- ⬌ 1¹/₂–2³/₄in (4–7cm)
- ◉ Lakes and rivers in North America; widely introduced elsewhere.
- 📖 Grayish brown coloration with a rounded tail and upward-pointing mouth.

Bad memories

Rainbow trout

Studies of rainbow trout seem to have disproved the myth that fishes do not have the brain power to feel emotions and suffer pain. They have pain receptors that respond to chemicals, heat, and pressure. When rainbow trout suffer painful stimuli, such as being injected with bee venom, they react as a mammal would, rubbing the afflicted area and breathing rapidly. They can also remember painful or stressful experiences. Studies have shown that fish that have previously been caught make distress sounds when they next see a fish hook or net. Rainbow trout also show nervous and fearful behavior when faced with a novel object—a useful response to have in the wild.

Oncorhynchus mykiss
- ⬌ up to 4 ft (1.2 m)
- ◉ Temperate freshwaters worldwide.
- 📖 Bluish green to brown back and sides, paler underneath, with black spots mainly on the back; spawning males develop a pink lateral stripe.

Fish school

French grunt

One definition of culture is a set of behaviors that are specific to a particular group, and are passed on to different groups or generations through learning. This seems to occur among French grunts. When a group of these fish is moved from one location to another, they adopt the schooling and migratory behavior patterns (such as the best routes to feeding grounds) of the fish of the same species in their new home. Resident groups of French grunts seem to include a "teacher" fish. When the teacher is removed, the new arrivals do not adopt the behavior of the residents. It seems, therefore, that the French grunts are truly learning rather than behaving by instinct or responding to the new environment.

Haemulon flavolineatum
- ⬌ 6–10in (15–25cm)
- ◉ Reefs in western Atlantic from Bermuda to the Gulf of Mexico and Brazil.
- 📖 Yellow tapered body with silver stripes, yellow fins, and a forked tail fin.

FOLLOWING THE TEACHER
French grunts gather in specific spots in Caribbean coral reefs before moving off to feed. Older individuals lead the migration to feeding spots and young fish learn from them where to go.

Finding shelter

Corn snake

Scientists have often regarded snakes as unintelligent because they are unable to remember how to negotiate a maze. Recently, however, it has been discovered that corn snakes are capable of learning as long as the task makes sense to them—such as finding a dark place to shelter in the heat of the day. Corn snakes were put in a large tub with eight holes cut in the bottom. One, marked with a brightly colored card, led to a hidden shelter. The snakes quickly learned which hole led to their hiding place, to which they rapidly retreated when a bright light was shone at them.

Elaphe guttata
- ⬌ 4–6ft (1.2–1.8m)
- ◉ Farmland, woodland, rocky hillsides in central and the southeastern US.
- 📖 Orange or brown with large, black-edged red blotches down the back and black and white markings underneath.

NORTHERN AMPHIBIAN
The tiny wood frog is North America's most northerly amphibian and the only frog found north of the Arctic Circle. It mainly eats small invertebrates such as spiders, beetles, slugs, and snails.

Fussy eater

Wood frog

Wood frogs have the ability to learn to avoid food that they find unpleasant. When researchers gave wood frogs hairy caterpillars to eat, the frogs attempted to swallow the caterpillars, then spat them out. The hungry frogs tried to eat the caterpillars a few times on the first day of the study and a couple of times on the second day, but by the third day the wood frogs had learned to avoid the insects. The researchers then tried to deceive the amphibians by dusting the caterpillars with colored powder but the frogs were not fooled. The capacity for this form of learning enables wood frogs to avoid types of prey that may harm them.

Rana sylvatica
- ⬌ ³/₄–2¹/₂ in (2–6 cm)
- ◉ Woodland in North America.
- 📖 Light tan to dark brown overall with dark spots and mottled sides; black "mask" across each eye; two ridges from the back of the head down the back.

Waiting in line

Nile crocodile

Crocodiles normally hunt alone, waiting submerged in water, in order to ambush their prey. However, in some places they have learned to hunt semi-cooperatively, which indicates a certain level of intelligence. In parts of Africa, Nile crocodiles have learned the regular crossing points across a river so that they can trap migrating animals, such as wildebeest or zebra. They assemble and line up near these sites to wait for their prey, and seem to act in concert to make a kill.

Socially, crocodiles lead relatively complex lives and relate to one another more like birds and mammals do, rather than reptiles. Most crocodile species have an extensive communication system using gestures, smell, and vocalizations. For instance, a head-slap on the water, jaw snapping, and tail thrashing all signal dominance, while head raising is a gesture of submission. Crocodiles have an acute sense of smell but their chemosensory communication is not well understood. Adults will come to the rescue of juveniles if they hear their distress calls, even if they are not their own.

DANGEROUS CROSSING
In Kenya's Masai Mara migrating wildebeest must cross two wide rivers, where Nile crocodiles await them. When the crocodiles spot a weak individual, they block its route back to the shore and start to close in.

Crocodylus niloticus
- ↔ 20 ft (6 m)
- ⊙ Waterways throughout Africa and western Madagascar.
- ▭ Dark khaki skin covered in thick scales; poweful, long, narrow snout.
- ≫ 220, 401, 464

FISHY FEAST
Saltwater crocodiles (*Crocodylus porosus*) are normally fiercely territorial, but groups of over 40 hunt alongside each other in the Mary River, Australia, to feed on migrating mullet.

Using bait

Green heron

The green heron is a patient and effective hunter. As in most herons, its normal mode of feeding is to stand motionless with its neck drawn in, staring into the water. If it spots prey, it makes a sudden, precise lunge with its thick, sharp bill. At other times, it will disturb the riverbed with its feet to stir up invertebrates, fishes, and frogs, which it can then snap up. However, the most interesting technique in the feeding repertoire of the green heron is its use of bait to lure prey to the surface. This bird employs a variety of lures, including mayflies, feathers, nuts, and even bread, probably scavenged from humans or their trash. Not all green herons use this technique to fish, and the origins of the behavior are not known. They do not appear to be copying humans, but have somehow learned an association between putting out the bait and seeing fish or other prey come to the surface to investigate.

Butorides virescens
- ↔ 14–18 in (35–45 cm)
- ⊙ Wetlands of North and Central America.
- ▭ Glossy, dark green cap and back, chestnut neck with a white line; dark, sharp bill; females smaller with more dowdy plumage.

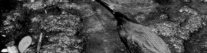

LAYING THE BAIT
≫01 A green heron has selected a nut as bait. ≫02 It lays the bait on the water surface and waits motionless until a fish or small animal comes closer to investigate. ≫03 The heron swiftly attacks and succeeds in seizing its target, a small fish.

≫01   ≫02   ≫03

Learning languages
Grey parrot

One of the most intelligent species of bird, the grey parrot is thought to have developed its impressive communication skills as a result of its habit of living in large flocks and feeding cooperatively in the wild. Most of the research on parrot intelligence, however, has come from studies of captive animals. Grey parrots can mimic and remember a large number human words and, taking the use of language a significant stage further, are also able to understand the meaning of some words, demonstrating this ability by using them appropriately. They are thought to have the same level of understanding as a five-year-old human child with the emotional acuity of a two-year-old.

Psittacus erithacus

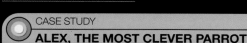

◧ 13 in (33 cm)

⊙ Secondary rain forest of West and Central Africa.

▥ Pale gray body feathers, white feathering around eyes, dark gray wings, red tail.

CASE STUDY
ALEX, THE MOST CLEVER PARROT

Alex, a grey parrot, was studied by Dr. Irene Pepperburg (pictured together below) for 30 years. Alex learned to identify 50 different objects, distinguish seven different colors, and five shapes. He understood concepts such as bigger, smaller, same, different, and the concept of zero, and he knew 150 words. Alex made up the word "banerry" (a cross between banana and cherry) to describe apples.

Long memory
Common pigeon

In addition to having excellent eyesight and the capacity to remember hundreds of images for long periods of time, the common pigeon, or rock dove, is also able to discriminate between different classes of object using abstract concepts (see panel, right). In the wild, common pigeons also have an extraordinary capacity for homing: being able to return to their nest from considerable distances. A combination of factors contribute to this remarkable ability: recognition of major visual landmarks, use of an internal magnetic compass, and, perhaps a memory of the signature smell of the area where they live.

Columba livia

◧ 11¹/₂–13 in (29–33 cm)

⊙ Widespread and common throughout Europe; also occurs in Africa, North America, South America, and Asia.

▥ Usually gray with iridescent pink and green feathers on neck and shoulders, but can vary from white to brown.

CASE STUDY
ART CRITICS

Pigeons are renowned for their ability to distinguish between and categorize objects. In one study they were trained to discriminate between individual paintings by the famous Cubist and Impressionist painters Picasso and Monet. They then generalized this ability to tell the difference between specific paintings by these two artists, to the ability to recognize paintings by these artists that they had not seen before, showing that they had learned the difference between a cubist and an impressionist painting.

The same scientists trained both human students and pigeons and found that their ability to tell Van Gogh from Chagall paintings that they had not seen before was remarkably similar. Because it would be nearly impossible to devise a simple rule to distinguish a Monet from a Picasso, it is suggested that pigeons have a similar ability to humans for categorizing objects or understanding abstract concepts.

Clever mimic
Superb lyrebird

This lyrebird has an astonishing ability to mimic artificial and natural sounds. As part of their courtship ritual, the males build an arena to dance in, display their beautiful tail feathers, and sing to the females. Their songs are spliced with a faithful rendition of other birds' calls and sounds they have heard, which could even include chain saws or car alarms. One superb lyrebird was discovered to have picked up songs played by a flutist who lived nearby, and incorporated them into his own calls. Female lyrebirds are also excellent mimics but are rarely heard. This species is difficult to see and often the only way of telling that it is present is if the sounds of many different bird calls are heard coming from a single area.

Menura novaehollandiae

 29–39 in (74–98 cm)

Wet forest of New South Wales, Victoria, and Tasmania, Australia.

Russet wings and bill, black legs; the adult male has ornate curved tail feathers in the shape of a lyre.

CAR CRUSHING
When cars stop at a red light, carrion crows place nuts on the road. As the lights change, the cars drive over the nuts, and crack them open. Later the birds can retrieve their nuts and access the flesh inside.

Nut cracker
Carrion crow

Crows are among the most adept tool users of the bird world and in Japan carrion crows have taken this ability a stage further by using vehicles to crack nuts (see left). A similar species, the New Caledonian crow (*Corvus moneduloides*) has been observed in the wild making and using a variety of tools fashioned from grass stems and twigs—for example, to extract grubs from rotting wood. Laboratory studies have confirmed the highly sophisticated tool-making abilities of the New Caledonian crow.

Corvus corone

 18½–20½ in (47–52 cm)

Open country and urban areas in Europe and Asia.

Black or gray and black feathers; stout, curved bill.

>> 314

Clean culture
Japanese macaques

Japanese macaques have been studied in the wild for over 50 years, longer than most other nonhuman primates. They lead complex social lives, living in groups of around 30 but sometimes up to 100 individuals. These monkeys are thought to have a rudimentary form of culture, a mark of intelligence, since they pick up new behaviors from each other. For example, they have learned how to make tiny snowballs in their hands and then roll them along the ground to create larger ones. This behavior does not seem to have a purpose other than enjoyment, but in some troops this playful behavior has spread rapidly. Other forms of culturally transmitted behavior include, famously, the habit

Dance class
Long-tailed manakin

All species of manakin are lek maters. During a lek the males perform an elaborate courtship in front of females, and the male who shows the most impressive display is able to mate with the greatest number of females. Normally lekking involves males competing with other males, but long-tailed manakin males actually cooperate during their display. Usually, two males, a dominant "alpha" male and a subordinate "beta" male, will form a partnership that can last for years. When there are females present, the males display with elaborate jumps, leapfrogging, and "butterfly" flights. The alpha male, who is normally the oldest, mates with the females. The only evolutionary advantage of this altruistic behavior for the beta male is that he may be learning how to court females more effectively, following a form of apprenticeship. He will eventually replace the dominant male when he dies.

Chiroxiphia linearis

 5 in (12.5 cm)

Subtropical or tropical dry or moist lowland forests throughout Central America.

Males black with brilliant azure patches and long central tail feathers; females olive green.

FOLLOW MY LEAD
The male long-tailed manakins summon the female by calling. They then leapfrog backward over a branch and make a butterfly-like flight. Once both males have performed, the dominant male will continue the butterfly flight on his own and then mate with the female if she is receptive.

among one troop of Japanese macaques on the island of Koshima of washing their food in the sea (see panel, below right). Another troop developed the habit of taking baths in the hot springs of their home territory.

Macaques in general are extremely hierarchical: females are dominant and daughters inherit their mother's rank. Often, new behaviors that are taken up by the troop are initiated by the females. Other distinctive features of Japanese macaque troops include regional differences in their vocalizations, or "accents," particularly for calls relating to food items, which they use to notify others of a particularly delicious find.

Macaca fuscata

- 19½–26 in (50–65 cm)
- Subtropical to subarctic forest in Japan (excluding Hokkaido).
- Red face, hands, and bottom, gray-brown fur, short tail.

>> 412

FOLLOW MY LEADER

Even though these "snow monkeys" are the most northerly living primates in the world, they hate deep snow. In Japan's Nagano Prefecture at an altitude of 2,600 ft (800 m), as much as three feet of snow can fall in a single night. One monkey will often lead the way, creating a path through the snow, which the others follow, eventually creating a network of snowy trails.

MACAQUE SAUNA

To keep warm in temperatures often below 5° F (-15° C), a troop of Japanese macaques sits in hot springs. The behavior was started by females and copied until the whole troop was taking hot baths.

WASHING POTATOES

Two new cultural practices were taken up by a troop of Japanese macaques in Koshima. Instead of using her hands to brush the sand off sweet potatoes offered to her on the beach, a female called Imo started dipping them in the nearby river. Her immediate family soon copied her, followed by the rest of the troop. Imo then started dipping her potato in the sea, biting it, and dunking it again—presumably because she liked the salty taste—and the others began to copy her. Later she took to washing wheat. She would pick up a handful and toss it in the water. The wheat floated on the surface where she could easily scoop it up free from sand. Again, the rest of the troop followed her example.

Tool kit

Tufted capuchin

Capuchin monkeys have long been regarded as one of the most intelligent groups of monkey because of their use of tools in laboratory conditions. However, tufted capuchins in the wild in the Caatinga forests of Brazil have been observed using stones to crack open seeds, and branches to dig for tubers. But the most common form of tool use recorded was the use of stones for digging; the monkeys pounded the earth with the stone with one hand while scraping away the soil with the other.

An unusual practice observed among capuchins in the wild is to rub millipedes across their fur. The insects' bitter body fluid acts as a natural insect repellent. Being able to use "tools" in this way could indicate that these monkeys appreciate the link between cause and effect, a skill that human infants also develop.

Cebus apella

- 14–16½ in (36–42 cm)
- Variety of forest types in northern South America.
- Brown fur; pale chest, stomach, upper arms, and face; black sideburns, cap, hands, feet, and tail tip.

CRACKING THE PROBLEM

>>01 A tufted capuchin selects a large rock for a hammer to crack a nut. >>02 The monkey lifts the rock over the nut placed on a stone anvil. >>03 It pounds the nut to break the shell. >>04 The monkey can now get at the edible part inside the shell.

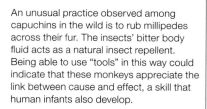

>>01 >>02 >>03 >>04

Master toolmaker

Chimpanzee

Chimpanzees exhibit several behaviors that are thought to be key indicators of intelligence, one of the most significant of which is their sophisticated use of tools. For example, at Gombe National Park, Tanzania, the chimpanzees have been observed to scrunch up handfuls of leaves and dip this "sponge" into pools of water that have collected in tree hollows. They then squeeze the leafy sponge into their mouths to obtain a drink. Approximately nine types of tool use have been documented in chimpanzees, including the use of sticks to extract insects from their nests. But the types of tool use prevalent in any one group of chimpanzees varies depending on the location of the group being studied, hence the idea that these apes possess a rudimentary form of culture that is passed on from one generation to the next.

Various studies have shown that chimpanzees can learn sign language. They are also capable of learning how to count and do simple mathematics, such as addition and subtraction. Chimpanzees can also recognize their reflections in a mirror, indicating that they have some level of self-awareness. Some studies have suggested that they have the basics of "theory of mind"—the ability to understand what another individual might be thinking.

Although chimpanzees are mainly vegetarian, these apes also eat other animals, usually monkeys, for which they hunt cooperatively. Chimpanzees live in large hierarchical social groups. One male is dominant but other males may form variable coalitions to oust him or to keep him in "power." Their society is more fluid than that of monkeys; chimpanzees will form friendships and alliances rather than always inheriting their rank. They are one of the few animal species capable of deception, often attempting to trick each other to obtain food or matings. Like most social animals, chimpanzees can be extremely violent.

Pan troglodytes

◀▶ 29–37 in (73–95 cm)

⊙ Gallery forest, rain forest, and woodland savanna across equatorial Africa.

▭ Black or pale pink bare skin on face, ears, palms, and soles; black hair over the rest of the body; forward-facing eyes and mobile lips; longer arms than legs.

≫ 174, 247, 454, 460, 465

FAMILY LEARNING
Even young chimpanzees, as pictured here, are adept at using sticks as tools to extract termites from their mounds.

A VARIETY OF TOOLS
Chimpanzees have been documented using many different types of tools, from the use of a stone as a nutcracker (above) to the use of a long stick as an arm extension to retrieve a banana from the water (left). It is interesting to note that the latter tool was found to be necessary even in this shallow water because chimpanzees hate getting wet.

⊙ CASE STUDY

UNDERSTANDING SIGNS AND SYMBOLS

The bonobo (*Pan paniscus*) is the only other species of the genus to which the chimpanzee belongs. In a study of language learning at Georgia State University, US, two bonobos, Kanzi (pictured below) and Panbanisha, have been taught to point to keys on a keyboard labeled with symbols of a variety of familiar objects and concepts to obtain food or initiate actions. Pressing the keys also produces the word sounds, which the bonobos have also learned.

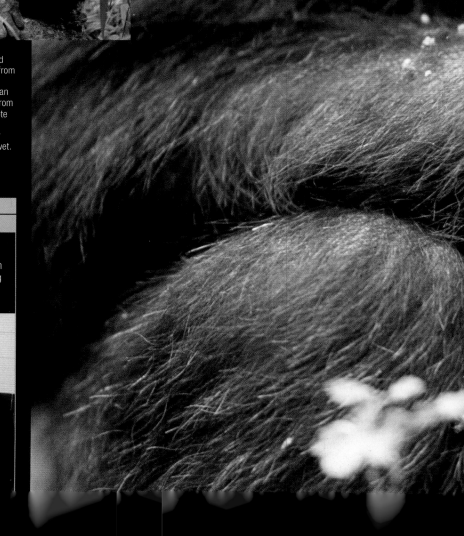

TERMITE FISHING
This chimpanzee has extracted termites—a favorite meal among chimpanzees—from their nest by sticking a twig into a hole in the mound. Chimpanzees use a similar technique to "fish" for ants using grass stems. As in humans, individuals exhibit a preference for using their left or their right hand for these manual tasks.

TRYING FOR TERMITES
>>01 The chimpanzee delicately inserts a fine stick that he has stripped of its leaves into a hole in the termite mound.   >>02 After a short time he removes the stick to which the termites have attached themselves and consumes them by sliding the stick through his mouth.   >>03 He is careful not to waste any of this delectible snack and is sure to eat all the insects that may be clinging to the end of stick.

>>01   >>02   >>03

ARE ANIMALS SELF-AWARE?
Whether or not animals other than humans have a
consciousness is a subject of much debate. There
is some evidence that chimpanzees can understand
the outcome of their actions and how these affect
other individuals, and that they can put themselves
in another individual's place. This at least suggests
they recognize their own identity and that of others.

Watch and learn
Orangutan

Although orangutans lead relatively solitary lives, they are very adaptable primates and can copy behavior they have seen in other orangutans or even humans. One orangutan was involved in a number of experiments, including one which showed that he could imitate 90 percent of the body movements that were performed in front of him. They are also able to use tools, such as twigs to poke out insects in trees and branches and to chisel open termite nests. For orangutans, leaves come in useful for a wide range of things—for example, for cleaning themselves, as a napkin when eating messy food, or to use as gloves when they have to handle prickly items, such as durian fruit. They have even been known to use pitcher plants as cups and drink from them. In captivity, orangutans have been taught to use a rudimentary language system with keys representing up to six items of food.

AN UNFAMILIAR ACTIVITY
At one primate rehabilitation center, some of the orangutans have copied humans by washing clothes with soap and water. One young female also sawed wood and hammered nails.

ALL-WEATHER PROTECTION
Most animals construct nests, but orangutans go a step further, using leaves to make a rain shelter or sun shade, or by creating an "artistic" nest lining from twigs placed with the leafy end sticking outward.

Pongo pygmaeus

⬌ 35 in–3 ft 3 in (90–100 cm)

⬥ Forest canopy in Borneo and Sumatra.

▥ Shaggy, orange coat; large hands and feet, very long arms. Adult males have heavy folds of skin on either side of their face and a throat pouch.

≫ 412

Forward thinking
Sea otter

The sea otter is one of only a few mammals that use tools. Its diet consists of a wide range of molluscks and crustaceans, as well as fishes and sea urchins, and it often uses stones to knock shellfish from rocks. It may need to use a force equivalent to 4,000 times its own body weight. It also uses stones to break open shellfish. A sea otter may balance a stone on its chest and pound the shellfish against it. It often keeps the same stone during a feeding session, which may well imply that it can think ahead, anticipating using it in the future. Although they forage on their own, sea otters usually rest in large groups. When resting, they prevent themselves from drifting out to sea by wrapping themselves in kelp to anchor them to the sea floor. They are vocal animals: females often coo when content and sea otter pups make a mewing call similar to that of a seagull.

Enhydra lutris

⬌ Up to 4¹/₂ ft (1.4 m)

⬥ Coastal waters of the North Pacific.

▥ Dense, brown fur, flattish, rudderlike tail, and large hind feet.

Sea otters have to eat **more than a third** of their own body weight in food each day just to survive.

SHELLFISH SUPPER
A sea otter tucks into a welcome meal of shellfish. It may have had to dive numerous times in order to dislodge the creature from the rock to which it was fixed.

CRACKING CLAMS
Lying on its back, this sea otter is using a stone as an anvil against which to smash a clam. It may take in the range of 35 blows to crack open the shell.

Spongy protection

Bottlenose dolphin

Highly social, big-brained animals, bottlenose dolphins live in groups, called pods, of around 12 individuals. In the wild they can show altruism, helping sick or injured dolphins, in addition to being compassionate toward other species. Bottlenose dolphins in Shark Bay, Australia, have started using marine sponges as tools. They balance them on the end of their noses to protect themselves when they are foraging. This technique was discovered by one female and spread throughout the population.

Scientists have taught dolphins sign language using hand and arm signals. They can still follow these commands when their trainer is on a television screen, showing that they understand the images as representations of the real world.

Tursiops truncatus

- 6¼–13 ft (1.9–4 m)
- Temperate, tropical, and subtropical coastal waters.
- Gray, torpedo-shaped body, pale flanks and belly.

>> 351, 461

New tricks

Californian sea lion

In the wild Californian sea lions are long-lived, social creatures. They travel great distances to breeding and feeding areas of which they need to remember the location. Long known for their ability to learn tricks (see panel, right), in recent years their intelligence levels have been tested scientifically. Scientists have discovered that sea lions have exceptionally good long-term memories, recalling concepts they were tested on up to ten years previously. Sea lions have also been taught gestures to represent words—

Zalophus californianus

- 1.8–2.1 m (5¾–7ft)
- Coastal waters of the eastern Pacific Ocean from British Columbia, Canada, to Mexico.
- Dark brown fur with light brown flanks and underside. Females smaller and usually paler in color.

mainly objects such as balls Z rings, as well as colors. So, for instance, one sea lion could understand complex commands such as "fetch the small black ball." Sea lions have been shown to recognize similarities in pictures shown to them.

PERFORMANCE ARTIST

Humans have exploited the intelligence of sea lions for many decades. They have long been major attractions in amusement parks and circuses, where they have been trained to catch balls, run up ladders, and honk horns. They have also been taught how to paint, using their mouths to hold brushes, an activity that prevents boredom in captive environments. The sea lion shown here is said to be able to write Chinese characters. The US military have also attempted to utilize their intelligence coupled with their underwater skills to counter enemy divers.

Hungry minds

Wild boar

Pigs have good long-term memories. In the wild, their food is unevenly distributed, meaning that they have to remember where the good foraging areas are. The ancestor of domestic pigs, wild boar are social animals, able to recognize individuals and their rank, and have a complex system of communication with grunts and squeaks that are used in different contexts. There is some evidence that they can learn from watching one another. Researchers suggest that, thanks to this skill, combined with their memory and problem solving abilities, pigs of all species are smarter than dogs and possibly equivalent to primates in intelligence. Scientists have tested their memory by training pigs to learn the meaning of simple words and phrases. When presented with them several years later, the pigs could still remember the instructions.

Sus scrofa

- 3–3½ ft (0.9–1.1 m)
- Woodlands of Europe, North Africa, and Asia.
- Dark gray, black, or brown coat with stiff bristles; large head; elongated canine teeth that form tusks.

>> 200

IN THE PUBLIC SERVICE

An Israeli mine-clearance expert has trained pigs to assist in the detection of buried antipersonnel mines. It is claimed that these pigs are more suited to this dangerous task than dogs because they are more intelligent, have a better developed sense of smell, and are easier to train. Soda (pictured here), is a one-year-old mini-pig. Here, she is indicating to her trainer that she has found a mine.

Emotional intelligence

African elephant

This species has the largest brain of any animal—twice the size of that of the largest whale—and is thought to be highly intelligent. Elephants are able to use tools, remember concepts over long periods, as well as showing other emotionally intelligent skills, such as grief, altruism, and self-awareness. One elephant in each herd, the matriarch, remembers the locations of food and water that may be great distances apart and imparts her knowledge to the others. When a member of the troop dies, the rest seem to mourn, standing quietly around the dead animal. Elephants are thought to show altruism, helping members of their own troop if they become incapacitated, as well as giving assistance to other species by, for instance, placing hurt humans in the shade and guarding them from predators.

Loxodonta africana

- 5.5–7.5m (18–24½ft)
- African savanna.
- Brownish gray hide, large ears, a trunk, which ends in two fingerlike projections, and a pair of tusks.

>> 295, 417, 466–67

IN MOURNING

Elephants often seem fascinated by elephant bones, turning them over and touching them with their trunks, as pictured here. They may be one of the few animals that have a concept of death.

GLOSSARY AND INDEX

Glossary

abdomen
The belly of a vertebrate or the hind part of the body of an arthropod.

adaptation
Any inherited feature of an animal's structure or behavior that helps fit it to its environment and lifestyle; also, the evolutionary process giving rise to such features.

advertisement
Any behavior by an animal that functions to announce its presence. Advertisement is often used by males, both to warn off other males and to attract females. See also *song*.

aggregation
A nonsocial gathering of animals, whether of the same species or multiple species, occurring, for example, if many animals arrive independently to feed at a food source. See also *congregation*.

algae
Any of a variety of simple photosynthetic life forms, including both single-celled species and larger forms, such as seaweeds. As the main food producers in the oceans, algae are vital to marine food chains. See also *plankton, protists*.

alpha, beta, gamma
In animal behavior, terms that apply to the position of an individual within its social group. An alpha male (and/or alpha female) is the dominant member of the group. Beta individuals are the next most dominant, while gamma individuals occupy a lower position in the group's hierarchy.

altruism
Behavior that benefits others at one's own expense, such as a parent putting itself at risk to defend its offspring. It is argued that true altruism cannot exist in animals since natural selection would weed it out, and that most apparent altruism can be explained as kin selection. See also *kin selection*.

ambush predator
Any predator whose main feeding strategy is to stay in one place and wait for suitable prey to approach. Also known as a sit-and-wait predator.

amniote
A reptile, bird, or mammal. The term derives from the fact that the embryo of these animals develops within a fluid-filled sac called an amnion. This occurs either inside an egg (reptiles and birds) or in a uterus (most mammals).

anadromous
Of fishes: living most of their lives at sea but entering rivers to breed. See also *catadromous*.

anisogamy
A condition in which the sex cells (gametes) are of two different kinds. Anisogamy occurs in all animals, with sperm cells (smaller) produced by males, and egg cells (larger) produced by females. Hermaphrodites produce both sperm and eggs. See also *gamete*.

apex predator
A predator at the top of its food chain, hunted by no other animal.

aposematic
Of colors and patterns on an animal: designed to warn potential predators that the animal is poisonous or otherwise dangerous.

appeasement
Any set of behaviors designed to deflect aggression coming from another member of the same species.

appendage
A limblike structure, which may be modified as legs, gills, swimming organs, or in other ways.

appetitive behavior
Any behavior of an animal when seeking a particular goal (not necessarily food), as distinct from its behavior when the goal is actually reached.

arachnids
The group of arthropods that includes spiders, scorpions, mites, and relatives. See also *arthropods*.

arthropods
A major group (phylum) of invertebrate animals with jointed legs and a hard outer skeleton. Arthropods include insects, arachnids, and crustaceans. There are more species of arthropods than all other animals put together.

asexual reproduction
Reproduction not involving sex. Examples include splitting or fragmenting the body, budding off new individuals from a larger "parent," or forming specialized reproductive structures, such as spores. See also *parthenogenesis*.

autonomic nervous system
The part of the vertebrate nervous system that deals with involuntary processes, such as controlling the body's glands and the muscles of the gut. In mammals it is further divided into the sympathetic nervous system, which tends to prepare the body for "fight or flight," and the parasympathetic nervous system, which acts to bring the body back to normal.

axon
A cablelike extension of a nerve cell (neuron) along which electrical signals are transmitted away from the cell.

bachelor group
A group formed by males of the same species that have no sexual partners. In lions, for example, young males may team up in a bachelor group to displace another dominant male.

Batesian mimicry
See *mimicry*.

behaviorism
An approach to analyzing human and animal behavior, most influential in the early to mid-twentieth century. Its theories focused strictly on external behavior patterns and the links between them, avoiding discussion of "unobservable" phenomena such as mental states.

benthic
Associated with the seafloor, or the bottom of a lake or river.

beta
See *alpha, beta, gamma*.

bioluminescence
The production of light by living organisms.

biome
A large-scale land ecosystem, or set of ecosystems, whose main characteristics are determined by climate. Deserts and tropical rain forests are both examples of biomes.

bivalves
Aquatic mollusks, such as clams, mussels, and oysters, that have a shell made up of two halves joined by a hinge. Most bivalves move slowly or not at all, and are filter feeders. See also *filter feeding, mollusks*.

bonding
The formation and maintenance of a strong, mutually helpful relationship between two or more members of the same species. It includes pair bonding, the attachment between male and female formed in monogamous species.

bony fishes
The group that includes most of the world's fish species, except for cartilaginous fishes (sharks, rays and their relatives) and jawless fishes (hagfishes and lampreys). See also *cartilaginous fishes, jawless fishes*.

brachiation
A method of movement characteristic of apes, such as gibbons, in which the body is swung through the trees by the arms.

brackish
Saltier than fresh water, but less salty than ocean water.

bryozoans
Small colonial sea-living animals, also called moss animals, that live attached to surfaces such as seaweed fronds. They are filter feeders.

caching
See *hoarding*.

calcareous
Made of or containing the mineral calcium carbonate; chalky.

camouflage
Colors or patterns that cause an animal to resemble its environment, so that it is not noticed by potential predators or prey, or both. See also *mimicry*.

cartilaginous fishes
A group of fishes, including sharks, rays, skates, and chimaeras, that have skeletons made of cartilage, not bone. See also *bony fishes, jawless fishes*.

catadromous
Of fishes: living most of their lives in freshwater but migrating to the sea in order to breed. Eels are an example. See also *anadromous*.

caudal
Relating to the tail or posterior part of an animal.

central nervous system (CNS)
The brain and spinal cord of vertebrates, as distinct from the nerves supplying the rest of the body. Also, similar concentrations of nerve tissue in some invertebrates.

cephalopods
A group of predominantly swimming mollusks that includes squid, cuttlefish, octopuses, and nautiluses. They have large brains and display complex behavior. See also *mollusks*.

cephalothorax
The front part of the body of some arthropods (arachnids and crustaceans) when not obviously divided into a separate head and thorax. See also *thorax*.

cerebellum
Part of the rear of the brain in vertebrates, responsible for coordinating the details of complex body movements.

cerebral hemispheres
Paired outgrowths of nervous tissue at the front of the brain in vertebrates. They reach their greatest size and importance in mammals, where they are the main regions integrating behavior and processing information. In humans there is division of labor between the two hemispheres, with language mainly being processed in the left hemisphere.

chemoreception
The ability to detect particular chemical substances, a fundamental ability common to all animals. Taste and smell are forms of chemoreception.

chitin
A tough, horny substance that is the main material of arthropod exoskeletons. See also *exoskeleton*.

chromosome
One of a number of structures found in the cells of all animals and plants, each consisting of a single DNA molecule combined with various proteins. A single chromosome may contain thousands of different genes, and between them they contain the animal's genome. There is an identical set of chromosomes in nearly all the cells of the body. See also *DNA, gene, genome, protein*.

circadian rhythm
An internal physiological rhythm in animals with a time period of about a day. It can be thought of as an internal "biological clock," kept accurate by reference to outside events such as day and night.

circannual rhythm
An internal physiological rhythm with a period of about a year.

clade
A group of species consisting of all the evolutionary descendants of a given ancestor. Mammals are a clade, for example. Reptiles, however, are not a clade unless birds are included within them, since birds are descended from dinosaurs, which are reptiles. Cladistics is the approach to classification that seeks to use only clades to classify organisms, and to avoid using other terms.

cnidarians
A major group (phylum) of aquatic invertebrate animals with simple bodies bearing stinging cells and tentacles that surround a single opening (mouth). Cnidarians include corals, sea anemones, and jellyfish, and are often colonial.

colonial
Of an animal: living in colonies. A colony can consist of separate individuals, as with ant colonies, or animals joined by strands of living tissue, as is the case of many marine invertebrates, such as corals. Individuals may be specialized for different roles, such as feeding, reproduction, and defense, in which case the colony may behave more like a single individual.

commensal
Living in close association with an animal of another species, for example by sharing its burrow, without either helping or damaging it. See also *mutualism, symbiosis*.

communication
Processes in which an animal gives out information intended to influence the behavior of another animal. Most communication is between animals of the same species, and can relate to social life, reproduction, territorial disputes, or other aspects of life. Communication between different species often involves deceit. See also *deceit, display, scent marking, song, vocalization*.

conflict (internal)
The state of being torn between conflicting motivations, such as between attacking and fleeing. An animal often demonstrates internal conflict by resorting to a displacement activity such as grooming. See also *displacement activity, motivation*.

congregation
Any genuine, intentional social gathering of animals, as distinct from a mere aggregation. See also *aggregation, flocking, herding, schooling*.

consciousness
Roughly, being aware that one exists and of one's physical sensations and feelings. Consciousness probably exists in a number of other animals as well as in humans, although it is difficult to prove

either way. Behavioral scientists are also interested in self-consciousness (for example, whether an animal is aware that it is one particular chimpanzee among others).

convergent evolution
The phenomenon in which unrelated organisms have evolved to look similar as a result of being adapted to similar environments or ecological niches. For example, marsupial mice in Australia look similar to mice found elsewhere, but are not related.

copulation
The sex act in which sperm cells are deposited within the body of a partner, usually by a penis or equivalent structure. Copulation is most common in land animals, where the alternative of releasing unfertilized sex cells into the water is not available. In some hermaphrodite animals, each partner deposits sperm within the other. See also *spermatophore*.

countershading
A type of camouflage pattern in which an animal is typically darker above and lighter beneath. It tends to counter the effect of shadows, making the animal more difficult to see.

crustaceans
The dominant group of arthropods (jointed-legged invertebrates) found in the oceans. Crustaceans include crabs, lobsters, shrimp, and barnacles. See also *arthropods*.

cultural transmission
The passing on of behavior patterns from one animal to another through learning, rather than via the animals' genes. For example, knowledge of migration routes in birds and mammals is often passed on by cultural transmission.

deceit
The process in which an animal sends misleading information to others. A bird pretending to be injured in order to lure a predator from its nest is an example. See also *mimicry*.

delayed implantation
The phenomenon found in some mammals where the development of a fertilized egg is put "on hold" at an early stage, before implantation (attachment of the embryo to the wall of the uterus) has taken place. Implantation may be delayed for months, allowing young to be born at a time more suitable to both mother and baby. See also *uterus*.

dendrite
A branchlike outgrowth of a nerve cell (neuron) that carries incoming electrical signals to that cell. A neuron usually has many dendrites.

desiccation
The process or result of losing moisture content; drying up.

detritus
The decaying fragments of dead organisms. A detritivore is an animal that feeds on detritus.

diapause
A period, which may last for months, in which development or growth is suspended; the term is commonly used in the context of insect eggs or pupae.

dispersal, dispersion
(1) The phenomenon in which animals or animal groups leave their birth area for another area. Dispersal usually involves a one-way trip, in contrast to migration. Depending on the species, it is often only young males or young females that disperse. An explosive spread of a species, for instance as a result of a population explosion and food shortages, is called an irruption. See also *migration, nomadic*. **(2)** Dispersion also refers to the static pattern of an animal population in its environment, for example whether it is regularly spaced out or clumped together in small areas.

displacement activity
An activity such as preening, when carried out not for its own sake but at a time when the animal is in a state of conflict between opposing motivations, such as attacking or fleeing. See also *conflict, motivation*.

display
A form of visual communication in which an animal uses body postures, movements, and particular patterns on its body to communicate, usually to another member of the same species. The behavior is typically stereotyped for a given species, and the purposes can include courtship and threat.

disruptive coloration
Color patterns on an animal, often bold stripes and blotches, that disguise its shape; a form of camouflage.

DNA
Short for deoxyribonucleic acid, a very long molecule made up of small individual units. DNA is found in the cells of all animals and other living things; the order of the small units "spells out" the genetic instructions (genes) of the animal. See also *chromosome, gene, genome*.

dominance
Phenomenon in group-living animals in which some members of the group have a higher status than others. Dominant animals have more access to resources such as food and mates. Which animal becomes dominant may be settled by actual fighting or by ritualized displays.

dorsal
Relating to the back or upper surface of an animal. See also *ventral*.

echinoderms
A major group (phylum) of marine invertebrates that includes starfish, brittle stars, sea urchins, and sea cucumbers. Echinoderms have bodies arranged in parts rather like the spokes of a wheel (so-called "radial symmetry"). They use a unique system of hydraulic "tube feet" for moving or capturing prey or both.

echolocation
A method of locating and characterizing nearby objects used by dolphins, bats, and

some other animals, that involves emitting sounds and interpreting their echoes.

ecosystem
Any community of organisms considered together with the interactions between them and their associated physical environment.

ectoparasite
A parasite that lives on the outside of an animal. A louse is an example. See also *endoparasite, parasite*

ectothermic
Deriving body heat mainly from the environment, for example by basking in the sun's rays. See also *endothermic*.

emotion
A complex term that can refer to the subjective feeling of being angry, fearful, or happy for example, and also the bodily and behavioral changes associated with such feelings. Animal behavior experts usually focus on the latter, which are easier to measure and assess.

endoparasite
A parasite that lives within an animal, rather than on the outside surface. See also *ectoparasite, parasite*.

endoskeleton
An internal skeleton, typically made of bone. Unlike an exoskeleton, this type of skeleton is able to grow along with the rest of the body. See also *exoskeleton*.

endothermic
Deriving body heat mainly from internal chemical reactions, rather than from the environment. The main endothermic animal groups (birds and mammals) are also homeothermic, meaning that they keep their bodies at a constant temperature. See also *exothermic*.

enzyme
Any of a large variety of different molecules (nearly always proteins) that promote a particular chemical reaction in the body.

estivation
A bodily state similar to hibernation but occurring typically in the summer, to avoid dry conditions, for example.

estrous cycle
A regular cycle that occurs in the bodies of nonpregnant female mammals: the length of the cycle varies from days to months depending on the species. Each cycle includes a short period called estrus, or being "in heat," where the female is fertile and sexually receptive. The menstrual cycle of women and other female primates is a modified estrous cycle, but with sexual receptivity not limited to a short period.

ethology
The scientific study of animal behavior, especially in relation to how animals live under natural conditions.

eusocial
A term applied to highly organized animal societies, such as those of ants and termites. In colonies of eusocial animals there is typically a single breeding female (the queen), with other nonbreeding

workers and sometimes "soldiers" serving the colony's interests.

evolution

In its straightforward modern definition, evolution is simply any change in the average genetic makeup of a population of living things between one generation and the next. By this definition, evolution is an observed fact for many species, both in the wild and in laboratories. What is often called "the theory of evolution" is based on the idea, supported by various lines of evidence, that such genetic change is not random but is largely the result of natural selection, and that the operation of such processes over time can account for the huge variety of species found on Earth. See also *natural selection*.

evolutionary psychology

An academic approach to psychology that seeks to explain psychological phenomena as functional adaptations that have arisen during evolution. See also *adaptation*.

exogamy

Breeding outside one's own social group. In animals this is commonly achieved by young females or young males (depending on the species) leaving their original group and joining another one.

exoskeleton

A skeleton found on the outside of an animal. The term is mainly used in relation to insects and other arthropods. Exoskeletons combine support with body protection. See also *arthropod*.

experimental psychology

An academic approach to psychology based upon experiments, in contrast to pre-twentieth-century philosophical approaches. Experimental psychologists have traditionally studied animals in isolated laboratory conditions, in direct contrast to ethologists. See also *behaviorism, ethology*.

fertilization

The union of a male and female sex cell (in animals, a sperm and an egg cell) as the first step in the production of a new organism by sexual reproduction. In external fertilization, common in marine animals, eggs and sperm are released into the sea to meet by chance, while in internal fertilization, the male transfers sperm directly into the female's body.

filter feeding

Feeding by collecting and separating small food particles from the environment. When the food particles are suspended in water, it is also called suspension feeding. Collecting and straining small particles from mud and sand is called deposit feeding.

fission–fusion society

A type of animal society in which a larger group splits into smaller groups for some purposes (for example, feeding) and comes together for others (such as sleeping or migration). Examples include many monkeys, apes, and dolphins.

fitness

In evolutionary theory, "fitness" is the sum total of the qualities that give an individual an increased chance of leaving descendants. What makes an animal "fit" can include features such as a male peacock's tail that may be inconvenient for daily life, but helps attract females to mate with, and thus results in the male peacock having more offspring.

flash coloration

A form of defense in which a normally hidden pattern or color, such as eye-spots, is suddenly revealed when the animal is threatened, to startle a potential predator.

fledging

Of a young bird: in the process of developing feathers big enough to fly with. A fledgling is a young bird that has just reached the stage of being able to fly.

flocking

Group-forming behavior in birds, corresponding to herding in mammals and schooling in fishes. Its functions may include group defenses through "safety in numbers" and more accurate direction-finding during migration. See also *aggregation, herding, schooling*.

foraging

Activities concerned with seeking and obtaining food.

frugivorous

Fruit eating.

gamete

A sex cell (in animals, either a sperm cell or an unfertilized egg cell). Gametes typically contain just one copy of each of the body's chromosomes (the structures that between them carry the genes), whereas normal body cells have two copies. When sperm and egg combine during fertilization, the two-copy condition is restored. See also *chromosome, meiosis*.

gamma

See *alpha, beta, gamma*.

gastropods

The group of mollusks that includes snails and slugs. See also *mollusks*.

gene

A length of a DNA molecule that contains a particular genetic instruction. Many genes are blueprints for making particular protein molecules; others have a role in controlling other genes. Between them, the thousands of different genes in the body provide the instructions for a single cell to grow into an adult, and for many essential activities of the body to be carried out. Nearly every cell of an animal's body contains an identical set of its genes.

gene pool

Each of the thousands of different genes in the body may come in several varieties: the "gene pool" of a population or species of animal is a measure of the variety in their genes. If animals are highly inbred, their gene pool may be smaller, meaning that they have less genetic variety to deal with unexpected challenges, such as new diseases.

genome

The complete set of genes of a given species of animal or other living thing. The human genome, for example, is thought to contain about 20,000–25,000 different genes.

genotype

The genetic makeup of a particular organism. Identical twins, for example, have the same genotype because they share identical versions of all their genes. See also *phenotype*.

gestation

Pregnancy. In animals that produce live young, the gestation period is the time between fertilization and birth of the young.

gizzard

A region of the gut in which food is ground down before digestion. Many animals have gizzards, including birds and some worms.

gonad

Any organ that produces gametes (sex cells). It may be an ovary, a testis, or both at once. See also *ovary, testis*.

grooming

Behaviors that keep body coverings, such as fur or feathers, in good condition. In social animals, individuals may groom each other for secondary reasons such as appeasement. See also *appeasement, displacement activity*.

habituation

The phenomenon in which an animal reacts less and less to a repeated stimulus, such as a noise or a shadow overhead, if no harm follows. Habituation is a simple form of learning.

harem

In animal behavior, a group of females controlled by a single dominant male, who will defend them against other males trying to mate with them. Harems occur in many species of deer and antelope, for example. See also *polygamy*.

herding

A term used for group-forming behavior in mammals, especially large plant-eating species such as deer and antelope. Large herds are most common in open habitats that lack hiding places, where many eyes make it easier to spot predators. See also *aggregation, flocking, schooling*.

hermaphrodite

An animal that is both male and female at some point in its life. Species that are both sexes at once are called simultaneous hermaphrodites. There are also sequential hermaphrodites, which start out as males and become females later, or vice versa. Some species change sex repeatedly.

hibernation

A state in which the bodily processes of some animals are drastically slowed down in winter, with the animals becoming completely inactive. The term is mainly applied to mammals and birds that let their temperatures fall close to those of their surroundings. Less drastic inactive states are called dormancy, while similar states occurring for short periods are called torpor. See also *estivation*.

hoarding

The practice of hiding food items for later use. An animal may either hide its food in a single "larder" (caching), or in small amounts in different locations (scatter hoarding).

homeostasis

The maintenance of stable conditions within the body, for example in terms of chemical balance and temperature.

home range

The area in which an animal carries out most of its activities. A home range may or may not also be a territory. See *territory*.

hormone

A circulating chemical messenger produced by one part of the body that affects other organs or parts.

hydroids

A group of simple aquatic animals (cnidarians) that grow as small, branching colonies attached to rocks or seaweed. See also *cnidarians*.

imitation

The ability to observe and copy what another animal does. See also *mimicry*.

imprinting

A type of learning that occurs during a "sensitive period" in the early life of many birds and mammals, whereby the young animal forms an attachment to a particular place or object, treating it as a parent. While in nature it would attach to its real parent, in captivity young animals can imprint on humans or even inanimate objects. See also *sensitive period*.

infrared

Radiation similar to light but with a longer wavelength. It is invisible to humans and most animals, although it can be detected as "radiant heat."

infrasound

Sound that is too low in pitch for humans to hear, but is used for communication by some other animals.

innate

Inborn, in contrast to being learned or acquired from the environment.

insight

In animal studies, a term used especially in relation to learning and problem solving: an animal is said to have insight if it solves a problem by understanding its nature, rather than by trial and error, for example.

instinct

Any unlearned, genetically inherited ability enabling an animal to act in a particular way—for example, nest building in most birds is instinctive.

intelligence

An ability to think and solve problems in a way that involves understanding, and is not completely automatic or preprogrammed. Although some animal species appear to be more intelligent than others, it is difficult to devise tests to compare the intelligence of different animals in an unbiased way.

intraspecific

Within a species, or between members of the same species.

invertebrate

Any animal without a backbone. Of the 30 or so major groups (phyla) that animals are classifed into, vertebrates (animals with a backbone) form only a part of one phylum; all the rest are invertebrates.

irruption

See *dispersal*.

isolation call

A call emitted by the young of some animals when separated from their parent(s) that tends to bring the parent to their aid.

isolation mechanism

Any feature of anatomy, physiology, behavior, or the environment that serves to prevent members of different animal species or populations from breeding with each other.

iteroparous

Breeding repeatedly as adults, as compared with once only. See also *semelparous*.

Jacobson's organ

An extra organ of smell, also called the vomeronasal organ, located in the roof of the mouth in most land vertebrates (although apparently not primates). When snakes flicker their tongues, for example, they are transferring molecules from the air to be detected by this organ.

jawless fishes

Two groups of primitive fishes, lampreys and hagfishes, that branched off the line of fish evolution before jaws had evolved. See also *bony fishes, cartilaginous fishes*.

kinesis

A simple form of behavior in which animals move more quickly in unsuitable habitats, thus tending to end up in suitable locations without directly seeking them. An example is wood lice or sowbugs, which are more active in dry, well-lit environments that are less suitable for them. See also *taxis*.

kin selection

A form of natural selection in which a genetic trait spreads if it benefits enough of an individual animal's relatives (which share many of the same genes with it), even if the individual itself leaves no direct descendants. Kin selection is thought to explain the existence of apparently unselfish behavior in some animals. See also *altruism*.

K-strategist

A species that competes with others by becoming dominant in a stable ecosystem over the longer term. *K*-strategist animals are typically larger, invest more energy in body growth than reproduction, and have longer life histories than the contrasting r-strategist species. See also r-strategist, strategy.

language, animal

True language is sometimes defined as requiring grammatical rules and a wide vocabulary, so that new messages never encountered before can be sent and understood. In this sense, some animals such as chimpanzees do appear to show language abilities, in addition to communication skills in the broader sense. See also *communication*.

larva

A young stage of an animal, when completely different in form from the adult. Caterpillars and tadpoles are examples.

learning

Gaining information or acquiring new skills as a result of experience. Learning in an animal may take place in various ways, such as by trial and error, observation, or insight. See also *habituation, imprinting, maturation*.

lek system

A mating system that involves males gathering communally and competing for the attention of females by performing displays, building mounds, or undertaking other "show-off" activities. Species that use lek systems include many birds, such as peacocks, and some species of antelope. See also *mating system, display*.

lineage

Any branch on an evolutionary "family tree," consisting of a species or group plus its forebears, traced back to an original ancestor. See also *clade*.

mangrove swamp

A forestlike ecosystem found on many sandy and muddy coastlines in the tropics, and based on the growth of saltwater-tolerant mangrove trees.

mantle

In mollusks, the layer of tissue, originally forming the upper surface of the animal, that secretes the mollusk's shell. See also *mollusks*.

mating system

The typical pattern of mating behavior for any particular species. Different mating systems include monogamy (a single male and female paired together, either for life or a single season), promiscuity (in which both sexes have multiple partners), and polygyny (one male with several females). The term also includes the methods by which individuals compete for partners, such as the lek system. See also *lek system, polygamy*.

matrix

A term used in various different senses, often with the meaning of "surrounding substance." In bone, cartilage, and other connective tissues, the term refers to the noncellular supporting material in which the cells are embedded.

maturation

The situation of new features or behaviors appearing as an animal grows older, especially behaviors that are inborn and do not depend on learning. See also *learning*.

medusa

One of the two main body forms of cnidarians. Unlike the other form (polyp), medusas are wide and saucer shaped, as well as usually free-floating and able to swim. A jellyfish is an example of a medusa. See also *cnidarians, polyp*.

meiosis

The way in which a cell nucleus divides during the process of making sex cells (gametes). Unlike in normal cell division, the cells formed as a result of meiosis contain only half the number of chromosomes found in the original cell. See also *chromosome, gamete, mitosis*.

memory

Scientists distinguish between various types of memory, including semantic memory (knowledge of facts), episodic memory (memory for personal events), and procedural memory (memory for how to do things, such as riding a bicycle) as well as between long-term and short-term memory. Studies of the brain have confirmed that these are real distinctions, with different types of memory associated with distinct areas of the brain.

metabolism

The sum total of all the chemical reactions taking place in the body.

metamorphosis

A process in which an animal's body undergoes a major change in structure between the young stage and adult. Metamorphosis occurs in many species, including crabs, starfish, frogs, and butterflies. In insects, complete metamorphosis involves a total change in shape during a resting phase, called a pupa. During incomplete metamorphosis, a series of smaller changes occur each time the animal molts.

metapopulation

Any population of organisms that is made up of a number of smaller, semi-isolated subpopulations scattered throughout a given area. Many animal species exist naturally as metapopulations.

migration

A regular, often annual, large-scale movement of animals of a particular species from one region to another and back again, often connected with seeking food or breeding sites. See also *dispersal, nomadic*.

mimicry

The phenomenon in which one species of animal has evolved to look very similar to another unrelated animal; the assumption is that the mimicking animal gains benefit from the resemblance, especially via predators avoiding it. Where a harmless animal mimics a dangerous or poisonous one, it is called Batesian mimicry; where two or more dangerous species resemble each other, Müllerian mimicry. See also *imitation*.

mitosis

The process by which chromosomes are copied and shared out during normal cell division. The two cells that are produced have the same number of chromosomes as the original cell. See also *chromosome, meiosis*.

mobbing

The harassing of a predator by a group of its potential prey, for example of a hawk by a group of small birds.

mollusks

A major group (phylum) of invertebrate animals that includes the gastropods (snails and slugs), bivalves (clams and relatives), and cephalopods (octopuses, squid, and relatives). Mollusks are soft-bodied and typically have hard shells, though some subgroups have lost their shell during their evolution.

montane

Relating to mountains, and especially to upland habitats where trees can still grow—that is, habitats lying below the tree line.

motivation

A mental or bodily condition (or both) within an animal causing it to do something; also, the goal toward which the animal's activity is aimed. See also *conflict*.

Müllerian mimicry

See *mimicry*.

musth

A phenomenon in which some male animals (especially elephants and camels) become aggressive at a particular time of year. Musth is caused by increased male sex hormones and is related to the breeding cycle.

mutualism

A close relationship between two different species in which both benefit.

natural selection

The evolutionary process by which the environment favors the fittest individuals in a given population, weeding out those that are less fit. Since fitness is partly inherited, this should result in a population or species changing genetically over time and (other things being equal) becoming better adapted to their environment. See also *fitness*.

neoteny

See *pedomorphosis*.

nerve net

A netlike arrangement of individually connected nerve cells (neurons), without a central brain. Some simple invertebrate animals rely only on nerve nets, but still show quite sophisticated behavior.

neuron

A nerve cell. A simple neuron consists of a rounded cell body, branchlike outgrowths called dendrites that carry incoming electrical signals to the neuron, and a single cablelike extension, called an axon, that transmits outgoing messages. In practice, however, many neurons are more complex than this. See also *dendrite*.

neurotransmitter

Any of various chemical substances released by nerve cells that stimulate other nerve cells or muscles. Drugs such as antidepressants often work by affecting the amounts of different neurotransmitters active in the brain. See also *synapse*.

niche

Roughly, the ecological role that an animal or other living thing plays; also the role itself (for example "small, tree-living insect-eater"). Ecological theory says that no two species can occupy exactly the same niche, because one should out-compete the other.

niche splitting

The phenomenon in which an animal takes over part of the niche of another animal. For example, an invading bird species may outcompete a native bird when hunting insects low down in a tree, but the native bird may still be at an advantage when hunting higher up; the original niche therefore becomes "split."

nomadic

Of an animal: wandering widely and irregularly as part of its lifestyle (for example, in response to food shortages), as distinct from undertaking regular migrations. See also *migration*.

nursery

A group formed by the young of several mothers, usually looked after by several adults. The young of penguins and of some mammals form nurseries.

omnivore

Literally, "eating all." An animal whose natural diet includes a wide variety of animal and vegetable food.

ontogeny

The development of any life form from individual cell up to adult.

operculum

A term with various applications in zoology, all related to the original Latin meaning of "covering" or "lid." It can mean: the horny or calcareous disk used by many snails to shut themselves into their shells; the flaps that cover the gills of bony fishes and tadpoles; or any of various other structures. An opercular cavity is the space beneath the operculum of a fish or tadpole.

opposable

Of a thumb or other digit: able to be pressed against other digits of the same hand or foot, allowing objects to be grasped.

orientation

Accurately keeping track of one's direction or position in the environment. Different animals have different ways of orientating themselves (often using more than one at a time). Examples include counting the number and angle of the steps they take (some ants), observing the sun, moon, and stars, and detecting the Earth's magnetic field. See also *migration*.

ovary

An organ in female or hermaphrodite animals that produces egg cells. It usually has other functions such as producing sex hormones that affect the animal's body.

oviduct

A tubelike anatomical structure that conveys eggs from an animal's ovary. In mammals, the oviduct is highly modified, with part of it expanded to form the uterus, or womb.

oviparous

Producing eggs, as distinct from live young. See also *ovoviviparous, viviparous.*

ovipositor

An egg-laying tube extending out from the body of some female animals, especially in insects.

ovoviviparous

Producing eggs that are allowed to hatch within the female's body, so that live young are produced. See also *oviparous, viviparous.*

parasite

Any organism that lives in or on the body of a organism and feeds off it for an extended period. See also *ectoparasite, endoparasite.*

parasitoid

An animal that, while a larva, feeds on or inside another animal usually killing this host, before emerging to become a mature, free-living adult. Most parasitoids are insects.

parasympathetic nervous system

See *autonomic nervous system.*

parthenogenesis

Literally "virgin birth." Reproduction from an unfertilized egg cell. Females of some invertebrates, such as aphids, produce young parthenogenetically only during the summer months, when food is abundant. A few species always reproduce in this way, and form all-female populations. Unfertilized parthenogenetic eggs typically already contain two copies of each chromosome (see *gamete*).

pedomorphosis

Also called *neoteny,* an evolutionary trend in which a larval or juvenile stage becomes sexually mature, and no longer develops into the original "adult"; also, the retention of formerly juvenile characteristics into adulthood.

pelagic

Associated with the waters of the open ocean, distant from both the shore and the sea bottom.

phenotype

The sum of the observable characteristics of an individual organism. For example, identical twins, sharing the same genetic makeup (genotype), may not look identical because of differences in diet or other aspects of lifestyle. See also *genotype*.

pheromone

An odor produced to communicate with others of the same species—to attract the opposite sex, for example.

phylogeny

The pattern of evolutionary history of a species or group of species, or of an individual feature such as the eye. Phylogenetic classification uses methods such as cladistics to classify animals based on their evolutionary history. See also *clade*.

phylum (pl. phyla)

The highest-level grouping in the classification of the animal kingdom. Each phylum has a unique basic body plan. Mollusks, arthropods, and echinoderms are examples of phyla.

placenta

A fleshy structure, rich in blood vessels, that develops on the wall of the uterus during pregnancy in most mammals.

It connects the growing embryo to the mother and allows nutrition and waste products to pass between the two. A similar structure is found in some other animals such as sharks.

plankton

Marine or freshwater life forms living in open water that cannot swim strongly and so drift with the currents.

play

Activities that are not immediately useful, but are seemingly done just for fun. They are associated mainly with young animals, and usually interpreted as being useful in practicing skills for later life, or for learning about the environment.

polarized light

Light waves that all vibrate in one particular direction or plane. Some animals can detect polarized light coming from the sun or sky, helping them navigate.

polygamy

Any mating system in which males or females or both have multiple sex partners. The term is sometimes used specifically to mean a system where one male controls and mates with a number of females, which is more strictly called polygyny. Where only females have multiple partners it is called polyandry; where both sexes do, promiscuity. See also *mating system*.

polyp

One of two main body forms of cnidarians (the other form being a medusa). A sea anemone or coral animal is a polyp. Polyps are typically tubular in form and attached at their base. See also *cnidarians, medusa.*

prehensile

Capable of grasping. The tails of many monkeys are prehensile, for example.

problem solving

Achieving a particular goal when the method of doing so is not immediately obvious. See also *insight, intelligence.*

proteins

Molecules found in the body, consisting of long, folded strands made up of small units called amino acids. Proteins are vital to life, and there are thousands of different kinds. Nearly all enzymes are proteins, as is the horny substance that makes up hair and nails. See also *enzyme*.

protists

A wide grouping of often unrelated, mainly microscopic organisms, traditionally classified as a single kingdom. Protists are single-celled, and include algal forms, which photosynthesize, and protozoans, which do not. Their cells contain nuclei, like the cells of animals and plants, but unlike those of bacteria. See also *algae*.

reflex

An involuntary response in the nervous system to certain stimuli, for example the "knee-jerk" response in humans. Some reflexes, called conditioned reflexes, can be modified by learning.

reproductive investment

The amount of effort—in terms of time or food resources, for example—that

parents devote to reproduction, or to their individual offspring.

respiration

(1) Breathing. (2) Also called cellular respiration, the biochemical processes within cells that break down food molecules to provide energy, usually by combining the food molecules with oxygen.

ritualization

An evolutionary process whereby an activity originally done for practical reasons—for example, grooming—comes to acquire a secondary function in communication. Many animal displays contain ritualized versions of other behaviors.

r-strategist

A species that survives and competes by devoting itself to prolific reproduction ("r") rather than to large body size. Such species typically have short life cycles and do well in less stable environments. See also *K-strategist, strategy.*

ruminant

A mammal such as a cow, antelope, or deer with a stomach in several compartments. The first compartment, the rumen, contains microorganisms that partially digest the animal's usually grassy diet, whose food value would not otherwise be available to the animal.

rut

The breeding season of deer, often occurring in the fall. The rut, or rutting season, is marked by intense rivalry between males. It often involves roaring ("rut" is an old word for roar) and fighting. The term may also be applied to the breeding seasons of other hoofed mammals.

satellite male

A male animal living unobtrusively within the territory of a larger or more dominant male, seeking the opportunity to mate with females that are attracted by the dominant animal.

scavenger

An animal that feeds by eating the remains of other animals, such as those killed and left by a predator.

scent-marking

The deposition of odors by an animal onto the environment, or sometimes onto itself or another animal. The odors are usually produced by specialized scent glands. They may be used to mark territory, but can also have other functions such as creating "landmarks" to follow after dark.

schooling

The tendency of many fish species to gather together in large groups. The schooling is probably done for a number of reasons, including confusing a predator trying to pick out one individual target among many. Schools formed by sea mammals, such as dolphins, tend to have other functions, such as cooperative hunting. See also *aggregation, flocking, herding.*

search image

A "mental picture" that predatory animals seem capable of developing, which helps them recognize a particular prey species.

selfish-gene theories

Evolutionary theories emphasizing that the individual genes of an organism may tend to favor their own spread, rather than any overall "good" of the individual, or of the species as a whole.

semelparous

Programmed to breed only once before dying. Examples include salmon, octopuses, and many insects.

sensitive period

A period in the life of a young animal in which it is particularly receptive to learning certain skills or information, such as details of its parents' bird song, in a young bird. See also *imprinting*.

sexual dimorphism

The condition in which the males and females of a species differ obviously in appearance, for example, in color, shape, or size.

sexual selection

A type of natural selection in which a feature has developed solely because of its advantages in furthering sexual reproduction. The two main types are male rivalry—resulting, for example, in the evolution of large antlers in male deer for fighting each other with—and female choice, in which features such as the male peacock's tail have apparently evolved because they attract females. In both cases, the features may be a nuisance or disadvantage for the rest of the animal's lifestyle.

social insects

Insects that live in colonies in complex societies. The main social insects are wasps, bees, ants, and termites. See also *eusocial*.

sociobiology

The study of the biological bases of social behavior, especially in an ecological and evolutionary context.

song

In studies of birds, "song" refers to a specific kind of communication distinct from other bird calls. The main purposes of bird songs, which are usually uttered by males, are thought to be territorial defense against rivals and attraction of a mate. See also *vocalization*.

spermatophore

A protective package containing sperm, produced by some animals including octopuses and spiders. Depending on the species, it is either transferred directly to the female or left for her to pick up.

sperm competition

Literally, the competition between sperm (of different males) to fertilize a female's egg cells within her body. Sperm competition is thought to be the evolutionary force behind many features of animals, such as the size of the testes in different species.

sporocyst

A nonmoving larval stage in some parasitic worms. Within each sporocyst, a number of embryos grow, each developing into the next larval stage—part of the process in which a single egg gives rise to many adult worms.

strategy

As used in biology, an overall pattern of living shaped by evolution that helps an organism survive (more fully, evolutionary strategy); it does not imply conscious thought. Different animals typically have different strategies: see for example *K-selection, r-selection*.

stress

An altered bodily state in an animal, especially a vertebrate, resulting from exposure to threatening or painful stimuli. Stress typically involves changes in the body's hormones and alterations in the animal's behavior.

supernormal stimulus

A stimulus greater than anything of its kind found in nature. For example, a male butterfly may find an unnatural, large model female more attractive than the real thing.

symbiosis

A close living relationship between two species, that may benefit both animals involved, or may be more exploitative. See also *commensalism, mutualism, parasite*.

sympathetic nervous system

See *autonomic nervous system*.

synapse

A close contact between two nerve cells (neurons) allowing information to be passed between them. Synapses can either be electrical (the information is transmitted electrically) or chemical (chemicals called neurotransmitters are released from one neuron and stimulate the next). See also *neurotransmitter*.

syrinx

The sound-producing organ of birds. In contrast to the larynx of mammals, the syrinx is situated at the bottom of the trachea (windpipe).

tactile

Relating to touch.

taxis

A directed movement of an animal toward a particular place. See also *kinesis*.

teneral

A term applied to a newly emerged adult insect in which the outer covering (exoskeleton) is still soft and the colors are yet to fully develop.

territory

A particular area or section of habitat defended by an animal or group of animals against rivals, usually of the same species. See also *home range*.

testis

An organ in male or hermaphrodite animals that produces sperm cells. It usually has other functions such as producing sex hormones, which affect the animal's own body.

thorax

The chest region of land vertebrates, containing the heart and lungs; also the middle body division of insects and other arthropods.

threat display

A form of display performed by an animal that is threatening aggression. The threat may be directed against members of the same species or against other species. See also *display*.

tool

An external object, such as a twig, used by an animal for a particular purpose. Some bird and mammal species regularly use tools, and may trim or alter them to make them more effective.

trachea

The windpipe of vertebrates; also, any of the air tubes in insects and other land arthropods.

tunicates

A group of mainly filter-feeding marine invertebrates related to backboned animals (vertebrates). They include both attached forms (sea squirts) and others that drift in the plankton.

ultrasound

Sound too high in pitch for humans to hear, although other animals may be able to hear it.

ultraviolet

Radiation similar to light but with a shorter wavelength. It is invisible to humans but can be seen by other animals, including many insects and birds.

unken reflex

A defensive posture adopted by many frogs and other amphibians, in which brightly colored skin, usually on the underside, is exposed to warn a predator that the animal is distasteful.

uterus

In mammals, the enlarged part of the female reproductive tract in which the young develop before birth.

ventral

Relating to the lower surface or belly of an animal. See also *dorsal*.

vertebrate

Any animal with a backbone, including amphibians, reptiles, birds, mammals, and almost all fishes. See also *invertebrate*.

viviparous

Giving birth to live young, especially when nourished by a placenta or similar structure, rather than developing from eggs hatched within the female's body. See also *oviparous, ovoviviparous, placenta*.

vocalization

Uttering sounds by means of a vocal organ, such as the larynx of mammals and the syrinx of birds. Animals also make use of nonvocalized sounds, for example the drumming of woodpeckers. See also *song, syrinx*.

vomeronasal organ

See *Jacobson's organ*.

worms

Any of various, usually nonswimming, invertebrate animals that are long, slender, and flexible, and lack shells. There are several major groups (phyla) of worms, including flatworms, roundworms, and segmented worms, such as earthworms and their relatives.

Index

Page numbers in **bold** indicate illustrated references.

Acknowledgments

Dorling Kindersley would like to thank the following people for their help in the preparation of this book: Dawn Techow, Anna Pikovsky, and Udayan Chattopadhyay at the American Museum of Natural History for their help in co-ordinating the project; Peter Laws for early design work; Jack Metcalf for administrative assistance; and Helen Gilks, Daniel Gilpin, and Rachelle Macapagal.

Charlotte Uhlenbroek would like to thank: Ben Anderson and Simon McCreadie for help with research; Julian Partridge of Bristol University and Bridget Waller of the University of Portsmouth for comments on the text; Dan Rees, for his support and patience; and Sheila Abelman for being a wonderful agent and helping to get this project off the ground.

For their help in supplying images, **Laura Barwick** would like to thank: all at DK Image Library; Martin Copeland and Jenny Baskaya for their in-house support; Rebecca Sodergren and Sarah Hopper for picture research cover; and, in particular, all the researchers at the main contributing agencies who helped turn over every stone to find the very best pictures for this title.

Sources for the illustrations listed below are as follows: **p.111** Cuvier's beaked whale diving graph: Peter Tyack et al, *Journal of Experimental Biology*, Vol. 209, p.4238; **p.121** Seismic signalling in mole rats: "Seismic signal transmission between burrows of the Cape mole-rat," P. M. Narins, O. J. Reichman, J. U. M. Jarvis, and E. R. Lewis, *Journal of Comparative Physiology*, 170:13-21, 1992; **p.127** Timelags in sound reception: www.nature.com/journal/v417/n6886/images/417322a-f1.2jp; **p.128** Echolocation in sperm whales: http://palaeo.gly.bris.ac.uk/Palaeofiles/whales/odontoceti.htm; **p.129** Echolocation by Australian cave swiftlets: "Hearing and echolocation in the Australian grey swiftlet", Roger B. Coles, Masakazu Konishi, and John D. Pettigrew, *Journal of Experimental Biology* 129, 365-371, 1987; **p.140** Territorial boundaries of the Malaysian giant ant: "Territoriality in the Malaysian giant ant Camponotus gigas," Martin Pfeiffer and Karl E. Linsenmair, *Journal of Ethology* Volume 19, Number 2, 75-85, December 2001; **p.149** Body fat and migration in birds: *The Complete Encyclopedia of Birds and Bird Migration*, Christopher M. Perrins and Jonathan Elphick, 2003, p.26; **p.194** Intestine length in starlings: F. Harvey Pough, Christine M. Janis, and John B. Heiser, *Vertebrate Life*, p.461; **p.214** Attacks by great whites: "Graphs of white shark attacks and percentage of fatal attacks by decade" (web publication), International Shark Attack File, Florida Museum of Natural History, University of Florida; **p.218** Stoplight loosejaw, red emission and sensitivity: "Dragon fish see using chlorophyll," R. H. Douglas, J. C. Partridge, K. Dulai, D. Hunt, C. W. Mullineaux, A. Y. Tauber and P. H. Hynninen, *Nature* 393, 423-424, 4 June 1998; **p.218** Pharyngeal jaws in moray eels: "Raptoral jaws in the throat help moray eels swallow large prey," Rita S. Mehta and Peter C. Wainwright, *Nature* 449, 79–82, 6 September 2007; **p.234** Electro-sensitivity in the bill of the duck-billed platypus: "Electroreception and the feeding behaviour of platypus," Paul R. Manger and John D. Pettigrew, *Philosophical Transactions: Biological Sciences* 347(1322):359–381; **p.241** Western pipistrelle attack sequence: "Echolocation by insect-eating bats," Hans-Ulrich Schnitzler and Elizabeth K.V. Kalko, *BioScience* July 2001/Vol.51 No.7; **p.241** Echo recognition in greater horseshoe bats: "Classification of insects by echolocating greater horseshoe bats," G. von der Emde and H-U. Schnitzler, *Journal of Comparative Physiology*, August 1990/Vol. 167 No.3; **p.246** Lobtail feeding in humpback whales: "Culture in whales and dolphins," L. Rendell and H. Whitehead, *Behavioural and Brain Sciences* 24 (2); **p.310** Plumage change in the willow ptarmigan: "Cryptic behaviour in moulting hen willow ptarmigan lagopus l. lagopus during snow melt," Johan B. Steen, Kjell Einar Erikstad, and Karsten Høidal, *Ornis Scandinavica*, Vol. 23, No.1 (Jan.–Mar., 1992), pp.101–104; **p.465** Kangaroo rat sonogram: J.A. Randall, *Acoustic Society of America*; **p.449** Grey reef shark: Richard H. Johnson and Donald R. Nelson, *Copeia*, Vol. No.1, 1973.

The publisher would like to thank the following for their kind permission to reproduce their photographs:

(Key: a-above; b-below/bottom; c-centre; f-far; l-left; r-right; t-top)

1 Christian Ziegler: (b). **2-3 naturepl.com:** Christophe Courteau. **4-5 National Geographic Image Collection:** Norbert Rosing (t). **6 Corbis:** Martin Harvey. **6 Corbis:** Steve Kaufman. **7 Alamy Images:** Roger Munns (cla). **Corbis:** Gary Bell/zefa (cr). **FLPA:** Andrew Forsyth (cl); Frans Lanting (cra); Martin B Withers (crb). **Getty Images:** Winfried Wisniewski/Image Bank (bl); Art Wolfe (clb). **National Geographic Image Collection:** Steve Winter (tl). **stevebloom.com:** (br). **8-9 stevebloom.com. 10-1 Corbis:** Steve Kaufman. **10-77 Corbis:** Steve Kaufman. **12 Ardea:** Jean Paul Ferrero (fcla). **FLPA:** Colin Marshall (br). **Getty Images:** James Balog (ftl); Bill Beatty (fclb); Ralph Lee Hopkins/National Geographic (crb); Jeff Lepore (bl). **naturepl.com:** Willem Kolvoort (fcra); Michel Roggo (cra); Jeff Rotman (fbl). **Gastone Pivatelli:** (clb). **Science Photo Library:** Gilbert S. Grant (fcrb). **SeaPics.com:** (tr) (cla). **stevebloom.com:** (tl) (fbr) (ftr). **13 Ardea:** Jean Michel Labat (cl). **Corbis:** Paul Souders (cr). **naturepl.com:** Nick Garbutt (crb). **Photolibrary:** Phototake Inc (tr). **Alex Wild/myrmecos.net:** (cra). **14 DK Images:** Jerry Young (bl) (bc). **15 Alamy Images:** Rolf Nussbaumer (br). **Ardea:** D. Parer & E. Parer-Cook (cr). **18 DK Images:** Colin Keates (c) Dorling Kindersley, Courtesy of the Natural History Museum, London (cra) (crb). **19 DK Images:** Colin Keates (c) Dorling Kindersley, Courtesy of the Natural History Museum, London (crb). **20 Alamy Images:** Nordic Photos (cb). **Shutterstock:** Michael J Thompson (bl). **21 Alamy Images:** Terry Whittaker (br/tworhino). **Photolibrary:** Mary Plage/OSF (br). **Shutterstock:** Stephane Angue (cb); John Carleton (cra); EcoPrint (crb/black rhino); Jan Gottwald (crb); Volker Kirchberg (tr); Snowleopard1 (crb/indian rhino); Elena Talberg (br/rhinos); Chris Turner (cr). **22 Alamy Images:** blickwinkel (cla). **Science Photo Library:** Peter Scoones (cr); Sinclair Stammers (br). **SeaPics.com:** (tl). **Shutterstock:** Ian Scott (ca) (cra). **23 Klaus Lang & WWF Indonesia:** (bl). **naturepl.com:** Rod Williams (clb). **Shutterstock:** Ziga Camernik (cl); Luis Louro (fcl); Victor Soares (c). **26 Andrew Martinez:** (cl). **Photolibrary:** N. M. Collins/OSF (fclb); Micromacro (bl). **Linda Pitkin/lindapitkin.net:** (cr) (clb). **27 Paul Kay:** (br). **Sue Scott:** (cr). **29 FLPA:** R. Dirscherl. **32 Oceanwide Images:** Gary Bell/oceanwideimages.com (bc). **SeaPics.com:** (cl). **34 Warren Photographic:** Kim Taylor (clb/mantis). **35 DK Images:** Frank Greenaway (c) Dorling Kindersley, Courtesy of the Natural History Museum, London (crb). **40 Ardea:** Becca Saunders (cr). **Corbis:** Brandon D. Cole (br). **imagequestmarine.com:** Kelvin Aiken/V & W (bc). **naturepl.com:** Brandon Cole (ca); Naturbild (cra). **41 imagequestmarine.com:** Peter Herring (cb); Masa Ushioda (cra) (ca). **naturepl.com:** Solvin Zankl (tl). **Photolibrary:** Rudie H Kuitel/OSF (tr). **John E Randall:** (cb). **Science Photo Library:** Peter Scoones (cb). **42 Alamy Images:** Stephen Frink Collection (ca). **John E Randall:** (cra). **SeaPics.com:** (tr). **43 Photolibrary:** Richard Herrman/OSF (crb). **46 Bruce Coleman Inc:** Jack Dermid (cb). **David M. Dennis:** (crb). **Chris Mattison Nature Photographics:** (cr). **NHPA/Photoshot:** Robert Erwin (clb); Pavel German (c). **47 Ardea:** Hans & Judy Besle (cb). **Dr W.R. Branch:** (cr). **Bruce Coleman Inc:** S. C. Bisserot (clb); Dr M. P. Kahl (c). **R.W. Van Devender:** (tc). **Chris Mattison Nature Photographics:** (tc). **NHPA/Photoshot:** Daniel Heuclin (cl). **48 fogdenphotos.com :** M & P Fogden (cl). **Chris Mattison Nature Photographics:** (bc); Chris Mattison Nature Photographics (tc). **49 Thomas Marent. 52 Photolibrary:** Randy Morse (br). **53 Ardea:** Jean Paul Ferrero (cl). **fogdenphotos.com :** M & P Fogden (ca). **naturepl.com:** Mike Wilkes (ca). **54 Dr Indraneil Das:** (ca). **Chris Mattison Nature Photographics:** (tr) (bc). **NHPA/Photoshot:** Daniel Heuclin (br). **Photolibrary:** Zig Leszczynski/OSF (cra). **55 DK Images:** Chris Mattison Photographics (cb). **Chris Mattison Nature Photographics:** (tc) (cra) (tl). **Mark O'Shea:** (cl) (clb). **Photolibrary:** M & P Fogden/OSF (br). **58 Alamy Images:** Genevieve Vallee (cla). **DK Images:** Peter Cross (c) Dorling Kindersley, Courtesy of Twycross Zoo, Atherstone, Leicestershire (cra). **Roger Wilmshurst:** (bl). **59 Ardea:** Jean Paul Ferrero (c). **DK Images:** Kim Taylor (br). **FLPA:** Panda Photo (cb). **Andre van Huizen:** (tc). **rspb-images.com:** Bill Paton (cr). **Roger Wilmshurst:** (clb). **60 David Barnes:** (tl). **Bruce Coleman Inc:** Christian Zuber (cr). **DK Images:** Chris Gomersall Photography (tc). **Chris Mattison Nature Photographics:** (bc). **rspb-images.com:** Carlos Sanchez Alonso (br). **61 Roger Wilmshurst:** (cla). **62 Chris Gomersall Photography:** David Tipling (tr). **Bruce Coleman Inc:** Werner Layer (cl). **David Tipling Photo Library:** A Morris (cr); David Tipling (fcra). **FLPA:** Don Smith (bl). **Chris Mattison Nature Photographics:** (cra). **rspb-images.com:** Dusan Boucny (cb). **Shutterstock:** Mike Rogal (bc). **63 Robert E. Barber:** (tc). **Roger De La Harpe/Africaimagery.com:** (bc). **Nigel Dennis:** (clb). **FLPA:** Yossi Fahhol (fcra); Jurgen & Christine Sohns (cr). **naturepl.com:** Pete Oxford (bl). **NHPA/Photoshot:** Kevin Schafer (tl). **Photolibrary:** Sean Morris/OSF (c). **Roger Wilmshurst:** (cra). **64 Ardea:** John S Dunning (cl) (bc). **Chris Gomersall Photography:** P J Ginn (tr); Morten Strange (crb); Ray Tipper (tc). **Nigel Dennis:** (br). **Hanne & Jens Eriksen:** (bl). **FLPA:** T & P Gardner (clb). **fogdenphotos.com :** M & P Fogden (cla). **Thomas Holden:** (cra). **NHPA/Photoshot:** A. N. T. Photo Library (tl) (cb); Haroldo Palo Jr (ftr) (c). **Vireo:** Doug Wechsler (ca). **Dave Watts:** (cr). **65 Ardea:** Pat Morris (tr). **Chris Gomersall Photography:** Mike Lane (tl); Gordon Langsbury (tc). **Nigel Dennis:** (br). **DK Images:** Gary Ombler (c) Dorling Kindersley, Courtesy of Paradise Park, Cornwall (bl). **NHPA/Photoshot:** Kevin Schafer (ca). **Colin Varndell:** (crb). **Vireo:** Doug Wechsler (cl). **Dave Watts:** (cla). **66 Ardea:** John S Dunning (cb). **John Cancalosi:** (bl). **DK Images:** Maslowski Photo (tc); George McCarthy (tl). **Hanne & Jens Eriksen:** (cr). **Jack Jeffrey:** (bc). **Chris Mattison Nature Photographics:** (tr). **70 John Cancalosi:** (clb/Rufus bettong). **DK Images:** Jerry Young (cra). **Dr C Andrew Henley/Larus:** (clb). **Chris Mattison Nature Photographics:** (cr) (br). **naturepl.com:** Tom Vezo (c). **Dave Watts:** (ca). **P. A. Woolley and D. Walsh:** (cb). **71 Ardea:** Kenneth W. Fink (cb/tamandua); Peter Steyn (tl). **BIOS Photo:** Jany Sauvanet (crb). **Nigel Dennis:** (tr). **DK Images:** Jerry Young (cb/armadillo). **Getty Images:** Theo Allofs/Photonica (br). **naturepl.com:** Doug Perrine (cr). **Galen B. Rathbun:** (tc). **72 Corbis:** Frans Lanting (bl). **Peter Cross:** (cr). **DK Images:** Frank Blackburn (c) Dorling Kindersley, Courtesy of the Marwell Zoological Park, Winchester (cra); Exmoor Zoo (ca/striped grass mouse); Rollin Verlinde (cl); Jerry Young (ca/spiny mouse). **FLPA:** Frank W. Lane (cla). **Mike Jordan:** (c). **Chris Mattison Nature Photographics:** (br). **73 André Bärtschi/wildtropix.com:** (ca). **DK Images:** Jerry Young (c) (cb) (crb). **Fotomedia:** E. Hanumantha Rao (tc). **Imagestate:** (clb). **Photolibrary:** Michael Dick/OSF (cl). **Dave Watts:** (c). **74 Bruce Coleman Inc:** Bill Wood (tc). **Nigel Dennis:** (br). **DK Images:** Frank Greenaway (c) Dorling Kindersley, Courtesy of the Natural History Museum, London (cr) (clb); Gary Ombler (C) Dorling Kindersley, Courtesy of Drusillas Zoo, Alfriston, West Sussex (tl); Rollin Verlinde (tr); Jerry Young (c). **NHPA/Photoshot:** Daniel Heuclin (cl). **75 William Bernard Photography:** (ca). **DK Images:** Jerry Young (c) (cb). **76 DK Images:** Frank Greenaway (c) Dorling Kindersley, Courtesy of the Marwell Zoological Park, Winchester (tl) (bc) (cb); Jerry Young (tr). **Fotomedia:** Joanna Van Gruisen (clb). **78-131 Corbis:** Martin Harvey. **78-9 Corbis:** Martin Harvey. **80 National Geographic Image Collection:** David Doubilet. **81 naturepl.com:** Nick Garbutt (br). **Science Photo Library:** Eye of Science (cl). **82 naturepl.com:** AFLO (bc); Jurgen Freund (cl) (bl); Jeff Rotman (fbl) (br); Sinclair Stammers (tr). **83 FLPA:** Reinhard Dirscherl (c). **Science Photo Library:** Susumu Nishinaga (tr). **84 Photolibrary:** Tobias Berhard/OSF (tr); Howard Hall/OSF (ca). **84-85 naturepl.com:** Jeff Rotman (bl). **85 DK Images:** Steve Gorton/Oxford University of Natural History (tc). **Photolibrary:** David Fleetham/OSF (br). **Science Photo Library:** Eye of Science (cl); M. I. Walker (tr). **86 naturepl.com:** Dave Watts (cra). **Science Photo Library:** Steve Gschmeissner (bc) (br); Susumu Nishinaga (bl). **86-7 Alex Wild/myrmecos.net:** Alex Wild/myrmecos.net. **87 naturepl.com:** Mark Payne-Gill (tc); Jose B. Ruiz (tl); Dave Watts (tr). **88 NHPA/Photoshot:** Martin Harvey. **89 Ardea:** Bill Coster (fcl); Ken Lucas (c). **fogdenphotos.com :** M & P Fogden (tr). **naturepl.com:** Staffan Widstrand (cr). **Photolibrary:** David M Dennis/OSF (cl); Bob Fredrick/OSF (cb). **SeaPics.com:** (crb). **90 Alamy Images:** imagebroker/Alamy (c). **Ardea:** Gavin Parsons (bc). **FLPA:** Mitsuaki Iwago/Minden Pictures (bl). **Getty Images:** Piotr Naskrecki/Minden Pictures (cl). **Sharon Heald:** (cb). **naturepl.com:** Ingo Arndt (cb). **91 shahimages.com :** Anup and Manoj Shah. **92 FLPA:** Mark Moffett/Minden Pictures (clb). **Science Photo Library:** Claude Nuridsany & Marie Perennou (cl); Andrew Syred (c). **92-3 Nick Garbutt. 93 Alamy Images:** A & J Visage (bl). **naturepl.com:** Philippe Clement (br). **NHPA/Photoshot:** Stephen Dalton (cr). **94 Alamy Images:** blickwinkel (tc) (cra). **naturepl.com:** David Shale (ca). **Still Pictures:** F. Hecker (tr). **94-5 NHPA/Photoshot:** Guy Edwardes. **95 naturepl.com:** Philippe Clement (tr). **NHPA/Photoshot:** Roy Walker (cla) (ca). **96 FLPA:** Michael Durham/Minden Pictures (cl). **naturepl.com:** Kim Taylor (bl). **96-7 naturepl.com:** Kim Taylor. **97 naturepl.com:** Todd Pusser (tr); Gabriel Rojo (bc); Markus Varesvuo (cb). **NHPA/Photoshot:** Stephen Dalton (cra). **98 FLPA:** Colin Marshall (bc). **naturepl.com:** Michael Pitts (bl). **99 FLPA:** B. Borrell Casals (cr); Chris Newbert/Minden Pictures (t). **naturepl.com:** Georgette Douwma (crb); Nature Production (clb) (bl). **100 stevebloom.com. 101 Alamy Images:** Andre Seale (bl). **Ardea:** Pat Morris (cr). **Getty Images:** Peter Sherrard (c). **naturepl.com:** Steven Kazlowski (br); Michael D. Kern (cb); Jason Smalley (clb). **Photolibrary:** OSF (bl). **102 Ardea:** Ken Lucas (bl). **naturepl.com:** Doug Perrine (c); Premaphotos (cl). **NHPA/Photoshot:** Martin Harvey (crb). **102-3 NHPA/Photoshot:** Martin Harvey. **103 Corbis:** Stuart Westmorland (br). **Getty Images:** David Burder (c); Tim Laman/National Geographic (bc). **104 Corbis:** Gallo Images (ca). **naturepl.com:** Premaphotos (fcl); Doug Wechsler (cl). **105 Alamy Images:** Arte Sub (fbl); Chris Mattison (fcra). **Corbis:** Robert Pickett (br); Jeffrey L Rotman (fclb); Paul Souders (cra); Winfried Wisniewski/Zefa (fbr). **Chris Mattison Nature Photographics:** (crb). **naturepl.com:** Georgette Douwma (bl); Tony Phelps (cr); Jeff Rotman (fcl). **NHPA/Photoshot:** Image Quest 3-D (tr); Mark O'Shea (c). **Photolibrary:** OSF (cl). **Science Photo Library:** Eye of Science (fcla). **106 FLPA:** Winfried Wisniewski/Foto Natura (tr). **Shutterstock:** Rick Thornton (clb). **Markus Varesvuo:** Markus Varesvuo/birdphoto.fi (crb). **107 Alamy Images:** franzfoto.com (bl); Nearby (c). **Corbis:** Gallo Images (bc); Staffan Widstrand (tr). **Getty Images:** Martin Harvey (crb). **NHPA/Photoshot:** Kevin Schafer (cl). **Science Photo Library:** British Antarctic Survey (tl). **108 Science Photo Library:** Gilbert S. Grant. **109 Alamy Images:** Visual & Written SL (cb). **FLPA:** Reinhard Dirscherl (br). **Still Pictures:** Jean-Jacques Alcalay/Biosphoto (cl). **110 Alamy Images:** Scott Camazine (cb). **David Bickford:** (c). **naturepl.com:** Jurgen Freund (tr). **Science Photo Library:** Microfield Scientific Ltd (bl). **110-1 Corbis:** Paul Souders. **111 Ardea:** B. Moose Peterson (br). **FLPA:** Chris Newbert/Minden Pictures (tr); Ariadne Van Zandbergen (cb). **112 Thomas Marent:** (clb). **naturepl.com:** Peter Bassett (br). **Photolibrary:** Phototake Inc/OSF (cla). **Science Photo Library:** Professors PM Motta & S Correr (tr); Dr Linda Stannard, UCT (ra). **113 FLPA:** Frans Lanting (bl); Mark Moffett/Minden Pictures (cb). **Photolibrary:** Satoshi Kuribayashi/OSF (tr). **114 Alamy Images:** Images of Africa Photobank (bc); Michael J. Kronmal (cb). **Ardea:** D. Parer & E. Parer-Cook (cra). **naturepl.com:** Mary McDonald (c). **114-5 FLPA:** Ariadne Van Zandbergen. **115 Alamy Images:** Steve Bloom Images (tr). **FLPA:** Frans Lanting (crb). **naturepl.com:** Hans Christoph Kappel (br). **Photolibrary:** Juniors Bildarchiv (cra). **116 Alamy Images:** Phototake Inc (ca). **Science Photo Library:** Dr John Zajicek (cra). **116-7 Science Photo Library:** D. Roberts. **117 Alamy Images:** Phototake Inc (ca). **naturepl.com:** Gary K. Smith (br). **Science Photo Library:** Thierry Berrod, Mona Lisa Production (tl); H. Raguet/Eurelios (bl). **118 stevebloom.com. 119 Ardea:** M. Watson (tr). **FLPA:** Fred Bavendam/Minden Pictures (clb). **naturepl.com:** Philippe Clement (bc); Andy Sands (c); Peter Scoones (fclb); David Shale (cl). **Science Photo Library:** D. Roberts (crb). **Still Pictures:** David Cavanaro (fcl). **120 naturepl.com:** Brandon Cole (bl). **Photolibrary:** Rodger Jackman/OSF (crb). **Science Photo Library:** Steve Gschmeissner (cr); Susumu Nishinaga (ca); Rod Planck (cla). **121 naturepl.com:** Geoff Dore (cla); Anup Shah (cb). **NHPA/Photoshot:** Peter & Beverly Pickford (cra). **122 Corbis:** Fritz Polking (crb). **naturepl.com:** Dave Bevan (tr); Andy Sands (cb). **NHPA/Photoshot:** Anthony Bannister (cl). **Photolibrary:** Owen Newman/OSF (br); Phototake Inc/OSF (c). **122-3 FLPA:** Derek Middleton. **123 naturepl.com:** Christophe Courteau (ca); Tony Heald (tr). **124 Alamy Images:** Martin Harvey (clb); Mike Veitch (cl). **naturepl.com:** Mark Carwardine (ca); Nick Garbutt (fclb); Alan James (fcl); Toby Sinclair (cb). **Christian Ziegler:** (c). **124-5 Corbis:** Visuals Unlimited. **125 Alamy Images:** blickwinkel (cr); imagebroker (ca). **Science Photo Library:** Leonard Lessin (bl) (bc); Omikron (tr). **126 Alamy Images:** Marrin Dembinsky Photo Associates (cl). **Science Photo Library:** J. C. Revy (cb). **126-7 Tony Heald. 127 FLPA:** Tim Fitzharris/Minden Pictures (fbr). **naturepl.com:** Premaphotos (bc); Shattil & Rozinski (br). **128 Ardea:** Augusto Stanzani (bl). **naturepl.com:** Doc White (cl). **128-9 Ardea:** Jean Paul Ferrero. **129 Alamy Images:** Danita Delimont (bc). **NHPA/Photoshot:** A. N. T. Photo Library (cr). **130 Ardea:** Pat Morris (cr). **FLPA:** Norbert Wu/Minden Pictures (bc). **naturepl.com:** Dave Watts (tl). **130-1 Photolibrary:** Chris & Monique Fallows/Apex Predators/OSF. **131 Alamy Images:** David Hosking (crb). **NHPA/Photoshot:** Martin Harvey (br). **Science Photo Library:** Catherine Pouedras (clb). **132-3 Corbis:** Charles O'Rear. **134-175 Alamy Images:** Roger Munns. **134-5 Alamy Images:** Roger Munns. **135 Alamy Images:** Lawrence Stepanowicz (b). **naturepl.com:** Jurgen Freund (c). **Photolibrary:** Animals Animals/Earth Sciences/OSF (t). **136 Corbis:** Frans Lanting. **137 Alamy Images:** Bryan & Cherry Alexander

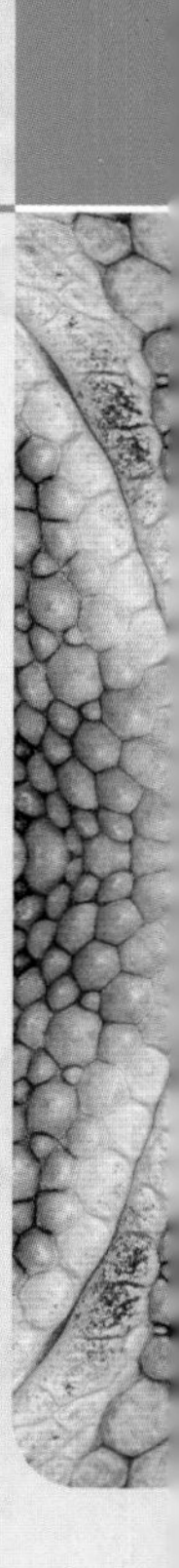

Photography (cl); Mark Conlin (br/fish); Gallo Images (br/side winding snake); Israel Images (ca); Juniors Bildarchiv (cr); Rolf Nussbaumer (tr). **imagequestmarine.com:** Peter Batson (crb). **Photolibrary:** Mary Plage/OSF (br/yak). **Science Photo Library:** Geroge Steinmetz (br/soda flats). **138 Alamy Images:** Steve Bloom Images (cb); Holmes Garden Photos (br). **naturepl.com:** George McCarthy (l). **139 Alamy Images:** Natural Visions (cla). **Ardea:** Tom & Pat Leeson (bl). **Thomas P Peschak/thomaspeschak.com:** (ca). **H. A. (Joe) Pase III, Lufkin , TX:** (cb) (br). **140 Alamy Images:** Wolfgang Polzer (bc). **Ch'ien C. Lee:** (tc). **NHPA/Photoshot:** Michael Patrick O'Neill (bl). **Photolibrary:** Animals Animals/Earth Sciences/OSF (crb). **140-1 Ch'ien C. Lee:** (t). **141 FLPA:** Larry West (bc). **Thomas Marent:** (clb). **142 Photolibrary:** Tui De Roy/OSF (tl). **142-3 Andy Rouse Wildlife Photography:** (b). **143 Alamy Images:** Rodney Hyett (bc). **Getty Images:** Geoff du Feu (tc). **naturepl.com:** Steven David Miller (cla). **NHPA/Photoshot:** John Shaw (crb). **144-5 shahimages.com :** Anup and Manoj Shah. **145 John Goodrich/WCS:** (ca). **naturepl.com:** Anup Shah (c). **146 fogdenphotos.com :** M & P Fogden (cl). **Thomas Marent:** (cra). **146-7 naturepl.com:** James Aldred (b). **147 naturepl.com:** Laurent Geslin (cb); David Kjaer (tr); Ian Redmond (bc). **148 Alamy Images:** Steve Bloom Images (br). **148-9 Photolibrary:** John Downer/OSF. **149 Alamy Images:** Terry Whittaker (cb). **Corbis:** Jonathan Blair (br). **150 Tom Biegalski:** Tom Biegalski/TTBphoto.com (clb). **naturepl.com:** Jurgen Freund (tc) (cra); Doug Perrine (c); Kim Taylor (br). **151 FLPA:** Frans Lanting (t). **Thomas Marent:** (cb) (cr). **152 Ardea:** Don Hadden (tc). **naturepl.com:** Hans Christoph Kappel (cl); Doug Perrine (cr); David Shale (crb). **SeaPics.com:** (clb). **153 Getty Images:** Joel Sartore/National Geographic (cr). **National Geographic Image Collection:** Paul Nicklen (fbl). **naturepl.com:** Michel Roggo (bl). **Photolibrary:** Daniel Cox/OSF (ca). **SeaPics.com:** (bc) (br). **154 Alamy Images:** Visual & Written SL (cr). **FLPA:** Frans Lanting (crb) (bl). **Leo P. Kenney:** (tl). **naturepl.com:** Michael Hutchinson (tr); George McCarthy (ca); Doug Perrine (clb). **Photolibrary:** Olivier Grunewald/OSF (br). **155 Alamy Images:** Nature PL (cla). **Getty Images:** Jason Edwards (cb). **Tomi Muukonen:** Tomi Muukonen/birdfoto.fi (cl). **naturepl.com:** Gertrud & Helmut Denzau (c). **Splashdowndirect.com:** Dave Hansford/Greenpeace (br). **156 USGS photo by Robert Gill:** (br). **naturepl.com:** Mike Read (t). **Keith Woodley, Miranda Shorebird Centre:** (clb). **157 Alamy Images:** blickwinkel (br). **FLPA:** Cyril Ruoso/JH Editorial (cr); Rodger Tidman (cl). **naturepl.com:** Tom Hugh-Jones (cra). **Photolibrary:** Mark Jones/OSF (bl). **Mark Trabue:** (tl). **158-9 FLPA:** Michio Hoshino/Minden Pictures. **159 National Geographic Image Collection:** Paul Nicklen (cr); Maria Stenzel (br). **naturepl.com:** Asgeir Helgestad (ca); Jeff Turner (cb). **160 Kieran Dodds/kierandodds.com:** (tr) (cra). **NHPA/Photoshot:** A.N.T. Photo Library (clb). **Science Photo Library:** Edward Kinsman (cl). **SeaPics.com:** (bl). **160-1 FLPA:** Reinhard Dirscherl (b). **161 naturepl.com:** Anup Shah (cra). **NHPA/Photoshot:** Jonathan & Angela Scott (tl). **162 Alamy Images:** Peter Arnold, Inc (cla). **FLPA:** Gerry Ellis/Minden Pictures (bl). **naturepl.com:** Gertrud & Helmut Denzau (cb). **162-3 National Geographic Image Collection:** Michael S. Quinton. **163 Alamy Images:** blickwinkel (cr). **Ardea:** Pascal Goetgheluck (cb). **FLPA:** Mitsuhiko Imamori/Minden Pictures (tr). **naturepl.com:** Jane Burton (crb); John Cancalosi (cra); Georgette Douwma (ca); Tom Vezo (bc). **NHPA/Photoshot:** T. Kitchin & V. Hurst (br). **164 FLPA:** Fred Bavendam/Minden Pictures (clb). **NASA:** NASA/visibleearth.nasa.gov (cr). **naturepl.com:** Michael Pitts (cl). **Photolibrary:** Neil Bromhall/OSF (cb); OSF (br). **165 Alamy Images:** Lawrence Stepanowicz (t). **166 Corbis:** Anthony Bannister (cla); Frans Lanting. **167 FLPA:** Mark Moffett/Minden Pictures (clb); Pete Oxford/Minden Pictures (cr); Krystyna Szulecka (crb). **David Maitland:** (tc). **Photolibrary:** Densey Clyne/OSF (bc). **168 Ardea:** Clem Haagner (crb). **fogdenphotos.com :** M & P Fogden (tr) (cra). **naturepl.com:** Steven David Miller (clb). **NHPA/Photoshot:** Martin Harvey (bc). **Photolibrary:** Mark Deeble & Victoria Stone/OSF (cla) (cl). **169 naturepl.com:** Jose B. Ruiz (tr) (c). **Photolibrary:** Ifa-Bilderteam Gmbh/OSF (bl). **170-1 FLPA:** Jim Brandenburg/Minden Pictures. **171 naturepl.com:** Dietmar Nill (cb); Dave Watts (cl) (c) (cr). **Photolibrary:** Juniors Bildarchiv/OSF (br). **172 FLPA:** David Hosking (bl); Winfried Wisniewski (br); Konrad Wothe/Minden Pictures (cla). **naturepl.com:** Terry Andrewartha (cr); William Osborn (cr); Philippe Clement (c). **173 Ardea:** Tom & Pat Leeson (tc). **FLPA:** Jim Brandenburg/Minden Pictures (bl). **NHPA/Photoshot:** Rich Kirchner (cla). **174 Ardea:** M. Watson (cl). **FLPA:** Jim Brandenburg/Minden Pictures (tc); Cyril Ruoso/JH Editorial (br). **M. C. McGrew/savethechimps.org:** (cb). **175 Thomas Marent:** (cla). **National Geographic Image Collection:** Paul Nicklen (tr). **Photolibrary:** Juniors Bildarchiv/OSF (clb); OSF (br). **176-271 FLPA:** Andrew Forsyth. **176-7 FLPA:** Andrew Forsyth. **177 Gerry Bishop:** (br). **FLPA:** S & D & K Maslowski (tr). **NHPA/Photoshot:** Martin Harvey (cr). **Science Photo Library:** Eye of Science (crb). **Still Pictures:** Reinhard Dirscherl/WaterFrame (cra). **178 naturepl.com:** Bence Mate. **179 FLPA:** Yossi Eshbol (bl). **Shutterstock:** Oksanaperkins (cl). **180 Alamy Images:** Lambie Brothers (bc). **Ardea:** Mary Clay (cr). **180-1 Denver Bryan:** (t). **181 Alamy Images:** Adrian Sherratt (crb). **182 Corbis:** M & P Fogden (cl); Momatiuk-Eascott (cb). **FLPA:** Nigel Cattlin (clb). **Photolibrary:** Animals Animals/Earth Sciences/OSF (bl). **Shutterstock:** Kitch Bain (c). **182-3 Corbis:** DLILLC. **183 FLPA:** Richard Brooks (cra); Jurgen & Christine Sohns (br). **NHPA/Photoshot:** Anthony Bannister (cb). **184 Alamy Images:** Philip Dalton (clb); Maximillian Weinzierl (tr). **Corbis:** Juan Medina/Reuters (cr). **Getty Images:** Norbert Wu/Minden Pictures (tc). **Photolibrary:** London Scientific Films (br). **185 Corbis:** Andreas Lander/dpa (cla). **Getty Images:** Bill Beatty (b). **PunchStock:** Digital Vision (tr). **188 imagequestmarine.com:** Roger Steene (cla). **Science Photo Library:** Georgette Douwma (cra). **188-9 FLPA:** Tui De Roy/Minden Pictures (b). **189 Alamy Images:** David Hosking (br); Nature PL (cr). **FLPA:** Tui De Roy/Minden Pictures (tl) (cl). **NHPA/Photoshot:** Daniel Heuclin (cla). **Still Pictures:** Tom Vezo (ca). **190 FLPA:** S & D & K Maslowski (t). **fogdenphotos.com :** M & P Fogden (br). **naturepl.com:** Staffan Widstrand (bl). **191 Alamy Images:** Arco Images (cr); Nature PL (clb). **Ardea:** Jean Paul Ferrero (bc); Duncan Usher (cl). **NHPA/Photoshot:** Stephen Krasemann (crb). **Markus Varesvuo:** Markus Varesvuo/birdfoto.fi (tl). **192 Getty Images:** Taylor S. Kennedy/National Geographic (clb). **National Geographic Image Collection:** Mattias Klum (crb). **Photolibrary:** Mark Hamblin/OSF (br). **Christian Ziegler:** (tr). **193 Alamy Images:** AfriPics.com (cl). **Getty Images:** Anup Shah (r). **naturepl.com:** Jurgen Freund (bl). **NHPA/Photoshot:** Ernie James (cr). **194 Alamy Images:** MJ Photography (cla); Panorama Media Ltd (ca); A & J Visage (cra). **Jean-Jacques Alcalay:** (b). **195 naturepl.com:** Sue Daly (tr). **Photolibrary:** Paul Kay/OSF (tl). **Science Photo Library:** Dr John Brackenbury (br). **SeaPics.com:** (bl). **196 naturepl.com:** Georgette Douwma (crb). **NHPA/Photoshot:** Mark Bowler (cb). **Photolibrary:** Rodger Jackman (bl). **196-7 SeaPics.com:** (t). **197 Corbis:** Jeffrey L. Rotman (bl). **FLPA:** Minden Pictures (cl). **naturepl.com:** Alan James (tc). **Photolibrary:** Animals Animals/Earth Sciences/OSF (c). **SeaPics.com:** (cra). **Still Pictures:** Reinhard Dirscherl/WaterFrame (br). **198 FLPA:** Fritz Polking (b). **Photolibrary:** OSF (cla). **199 FLPA:** S Charlie Brown (bc); Tui De Roy/Minden Pictures (br); Frans Lanting (tr). **naturepl.com:** David Kjaer (crb). **200 Alamy Images:** Roger Bamber (cl). **Ardea:** Stefan Meyers (crb). **Corbis:** Joe McDonald (cla). **FLPA:** M & P Fogden/Minden Pictures (ca). **naturepl.com:** Doc White (br). **201 Alamy Images:** Stock Connection Distribution (ca). **Corbis:** Joe McDonald (cla). **Still Pictures:** Klein J.- L & Hubert M.-L/Biosphoto (b); Bruce Lichtenberger (cra). **202 Alamy Images:** Steve Bloom Images (bl). **FLPA:** M & P Fogden/Minden Pictures (c). **203 FLPA:** Gerry Ellis/Minden Pictures (cl). **naturepl.com:** Meul/ARCO (tc); Rod Williams (tr). **204 FLPA:** Martin B Withers (crb). **NHPA/Photoshot:** Daniel Heuclin (br). **204-5 FLPA:** Jim Brandenburg/Minden Pictures (t). **205 Alamy Images:** WildPictures (tr). **FLPA:** Pete Oxford/Minden Pictures (cr). **naturepl.com:** Alan James (bl); Steven Kazlowski (crb); Constantinos Petrinos (fclb); Mike Read (cb); Lynn M. Stone (bc); Dave Watts (br); Doug Wechsler (cra). **NHPA/Photoshot:** Mark Bowler (cl). **206 FLPA:** Fred Bavendam/Minden Pictures (br). **National Geographic Image Collection:** David Doubilet (tl). **naturepl.com:** Rod Clarke/John Downer Productions (cl). **207 David Bygott:** (bc). **imagequestmarine.com:** Peter Parks (c). **Photolibrary:** Densey Clyne/OSF (cr) (bl). **SeaPics.com:** (tl) (ftr) (tc) (tr). **seashell-collector.com:** David Touitou (cl). **208-9 naturepl.com:** Ingo Arndt. **210 naturepl.com:** Premaphotos (ca). **Photolibrary:** Satoshi Kuribayashi/OSF (tr); Phototake Inc/OSF (tl). **211 FLPA:** Mitsuhiko Imamori/Minden Pictures (c) (cr) (fcr). **Tim Green:** (tl). **Science Photo Library:** Christian Laforsch (tr). **212 naturepl.com:** Kim Taylor (clb). **NHPA/Photoshot:** Anthony Bannister (bc) (crb). **Still Pictures:** Thierry Montford BIOS (t). **213 Natural Visions:** Andrew Henley (cla). **naturepl.com:** Martin Dohrn (br). **Jerome Orivel, CNRS:** (cl) (c) (cr) (fcr). **Photolibrary:** Satoshi Kuribayashi/OSF (tr). **Alex Wild/myrmecos.net:** (bl) (bc). **214 Chris & Monique Fallows/Apexpredators.com:** (cla) (ca) (cra) (r). **215 FLPA:** Fred Bavendam/Minden Pictures (fcra). **National Geographic Image Collection:** David Doubilet (tl). **naturepl.com:** Doug Perrine (cra). **NHPA/Photoshot:** Stephen Dalton (br). **Photolibrary:** Kathie Atkinson/OSF (bl). **SeaPics.com:** (c). **216-7 Thomas P Peschak/thomaspeschak.com:** (c). **218 Ardea:** Jean Michel Labat (crb). **imagequestmarine.com:** Peter Herring (clb). **Photolibrary:** Tobias Bernhard/OSF (tl). **219 naturepl.com:** Doug Perrine (cr); Kim Taylor (clb). **NHPA/Photoshot:** B Jones & M Shimlock (tr). **Photolibrary:** Paulo De Oliveira/OSF (bc). **220 FLPA:** Cyril Ruoso/JH Editorial (cra). **naturepl.com:** Suzi Eszterhas (cr). **Photolibrary:** Mauritius Die Bildagentur Gmbh/OSF (tl). **Winfried Wisniewski:** (b). **221 Getty Images:** Christian Ziegler/Minden Pictures (bl). **naturepl.com:** Michael D. Kern (tr). **NHPA/Photoshot:** Ken Griffiths (c); Daniel Heuclin (tl). **Photolibrary:** Brian P. Kenney (br). **David Wright:** (cr). **222-3 NHPA/Photoshot:** Stephen Dalton. **224 Ardea:** John Daniels (crb); Clem Haagner (bl). **FLPA:** Tui De Roy/Minden Pictures (ca); David Hosking (br). **fogdenphotos.com :** M & P Fogden (tl) (tc) (tr). **224-5 Mart Smit/martsmit.nl:** (t). **225 FLPA:** John Watkins (br). **226-7 Ardea:** Thomas Dressler. **227 Ardea:** M. Watson (br). **Corbis:** M & P Fogden (c). **NHPA/Photoshot:** Anthony Bannister (cra). **228 FLPA:** Jan Baks/Foto Natura (cl). **naturepl.com:** Vincent Munier (cr); Tom Vezo (tl). **SeaPics.com:** (bl). **229 Alamy Images:** Westend 61 (tl). **FLPA:** Wendy Dennis (br); Frans Lanting (tr) (clb). **230 Alamy Images:** Malcolm Schuyl (cl). **Ardea:** Karl Terblanche (cr). **Corbis:** Stephanie Pilick/dpa (tc). **naturepl.com:** Kim Taylor (bl); Dave Watts (bc). **230-1 naturepl.com:** Charlie Hamilton-James. **231 naturepl.com:** Charlie Hamilton-James (tl) (ftr) (tc) (tr). **232-3 National Geographic Image Collection:** Paul Nicklen. **233 National Geographic Image Collection:** Paul Nicklen (c) (cr) (crb). **www.skullsunlimited.com:** (br). **234 FLPA:** Jurgen & Christine Sohns (bl). **fogdenphotos.com :** M & P Fogden (br). **naturepl.com:** Richard du Toit (crb); Dave Watts (t). **235 National Geographic Image Collection:** Norbert Rosing (bl) (bc) (br). **naturepl.com:** T. J. Rich (tl). **stevebloom.com:** (ca). **236 Alamy Images:** Chris McLennan (clb). **naturepl.com:** Peter Blackwell (tl). **236-7 NHPA/Photoshot:** Martin Harvey. **237 naturepl.com:** Martin Dohrn (br). **NHPA/Photoshot:** Martin Harvey (cl) (c) (cr). **238 Corbis:** Stephanie Pilick/dpa (t). **238-9 National Geographic Image Collection:** Chris Johns. **240 FLPA:** David Hosking (c). **National Geographic Image Collection:** Chris Johns (b). **naturepl.com:** Pete Oxford (cr). **241 FLPA:** Michael Durham/Minden Pictures (t). **Frank Greenaway:** (b). **242-3 Christian Ziegler. 244 naturepl.com:** Mark Carwardine (cb) (bl); Doug Perrine (tc). **Christian Ziegler:** (cl). **244-5 Ardea:** Francois Gohier. **245 Photolibrary:** Rick Price/OSF (cr). **SeaPics.com:** (tl) (crb). **246 FLPA:** Mitsuaki Iwago/Minden Pictures (cb). **National Geographic Image Collection:** Ralph Lee Hopkins (crb). **naturepl.com:** Brandon Cole (t). **247 FLPA:** Dembinsky Photo Ass (bl); Frans Lanting (cra). **naturepl.com:** Barrie Britton (tc); Anup Shah (br). **NHPA/Photoshot:** Stephen Dalton (tl). **248-9 Göran Ehlmé. 250 Alamy Images:** blickwinkel (br). **naturepl.com:** Bruce Davidson (br); Anup Shah (cra). **NHPA/Photoshot:** Daniel Heuclin (cl). **Still Pictures:** H. Schmidbauer (ca). **251 Alamy Images:** Jon Massie (br). **FLPA:** Nigel Cattlin (tl); Frans Lanting (tr). **NHPA/Photoshot:** Ken Griffiths (bl). **Science Photo Library:** Eye of Science (cl). **252 Alamy Images:** Robert Fried (cra). **Kurt Jay Bertels:** (tc). **FLPA:** Mark Moffett/Minden Pictures (cr); André Skonieczny/Imagebroker (fcl). **naturepl.com:** Neil Bromhall (cl) (c); Brent Hedges (cb); Nature Production (bl); Jose B. Ruiz (br). **Science Photo Library:** Barbara Strnadova (tl). **253 naturepl.com:** Bernard Castelein (bl); Pete Oxford (br). **SeaPics.com:** (cl) (cr). **254-5 Juan Manuel Hernández. 255 naturepl.com:** Ron O'Connor (crb); Lynn M. Stone (br). **Still Pictures:** Sylvain Cordier/Biosphoto (cra). **256-7 naturepl.com:** Christophe Courteau. **258 naturepl.com:** Michael Durham (cl); Anup Shah (cb); Dave Watts (tl). **258-9 Howie Garber/WanderlustImages.com. 260 FLPA:** Frans Lanting (tr); Colin Marshall (clb); Mark Newman (ca). **Photolibrary:** Les Stocker/OSF (bc). **Still Pictures:** Darlyne A. Murawski (bl). **260-1 SeaPics.com. 261 NHPA/Photoshot:** N A Callow (tr). **262 Alamy Images:** Martin Harvey (ca); Medical-on-Line (tl). **Oceanwide Images:** Gary Bell/oceanwideimages.com (bl). **Photoshot:** Newscom (cra). **263 Alamy Images:** blickwinkel (tc). **Gerry Bishop:** (br). **Corbis:** Anthony Bannister (cla). **FLPA:** Mark Moffett/Minden Pictures (cl) (cb). **NHPA/Photoshot:** Stephen Dalton (tr). **264-5 FLPA:** Minden Pictures/Tui De Roy. **266 Alamy Images:** blickwinkel (cla) (ca) (crb); David Fleetham (tr); Jeff Rotman (bl). **Getty Images:** Bill Curtsinger/National Geographic (cr). **iStockphoto.com:** Anne de Haas (cl). **267 Alamy Images:** blickwinkel (cb). **Photolibrary:** Max Gibbs (Goldfish Bowl)/OSF (cla). **Still Pictures:** Klein/WaterFrame (cra). **268 Photoshot:** Bence Mate. **269 Alamy Images:** Danita Delimont (cr); Imagestate (cra); Mike Lane (tl). **Getty Images:** Beverly Joubert/National Geographic (br). **270 Ardea:** D. Parer & E. Parer-Cook (tc). **FLPA:** Jim Brandenburg/Minden Pictures (b). **271 naturepl.com:** Nick Gordon (c); Anup Shah (br). **NHPA/Photoshot:** Daniel Heuclin (crb). **SeaPics.com:** (tl) (ca). **272-3 Getty Images:** Art Wolfe. **272-321 Getty Images:** Art Wolfe. **273 FLPA:** Gerry Ellis/Minden Pictures (c); Fred Bavendam/Minden Pictures (b). **National Geographic Image Collection:** Joel Sartore (t). **274 Getty Images:** John & Lisa Merrill. **275 Alamy Images:** Matthew Doggett (cl). **Getty Images:** Norbert Wu/National Geographic (tr). **naturepl.com:** Premaphotos (bl); Anup Shah (br). **276 Alamy Images:** E. R. Degginger (bl). **FLPA:** Mitsuaki Iwago/Minden Pictures (tl); Mike Lane (cla). **NHPA/Photoshot:** Roger Tidman (clb). **SeaPics.com:** (cl). **276-7 Alamy Images:** Danita Delimont. **277 FLPA:** Simon Litten (br). **Thomas Marent:** (t). **naturepl.com:** Martin Gabriel (cb); Pete Oxford (bc); Phil Savoie (crb); Claudio Velasquez (cra). **278 Getty Images:** Fred Bavendam/Minden Pictures (cr). **naturepl.com:** Constantinos Petrinos (cl). **Photolibrary:** OSF (bl). **Scubazoo.com:** Roger Munns (tr) (cra). **SeaPics.com:** (cla). **279 imagequestmarine.com:** Mark Blum (tc); Roger Steene (cla). **Photolibrary:** David Fleetham/OSF (b). **SeaPics.com:** (c). **280 Ardea:** Auscape (cl). **Getty Images:** Heidi & Hans-Jurgen Koch/Minden Pictures (tr). **imagequestmarine.com:** Valda Butterworth (cb); Jim Greenfield 2004 (crb); Roger Steene (bl). **NHPA/Photoshot:** Joe Blossom (tl). **Still Pictures:** Eichaker Xavier/Biosphoto (cr). **281 Tom Eiser, Cornell University:** (cra). **Getty Images:** Piotr Naskrecki/Minden Pictures (cla). **Thomas P Peschak/thomaspeschak.com:** (b). **Photolibrary:** Satoshi Kuribayashi/OSF (c). **282 FLPA:** Reinhard Dirscherl (bl). **imagequestmarine.com:** Peter Parks (cla); Jez Tryner (cl). **SeaPics.com:** (cra). **283 naturepl.com:** Doug Perrine (clb). **SeaPics.com:** (br). **284 Alamy Images:** Jack Picone (bc). **Edmund D. Brodie, Jr.:** (tr). **naturepl.com:** Christophe Courteau (fcla) (ca) (cla) (cra); George McCarthy (cb); Mark Payne-Gill (bl). **285 FLPA:** ZSSD/Minden Pictures (t). **Thomas Marent:** (bl) (cb). **naturepl.com:** Nick Gordon (br). **286 Corbis:** Rod Patterson (crb). **Edmund D. Brodie, Jr.:** (cla). **naturepl.com:** John Cancalosi (clb). **Photolibrary:** Animals Animals/Earth Sciences/OSF (bc); Waina Cheng (cl). **Still Pictures:** Ed Reschke (tc) (cra). **287 Alamy Images:** Phototake Inc (br). **Ardea:** Pascal Goetgheluck (tr); Jean Paul Ferrero (cl). **National Geographic Image Collection:** Joel Sartore (bl). **NHPA/Photoshot:** Anthony Bannister (cr). **288 Joe McDonald:** (cl). **NHPA/Photoshot:** Stephen Dalton (cb). **288-9 NHPA/Photoshot:** Stephen Dalton Production. **290 naturepl.com:** Tony Heald (cra); Markus Varesvuo (c). **290-1 FLPA:** Peter Davey (b). **291 FLPA:** Flip De Nooyer/Foto Natura (cl). **naturepl.com:** Barry Mansell (cra). **292 naturepl.com:** Mark Payne-Gill (fcl) (c) (cl) (cr). **NHPA/Photoshot:** Nigel Dennis (tl). **292-3 Getty Images:** J. Sneesby/B. Wilkins (b). **293 Ardea:** Tony Beamish (cl). **IFAW, International Fund for Animal Welfare:** T Samson (br). **National Geographic Image Collection:** Peter G. Veit (cr). **naturepl.com:** George McCarthy (tc). **Still Pictures:** Alain Compost/Biosphoto (tr). **294 Corbis:** John Conrad (cl); Martin Harvey (br). **Getty Images:** (bl). **naturepl.com:** Niall Benvie (tc). **295 Afripics.com:** Daryl Balfour (b). **Alamy Images:** Kitch Bain (tr). **296 Alamy Images:** Neil Hardwick (cr). **DK Images:** Philip Dowell (ca). **FLPA:** Frans Lanting (bc) (br). **naturepl.com:** E. A. Kuttapan (tr). **SeaPics.com:** (cl). **296-7 National Geographic Image Collection:** Tim Laman. **297 FLPA:** Michael Quinton/Minden Pictures (tl). **naturepl.com:** Georgette Douwma (cra); David Shale (ca). **José Roberto Peruca:** (bc). **Still Pictures:** Francois Gilson/Biosphoto (br). **298 FLPA:** Frans Lanting (c); Chris Newbert/Minden Pictures (tc); Norbert Wu/Minden Pictures (cla). **Getty Images:** Patricio Robles Gil/Minden Pictures (crb). **naturepl.com:** Pete Oxford (bl). **299 Getty Images:** Jeff Lepore (br). **Thomas Marent:** (tc) (c). **NHPA/Photoshot:** James Carmichael Jr (bl). **Senckenberg, Messel Research Department, Frankfurt a. M. (Germany) :** (cra). **300 NHPA/Photoshot:** Trevor McDonald (clb) (bc) (bl) (cb). **300-1 NHPA/Photoshot:** Trevor McDonald. **301 Lydia Mäthger (permission from Biology Letters) :** (bl) (bc). **SeaPics.com:** (ca) (cr). **302-3 Art Wolfe. 304 FLPA:** Reinhard Dirscherl (cb). **naturepl.com:** Dave Bevan Photography (cra). **Photolibrary:** Waina Cheng (cla). **SeaPics.com:** (tc) (br). **305 Alamy Images:** Visuals & Written SL (cra). **FLPA:** Fred Bavendam/Minden Pictures (tr). **naturepl.com:** Sue Daly (cb). **Photolibrary:** David Fleetham/OSF (c). **SeaPics.com:** (bl). **306 FLPA:** Gerry Ellis/Minden Pictures (tr). **fogdenphotos.com :** M & P Fogden (c). **Nick Garbutt:** (cra). **naturepl.com:** Doug Wechsler (cla) (cl). **NHPA/Photoshot:** Chris Mattison (tc). **306-7 Thomas Marent:** (b). **307 Alamy Images:** Martin Harvey (cra). **Corbis:** M & P Fogden (tr). **Thomas Marent:** (br). **naturepl.com:** Pete Oxford (cla). **308-9 Anna Henly Photography. 310 Ardea:** Tom & Pat Leeson (ca). **FLPA:** Thomas Mangelson/Minden Pictures (tl); Derek Middleton (br); Chris Schenk/Foto Natura (clb). **naturepl.com:** Peter Reese (bc). **311 naturepl.com:** Sue Flood (crb); Paul Johnson (cra); Pete Oxford (tl); Philippe Clement (clb). **Photolibrary:** David Fleetham/OSF (br). **312 Alamy Images:** Steve Bloom Images (b). **Corbis:** D. Robert & Lorri Franz (tr). **Getty Images:** Mike Kelly (tc); Peter Lilja (cla). **313 Alamy Images:** Andrew Darrington (bl). **FLPA:** D. P. Wilson (cla); Konrad Wothe/Minden Pictures (br). **Getty Images:** Mark Moffett/Minden Pictures (cl). **A.Stabentheiner/H.Kovac/S.Schmaranzer:** (cra) (cr) (fcr) (fcra). **Wikipedia, The Free Encyclopedia:** (tr). **314 Alamy Images:** Duncan Usher (crb). **Ardea:** Valerie Taylor (cra) (cr). **FLPA:** Fred Bavendam/Minden Pictures (tr) (fcla). **Joyce Gross:** (bl). **315 José Luis Gómez de Francisco:** (bl). **Manual Presti:** (cla) (ca) (cra). **316-7 Douglas David Seifert. 317 Alamy Images:** Hornbill Images (c). **318-9 National Geographic Image Collection:** Mattias Klum. **319 Getty Images:** Mattias Klum/National Geographic (ca) (br). **NHPA/Photoshot:**

Nigel Dennis (cr). **320 Alamy Images:** Stockbyte (br). **Corbis:** Steve Kaufman (tr); Jacques Langevin/Corbis Sygma (crb). **naturepl.com:** Bruce Davidson (bl); Rolf Nussbaumer (ca). **Still Pictures:** S. E. Arndt/Wildlife (cla). **321 FLPA:** Pete Oxford/Minden Pictures (cla) (ca) (cra). **National Geographic Image Collection:** Beverly Joubert (b). **322-3 Getty Images:** Winfried Wisniewski/Image Bank. **322-375 Getty Images:** Winfried Wisniewski/Image Bank. **323 Ardea:** D. Parer & E. Parer-Cook (tr). **FLPA:** Michio Hoshino/Minden Pictures (cra). **Chris Mattison Nature Photographics:** (crb). **naturepl.com:** Terry Andrewartha (cr); Anup Shah (br). **324 Still Pictures:** Manfred Danegger. **325 Alamy Images:** cbimages (cla). **Science Photo Library:** D. Phillips (cra). **326-7 Photoshot:** Andy Newman/Woodfall Wild Images. **327 Alamy Images:** blickwinkel (cr). **naturepl.com:** Michael Pitts (cra). **328 Alamy Images:** Holt Studios International Ltd (cr). **Ardea:** Steve Hopkin (b). **Corbis:** Visuals Unlimited (fcl). **imagequestmarine.com:** Valdimar Butterworth (cl). **Reuters:** Phil Noble (tr). **Science Photo Library:** Sinclair Stammers (c). **329 FLPA:** Fritz Siedel (cla); D. P. Wilson (bl). **SeaPics.com:** (crb). **Still Pictures:** Joel Bricout/Biosphoto (tc). **Grahame Teague Photography:** (tr). **330 Ardea:** D. Parer & E. Parer-Cook. **SeaPics.com:** (bl). **331 Ardea:** Auscape (br). **Ben Chapman:** (cr). **naturepl.com:** Willem Kolvoort (tl); Kim Taylor (tc) (tr). **SeaPics.com:** (bl). **D. Scott Taylor:** (c). **332 FLPA:** M & P Fogden/Minden Pictures (ca); Frans Lanting (b); Albert Visage (cla). **naturepl.com:** Hanne & Jens Eriksen (tc); Mike Wilkes (cra). **333 FLPA:** Norbert Wu/Minden Pictures (tr). **Getty Images:** Piotr Naskrecki/Minden Pictures (bl). **naturepl.com:** Kim Taylor (crb). **PA Photos:** Matthew L. M. Lim & Daiqin Li (c). **Scubazoo.com:** Matthew Oldfield (cla) (ca) (cra). **334 FLPA:** Michael Durham/Minden Pictures (t). **Brian Kenney:** (br). **naturepl.com:** Kim Taylor (ca). **Photolibrary:** OSF (c). **335 Ardea:** Ken Lucas (cr). **Anthoni Floor / seafriends.org:** (br). **336 Alamy Images:** Peter Arnold Inc (bl). **FLPA:** Paul Hobson (crb). **fogdenphotos.com :** M & P Fogden (cr). **naturepl.com:** Rolf Nussbaumer (tl); Todd Pusser (bc). **NHPA/Photoshot:** James Carmichael Jr (tr). **337 Tasha L. Metz/seaturtle.org:** (crb). **Photolibrary:** David Fleetham/OSF (t). **SeaPics.com:** (bc). **338 Ardea:** John Cancalosi (br); M. Watson (bc). **Chris Gomersall Photography:** (tr). **FLPA:** Neil Bowman (cr) (cra); Konrad Wothe/Minden Pictures (cl). **naturepl.com:** Jorma Luhta (tl). **SeaPics.com:** (clb). **339 Ardea:** D. Parer & E. Parer-Cook (br). **FLPA:** Michio Hoshino/Minden Pictures (tc) (c) (tr). **SeaPics.com:** (bc). **340 FLPA:** Mitsuaki Iwago/Minden Pictures (cl); Frans Lanting (cla). **Photolibrary:** Satoshi Kuribayashi/OSF (bc). **340-1 naturepl.com:** John Cancalosi. **341 naturepl.com:** Nature Production (c). **NHPA/Photoshot:** Jonathan & Angela Scott (crb); Alan Williams (cra). **Photolibrary:** Clive Bromhall/OSF (bc). **342 FLPA:** Mark Moffett/Minden Pictures (c) (cr); Chris Newbert/Minden Pictures (cl). **National Geographic Image Collection:** Jozsef Szentpeteri (bl). **naturepl.com:** Georgette Douwma (tl). **NHPA/Photoshot:** Karl Switak (cra). **343 FLPA:** B. Borrell Casals (c); Mark Moffett/Minden Pictures (br). **naturepl.com:** Nick Garbutt (cl). **NHPA/Photoshot:** Anthony Bannister (bl). **Photolibrary:** M & P Fogden/OSF (t). **345 FLPA:** Mark Moffett/Minden Pictures (ca) (bl) (cl). **345-6 FLPA:** Mark Moffett/Minden Pictures. **346 FLPA:** Mark Newman (bl). **NHPA/Photoshot:** T. Kitchin & V. Hurst (ca); Linda Pitkin (tl). **SeaPics.com:** (cra). **346-7 fogdenphotos.com :** M & P Fogden (b). **347 fogdenphotos.com :** M & P Fogden (tl). **Photolibrary:** M & P Fogden/OSF (ca). **348 FLPA:** Jim Brandenburg/Minden Pictures (b). **naturepl.com:** Rupert Barrington (tc); Kim Taylor (tr). **NHPA/Photoshot:** Eric Soder (cr). **349 Ardea:** M. Watson (tl) (bc). **naturepl.com:** Barrie Britton (c); Pete Oxford (clb). **Science Photo Library:** Kenneth W. Fink (br). **350 Alamy Images:** blickwinkel (bc). **FLPA:** Tim Fitzharris/Minden Pictures (t); Frans Lanting (cb); Mark Newman (br). **351 FLPA:** Cyril Ruoso/JH Editorial (tc); Jan Vermeer/Foto Natura (tr). **naturepl.com:** Terry Andrewartha (cr). **SeaPics.com:** (bl) (bc). **www.skullsunlimited.com:** (br). **Still Pictures:** Michel & Christine Denis-Huot/Biosphot (cl). **352 Lydia Fucsko/lydiafucsko.com:** (clb). **naturepl.com:** Bengt Lundberg (crb). **Photolibrary:** OSF (bc). **Science Photo Library:** James H. Robinson (tr). **352-3 Ardea:** Duncan Usher. **353 naturepl.com:** Jose B. Ruiz (bc) (br). **Photolibrary:** Mark Hamblin/OSF (tc). **354 FLPA:** Richard Becker (bl). **naturepl.com:** Meul/ARCO (tr). **Premaphotos Wildlife:** Ken Preston-Mafham (br). **355 Oceanwide Images:** Rudie Kuiter/oceanwideimages.com (cb). **Photolibrary:** Joaquin Gutierrez Acha/OSF (tl). **SeaPics.com:** (tr) (bl) (br) (cr). **356 naturepl.com:** Kim Taylor (cra); Solvin Zankl (tr). **Photolibrary:** David M Dennis/OSF (cla). **356-7 Ulrich Doering. 357 FLPA:** Ingo Arndt/Foto Natura (tl). **naturepl.com:** Anup Shah (cl); Solvin Zankl (ca). **Fred Siskind:** (tr). **358 FLPA:** Frans Lanting (c). **Nick Garbutt:** (cra). **naturepl.com:** Pete Oxford (tc); Phil Savoie (bc); Artur Tabor (bl); Tom Vezo (cr). **359 Photolibrary:** Eliott Neep/OSF (bl) (bc) (br). **rspb-images.com:** Chris Knights (r). **360-1 FLPA:** Tui De Roy/Minden Pictures. **362 Auscape:** David Parer & Elizabeth Parer-Cook (cb). **Chris Mattison Nature Photographics:** (tl). **National Geographic Image Collection:** Jason Edwards (clb). **naturepl.com:** Phil Savoie (br). **363 Ardea:** Stefan Meyers (cra). **Corbis:** Tom Brakefield (tl). **FLPA:** Gerry Ellis/Minden Pictures (ca); David Hosking (cr). **Sharon Heald:** (b). **364 FLPA:** Mark Newman (l); Terry Whittaker (cr). **naturepl.com:** Wegner/ARCO (cra). **365 National Geographic Image Collection:** Joel Sartore (tr). **naturepl.com:** Mark Carwardine (crb). **NHPA/Photoshot:** Ernie James (c). **Photolibrary:** Tony Martin/OSF (bl) (bc) (br). **Still Pictures:** A. Buchheim (ca). **366 FLPA:** Silvestris Fotoservice (c). **naturepl.com:** Premaphotos (crb). **Photolibrary:** Martyn Colbeck/OSF (bl). **Science Photo Library:** Dr George Beccaloni (ca). **Scubazoo.com:** Roger Munns (tr). **367 FLPA:** Fred Bavendam/Minden Pictures (ftr). **naturepl.com:** Nigel Bean (cl); Constantinos Petrinos (br); Premaphotos (c). **David Nelson:** (ftl) (tc) (tl) (tr). **368 FLPA:** Robin Chittenden (tl). **naturepl.com:** Meul/ARCO (c). **NHPA/Photoshot:** Anthony Bannister (ca). **Photolibrary:** OSF (tr). **368-9 Thomas Endlein:** (b). **369 Ardea:** Jean Michel Labat (cr). **Photolibrary:** Clive Bromhall (br). **Science Photo Library:** Andrew Syred (cl). **SeaPics.com:** (fcla) (cla) (ca) (cl). **370-1 Ruben Smit. 372 Ardea:** M. Watson (cla). **FLPA:** B. Borrell Casals (cr); Derek Middleton (cb). **National Geographic Image Collection:** George Grall (tr). **naturepl.com:** Willem Kolvoort (b). **373 Alamy Images:** Reinhard Dirscherl (cr). **Ardea:** Steve Downer (t). **National Geographic Image Collection:** Bianca Lavies (br); Norbert Rosing (bl). **NHPA/Photoshot:** Alberto Nardi (bl). **374 Auscape:** C. Andrew Henly (bc) (br). **Graham Catley:** (fcl) (c) (cl) (cr). **FLPA:** Neil Bowman (ca). **naturepl.com:** Jorma Luhta (tr). **NHPA/Photoshot:** Alan Williams (tl). **375 Alamy Images:** Terry Whittaker (br). **Corbis:** Tom Brakefield (cr). **FLPA:** Cyril Ruoso/JH Editorial (tr). **naturepl.com:** Anup Shah (cl). **376-417 FLPA:** Frans Lanting. **376-7 FLPA:** Frans Lanting. **377 Suzi Eszterhas Photography:** (b). **naturepl.com:** Tom Mangelson (c). **378 Getty Images:** Anup Shah/Image Bank. **379 naturepl.com:** Peter Blackwell (br); Georgette Douwma (tr); Doug Perrine (bc). **Science Photo Library:** Science Source (fcla) (c) (ca) (cl) (cla) (cr) (cra) (fcl). **380 FLPA:** Michael Durham/Minden Pictures (cl) (c). **380-1 FLPA:** Michael Durham/Minden Pictures. **381 Alamy Images:** ARCO Images GmbH (bl). **FLPA:** Sumio Harada/Minden Pictures (ca). **naturepl.com:** Ingo Arndt (clb); Anup Shah (c) (br). **NHPA/Photoshot:** George Bernard (cla); Stephen Dalton (tr). **382 Anthoni Floor / seafriends.org:** (br). **FLPA:** Norbert Wu / Minden Pictures (cr). **Christian Fuchs:** (tl). **naturepl.com:** Kim Taylor (clb). **Photolibrary:** Phototake Inc / OSF (tc). **SeaPics.com:** (ca). **383 Alamy Images:** Guy Huntington (cra); NaturePics (tr). **naturepl.com:** Ross Hoddinott (b). **NHPA/Photoshot:** Stephen Dalton (tc). **384-5 FLPA:** Reinhard Dirscherl. **386 Thomas Marent:** (l) (cb) (crb). **387 Thomas Marent:** (clb) (cb) (r). **388 FLPA:** Nigel Cattlin (tr). **fogdenphotos.com :** M & P Fogden (b). **Getty Images:** National Geographic (tc). **National Geographic Image Collection:** Darlyne A. Murawski (tl). **naturepl.com:** Andrew Parkinson (cl); Kim Taylor (cr). **389 Jose Castro:** (cl). **National Geographic Image Collection:** David Doubilet (tr). **SeaPics.com:** (cb). **390 FLPA:** Reinhard Dirscherl (ca); Foto Natura Stock (cl) (cr); Jean Hall (c). **Thomas Marent:** (clb) (bl). **naturepl.com:** George McCarthy (crb); Kim Taylor (tl); Doug Wechsler (tr). **Papiliophotos:** Robert Pickett (cb). **391 Conservation International:** Robin Moore (cb). **Corbis:** David A. Northcott (cr). **Thomas Marent:** (clb). **naturepl.com:** Jane Burton (tl). **NHPA/Photoshot:** Laurie Campbell (br); Daniel Heuclin (cra). **392 Ardea:** Duncan Usher (tr). **naturepl.com:** Doug Allan (clb); Matthew Maran (tl). **Photolibrary:** David Tipling (bc). **392-3 naturepl.com:** Doug Allan. **393 Ardea:** Hans & Judy Beste (ca). **FLPA:** Foto Natura Stock (tl). **Getty Images:** Pete Oxford/Minden Pictures (crb). **Photolibrary:** Kathie Atkinson/OSF (cra). **394 Ardea:** D. Parer & E. Parer-Cook (bl) (cb). **FLPA:** S & D & K Maslowski (br). **NHPA/Photoshot:** Kevin Schafer (tr). **Still Pictures:** Regis Cavignaux/Biosphoto (tc). **395 Christophe Couteau:** (clb). **naturepl.com:** Andrew Cooper (ca); Anup Shah (br). **NHPA/Photoshot:** Yves Lanceau (cra). **396 Corbis:** M & P Fogden (cl); Christophe Karaba/epa (tr). **FLPA:** Michael Gore (bl); Winfried Wisniewski/Foto Natura (cr). **Sharon Heald:** (br). **naturepl.com:** John Cancalosi (cb). **397 FLPA:** Phil McLean (c). **2002 MBARI:** (bl). **naturepl.com:** Kim Taylor (br). **SeaPics.com:** (cla) (tr). **398 Ardea:** Alan Weaving (tc). **FLPA:** Heinz Schrempp (br). **Natural Visions:** Jeremy Thomas (clb). **naturepl.com:** Nature Production (c). **399 FLPA:** Norbert Wu/Minden Pictures (tl). **Photolibrary:** Pacific Stock/OSF (b). **SeaPics.com:** (tr). **400 naturepl.com:** Mark Payne-Gill (clb); Constantinos Petrinos (tr). **SeaPics.com:** (tl). **400-1 naturepl.com:** Anup Shah. **401 Alamy Images:** Digital Vision (cr). **Ardea:** M. Watson (clb). **FLPA:** Silvestris Fotoservice (tr). **naturepl.com:** Anup Shah (cb). **photographersdirect.com:** AfriPics Images (crb). **Photolibrary:** Animals Animals/Earth Sciences/OSF (cla). **402 Photolibrary:** Alan Root/OSF. **403 FLPA:** Tui De Roy/Minden Pictures (cl); Adri Hoogendijk/Foto Natura (bl); Mitsuaki Iwago/Minden Pictures (crb). **naturepl.com:** John Cancalosi (cla); Dave Watts (tr). **404-5 FLPA:** Frans Lanting. **406 Ardea:** Nick Gordon (cra). **Bat Conservation International:** Merlin D. Tuttle (cr). **naturepl.com:** David Kjaer (tl); Tom Mangelson (bl). **NHPA/Photoshot:** Daniel Heuclin (cl). **407 Ardea:** Tom & Pat Leeson (tr). **FLPA:** Flip Nicklin/Minden Pictures (cl); Michio Hoshino/Minden Pictures (br). **naturepl.com:** Pete Oxford (tc); Anup Shah (bl). **408 Ardea:** Jagdeep Rajput (bc). **FLPA:** Gerry Ellis/Minden Pictures (br). **naturepl.com:** Doug Perrine (bl); Anup Shah (tr); Tom Vezo (cl); Carol Walker (cb). **NHPA/Photoshot:** Joe Blossom (crb). **409 Alamy Images:** imagebroker (bl). **FLPA:** Neil Bowman (cr); Andrew Forsyth (bc). **Getty Images:** T. Kitchin & V. Hurst (cla). **Photolibrary:** Aldo Brando/OSF (tr). **410-1 NHPA/Photoshot:** Andy Rouse. **412 FLPA:** R P Lawrence (tc); Pete Oxford/Minden Pictures (cra); Fritz Polking/Foto Natura (crb); Inga Spence (cl). **naturepl.com:** Anup Shah (bl). **413 Ardea:** Jean Michel Labat (clb); Tom & Pat Leeson (t). **Suzi Eszterhas Photography:** (br). **414-5 naturepl.com:** Anup Shah. **416 Ardea:** Francois Gohier (crb). **brandoncole.com:** Brandon Cole (bc). **FLPA:** Michael Quinton/Minden Pictures (cr). **Cathy & Gordon ILLG/advenphoto.com:** (tr). **Mark Wallner:** (cl/otter). **417 Alamy Images:** Robert W. Ginn (br). **Suzi Eszterhas Photography:** (bl). **FLPA:** Gerry Ellis/Minden Pictures (t); Frants Hartmann (c). **418-439 Corbis:** Gary Bell/zefa. **418-9 Corbis:** Gary Bell/zefa. **421 Alamy Images:** Ryan Ayre (crb); blickwinkel (br); Holt Studios International Ltd (cl); Michael Patrick O'Neill (cra/fish); Top-Pics TBK (cra/lions). **FLPA:** Flip De Nooyer/Foto Natura (clb); Mark Hosking (cl); Pete Oxford/Minden Pictures (fcl). **Getty Images:** Tohuku Color Agency (crb/birds). **naturepl.com:** Christophe Courteau (fclb); Nature Production (c). **Photolibrary:** Survival Anglia/OSF (cb). **Shutterstock:** Craig Hosterman (tr). **422 Alamy Images:** Penny Boyd (cla); dbimages (cra). **Getty Images:** Mitch Reardon/Riser (b). **423 Alamy Images:** WaterFrame (cr). **FLPA:** J. W. Alker/Imagebroker (cla); Colin Marshall (bl). **Pauline Montecot:** (cb) (crb). **424-5 FLPA:** Pete Oxford/Minden Pictures. **425 FLPA:** Fritz Polking (br). **Hugh Schermuly:** (ca). **426 naturepl.com:** Willem Kolvoort (bl); Kim Taylor (cl). **SeaPics.com:** (cr) (crb). **Alex Wild/myrmecos.net:** Alex Wild (tc) (cra). **427 Photolibrary:** Tobias Bernhard/OSF. **428-9 Béla Násfay. 430 Alamy Images:** Danita Delimont (c). **Getty Images:** Roy Toft/National Geographic (cra). **naturepl.com:** Anup Shah (cl). **NHPA/Photoshot:** Jari Peltomaki (bc). **Photolibrary:** Konrad Wothe/OSF (tl). **430-1 FLPA:** Suzi Eszterhas/Minden Pictures (b). **431 Corbis:** Keren Su (tr). **Getty Images:** Harald Sund/Photographers Choice (crb). **432-3 naturepl.com:** Jose B. Ruiz. **434 Alamy Images:** Tom Uhlman (crb). **FLPA:** Frans Lanting (bl); Mark Newman (tr); Tom Vezo/Minden Pictures (br). **naturepl.com:** Chris Gomersall (cl). **435 Ardea:** Dennis Avon (cra). **Arto Juvonen/Birdfoto.fi:** (cl). **naturepl.com:** Neil Bromhall (crb) (br); Bruce Davidson (tl). **436 Corbis:** Kevin Schafer (tc). **FLPA:** Andrew Forsyth (tr); David Hosking (b). **NHPA/Photoshot:** David Higgs (br). **Still Pictures:** A & J Visage (cla). **437 Alamy Images:** Worldfoto (cb). **FLPA:** Tim Fitzharris/Minden Pictures (br); Mark Newman (cr). **Getty Images:** Manoj Shah/Stone (cl). **naturepl.com:** Karl Ammann (tl). **NHPA/Photoshot:** David Higgs (cr). **438 FLPA:** Jurgen & Christine Sohns (tl). **NHPA/Photoshot:** Martin Harvey (cra). **Still Pictures:** MCPHOTO (ca). **438-9 FLPA:** Yva Momatiuk & John Eastcott/Minden Pictures (b). **439 Alamy Images:** blickwinkel (tl). **FLPA:** Frans Lanting (tr). **naturepl.com:** Huw Cordey (c); Doug Perrine (br). **440-1 FLPA:** Martin B Withers. **440-467 FLPA:** Martin B Withers. **441 Alamy Images:** Amazon Images (crb). **fogdenphotos.com :** M & P Fogden (tr). **naturepl.com:** Kim Taylor (br). **SeaPics.com:** (cra). **442 Corbis:** Daniel J. Cox. **443 fogdenphotos.com :** M & P Fogden (bc). **naturepl.com:** John Cancalosi (br); Jose B. Ruiz (bl); Francois Savigny (fbr); Anup Shah (cra). **444 Alamy Images:** Michael Patrick O'Neill (tr). **FLPA:** Nigel Cattlin (cr). **naturepl.com:** Mark Brownlow (br); Pete Oxford (cb). **Photolibrary:** Keith Porter/OSF (ca). **Science Photo Library:** Stuart Wilson (bl). **445 Alamy Images:** Maximillian Weinzierl (tl). **Ardea:** Chris Martin Bahr (clb). **FLPA:** Mark Moffett/Minden Pictures (br). **fogdenphotos.com :** M & P Fogden (tr). **Photolibrary:** Juniors Bildarchiv/OSF (bc). **Premaphotos Wildlife:** Ken Preston-Mafham (cl). **446 Ardea:** Francois Gohier (bl); M. Watson (cl). **fogdenphotos.com :** M & P Fogden (tl). **naturepl.com:** Hermann Brehm (tr). **NHPA/Photoshot:** Christophe Ratier (br). **447 Alamy Images:** Nick Greaves (tr). **FLPA:** Gerald Lacz (clb). **naturepl.com:** Solvin Zankl (cl). **NHPA/Photoshot:** Jonathan & Angela Scott (tl). **Still Pictures:** Reinhard Dirscherl/WaterFrame (br). **Ingrid Wiesel/Brown Hyena Research Project:** (cr). **448 Alamy Images:** Arco Images GmbH (bl); Isita Image service (r); Peter Llewellyn (L) (bc). **Science Photo Library:** Tim & Alistair Lionel (c). **SeaPics.com:** (cla). **449 Ardea:** Peter Steyn. **FLPA:** Mark Moffett/Minden Pictures (tl). **Natural Visions:** Peter David (cl). **naturepl.com:** Nature Production (cr); Doug Perrine (b). **450 Ardea:** Jean Paul Ferrero (br). **fogdenphotos.com :** M & P Fogden (bl). **SeaPics.com:** (tr). **451 Ardea:** John Daniels (tc). **Getty Images:** Norbert Rosing/National Geographic (ca). **Still Pictures:** S. Weber (r). **452 FLPA:** John Hawkins (cla); SA Team/Foto Natura/Minden Pictures (crb). **Photolibrary:** Kathie Atkinson/OSF (bl). **453 naturepl.com:** Pete Oxford (tr). **stevebloom.com. 454 Alamy Images:** Jeff Minter (cl). **naturepl.com:** Christophe Courteau (bl); Anup Shah (br). **NHPA/Photoshot:** David Higgs (tr); Martin Harvey (tl). **Photolibrary:** Clive Bromhall/OSF (c) (cr). **455 Alamy Images:** Enrique R. Aguirre Aves (bl). **Ardea:** Duncan Usher (t). **FLPA:** Mark Raycroft/Minden Pictures (br). **naturepl.com:** Doug Allan (bc). **Still Pictures:** BIOS Bios (c). **456 Alamy Images:** Steve Bloom Images (cla). **FLPA:** M & P Fogden/Minden Pictures (ca). **Gastone Pivatelli:** (r). **457 Ardea:** Pat Morris (cb). **Corbis:** Anthony Bannister/Gallo Images (tl). **fogdenphotos.com :** M & P Fogden (bc). **naturepl.com:** Meul/ARCO (cra); Kim Taylor (c). **Photolibrary:** Animals Animals/Earth Sciences/OSF (clb). **458 Getty Images:** Tom Hopkins/Aurora (tl). **Björn Lardner:** (bl). **naturepl.com:** Gary K. Smith (bc). **Photolibrary:** Sojourns in Nature/OSF (ca). **459 Alamy Images:** f1 online (bc). **Ardea:** Chris Knights (tr); Sid Roberts (bl). **Corbis:** Theo Allofs (cla). **NHPA/Photoshot:** Tony Crocetta (cr). **Photolibrary:** Konrad Wothe/OSF (ca). **460 Alamy Images:** Amazon Images (c); Arco Images GmbH (clb); Rick & Nora Bowers (cra). **Courtesy of Jane Goodall Institute:** (bl) (bc) (br). **naturepl.com:** Anup Shah (crb). **NHPA/Photoshot:** Ernie James (cl). **Photolibrary:** Juniors Bildarchiv/OSF (tl). **461 Alamy Images:** Alaska Stock LLC (tl). **FLPA:** Flip Nicklin/Minden Pictures (b). **462 Ardea:** Pat Morris (c). **FLPA:** Tim Fitzharris/Minden Pictures (cl); Pete Oxford/Minden Pictures (tr/thorn bug). **fogdenphotos.com :** M & P Fogden (tr/golden mole). **naturepl.com:** Anup Shah (b); Kim Taylor (cra). **463 Alamy Images:** Simon de Glanville (tc). **Ardea:** John Mason (ca). **FLPA:** Richard Becker (tl). **Getty Images:** Time & Life Pictures (crb). **naturepl.com:** Kim Taylor (br). **464 Ardea:** Brian Bevan (tr). **Getty Images:** Wil Meinderts/Foto Natura (ca). **naturepl.com:** Niall Benvie (crb); Steven David Miller (b). **Tom Richardson/Nigel Franks:** (tl). **465 FLPA:** Jurgen & Christine Sohns (tl). **fogdenphotos.com :** M & P Fogden (cra). **shahimages.com :** Anup and Manoj Shah (bl) (bc). **Still Pictures:** H. Brehm (br); Cyril Ruoso/Biosphoto (cl). **466-7 FLPA:** Gerry Ellis/Minden Pictures. **467 Alamy Images:** Images of Africa Photobank (cra). **naturepl.com:** Anup Shah (cr) (br) (crb). **468 stevebloom.com. 468-485 stevebloom.com. 470 stevebloom.com. 471 Alamy Images:** Wayne Hutchinson (crb). **Corbis:** R. P. G./Corbis Sygma (fcrb). **Getty Images:** Bill Curtsinger/National Geographic (bl). **naturepl.com:** Tony Heald (tr). **Science Photo Library:** Thierry Berrod, Mona Lisa Production (clb) (cb); CNRI (fcl); Philippe Psaila (fclb). **472 FLPA:** Jurgen & Christine Sohns (c). **naturepl.com:** George McCarthy (br); Solvin Zankl (t). **473 Ardea:** Becca Saunders (cla). **FLPA:** Maurice Nimmo (cra). **imagequestmarine.com:** Michael Aw (cr). **National Geographic Image Collection:** Robert Sisson (br). **naturepl.com:** Constantinos Petrinos (bl). **SeaPics.com:** (tc). **474 FLPA:** Mark Moffett/Minden Pictures (tl) (c). **naturepl.com:** Premaphotos (b). **Matthias Wittlinger:** (cr). **475 naturepl.com:** Doug Perrine (c); Michel Roggo (tr); Doug Wechsler (bl). **Photolibrary:** Animals Animals/Earth Sciences/OSF (br); Brian P. Kenney/OSF (tl). **476 FLPA:** Suzi Eszterhas/Minden Pictures (cla). **National Geographic Image Collection:** Robert Sisson (bl) (bc) (br). **NHPA/Photoshot:** Martin Harvey (tl). **476-7 FLPA:** Suzi Eszterhas/Minden Pictures. **477 Ardea:** Steve Hopkin (bc). **Corbis:** Rick Friedman (cr). **naturepl.com:** Lynn M. Stone (cra). **478 naturepl.com:** Miles Barton (ca) (cl). **Photolibrary:** Picture Press/OSF (tl). **Photoshot:** Marie Read/Woodfall Wild Images (bc). **478-9 FLPA:** Pete Oxford/Minden Pictures (b). **naturepl.com:** Ingo Arndt (c). **479 FLPA:** Pete Oxford/Minden Pictures (bl) (bc) (br). **Yukihiro Fukuda:** (tc). **naturepl.com:** Miles Barton (cl). **480 FLPA:** Cyril Ruoso/JH Editorial (c). **National Geographic Image Collection:** Michael K. Nichols (bl). **stevebloom.com:** (tr). **Still Pictures:** Cyril Ruoso/Biosphoto (cb). **480-1 naturepl.com:** Anup Shah. **481 Photolibrary:** Stan Osolinski/OSF (bl) (bc) (br). **482 Ardea:** Tom & Pat Leeson (b). **FLPA:** Norbert Wu/Minden Pictures (cr). **naturepl.com:** Andrew Murray (tr); Anup Shah (cla). **483 Alamy Images:** Paul Glendell (cb). **FLPA:** Reinhard Dirscherl (tl). **Getty Images:** APF (c); David Silverman (bc). **naturepl.com:** Richard du Toit (br); Hugh Pearson (c). **484-5 stevebloom.com. 486-7 naturepl.com:** Yuri Shibnev (b)

Jacket images: *Front:* **naturepl.com:** Anup Shah. *Back:* **naturepl.com:** Anup Shah. *Spine:* **naturepl.com:** Anup Shah ; Front Endpapers: **Ben Osborne/benosbornephotography.co.uk**; Back Endpapers: **Ben Osborne/benosbornephotography.co.uk**

All other images © Dorling Kindersley
For further information see: www.dkimages.com

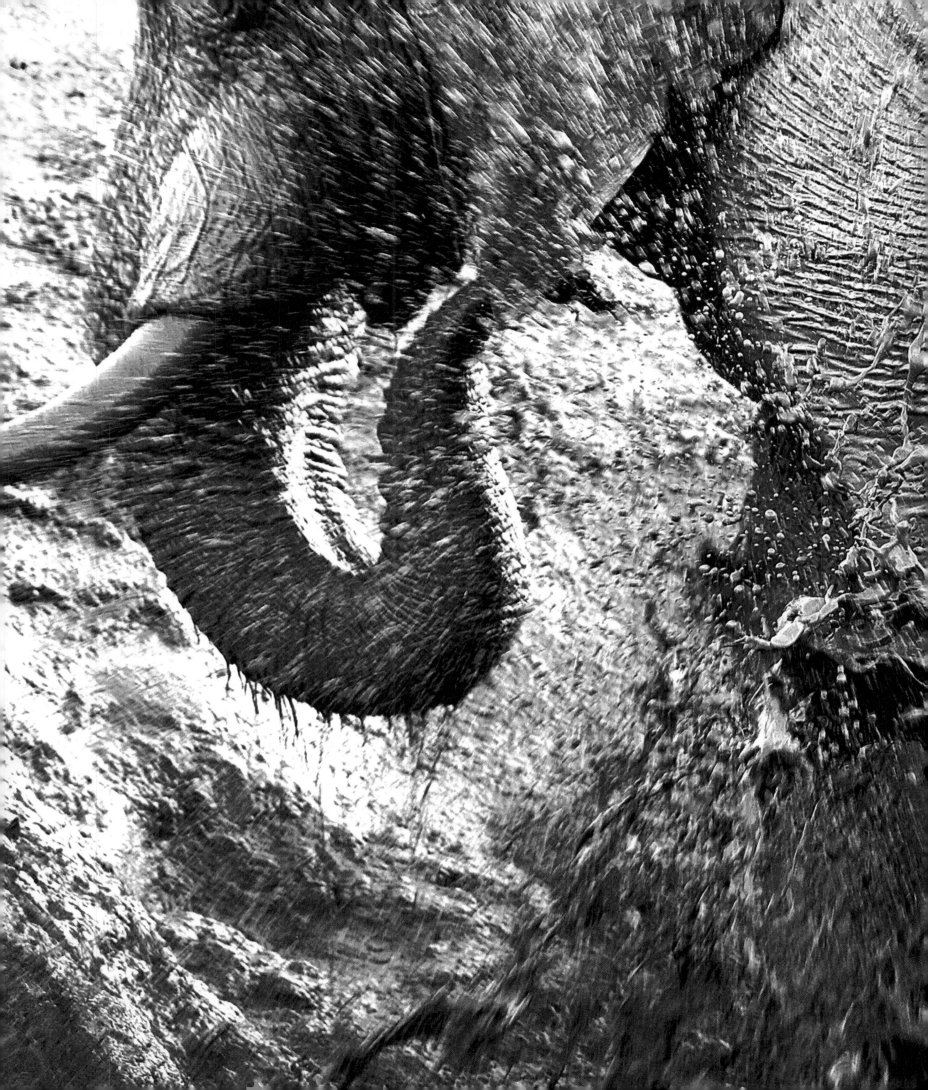